PHILOSOPHY BETWEEN THE LINES

PHILOSOPHY
Between
THE LINES

The Lost History of Esoteric Writing

ARTHUR M. MELZER

University of Chicago Press
Chicago & London

ARTHUR M. MELZER is professor of political science at Michigan State University, where he is also cofounder and codirector of the Symposium on Science, Reason, and Modern Democracy. He is the author of *The Natural Goodness of Man*.

The University of Chicago Press, Chicago 60637
The University of Chicago Press, Ltd., London
© 2014 by The University of Chicago
All rights reserved. Published 2014.
Printed in the United States of America

23 22 21 20 19 18 17 16 15 14   2 3 4 5
ISBN-13: 978-0-226-17509-6   (cloth)
ISBN-13: 978-0-226-17512-6   (e-book)
DOI: 10.7208/chicago/9780226175126.001.0001

Library of Congress Cataloging-in-Publication Data
Melzer, Arthur M., author.
Philosophy between the lines : the lost history of esoteric writing / Arthur M. Melzer.
pages cm
Includes bibliographical references and index.
ISBN 978-0-226-17509-6 (cloth : alk. paper) — ISBN 978-0-226-17512-6 (e-book)
1. Philosophical literature—History and criticism. 2. Methodology. 3. Hermeneutics.
4. Censorship. 5. Secrecy. I. Title.
B52.66.M45 2014
190—dc23

2014016966

♾ This paper meets the requirements of ANSI/NISO Z39.48-1992 (Permanence of Paper).

For
Shikha and Prateik

There is not a truth existing which I fear . . . or would wish unknown to the whole world.

—THOMAS JEFFERSON

Must one be senseless among the senseless? No; but one must be wise in secret.

—DIDEROT

[CONTENTS]

EXOTERIC and ESOTERIC, adj. (History of Philosophy):
The first of these words signifies *exterior*, the second, *interior*.
The ancient philosophers had a double doctrine; the one ex-
ternal, public or *exoteric*; the other internal, secret or *esoteric*.
—*Encyclopedia* of Diderot

. . . the distinction between the two doctrines so eagerly received by all the Philosophers, and by which they professed
in secret sentiments contrary to those they taught publicly.
—JEAN-JACQUES ROUSSEAU

We moderns are believers in progress. But as even we must admit, the passage of time brings not only intellectual advance but also decline—discovery
but also ossification, denial, and forgetting. There is a natural tendency, however, to notice and be impressed with the former, to neglect the latter. Discoveries stand out, while forgettings are invisible.

Countless books have been written celebrating the discovery of some important phenomenon. The present work examines the forgetting of one.

A LOST METHOD OF WRITING—AND READING

In a letter to a friend, dated October 20, 1811, Johann Wolfgang von Goethe speaks of an act of forgetting taking place before his eyes: "I have always considered it an evil, indeed a disaster which, in the second half of the previous century, gained more and more ground that one no longer drew a distinction between the exoteric and the esoteric."[1] The intellectual life of the West, Goethe reports here, has gradually been undergoing a strange and unfortunate transformation. Through a slow act of collective amnesia, a well-known phenomenon has quietly been dropping out of awareness: the philosophic practice of esoteric writing. By this is meant the practice of communicating one's unorthodox thoughts primarily "between the lines," hidden behind a veneer of conventional pieties, for fear of persecution or for other reasons.

Although unheeded, Goethe's warning turned out to be remarkably prescient, pointing to a philosophical forgetting that would continue to spread and deepen for another hundred years. For during the first half of the eighteenth century, esoteric writing was still very well known, openly discussed, and almost universally practiced (as it had been since ancient times), as can be seen from the epigraphs. These two statements could be multiplied a hundred times—and will be. And yet this well-established phenomenon was somehow slowly forgotten in the course of the nineteenth century and, in the twentieth, confidently declared a myth.

It was rediscovered principally by Leo Strauss—the University of Chicago political philosopher—who began publishing on the subject in the late 1930s. As Alexandre Kojève declared in recognition of this achievement: "Leo Strauss has reminded us of what has tended to be too easily forgotten since the nineteenth century—that one ought not to take literally everything that the great authors of earlier times wrote, nor to believe that they made explicit in their writings all that they wanted to say in them."[2] Still, Strauss's efforts at recovery also went largely unheeded.

The present study is an exercise in historical recollection and retrieval. It attempts to more clearly display, document, and, above all—if possible—*reverse* this extraordinary act of forgetting. It aims to reestablish a general recognition of the several reasons for and the near-universal prevalence of esoteric writing among the major philosophical writers of the West prior to the nineteenth century. My goal here is not to get people to like esotericism (I am no great lover of it myself), or to engage in it themselves (as I do not), but simply to recognize, understand, and accept it as a historical reality— indeed a monumental one affecting the whole conduct of intellectual life in the West over two millennia. I seek a restoration not of esoteric writing but of esoteric *reading*—the recovery of a crucial but long-lost element of philosophical literacy.

What I also do *not* attempt to do is determine the particular esoteric teaching of everyone (or anyone) in this long line of thinkers—something that cannot be done in a general work of this kind, but only with meticulous care, one philosopher at a time. My book is not: *The Esoteric Secrets of All Ages Revealed!* It is simply, if you like: *Awareness of the Forgotten Practice of Esoteric Writing Restored.* That is project enough.

WHAT IS AT STAKE

Naturally, the reader, who has yet to be shown much evidence for the reality of this strange practice, will want to reserve judgment on the merits of the project. Still, the great importance of the issue itself should at least be clear. Here is what is at stake.

If it turns out to be true that most philosophers of the past routinely hid some of their most important ideas beneath a surface of conventional opinions, then surely we had better know that. If they wrote esoterically and we do not read them esoterically, we will necessarily misunderstand them. We will systematically cut ourselves off from their thought precisely in its most unorthodox, original, and liberating part.

But the damage, great as it is, does not stop there. Not only will we misunderstand all these thinkers as individuals, but through the accumulation of such errors, we will also form mistaken ideas about the relations among thinkers, about how ideas develop over time, about the whole movement and meaning of Western intellectual history. This misunderstanding would be especially damaging to modern philosophy, which tends to rest, implicitly or explicitly, on a "theory of history," an interpretation of the stages and trajectory of philosophical thought.

But the damage may, in fact, extend yet one crucial step further. If, for these reasons, we misunderstand earlier philosophers and, because of that, the history of philosophical thought, don't we also run a great risk of finally misunderstanding the character of human reason as such—especially how it relates to the political and cultural environment in which it is embedded? For we can know how the faculty of reason works and what it is capable of primarily by seeing what it has done—by its history, its concrete record of failures and achievements. Thus, to systematically misconstrue the history of reason puts one in great danger of misunderstanding reason itself.

It is this fear that, for example, particularly animates Strauss's great pre-occupation with the issue of esotericism. Let me illustrate with one strand of his complex argument on this issue. The ignorance of esoteric writing, which causes us to misinterpret the history of philosophy, does not do so, he argues, in simply random ways. In addition to the various particular errors we may make regarding particular thinkers, there is also a common mistake that we commit again and again in our interpretation of all thinkers. We mistake the philosopher's surface, exoteric teaching for his true one. And again, these surface teachings, however much they may vary from thinker to thinker, all have one essential thing in common: they are carefully designed to create the false appearance of conformity to the most powerful dogmas of the time, which it is too dangerous to question openly.

Therefore, the established custom of reading esoteric writers nonesoterically has a very precise and predictable effect on the practice of scholarship. It gives rise to a systematically recurring misimpression: everywhere we look, we see the dispiriting spectacle of the human mind vanquished by the hegemonic ideas of its times. It appears that even our most celebrated geniuses—our Aristotles and Shakespeares—with all their extraordinary gifts and agonized efforts, always end up just confirming the myths of their particular "cave." It is difficult to overstate the profound influence of this recurring experience. It forms a crucial but unseen part of the intellectual background of our times, motivating the late modern or postmodern pre-disposition to the radical critique and disempowerment of reason. In the age of the forgetfulness of esotericism, it comes to seem obvious to everyone that the human mind is not free but wholly contextualized, culture-bound, socially determined. And if that is so, then all our truths are ultimately local, accidental, and temporary; our highest wisdom, only the hometown ethnocentrism polished up.

The awareness of esotericism, by contrast, reveals the falseness, the calculated insincerity of this ubiquitous facade of philosophical conformity—which now comes to sight as an ironic and artful act of resistance. Behind this defensive wall, sheltered and encouraged by it, thrives a secret underground of daring and dissent, a freewheeling speak-easy of the mind. But we, who should celebrate this, are somehow reluctant to believe it. Yet, as an old Ethiopian proverb observes, "When the great lord passes, the wise peasant bows deeply—and silently farts." Every subject class has its silent arts of resistance—the philosophers too. For where force is lacking, fraud and secrecy are the primary agents of freedom.[3] If modern scholars thought more like wily peasants, they would be less resistant to the essential truth that there is always more freedom in the world than the compliant surface of things would lead one to suppose.[4] Thus, the true history of human reason is of necessity a secret history: when the practice of philosophic secrecy is once seen, then the faculty of human reason no longer appears quite as servile and culture-bound as it inevitably does to us.

In short, the ignorance of esotericism, by blinding us to the hidden world of freedom, keeps us in ignorance of ourselves—of the surprising power and independence of the human mind, of its unsuspected capacity to resist time and place.[5]

One last point. If it should turn out that this tradition of philosophical esotericism is indeed a reality, that immediately brings to light a second crucial reality: the fact of our long blindness and denial regarding the first. We are compelled to wonder: how in the world could we have missed something so big and so (formerly) well-known? In other words, at stake, finally, in the question of esotericism is also a crucial question regarding *ourselves*: what are the particular defects or biases of the modern worldview such that we became incapable of seeing a reality as massive and important as this one?

As phenomena to be studied, discoveries are interesting, but forgettings are profound. Through the one, we explore and celebrate our insights, but through the other we discover our blindness. It is only through the encounter with a reality that we could not perceive that we see the limitations of our perception—and so begin the slow process of transcending them.

As intriguing as all of this might seem, however, many will object that a long-forgotten tradition of secret writing by Western philosophers sounds rather fanciful. It seems less like a forgotten truth and more like an academic urban legend started, perhaps, by scholars too steeped in medieval ideas or Talmudic habits or longings for privileged access to secret wisdom.

The exchange of charges and countercharges on this issue has been heated. But amid all this controversy, three things may be said to be certain: First, if the theory of esotericism is true, it is a matter of the greatest importance. Second, we today are viscerally inclined to believe that it is false. And thus third, there is urgent need for a new, more considered examination of the question.

The stars, moreover, seem well aligned for this venture. The last few decades have seen a veritable explosion in hermeneutical theory. Everywhere there is a heightened consciousness of rhetoric, audience, reader response, playfulness, and other new or long-forgotten issues of textual interpretation. All our Enlightenment presuppositions about the nature of writing, reading, and publication—about the whole relation of thought to life—have been subjected to a searching critique. The crumbling of long-impregnable paradigms has freed the current age for a new, more original encounter with the question of esotericism.

The present work attempts such a reexamination, first by gathering and displaying the concrete historical evidence for esotericism, second by exploring the broad background of philosophical assumptions underlying this practice, and third by examining the contrary assumptions underlying the powerful modern denial of its existence.

[ACKNOWLEDGMENTS]

My friends and colleagues all regard it as curious that I should be the one to write this book. There are people who have a real love for esoteric interpretation and a real gift for it. I am not one of them. My natural taste is for writers who say exactly what they mean and mean exactly what they say. I can barely tolerate subtlety. If I could have my wish, the whole phenomenon of esoteric writing would simply disappear.

But it will not. And it is strange that it has not been given the serious attention it deserves, especially in view of both the monumental importance of the phenomenon and the mountain of evidence attesting to it. Yet that evidence, it must be conceded, has never been collected, displayed, and explained as well as it might. Having spent a long time grumbling that somebody ought to do so, I have finally decided to do it myself. Perhaps it will be done better by someone with at least a temperamental sympathy for the skeptics.

I am greatly indebted to many people for their help. Most of the ideas presented here were developed in conversation with my good friends and colleagues Jerry Weinberger, Dick Zinman, Steven Kautz, and David Leibowitz. They also read various parts of the manuscript—Zinman and Kautz, the whole thing. Their copious and probing comments have been invaluable. Among others who have given generously of their time and expertise, reading the manuscript in part or whole, I would particularly like to thank Rafe

Major, John Tryneski, my editor at the University of Chicago Press, and Sara Melzer, my sister and editor-for-life. Many of my oldest friends and teachers provided essential encouragement through their bibliographical suggestions, textual finds, philosophic and linguistic expertise, and lively and long-sustained interest in the project. It is a pleasure to mention Robert Kraynak, Harold Ames, Clifford Orwin, Thomas Pangle, Abe Shulsky, Hillel Fradkin, Jim Nichols, Marc Plattner, Jim Ceaser, Richard Velkley, Jeremy Rabkin, Bill Kristol, Charles Fairbanks, Chris Bruel, Harvey Mansfield, Werner Dannhauser, and the late Allan Bloom and Ernest Fortin. For similar help and contributions I would also particularly like to thank Till Kinzel and Sherm Garnett, as well as David Janssens, Michael Zuckert, Catherine Zuckert, Paul Cantor, Ralph Lerner, Tom Shul, Eric Petrie, Chris Nadon, Daniel Tanguay, Chris Kelly, Tobin Craig, Fred Baumann, Steve Lenzner, Heinrich Meier, Ken Weinstein, Damon Linker, Timothy Burns, Svetozar Minkov, Forrest Nabors, Joseph Knippenberg, Paul Stern, Alex Orwin, Stewart Gardner, Brad Jackson, Anas Muwais, and Andrew Bibby. I must make particular mention of Paul Rahe, whose writings—especially his encyclopedic *Republics Ancient and Modern*—are an important resource for the philosophic testimony to esotericism. I also owe a special debt to Jenny Strauss Clay for her generous contributions of effort and enthusiasm, her excellent Greek and Latin translations, and other help in finding and interpreting passages in classical literature. I would like to thank Jack Byham, my research assistant, for his help with the notes and bibliography. It goes without saying, of course, that no one of these individuals agrees entirely with what I have written.

My greatest and fondest debt is to Shikha Dalmia, my wife and companion, through whose encouragement, advice, and artful interventions I found the means to keep going in an endless project, as well as the strength, finally, to stop.

For financial support, I am very grateful to the Earhart Foundation, the National Endowment for the Humanities, and the Program on Constitutional Government at Harvard University.

An earlier version of chapter 7 originally appeared as "On the Pedagogical Motive for Esoteric Writing," *Journal of Politics*, November 2007. Parts of chapter 10 were originally published as "Esotericism and the Critique of Historicism" in *American Political Science Review*, May 2006. An earlier version of portions of chapter 6 can be found in "On the Inherent Tension between Reason and Society," in *Reason, Faith, and Politics: Essays in Honor of Werner J. Dannhauser*, ed. Arthur M. Melzer and Robert P. Kraynak (Lanham, MD: Lexington Books, 2008).

What Is Philosophical Esotericism?

It is said that Anacharsis the Scythian [a sixth-century BC philosopher], while asleep, held his secret parts with his left hand, and his mouth with his right, to intimate that both ought to be mastered, but that it was a greater thing to master the tongue than voluptuousness.

—CLEMENT OF ALEXANDRIA, *Stromata*

Forgotten fields, like unweeded gardens, grow a bit wild. Thus, it is necessary to begin by trying to state with greater precision the thesis being defended here. "Philosophical esotericism" needs to be distinguished from the profusion of related phenomena that surround it—after which its internal divisions or variations need to be clearly identified.

In common parlance, "esoteric" is often used synonymously with "recondite" or "abstruse," simply to denote any kind of knowledge that, by virtue of its inherent difficulty, profundity, or specialized focus, surpasses the understanding of most people—like quantum mechanics. But in a stricter sense—and the one intended here—it is something difficult to understand because hidden or secret. The term derives from the Greek *esoterikos*, meaning inner or internal. An esoteric writer or writing would involve the following characteristics: first, the effort to convey certain truths—the "esoteric" teach-

ing—to a select group of individuals by means of some indirect or secretive mode of communication; second, the concomitant effort to withhold or
conceal these same truths from most people; and third (a common but not
strictly necessary characteristic) the effort to propagate for the sake of the
latter group a fictional doctrine—the "exoteric" teaching—in place of the
true doctrine that has been withheld.

On this understanding of the term, there are a variety of movements that
today and for centuries have pointedly emphasized a long Western tradition
of "esotericism." All the most prominent of these are forms of mysticism:
Theosophy, Gnosticism, Hermeticism, Rosicrucianism, Kabbalah, Neoplatonism, Neo-Pythagoreanism, and others. In one manner or another, all
of these movements hold that there exists a single, secret body of "Esoteric
Knowledge" that is of a mystical or occult nature and that links together the
brotherhood of esoteric thinkers across the ages.

When Leo Strauss began writing about esotericism in the late 1930s, he
was acutely aware that the only unbroken remembrance or living awareness of the phenomenon was in the mystical tradition. As he put it, in the
present age "the phenomenon in question [esotericism] . . . is discussed
under the title 'mysticism'"[1]—a statement that, despite the efforts of Strauss
and others, still remains largely true today. If one does an internet search or
a title search in the Library of Congress catalog for "esotericism," the overwhelming majority of replies concern Theosophy.

But the mystical version of esotericism is a very small part of a larger phenomenon. Esotericism is actually a practice to be found throughout the
mainstream Western philosophical tradition and the mainstream literary
and theological traditions as well. This larger phenomenon is the esotericism that Strauss may be said to have rediscovered.[2]

In this larger sense, esotericism does not imply (as the mystical sense
does) that there is a single "Esoteric Philosophy" linking all genuine esotericists. Here "esoteric" denotes not a particular body of secret or occult knowledge but simply a secretive mode of communication—not a specific set of beliefs, but the practice of partly revealing and partly concealing one's beliefs,
whatever they may be. It is not a philosophical doctrine but a *form of rhetoric*, an art of writing (although the belief that it is necessary to employ such
rhetoric *is* typically rooted, as I will argue, in larger, philosophical views).

In this broader sense, esoteric writers will naturally differ from one another far more widely than in the mystical sense: they will all employ a secretive art of communication but on behalf of different doctrines, moved by

different motives and purposes, and employing different esoteric techniques and strategies.

Furthermore, within the subcategory of philosophical esotericism, which is our interest here, there are important differences. The primary source of these differences is to be found in the larger philosophical views just alluded to. For philosophical esotericism, while not a mystical phenomenon, is also not simply a literary or rhetorical one either — not merely a technique employed to deal with an occasional, practical problem (such as persecution). In its several distinct forms, it grows out of the fundamental and abiding philosophical problem of theory and praxis — especially the question of the relation between philosophic rationalism and political community, or between "the two lives": the *vita contemplativa* and the *vita activa*. Are the two fundamentally harmonious (essentially the Enlightenment view) or antagonistic (the dominant classical view)? Clearly, a thinker's position on this philosophical question will largely determine his stance regarding the act of writing — his stance, that is, regarding the true purpose of and the proper rhetorical method for the public communication of philosophical thought.

In writing their books, most thinkers during and after the Enlightenment, for example, were motivated largely by the belief that philosophy, properly communicated, could remake the practical sphere in its own image: it could bring the political world into harmony with reason. And based on this harmonizing motive and assumption, they tended to employ a certain form of esotericism — a relatively loose concealment or dissimulation — for two reasons: partly as a propagandistic rhetoric to aid them in their ambitious projects for political and religious transformation and partly as a defensive expedient to shield them from the persecution that these revolutionary projects would inevitably (but only temporarily) provoke.

Classical and medieval thinkers, by contrast, tended to practice a more concealed, more thoroughgoing esotericism — esotericism in the fullest sense — because they were motivated, not by the hope that philosophic rationalism could enlighten and reform the political world, but by the fear that, to the contrary, rationalism, if openly communicated, would inevitably harm that world by subverting its essential myths and traditions. And, again, they were also motivated by fear of the persecution that this harm would naturally provoke. Their purpose for publishing books of philosophy was rooted not primarily in political schemes, as with the Enlightenment thinkers, but in educational aims. And these aims in turn gave them a further, pedagogical motive for esotericism: a text that presents hints and riddles instead of answers practices the closest literary approximation to the Socratic method—it forces readers to think and discover for themselves.

We may distinguish, then, four primary kinds of philosophical esotericism. To state the point in more analytical fashion, a philosophical writer will purposely endeavor to obscure his or her true meaning either to avoid some evil or to attain some good. The evils to be avoided are essentially two: either some harm that society might do the writer (persecution) or some harm that the writer might do society ("dangerous truths"), or both. The effort to avoid these two dangers gives rise to what I will call *defensive* and *protective* esotericism, respectively.

But of course a still easier way to avoid the dangers of writing would be to avoid the act of writing. If philosophers choose to publish in spite of these considerable dangers, it is for the sake of some good, of which there are primarily two: either the political (cultural, intellectual, religious) reform of society in general or the philosophic education of the rare and gifted individual (or both). And each of these positive aims also turns out to require an artful rhetoric—either propagandistic or educational. From these arise what I will call *political* and *pedagogical* esotericism.

Not only has the *motive* for employing esoteric concealment varied from thinker to thinker, but so also has the basic *form*. A philosopher might write nothing at all, for example, and confine himself entirely to oral teaching, saying one thing in public and another to initiates, as Pythagoras was widely reputed to have done. He might confine his true views to an oral teaching but write books setting forth a salutary public or exoteric doctrine. He might produce two different sets of writings for different audiences, one exoteric, the other esoteric (although, given the easy transmissibility of books, the esoteric writing could not dare to be completely open). Or his writings may contain multiple levels, with an exoteric teaching on the surface and an esoteric one conveyed "between the lines," that is, indirectly, through hints and insinuation.

The primary focus in what follows will be on multilevel writing, which seems to have been the most prevalent form of esotericism. But it is important to keep all these possibilities in mind.[3]

Esotericism also varies widely in *degree*. In some cases, the exoteric doctrine may merely be a popularized or sanitized version of the esoteric doctrine. In others, it will be radically different, even opposite. Again, some esoteric authors will withhold or conceal parts of the truth (as they see it), but say nothing *contrary* to it. They will not tell "the whole truth," but they will tell "nothing but the truth." They will, if you like, be esoteric but not exoteric. Other authors will both conceal the truth and present falsehoods or "noble lies" as if they were true.

Although the particular content, motive, form, and degree of esotericism has thus varied, the existence of esotericism of *some* kind has nevertheless been strikingly constant. Virtually all scholars today are willing to admit that, here and there, a philosopher or two can be found who engaged in esoteric writing. It is almost impossible to avoid such an admission because, as will be seen, there is such widespread evidence in the philosophic tradition for esoteric writing that there is almost no spot where a scholar may dig without eventually unearthing some tattered piece of testimony to this practice. But the typical response to such finds is to declare esotericism a real but rare, strange, and uncharacteristic practice that arises now and then from eccentric circumstances. In this way, we tend to dismiss the practice in the very act of acknowledging it. It is our most common way of denying the real phenomenon.

To repeat, the real phenomenon, the idea that was once well-known and now forgotten, is this: through most of history, philosophical esotericism has *not* been a curious exception—it has been the rule. It has been a near-constant accompaniment of the philosophic life, following it like a shadow. Furthermore, it has had such relative universality precisely because it derives not from occasional or eccentric circumstances but somehow from the inherent and enduring character of philosophy itself in its relationship to the practical world—from the issue of "theory and praxis."

That, at any rate, is the thesis of this work. The question is: Is this a curious myth or a strangely forgotten truth?

HOW TO DEMONSTRATE THE EXISTENCE OF ESOTERICISM

Proving the reality of philosophical esotericism in a manner that will be convincing to most scholars presents a daunting task, and for at least two reasons. First, as a secretive activity, esotericism is obviously resistant, by its very nature, to open and clear disclosure. Most evidence pertaining to it is likely to fall far short of perfect clarity and thus to require, on the part of the investigator, a high degree of sensitivity, judiciousness, and sympathy. But, second, as a secretive activity—as well as an alien, deceptive, and elitist one—it inspires in most people today the very opposite of these necessary sentiments. Thus, it has a particularly hard time getting the fair and sympathetic hearing that it particularly requires.

In view of these difficulties and especially the uncertainty of the evidence, it is clearly necessary to address the issue of esotericism carefully, one philosopher at a time, so that the evidence can be sifted as closely as possible, placed in historical context, and evaluated in dialogue with the secondary literature. Such work has been going on for some time now and is making real if slow progress.[4]

But the one-philosopher-at-a-time approach, while necessary, also has inevitable shortcomings. It needs to be guided as well as supplemented by the opposite method: an effort to display the phenomenon of esotericism as a whole, in its full theoretical and historical sweep. That is what I attempt to do here. For the evidence concerning a particular philosopher will often remain stubbornly ambiguous when examined—no matter how carefully—in the context of that thinker alone. But it can take on new dimensions when linked to similar evidence in other thinkers. There are patterns in the big picture invisible at the level of individual works.[5]

Furthermore, this more synoptic perspective allows one to see how the practice of esotericism has changed over time and, conversely, to see what is enduring and essential in it—its underlying basis and unity. Finally, it is essential to realize that a person's judgment on the question of esotericism is ultimately not a freestanding thing. It is inseparably tied to a larger worldview—to deep assumptions regarding the nature of philosophic truth, political life, and the communication of the one to the other. Thus a persuasive case for esotericism ultimately requires a larger philosophical narrative that is able to address these deep assumptions. It demands something like a Kuhnian paradigm shift.

Thus, in attempting the more global approach, I make use of three primary forms of evidence or argument. First, on the empirical level, I present explicit "testimonial evidence": the hundreds of statements by philosophers from every historical period openly testifying to the use of esoteric writing, either in their own works or in those of others. This massive body of empirical evidence forms the foundation for the rest of the argument.

Second, on the philosophical level, I try to *explain* this surprising evidence: what causes could have led so many philosophers in such different times and places to engage in such strange behavior? I explore the enduring philosophical concerns—the fundamental tensions and contradictions subsisting between thought and life, philosophy and society, theory and praxis—that motivate philosophical esotericism in all its various forms.

But a third level of analysis is necessary owing to that other historical fact from which we began: our *forgetting* of esotericism. This remarkable event is strong evidence for the suggestion, made above, that the modern worldview somehow involves a deep aversion to esotericism that will not easily be dispelled by the facts and explanations presented on the first two levels. Thus it is necessary, on what might be called the "self-knowledge level," to turn our gaze back on ourselves and attempt to identify, address, and overcome the sources of this cultural resistance.

In what follows, chapters 1, 3, and 4 present these three different levels of evidence or argument. (Chapter 2, a short interlude, supplements this effort by providing two brief examples of esoteric writing and reading—to make the phenomenon under discussion a bit more concrete.) Yet these three chapters remain on a somewhat abstract level because, to avoid needless complexity at the beginning, they speak about philosophical esotericism in general, without separating it out into its several distinct varieties. Chapters 5 through 8 descend from this abstract plane to explore the four distinct forms of esotericism—defensive, protective, pedagogical, and political. Here, the description and proof—which combines all three levels of argument—can become more fine-grained and concrete.

Chapters 9 and 10, proceeding on the assumption that some readers will have found these arguments for the reality of esotericism persuasive, go on to draw the consequences. What exactly follows if the tradition of philosophical esotericism is real? Chapter 9 elaborates the *practical* consequence by providing some introductory instruction in the art of esoteric reading. This exercise will also help to give a more concrete picture of esotericism, showing what this practice looks like and how it works.

Chapter 10 turns from the practical to the *philosophical* consequences of the recovery of esotericism. Drawing upon the thought of Leo Strauss, it explores how this rediscovery, if correct, changes the whole philosophical landscape in important ways. In particular, it shows how it makes possible, in Strauss's view, a new defense of reason or philosophic rationalism against the powerful modern forces threatening to undermine it, especially radical historicism.

There is no doubt that this work brings unwelcome news. If it really is true that the strange practice of esotericism was, through most of history, as widespread and important a phenomenon as is claimed here, that will pose a whole new set of problems for scholarship. Still, if it is true, we had better get used to it.

And there is, after all, a bright side to it. A veritable lost continent has been rediscovered in our time. Against all odds, here in our jaded, seen-it-all postmodernist world, suddenly a fresh new frontier lies open before us, a practically untouched field of study where there is much groundbreaking work to be done by those with the ambition to do it. Large issues need to be reopened: the relation of philosophical truth to political life, the purpose of philosophical publication, the role of ideas in history, the true character of philosophical education, the forgotten premises of modern "progress-philosophy," and many other weighty matters. The whole course of Western philosophical thought is not so well-known and settled as we have long thought it to be. Beneath its conventional exterior, it is more daring, original, and alive.

> "Listen; there's a hell of a good universe next door: let's go."
> —E. E. CUMMINGS

PART ONE

The General Evidence and Argument
for the Reality of
Philosophical Esotericism

The Testimonial Evidence for Esotericism

The world is full of obvious things which nobody by any
chance ever observes.
—SHERLOCK HOLMES

If a long and now-forgotten tradition of philosophical esotericism really
did exist in the West, how could we ever prove that? How could we even
know it?

The surest way would be if the philosophers themselves told us. And so
they have. For what is necessarily secret in esotericism is the content of the
hidden doctrine, but not its existence. For a whole variety of reasons, one
philosopher may choose to report on the esoteric practices of another. And
sometimes, less often to be sure, a philosopher may speak of his own esotericism. He might be moved to do so, for example, to explain to those who
would dismiss his text as problematic and contradictory that these defects
are not accidental, or to positively encourage his readers to pay closer attention and find the secret teaching if they can, or to give them some small
guidance regarding how to go about it. Of course, all of this would be visible
to the censors too—but not necessarily in a way that would allow them to
prove anything. Moreover, in certain sophisticated times or indulgent ones,
such an acknowledgment might even be reassuring to the ruling class, being

an open display of the author's deference to their authority and a declaration of his commitment to hide from the impressionable multitude anything that might be misunderstood or corrupting. There is no *necessary* inconsistency in speaking openly about secrecy.

Thus, philosophic testimony to esotericism is definitely possible. The only question is: does it actually exist—beyond some isolated instances? Once one makes up one's mind to go looking for it, it turns out to be surprisingly easy to find. There are hundreds of such statements, stemming from every period and strain of Western thought, testifying to the reality of esotericism.

Since it would be tedious to read a long list of such quotations, I will present here just a brief representative sample running to about thirty passages that roughly cover the span of Western philosophical thought prior to 1800. Many more passages will be found woven into the argument of the chapters to follow. And in an online appendix (available at http://www .press.uchicago.edu/sites/melzer/), I present the full, chronological compilation of the testimony that I have been able to find up to this point. Although certainly not exhaustive, it runs to well over seventy-five pages. Almost every major thinker from Homer to Nietzsche is included, as either the source or the subject of such testimony (or both).

To be sure, quotations of this kind presented with little context will lack the scholarly solidity and persuasive force of more detailed and contextualized presentations. For present purposes, I do not even distinguish among the four different variants of or motives for esoteric writing (although, I do select one example—Aristotle—to discuss in fuller detail). These shortcomings will be remedied (to the extent possible in a synoptic work of this kind) in chapters 5 through 8 with their greater concreteness and specificity.

But for the moment, I rely on the sheer power of numbers. One contextless quotation will lack persuasive power; but if it is followed by another and still another, all making the same general point, the effect becomes cumulative. The effect is also retrospective: the solidity of the whole lends new plausibility to each component part. On a second reading, we are less reluctant to take each passage at face value. Dots can be powerful when connected.

Let us consider the evidence then. Afterward we will press the question of what it does and does not prove.

A SURVEY OF THE TESTIMONIAL EVIDENCE

Perhaps the most obvious way to begin our search for the open acknowledgment of esotericism is to proceed as any schoolchild would: let us look it up in the encyclopedia. That is where one hopes to find, not the possibly idiosyncratic or obscure speculations of some one thinker, but what a larger group, even a given society holds to be general knowledge. Yet, if one looks at contemporary encyclopedias, or even goes back a century, one will not find much or anything about esoteric writing. This is the period of the great forgetting.

But if one goes back to around 1750, to the famous *Encyclopedia* written and edited by Diderot and other leading figures of the French Enlightenment, suddenly the situation is completely different. This influential work, the centerpiece of the Enlightenment, makes mention of esotericism in no less than twenty-eight different articles, by many different authors, including one expressly devoted to the subject and bearing the title "Exoteric and Esoteric." The thesis of this article, from which we have quoted before, is that "the ancient philosophers had a double doctrine; the one external, public or *exoteric*; the other internal, secret or *esoteric*."[1] What is more, the author, one Samuel Formey, appears to see no need—and indeed makes no effort—to marshal evidence for this assertion. He treats it as noncontroversial, a matter of general knowledge—which indeed it was. If one consults, for example, the *Dictionary of the Academy Française*, fifth edition (1798), under the word *exoteric* one finds a brief definition—"exterior, public"—to which is appended a short phrase to help illustrate the use of the term. The phrase chosen is: "The exoteric dogmas of the ancient philosophers."

More evidence of this practice as an item of common knowledge will be seen if we continue to work our way backward in time. In England, about a decade before the *Encyclopedia*, we find a short but perfectly explicit disquisition on esotericism, running to about twenty-five pages, contained within Bishop William Warburton's *Divine Legation of Moses Demonstrated* (1738), a famous critique of Deism. Warburton argues at length that "the ancient Sages did actually say one Thing when they thought another. This appears from that general Practice in the Greek Philosophy, of a two-fold Doctrine; the External and the Internal; a vulgar and a secret."[2] Today it may seem unremarkable that this statement, indeed this lengthy disquisition, appeared in Warburton's book, which has now been forgotten along with its author. Thus, it is important to recall: this book was one of the single most influential and widely read works of the eighteenth century.[3]

About twenty years before that, John Toland, an important English Deist and friend of Locke, published an entire treatise on esotericism. A short work, it bore the lengthy title: *Clidophorus, or, of the Exoteric and Esoteric Philosophy; that is, Of the External and Internal Doctrine of the Ancients: The one open and public, accommodated to popular prejudices and the Religions established by Law; the other private and secret, wherein, to the few capable and discrete, was taught the real Truth stripped of all disguises* (1720). According to Toland, esotericism "was the common practice of all the ancient philosophers."[4]

A bit earlier, in Germany, we find the philosopher Leibniz speaking along the same lines: "The ancients distinguished the 'exoteric' or popular mode of exposition from the 'esoteric' one which is suitable for those who are seriously concerned to discover the truth" (1704).[5]

Earlier still, a similar claim can be found in Pierre Bayle's encyclopedic *Historical and Critical Dictionary* (1695–97). In his article on Aristotle, he states: "the method of the ancient masters [i.e., philosophers] was founded on good reasons. They had dogmas for the general public and dogmas for the disciples initiated into the mysteries."[6]

At about the same time (1692), Thomas Burnet, the English cosmological and theological thinker, much admired by Newton, published his *Archæologiæ philosophicæ*, in which he remarks:

> *It is well known*, that the ancient wise Men and Philosophers, very seldom set forth the naked and open Truth; but exhibited it veiled or painted after various manners; by Symbols, Hieroglyphicks, Allegories, Types, Fables, Parables, popular Discourses, and other Images. This I pass by in general *as sufficiently known*.[7]

Finally, in 1605, Francis Bacon, while using a very different vocabulary, makes essentially the same point. The ancients, he claimed, employed two different manners of writing, the "Enigmatical and Disclosed." "The pretense [of the Enigmatical] is to remove the vulgar capacities from being admitted to the secrets of knowledges, and to reserve them to selected auditors, or wits of such sharpness as can pierce the veil."[8]

In sum, with perfect explicitness, all these early modern writers—spanning three countries and one hundred fifty years—attribute esotericism to virtually *all* ancient philosophers and philosophic poets and seem to regard this fact as well-known. But what was their view of modern philosophers—regarding whom, after all, their testimony might be held to be more reliable? In keeping with a common practice, most of these writers maintain a discreet silence about thinkers closer to their own time. But this silence is broken by John Toland toward the end of *Clidophorus*, his treatise on esotericism: "I have more than once hinted that *the External and Internal Doctrine* are as much now in use as ever." In another work, he repeats that esotericism is "practiced not by the Ancients alone; for to declare the Truth, it is *more* in Use among the Moderns, although they profess it is less allowed."⁹

For example, according to Leibniz:

Descartes took care not to speak so plainly [as Hobbes] but he could not help revealing his opinions in passing, with such address that he would not be understood save by those who examine profoundly these kinds of subjects.¹⁰

Toland's claim about the virtually *universal* use of esotericism among the moderns (as well as the ancients) is supported more broadly by an important letter written by Diderot in 1773, which we will have occasion to quote again. It is addressed to François Hemsterhuis, a minor Dutch author whose book—which apparently employed esoteric restraint to avoid persecution—he had just read:

You are one example among many others where intolerance has constrained the truth and dressed philosophy in a clown suit, so that posterity, struck by their contradictions, of which they don't know the cause, will not know how to discern their true sentiments.

The Eumolpides [Athenian high priests] caused Aristotle to alternately admit and reject final causes.

Here Buffon [the eighteenth-century French naturalist] embraces all the principles of materialists; elsewhere he advances entirely opposite propositions.

And what must one say of Voltaire, who says with Locke that matter can think, with Toland that the world is eternal, with Tindal that freedom is a chimera [i.e., three irreligious theses], but who acknowledges a punishing and rewarding God? Was he inconsistent? Or did he fear the doctor of the Sorbonne [the church]?

Me, I saved myself by the most agile irony that I could find, by generalities, by terseness, and by obscurity.

I know *only one modern author* who spoke clearly and without detours; but he is hardly known.¹¹

In this remarkable letter, Diderot—who stood at the very center of the Enlightenment "republic of letters"—essentially claims that, with the exception of one writer (he means Holbach, who was, among other things, a more or less open atheist and materialist), *all* modern thinkers known to him wrote esoterically—including himself. What is more, with extraordinary prescience, he conjectures that future readers, living in a world in which intolerance and persecution will have been overcome, will no longer understand the cause of the curious contradictions and detours they find in these writers and so "will not know how to discern their true sentiments." In short, he predicts precisely the intellectual "misfortune," the forgetfulness of esotericism, that, by 1811, Goethe had begun to observe, and that today holds us firmly in its grip. A large part of the thesis of the present book is contained in this one letter.

The ubiquity of esotericism in modern as well as ancient times is also described in numerous passages of Condorcet's *Sketch for a Historical Picture of the Progress of the Human Mind* and, as we have already seen, by Rousseau, who speaks of "the distinction between the two doctrines so eagerly received by *all* the Philosophers, and by which they professed in secret sentiments contrary to those they taught publicly." Rousseau also openly acknowledges that he himself wrote esoterically.[12]

Resuming our backward march, we hear Erasmus, the Dutch humanist, declare, in a letter of 1521:

> I know that sometimes it is a good man's duty to conceal the truth, and not to publish it regardless of times and places, before every audience and by every method, and everywhere complete.

In this spirit, he criticizes Martin Luther in another letter for "making everything public and giving even cobblers a share in what is normally handled by scholars as mysteries reserved for the initiated."[13]

Also consider the early Italian humanist and poet Boccaccio who, in his *Life of Dante* (1357), asserts that all great poets write on two levels—for the "little lambs" and the "great elephants." The same narrative passage will present

> the text and the mystery that lies beneath it. Thus, it simultaneously challenges the intellect of the wise while it gives comfort to the minds of the simple. It possesses [i.e., presents] openly something to give children nourishment and yet reserves in secret something to hold with fascinated admiration the minds of the deepest meditators. Therefore, it is like a river, so to speak, both shallow and deep, in which the little lamb may wade with its feet and the great elephant may swim freely.[14]

Moving back to the medieval period, let us briefly survey the big four philosopher/theologians: Thomas Aquinas, Maimonides, Alfarabi, and Augustine. They, again, are very explicit. Aquinas recommends the use of esotericism, arguing (in 1258):

> Certain things can be explained to the wise in private which we should keep silent about in public. . . . Therefore, these matters should be concealed with obscure language, so that they will benefit the wise who understand them and be hidden from the uneducated who are unable to grasp them.[15]

Similarly, Maimonides, writing in the twelfth century, declares:

> These matters [of theology] are only for a few solitary individuals of a very special sort, not for the multitude. For this reason, they should be hidden from the beginner, and he should be prevented from taking them up, just as a small baby is prevented from taking coarse foods and from lifting heavy weights.

Therefore, he openly states in the *Guide of the Perplexed* that in discussing such matters he will not offer anything beyond what he calls "the chapter headings." And, he continues:

> Even those are not set down in order or arranged in coherent fashion in this Treatise, but rather are scattered and entangled with other subjects. . . . For my purpose is that the truths be glimpsed and then again be concealed.[16]

The tenth-century Arabic philosopher Alfarabi states in his commentary on Plato's *Laws*:

> The wise Plato did not feel free to reveal and uncover the sciences for all men. Therefore, he followed the practice of using symbols, riddles, obscurity, and difficulty, so that science would not fall into the hands of those who do not deserve it and be deformed, or into the hands of one who does not know its worth or who uses it improperly. *In this he was right.*[17]

Finally Augustine, who speaks frequently of esotericism, asserts (in 386) that the pure stream of philosophy should be guided through shady and thorny thickets, for the possession of the few, rather than allowed to wander through open spaces where cattle [i.e., the "common herd"] break through, and where it is impossible for it to be kept clear and pure. . . . I think that that method or art of concealing the truth is a useful invention.[18]

Let us turn, last, to Greek and Roman antiquity. We have seen some solid evidence that the awareness and practice of esoteric writing were quite common in the early modern period and in medieval times as well. Thus, there would be nothing odd if the ancients were also esoteric. Indeed, it would be surprising if they were exceptions to this very broad trend. Furthermore, we have heard the testimony of a wide range of both modern and medieval thinkers expressing their considered view that virtually all of the ancient philosophers wrote esoterically, that the classical world was in fact the true home and original model of philosophical esotericism. Still, the open acknowledgment by philosophers of their own esotericism was less common in the ancient world than it became in medieval and modern times. In view of this fact, as well as the central importance of the classics in the history of esotericism, it will help to proceed a bit more slowly through the big three: Cicero, Plato, and especially Aristotle, to whom I will devote a separate section.

In *De natura deorum*, Cicero explicitly acknowledges and defends (on pedagogical grounds) his unwillingness to state his philosophical opinions openly. The same point is made in his *Tusculan Disputations*, where he relates this behavior to that of Socrates. Among the many warring philosophical sects, he states:

> I have chosen particularly to follow that one [the New Academy] which I think agreeable to the practice of Socrates, in trying to conceal my own private opinion [and] to relieve others from deception.[19]

Indeed, in his dialogues *De finibus* and *The Laws*, Cicero presents himself as a proponent of Stoicism and takes on the role of defending it, even though, as we know from other writings, he was actually an adherent of the New Academy—which rejected Stoicism.

Along these same lines, Augustine argues that Cicero was a nonbeliever and sought to convey that view.

> That, however, he did not do in his own person, for he saw how odious and offensive such an opinion would be; and, therefore in his book on the

nature of the gods [*De natura deorum*], he makes Cotta [defend this view] against the Stoics, and preferred to give his own opinion in favor of Lucilius Balbus, to whom he assigned the defense of the Stoical position, rather than in favor of Cotta, who maintained that no divinity exists.[20]

Diderot agrees (as does Rousseau) in seeing Cicero as a particularly transparent esotericist, especially in matters of religion (although he would seem to exaggerate the obviousness of Cicero's atheism here):

[Cicero's] books *On Divination* are merely irreligious treatises. But what an impression must have been made on the people by certain pieces of oratory in which the gods were constantly invoked . . .where the very existence of the pagan deities was presupposed by orators who had written a host of philosophical essays treating the gods and religion as mere fables![21]

Not only in Cicero, but in almost all classical thinkers the case for esotericism is clearest—indeed, almost impossible to deny—with respect to religion, for in the ancient, pagan world, the gulf between philosophy and the prevailing religion was obviously far greater than in the Christian world. Consider Gibbon's view of the whole matter, which is fairly typical:

How, indeed, was it possible that a philosopher should accept, as divine truths, the idle tales of the poets, and the incoherent traditions of antiquity; or, that he should adore as gods, those imperfect beings whom he must have despised as men?

Not only were the superstitious roots of the reigning religion more obvious at that time but so was its political use and function. Therefore, Gibbon continues:

The various modes of worship, which prevailed in the Roman world, were all considered by the people as equally true; by the philosopher as equally false; and by the magistrate as equally useful.

But of course the philosophers—like the magistrates—did not openly display their skepticism. Rather:

Viewing, with a smile of pity and indulgence, the various errors of the vulgar, they diligently practiced the ceremonies of their fathers, devoutly fre-

quented the temples of the gods; and sometimes condescending to act a
part on the theatre of superstition, they concealed the sentiments of an
Atheist under the sacerdotal robes.[22]

And if we look ourselves, we do seem to find that the classical philosophers
constantly contradict themselves on the subject of religion, sometimes supporting the official gods, superstitions, and rituals of the city, sometimes suggesting piecemeal reforms, sometimes speaking of an abstract metaphysical
god, and sometimes hinting at a still more extreme skepticism.[23]

Turning to Plato, we note that the writings we possess consist of the dialogues and some letters of uncertain authenticity, his lectures or treatises
having been lost. But in his dialogues, unlike Cicero's, Plato is never a speaking character, so it is only in the letters that we may possibly find a first-
person account of how Plato writes. On the other hand, actions often speak
louder than words, and the simple fact that, in almost all the dialogues, Plato
has chosen Socrates for his main spokesman surely tells us something about
his taste in the matter of communication. In the *Republic* (337a), Socrates's
communicative habits are described by Thrasymachus:

> Here is that habitual irony of Socrates. I knew it, and I predicted to these
> fellows that you wouldn't be willing to answer, that you would be ironic and
> do anything rather than answer if someone asked you something.[24]

Socrates is famous for his irony—just as Plato is famous for his dialogues.
Perhaps Plato (and Xenophon) developed the dialogue form as (among
other things) a means of carrying on, in the medium of writing, their master's notoriously elusive manner of speaking. That, at least, was the conclusion reached by Augustine:

> For, as Plato liked and constantly affected the well-known method of his
> master Socrates, namely, that of dissimulating his knowledge or his opinions,
> it is not easy to discover clearly what he himself thought on various matters,
> any more than it is to discover what were the real opinions of Socrates.[25]

Many others have formed a similar impression. Nietzsche speaks of Plato's
"secrecy and sphinx nature."[26] Montaigne points out the obvious fact that

> [s]ome have considered Plato a dogmatist, others a doubter. . . . From Plato
> arose ten different sects, they say. And indeed, in my opinion, never was a
> teaching wavering and noncommittal if his is not.[27]

Finally, there is the well-known passage in Aristotle's *Physics* (209b) where he alludes in passing to Plato's "unwritten doctrines."

With all of this as introduction, let us turn to the vexed issue of Plato's letters. There, it turns out that we find openly stated by Plato—and more than once—the same view we have just been discussing. There are several passages in the Seventh Letter and again several in the Second Letter explicitly claiming that he purposely avoided an open disclosure of his deepest thought as something that would be harmful to most people (to "the many"). But, as he implies in a famous statement from the Seventh Letter, he did leave "small indications" for the "few" for whom such hints would be sufficient as well as beneficial. Here is the crucial passage:

> If it seemed to me that these [philosophical] matters could adequately be put down in writing *for the many* or be said, what could be nobler for us to have done in our lifetime than this, to write what is a great benefit for human beings and to lead nature forth into the light for all? But I do not think such an undertaking concerning these matters would be a good for human beings, unless for some *few*, those who are themselves able to *discover them through a small indication*; of the rest, it would unsuitably fill some of them with a mistaken contempt, and others with lofty and empty hope as if they had learned awesome matters.[28]

There is no solid consensus—because little solid evidence—concerning the authenticity of the letters, although the seventh is widely seen as the strongest candidate. It would be dogmatic to simply accept them as real—or to simply dismiss them.

Amid this uncertainty, one way of proceeding is to consider that this letter may be a faithful or knowledgeable account of Plato's views regardless of who wrote it. In particular, the crucial passage above takes the form, not of a bald assertion, but of a reasoned argument. And each stage of the argument can be seen to be based upon premises well attested in the dialogues. Only the conclusion takes us into new territory. Yet it does so only by showing that these familiar Platonic theses, when connected together and thought through logically, point to this previously unstated conclusion—to the use of esoteric communication—as an almost inevitable consequence.[29]

The passage begins, for example, with the classic Platonic view that philosophic knowledge is the supreme good of life and that helping others to acquire it is, where possible, an act of the highest beneficence. But the inevitable consequence of locating the human good in something so lofty and difficult, indeed almost superhuman, is that it will be far beyond the reach of most people. It thus leads directly to the very stark distinction, employed in this passage and familiar from the dialogues, between the "many" and the philosophic "few"—as described, for example, in the famous cave analogy of the *Republic*. As it is put in the *Timaeus* (28c) (echoes of which one hears in the above passage):

> To discover the maker and father of this universe were a task indeed; and having discovered him, to declare him unto all men were a thing impossible.

But the passage goes on to point out that philosophy is not only impossible for most people but also positively harmful and corrupting to them, producing a misplaced contempt in some, an unwarranted arrogance in others. And this idea too—the danger of knowledge in the wrong hands—is a recognizable Platonic theme. It is a crucial element, for example, in his critique of sophistry. As Socrates states in the *Republic*:

> When men *unworthy of education* come near her and keep her company in an unworthy way, what sorts of notions and opinions will we say they beget? Won't they be truly fit to be called sophisms? (496a, emphasis added)

And therefore:

> "Don't you notice," I said, "how great is the harm coming from the practice of dialectic these days?" . . . "Surely its students . . . are filled full with lawlessness." (537e)

Furthermore, in Plato's view, this harm and corruption cannot be left unaddressed. Plato famously argues—most memorably in his critique of the poets in the *Republic*—that to avoid the danger of corruption there must be *censorship*, including, in the best case, self-censorship.[30] And as presented in the passage above, it is precisely such reasoning that caused Plato to censor his own compositions, to refrain from all attempt to "put down in writing for the many" the wondrous things that he knew. This is the passage's crucial conclusion, which does go beyond anything openly stated in the dialogues—but which does seem to follow with strict necessity from premises that are clearly stated there.

Further evidence for this conclusion can be seen in the aspect of the dialogues from which we began. While they never openly address Plato's own

manner of communicating, they constantly call our attention to Socrates's—
he is depicted as the greatest of self-censorers. Think about it: not only is this
great ironist unwilling to talk straight, but he is unwilling to write at all. In
the dialogues, Socrates never openly explains the first of these famous facts
about himself, but in the *Phaedrus* (275d–e) he does say why he opposes and
avoids writing. And his explanation is essentially the same as the one given
in the above passage: a written text is too univocal, it says the same things to
all people whether they can understand and appreciate it or whether they
would be corrupted by it.

Yet this confirmation of the passage's central argument points to an obvious puzzle. Socrates duly refrained from writing, but Plato did not. If we
follow the above reasoning, this would make sense only if Plato felt that he
had overcome the problem of the univocity of writing by finding a form of
composition that spoke differently to different people. And that is precisely
what is suggested in the above passage when "Plato" implies that commit-
ting his deepest thoughts to writing—which he clearly longs to do—would
be permissible and beneficial if these writings were fully understandable
only to "some few" who might catch on through a "small indication." This is
clearly the view of Plato's writing held by Alfarabi. Plato, he writes,

> resorted to allegories and riddles. He intended thereby to put in writing his
> knowledge and wisdom according to an approach that would let them be
> known only to the deserving.[31]

Diogenes Laertius came to a similar conclusion: "Plato has employed a
variety of terms in order to make his system less intelligible to the ignorant."[32]

But as strictly logical as all of this might be, someone still might ask—as
certain scholars have—whether such esoteric practices were really something that Plato could have conceived in his time. Aren't we just reading
later, Neoplatonist concepts and practices back into his mind?[33]

The answer to this question admits of no uncertainty. In several of the
dialogues, both Socrates and Protagoras explicitly speak of an earlier tradition of esoteric writing, attributing it to Homer, Hesiod, and several other
poets: these writers used the mythical form, they claim, to express their
Heraclitean philosophical opinions in a hidden way for the sake of the few.
It is, as Socrates explains in the *Theaetetus*, "a tradition from the ancients who
hid their meaning from the common herd in poetical figures."[34] Again, Socrates says something similar of Protagoras himself:

Can it be, then, that Protagoras was a very ingenious person who threw out this dark saying for the benefit of the common herd like ourselves, and reserved the truth as a secret doctrine to be revealed to his disciples?

The answer to this rhetorical question is clearly "yes," in Socrates's view, as becomes clear a few pages later when he promises to help Theaetetus to "penetrate to the truth concealed in the thoughts" of Protagoras.[35] Again, in the *Laws* (967a–d), the Athenian Stranger asserts that most of the pre-Socratic philosophers were actually atheists—although they all certainly claimed to be believers of some kind. It is certain, then, that Plato was well acquainted with various forms of esotericism.[36]

Furthermore, he expresses no disapproval of the practice. On the contrary, the author of the infamous term "noble lie" obviously believed in the moral propriety of socially salutary fictions. And the author of the *Apology* was obviously very much preoccupied by the great danger of persecution that philosophers typically face. There is no good reason to insist, therefore, that Plato would have stopped short of the logical conclusion of his strongly held beliefs.

At a minimum, it seems fair to say that the above passage of the Seventh Letter—*regardless* of who wrote it—makes a cogent argument to the effect that various well-attested Platonic views, when thought through together, point directly to esotericism, a practice clearly well-known and acceptable to Plato. But on this basis one might also hazard a further step, for if this minimalist position is true, that also significantly strengthens the case for the maximal one—for the genuine Platonic provenance of the letter—since the main obstacle to its acceptance has always been the putative implausibility of its content.[37]

THE CREDIBILITY OF THIS EVIDENCE

I have presented here only a small sample of the perfectly explicit statements that can be found attesting to the use of philosophical esotericism. It is important be clear about what this evidence proves and does not prove. Certainly, nothing has been established definitively and beyond question. But many readers, I imagine, will feel reluctant to grant this evidence much credence. Let us interrogate these feelings by examining what misgivings one might reasonably have about the evidence—and what replies can be made.

First and most obviously: these are just bare quotations. There could be

significant problems of translation, authenticity, context, and interpretation.

That is all true enough (although, to be fair, most of the statements are
rather short, clear, and straightforward). But where there is so much smoke,
it becomes increasingly questionable to claim that there is no fire. Indeed,
in the full compilation, the numbers are sufficiently large so that even if a
scrupulous analysis led one to eliminate—to take an extreme case—fully
half the testimony owing to problems of translation, context, and the like,
still the remaining evidence would be more than sufficient to show that esotericism was a very real, widely practiced, and frequently discussed phenomenon.

To this one might reply that the sheer quantity of evidence cannot completely settle the issue. Also crucial is distribution. If the testimony, great as
it is, primarily derives from a few atypical places, like the late empire period
with its mystical tendencies or sixteenth-century Europe with the increased
persecution accompanying the Protestant Reformation, then the results
would not be generalizable.

But the facts quickly dismiss this concern. The single most striking thing
about the testimonial evidence is in fact not its quantity but its universality:
it just shows up everywhere. It is there in fifth-century Athens and first-
century Rome, in fourth-century Hippo (Algeria), twelfth-century Cor-
doba, thirteenth-century Paris, sixteenth-century Florence, seventeenth-
century Amsterdam, and eighteenth-century London; it is there among the
pagans, the Jews, the Christians, and the Muslims; it is found with the Platonists and the Aristotelians, the Stoics and the Epicureans, the nominalists
and the realists, the mystics and the materialists. It is in fact difficult to name
a single major philosopher from any time or place before 1800 who did *not*
somewhere make open and approving reference to this practice, regarding
either his own writings or those of others (or both).

Another obvious misgiving one might have is that much of the testimony
is in the "third person": it involves one philosopher reporting on the esotericism of another. In such cases, the reporter can always be mistaken.

That is surely true, but once again one must consider both the large quantity and wide distribution of such reports. Why do so many philosophers in
so many different circumstances all agree in attributing this particular practice to other philosophers? This is the phenomenon one must explain—or
explain away—if one wishes to overturn the testimony.

The most common candidate, indeed virtually the only one, for such an

e claim that esotericism is a "legend." The whole idea of
tericism, the argument goes, was thought up in some par-
)lace where it became the accepted view. In the classic ver-
der Grant, for example:

he later empire, who were accustomed to the idea of mystical and hierophantic teachings, as professed by the neo-Platonic and
neo-Pythagorean sects . . . created the fable that Aristotle had a double
doctrine.[38]

As time passed, this view became an authoritative tradition. Philosophers in
later and very different intellectual climates continued to repeat its claims
because they accepted the authority of that longstanding tradition whose
questionable origins and evidentiary basis had long been forgotten. That is
why there now exists this large but mistaken body of third-person testimony
to esotericism. As George Boas states, esotericism is "just another legend
dating from the time when superstition was taking the place of reason."[39]

But there are a number of problems with this argument, any one of which
would suffice to refute it. First, the testimony to esotericism long predates
Neoplatonism. Second, most of the testimony we have that postdates it concerns forms of esotericism that have nothing to do with mystical, Neoplatonist themes. When, in the letter quoted above, Diderot attributes esotericism to Aristotle, he is imputing to him not a mystical esoteric doctrine but
something closer to a materialistic one — disbelief in final causes (something
that Hobbes too suspects him of), which, they think, Aristotle has hidden
primarily to appease the religious authorities of his time. Whether correct or
incorrect, how could this suspicion derive from reliance on early medieval
legends of Aristotelian mysticism? In fact, virtually none of the testimony
quoted in this chapter thus far is about mystically motivated esotericism.
It all concerns the four motives discussed above — defensive, protective,
pedagogical, and political (none of which Grant et al. ever acknowledge or
evaluate).[40]

Third, not all the testimony to esotericism is of the third-person kind.
There are many first-person cases, where philosophers openly acknowledge
their own esotericism — such as Rousseau, Diderot, Erasmus, Aquinas, Maimonides, Cicero, Lucretius, Plato (if the Seventh Letter is authentic), and
others. Indeed, there are enough such cases to establish on this basis alone
the reality and pervasiveness of esotericism — and thereby also to demonstrate that the third-person report of it is trustworthy and no mere legend.

Furthermore, concerning the testimony that is third person, it is implausible to attribute to all these philosophers a blind adherence to ancient legends on a question like this. After all, that is not how the scholars who promote the "legend" theory themselves reason. Here, for example, is what Eduard Zeller, the celebrated German classicist and philosopher, says in his critique of Aristotelian esotericism:

> The idea that [Aristotle] designedly chose for [his theoretical works] a style obscure and unintelligible to the lay mind is disproved by the visible characteristics of the texts themselves. . . . Besides it is obvious that any such theory attributes to the philosopher a very childish sort of mystification, wholly destitute of any reasonable motive.[41]

Zeller states that he relied on two things for his own assessment of the plausibility of classical esotericism: first, his own reading of the philosophical texts, and, second, his general understanding of what a philosopher is, what esotericism is, and whether there could be any reasonable motive for philosophers to engage in such behavior. This method is only commonsense. And I submit that the many philosophers testifying to earlier esotericism were probably no less sensible.

Such thinkers as Bacon, Bayle, Leibniz, Diderot, and Rousseau were not mindlessly repeating some legend inherited from medieval times about the books sitting before them. They opened those books and studied them for themselves. And when they declared them esoteric with such confidence, that is because they actually *found* them esoteric. They saw for themselves, that is, the manifest problems and puzzles on the surface of the text. They experienced for themselves the real progress one could make in slowly resolving those problems if one allowed the supposition that the author might sometimes be employing irony and indirection. Esotericism, for these thinkers, was not a "legend": it was a personal literary experience.

But why, one might ask, did these thinkers have these interpretive experiences of earlier philosophical texts when later readers like Zeller and Grant did not? The most likely answer is that, as Zeller himself emphasizes in the second part of his statement, later readers regarded esotericism as a "very childish sort of mystification" that was "wholly destitute of any reasonable motive." Similarly, Grant was repelled by "all the nonsense about [Aristotle's] double doctrine."[42] Ingemar During regarded ancient testimony to esotericism as so much "pretentious nonsense."[43] Under the influence of a late-Enlightenment view of philosophy and its role in the world and also a narrow, primarily mystical understanding of esotericism, these thinkers could not really take the idea of philosophical esotericism seriously. If the text they were reading happened to be esoteric, they would be the last to know it.

By contrast, the long line of earlier philosophers who gave their third-person testimony to esotericism seem to have had a broader and more representative understanding of both philosophy and esotericism such that philosophical esotericism struck them as something sensible if not indeed necessary. After all, as we know from the first-person testimony, many of them chose to practice esotericism themselves. It was thus something the value of which—and the concrete workings of which—they understood on their own and from the inside, not from ancient legends. Thus, third-person philosophical testimony to esotericism, while obviously less reliable than first-person confessions, is not to be dismissed as the product of legends or of external guesswork. It is powerful evidence from a genuinely privileged source—especially when there is a large consensus.

What further reasonable objections could be raised against the testimonial evidence for esotericism? There are, to be sure, no absolute certainties here—but that was never to be expected. The issue has always been: is the evidence for esotericism stronger than the evidence against it?

So let us now address the other half: what is the pre-1800 philosophical testimony *against* esotericism? Which philosophers constitute the "other camp"? Who are the Grants and Zellers of earlier ages seeking to rescue philosophy from this tiresome legend they find repeated all around them? Strangely, that is a question that is never posed. But the answer is: there is no such other camp, and with one or two exceptions, there is no counter-evidence. All of the voluminous philosophical testimony to the existence of esotericism throughout history, which we have been sampling, stands more or less uncontradicted.

The one major exception I have found is Adam Smith, who, around 1750, in an essay entitled *The History of the Ancient Logics and Metaphysics*, angrily denounces the Neoplatonist claim that Plato's true, esoteric teaching concerning the Ideas was that they are not self-subsistent beings after all but rather thoughts in the Divine Mind. And in this context he goes on to criticize

that strange fancy that, in his [Plato's] writings, there was a double doctrine; and that they were intended to seem to mean one thing, while at bottom they meant a very different, which the writings of no man in his senses ever were, or ever could be intended to do.[44]

This striking statement—occurring in a footnote to a short essay of his youth which he never published—is the only mention Smith ever makes of the subject. Thus, it is difficult to say whether this continued to be his view in his later years and also whether it involves a rejection of all esotericism—of every kind and degree—or only the more extreme forms found in the Neoplatonists and their followers.[45] Whatever the case, this brief statement—so far as I am aware—constitutes the whole of the "other side" in this debate.

That is a bit surprising. It is not as if, throughout history, esotericism has not been discussed and debated. One finds plenty of heated disputes on the subject. There are disagreements (for example, between Toland and Warburton, along with their followers) about what has been the primary motive throughout history causing thinkers to write esoterically. There are disputes about the proper technique for interpreting a given esoteric writer and thus also about the true content of his esoteric teaching (as with the nearly universal indignation aroused by the Neoplatonists and their mystical esoteric readings). There are debates about whether esoteric writers merely conceal the truth or tell outright lies (as we will soon see among the Aristotle commentators). Not infrequently, certain esoteric writers will criticize others of their kind for being too open or, conversely, too timid. But there is no evidence of dispute over the *historical reality* of esotericism.[46]

To be sure, there may well be such thinkers and I have just not yet come across their writings, or these writings may have been lost. Nevertheless, if such thinkers of any significant weight and number existed, surely some sign of it would already have shown up in the myriad writings that we do have on the positive side of the issue: some reference to these naysayers, to the "other side," and some considered effort to prove them wrong. But, as best I can tell, no such discussions exist either. Books defending the existence of esotericism against its deniers, like those denying it, are a genre unique to our age.

In sum, the testimonial evidence for esotericism—these bare quotations—turns out to be far more solid than one might initially be inclined to think. The reasonable objections that can be raised against it can all be easily rebutted. Three striking features make the testimony peculiarly powerful: it is massive in extent, universal in distribution, and virtually uncontradicted.

ARISTOTLE, THE "CUTTLEFISH"

After so quick a run through two millennia of Western philosophy, it would obviously be desirable, if not obligatory, to pick at least one thinker for a sustained examination. For a variety of reasons, the best candidate for this illustrative exercise is Aristotle.

First, he is, I think, the hardest case, the (pre-1800) thinker least likely to be esoteric. There are philosophers whom one can at least picture engaging in this practice. Maimonides, for example, is so open about his esotericism and so obscure in other ways—so generally "medieval"—that people incline to think that anything is possible with him. But Plato's writings too are so manifestly playful, poetic, and puzzling that scholars have found it difficult to entirely rule out the possibility of esotericism.[47] Aristotle is altogether different. He seems to be so straight and literal-minded, so intent on avoiding all misunderstanding, so eager to be clear, precise, and methodical at all times—as if writing for a contemporary philosophy journal—that claims of his esotericism seem utterly absurd.[48] Being the hardest case, he is also the test case. One feels that if Aristotle, of all thinkers, was esoteric—well, then anyone can be.

On the other hand, Aristotle is also the philosopher with the single largest "secondary literature." Beginning in ancient times, there has been a long, largely unbroken tradition of commentary on his writings. And up through the early modern period, a near-constant feature of this tradition has been talk of his esotericism. So with Aristotle there is broader evidence and testimony to explore than with any other thinker.

Finally, the combination of these two factors has made modern Aristotle scholarship unique in ways that are crucial to our investigation. Owing to the second factor, modern scholars found that with Aristotle, unlike other thinkers, it was impossible to simply ignore or "forget" the issue of esotericism. The historical testimony was just too explicit, widespread, and long-standing. But owing to the first factor, they also found it impossible to accept this testimony. Thus, for a brief but crucial period starting in the nineteenth century and continuing into part of the twentieth, classical scholars of the first rank felt compelled to devote fierce and sustained attention to the otherwise-neglected issue of esotericism. They sought to apply all the tools of modern philology to the task of dismissing esotericism, once and for all, as a foolish legend. In short, with Aristotle, we have the best and almost the only opportunity to witness an elaborate prosecution of the missing side—the case against esotericism—conducted at the highest levels of scholarship.⁴⁹

For all these reasons, Aristotle is the standout candidate for careful analysis. Having, to this point, conducted a breezy, high-altitude survey of the philosophical landscape, we descend, for the length of this section, to a slow and punctilious crawl. As before, but at greater length, we will focus on the historical testimony to Aristotle's esotericism. But in addition we will examine the scholarly critique of that testimony. Last, through a brief look at some of Aristotle's writings, we will try to reach a final verdict on the historical testimony and the scholarly critique of it.

The "Exoteric" vs. the "Acroamatic" Writings of Aristotle

Prior to the nineteenth century, as I have said, there was incessant talk of Aristotle's esotericism. Indeed, since ancient times, he was seen, not as the hardest case, but as the classic case. In the second century AD, for example, he was so well-known for his esoteric doubleness that this trait is identified as one of his most distinctive characteristics by the Greek satirist Lucian (117–c. 180 AD). In his comic dialogue *The Sale of Lives*, Lucian depicts a slave auction of philosophers arranged by Zeus, with Hermes as the auctioneer. We pick up the action after the sale of Pythagoras, Diogenes, Heraclitus, and some others.

> ZEUS: Don't delay; call another, the Peripatetic.
> HERMES: . . . Come now, buy the height of intelligence, the one who knows absolutely everything!
> BUYER: What is he like?
> HERMES: Moderate, gentlemanly, adaptable in his way of living, and, what is more, he is double.
> BUYER: What do you mean?
> HERMES: Viewed from the outside, he seems to be one man, and from the inside, another; so if you buy him, be sure to call the one self "exoteric" and the other "esoteric."⁵⁰

The initial source and ground of all this emphasis on Aristotle's esotericism is the once famous and still undeniable fact that on nine distinct occasions in the extant writings, he refers in passing to "the exoteric discourses" (*exoterikoi logoi*).⁵¹ In the *Nicomachean Ethics*, for example, he says:

But some points concerning the soul are stated sufficiently even in the exoteric arguments, and one ought to make use of them—for example, that one
part of it is nonrational, another possesses reason. (1102a26)[52]

Again, in the *Eudemian Ethics*, in the context of a brief discussion of Plato's
doctrine of the ideas and his objections to it, Aristotle remarks:

the question has already received manifold consideration both in exoteric
and in philosophical discussions. (1217b20)[53]

A massive scholarly literature has grown up to interpret these nine brief
passages—but without ever reaching a clear consensus. The reason would
seem to be that Aristotle does not use the term "exoteric" (literally, "external," "outside") with the precision or specificity that we are looking for and
that it later came to possess. In some cases (most clearly *Politics* 1323a22), he
is clearly referring to certain of his own writings that are of a more popular,
subphilosophic character. But in other cases (see especially *Physics* 217b31)
Aristotle seems to be referring to writings of this kind produced by other
thinkers and perhaps even to the informal theories and thoughtful discussions of educated men at large. In most of the remaining cases, it is impossible to say with certainty which of these he meant. Thus, as Grant emphasizes, the only solid generalization that can be made about this infamous
term is that, in Aristotle, "exoteric" refers to a simplified, popular, subphilosophic account of some kind, given by someone.[54] Thus, on this understanding, an exoteric account is not necessarily false or fictional or defined against
something "esoteric" in the sense of secret or concealed—although it can be.
And by itself, the term tells us virtually nothing about the character or systematic divisions of Aristotle's writings.

But looking beyond these passages that have stolen so much scholarly
attention, we can find more fruitful ground. For virtually everyone agrees,
based on much other evidence, that Aristotle's corpus (putting aside the letters, poems, and collections) was indeed divided into two broad categories
of writings: a set of earlier, popular works, addressed to a wide audience (the
now-lost dialogues and perhaps some other writings) and the more exacting, strictly philosophical works, addressed to the Lyceum's inner circle and
probably composed, originally, in connection with oral presentation there,
which includes virtually all the works we now possess. And the names for
these two categories of writings—at least according to later, ancient think-

ers and editors—were, respectively, "exoteric" and "acroamatic" or "acroatic" (literally, "designed for hearing only").[55]

I would suggest that it is possible to further refine this distinction as follows. It seems that the category of "acroamatic" is susceptible of degree, that some works in this grouping are more acroamatic than others. Some works—like the *Ethics* and *Politics*—were beyond the reach of popular audiences only through their more advanced and exacting philosophical method, but others—like the *Metaphysics* and *Categories*—transcended the popular level also through the abstruseness of their very subject matter. Indeed, we can see for ourselves that the latter two works clearly address a more specialized audience than the well-educated citizenry addressed in the former two, although all alike fall within the acroamatic category. Further evidence for this distinction can be seen in the fact that, so far as we know, Aristotle devoted few if any dialogues or other exoteric writings to these more abstruse subjects (the main exception being the dialogue *On Philosophy*). But concerning subjects of broader concern—ethics, politics, and rhetoric, for example—he produced extensive exoteric as well as acroamatic treatments.[56]

Two Distinct Forms of Esotericism

All of this is relatively noncontroversial. The critical questions concern both the relation between these two broad categories of works and their internal character. On the most general level, the question is this. Should these works be understood—as modern scholars insist—on the model familiar to us from contemporary thinkers who have written both popular and technical works? Then there would be no question of esotericism—no issue of intentional concealment or secret communication or noble lies. On this view, the two sets of writings would present the same essential doctrine, only the one in a more elementary and popular way, appropriate for beginners or laymen, the other in a precise and scientific manner, suitable for more advanced and dedicated students. Or, alternatively, should the character and relation of these works be understood in terms of esoteric motives and techniques? But here things become a bit complex. There are two distinct forms of esotericism that Aristotle may be employing here, so this general question needs to be resolved into two subquestions (which themselves will have subparts). Much misinterpretation of the historical record has arisen from the failure to make this distinction.

First, do the two different categories of works present, not two versions of the same doctrine, one elementary, the other advanced, but rather—to begin with the extreme case—two altogether different doctrines, one false and the other true: an exoteric teaching for the benefit of popular audiences, which makes crucial concessions to political needs and prevailing prejudices, and an acroamatic one reserved for the philosophic reader, which resolutely rejects every such concession? This first kind of esotericism, however, can also take a less extreme form, in which the exoteric doctrine is different from the acroamatic but only by being incomplete, not positively deceptive: it leaves out or conceals certain ultimate truths deemed harmful to most, but it does not propagate an alternative, mythical doctrine.

Second, one must also raise a question about the internal character of each group of writings, regardless of the relation between them. Even if the teaching of the two sets of writings is fundamentally the same (or if there is only one set), one still needs to ask whether, within each set, that teaching is presented openly or hidden between the lines. Similarly, if the two sets of writings present different teachings, the same question needs to be raised. Do the acroamatic writings, which contain the true philosophic teaching, present that teaching right on the surface or only beneath it? And conversely, do the exoteric writings wholly confine themselves to the exoteric teaching or do even these more popular works also contain something between the lines that would point the careful reader in the direction of the philosophic teaching?

In other words, there are two entirely distinct ways in which a writer may contrive to speak differently to different audiences: either by giving each audience its own separate set of works (although, over the long run, it is nearly impossible to maintain this separation) or by conveying, within the same work, one teaching on the surface and the other beneath it—multilevel writing. Teachings can be separated either by work or by level. In exploring Aristotle's manner of communication, we need to ask about both techniques, as well as the—not unlikely—possibility that he combines the two (given the inherent difficulties of the first technique).

In what follows, I will argue for the latter possibility, that Aristotle puts forward two distinct teachings, separated by both level and work. The testimonial evidence from the ancient commentators, we will see, is virtually unanimous and uncontradicted in depicting Aristotle as a multilevel writer. It is divided, however, on the question of whether Aristotle assigned distinct teachings to the two sets of works. Yet that question can be answered in the affirmative, I will argue, by consulting the evidence of the texts themselves.

The Earliest Testimony concerning These Questions

One thing making it difficult to answer these questions is that we do not possess any of the exoteric works, but know of them only by report. On the other hand, we are aided by the existence of a huge ancient and medieval literature of commentary on Aristotle. Just the ancient Greek commentaries alone run to over fifteen thousand pages. Yet two problems threaten to undermine their usefulness. They disagree regarding at least one of our questions. And, as modern scholars emphasize, most of them were influenced by neo-Pythagoreanism, Neoplatonism, and other mystical tendencies in the later empire period, which may have significantly biased their views on these questions. We need to consult this voluminous evidence, then—but with caution.

The first clear statement on these issues that has come down to us is found in Plutarch (46–120 AD) and seconded, several decades later, by Aulus Gellius (c. 125–after 180 AD)—both of whom are relying, as the latter indicates, on Andronicus of Rhodes (c. 60 BC), a philosopher and the authoritative ancient editor of Aristotle's works.[57] Plutarch claims that the second, less popular category of Aristotle's writings concerns the "secret [*aporrata*, not to be spoken] and deeper things, which men call by the special term acroamatic and epoptic and do not expose for the many to share."[58] (He is especially speaking here of what I've called the "more acroamatic" writings on nature and logic.) He continues that when Alexander the Great, Aristotle's former pupil, heard that his teacher had decided to publish some of the acroamatic discourses, he wrote to him in protest. Aristotle then replied in the following letter, which is featured in Andronicus's edition of his writings, and which Plutarch carefully describes and Gellius quotes in full:

> Aristotle to King Alexander, prosperity. You have written me about the acroatic discourses, thinking that they should be guarded in secrecy. Know, then, that they have been both published and not published. For they are intelligible only to those who have heard us.[59]

The authenticity of this letter is doubtful. But regardless of who wrote it (During conjectures that it was Andronicus himself), it may well present an informed account of the character of Aristotle's writings. What we do know is that a thinker and historian of the stature of Plutarch finds the *content* of the letter accurate in light of his own personal reading of Aristotle. For, as he goes on to explain:

To say the truth, his books on metaphysics are written in a style which makes them useless for ordinary teaching, and instructive only, in the way of memoranda, for those who have been already conversant in that sort of learning.[60]

These statements directly address—if only partially—our two questions. Regarding the first, Plutarch and Gellius (and probably Andronicus, their source) clearly embrace the view that the distinction between Aristotle's exoteric and acroamatic writings is not simply reducible to elementary vs. advanced, as our scholars claim. It obviously involves something esoteric: a firm desire to conceal from most people certain of his deepest views (by excluding these views from the exoteric works), while also revealing them to others (by including them in his distinct, acroamatic works).

But Plutarch et al. also clearly affirm that Aristotle employs the second, multilevel form of esotericism as well—in answer to our second question. While the "secret and deeper things" are contained only in the separate, acroamatic writings, even there they are not presented openly but secreted behind a veil of artful obscurity. The acroamatic works are both "published and not published": they are multilevel writings that speak to some people and not to others.[61]

Let us momentarily put aside the first question (concerning the two sets of works), since it is the more complicated, and continue to explore the ancient testimony regarding the second question, as well as the critique of that testimony by modern scholars.

The Evidence concerning the Second Question: Is Aristotle a Multilevel Writer?

Several scholars, seeking to impeach this earliest testimony to Aristotle's esotericism, have attributed it to the influence on Plutarch of neo-Pythagorean ideas prevalent in his time.[62] It would be as difficult to sustain as to refute such a claim, since Plutarch's relation to neo-Pythagoreanism is complex and poorly understood. But there appears to be no evidence of neo-Pythagoreanism in the case of either Gellius or Andronicus.

However that may be, Grant also turns to a second, more direct line of attack, ridiculing Plutarch's reading of Aristotle and his testimony (just quoted) reporting the intentional obscurity or multileveled character of Aristotle's writing. Grant asserts: "Such a statement does not require refutation."

Here, he is drawing upon the deep and indignant skepticism that, as mentioned at the beginning, is aroused in modern times at the very suggestion of Aristotelian esotericism. Still, to buttress his point, he adds confidently:

> After the Renaissance, when the works of Aristotle in their original form were widely studied, all the nonsense about his double doctrine was at once dissipated; and the simple, plain-sailing character of his philosophy was admitted on all hands.[63]

But here we may say that Grant, in his supreme confidence, is entirely mistaken. The evidence he summons to support his view speaks powerfully against it. From the Renaissance to about 1800, the esoteric character of Aristotle's philosophy was acknowledged by almost everyone who discussed the subject.

In turning now to the other ancient and medieval commentators on Aristotle we will find exactly the same thing (although, again, modern scholars have tried to argue the contrary).[64] Simplicius of Cilicia (c. 490–c. 560), who, though a Neoplatonist, is widely regarded as the most learned and reliable of the Greek commentators (after Alexander of Aphrodisias), remarks in his commentary on the *Physics* that in Aristotle's acroamatic works, "he deliberately introduced obscurity, repelling by this means those who are too easy-going, so that it might seem to them that they had not even been written."[65] He is clearly endorsing as well as elaborating the view reported by Plutarch. Similarly, Themistius (317–c. 390), who was only tangentially related to neo-Platonism, states in his paraphrase of the *Posterior Analytics* that "many of the books of Aristotle appear to have been contrived with a view to concealment."[66] The Neoplatonist Ammonius (c. 440–c. 520), in the first paragraph of his commentary on the *Categories*, lists ten questions that must be addressed before beginning the study of Aristotle's book. The eighth is: "Why has the Philosopher obviously made a point of being obscure."[67] He gives his answer a few pages later:

> Let us ask why on earth the philosopher is contented with obscure [*asaphes*] teaching. We reply that it is just as in the temples, where curtains are used for the purpose of preventing everyone, and especially the impure, from encountering things they are not worthy of meeting. So too Aristotle uses the obscurity of his philosophy as a veil, so that good people may for that reason stretch their minds even more, whereas empty minds that are lost through

carelessness will be put to flight by the obscurity when they encounter sentences like these.[68]

In the Islamic tradition as well, we hear Alfarabi claiming:

> Whoever inquires into Aristotle's sciences, peruses his books, and takes pains with them will not miss the many modes of concealment, blinding and complicating in his approach, despite his apparent intention to explain and clarify.[69]

Alfarabi sees perfectly well what we see—that Aristotle often displays a meticulous effort "to explain and clarify"—but he and the others also see that that is not the whole story.[70] Among the Greek commentators, artful obscurity was in fact so well established as a major characteristic of Aristotelian writing that, in their discussions and disputes over the authenticity of various manuscripts, they used this quality as a crucial marker of authenticity. Thus, we find the Neoplatonist Olympiodorus the Younger (c. 495–570) arguing:

> Some people have condemned the first book [of the *Meteorologica*] as spurious, in the first place because it goes beyond Aristotle himself and practices clarity [*sapheneia*]. Against them I shall maintain that there is a great deal of unclarity [*asapheia*] in the book.[71]

If it is lacking in obscurity, it cannot be genuine Aristotle. Similarly, among writers in the sixteenth and seventeenth centuries—including such confirmed non-Neoplatonists as Pierre Gassendi and Joseph Glanvill—it became something of a standard trope to liken Aristotle to a cuttlefish, for, like the squid, the cuttlefish squirts ink as a defensive measure.[72] In sum, concerning the question of multilevel writing—our second question—there is impressively clear, widespread, and uncontradicted testimony that the use of intentional obscurity to convey different messages to different readers is one of Aristotle's most characteristic features as a writer.[73]

The Evidence concerning the First Question: The View of Alexander of Aphrodisias

Let us return then to the first question: is there also a fundamental difference of doctrine between the two sets of writings, exoteric and acroamatic? Thus far, we have seen the partial answer of Plutarch and Gellius (and perhaps Andronicus): Yes, in the sense that only the acroamatic writings contained what Plutarch called the "secret and deeper things, which men ... do not expose for the many to share." Yet, this answer leaves unclear the precise character of the difference between the two kinds of writings. Specifically, are the exoteric works simply *incomplete*—simply *silent* on the subject of these excluded "deeper things"—or do they go on to present an alternative, fictional doctrine in their place? In other words, do Aristotle's writings present a full-blown "double doctrine," one fictional and the other true? On this particular aspect of the first question there is important disagreement among the commentators (in contrast to the unanimity regarding the question of multilevel writing).

The most important statement on the issue was made by Alexander of Aphrodisias (c. 200), and it strongly supports the "double doctrine" thesis. Unfortunately, the work in which he states his view—most likely his commentary on *De anima*—is not among those that have come down to us. We know his position only from the report of his chief opponents—three Neoplatonist commentators, Ammonius, Olympiodorus, and Elias (sixth century). According to Elias's account, the latest and most fully elaborated of the three, Alexander claimed that "in the acroamatics, he [Aristotle] says the truth and what seems true to him, but in the dialogues, falsehoods that seem to be true to others."[74]

This statement carries great weight because Alexander of Aphrodisias is perhaps the most authoritative source we possess on Aristotle after Aristotle himself. Known for over four centuries, among pagans, Christians, and Muslims alike, as simply "the Commentator," he is the most informed, judicious, and philosophic of the Greek interpreters of Aristotle. His importance regarding our issue is all the greater in view of the fact that he may well be the last commentator to actually have had full and direct access to the exoteric as well as the acroamatic writings.[75] Finally, he is also the last ancient commentator to be wholly free of Neoplatonist influence. There is no trace in him of either the syncretistic or the mystical and spiritualistic tendencies powerfully emerging in his time.

One would therefore expect that the modern scholars of this issue—having identified Neoplatonist bias as *the* great obstacle to the accurate assessment of Aristotle's manner of writing—would seize upon this claim of Alexander's as the single most important piece of evidence we possess. Instead, most of them completely ignore it.[76]

The great exception is During, who focuses intently upon it—in order to prove that Alexander never made such a claim. We know of this claim, after all, only from the report of the three commentators, who could always be mistaken. Therefore, During makes bold to prove that the commentators, in reading Alexander's text, grossly misinterpreted it (a text that During himself has of course never seen). His argument proceeds on a conjecture: What Alexander really asserted in his lost commentary is only the obvious point that in the acroamatic writings, which are treatises, Aristotle speaks in his own name, whereas in the exoteric writings, which are dialogues, he includes different characters expressing their own opinions. But Elias, somehow not comprehending this simple point, mistakenly ascribed to Alexander the very different claim quoted above, that in the exoteric works, Aristotle endorses false opinions.[77] And that is how this erroneous report arose.

During's conjectural reconstruction of these distant events seems farfetched on a number of counts. First, it is hard to see how the mistake he attributes to Elias could be made by any person of ordinary intelligence, let alone by a brilliant and renowned commentator, rigorously trained in the art of close textual analysis. Second, it is necessary to assume that this quirky mistake was made not just once, but three times, first by Ammonius, then by Olympiodorus, and finally by Elias—since all three give essentially the same report of Alexander.[78]

Furthermore, Elias and Olympiodorus make it perfectly clear that their understanding of Alexander's view in no way hinges—as During assumes here—simply on the interpretation of a few sentences spoken about Aristotle's manner of writing. Rather, it is firmly rooted in Alexander's whole interpretation of Aristotle. As they explain—with stern disapproval—Alexander denies the immortality of the soul and believes that that is also the genuine Aristotelian view. The acroamatic works, including *De anima*, can (arguably) be interpreted in that manner, but the exoteric works manifestly cannot for they "loudly proclaimed the immortality of the soul," as Olympiodorus puts it.[79] Therefore, it is perfectly obvious from the *content* of Alexander's interpretation of Aristotle that he did indeed believe that the acroamatic writings presented Aristotle's genuine doctrine, while the exoteric writings conveyed a fundamentally different teaching, closer to popular beliefs. And this view of Alexander's is the best evidence we possess concerning the precise relation of the two sets of Aristotle's writings.

The Great Debate: Alexander vs. the Neoplatonists

Thus, if During and the others want to defend their strict anti-esoteric stance regarding Aristotle, they cannot simply dismiss Alexander's contrary view with the dubious claim that he did not really espouse it. They will have to confront and *refute* that view—by appealing to the testimony of the three commentators who explicitly contradict Alexander: Elias, Olympiodorus, and Ammonius (buttressed by some others like Philoponus). But before this confrontation, two initial observations.

First, one must note the great irony that the anti-esoteric scholarly camp, which began by attributing all the talk of esotericism to the malign influence of Neoplatonism, must now stake its whole case on the hope to use these neo-Platonist commentators to refute the one commentator who remained wholly free of Neoplatonist influence.

Second, During seems to believe that, however it turns out with Alexander, at least these three commentators are wholly on his side and against the esoteric interpretation of Aristotle. But even that is not true. If one is looking at the first question—whether the exoteric and the acroamatic writings both teach the same doctrine—then these interpreters do indeed argue for the anti-esoteric answer: the teachings of both sets of writings are essentially the same. But During seems to be unaware or somehow neglects that esotericism can take a second form, multilevel writing. And, as we have seen, there is a very large consensus of philosophers and commentators—pagan, Neoplatonist, Islamic, and Christian—affirming that Aristotle did practice this second form of esotericism. It turns out, moreover, that the three Neoplatonist commentators on whom During must rely are themselves *all firm members of that consensus.* Indeed, I have already quoted from Ammonius and Olympiodorus above when illustrating that view. As for Elias—of the three thinkers, the most open and fervent critic of esotericism of the first type (different doctrines in different sets of writings)—here is what he says, eleven pages later, concerning the second, multilevel type:

> When Alexander [the Great] blamed him for publishing his writing, Aristotle said, "they are published and not published," hinting at their lack of clarity . . . [which is like] what Plato said [in the Second Letter, 312d8]: "if something should happen to the tablet [i.e., the writing] either on land or on sea, the reader because of its obscurity would not understand its contents." Thus [one should write] in order to hide; in order to test those fit and those unfit, so that the unfit should turn their backs on philosophy.[80]

Thus, the three commentators whom During considers to be on his side are in fact all firm believers in Aristotelian esotericism—just not the kind that Alexander is speaking of, the first kind.[81] Indeed, the record of commentary on Aristotle is full of heated debates regarding these subsidiary questions of esoteric technique. But, so far as I can tell, there is no debate at all about whether Aristotle was esoteric in some form. That is accepted on all sides.

So in the intracommentator debate to which we now briefly turn, all parties agree that Aristotle uses obscurity to withhold certain higher truths from most readers. The disagreement concerns whether—especially in the exoteric writings, but possibly in the acroamatic to some extent as well—he goes beyond the *withholding of truth* to the positive *endorsement of falsehoods*, that is, to the provision of an "exoteric doctrine" in the strict sense of an alternative, fictional teaching, a "noble lie." To restate the question in terms of its practical meaning: if we are trying to read Aristotle esoterically, should we simply be looking for subtle hints of unstated ideas or should we also be questioning the sincerity of the doctrines he openly affirms and argues for?

The three Neoplatonist commentators all take the less extreme of the two alternatives: Aristotle leaves much unsaid, but what he does say, he believes; he conceals but does not lie. He seeks to exclude part of his audience but not to deceive them.[82] This view is crucial to the commentators because, as Neoplatonists, they interpret Aristotle in a religious or spiritualistic manner, and themes of that kind figure more prominently in the exoteric than in the acroamatic writings. Thus they are eager to maintain that the former works, although more popular than the acroamatic, nevertheless propound the same doctrine and so are equally valid and in some respects more useful. In their own writings, they certainly make crucial use of them.[83] Alexander, by contrast, has a more skeptical, naturalistic interpretation of Aristotle's ultimate doctrine and thus maintains—as he would have to—that the more spiritualistic exoteric writings contain much that is "merely exoteric" or pious fiction.[84]

So who is right? I have already argued above that, for a variety of reasons, Alexander is regarded as the far more reliable source in general. But perhaps we can also judge between the contradictory claims of these commentators by examining Aristotle's texts for ourselves. This is difficult to do in a definitive manner since we do not possess any of the exoteric writings.[85] But we have some knowledge of them and, at least regarding one crucial issue, the immortality of the soul, we are able to make a fairly reliable comparison of how the two different categories of works treat a major philosophical question.

Concerning the exoteric writings, Elias informs us that "the dialogues very much seem to herald the immortality of the soul," a claim also made by many others, like Proclus and, as we have already seen above, Olympiodorus.[86] What is more, we possess, in fragmentary form, large parts of the *Eudemus*, Aristotle's famous dialogue on the soul and the afterlife, loosely modeled on Plato's *Phaedo*. And these fragments clearly seem to substantiate the claims of the commentators. Specifically, Aristotle appears to assert the immortality of the soul, meaning the personal or individual soul, which, as such, includes the memory of one's former self and life on earth.

But if we turn to the other set of works, we find that nowhere in the entire corpus of the acroamatic writings does Aristotle ever make a comparable assertion. In two famously brief and obscure passages in *De anima* (408b18–29, 430a23), he asserts the immortality of a small part of the soul, the "active intellect," but he leaves very unclear what this is and how we know it is immortal. Still, it seems clear from what he does say that, once the body dies, there is no continuation of our personal memory, since this is not an operation of the active intellect. So there is no true "personal immortality."

If, to gain greater clarity on this crucial issue, we turn to the *Nicomachean Ethics*, Aristotle's work dedicated to exploring the fundamental questions about how we should live, we find, remarkably, that he never once raises the question. The closest he comes is in book 1, chapter 10, which considers a related but much smaller question: can a man who lives a happy life to the end be said to become unhappy when, after his death, utter ruin befalls his family and estate? With the deftness of a tightrope walker, Aristotle manages to explore all the many ins and outs of this conundrum without ever once tipping his hand on the larger question that it inescapably points to: is there or is there not an afterlife of some kind? In its teasing evasiveness, the discussion seems to show us, without telling us, that he is unwilling to openly address this question. Two books later, however, in a very different context, Aristotle does remark in passing: "Wish [as distinguished from choice] may be for things that are impossible—for example, immortality" (1111b22).

These brief textual observations certainly do not settle the question of Aristotle's view of immortality. They do suffice, however, to make a fairly strong case for the Alexandrian position in our debate: the two kinds of Aristotelian writings do not present the same teaching. There is a "double doctrine." On this most important issue of life, the exoteric writings clearly proclaim a quasi-religious doctrine of personal immortality that is more in tune with political needs as well as popular wishes and longings. By contrast, the acroamatic or philosophic works studiously avoid *any* clear declaration on the issue. At the same time, they also seem to point, quietly and obscurely, toward a much more skeptical view that, whatever its precise details, denies personal immortality.[87] It seems clear that, in the exoteric writings, Aristotle is indeed willing to endorse fictions, to affirm and even argue for—with all his characteristic earnestness and precision—doctrines that he does not believe.

Still, this argument is not ironclad. How could it be when relying solely on fragments and ancient reports for its understanding of the exoteric writings?[88] What would be very helpful is confirming evidence of some sort in the texts that we actually do possess. This is not an unreasonable hope since, as we have seen, the acroamatic works are multilevel writings employing obscurity to conceal the truth. It is entirely possible, then, that they also engaged in the further practice—at issue in the current debate—of endorsing, on the surface, doctrines that Aristotle ultimately rejected, either beneath the surface of that same work or in some other, "more acroamatic" work. In other words, we can confirm our suspicions about the lost exoteric works if we can show that the acroamatic works themselves contain a surface layer of teachings that are "merely exoteric."

Exoteric Teachings in the Acroamatic Works

That turns out to be surprisingly easy to do. Let us turn, for example, to another absolutely fundamental question: is there a god or gods? As everyone knows, in the "theology" discussion of *Metaphysics* 11, Aristotle answers this question through his doctrine of the unmoved mover: a perfect, unitary, and unchanging being that lives a completely contemplative life—thought thinking itself. But everyone also knows that the *Nicomachean Ethics* and *Politics* are full of respectful references to the traditional gods of the city, which describe, for example, who it is that the gods love and reward most (*Ethics* 1179a23–34), that they are owed honor (*Ethics* 1165a23), and that one of the most crucial elements of a city, without which it cannot exist, is that part—the priesthood—that attends to the divine (*Politics* 1328b2–13).[89] To be sure, Aristotle speaks much less frequently and reverently of the gods than does Plato, and he often does so in a somewhat conditional manner, and occasionally he gives hints of a higher conception of "the god," but still it is very hard to deny that what he does affirm in these works is in stark contrast to the teaching of the *Metaphysics*. Thus, Sir David Ross, who begins his classic work *Aristotle* by dismissing in a sentence the legend that the exoteric/acroamatic distinction involves "the practice of an economy of truth toward the public," must nevertheless acknowledge later on that in most of these religious passages Aristotle "is clearly accommodating himself to the views of his age." And even Grant himself is compelled to admit that in these works "there are several popular and exoteric allusions to 'the gods.'"[90] To put it in a less grudging and more accurate way, if the *Metaphysics* presents Aristotle's true view of theology, then almost the entire treatment of the gods in these two works is "merely exoteric."[91]

If we go on to take up the related question of providence, we see a similar pattern. It has seemed obvious to many of Aristotle's interpreters, not unreasonably, that since his god is purely contemplative, indeed self-contemplative, there is no basis in Aristotle's thought for particular providence. But Aristotle himself refrains from ever drawing that conclusion—or indeed any other conclusion on the matter. Here is another major question of life regarding which the Philosopher maintains a studied and nearly total silence. Still, here and there, when he does take a stand, it is not to support the position that the *Metaphysics* would lead one to expect. Rather, he affirms the existence of divine providence, albeit with a statement so abstract or so hedged with conditionals that it makes a rather weak impression. Thus, in *On the Heavens* (271a33) he declares: "God and nature do nothing in vain." In the *Nicomachean Ethics* (1099b13), he states that happiness comes from the gods—or at least it would be *fitting* for it to do so. And later (1179a23) he suggests that the gods love and reward the philosophers—*if* they love and reward anyone. Taking all of this into account, Ross—once again, an esoteric reader in spite of himself—reasonably concludes:

> But it is remarkable how little trace there is of this [providential] way of thinking, if we discount passages where Aristotle is probably accommodating himself to common opinions.[92]

It seems fair to say, in sum, that Aristotle probably rejects providence, but, if he does, he deliberately conceals that conclusion. He generally evades the subject as much as possible, but occasionally speaks exoterically (but tepidly) in favor of providence.

We have now seen the same pattern of behavior regarding three topics—God, providence, and the afterlife. Still, someone might try to object that, as important as these topics are, they do not seem to be central to Aristotle's philosophical activity. Thus, it would be more impressive and dispositive if we could catch Aristotle speaking exoterically about matters closer to his heart. Let us turn, then, to what is arguably Aristotle's central theoretical teaching: his doctrine of natural teleology. As is well recognized, a defining characteristic of Aristotelian teleology is that it is an "immanent" or "pluralistic" teleology. "The end of each species," to quote Ross again, "is internal to the species; its end is simply to be that kind of thing."[93] It is not an "extrinsic" teleology, where one species exists for the sake of another or for the whole, and still less an "anthropocentric" teleology, where all things exist for the benefit of man. Horses do not exist for men to ride. That is the consistent claim of Aristotle's teaching in all of the acroamatic works.

Except in the *Nicomachean Ethics* and the *Politics*. In the former (1106a20), Aristotle states that the natural excellence or perfection of a horse is to be good at carrying its rider. Similarly, in the *Politics* (1256b16), he asserts—and even supports his assertion with arguments—that the plants exist for the sake of the animals and the animals for the sake of man. So, even with respect to this theoretical doctrine so central to Aristotle's whole thought, he clearly seems willing to speak exoterically here, to falsify his doctrine.[94]

Related to this exoteric anthropocentrism in the *Politics* is an exoteric ethnocentrism. On the second page of the book (1252b4), Aristotle unabashedly endorses the reigning dogma that the Greeks are the natural rulers of the barbarians, that is, of all non-Greeks, because the latter are naturally slavish. (Among other things, this claim is crucial to the defense of his theory—also exoteric I would suggest—that nature has conveniently divided the human species into natural masters and natural slaves.) But later, in book 2, where Aristotle devotes himself to examining the three existing cities that are the best, he quietly includes among them Carthage—a barbarian city.[95]

In conclusion, this brief examination of certain topics in the acroamatic writings lends strong support to the position of Alexander of Aphrodisias in his debate with the three Neoplatonist commentators. Not only is Aristotle a multilevel writer who hides some of his doctrines through intentional obscurity—as all parties are agreed—but he also propagates certain salutary fictions or noble lies. He does so especially—characteristically—in the exoteric writings, but also to some extent in the acroamatic. In short, he deploys a full-blown "double doctrine."

And this claim, moreover, can no longer be dismissed as Neoplatonist nonsense—as During, Grant, and the others have long tried to do—because, as we have come to see, precisely the opposite is the case. The view of Aristotle as propagating a double doctrine in his two sets of writings is precisely a *rejection* of the Neoplatonist view.

To us today, Aristotle may seem like the "hardest case" regarding esotericism. But we have now seen how and why through most of history he was seen as the classic case.[96]

THE PREVALENCE OF ESOTERIC COMMUNICATION
AMONG NON-WESTERN PEOPLES TODAY

The mounting testimonial evidence for the practice of esotericism, powerful as it is, still faces two tenacious obstacles. First, there is the problem facing all historical as distinguished from social science research: the evidence is all static, rooted in the distant past. There is no opportunity to question, clarify, and cross-examine. And second, whatever the evidence and arguments may say, there is also a voice deep within us that keeps repeating the same thing: esotericism is strange behavior—plain and simple. It just doesn't pass the smell test.

To address these obstacles, it may help to turn briefly to a very different kind of evidence: recent social science studies of how ordinary people in different cultures communicate. For here the testimony and research are very much contemporary, responsive, and ongoing. And, as it happens, what this living testimony shows is that esoteric modes of communication—strange as they smell to us—are actually part of the daily diet of most of the rest of the world (and this is the case, not simply for rarified, intellectual discourse, but also for plain, everyday parlance). Thus a brief immersion in this field of research may help us to gain some much-needed distance on our ingrained tastes and reactions.

Among the most important ways in which cultures differ is in their modes and styles of communication. Yet the study of these differences has long been neglected. Fortunately, it has recently become a high-priority field, largely owing to the explosive rise of globalization. Research is moving ahead rapidly in an impressively large and diverse collection of disciplines.

On the purely theoretical level, "comparative rhetoric" has become a growing field within comparative literature. In the social sciences, the growing practical concern for cross-cultural understanding and cooperation has given birth to the field of "intercultural communication," which has become a high-growth industry within sociology, communications, and anthropology. On a still more practical level, business schools and especially the growing subfield of international public relations have also been devoting ever-increasing attention to the great differences in communication styles across cultures. The same is true of international relations programs within political science departments, especially those with specializations in diplomacy. Finally, international volunteer organizations like the Peace Corps have become sources as well as users of our growing understanding of these all-important cultural differences. Ironically, this burgeoning new field—which has arisen to help us correctly interpret and connect with the communicative practices of other cultures—may also help us to correctly interpret and reconnect with the writings of our own past. For the latter, in many important respects, have more in common with non-Western cultures today than with our own.

Perusing this large new literature, one is struck by the fact that despite its great diversity—its dispersal over such widely differing disciplines, with distinct motives and methodologies—everywhere one hears almost the identical characterization of the Western communicative style and its differences from that of other cultures. Anthropologist Edward T. Hall, for example, probably the most famous and influential writer in the field, distinguishes between what he calls "low context" societies like the United States and Europe and the "high context" societies found throughout most of the developing world. In the former, when one communicates with others—whether orally or in writing—one is expected to be direct, clear, explicit, concrete, linear, and to the point. But in most of the rest of the world, such behavior is considered a bit rude and shallow: one should approach one's subject in a thoughtfully indirect, suggestive, and circumlocutious manner.[97]

The very same contrast is to be found in *The Peace Corps Cross-Cultural Workbook*. This is a field manual developed by the Peace Corps—drawing upon long years of hands-on experience in many different cultures—to help prepare its volunteers to understand the communicative customs of their host countries. In the United States and other Western countries, it emphasizes, we are accustomed to a "direct" style of communication:

> People say what they mean and mean what they say; you don't need to read between the lines; it's important to tell it like it is; honesty is the best policy.

But American volunteers need to understand that outside the West, cultures incline, in varying degrees, to an "indirect" communicative style: "People are indirect; they imply/suggest what they mean; understatement is valued; you need to read between the lines."[98]

This is certainly true among the preliterate Wana peoples of Indonesia, according to George Kennedy's *Comparative Rhetoric: An Historical and Cross-Cultural Introduction*. Among the Wana, frequently "speakers disguise their meaning . . . and say something indirectly in an elegant way to one who understands."[99] As Joy Hendry and C. W. Watson explain in the introduction to their edited volume *An Anthropology of Indirect Communication*, this kind of communicative style has been documented by many researchers in myriad primitive societies, such as the peoples of Malay, the Trobriand Islands, Papua New Guinea, the Marquesan Islands, Sulawesi, the Azande tribe of north central Africa, and the Wolof people of Senegal.[100] Among the many reasons for this common practice, they list:

> To avoid giving offence, or, on the contrary, to give offence but with relative impunity; to mitigate embarrassment and save face; to entertain through the manipulation of disguise; for aesthetic pleasure; to maintain harmonious and social relations; to establish relative social status; to exclude from a discourse those not familiar with the conventions of its usage and thereby to strengthen the solidarity of those who are.[101]

Examples can also be found in the more developed world. A leading characteristic of Chinese culture, according to communications scholars Ge Gao and Stella Ting-Toomey, is *han xu* or "implicit communication." This is speech that is "contained, reserved, implicit, and indirect."

> *Han xu* is considered a social rule in Chinese culture. . . . To be *han xu*, one does not spell out everything but leaves the "unspoken" to the listeners.

It follows that, much more than in the West, "the ability to surmise and decipher hidden meanings is highly desirable in Chinese culture." Indeed, among the main purposes or effects of this style is this:

> When the Chinese vaguely express an idea, an opinion, or a suggestion, they expect their conversational partner to be highly involved and to take an active role in deciphering messages. . . . A hesitant and indirect approach serves to grant the listener an equal footing with the speaker in conversation.[102]

Opposite to our Western expectations, ambiguity draws the listeners in. It heightens their involvement, making them complicit in what is being said. An esoteric style, although its most obvious use is as a means for *excluding* unwanted listeners (its "defensive" and "protective" roles), also functions as a means of *inclusion*, tightening the bond between speaker and hearer, writer and reader (its "pedagogical" role).

Moreover, this indirect style is practiced, not only in polite conversation, but also in matters of the greatest importance. Henry Kissinger, recounting in his memoirs the momentous negotiations for the opening to China, was quite struck by Mao's elliptical mode of communication:

> His meaning emerged from a Socratic dialogue that he guided effortlessly and with deceptive casualness. . . . The cumulative effect was that his key points were enveloped in so many tangential phrases that they communicated a meaning while evading a commitment. Mao's elliptical phrases were passing shadows on a wall; they reflected a reality but they did not encompass it.[103]

Switching to a very different part of the world — the Middle East — and to a very different scholarly discipline, public relations, we find a remarkably similar account. In "Understanding Cultural Preferences of Arab Communication Patterns," published in the *Public Relations Review*, R. S. Zaharna states that "the Arab cultural preference is for indirect, vague, and ambiguous statements." The key thing that U.S. public relations professionals working in Arab countries must be brought to appreciate is that

> [t]he burden for understanding falls not on the speaker speaking clearly, but on the listener deciphering the hidden clues. In fact, the better the speaker, the more skillful he may be in manipulating the subtlety of the clues. The Arab audience, which is participatory, delights in finding these hidden clues.[104]

Again, according to Milton J. Bennett, executive director of the Intercultural Development Research Institute, Japanese culture also tends to demand that

> its speakers imply and infer meaning from the context of relatively vague statements — the way it is said, by whom, to whom, where, at what time, and just before or after what other statement.[105]

The effect of this ambiguity and indirection is described by Sheila J. Ramsey as follows:

> Rather than expressing a judgment or opinion, Japanese often prefer to give the other person space to react and draw his or her own conclusions. This preference is evident in the purely descriptive poetry form of haiku, in which the poet presents experience and observations rather than evalua-

tion. In reacting and filling in the gaps, the reader is drawn in. . . . This emphasis upon the receiver's role is at the heart of different approaches to media advertising in the two cultures [Japan and the United States].[106]

Finally, we may cite an article in the *New York Times* entitled "Iranian 101: A Lesson for Americans—The Fine Art of Hiding What You Mean to Say." Foreign correspondent David Slackman finds that

> Americans and Iranians speak two different languages. Americans are pragmatists and word choice is often based on the shortest route from here to there. Iranians are poets and tend to use language as though it were paint, to be spread out, blended, swirled.

Thus, in Iran,

> "[y]ou have to guess if people are sincere, you are never sure," said Nasser Hadian, a political science professor at the University of Teheran. "Symbolism and vagueness are inherent in our language."
>
> "Speech has a different function than it does in the West," said Kian Tajbakhsh, a social scientist who lived for many years in England and the United States before returning to Iran a decade ago. "In the West, 80 percent of language is denotative. In Iran 80 percent is connotative." . . . In Iran, Dr. Tajbakhsh said, listeners are expected to understand that words don't necessarily mean exactly what they mean. "This creates a rich, poetic linguistic culture . . . where people are adept at picking up on nuances."[107]

These examples could easily be multiplied, but the point is clear enough. We in the West are accustomed to a plain and direct mode of speech, which we think of as normal. Indirect speech strikes us as something improbable and aberrant. But outside the modern West, people incline to a kind of esotericism of everyday life. Whether in preliterate tribes or sophisticated civilizations, whether in Asia, Africa, Latin America, or the Middle East, almost everywhere one finds the considered embrace of reserve, indirection, and ambiguity. Whatever the reasons for it (a question to be pursued later), that is the plain, empirical fact.[108]

It is a fact, however, that people in the West find very difficult to accept and adjust to. To be sure, we are all good multiculturalists now, and when it comes to most other matters of culture—to dress, cuisine, social mores, religious customs, and so forth—we are eager to respect the customs of others and to imagine how "other" we ourselves must seem in their eyes. But for some reason the issue of speech and communication—perhaps because it is so basic to our humanity—awakens in us a stubborn and atavistic ethnocentrism. As many scholars of intercultural communication have in fact reported, when otherwise open-minded Westerners have to deal with the indirect and ambiguous manner of speaking practiced in, say, China, Mexico, or the Middle East, they tend to react with simple indignation. It is somehow deeply upsetting. This way of speaking strikes them as just plain wrong—as illogical, devious, cowardly, inscrutable, and childish.[109] They almost can't believe it's real.

And that, of course, is very much how Zeller and other modern scholars have reacted when confronted with earlier esotericism. Notwithstanding all the evidence, they feel in their bones that it is a bizarre and demeaning practice that cannot be real.

On this issue, there is a stubborn ethnocentrism in us all. Needless to say, it is crucial to overcome it and to penetrate the rhetorical customs of other cultures—crucial not only for Peace Corps volunteers, public relations professionals, and diplomats, but also for students of the philosophical history of the West. The present work is, as it were, a Peace Corps field manual for Western scholars that aims to promote connection with the communicative customs of our distant past.

Interlude: Two Brief Examples

If you have to be told everything, do not read me.
—JEAN-JACQUES ROUSSEAU, *Emile*

If, based on the evidence seen so far, the phenomenon of esotericism has, as it were, finally gotten our full attention, it might be helpful to pause here to examine—more closely than we previously had the patience to do—just what esoteric writing is, what it looks like, and how it works. Two brief illustrations will help to make the phenomenon both more intelligible and less forbidding. They will also help to confirm the *testimonial* evidence we have seen so far with at least a small sampling of *textual* evidence.

As a rule, philosophical esotericism does not take the form of a secret code or other arcane contrivance that is impenetrable to all except those possessing a special key. On the contrary, esoteric writers tend to employ techniques that are quite intuitively accessible, at least for people who have spent a little time imagining how they themselves might go about hinting at an idea without openly stating it. Everyone knows how to drop a hint. Allusion, metaphor, insinuation, symbolism, riddle, irony—all of these are essential parts of the normal repertoire of civilized human discourse, as the intercultural communication literature powerfully indicates. Esoteric writing should be thought of, not as something wholly alien and artificial, but as

a more concentrated and refined use of techniques that are relatively familiar to us from ordinary parlance (even in our "low context" culture).

To illustrate, I will discuss one example of philosophical writing from
the classical period—Plato's *Republic*—and one from the modern period,
Machiavelli's *Discourses* and *Prince*. From the historical evidence just presented, we see that there is considerable historical testimony to the esotericism of Plato. As for Machiavelli: Bacon, Spinoza, Rousseau, and Diderot
all explicitly describe him as esoteric.[1] And he himself declares in a letter to
Guicciardini: "For some time, I never say what I believe and I never believe
what I say; and if it sometimes occurs to me that I say the truth, I conceal it
among so many lies that it is hard to find it out."[2] I will try to bear out these
testimonial claims by giving a short esoteric reading of something in each of
their writings.

But a quick caveat. In a short space, it is impossible to marshal the kind
of evidence and argumentation that would be needed to make an esoteric
interpretation broadly persuasive. It should be understood, then, that these
brief examples are meant here as suggestive and illustrative—not demon-
strative. (For examples that are more fully elaborated, see the "suggestions
for further reading" given in chapter 9.) For present purposes, it will suffice
if these short discussions are plausible enough to convince the reader that
something esoteric is going on in these texts, even if the precise interpretations suggested are not completely persuasive.

Let me begin on the broadest level by simply listing some of the more
commonly employed esoteric techniques. If an author should seek to criticize covertly the reigning government or the dominant religious or philosophical beliefs, one obvious way of doing so would be to write allegorically,
directing his criticisms at some other object, distant in time or place (or perhaps an animal of some kind), while hinting at a connection to his true target. Or he might openly report his criticisms, but put them in the mouth of
some other character of whom he expresses stern disapproval. Or he might
openly report them, but for the necessary purpose of refuting them, which
he does in a notably unconvincing manner.

More generally, a thinker can hint at an idea without expressly stating it
by presenting it in an obscure manner, or very tersely, or ambiguously. He
can break the idea down into its constituent parts and then disperse these
parts over a long work. Or he can openly state the whole idea, but only in
passing and in some obscure corner of his book, while proclaiming the contrary view a dozen times over in prominent places. He can make use of irony,
paradoxes, parables, stories, symbols, and myths. Or he can place stumbling

blocks in the reader's path that compel him to stop and wonder what the writer is really up to, such as unexplained digressions, surprising omissions, unnecessary or slightly altered repetitions, and implausible blunders, such as errors of fact, patent contradictions, and misquotations.

This brief list is obviously not meant to be exhaustive. It is also not universal: different writers employ different techniques. For that reason, writers will sometimes attempt to give the reader some guidance by hinting at—in some cases, even openly stating—some techniques they have employed.

MACHIAVELLI AND THE POLITICAL PROBLEM OF CHRISTIANITY

We find an example of this in Machiavelli's *Discourses*. The next to last chapter of this book (3.48) bears the title: "When one sees a great error made by an enemy, one ought to believe that there is deception underneath."[3] This would seem to point to the last technique on our list: implausible errors or blunders. It is true that, on the surface, Machiavelli is speaking here about military tactics, but obviously the same technique can apply in the literary realm. It must also be kept in mind that, as Machiavelli explicitly declares, he is engaged—like all the later, Enlightenment thinkers—in a great struggle aimed at overthrowing prevailing modes of thought and practice. And the primary weapons in this battle are books. Therefore, as I believe a longer analysis could show, Machiavelli often speaks of military strategy as a way of covertly discussing literary strategy.

Some support for this idea can be found in Alexander Pope's *An Essay on Criticism*, where we find the exact same conflation of military and literary strategy—as well as the identical warning concerning seeming errors:

> A prudent chief not always must display
> His pow'rs in equal ranks, and fair array
> But with th'occasion and the place comply
> Conceal his force, nay seem sometimes to fly,
> *Those oft are stratagems which errors seem*,
> Nor is it Homer nods, but we that dream.[4]

Among other things, then, we should be on the lookout for intentional "great errors" as we read Machiavelli.

There turn out to be many such errors, but let us briefly examine two. The first involves a uniquely important quotation. Machiavelli's works are of course full of quotations, as well as allusions and references to ancient historians, poets, and philosophers. But what about the Bible? Surprisingly, although there are many allusions to biblical stories, in the whole of the *Prince* and the *Discourses*, there is just one, single quotation from the Bible. Furthermore, this quotation occurs in a uniquely important chapter, book 1, chapter 26: the single chapter in the whole of the *Discourses*—a work devoted to the analysis and restoration of republican government—that is expressly dedicated to tyranny, to the greatest enemy of republican liberty. It is fair to say, then, that at least for the careful reader, a double spotlight, as it were, falls on this short quotation.

Machiavelli employs it in the course of explaining that if a man should rise from private life to be the sole ruler of a city or province, especially an unruly one, then the only sure means for holding onto it is to "make everything new." What this simple-sounding phrase means is something extraordinarily tyrannical:

> to make in cities new governments with new names, new authorities, new men; to make the rich poor, the poor rich, as did David when he became king—"who filled the hungry with good things and sent the rich away empty"; besides this to build new cities, to take down those built, to exchange the inhabitants from one place to another.

Machiavelli himself goes on to remark:

> These modes are very cruel, and enemies to every way of life, not only Christian but human; and any man whatever should flee them and wish to live in private rather than as king with so much ruin to men.[5]

In his description, Machiavelli attributes this brutally tyrannical behavior to David, backing up his claim with a quotation—his one and only quotation from the Bible (Luke 1:53). But as almost any annotated edition of the *Discourses* will inform you, Machiavelli has made a bizarre mistake here. The quotation he recites is not about David at all. It is describing—God!

What are we to make of this? No one is infallible; and surely it is possible that it is an innocent mistake, a random error. But just as surely, that is not the most likely interpretation. For, first, it concerns the sole quotation from the Bible, which occurs in the sole chapter explicitly devoted to tyranny. Second, the consequences of the error are not random, but highly significant. Third, the quotation that Machiavelli mischaracterizes is not some obscure, seldom-quoted line, but one of the best-known passages of the Gospels. It is part of the Magnificat or Song of Mary, a canticle sung or recited in Vespers, the evening prayer service, which Machiavelli would have heard many hundreds of times. And fourth, he has explicitly alerted us (as Pope did after him) to watch out for this very kind of trick. He has committed a "great error," and therefore, following his own admonition, we ought to "believe that there is deception underneath." Specifically, through the error in this unique quotation, Machiavelli would seem to be covertly communicating a crucial and dangerous message: that the God of the New Testament is a great tyrant or, more broadly, that the Christian religion is perhaps the true cause of the loss of the ancient republican liberty that he, Machiavelli, is striving in this book to revive.[6]

What adds to the plausibility of this interpretation is that it is supported by a second example, which uses the exact same technique—and to convey the same lesson. In the *Prince*, too, Machiavelli discusses the loss of liberty in the postclassical world. In one of his most famous teachings, he asserts that the modern world has become weak and enslaved primarily owing to the reliance on mercenary and auxiliary troops—on outside forces. This military problem—and not Christianity—would seem to be the central cause of the loss of liberty. To remain strong and free, one must always rely on "one's own arms." To prove and illustrate this core principle of self-reliance, Machiavelli gives a number of examples, culminating in the famous biblical story of David and Goliath. In Machiavelli's telling:

> Saul, to give [David] spirit, armed him with his own arms—which David, as soon as he had them on, refused, saying that with them he could not give a good account of himself, and so he would rather meet the enemy with his sling and his knife.[7]

But here again there is a "great error." As most everyone knows, David did not take a knife or sword with him, but only his sling (hence, when he cut off Goliath's head, he had to use the latter's sword). This may seem a small point, but the Bible is quite insistent about it:

> So David prevailed over the Philistine with a sling and with a stone, and struck the Philistine, and killed him; there was no sword in the hand of David.[8]

This small detail is given such great emphasis because it conveys the core meaning of the story. As the smaller and poorly-armed David explains, standing before Goliath: "You come to me with a sword and with a spear and with a javelin; but I come to you in the name of the LORD."[9] The whole point of the story—indeed, the whole point of the Bible—is that we should *not* rely on ourselves or our own arms: we must put our whole faith and trust in the Lord, who alone can deliver us from our enemies as from all evil.

Thus, when Machiavelli incorrectly puts a knife in David's hands—and in the very context of discussing the need for "one's own arms"—it is extremely unlikely that this is an innocent mistake, not only because it concerns a very significant and well-known detail, but also because it forms part of a larger, even more striking "error": the use of this famous biblical story to prove the very opposite of its meaning.

Far more likely is that Machiavelli is being here, well . . . Machiavellian. He introduces the David and Goliath story in order to be able to claim, on the surface, that his new teaching is consistent with the Bible. But he changes— he reverses—the all-important detail of the knife in order covertly to announce the very opposite message: that his central new teaching of military self-reliance—and ultimately of human self-reliance—is diametrically opposed to the central teaching of the Bible. As in the first example, Machiavelli seeks here to proclaim, just a bit beneath the surface, his true, humanistic project, which is to subvert and replace the whole biblical orientation, which is the true cause of our loss of freedom. For the Christian teaching of passivity and trust in the Lord, in his view, has disarmed the world, making it weak and ripe for tyranny. Machiavelli would contribute to the restoration of ancient republican liberty by putting a sword back in human hands.[10]

It goes without saying that the esoteric interpretation of two isolated passages, even if quite plausible, cannot stand alone. These readings need to be integrated into a careful interpretation of the whole of Machiavelli's writings. Still, I do believe that at least this much is relatively clear: First, there are manifest difficulties or puzzles on the surface of these texts. Second, Machiavelli has openly alerted us to the character of certain of these difficulties, declaring that there is "deception underneath." And third, these puzzles can be plausibly resolved in ways that help to make sense of his larger philosophical and literary activity.

PLATO AND THE NATURAL LIMITS OF POLITICS

This reading of Machiavelli, while perhaps controversial, is not so far outside the mainstream of scholarly interpretation as to shock anyone. For an illustration of esoteric reading that yields an interpretation fully opposite to the dominant one, we turn to Plato's *Republic*. Here we must rely not on two simple passages, as we did above, but on a lengthy series of dots that need connecting.

For two millennia the *Republic* has stood as the classic representative of ancient utopianism: the fullest expression and exploration of the idealistic longing for perfect justice on earth. But, on the other hand, it is hard for the reader not to feel some distaste, even horror, with respect to some of the characteristic institutions of this "perfect society," such as the "noble lie," the abolition of the family, the use of eugenics, or the proposal that the philosopher-king, on first coming to power, should wipe the cultural slate clean, as it were, by expelling everyone over the age of ten. It is for reasons like these that readers often see the *Republic* as—contrary to Plato's intention—an *anti*-utopia, a classic demonstration of the totalitarian excesses that can grow out of a too great demand for perfect justice.

It is strange and puzzling that a single text—and one so brilliant, artfully written, and long revered—should inspire diametrically opposite reactions of this kind. One is moved to wonder: could it somehow be possible that this twofold reaction represents, not the abject failure of Plato's art, but its fullest intention? I would suggest that if readers are simply *aware* of esotericism as a historically common practice, they will be open to noticing what otherwise they will unfailingly overlook: that the *Republic* actually contains numerous hints, some of them quite open and obvious, suggesting that Plato himself did intend both of these opposite reactions to his book.

Without doubt, on the surface level of the text, the *Republic* is an idealistic quest for the perfectly just society, which it reaches gradually in three ascending stages. At no point does it openly renounce this quest or declare it a failure. When the final element of the proposed society—the rule of philosopher-kings—is put in place in book 6, Socrates still states that this is necessary for the city to "become perfect" (499b).

But it is almost equally undeniable, I think, that, throughout the book, in a kind of contrary, downward movement, Socrates quietly introduces institutions and descriptions that—if the reader connects the dots—increasingly point to the very grave and inescapable imperfections of this "perfect" city and thus of political life as such. On this level, the book is about, not the utopian possibilities, but the strict natural limits of politics. Among the many instances of this countermovement, let me cite three that are particularly explicit.

In book 3, after some initial reluctance, Socrates openly declares that their utopia in the making will require a "noble lie," a grand justifying myth

(414b–15d). The city, even the *best* city, it now suddenly appears, cannot rest on rationality and truth. Politics somehow requires illusion and deception. Then later, in book 5, when Socrates is arguing for the communal possession of spouses and children, he openly acknowledges that this institution—truly just, but profoundly disliked—will require the rulers to employ a "throng of lies and deceptions" (459a–460d). The ideal city, it seems, requires, not just a grounding myth, but the daily use of deception and manipulation by the rulers. The culmination of this contrary, downward trend is reached in book 7 in the famous image of the cave. In the context of explaining the true character of philosophy, Socrates compares the city, even the best city, to a cave, a subterranean pit of ignorance and illusion, where the citizens, imprisoned and enchained, spend their lives as if in a dream, taking shadows for reality (514aff.). In view of these three plain examples—all of them making the same point: the inescapable opposition between the city and truth—it seems to me extremely difficult to deny that the *Republic*'s dominant utopian narrative is repeatedly subverted by critical, even anti-utopian reflections.

On this interpretation, then, the *Republic* is, on one level, an attempt to arouse and specify with precision our utopian political longings, so as, on another, to confront all the ways in which human nature renders these longings ultimately impossible. And it conveys this lesson not only in order to tame and moderate the political realm but also to redirect our thwarted idealistic energies, using them as a springboard into the philosophical realm where they may find their true and proper satisfaction.

Let me try to give a somewhat fuller, more substantive account of this second, critical message of the *Republic*, while also supplying a wider range of examples of how Plato communicates it between the lines.

To begin with, how does Socrates ever get started on his famous utopian mission in the *Republic*? It is not his own idea but his response to the request of Glaucon and Adeimantus, Plato's brothers, who beg him to explain the true nature of justice and to demonstrate that it alone is the supreme good of life. Readers naturally assume that, in the lengthy discussion that follows, Socrates surely means to satisfy that request. However, this assumption is not at all supported, it is openly contradicted, by Socrates's immediate reply to the brothers' plea:

> On the one hand, I can't help out. For in my opinion I'm not capable of it. . . . On the other hand, I can't not help out. For I'm afraid it might be impious. . . . So the best thing is to succor her [justice] as I am able.[11]

This is Socrates's rather hedged characterization of how he will approach the whole discussion of justice to follow. Most readers pass over it without pause, dismissing it as a bit of self-deprecating Socratic irony. But one of the advantages of Socrates's reputation for irony is that it allows him occasionally to state shocking things quite openly without being taken seriously. In this case, I believe that Socrates states very accurately here just what he will be doing in the whole remainder of the *Republic*: defending the brothers' utopian longings for justice *as best he is able*, while knowing that it is *not* ultimately possible to succeed. Some further evidence of this can be found in the action, the dramatic dimension of the dialogue, Throughout the whole conversation, what is Socrates's dominant attitude? He is depicted not—as one might expect—as a moral idealist eager to describe his perfect society, but rather as a most reluctant participant, eager to get away with saying as little as possible (327c, 357a, 449a–450b). In other words, not only does he explicitly *say* that he is somehow dubious about this whole pursuit of utopia, but he is repeatedly shown to *act* that way too.

Less than four pages later, this reading receives some strong confirmation. Socrates and the two brothers have set out to describe—to construct in speech—a society that is "perfectly good" (427e, 499b), which they do in three stages or three stabs. In the first, they describe the fundamental principle of social union—the division of labor—and the most basic society built upon it. People are not all the same, Socrates explains, but some are best at one art, others at another. So let the naturally best farmer devote himself to nothing but farming (thereby also perfecting his art), and the best shoemaker to shoemaking, and so on for all the necessary arts—"one man, one job." After they have exchanged goods with one another, all their needs will be met and in the best possible way: each individual will profit as if he himself possessed the perfected talents of all. The common good and the good of each individual will both be maximized.

After they are done constructing this elementary society, Socrates, seeking to clarify the precise nature of its justice, asks: "Where in it, then, would justice be?" Or rather, that is what we expect him to ask. Instead he asks: "Where in it, then, would justice *and injustice* be?" (371e; see 427d). A surprising question. Their whole effort has been to construct a purely good and just society. And since they are constructing it "in speech," they can make whatever arrangements they like. They are totally in control. And yet Socrates very quietly but clearly signals that their city—the most basic city possible—already contains injustice. Somehow, four pages into the project, the hope for perfect justice has *already failed*—just as Socrates had implied it would.

Where, then, is the injustice? Socrates does not tell us: he quickly changes the subject. But Plato, having planted this question in our minds, does not leave it wholly unaddressed. He indicates an answer between the lines.

In the whole discussion of the first city, Adeimantus is Socrates's sole interlocutor, and he is a man of few words. "Certainly." "Most certainly." "Of course." "That's so." In this section, he speaks over thirty times, but rarely with more than three words and never with more than a line—except once, when he delivers himself of a major address: six lines! It would seem that something is suddenly bothering Adeimantus about this city. What is it?

Shopkeepers. Society is built on the division of labor, and the division of labor requires exchange, and exchange requires markets, and markets require shopkeepers—so that the producers do not have to wait around for the arrival of buyers, neglecting their craft, but can sell to the shopkeeper who sells to the buyers. So Socrates simply asks Adeimantus whether their city will need shopkeepers—just as he asked him before about shepherds and carpenters—when suddenly Adeimantus launches into his long speech. He acknowledges the timing problem and the need for shopkeepers, saying:

> There are men who see this situation and set themselves to this service;
> in rightly governed cities, they are usually those whose bodies are weak-
> est and useless for doing any other job. They must stay there in the mar-
> ket and exchange things for money with those who need to sell something
> and exchange, for money again, with all those who need to buy something.
> (371c–d)

What appears to be on Adeimantus's mind—though he refrains from expressing it openly—is that he (like most members of traditional, noncommercial societies) regards this as a demeaning job: shopkeepers must sit around all day in the market, doing nothing, producing nothing, moving money around, profiting from the work of others.

And this unstated problem, which drives Adeimantus to speak—call it the problem of "bad jobs"—is also the one responsible for the surprising presence of injustice in this seemingly well-ordered city. The division of labor, through which each spends his whole day and his whole life at a single task, is perfectly just and advantageous for all so long as all the jobs that society requires are reasonably good ones—at least as good as or better than what one would be doing if there were no specialization. But in fact there are bad jobs—shopkeepers or, if you like, garbage men, coal miners, infantry-men, ditchdiggers, etc.—and still it is *necessary* for society that *someone* do these jobs. These unlucky people are condemned by the system of special-ization to pass their whole lives engaged in a stunting, unhealthy, slavish, or dangerous activity. In this way, the common good of the whole is inseparable from the systematic exploitation of some of its members.

Adeimantus delivers his long speech because he is attempting to reply to or minimize this unstated difficulty. His reply is: "in rightly governed cities, they [shopkeepers] are usually those whose bodies are weakest and useless for doing any other job." If this is really the case across the board, if they are incapable of doing any better job, then there is no injustice in constraining them to do this one. But his use of the word "usually" shows that he knows this will not always be the case.

Socrates, of course, knows exactly what is bothering Adeimantus and, in his reply, goes on himself to make use of this justifying argument that the latter has just introduced. Socrates now adds to the city one final category of citizens that it seems he was hesitating to mention or at least saving for last, the worst of the jobs: servants or menial laborers.

> There are, I suppose, still some other servants who, in terms of their minds, wouldn't be quite up to the level of partnership, but whose bodies are strong enough for labor. (371e)

Like Adeimantus, Socrates tries to resolve or mitigate the problem of bad jobs—without ever openly describing it. These jobs can be justified by virtue of the natural defectiveness of certain individuals, some in body (shop-keepers), some in mind (laborers), which makes them incapable of any better job. But obviously nothing guarantees that such individuals will be supplied in the right kind and number required. In actuality, a certain level of systematic injustice or exploitation would seem to be inseparable from even the most basic city.

Moving on to the second city, we find further evidence of the *Republic*'s anti-utopian substratum. Here, we come across the noble lie. But while Soc-rates is open, as we have seen, in calling for the use of this lie, he never really makes clear why this radical expedient is so necessary. He thus leaves hidden the most troubling aspect of the lie: the fundamental defects of the city that the lie is needed and designed to cover over. In describing the myth, he tells us the "solution," while leaving it to us to figure out the problem.

According to the myth, the citizens are "autochthonous": they have all

been born together from the land, which is their common mother. Furthermore, they come in three different races: golden, silver, and iron or bronze,
which correspond to the three classes needed by the city—rulers, guardians,
and artisans/farmers. Also, each is born together with the tools of one of the
particular jobs required by the city.

As I will argue at greater length in chapter 6, this elaborate lie is constructed to hide from view four essential defects afflicting the city—every
city. The first part of the lie, concerning autochthony, gives a mythical reply
to two otherwise unanswerable questions: what legitimizes the city's occu-
pation of the land on which it sits and what justifies its inclusion of just these
particular human beings to the exclusion of all others? These problems point
to the inescapable arbitrariness and injustice of any city that falls short of a
world state (as all must). These are significant new difficulties quietly pointing to the impossibility of perfect justice.

But what most concerns us here are the other two defects—those concerning the internal division of the citizens into distinct classes and jobs—
since these connect with the problem of the division of labor that we have
been discussing. Let me try to place all these interconnected issues in a
somewhat larger context.

By justice we mean two distinct things: serving the common good and
giving to each individual what he is owed or what is good for him. A just society must combine the two. A society is not just if it achieves the common
good but only through the oppression of some individuals, nor if it scrupulously protects the good or rights of individuals but at the sacrifice of the
common good. A just society is one in which there is a complete harmony
between the communal and the individual good, with neither being sacrificed to the other. In Marx's phrase (to quote a *genuine* utopian), it is "an association in which the free development of each is the condition for the free
development of all."[12] This means that the activity that perfects and fulfills
me as an individual happens to be the exact same thing as what the community needs for me to do and be for the perfection of the common good. My
personal calling as an individual coincides with my duty or role as a citizen.
In Aristotle's formula, in such a society the good man and the good citizen
are the same. Here the socialization of the individual, through which he is
molded to the needs of society, constitutes a process not of alienation or in-
doctrination but of self-actualization. My social role corresponds to my true
natural self. That is a just social order in the strict and full sense.

The crucial question—which is the true subject of the *Republic*—is
whether human beings are so constituted by nature as to make such a social

order possible. Now, the common good requires that the city contain certain "parts" adapted for the performance of the essential social tasks—economic production, military defense, and wise political leadership—just as the good functioning of a beehive requires the presence of different kinds of bees specializing in the performance of the various necessary functions. But is there any reason to believe that human individuals are, like bees, born to be one of these social parts? With respect to their abilities, are all individuals naturally gifted at one of these necessary tasks, so that they are either natural workers, natural fighters, or natural rulers? And psychologically, are they so constituted by nature that their true fulfillment as individuals coincides with one of these socially necessary functions?

Socrates clearly, but tacitly, indicates that the answer to this necessary question is no. He does so by asserting that we must make use of a myth, an elaborate *lie* in order to affirm that the answer is yes. The myth of the metals (that we are born for one of the classes) and the myth of the tools (that we are born for one of the jobs) are needed precisely to cover over the problematic truth, the fundamental defect of human political life, that there is no such complete harmony between the needs of society and the good of each individual (although there is certainly a partial harmony). There is an unavoidable mismatch between the whole and its parts. That is the crucial, unstated problem to which these elements of the noble lie are the "solution."

The first and clearest manifestation of this mismatch is the problem we encountered in the first city: while most jobs are good, there are certain jobs absolutely necessary for the common good that are bad for the individual. (And Adeimantus's long speech addressing this problem amounts to a first, crude statement of the noble lie.) If there were time to work our way carefully through the rest of the *Republic*, we would find that other manifestations of the mismatch repeatedly crop up.

I will just quickly describe—without trying to elaborate on or substantiate—the two most obvious. At the beginning of book 5, the interlocutors "arrest" Socrates again and compel him to explain the best city's arrangements with respect to love, family, and children, which they accuse him—correctly—of having tried to ignore. We soon see why.

Love and family life, Socrates now claims, are forms of injustice, because these powerful private attachments diminish and conflict with our dedication to the common good. Indeed, the whole principle of family life—blood, kinship—conflicts with the principle of justice, which is merit. It systematically resists the effort to place each person born into society in the job and class to which he naturally belongs. Perfect justice, then, requires the

abolition of love and family, the communal possession of spouses and children, and the regulation of mating through a state-run eugenics program. In
utopia "neither will a parent know his own offspring, nor a child his parent"
(457d). Now, as mentioned above, this is where many readers turn against
Plato, for this institution seems horrible and inhuman. I can only assert here,
however, that beneath the surface (and not that far beneath), Plato indicates in various ways that he himself understands and embraces this objection. The private family, although indeed unjust, is nevertheless natural to
us and necessary to the happiness of most people. There is a natural incompatibility between the genuine needs of the communal order and those of
its individual human parts.

The ultimate expression of this incompatibility, however, is to be found
in the crowning institution of the third city and of the whole *Republic*: the
rule of philosopher-kings. The highest need of the community is for the philosopher to return to the "cave," the city, and rule it with his great wisdom;
but the highest need of the philosopher is to detach himself from the city
as from all mortal things and to contemplate the eternal. The last thing he
would want is to entangle himself in ruling the sunless, shadow-world of the
cave. For philosophers, it is the ultimate "bad job"—and not justified, as with
the shopkeepers and menial laborers of the first city, by some natural defect
that makes them incapable of anything better. Thus, the fullest perfection
of the community is possible only through arresting and exploiting the fully
perfected individual—a conclusion adumbrated in the very opening lines
of the dialogue, where Polemarchus and the others playfully arrest Socrates
and force him to stay down with them in the Piraeus when he intended to
go back up (327a–328b; see 449a–450a).

In sum, we are not bees. A genuine whole cannot be formed of these parts.
The practical lesson is that while the political world is certainly capable of a
better and a worse, it is both futile and dangerous to try to give to it a perfection that it is not capable of receiving. Still, our strong desire to do so is not
simply a mistake. It stems from important and admirable qualities. But these
can find their true satisfaction only when—embraced and worked through
to their end—they are steered into a different realm altogether, into the
transpolitical life of philosophy.

This quick race through the *Republic*, a long work of extraordinary complexity, naturally stands in need of a hundred clarifications, qualifications,
and replies to potential objections—none of which can be supplied here.
But my purpose has not been to establish this interpretation as the demon-
stratively correct one. Let it be incorrect. Here, as with the Machiavelli in-

terpretation, I have simply sought to provide the reader with a concrete and reasonably plausible *illustration* of what sorts of things are meant by reading between the lines. In particular, I wanted to show that it is not anything so terribly arcane or out of reach.

Beyond that, I have tried to exhibit enough specific cases of genuine puzzles on the surface of the text to provide some *textual* evidence for what we have found constantly repeated in the *historical* evidence: that *something* is going on beneath the surface of these works, that they stand in need of an esoteric interpretation of *some* kind, even if the precise one offered here should be found wanting.

The Theoretical Basis of Philosophical Esotericism:
The "Problem of Theory and Praxis"

Man is the rational animal.
—ARISTOTLE

Man is the political animal.
—ARISTOTLE

The empirical evidence for esotericism—this large collection of quotations—indicates that esoteric communication was a nearly universal practice among Western philosophers prior to the late modern era. Yet this evidence would carry greater plausibility if it *made sense*—if we understood the motives or theoretical rationale behind these reported facts. What feature of the human condition could have induced so many philosophers in such different times and places to engage in this same strange behavior? As we have briefly seen, there are actually four related but distinct motives behind philosophical esotericism. Each is different and needs to be discussed separately. But first they need to be discussed together. Before immersing ourselves in the details of its variants, we need to understand what esotericism is in itself, in its underlying unity and theoretical core—if it has one.

Perhaps it does not. Esotericism is just a particular technique of communication, and different people can make use of it for totally unrelated purposes. Throughout history, as we have seen, the technique of esoteric communication has been a surprisingly widespread phenomenon, and if all these instances are included, it is very unlikely that there is any fundamental underlying unity to be found.

But our subject is *philosophical* esotericism, and here there is more reason to expect a unifying core. To anticipate, I will argue that philosophical esotericism in all its forms ultimately grows out of a single, enduring problem of the human condition: the fact that we are not pure minds, the essential *dualism* of "theory" and "praxis," of reason and its nonrational preconditions. In its philosophical use, the technique of esotericism—which is *dualistic* in its effort to send two messages at once—is an outgrowth of the essential dualism of human life.

THE TWO LIVES

Esotericism, as it first comes to light, is simply a somewhat offbeat manifestation of the art of writing. It is a particular form of *rhetoric*. And, as such, it seems to be a purely practical and literary matter—not a philosophical one.

But rhetoric, as employed by philosophers, is never simply a literary matter, a mere question of taste, style, or effectiveness. For the ultimate ground of rhetoric is something more fundamental: the whole relationship that subsists between the writer and the reader. This crucial issue is most often invisible because one takes for granted that the writer and the reader are not *fundamentally* different. It comes into play when they are—as when an adult tries to explain something difficult to a child (to take the starkest case), or a Buddhist sage addresses a beginning student, or a philosopher speaks to nonphilosophers. Thus, the overriding issue and determinant of *philosophical* rhetoric, at work in all the older books of philosophy, is this crucial question: how should the theoretical human being relate to (and thus address) the practical human being?

This statement requires some unpacking. For starters, it rests on a premise that rings strangely in our ears: that there exist fundamentally different types of human beings or ways of life—and they are unequal. This is an idea that, in our relatively egalitarian and homogeneous world, people incline to dismiss, if they raise it at all. One powerful indication of this tacit rejection is that the various competing hermeneutical theories prevalent today, however much they may disagree in other respects, mostly agree in this, that they speak about "the reader"—as if it should go without saying that all readers are essentially the same and, what is more, that all past writers have proceeded on this assumption. This unspoken assumption effectively excludes from the start all serious consideration of the core idea structuring philosophically esoteric rhetoric: the multiplicity of human types and thus of reader types. This core belief may of course be incorrect—the misguided attitude of an inegalitarian and heterogeneous world. It is certainly distasteful to us, but that cannot detain us. Precisely our purpose here is to achieve a sympathetic understanding of the historical practice of esotericism, and therefore it is important to put ourselves in mind of the conception that prevailed in the earlier "esoteric ages," especially in the classical period.

The crucial point concerns what is meant by a "philosopher."[1] In the older view, it is not simply a person like "you and me," only with a particular interest in philosophy (although there are such people too, of course), any more than a saint is a person with a peculiar liking for religion. Again, philosophy is not a specific subject matter like botany or geology, or a particular technique or expertise, as in the contemporary phrase "a professional philosopher." It is above all a distinct *way of life*—something that makes one a different *type of human being.* One is a philosopher not so much because of what one does or is able to do as because of what one most fundamentally loves and lives for. The philosopher is the person who, through a long dialectical journey, has come to see through the illusory goods for which others live and die. Freed from illusion—and from the distortion of experience that illusion produces—he is able, for the first time, to know himself, to be himself, and to fully experience his deepest longing, which is to comprehend the necessities that structure the universe and human life as part of that universe. This is the famous *vita contemplativa*, an ideal of life found, in one form or another, among virtually all classical and medieval thinkers and still powerful among many modern thinkers as well.

We of course know all about this contemplative ideal but have a tendency to misunderstand by assimilating it to the intellectual models that dominate today, such as the scientist, the scholar, and the intellectual. In some important respects, the classical philosophical ideal has more in common with certain Eastern conceptions, such as the Buddhist sage, than with modern Western ones. Today, we admire the great scientist, scholar, and intellectual primarily for their extraordinary ability, for what they can do, not for their unique way of living and being. The emphasis is on their external achievements, not their attainment of an inner enlightenment, their reaching some higher or purer state of being. Such claims make us suspicious. We believe in intelligence but not in "wisdom"—not in a use of the mind that leads to the transcendence of ordinary life. We greatly respect experts but no longer speak of sages and wise men.

Thus, what we tend to exclude from serious consideration, to say it again, is the crucial idea that the philosopher is a fundamentally different type of human being. To be sure, we are multiculturalists and love to celebrate diversity, but precisely on the premise that these picturesque cultural differences do not go all that deep. For deeper levels, we tend to revert to our older principle: "underneath, we're all the same." We are, as it were, existential monists: there is only one kind of human life. Let me try, then, to make this earlier claim of fundamental difference or existential dualism more precise.[2]

If one person lives predominantly for honor and another for money, they live different lives, but not yet in the radical sense in which the philosopher's life is different from both of theirs. For (typically) the honor-lover has not arrived at his life through the examination and transcendence of the money-lover's life. But that is the case with the philosopher who—much like the Buddhist sage—becomes what he is only by undergoing a wrenching "turning around of the soul" (in Plato's phrase, *Republic* 521c), a kind of philosophic "conversion" or "rebirth," by coming to see the unreal character of the goods on which all nonphilosophic lives are based. Thus, the philosophic life is "different" from other lives, not because it is one alternative among a number of equally valid alternatives, or even because it represents a higher stage of development along the same, continuous path of life. It is the product of a radical break with nonphilosophic life, a discontinuity—a *turning around* of the soul. In the famous discussion of the cave in the *Republic*, Plato depicts the philosopher as living in an entirely different world from the nonphilosopher. Aristotle's account is no less extreme, suggesting that the philosophic life stands to the nonphilosophic as the divine to the human.[3] This is the classical theory of "the two lives": the *vita contemplativa* and the *vita activa*, the lives of theory and praxis.[4]

Now, whether correct or incorrect, this strong dualism obviously has a number of important consequences concerning the *communication* of philosophical understanding, especially through writing. Impressed by the radical distinctness of the philosophic life, earlier thinkers were particularly appreciative of oral communication since it allows one to say appropriately different things to fundamentally different types of people as well as to those in different stages of their development. But these same concerns obviously point to a grave difficulty with written communication.

Writing is a remarkably useful invention, but it involves a fateful trade-off: it makes it possible to address people distant in place and time, but at the price of losing strict control over whom one addresses. It typically forces one to say the same thing to everyone. This is the point that Socrates, who refused to write, most emphasizes in his famous critique of writing in the *Phaedrus*, "every [written] speech rolls around everywhere, both among those who understand and among those for whom it is not fitting, and it does not know to whom it ought to speak and to whom not."[5] Today, although we can certainly understand this claim, we do not see much of a problem here. Socrates does—the univocity of writing is in tension with the duality of lives.

When a philosopher publishes a book—even if it is with the primary intention of addressing other philosophers—he inevitably crosses an essential divide. He displays his life and thought to lives fundamentally different from his own. A "philosophic book" is, as it were, a perpetually open door connecting two alien worlds. It is thus not at all a natural or obvious thing, to be taken for granted ("of course philosophers will write books"). It is strange, a combining of things naturally distinct—a sort of hybrid being, the healthiness of which is a great and open question.

In the end, to be sure, most philosophers have made the choice to engage in publication, but not without protracted and profound reflection about whether to do so, and for what precise purpose, and then finally: *how*—with what *rhetoric*. And each philosopher's answer to this series of questions has ultimately depended on his particular understanding of the relationship—harmonious or antagonistic—subsisting between the two different lives. All the famous books of philosophy lining our shelves were conceived and rhetorically crafted, each in its own unique way, on the basis of some answer to the inescapable "literary" question: what is the proper posture of those who live for truth toward those who live for something other than truth?

Over the last two centuries, philosophers have increasingly moved toward the view that the lives of theory and praxis are ultimately harmonious and—more—essentially the same (our "monist" tendency), and therefore that a philosopher should write openly about all matters, saying the same things to all people. This has now come to seem normal.

But in earlier centuries and especially the classical and medieval periods, thinkers tended strongly to the opposite view: there are certain important truths that those not living a purified, philosophic life will find useless, or harmful, or intolerable. Thus, it is important to avoid saying the wrong thing to the wrong person. One must be a "safe speaker" (as Xenophon called Socrates)—a concept that sounds strange in our garrulous and loose-lipped age.[6] As Diogenes Laertius reports in his "life of Anacharsis": "To the question, 'What among men is both good and bad?' his answer was 'The tongue.'"[7] In general, philosophers have tended to agree with Socrates that the great problem of writing is that it is *univocal*: it says the same thing to all people. And the only solution to this problem—other than the avoidance of writing—has been to write multivocally, to develop a special rhetoric that enables a writing to say different things to different people. Esoteric writing.

We have traced the rhetorical art of esotericism back to the underlying issue of the two lives, the dualism of theory and praxis (especially as it confronts the univocity of writing). But this issue itself is in need of elaboration, for it is something that we imperfectly understand. The dualism of theory and praxis is, for some reason, rarely recognized and thematized today as one of the basic "problems of philosophy" that should structure our thinking—and our reading of earlier philosophers. There is not even a generally accepted understanding of what "the issue of theory and praxis" is. But if we have proved to be blind to esotericism, that is probably because we do not see clearly the problem to which it is the response.

Let me hazard a quick outline of the issue, tracing it from its most obvious and elementary beginnings through its historical transformations in order to see how it gives rise to the practice of philosophical esotericism in its four distinct forms. This very broad-brush discussion will prepare the chapters to follow, where it will be fleshed out and substantiated. For the whole book is essentially an effort to redescribe the history of Western philosophical thinking and writing as it appears when viewed from the standpoint of this fundamental but neglected problematic of theory and praxis.

THE DUALISM OF HUMAN NATURE:
THEORY AND PRAXIS

To begin at the beginning: we all seek to know what is good for us, what will make us happy. But to pursue this question, it is above all necessary to ask what we are, how we are put together. "What is healthful and good," says Aristotle, "is different for human beings and for fish."[8] What is good for a being is *relative*—to its nature or constitution. So what is our nature as humans? That is a famously problematic question. Without aspiring to an answer (or even a full defense of the question), we can review certain classic first moves in an effort to clarify the structure of the issue—which is our limited purpose here. We just want to see how this most basic question leads directly to the problem of theory and praxis.

Aristotle states the classic answer: "Man is the rational animal." This means, not that we are perfectly reasonable, of course, but that we possess the faculty of reason. And to this much, presumably, everyone will agree. Beyond this, the formula means that we naturally incline to make use of this faculty, and that we take inherent delight in doing so, just as we delight in the use of our faculty of sight for its own sake, independent of utility. Still further, it means that we identify our very existence with this faculty. If, through some accident, a person were to lose his opposable thumbs or his ability to walk on two legs, his life as a human being would still remain. But if he were to lose all higher mental functioning, then we would say that the human being we once knew is no longer there. His life—his human existence—is gone, even if his body thrives, all his practical needs are met, and he is rich and famous. For human beings, being truly alive is inseparable from awareness and understanding. I am because I think. Accordingly, Aristotle's formula also means or at least suggests that our highest aliveness and flourishing is to be found in the greatest actualization of this faculty that is most us—in the life of fullest rational awareness, of greatest awakeness, of pure "theory."[9]

But, true as all of this (or some of this) may be, Aristotle's classic answer is manifestly incomplete, because there is more to us than our minds and more to life than thinking. Do we not have bodies, do we not eat, work, fight, and make love? We are not gods. If a mindless body is not a human being, neither is a disembodied mind. Thus, the same philosopher announces with equal pregnancy: "man is the political animal." This is his term for all the rest of us—the part that is not pure mind (which includes the practical or non-contemplative uses of reason). To be sure, in the narrowest sense, it refers to only one particular need: we naturally seek and delight in the company of other human beings for its own sake. But more important, it refers to our general way of approaching all of our needs. As social animals, we pursue our needs not directly, as separated, self-sufficient units, but indirectly and communally, through the formation of cooperative groups where we divide labor for production and join forces for defense.

On a still deeper level, we are political beings because the fullest development of society—which is *political* society, the *polis* or city—not only helps us to satisfy these preexisting, bodily or economic needs but stimulates within us the growth of new and higher needs, it summons us to our higher selves. Political society comes into being for the sake of mere life, according to Aristotle, but exists for the sake of the good life. In the beginning, we create it; after that, it creates us. It turns us from primitive hunter-gatherers into civilized human beings. Rousing us from tribal slumber, it causes the mind to develop and the heart to expand. It transforms us from bodily, economic creatures and clannish family beings into moral beings and citizens. It opens us up to a new world of realities, teaching us to seek honor, love justice, and long for noble and sacred things. The *polis* constitutes the lifeworld within which civilized humanity can fully unfold. We are deeply political animals, then, because only in and through the political community—this new, moralized, and sanctified world—can we truly become all that we are and experience our full human potential.[10]

It would seem, then, that the full Aristotelian view of human nature is dualistic (although not necessarily in a metaphysical sense): two related but quite distinct and potentially rival things make us human: rationality and politicality, that is, knowing and belonging, contemplation and citizenship, thought and action, intellect and morality—*theory and praxis*. We are human by virtue of reason, a unique capacity to connect with objective reality—but also through a unique capacity to connect with our fellow human beings. We humans are strangely composite beings, combining together two different natures—like centaurs or, perhaps, schizophrenics.

If this simple account strikes the reader as too Aristotelian or essentialist, let me cite a passage from Richard Rorty's classic essay "Solidarity or Objectivity," which presents the same basic idea of human dualism in a more postmodern idiom:

> There are *two principal ways* in which reflective human beings try, by placing their lives in a larger context, to give sense to those lives. The first is by telling the story of their contribution to a community. . . . The second way is to describe themselves as standing in immediate relation to a nonhuman reality [i.e., some objective truth]. . . . I shall say that stories of the former kind exemplify *the desire for solidarity*, and that stories of the latter kind exemplify *the desire for objectivity*.[11]

"Objectivity and solidarity" or "rational animal and political animal"—for our general purposes these may be equated. Indeed, in different times and philosophical circumstances, thinkers have employed a wide variety of vocabularies pointing to a fundamental dualism of human life: pure reason and practical reason, mind and body, reason and *existenz*, knowing and doing, truth and life, or, in Strauss's terminology, the philosopher and the city. These dualisms are all different but have a certain fundamental base in common. We are clearly rational beings; and just as clearly, we are not purely rational—not disembodied minds with nothing but theoretical thoughts and contemplative needs. Our minds come attached to something very different: to bodies, which give us *practical* needs, which then drive us together with our fellow human beings in a social solidarity that ultimately stimulates our development as moral and political beings. I use the purposely general term "theory and praxis" to refer to this very broad dualism.

THE PROBLEM OF THEORY AND PRAXIS

From this basic human duality, there arise a number of abiding philosophical questions—I would emphasize five in particular—which form the core of "the problem of theory and praxis."

The most obvious and fundamental concerns the question with which we began. If we are double beings, then in what does our true good consist: theory or praxis (or some mix of the two)? Is happiness to be found in the fullest actualization of our rationality or of our politicality, in the detached quest for theoretical truth for its own sake or in active participation within the moral/political/religious community, in the *vita contemplativa* or in the *vita activa*? The primary issue for almost all classical political philosophers is the exploration of this question—an exploration that culminates, for almost all, in a clear preference for the philosophic life. Ultimately, we do not think in order to act, but act in order to think. In modern thought, there is a strong (but not always dominant) tendency toward the reversal of this conclusion, toward the supremacy of practical life in some sense—which one sees most clearly in Hobbes, in the form of bodily security, Marx, in the form of productive life, and Kant, in the form of moral life.

But there is also a second, closely related question that necessarily arises from our natural duality: Regardless of which element is primary for our happiness, how do the two distinct elements fit together? How does our rationality relate to our politicality, the theoretical human being to the practical human being? What function can philosophic reason perform in the world of practice? As we say today: "what is the proper role of the intellectual?" or "what influence do ideas have in history?"

But the real question here is much larger than the ones we are accustomed to ask. Above all, the issue is: Are the two elements of our nature essentially antagonistic or harmonious? Do they somehow conflict with one another—within either the individual or society—so that humans need to combat one part of their nature (or one part of society) in order to fulfill the other? Does the dualism of theory and praxis constitute, in this way, a tragic flaw in the human condition, a natural obstacle to harmony and happiness in the individual or society? Or, conversely, do the two elements ultimately complement and aid one another, perhaps even merge together, resolving the dualism into monism, so that the human problem, although a bit messy and complex, is in principle capable of harmonious resolution?

Third, this latter, harmonistic possibility produces an important subquestion: If unity is ultimately achievable, is that primarily due to the conformity of praxis to theory or of theory to praxis? Does reason somehow come to rule over political life, bringing it into harmony with its rational demands, or, conversely, does our sociality, being deeper and more powerful than reason, mold the latter in accordance with its needs? To put it simply, does thought shape history or history shape thought (assuming that they do not go their separate, antagonistic ways)?

Fourth, if the latter should prove to be the case, if theory and praxis are harmonious because praxis or history shapes thought, then we get this further question: Is what we mean by "theory"—the capacity for "rationality" or "objective truth"—really possible in the end? If all thought is conditioned by and relative to our particular practical interests or the concepts and assumptions posited by the practical sphere—such as the local language, economic structure, or power hierarchy—then can human reason ever escape historical or cultural relativism? The status of reason, the whole possibility of knowledge is, in this way, ultimately at stake in the question of theory's relation to praxis. If we are not disembodied minds, then how can thought ever be "unconditioned"?

Fifth and finally, these issues also lead to a crucial practical question. If theory and praxis are fundamentally antagonistic, then one of the central issues of political philosophy must be to find the best means through which this conflict, which can never be eliminated, may at least be managed and mitigated. Conversely, if the two elements are ultimately complementary, then the crucial issue becomes rather to find the best means for realizing this potential harmony.

These five precise questions follow with fairly strict necessity once you grant the basic premise that we are not pure minds but dual beings of some sort. But all major philosophers grant that premise. Thus, it makes sense to try to approach the history of political philosophy as, in major part, an effort—explicit or implicit—to answer these five questions. This approach is certainly necessary in order to understand esotericism. The second, third, and fifth questions, in particular, will eventually lead us back to our main topic here, the motive for philosophical esotericism. (The fourth will be crucial to the effort, pursued in the last chapter, to understand the philosophical consequences of esotericism.) Let us try, then, in the space of a few pages, to elaborate these questions and the history of reply to them, starting with the second: how do rationality and sociality relate to each other?

THE RELATIONSHIP BETWEEN OUR RATIONAL AND POLITICAL BEING

Obviously on the most elementary level, reason and sociality depend on and support each other, even to the point of being inseparable. Reason cannot flourish or even develop at all without society, for reason requires language and it greatly benefits from the knowledge imbedded in society's technical, moral, and political traditions and transmitted through its educational practices. Conversely, political life cannot develop and flourish without reason, since it requires a high development of the productive arts and of moral and political understanding.[12]

But as these two elements develop over time, the relation between them does not necessarily remain the same. When and where reason finally comes fully into its own, when it conceives the radical project of relying entirely on its own powers in making sense of the universe without taking anything on faith or tradition, when, in short, it rises to the level of philosophy, rationalism, or science, then this harmony finally turns to opposition. Reason, nurtured in its initial stages by society, now finds its primary obstacle in the fundamental conventions, traditions, and prejudices of society. Conversely, society, initially provisioned and counseled by reason, now finds a primary danger in philosophy's relentless drive to question all of the dogmas upon which it is based. In this second stage, then, philosophy appears essentially antinomian or antisocial, and society seems fundamentally anti-intellectual, antirational, or, in Plato's term, misological ("reason-hating"). There is a head-on collision between the two elements.

But what happens next? That is the crucial question.

Is this second stage the final one—because based on the full development of both reason and society—so that, tragically, the fundamental conflict between the two elements constitutes their true and permanent condition? This conflictual view is the one taken by most classical thinkers. Versions of it can be found expressed (with important differences) in such ancient texts as Sophocles's *Oedipus tyrannus*, Aristophanes's *Clouds*, Plato's *Apology*, the myths of Prometheus, the Sirens, and Pandora, and even in the biblical tales of the Tree of Knowledge and the Tower of Babel. On this view, the two defining elements of human life do not fit together.

Alternatively, perhaps there is a later historical stage—rooted in some further progress of reason or society or both—in which these warring elements return to mutual support and harmony. That is the harmonist view dominant within modern thought, with its humanist optimism and faith in progress.

Notwithstanding its fundamental importance, however, the revolutionary character of this modern shift in philosophical orientation became obscured in later centuries. Indeed, the whole classical, conflictual alternative has largely become lost to view—and with it the relevance and drama of this (second) question of theory and praxis. And all of this for a variety of reasons.

First, the humanistic and progressive character of modern thought not only pushes it toward the harmonist view but eventually causes it to lose all sense of the alternative (as will be seen at greater length in the next chapter). In addition, the conflict between the modern view and the classical alternative has been hidden by the noisy and diverting subconflict that the modern view has generated from within itself. For, as we have just seen, the harmonist view logically divides into two opposite versions. The harmony of the two elements can be established by either the rule of theory over praxis or the reverse. And the whole history of modern thought has largely been driven by the riveting battle centering on this very issue—the "third question" of theory and praxis, which has eclipsed the second.

RATIONALITY AND POLITICALITY IN MODERN THOUGHT: THE ENLIGHTENMENT VS. THE COUNTER-ENLIGHTENMENT

The battle referred to is the familiar conflict between the Enlightenment and the counter-Enlightenment, which may be understood as a contest between the two rival elements of our nature to be the dominating element that restores unity. The Enlightenment champions reason as the controlling phenomenon, and the romantic counter-Enlightenment (in its many incarnations) gives primacy to our social being, our profound political or historical imbeddedness. In other words, just as the medieval period was dominated by the great struggle between reason and revelation, so the modern period has been largely characterized by the battle between reason and various kinds of *secular* antirationalism, all of which ultimately stem from the needs of our nonrational nature, the needs of our practical existence.[13] The battle has gone something like this.

Starting with Bacon, Hobbes, and Descartes and continuing through the Enlightenment even to the present day, the dominant strain of modern philosophy has embraced reason and rationalism, but of a new kind—one that has moved an important step closer to praxis, having sacrificed the more detached and contemplative claims of reason in favor of a more activist as well as more instrumental or technological understanding of rationality. But this modern reform of rationalism was made for the express purpose of rendering it more able to conquer and rationalize the realm of practice, that is, the political world (through enlightenment and revolution) and the physical world (through scientific technology).

This whole strain of thought, which we may loosely call "Enlightenment rationalism," holds, in the first place, that reason, although initially overpowered by the superstitions and prejudices imbedded in the realm of praxis, is able progressively to free itself. As in Plato, philosophic reason possesses the power to escape the cave of social illusion and ascend to an objective, universal, and timeless truth.

But this new Enlightenment rationalism goes decisively beyond Plato and classical rationalism by claiming that theory can not only free itself from praxis but ultimately return to, rule, and rectify praxis. The philosopher, once liberated from society and its prejudices, can, through a process of popular enlightenment, eventually liberate society itself from its illusions and bring it into final harmony with reason, including the public embrace of the philosophic or scientific enterprise. The Enlightenment, broadly construed, includes a number of alternative accounts of how reason might come to rule the world in this way: it might be through the direct action of enlightened rulers, tutored by philosophers, or, more indirectly, through the gradual spread of popular enlightenment promoted by a large new class of "intellectuals" united in the "republic of letters," or, finally, through the impersonal and automatic unfolding of the inherently rational historical process. But, through whatever precise means, philosophers can eventually create an "age of reason" where the dual demands of rationalism and social existence are finally in complete, monistic harmony—unified by and around reason.

But this modern, crusading rationalism soon gave rise, of course, to a reaction—a powerful and continually recurring reaction: the so-called counter-Enlightenment, which, in successive and increasingly radical waves, has been termed "romantic," "pragmatist," "existentialist," "poststructuralist," or "postmodern." The counter-Enlightenment, in its various manifestations, primarily emphasizes the power and value of the other, nonrationalist side of our nature: our life as social and amorous beings, our world of particular attachments, our longings for the noble and the beautiful. And from this nonrational standpoint, it highlights the many ways in which human reason is often a corrosive and destructive force.

Reason is universal, but life is particular. This is especially the case with political life with its basis in local traditions, accidental circumstances, arbitrary practices, and historical memories and legends. Thus, reason's abstract universalism alienates us from the particular attachments that ground communal loyalty and give life all of its sweetness and depth. Again, reason can be dry, analytical, abstract, and static. It puts us out of touch with concrete reality in its irreducible specificity and constant flux. Real life involves a world of intuitions, sentiments, and feelings that reason knows nothing of. Furthermore, reason often tends to a dangerous skepticism that paralyzes action, undermines shared dogmas, and debunks our loftiest ideals. On the other hand, as the French, Russian and other modern revolutions powerfully demonstrate, rationalism in its crusading, Enlightenment form also tends to an opposite danger: to a rigid doctrinairism, dogmatic universalism, ideological imperialism, political fanaticism, and ruthless totalitarianism. Finally, the manipulative, conquering, technological aspect of Enlightenment rationalism has its "Frankenstein" aspects, unleashing forces that then escape its control, creating military and environmental dangers. And, more deeply, it disrupts the posture of grateful acceptance and receptivity necessary for the proper relation toward nature or being.

This counter-Enlightenment critique of reason as harmful to practical life could seem like a return to the classical, conflictual view of theory and praxis, but at bottom it is very different. First, the specific criticisms are somewhat different, since the dangers of Enlightenment rationalism, which is activist and technological, differ from those of classical rationalism, which is detached and contemplative.

More fundamentally, the modern critique of reason (at least in its dominant strain) still recoils from conflictualism. It continues to be driven by the modern assumption that theory and praxis must somehow be harmonious. Therefore, from the harm that Enlightenment rationalism does to society, it concludes, not that there is a tragic and incurable conflict, but that the Enlightenment simply embraced a false—a distorted and defective—form of rationalism. And this conflict of distorted rationalism and society is only temporary and will be cured when we achieve a deeper understanding of the character of true rationality, some kind of "new thinking," especially through what may be called the politicization or historicization of reason.

The counter-Enlightenment, like the Enlightenment it counters, is still reformist and harmonist, only it sees the primary need as the reform, not of society, but of philosophy.

Edmund Burke, for example, writes in order to combat the new dangers brought into the world by the French Revolution and the abstract Enlightenment rationalism that stands behind it. He does so, partly by accepting the Enlightenment mode of reasoning and simply urging the practical inapplicability of its abstract conclusions. But he also goes further, suggesting the need for a kind of new thinking, one more historically imbedded. He argues that the philosopher, in the derivation—and not merely the application—of his principles, must be far more respectful of the local mores and established customs of society. He must take his standard not from abstract, universal reason but from "prescription," from the genuine moral legitimacy that accrues to an established practice, simply because it is established, however arbitrary it may be from the standpoint of abstract reason.[14]

Later, in its more radical, historicist forms, the counter-Enlightenment extends this effort to subordinate reason to society, theory to praxis. It denies to the philosopher any escape from the communal cave. It holds that proud reason is in fact entirely a creature of society—conditioned by and relative to it—so that there are no timeless, culturally independent meanings or truths. Thus, it fully reverses the Enlightenment view: not only is reason incapable of ruling society, it cannot even escape or transcend it; and this means that ultimately it is social life that rules reason. Society determines what will count as "rationality." For reason is a manifestation of life and not the reverse. All philosophy, even the most abstract and airy theorizing, is ultimately rooted in practical life. It is "ideology" of one kind or another, responding to the social needs, the shared commitments, the unthought assumptions of the political community. Thus, not reason but sociality is the deepest and strongest thing in us, and, when this lesson is properly assimilated, the latter can become the true basis for harmonizing thought and action.

Although today, in our postmodern era, this historicist view seems clearly ascendant, the battle very much continues. Yet amid all this conflict, everyone today seems at least to agree on this: these Enlightenment and counter-Enlightenment positions (or rationalist and antirationalist, or modern and postmodern) are opposites that, together, exhaust the possible views on the crucial question of reason and social life. If the answer is still open to debate, at least the question is certain. No important alternative has been neglected.

Yet, as I have been arguing, this view involves a considerable blindness, for in the heat of this subconflict something crucial has indeed been largely neglected. If the camera pans back, suddenly these "opposite" modern positions, locked for centuries in momentous battle, stand revealed as belonging together on the same side of a larger dichotomy: harmonist vs. conflictual. The two modern positions agree in excluding the conflictualist view, in embracing the humanistic imperative that *somehow* theory and praxis *must* be reducible to harmony. They disagree only as to how: the Enlightenment camp standing for the rationalization of political life, the counter-Enlightenment for the politicization of reason. But this noisy disagreement has served to hide from view the more fundamental alternative—the classical, conflictual view. In other words, in modernity, the third question of theory and praxis (the intraharmonist battle) has tended to eclipse the more fundamental second one (harmonist vs. conflictual), so that we barely raise it anymore.

TWO QUALIFICATIONS

I have elaborated this general schema concerning theory and praxis in the belief that it is essential for rendering fully intelligible the theoretical basis of philosophical esotericism in its four forms as well as in its historical mutations. Before employing it for that purpose, however, it is necessary to record some qualifications as well as to address an obvious objection.

I have argued that the dualism in our nature (rationality vs. politicality) gives rise to a duality of views concerning their relationship—conflictualism vs. harmonism (with the latter itself then dividing in two). I then identified these theoretical views with historical periods of thought: conflictualism with classical and medieval philosophy, harmonism, in its two forms, with modern philosophy in its two forms of Enlightenment and counter-Enlightenment thought. Having painted this picture with stark precision, for the sake of a clear theoretical overview, I must now point to the most important ways in which, in practice, these distinctions become blurred or compromised.

The first concerns the harmonist-conflictual distinction. The question of how philosophic rationality and politicality fit together is a complex one, not easily reducible to a binary opposition. Since the tensions between these two things are subject to degree, there will naturally be a continuum running from the extreme conflictual to the extreme harmonist position. Moreover, a given thinker may occupy one point on that continuum regarding some issues of potential conflict and another regarding other issues. It must be kept in mind, then, that although these two broad categories are reasonably coherent theoretically and also practically useful for understanding the general posture of a philosopher toward the world of practice and toward the act of writing, nevertheless each contains a good deal of room for internal variation.

That is why even among those in the same broad camp, no two thinkers employ exactly the same practical posture and rhetoric (consider Plato and Aristotle, for example). Furthermore these differences can easily ripen into conflict, as becomes particularly clear in the modern period (as will be seen at length in chapter 8). There is considerable tension, for example, between those, like Condorcet, who think the harmonist project of "universal enlightenment" can be genuinely universal and those, like Voltaire, who think it must be limited, in practice, to the middle and upper classes; or, again, between those, like Holbach, who believe that society can get beyond the need for religion of any kind and those, like Rousseau, who think that some sort of bare bones, rationalized religion will always be necessary.

The second qualification concerns the ancient-modern distinction. This too must not be understood in too rigid a manner. First, as with the previous distinction, each of these broad categories contains a world of variation and disagreement. But furthermore, not every chronologically modern thinker was "a modern" in the sense of participating in the very broad but still far from universal movement of the Enlightenment (or the counter-Enlightenment). There were certainly ancients among the moderns.[15] What is less clear is if there were genuine moderns among the ancients—thinkers, for example, who favored a philosophical movement to promote something like universal enlightenment as well as the technological conquest of nature.

Having registered these qualifications, we turn to an obvious objection concerning the claimed connection between these two distinctions.

THE PREVAILING IMAGE OF CLASSICAL
AND MODERN THOUGHT

Someone will object that to call the modern period harmonist and the classical one conflictual is, in fact, to reverse the long-prevailing conceptions of both of these eras. We think of the modern age as decentered and turbulent in comparison with the serenity of the classical era, the age of order and harmony, of "noble simplicity and quiet grandeur," in Winckelmann's famous phrase. Certainly it was in the modern period and not the classical that the conflict between reason and society came most to the fore. It was the Enlightenment philosophes, after all, who established the well-known paradigm of the modern philosopher or intellectual who is defined precisely by his opposition to society, his culture criticism, his bold adversarial stance. This reaches its peak in Marx: "Workers of the world unite, you have nothing to lose but your chains." A philosophical call to violent social revolution—now that is *real* conflict between philosophy and society. And it is characteristically modern. It is not a sentence one could ever imagine Aristotle or any major premodern philosopher uttering. It is obvious, then, that it is actually classical thought, with its famous emphasis on order, balance, and harmony, that has tended to exclude the conflictual view of theory and praxis. Modern thought is guilty of no such neglect: the conflictual view is rather its particular specialty.

All of this is very true, in a sense, but misleading. It is true that the Enlightenment philosophers believed reason and truth to be in conflict with *existing* society, but—unlike the classics with their genuinely conflictual view—not with society as such. They viewed this conflict not as natural and permanent, as did the classics, but as historically contingent, solvable, and so ultimately reducible to harmony.

What is more, it is precisely this underlying harmonism that produced the appearance of great conflictualism. The Enlightenment philosophers pushed their rationalist critique of existing society so openly and aggressively only because they expected, through this temporary heightening of conflict, to bring about a future society that would be in genuine harmony with reason. Enlightenment intellectuals are indeed against their times, but only because ahead of them. Thus, their famous emphasis on conflict and bold opposition and even their call for violent revolution all derive from a powerful new harmonism (as is particularly obvious in Marx). Modern "conflictualism" is really a consequence and sign of its opposite: it is war heightened precisely by a new hope to end all war. It is *pseudo*-conflictualism. The real thing conducts no such crusades because it entertains no such harmonist hopes. It is quietly resigned to (measured) conflict as something that can never be overcome.

This same structure of thought—a temporarily heightened conflict deriving from increased faith in harmony—also characterizes the alternative camp within modernity, the counter-Enlightenment. From Burke to Foucault, it emphasizes and heightens the conflict between reason and society, although now putting primary blame on the former instead of the latter. In its different incarnations, we have seen, it attacks rationalism for such varied social evils as political doctrinairism and utopianism, the uprooting of tradition and inheritance, violent revolution, intolerance, persecution, colonialism, and totalitarianism. But, again, it engages in this political critique of reason, heightening the conflict between rationalism and society, precisely because, rejecting classical dualism, it is moved by the powerful monist faith that this conflict is somehow an aberration, a mistake, another problem to be solved. Harmony is possible. But it will be achieved, not in Enlightenment fashion by changing society to match the demands of reason, but rather the reverse: by forcing reason to realize that its fundamental principles have no other source or ground than the conventions or shared commitments of the particular society in which fate has placed it. As Rorty puts it, this movement "reinterprets objectivity as intersubjectivity, or as solidarity."[16] Thus, all its noisy confrontations notwithstanding, the counter-Enlightenment camp holds that, properly interpreted, rationality and social consensus or solidarity are so far from being in fundamental conflict that they are, at root, the same thing.[17]

Furthermore, just as the harmonist modern period in both its forms is in this way broadly misunderstood as conflictual, so the conflictual classical period is commonly misinterpreted as harmonist. Genuine conflictualism tends to be rather quiet and understated. Since it sees no solution, since it entertains no activist hopes for overcoming the opposition of reason and society, it does nothing to call undue attention to the issue, to provoke confrontation, to raise consciousness, to rally the troops—all of the steps, so familiar to us, of modern movement politics. And since we "solutionists" tend to believe that where there is a problem, there will be a movement, when we see no movement, we suspect there is no great problem. But here the opposite is more nearly the truth: the classics speak and act with more reserve concerning the conflict between theory and praxis precisely because they regard it as so great a problem. In their eyes, it is a permanent flaw in the human condition that can never be overcome but must simply be lived with, managed, endured. And one obvious aspect of managing it is not to constantly call people's attention to it, but rather, when possible and useful, to keep it quiet and under the rug.

This curious tendency of the two rival views of theory and praxis to appear as their opposites is responsible for a great deal of confusion concerning the true spirit of classical and modern thought. But above all, the pseudo-conflictualism of modern thought has helped to conceal—and so perpetuate, by sheltering from criticism—the modern tendency to ignore the genuine conflictual alternative.

THE PRACTICAL MEANS FOR MANAGING THE
THEORY/PRAXIS TENSION: "PHILOSOPHICAL POLITICS"

Having discussed how our rationality and politicality relate to one an-other—as posed by the second and third questions—we turn to the fifth and more practical issue: How is that relation to be handled in practice? If the relation is antagonistic, how is the conflict to be managed? If potentially harmonious, how is the potential to be realized? These very general questions quickly translate into a myriad of smaller ones of every kind.

The classical, antagonistic view, to start there, leads directly to such questions as these. While the philosopher is in tension with "society" as a whole, he will presumably be in more conflict with some of its parts than others. With what elements in society, then, should he seek to ally himself: the aristocrats, the oligarchs, the middle class, the demos? And what does he have to offer such people? What form of government is best from the standpoint of the interests of the philosophical life? Should he engage in politics himself? What should be his posture toward the prevailing religion and its authorities? What other institutions and movements are around at the time—religious, political, moral—that might constitute particular opportunities or dangers for him and his kind? How should he make a living? How can he win over the most talented of the young to the philosophical life without enraging the city? Should he attempt to establish a philosophical school, as Plato was the first to do with the Academy? Should he write books? And with what form and rhetoric? What places are available to go into exile if necessary? Should he cultivate friendly tyrants or monarchs for this purpose? Obviously the answers and even the questions will vary considerably from one time and place to another.

To give a name to this wide-ranging set of questions, one might call it "philosophical politics," which may be defined as the effort to secure the practical interests of the theoretical life—the safety and the propagation of philosophy—in the face of the natural hostility of the nonphilosophical community. Among other things, this concept helps one to understand how even those classical philosophers who most celebrate the apolitical ideal of pure contemplation may still be found engaging in political activity (either directly or through their writings and teaching). For the more a contemplative philosopher understands his own life to be based on the radical rejection and transcendence of the ordinary, political life of those around him, the more he must feel isolated and fear the potential hostility of that community, and thus the more he will be brought around to the practical necessity of philosophical politics. But this political activity, as real as it is and as elaborate as it may sometimes become, still remains very different from the sort of political activism by philosophers that emerges in the modern period under the influence of the harmonist idea, as will become clear in chapter 8.[18]

The modern, harmonist view leads to a basic transformation in the philosopher's practical aim: it is no longer to manage but to overcome the tension between theory and praxis, to actualize their potential unity. But here, as we have seen, there are the two rival camps, and they have very different, almost opposite practical concerns. Enlightenment philosophers seek the best ways to address and transform the political world, in order to bring it into harmony with reason. Counter-Enlightenment philosophers seek the best ways to address and transform other philosophers, in order to bring them and their reasoning into harmony with the political world.

From a practical standpoint, the latter project is much more straightforward. Such thinkers just need to teach and write books. Their highest practical need is for a new rhetoric that is somehow able to penetrate and humble the Enlightenment mind.

By contrast, Enlightenment philosophers, since their target is the political world, have many more practical concerns. Most of the questions raised by premodern thinkers continue to be relevant for them, but important new issues also arise, especially concerning how they can give their philosophical ideas increased practical effect. In different times and circumstances, they will confront such questions as these. Can the effort of modern natural philosophy to "conquer nature" and generate new technologies useful to ordinary life finally win for the philosophic life a broad respectability and status—even among the suspicious masses—that it never dreamt of in the past? Has the particular invention of printing changed in significant ways the situation of the philosopher or the power of philosophical doctrines in the world? Are there also significant lessons to be learned from the example of the Christian church, which has achieved great power in the world through nonpolitical and nonmilitary means—and largely through the power of a book? Should the philosopher try to strengthen his position by uniting somehow with other philosophers, as the clergy did in the church? Given the systematic danger that the Christian church has posed to the power of the state, does this give the philosophers new opportunities—lacking in antiquity—to make themselves useful to the latter? Can philosophers hope to transform the world through this sort of influence over enlightened rulers, like Frederick II of Prussia and Catherine the Great of

Russia? Or should they rely, instead, on the power they possess to shape the world indirectly, enlightening it through their books and through the dissemination of their ideas by a large new class of intellectuals and men of letters? Has the rift within the church created by the Protestant Reformation given them still other new ways to make themselves useful and powerful? Are there other movements around, like Freemasonry, that can help them spread their ideas and influence? Or is it rather the case that there is a rational "historical process," operating behind the scenes, that will bring about the triumph of reason in history? And in that case, what becomes of the role of the philosopher and intellectual? Are they reduced to being the "vanguard' of this impersonal process, announcing, explaining, and clearing the way for it?

Entire books could be written about any of these questions. The present book is about this one: How should the philosopher communicate his thought? In particular, how should he write?

PHILOSOPHICAL ESOTERICISM IN ITS FOUR FORMS

If we return, with this question in mind, to the classical, antagonistic position, the answer is pretty obvious. The conflictual view of theory and praxis leads directly to the need for esotericism—and in three distinct ways.

First, on this view, philosophy or rationalism poses a grave danger to society. For reasons that we have partly seen and that will be elaborated in chapter 6, all political communities are ultimately based, not on reason, but on some form of unexamined commitment or illusion. A fully rational and enlightened society is not possible. Thus, there is a fundamental tension between truth and political life—a conflict that no reform can ever cure. To manage this conflict and protect society from harm, then, the philosopher must conceal or obscure his most subversive ideas, while also, perhaps, promoting salutary ones—practicing *protective esotericism.*

Second, society likewise poses a grave danger to the philosopher. There are a great many sources of intolerance and persecution in the human heart, and the philosopher, being particularly strange, skeptical, aloof, exposed, and superior in intelligence, can easily trigger all of them. But given the point we have just considered—the genuine danger that philosophy poses to society—the hostility of society to the philosopher is also not entirely unreasonable. It is not simply a product of vulgar ignorance and misunderstanding that might be dispelled someday by greater education and familiarity, as the harmonist Enlightenment view would maintain. The danger of persecution is structural and permanent. To defend himself against it, the philosopher must conceal his more provocative or heterodox ideas, while possibly also seeking positive ways to make himself seem more acceptable — engaging in *defensive esotericism.*

But if philosophical publication is thus dangerous to both the writer and the general reader, what is the point of writing at all? Since the conflictual view excludes any hope for fundamental political transformation through the genuine and lasting enlightenment of the general population, that cannot be the purpose (although more limited hopes for partial and temporary reform might be an aim). Thus, the primary purpose of writing philosophical books is reduced to this: the education of the gifted, potentially philosophical individual.

But the conflictual view also has important implications for how this philosophical pedagogy must be carried out. A philosophical education is not simply intellectual, a pure matter of learning. It involves facilitating a transition from one way of life to another—indeed, to a life that is, on the conflictual view, fundamentally different from and opposed to the life one starts with. It requires a difficult conversion that shakes one to the core. If that is the case, then an open and straightforward approach to education that simply lays out the truth will not work. The student must be moved along gradually, artfully, in appropriate stages. This dialectical process will require withholding or managing the truth, so that the student is compelled to find it for himself, at his own pace, and in a form he can, at each stage, digest. In this way, the conflictual view naturally leads to the necessity for *pedagogical esotericism.* In other words, the same thing that makes protective esotericism necessary for the general reader—the tension between truth and ordinary life—makes pedagogical esotericism necessary for the potential philosophers.[19]

These three forms of esotericism, flowing as they do from the same premise, are typically found together. And thus united, they constitute what I will call *classical esotericism*, meaning, not only the esotericism characteristic of the classical thinkers, but also the fullest, "classic" development of the phenomenon of philosophical esotericism.

When we turn to the modern, harmonist view of theory and praxis in its Enlightenment form, the consequences for writing are quite different, but equally unmistakable. The harmonist premise, by holding out the hope for a convergence of reason and society, inspires the philosopher to take a more activist stance, to promote the creation of a rational world. This activist stance, in turn, leads directly to esotericism—if of a more limited, less thoroughgoing kind—and in two ways.

First, in becoming engaged in a project for fundamental political transformation, philosophy inevitably takes on in some degree the political tendency to prefer powerful ideas to true ones, to shape public doctrine in accordance with what people in a given time and place will be willing to believe and follow—in a word (if a later one) to become propagandistic. But the new rhetorical demands on the Enlightenment philosophers concern not only their quest for power and political efficacy, but also the responsible use of that power. They seek to subvert and transform traditional society, but in a gradual and orderly way, and this too requires the careful management of what they say and of how and when they say it. In switching from primarily pedagogical goals to political ones, in short, Enlightenment philosophers replace pedagogical esotericism with a *political esotericism*.

Second, as we have already seen, the activist, rationalizing stance of the Enlightenment philosophers inevitably led to a great, if temporary, increase in the tension between philosophy and society and therewith to a great increase in the danger of persecution, and thus to a heightened need for defensive esotericism.

It is not without irony, of course, that the belief in the potential harmony of theory and praxis should lead to a new form of esotericism as well as to the intensification of an old one. But both are made necessary, not by the existence of that harmony, but by the political activism needed to bring it into being. Thus, over the last two centuries, as that activism has slowly approached its goal, this esotericism has inevitably faded away.

In conclusion, if the historical testimony presented earlier showed esotericism to be, not an occasional or ad hoc practice, but one of the most constant features of the philosophic life, the present chapter shows why. Philosophical esotericism, especially in its classical but even in its modern, Enlightenment form, is a practical response to one of the most fundamental features of human life, the dualism and potential conflict of theory and praxis. Philosophical esotericism is a "doublespeak" elicited by the doubleness of life itself.

ESOTERICISM, ENLIGHTENMENT, AND HISTORICISM

The foregoing discussion not only helps to clarify what philosophical esotericism is in itself, but also to situate it in relation to other intellectual movements. Specifically, it shows the surprising inner connection among esotericism, historicism, and Enlightenment.

The connection of the first two will play a crucial role in chapter 10, where we explore the philosophical consequences of the theory of esotericism and in particular the central use that Strauss makes of this theory in his efforts to mount a new response to the challenge of historicism. What we have seen here is that these two seemingly unrelated phenomena are closely connected, for both are responses to the same problem of theory and praxis. In one sense, they are opposite responses, in that historicism is a form of the harmonist view and esotericism (in its premodern form) is an outgrowth of the conflictual view. The former claims that philosophy is necessarily a manifestation and support of the society in which it is imbedded, the latter that it is necessarily antagonistic to that society.

In another sense, however, the two stand together in opposition to the third alternative, the other form of the harmonist view—the universalistic rationalism of the Enlightenment. Both regard the latter as dangerous to the political world. But esotericism would render philosophic reason less dangerous through *rhetorical* means, by simply hiding some of its conclusions or adjusting the expression of them to local circumstances, whereas historicism would do so through *epistemological* means, by attacking reason itself and its aspirations to universal validity. From this point of view, historicism comes to light as a kind of radical replacement for esotericism.

OUR RESISTANCE TO THE CONFLICTUAL VIEW— AND TO ESOTERICISM

One further set of conclusions emerges from this discussion. In the effort to clarify and defend the foregoing account of theory and praxis—especially the history of the rival views of their relationship—it has been necessary to briefly discuss the ways in which modern thought has turned away from and ignored the conflictual view of theory and praxis, the view that forms the essential basis of esotericism (in its classical form). We have also seen how this modern neglect of the antagonistic view has itself become hidden from view. These points will play a crucial role in the next chapter, on the phenomenon of our blindness and resistance to esotericism.

[4]

Objections, Resistance,
and Blindness to Esotericism

> Everyone is forward to complain of the prejudices that mis-
> lead other men or parties, as if he were free and had none of
> his own. This [inconsistency] being objected on all sides, it is
> agreed that it is a fault and a hindrance to knowledge. What
> now is the cure? No other but this, that every man should let
> alone others' prejudices and examine his own.
> —JOHN LOCKE, *Conduct of the Understanding*

We have seen substantial testimony showing that—for some reason or
other—philosophers frequently engaged in esoteric writing. And then we
have examined their reasons for doing so. It remains to ask: what are our
reasons for feeling that they could not have done so? For, a crucial part of our
effort to understand esotericism sympathetically is to understand our long
lack of sympathy with it.

That readers should have questions about and objections to the arguments presented here is to be expected. I will try to address some of them in
the present chapter, others later. But the phenomenon at issue here extends
well beyond routine reservations. As we have partly seen, there are various
signs and indications that modern culture harbors a powerful resistance to

esotericism that lies deeper than facts and arguments. It is this above all that must be addressed before we can usefully move on.

ESOTERICISM AND MODERN CULTURE

What are the "signs and indications" of this resistance? For starters, as the evidence for philosophical esotericism slowly accumulates and one begins to truly take seriously the possibility that it is, after all, real—and more than real, a major historical phenomenon—one is likely to be struck, eventually, by the following reflection. How could there possibly have been such an important, almost universal practice going on in the world and we didn't even know about it? How could we have missed something so big? Of course, if the evidence for esotericism were extremely obscure, there would be no puzzle. But it is not. It has been sitting there in relative plain sight for centuries. So why have we not seen it? One is all but compelled to wonder: Has something been impeding our vision? Is there something wrong with the way that we look at the world?

This hypothesis grows stronger when one reflects on the fact that we were not always unaware of esotericism: it *became* unknown in the course of the nineteenth century (as Goethe was reporting). But how does a whole culture suddenly lose awareness of a practice that was, until relatively recently, so widespread, so openly discussed, so long enduring, so crucially important, and so thoroughly documented in the historical record? It is not easy to think of a comparable episode of philosophical forgetting, of intellectual expungement. Mustn't powerful cultural forces of some kind be at work here?

Then there is the next twist in the unfolding story: In the mid-twentieth century, Leo Strauss and others attempt to revive the understanding of esotericism. And, again, we see something unusual: these efforts are met with a resistance that seems to go beyond the usual sorts of scholarly disagreement and skepticism. To be fair, there were important exceptions: Alexandre Kojève, Arnaldo Momigliano, Gershom Scholem, Hans-Georg Gadamer, and a few others expressed real interest and admiration for Strauss's discoveries.[1] But for the most part—and especially in the Anglo-American world—the idea was treated as wrongheaded in the extreme, not to say crazy. We confine ourselves to scholars who in other respects express real appreciation for Strauss's work. Stephen Holmes writes: "We can confidently assume that Strauss's obsession with esotericism and persecution had its roots not in scholarship, but in the unthinkable tragedy of his generation [i.e., the holocaust]."[2] Gregory Vlastos sadly laments Strauss's "delusion that the classics of political philosophy were meant to be read as palimpsests—strange aberration in a noble mind."[3] And George Sabine fears that esotericism simply amounts to "an invitation to perverse ingenuity."[4] These are honest assessments by thoughtful scholars who, in their dismissive characterizations of esotericism—"obsession," "delusion," "aberration," "perverse"—give accurate expression to the predilections of our time concerning this issue.[5]

But the clearest evidence pointing to a unique resistance in modern culture emerges from the comparison of our attitudes toward esotericism with those of other places and times—the comparative study of "esotericism reception." It is a simple, empirical fact, such comparisons show, that no other culture has shared our peculiarly negative instincts in this matter—our firm disapproval and disbelief.

This was the clear finding, for example, of the intercultural communication literature discussed in chapter 1. Virtually all societies outside the modern West embrace a "high context" communicative style that emphasizes indirection and speaking between the lines. We, by contrast, are a uniquely "low context" culture that not only rejects indirect communication for ourselves but tends to regard those who do practice it with incomprehension bordering on denial.

The exact same picture emerges from the historical evidence. The examination of the philosophical testimony regarding esotericism expressed over the last two millennia of Western history shows that the broad rejection of the reality of esotericism is a thesis unique to late Western modernity. (And it is not as if we have a lot of important new information on the subject to justify this break with the judgment of all other ages.)

What is in some ways even more striking is that, in the two millennia of Western philosophy prior to 1800, not only is the denial of esotericism extremely rare, but no one even expresses great dislike or disapproval of the practice either. To be sure, here and there, one finds concern about the dishonesty involved or the potential for abuse or the difficulty created for interpretation. But nowhere does this rise to the level of outright condemnation or the refusal to practice it. During the long history of Western thought prior to our time, amid all the changes of politics, religion, and culture, virtually everyone essentially approves of or accepts esotericism. The long, angry list of objections to it—be detailed momentarily—that forms the ground of our confidence that this repugnant practice could not possibly have been widespread somehow did not affect the people of earlier times in the same way.

In short, both the denial and the strong disapproval of esotericism—which feel to us so natural and self-evident—actually turn out to be rather local attitudes, the unique and quite eccentric response of our tiny little corner of history. While all other ages seem naturally to appreciate that the philosophers typically approach the act of writing with a good deal of caution, irony, and artfulness, we alone scrutinize their manuscripts with earnest literal-mindedness. For some reason, when it comes to this particular issue, we moderns, in all our sophistication, play the rubes and clueless provincials, with everyone else, as it were, chuckling behind our backs. We clearly have issues here.

THE EXAMPLE OF JESUS' PARABLES

Given the importance of this phenomenon, it will help to consider a concrete illustration. It concerns the most famous practitioner of riddling speech in the Western tradition—although not a philosopher.

As everyone knows, the New Testament depicts Jesus as employing a very specific form of rhetoric in addressing the people (as distinguished from his disciples): he speaks in *parables*. "He did not speak to them [the people] without a parable, but privately to his own disciples he explained everything."[6] Yet parables can be used to make things either more clear and concrete or more obscure and challenging. We today would of course assume that Jesus had only the former intention. Surely he must have sought to make himself as clear and accessible as possible to everyone. But our faith in plainspeaking openness is by no means as universally self-evident as we blithely assume. Typically, prophets do not share that faith. In a very different spirit, Jesus sternly declared: "Give not that which is holy to dogs; neither cast ye your pearls before swine" (Matt. 7:6). In Matthew and elsewhere, he explicitly states his reason for speaking as he does—and it is not to make things more clear and accessible:

> Then the disciples came and said to him, "Why do you speak to [the people] in parables?" And he answered them, "To you it has been given to know the secrets of the kingdom of heaven, but to them it has not been given. For to the one who has, more will be given, and he will have an abundance, but from the one who has not, even what he has will be taken away. This is why I speak to them in parables, because seeing they do not see, and hearing they do not hear, nor do they understand." (Matt. 13:10–12; see also Matt. 7:6, 19:11, 11:25; Col. 1:27; 1 Cor. 2:6–10; 1 John 2:20, 2:27; Prov. 23:9; Isa. 6:9–10)

Again, in Mark 4:11, Jesus tells the disciples: "To you has been given the secret of the kingdom of God, but for those outside everything is in parables." In a similar spirit, Jesus "strictly charged the disciples to tell no one that he was the Christ [i.e., the messiah]" (Matt. 16:20; see Matt. 12:16; Mark 8:30; Luke 9:21). Even with the disciples, Jesus was not completely open: "I have yet many things to say to you, but you cannot bear them now" (John 16:12). Moreover, we can easily see for ourselves the truth of what Jesus claims about the parables, for most of them are indeed not clarifying but rather difficult to understand. Even the disciples are depicted as having great trouble interpreting them. We have, then, extensive, unambiguous, and uncontested textual evidence that Jesus spoke to the people in a riddling, esoteric manner (even if his precise reasons for doing so remain somewhat unclear).

Now, in addition to these biblical texts, we also have a second, very large body of texts showing how earlier ages read and interpreted the first set. This is what we are particularly interested in. We want to see concretely how readers of very different periods *reacted to* these same biblical texts, with their explicit claims of esotericism. Did they find them plausible? Did they accept or deny, approve or disapprove of esotericism? The long, unbroken tradition of biblical commentary that we possess enables us to conduct this experiment in esotericism reception over a period of almost two thousand years.

Thus, to begin with Thomas Aquinas, in an article of the *Summa Theologica* entitled "Whether Christ Should Have Taught All Things Openly?" he explains that the people to whom Jesus spoke were "neither able nor worthy to receive the naked truth, which He revealed to His disciples" and that is why he "spoke certain things in secret to the crowds, by employing parables in teaching them spiritual mysteries which they were either unable or unworthy to grasp."[7] Similarly, Calvin, in his *Commentaries*, remarks:

> Christ declares that he intentionally spoke obscurely, in order that his discourse might be a riddle to many, and might only strike their ears with a confused and doubtful sound. . . . Still it remains a fixed principle, that the word of God is not obscure, except so far as the world darkens it by its own blindness. And yet the Lord conceals its mysteries, so that the perception of them may not reach the reprobate.[8]

Grotius explains:

> He spoke to the people through the indirectness of parables, that those who heard Him might not understand, unless, that is, they should bring thereto such earnestness of mind and readiness to be taught as were required.[9]

In addition, Augustine maintains:

> the Lord's meaning was therefore purposely clothed in the obscurities of parables, that *after His resurrection* they [the parables] might turn them to wisdom with a more healthy penitence.[10]

And, for one more example, John Locke, emphasizing the political element, argued that Jesus "perplex[ed]" his meaning to avoid being arrested before he could complete his mission:

> For how well the chiefs of the Jews were disposed towards him, St. Luke tells us, chap 11:54, "Laying wait for him, and seeking to catch something out of his mouth, that they might accuse him," which may be a reason to satisfy us of the seemingly doubtful and obscure way of speaking, used by our Savior in other places—his circumstances being such, that without such a prudent carriage and reservedness, he could not have gone through the work which he came to do.[11]

From these very brief excerpts, we see that there was some ongoing and lively disagreement about the precise purpose of Jesus' practice of esotericism but that there was no trace of dispute concerning its existence. This was accepted as beyond question.

If one expanded this brief survey to include the entire two-thousand-year tradition of Bible commentary, essentially the same results would be found—until, that is, one gets to the last century and a half. For, as soon as one crosses over into our strangely enchanted era, everything suddenly changes. Now, for the first time in history, one finds the widespread denial of Jesus' esotericism—notwithstanding the extremely solid textual basis for it and the concurrence of virtually all commentators of all previous ages. Our experts float one loosely grounded philological speculation after another— primarily conjectures concerning the adulteration of the texts—in an effort to prove that Jesus actually spoke as we modern-day Westerners would have expected him to, with plainspeaking openness. Here the alien, outlier status of our anti-esoteric culture becomes plain for all to see, clearly marked out in the single densest, richest, and longest tradition of textual commentary in Western history.

As the distinguished literary critic Frank Kermode remarked with some wonder in his 1978 Charles Eliot Norton lectures on the hermeneutics of biblical commentary:

For the last century or so there has been something of a consensus among experts that parables of the kind found in the New Testament were always essentially *simple*, and always had the same kind of point, which would have been *instantly taken* by all listeners, outsiders included. Appearances to the contrary are explained as consequences of a process of meddling with the originals [i.e., textual alteration] that began at the earliest possible moment. The opinion that the parables *must* originally have been thus, and only thus, is maintained with an expense of learning I can't begin to emulate, against what seems *obvious*, that "parable" does and did mean much more than that. When God says he will speak to Moses openly and not in "dark speeches," the Greek for "dark speeches" means "parables." . . . "Speak in parables" is the opposite of "openly proclaim."[12]

Without knowing it, what Kermode has run up against here, to his bewilderment and chagrin, is our eccentric modern resistance to esotericism. His simple observations of how, with a vast "expense of learning," modern experts strive to overturn the obvious, driven by "the opinion that the parables *must* originally have been" simple and transparent—all of this is paradigmatic for our unique age.[13] Wherever it is a matter of esotericism, in the sphere of religion no less than in philosophy, our age stands stubbornly in opposition—and utterly alone against all the rest of history.

In view of all this, it becomes necessary to turn the spotlight around, so to speak, and momentarily shift the focus from esotericism to ourselves and our habits of thought—in the hope of identifying, confronting, and overcoming the sources within us of this resistance.

But this effort at self-examination is also vitally important for its own sake—not just to understand esotericism but, even more, to know ourselves. For the blindness to esotericism—which has deep theoretical roots—is actually one of the most profound and revealing features of modern thought as such. In other words, if the modern mind (like the mind of every age) wears certain blinders of which it is unaware, it has no means to discover those blinders except by bumping into some important reality that it has been unable to see. The phenomenon of esotericism serves that function. It constitutes, for us, a kind of disclosive device that lights up many of the concealed assumptions that have long conditioned and limited our thinking. It provides, strange to say, a unique window on our souls.

It should be kept clearly in mind, however, that the question under examination here is not why we ourselves do not write esoterically (or whether we are correct in making this choice), but why we feel so certain that others did not do so. What is the source of our resistance to the *historical reality* of esotericism?

THE SOURCES IN MODERN CULTURE OF
THE DENIAL OF ESOTERICISM

There is a long list of reasons, some obvious, some less so, why the idea of esotericism strikes us instinctively—that is, prereflectively and profoundly—as something unsavory or harmful or, at any rate, fundamentally implausible.

The most profound (but least obvious) reason concerns, not the visible characteristics or consequences of esotericism, but its source, its essential premise—the antagonistic view of theory and praxis. Somehow, there is something essential to the modern mind that stands in indignant opposition to this view. Let me sketch out a suggestion for how to understand this.

Consider, for a starting point, the oft-repeated observation that modern man lacks a sense of tragedy. If true, this would constitute a crucial blinder, hindering access to the conflictual posture, which obviously has much in common with the tragic view of life. Sophocles's *Oedipus tyrannus*, arguably the most powerful and representative of ancient Greek tragedies, was precisely a tragedy of theory and praxis, of the incurable conflict of truth and political life. It tells of a wise king, a man of unique vision, who, having been led to violate the most sacred taboos, brings a plague upon the political community until finally he ends it—by blinding himself. Today, while people are often intrigued by this play, it does not seem to speak to them, to address a problem that they themselves address. Quite the opposite: for us, "Oedipus" names a classic psychological disorder, present at our imperfect beginnings but more or less *curable* through the science of psychotherapy, through the life-healing power of truth. This reversal of the tragic tale is typically modern: the very idea that life could have an incurable problem at its core—that the two essential elements of our nature, rationality and sociality, could be permanently at war—strikes people today as simply too tragically disordered to be true.[14]

So where does this modern resistance to tragedy—and thus to conflictualism and therewith to esotericism—come from? Why do we find fundamental disorder implausible? Certainly not because of a naive idealism of some kind, a faith in the divine or natural order of the universe—"it all fits together." For a tough-minded realism about the accidental and radically imperfect character of the world is another prominent feature of modern thought. Somehow, we are just as inclined to be skeptical of idealism as of tragedy—of order as of disorder.

The source of our resistance to tragedy would thus seem to be something new and more complex: a novel kind of idealism that emerges precisely on the basis of modern realism—secular *humanism*. It is the faith, not in God, and not in nature, but in man—in his ability to triumph, sooner or later, over the grave imperfections of his received condition. It is the faith in progress and human conquest. The humanist mind rejects the vision of a fixed order—as well as of fixed disorder. The vision that defines it is rather this: the world has an original disorder that can progressively be controlled and cured through human effort.

If we continue to seek the source, in turn, of this new humanistic posture, we find that it is plausible and attractive from a number of different points of view. But this precise formula would seem to be crucial above all for the anti-clerical and secularizing quest to liberate us from the rule of a higher power. For if the world is originally well ordered, then God is needed to explain that order. And if it is incurably disordered, then God is needed to save us from that disorder. Only if life is originally bad but fixable through human effort is it the case that God is neither a necessary hypothesis nor a fundamental need. That is why this specific humanistic posture seems to be the product, not so much of some new discovery about the world, as of a need, a demand, an imperative. The humanist credo that life has no fundamental problems that we cannot cure has the character less of a calm, settled belief than of a mixture of hope and insistence.[15] This secularizing imperative, then, would seem to be the ultimate ground of our determined disbelief in the tragic view of life, in the antagonistic relation of theory and praxis, and therewith in the reality of philosophical esotericism.

Some simple evidence for these admittedly large claims can be seen in the basic trajectory of modern philosophy. When we look back at the origins of modern thought, one of the most striking things is that its enthusiastic embrace of the project to harmonize theory and praxis was based more on a leap in the dark than on any solid evidence that it was reasonable and likely of success. In the realm of natural philosophy, for example, when thinkers like Bacon, Hobbes, and Descartes proclaimed their intention to redirect contemplative philosophy to the practical end of the "relief of man's estate" (Bacon) by making man "the master and owner of nature" (Descartes), they did so long before the progress of science proved that such far-reaching technological mastery was actually possible.

One sees the same leap in political philosophy: the early Enlightenment thinkers eagerly embarked on their unprecedented effort to enlighten and rationalize the political world well before there was any solid historical evidence that such a radical transformation of public consciousness would be possible or salutary.

What is more, as this enlightening effort proceeded, it soon became clear that, notwithstanding its partial successes, it was indeed dangerous in a variety of ways to social health, as the thinkers of the counter-Enlightenment thunderously proclaimed. Yet once again one sees something remarkable: these latter thinkers, obsessed as they were with the dangers of Enlightenment harmonism, were nevertheless not tempted to return to the conflictual view and to classical esotericism. Still driven by the spirit of humanist harmonism, they chose instead to continue the pursuit of unity—only in the reverse manner by subordinating theory to practice. They willingly replaced the rationalization of politics with the politicization of reason. But of course this move involved great dangers of its own, culminating eventually in the radical historicist view that wholly relativizes reason. So powerful, in other words, is the modern harmonist imperative that, rather than return to classical dualism and esotericism, one philosopher after another pursued this goal even at the price of gravely undermining the claims of reason.

It seems clear, in sum, that there exists in modern thought a *fundamental* resistance to classical esotericism—and fundamental in two respects. It is modern thought at its *deepest* level—the secularizing, humanist, progressivist, solutionist, "antitragic" project—that stands in direct opposition to esotericism at *its* deepest level: the tragic, conflictual position on theory and praxis. We not only reject the esoteric view for ourselves but indignantly resist the thought that the great minds of earlier ages could ever have embraced it either. We quietly erase it from the history of philosophic thought.[16]

FURTHER SOURCES OF DENIAL

If the progressive, activist spirit of modern thought has tended to close our minds to the phenomenon of classical esotericism, that spirit nevertheless remains compatible with, indeed productive of, modern, political esotericism—the combination of manipulative and defensive rhetoric needed by the early modern thinkers in their dangerous efforts to transform and rationalize the political world. So the second most important source of the forgetting of esotericism, especially in the last two centuries, has been the gradual success of the modern movement, which finally rendered this activist and defensive esotericism unnecessary.

What is more, the success of this movement created a new world—one in which it is particularly easy to forget that such rhetoric was ever necessary. We in the modern West have been blessed, for many generations now, to live under liberal democratic regimes that defend freedom of speech and thought as a matter of principle. But great blessings enjoyed over long periods often carry a curse: the loss of appreciation and even of understanding of the blessings one has been given. Coddled by good fortune, we forget—in our bones if not our minds—that the natural condition of "thought" is grave weakness and insecurity, as one sees virtually everywhere else in history. Philosophy, in particular, has always dwelled in extreme danger. Thus in all prior ages, people have instinctively understood the necessity of (at a minimum) defensive esotericism. Only we, cursed by unique good fortune, have lost palpable touch with this old necessity and so incline to deny that it was ever much of an issue.

Furthermore, unimpressed by the necessity for such esotericism, we have naturally been more struck with the inherent and undeniable problems with it—problems that have also become particularly magnified in our eyes because we see them through the lens of various other aspects of our unique liberal-democratic-Enlightenment worldview. Indeed, the idea of esotericism would seem to systematically violate every cherished moral and intellectual ideal of our time.

Its evident *elitism* offends our democratic egalitarianism.

Its *secrecy* contradicts our liberal commitment to openness and transparency, as well as the Enlightenment project of demystification and disenchantment.

Its *dishonesty* violates our moral code of truthfulness, our scholarly and scientific code of the open sharing of results, as well as our cultural ideal of sincerity or authenticity.

Its *caution* or *"prudence"* in making such great accommodation to the demands of censors and persecuting authorities strikes us as cowardly in comparison with the modern ideal of the Enlightenment intellectual, risking everything to speak truth to power.

Its intentional embrace of *obscurity* sins against our scientific culture of literalness, clarity, and systematic rigor.

Its effort to *cloister knowledge* for the appreciation of the elite few, while leaving prejudice and illusion unmolested in their reign over everyone else, contradicts the great project for the universal dissemination of knowledge and enlightenment that is inseparable from the modern ideal of progress—moral, social, and intellectual.

The curious *childishness* of its playing with puzzles and riddles clashes with our ideal of philosophical seriousness and gravity.

Finally, the claim that, between the lines, the philosophers *reject the reigning ideas of their society*, even though these ideas are strongly embraced on the surface of their writings, collides with our historicist or contextualist certainty that no mind is able to free itself from the background assumptions and shared commitments of its time and place.

It would be difficult indeed to point to another institution that offends us in so many different ways.

Still, if the institution in question concerned the historical activities of kings, aristocrats, generals, or businessmen, then its extreme offensiveness would not necessarily incline us intellectuals to deny its reality. Quite the contrary. But esotericism concerns the intellectual life—our life. And many of us pursue that life precisely in the hope of finding something more honest, something purer and loftier. Thus to charge philosophers, of all people, with esotericism—with behavior that we find so childish, cowardly, deceitful, elitist, inauthentic, and so forth—strikes us intellectuals as both demeaning and implausible in the extreme. Surely esotericism is a practice to be expected of mystics, astrologers, and alchemists, not genuine philosophers.

Moreover, esotericism appears not only demeaning to the intellectual life in all these ways, but also dangerous to it, because so easily abused—and this by both writers and readers alike. In the case of writers, this practice can only encourage intellectual charlatans of all kinds who will use it to conceal their fraud and vanity behind high-sounding nonsense. This fact has led one scholar, writing in the *Times Literary Supplement*, to venture the following assertion: "Would it not be true to say that all the normal motives for esotericism—for instance self-aggrandizement, power-mongering, snobbery and fraud—are bad and vicious?"[17]

But esotericism will be abused not only by writers, but by readers and interpreters. For this theory destroys all possibility of exactness and certainty in the interpretation of texts. And this uncertainty would have the further result of leaving the door permanently open to every young genius with an active imagination and conspiratorial turn of mind. The whole theory is, to repeat Sabine's remark, an open invitation to "perverse ingenuity."

Furthermore, for a variety of reasons, we live in an age of extreme hermeneutical pessimism. We despair of the possibility of reaching the "true interpretation" of even the simplest of texts. In such an environment, the idea that earlier thinkers wrote esoterically is a most unwelcome suggestion, threatening to burden the practice of scholarship with all kinds of new and intractable demands. Exactly *how* is one to read "between the lines," and how is one ever to know that one has reached the author's true, esoteric teaching? Every such difficulty, real as it may be, grows in our eyes into a sheer impossibility. In our hermeneutical malaise, this theory feels to us altogether unmanageable, unbearable, unacceptable.

Finally, the idea of esotericism has, ironically, been tarnished to some extent by association with its principal rediscoverer, Leo Strauss. Many of his writings (especially the later ones) are extremely obscure, often more so than the works they are meant to gloss—a poor advertisement for his interpretive methods. More generally, Strauss's obscurity when put together with the inherently suspect topic of esotericism has—perhaps inevitably—made people rather suspicious. Scholars might have been less reluctant to give a serious hearing to his theory, as radical and unconventional as it is, if he had given them a clearer idea of exactly where he was going with it. But as it is, with all this dark emphasis on hidden teachings and noble lies, people understandably wonder: exactly what are Strauss and his followers trying to do? Speculation has proliferated, most of it political, some of it rather extravagant and conspiratorial—what Peter Minowitz ventures to call Straussophobia.[18]

With so many and such powerful forces arrayed against it, it is perhaps no wonder that the understanding of esotericism has been all but expunged from the Western mind over the last two hundred years. In the remainder of this chapter, I will attempt to respond to some of these objections. Others will be better addressed in other chapters where they can be examined side by side with the very different attitudes that moved earlier thinkers to embrace esotericism.[19]

THE STRAUSS PROBLEM

To begin with the last stated issue, one certainly does not have to be a Straussian, even a fellow traveler, to believe in the reality of esoteric writing—any more than one needs to be a particular admirer of Columbus to believe in the existence of America. The arguments and evidence for esotericism stand (or fall) on their own. Indeed, some of the best recent research on this topic has been done by non-Straussian scholars.[20] So, if you don't like Strauss, well, just try not to think about him.

It is definitely possible to solve the Strauss problem in this genial manner. But it is not altogether optimal. One does not need Strauss to see the reality, historical pervasiveness, and basic importance of esotericism, but in the end, one does need him—or so I would argue—if one wants to explore the fullest philosophical meaning of this phenomenon and especially its relevance for us today, its crucial significance for the trajectory of modern and postmodern thought. I will examine Strauss's rather complex views on these issues in some detail at the end, in the tenth chapter. Naturally, not everyone will find them persuasive. But, in the time-honored language of dust jacket blurbs, I believe that they do constitute "essential reading" on this particular subject.

So it is not so easy to sidestep Strauss altogether. But it is my hope that by the time readers reach that final chapter, having been convinced of the essential correctness of the once-despised theory of esotericism, they may incline to view Strauss too with somewhat less suspicion. But to that end, it would also help to furnish here a preliminary reply—however summary and unargued—to the main question animating that widespread suspicion: with his mysterious obsession with secrets and lies, just what was Strauss really up to?

It is true that Strauss was up to something. He wasn't just writing books about things that chanced to interest him. There is a single, unified purpose—a project—that he pursued throughout his career and in all his far-flung researches, from Plato, Thucydides, and Aristophanes, to Alfarabi, Maimonides, and Marsilius, to Spinoza, Burke, and Heidegger.

But the beginning of wisdom regarding Strauss is to realize that this project concerned not politics, as is almost universally assumed, but philosophy. Indeed, his project involved precisely the effort to overturn the pervasive modern tendency to subordinate philosophy to politics. It is true that he was a "political philosopher," a fact upon which he laid great emphasis. But he understood this pursuit in the classical way, not as the philosophical guidance of politics (which is only minimally possible), but as the political pathway to and defense of philosophy. In other words, the highest subject of "political philosophy" is not, as we today would assume, the political life. On the contrary:

> The highest subject of political philosophy is the philosophic life: philosophy—not as a teaching or as a body of knowledge, but as a way of life— offers, as it were, the solution to the problem that keeps political life in motion.[21]

Political passion is only the necessary first rung in a ladder of dialectical and pedagogical ascent, the last rung of which is philosophical passion. This view of ancient political thought derives from Strauss's esoteric reading of works like the *Republic*—a reading akin to the one we saw illustrated in chapter 2. It will of course be objected that this paradoxically "apolitical" understanding of classical political philosophy seems implausible and surely runs counter to the prevailing scholarly view. But our purpose at the moment is to establish what Strauss thought, not whether it is true or false. Moreover, the very unconventionality of his view only strengthens my point: the radical subordination of politics to philosophy is one of the most distinctive and defining themes of Strauss's thought.

Thus, Strauss's preoccupation with esotericism in particular has nothing to do with a political agenda. If you read *Persecution and the Art of Writing* from cover to cover, his most thematic discussion of the issue, you will find that it is not at all about the use of "noble lies" by rulers to control the people (although that is a genuine phenomenon), but about the use of esoteric writing by philosophers to escape control by the rulers. More generally, in his view, the truest purpose of esotericism, which is found in its highest form in Plato, is precisely to *separate* philosophy and politics, theory and praxis—to insulate each from the other, that being best for both. For most of the evils of the modern world, in Strauss's view, ultimately stem from the improper relation of theory and praxis, specifically from the compulsion to bring them together, which eventually deforms each, producing ideologized politics and politicized philosophy. That is why he admiringly wrote of Plato's esotericism:

> Plato composed his writings in such a way as to prevent for all time their use as authoritative texts. . . . His teaching can never become the subject of indoctrination. In the last analysis, his writings cannot be used for any purpose other than for philosophizing. In particular, no social order and no party which ever existed or which ever will exist can rightfully claim Plato as its patron.[22]

Strauss's writings, too, were for the sake of philosophizing—not any political party. Of course, even philosophers have to live in political communities, and thus, as a *citizen*, Strauss had serious political concerns and opinions—primarily conservative—which he expressed sparingly, but forcefully. But they were not the subject of his guiding intellectual project, not what he

was "up to"—and definitely not the source of his preoccupation with esotericism.

This fact should be obvious from his writings: he wrote about fifteen
books and not a single one of them was about the contemporary political
scene and what should be done. The same is true of his courses at the University of Chicago and elsewhere (which are now being made available on
line).[23] If you compare him to some of his well-known contemporaries like
Hannah Arendt or Herbert Marcuse, it is obvious that he was much less politically engaged than they. His project, to say it again, was philosophical—
and directed, in particular, at the reasoned liberation of philosophy from
politics, with all its distorting hopes and illusions.

What, then, more specifically, was his philosophical project? The starting point of Strauss's path of thought was the observation that in our time
the whole legitimacy of western science, philosophy, and rationalism was
being radically challenged—and at the hands of two opposite but mutually
reinforcing movements: the "postmodern" force of historicism or cultural
relativism and the ancient force of religious orthodoxy, now newly embold-
ened by reason's self-destruction. This is the great intellectual predicament
of our age, the "crisis of modernity."

Strauss's project was simply to defend philosophy or rationalism—albeit,
a minimalist, skeptical, Socratic rationalism—from this twin attack. His
thought falls under the category of "philosophic apologetics": he was less
concerned to elaborate a philosophical system (still less, a political one)
than to ground the legitimacy of rationalism as such. He saw this as the first
and deepest philosophical issue.

In his view, the rediscovered phenomenon of esotericism constituted the
great key to mounting a new, more successful defense against rationalism's
two, near-victorious opponents—and that in a variety of different ways. To
give one example—one prepared by the previous chapter—historicism and
esotericism are ultimately rival answers to the same fundamental question:
what is the relation between theory and praxis. The theory of esotericism
(in its classical form) argues for the inherent and inescapable tension between reason and society. As such, it constitutes a critique of the historicist assumption of their underlying unity, of the inherent subordination of
reason to society and its fundamental commitments. Esotericism thus challenges historicism at its core.

Strauss is so "obsessed" with esotericism, in sum, because he is engaged in
the philosophical project of defending rationalism, and he believes that his
recovery of this long-forgotten phenomenon has suddenly opened up new

paths of thought that offer the best hope for overcoming the contemporary crisis of reason.

Needless to say, after hearing him out at length, some will be sympathetic to Strauss's project and others not. Some will reject the whole problematic of crisis upon which it rests. But, at a minimum, it should be clear—in response to the various suspicions that surround him—that his great preoccupation with esotericism was not for the sake of any political scheme.[24]

And, to end where we began, it should always be firmly kept in mind that whatever one's final view of the complex philosophical issues raised by Strauss, both the historical existence and the scholarly importance of esotericism are facts that stand squarely on their own.

THE SCHOLARLY MISGIVINGS ABOUT ESOTERICISM

Let us turn to the more substantive aspects of our difficulty with esotericism. There is first of all the vexing question of exactly *how* one is to read a text between the lines. Can this really be done in a responsible manner? This is a necessary and difficult question. It will be taken up at length in the ninth chapter, which offers an introductory guide to esoteric reading, where I hope to show that it can be addressed in a reasonably nonarbitrary way, especially by continuing our reliance, where possible, upon the explicit testimony of past writers and readers.

Yet even if it is granted, for the moment, that esoteric interpretation can be conducted in a responsible way, it still remains the case that such interpretations rarely if ever permit of a great degree of certainty. This is surely true and very unfortunate. But it is not a problem that can be escaped. For if a book has been written esoterically and if, to avoid uncertainty, we refuse to read it that way, then we will surely misunderstand it. That is, if you like, the one certainty here.

Someone might reply, however, that this statement would be more compelling if the converse were also true: if we do read the book esoterically, then we are guaranteed—or at least likely—to understand it. But this is far from the case. And if we do a particularly bad job of esoteric reading, we may well misunderstand the book more grossly than if we had stuck to a strictly literal reading. For, esoteric interpretation is unusually difficult to do right and very easy to get wrong—very wrong. By freeing readers from the literal meaning of the text, it exposes them to various inevitable temptations and corruptions. It will open the door to Sabine's "perverse ingenuity."

To this charge, one can only reply: indeed it will. It must. It already has.

And if the present work is successful in winning broader recognition for the necessity of this manner of reading, it will surely contribute to an increase in the number of bad esoteric interpretations—that being the price to be paid for a few good ones. It cannot be denied that this is a grave disadvantage.

But to continue in this spirit of realism, it should also be acknowledged that the strictly literal approach to the reading of texts in the history of philosophy (and literature) has not succeeded in producing much agreement and certainty either. For some puzzling reason, grave and nagging problems of interpretation have always continued to exist. And over the last century in particular, these problems have led to a dizzying proliferation of non-literal interpretive approaches: Hegelian, Marxist, Freudian, Jungian, structuralist, poststructuralist, feminist, deconstructive, new historicist, and so forth. And it is fair to say, I believe, that the great majority of these new approaches are also invitations to uncertainty and to perverse ingenuity.[25]

In fact, aren't they even more so than the theory of esotericism? For if the latter, like all its rivals, releases the reader from the authority of the literal text, still, it does so, unlike all its rivals, only in the name of finding a still more authoritative and intelligent level of the text, and one that is still attributable to the author in his or her wisdom and artfulness. Thus, the theory of esotericism is ultimately quite hermeneutically conservative in that it produces a heightened level of deference toward the text—of caution, exactness, and mastery of detail. It just sees the text as a multileveled phenomenon, artfully produced by the author's multileveled intention. By contrast, most of the other hermeneutical theories encourage a sense of liberation from the text as a whole, and certainly from its author's intentions; and they allow (where they do not positively celebrate) a more freewheeling sense that the text is ours to make of what we will.[26]

There is also another important way in which, from the standpoint of these criteria of certainty and scholarly sobriety, the theory of esotericism is superior to its rivals: it is not simply rooted in *theory*. It—and it alone—is susceptible of empirical proof. The claim that many older thinkers wrote esoterically can be factually demonstrated through reference to the explicit testimony of those thinkers. And at least some of the techniques for esoteric reading can be similarly grounded.

Here is a statement by Rousseau, for example, expressly telling us how he wrote—and thus how we should read—his *First Discourse*:

> It was only gradually and always *for few readers* that I developed my ideas.
> . . . I have often taken great pains to try to put into a sentence, a line, a word

tossed off as if by chance the result of a long sequence of reflections. Often, *most of my readers* must have found my discourses badly connected and almost entirely rambling, for lack of perceiving the trunk of which I showed them only the branches. But that was enough for *those who know how to understand*, and I have never wanted to speak to the others.[27]

With an explicitness and clarity that could hardly be improved upon, Rousseau confirms here the basic points of the theory of esotericism. First, he did not think of all his readers as alike, but made a fundamental distinction between the "few readers"—that is, "those who know how to understand"—and "most of my readers." Second, in his writing, he was trying to speak to the former and to exclude the latter, to whom he "never wanted to speak." And third, he sought to accomplish this feat of saying different things to different readers within one work by obscuring and merely hinting at his true ideas in such a way that "most of my readers" would merely see a text full of problems—"badly connected and almost entirely rambling"—but that the "few" would succeed in perceiving the "trunk."

Thus, one can say with virtually complete certainty that at least for the interpretation of this work of Rousseau's, the esoteric method is absolutely proper and necessary. This conclusion is not based on abstract literary theory; it is Rousseau's own explicit assertion (although no such certainty would attach, of course, to the particular result of that interpretive effort). This kind of confirmatory evidence is possible for the theory of esotericism—and it alone—because esotericism explains the difficulties in the text through reference to the author's *conscious intention*, which he may choose to openly reveal, as Rousseau does here. It is in the nature of almost all the other prevailing hermeneutical theories—which are far more skeptical of authors and which rely upon unintentional or unconscious forces to explain the text—that they can never bring forward in their own justification anything like this kind of empirical, testimonial evidence. They are inescapably theoretical.

One can go still further: the empirical evidence available to support esotericism also tends at the same time to undermine these theoretical arguments for the other nonliteral interpretive methods. When people argue in justification of these other methods, they must all ultimately begin from the same crucial beginning point: the failure of the literal interpretation. Without that, they have no right to get started. It is the manifest *problems* in the surface argument of the text—the contradictions, the missing connections, the lack of order—that legitimate the quest for other, hidden causes of the text, such as the author's religious upbringing, cultural milieu, political class, economic position, psychological makeup, sexual orientation, gender identity, the problems inherent in language and in writing, and so forth. But in the above passage, the author, Rousseau, demonstrates that these problems do not in fact derive from unconscious forces—because he himself accurately describes them. And then he explains where they do come from: he has deliberately created them as part of his effort to communicate esoterically. In thus explaining away the surface problems of the text, Rousseau is denying legitimacy to all these other interpretive approaches—at least until it can be shown that there are still other major problems in the text, which are not attributable to his esotericism.

In other words, the empirical evidence for esotericism points also to the following possibility. Perhaps it has been the esotericism of the philosophers—which works precisely by intentionally planting suggestive *problems* in the text—that has been primarily responsible all along for the famous failure of the literal approach to interpretation. And thus, ironically, it is the practice of esoteric writing that has also given rise to all these other, rival interpretive theories, which were invented to explain the source of these textual problems once their true source in esotericism had been forgotten. There is some evidence for this suggestion in the very curious fact that, although these problem-laden texts have existed for centuries, even millennia, it is only in the last two centuries or so—only in the period of the forgetfulness of esotericism—that scholars were suddenly moved by the textual problems to formulate these new theories of interpretation. There is only one nonliteral hermeneutical theory that preexists this period—and that is the theory of esotericism, which is twenty-five hundred years old. Without denying, then, that a great and problematic uncertainty attaches to all nonliteral interpretive approaches, we have strong grounds for suggesting that the theory of esotericism is at least more firmly grounded than its major nonliteral rivals.

OF RESISTANCE AND BLINDNESS

Strictly speaking, however, all of the arguments just made are completely beside the point. For even if they were wrong, even if the disadvantages of esotericism for scholarship were every bit as grave as is claimed, exactly what would follow? That thinkers of the past therefore did not write esoterically?

Obviously, the proper response to *all of the objections* raised above, moral as well as scholarly, should be this: the question before us is not whether we *like* the practice of esotericism (still less whether we like Leo Strauss or his students) but simply whether, in fact, it is *real*. And precisely if, for the long list of reasons recounted above, we have a deeply rooted aversion to the practice of esotericism, we have a good reason to be suspicious, not of the historical reality of esotericism, but of ourselves—of the very real danger that we have, for two hundred years now, been denying the truth about it.

To further this salutary suspicion and self-criticism, it is helpful to think about exactly how this denial works. If we have objections to esotericism or find it repugnant, it is easy to see how that would lead us to avoid practicing it ourselves, but precisely how does it cause us to deny that earlier thinkers ever practiced it either? We abhor slavery but do not deny that it ever existed. There would seem to be two different routes to this further conclusion.

The first is "resistance." Not wishing philosophy, which we admire, to be tainted with this practice, which we despise, or, conversely, this practice to be legitimated by philosophy, we avert our eyes from the facts. From simple wishful thinking, we seize upon every opportunity to question, discount and dismiss the evidence. The cure for this resistance is simply to bring our various motives and biases to the surface, to fuller awareness—as this chapter has been trying to do.

The second and more profound form of denial is "blindness." Here, the flaw is not wishful but anachronistic thinking. We take our own particular aversions and ahistorically or ethnocentrically impute them to earlier ages; then we reason that the great thinkers of the past could hardly have engaged in such obviously repugnant behavior. We wouldn't do it, therefore they couldn't have done it. But in reasoning this way, we underestimate the historical uniqueness of our world, forget how far we have drifted from the attitudes and beliefs of past times. Owing to this drift, our own objections and aversions turn out to be surprisingly untrustworthy guides to past attitudes, especially in the matter of esotericism. Indeed, earlier ages do not seem to have felt as we do about virtually any of the fervent objections to esotericism listed above, or so I will argue. The cure, then, to the problem of blindness and ethnocentrism is again a greater knowledge of ourselves in our uniqueness, our historical particularity—which then frees us for a more genuine and accurate understanding of the past, whose distinct attitudes and actions we are trying to understand.

With all of this in mind, let us consider the three most obvious and potent of our moral objections to the practice of esotericism: the issues of elitism, secrecy, and dishonesty.

THE INEGALITARIANISM OF THE OLD WORLD

The first thing that puts people off from esotericism is its snooty, almost cartoonish elitism. When it is gravely explained that an esoteric book is one written to secretly address "the few" or "the wise," while excluding "the many" or "the vulgar," who today can bear such talk? We live in a democratic age and view the world through an egalitarian lens. In such times, as Tocqueville points out, "the general idea of the intellectual superiority that any man whatsoever can acquire over all the others is not slow to be obscured."[28] We naturally incline to dismiss the whole theory of esotericism as impossibly arrogant and elitist.

But of course, only a few short centuries ago, all the world was ruled by monarchs and aristocrats. Most of the philosophers, too, held that the best form of government was some sort of aristocracy. In these ages, a vast chasm separated the leisured, educated elite from the toiling and illiterate masses. A sense of rank and inequality suffused every aspect of life. It is oddly anachronistic to think that this earlier world, exquisitely elitist, would, like us, have recoiled in egalitarian horror at the idea of esotericism.

If we incline to this mistake, it is because, while it is easy to see that the past was more inegalitarian than the present, it is very hard to take the full measure of this fact. For in democracies, as Tocqueville points out, people tend to stare obsessively at the few inequalities still remaining while ignoring the vast world of inequalities overcome.[29] This means that egalitarian societies incline to misunderstand themselves: they systematically underestimate their own egalitarianism. Thus, they underestimate, in particular, how utterly different all their perceptions and sensibilities have become from those of earlier, nonegalitarian ages. In other words, we citizens of the modern West have gradually undergone a great democratization of the mind of which we are scarcely aware. This hinders us from appreciating how very different—how shockingly different—attitudes were in earlier, inegalitarian times. Consider a few examples.

"In an aristocratic people," Tocqueville explains, "each caste has its own opinions, sentiments, rights, mores, and separate existence. . . . They do not have the same manner of thinking or of feeling, and they scarcely believe themselves to be a part of the same humanity."[30] Thus, Pierre Charron does not hesitate to assert that a wise man "is as far above the common sort of men as a common man is above the beasts."[31] "To speak of the people," remarks Guicciardini, "is really to speak of a mad animal, gorged with a thousand and one errors and confusions, devoid of taste, of pleasure, of stability."[32] Livy affirms that "nothing is so valueless as the minds of the multitude."[33] Spinoza speaks of "the masses whose intellect is not capable of perceiving things clearly and distinctly."[34] And Cicero goes so far as to claim that the very faculty of reason is "disastrous to the many and wholesome to but few."[35]

Naturally, these great inequalities were seen as having crucial consequences for the issue of communication. According to Montaigne, "Aristo of Chios had reason to say long ago that philosophers harmed their listeners, inasmuch as most souls are not fit to profit by such instruction."[36] Galen, the Greek physician and philosopher, wrote: "My discourse in this book is not for all people; my discourse is for a man among them who is equal to thousands of men, or rather tens of thousands."[37] Similarly, Maimonides declares in the introduction to the *Guide of the Perplexed* that he "could find no other device by which to teach a demonstrated truth other than by giving satisfaction to a single virtuous man while displeasing ten thousand ignoramuses—I am he who prefers to address that single man by himself, and I do not heed the blame of those many creatures."[38] In a similar spirit is the famous verse of Horace: "I loathe the mob impure and forbid it place. Let tongues be silent!"[39] Again, Synesius of Cyrene asks: "For what do the many and philosophy have to do with one another? The truth must be left secret and unspoken, for the multitude are in need of another state of mind."[40] Similarly, Seneca quotes Epicurus as having said: "I have never wished to cater to the people; for what I know they do not approve, and what they approve I do not know." But Seneca then goes on to remark: "this same watchword rings in your ears from every sect—Peripatetic, Academic, Stoic, Cynic."[41] La Mettrie expresses a similar attitude:

> Whatever may be my speculation in the quiet of my study, my practice in society is quite different. . . . In the one place, as a philosopher, I prefer the truth, while in the other, as a citizen, I prefer error. Error is more within everyone's grasp; it is the general food of minds of all ages and in all places. What indeed is more worthy of enlightening and leading the vile herd of mindless mortals? In society I never talk about all those lofty philosophical truths which were not made for the masses.[42]

Nietzsche translates these observations into a crucial—but counterintuitive—generalization about writing:

> *On the question of being understandable*—One does not only wish to be understood when one writes; one wishes just as surely *not* to be understood. It

is not by any means necessarily an objection to a book when anyone finds it impossible to understand: perhaps that was part of the author's intention—he did not want to be understood by just "anybody." All the nobler spirits and tastes select their audiences when they wish to communicate; and choosing that, one at the same time erects barriers against "the others." All the more subtle laws of any style have their origin at this point: they at the same time keep away, create a distance, forbid "entrance," understanding, as said above—while they open the ears of those whose ears are related to ours.[43]

Finally, bringing this all back to the issue of equality, Nietzsche speaks of

[t]he difference between the exoteric and the esoteric, formerly known to philosophers—among the Indians as among the Greeks, Persians, and Muslims, in short, wherever one believed in *an order of rank and not in equality and equal rights.*[44]

One might object, of course, that, this list of quotations notwithstanding, there were also exceptions to this inegalitarian bent in Western philosophy. Indeed, there were. But in the period prior to 1800, which is at issue here, egalitarian voices were relatively few, and, more to the point, even they do not seem to have opposed esotericism on egalitarian grounds. In this period, the most open, heartfelt, and determined egalitarian was doubtless Rousseau. Therefore, he makes a good test case in the effort to determine whether in fact *any* earlier thinkers can be found who, like us, reject esotericism as too elitist. But of course the results are already in. Rousseau has stated as plainly and unabashedly as one could want that he is a proudly esoteric writer who seeks to address the "few," "those who know how to understand," while excluding all the others.

Clearly it is an anachronistic fallacy, then, to project our own egalitarian objections to esotericism back on earlier ages. Truth to tell, earlier ages seem for the most part to have regarded the elitist character of this practice as a point in its favor.

That said, it should also be pointed out that three of the four motives for esotericism—the desire to escape persecution, promote political change, and teach in a Socratic way—can all be defended in essentially egalitarian terms. It is only protective esotericism—the hiding of dangerous truths from those not ready for them—that is inherently elitist.

THE NORMALITY AND UBIQUITY OF SECRECY

The theory of esotericism also strikes us as manifestly improbable because it involves attributing to the great philosophers of the past behavior that is secretive and mysterious. Such behavior strikes the contemporary mind as both immoral and childish. When we picture in our minds men of the stamp of Aristotle, Thomas Aquinas, or Descartes, gravely bent over their writing desks, we simply cannot imagine that they were hard at work playing hide and seek with their most treasured insights. The whole suggestion is bizarre and demeaning.

But once again, this objection presupposes that earlier ages viewed the phenomena of hiddenness, secrecy, and reserve in essentially the same way we do—and, once again, this is a very unhistorical assumption. As soon as one looks beyond the narrow borders of our liberal-democratic universe to what may loosely be called "traditional society," one finds a world that is steeped in secrecy and that *honors* reserve and indirection (as one can already see in many of the above quotations).

We live in and cherish the "open society," where secrecy and reserve are fundamentally suspect phenomena. We practice a morality, an epistemology, even a metaphysics of liberal democratic openness, attributing the highest value, the truest knowledge, and the greatest reality to that which is public, disclosed, and available to all. In politics we seek "transparency," in business "publicity," in academics "publication." And as to our personal lives, we live in an increasingly expressive society—a sincerity culture, also a therapeutic culture—where people bare their hearts to strangers on a plane or on live television or on the internet. We enthusiastically celebrate openness—partly as confession, partly as exhibitionism—full of strange hopes that it will grant us healing and connection. And we have gotten so used to all of this that we can imagine no legitimate alternative. It's the most natural thing in the world.

We are thus profoundly estranged from the traditional inclination for reserve and concealment. This inclination strikes us as something requiring treatment. It is almost beyond our capacity to comprehend that in many earlier societies, indeed in much of contemporary India and Japan, husbands and wives, parents and children can pass their whole lives without ever once openly saying: I love you.

Conversely, most traditional cultures would find it difficult to comprehend the modern idea that if one has come into the possession of some profound knowledge, one should lay it open for the perusal of every passing eye. That would seem both foolish and unseemly. Indeed, during most of history, what would have raised skeptical glances—what would have required lengthy tomes of apology, explanation, and proof like this one—is not the practice of esotericism, but our modern, Western concepts of openness and publication.

In a traditional society, after all, the highest knowledge both concerns and derives from the divine, and such sacred knowledge is not to be profaned by being disclosed to the unworthy. According to an account of the Pueblo Indians, "one reason often adduced for secrecy by Pueblo leaders is that religious ceremonies lose their power if they are known by the wrong people. This is certainly an attitude commonly encountered in many parts of the world."[45] And as we have just seen, this instinct for reserve is not only to be found among pagans and polytheists: "Give not that which is holy to dogs; neither cast ye your pearls before swine."

Strabo, the Greek geographer and historian, explains this widespread inclination to religious secrecy as follows: "it is in accordance with the dictates of nature that this should be so." For secrecy "induces reverence for the divine, since it imitates the nature of the divine, which is to avoid being perceived by our human senses."[46] Does it not, in short, make a kind of perfect sense that the proper condition of the highest knowledge, like that of the highest Being, is to be hidden?[47]

At the same time, on a more secular and utilitarian level, if knowledge is power, then secrecy is the husbanding and maintenance of power. The rulers, the priests, the warriors, the craftsmen and fine artists, the healers and medicine men, the merchants, the medieval guilds—all had and needed their trade secrets. Rare indeed is the man who finds his interest in freely telling everything he knows.[48]

In premodern society, in a direct reversal of our instincts, when something is "published" or openly disclosed, it becomes in important respects diminished in power and worth. Thus, traditional life was suffused with reserve, exclusion, and concealment. Not openness, but secrecy—the compartmentalization of knowledge—was the *normal* state of things, the default position. Here, one needed a special reason to be open amid so many instincts and habits of secrecy.

In such a world, the secretive practice of philosophical esotericism— though it strikes us as childish, immoral, and thus highly implausible—had the character less of an exception than of a rule. *Of course* the philosophers had their secrets too.

Consider only one brief example—the *representative* example of the philosophic life in the Western tradition: Socrates. In the Platonic dialogues, he is
depicted as renowned throughout Athens for never giving anyone a straight
answer. Indeed, he has gone down in history as a man with a form of irony
named after him.

With the issue of secrecy, just as with that of elitism, we have clearly been
misled by the anachronistic assumption that earlier generations shared our
own moral habits and instincts. Think about it: the two greatest teachers of
the Western tradition were Jesus and Socrates. And both were famous for
their secrecy and indirect speech.

ON SALUTARY LYING

Esotericism is fundamentally dishonest. Is it really believable that the greatest truth seekers of the past were in actuality all bald-faced liars? This is perhaps the most disturbing challenge to esotericism.

It is one that our age, to its credit, regards with particular seriousness. In
his classic *History of European Morals*, W. E. H Lecky argues that "veracity is
usually the special virtue of an industrial nation," because in market societies with great economic specialization people are so interdependent that
trustworthiness becomes the paramount virtue.[49] A related point is made
by Hannah Arendt, who points out that "except for Zoroastrianism, none
of the major religions included lying as such, as distinguished from 'bearing
false witness,' in their catalogues of grave sins." This changed only in modern
times, she continues, owing largely to the rise of *intellectual* specialization,
that is, "the rise of organized science, whose progress had to be assured on
the firm ground of the absolute veracity and reliability of every scientist."[50]
To this, one could add that in a democratic regime, one that is also an "information society" and that is faced with complex issues of monumental proportions, like nuclear warfare and environmental degradation, it is more important than ever that scientists and experts speak truth to the public in as
clear and scrupulously honest a manner as possible. We are rightly disturbed,
then, by the dishonesty of esotericism.

In the particular case of *defensive* esotericism, where writers are driven by
the fear of persecution or even execution, most people would grant that the
use of deception can be legitimate. The far more difficult case concerns the
propriety of so-called "salutary" or "noble" lies, where one deceives others
for their own benefit, whether ideological, pedagogical, or political. Can
these ever be legitimate? Fortunately, the task before us here is to settle not

this complex moral question but rather the relatively simple historical question of how thinkers of the past tended to answer that moral question.

It is fairly easy to show that a very large and wide-ranging group of earlier thinkers regarded the use of salutary lies or at least of concealment of some portion of the truth as just or allowable under the right circumstances. This is not unrelated, of course, to their much greater belief in human inequality as well as their respect for secrecy.

For starters, the position of Plato and (his) Socrates on the propriety of noble lies is well known. Regarding Xenophon, Dio Chrysostom writes that from a very careful reading of his *Anabasis* one will learn how "to deceive one's enemies to their harm and one's friends to their advantage, and to speak the truth in a way that will not pain those who are needlessly disturbed by it."[51] As for the Stoics, Plutarch quotes Chrysippus as saying: "Often indeed do the wise employ lies against the vulgar."[52] And Grotius writes: "If we may trust Plutarch and Quintillion the Stoics include among the endowments of the wise man the ability to lie in the proper place and manner."[53]

In the medieval period, we find Maimonides declaring:

These matters [of theology] are only for a few solitary individuals of a very special sort, not for the multitude. For this reason, they should be hidden from the beginner, and he should be prevented from taking them up, just as a small baby is prevented from taking coarse foods and from lifting heavy weights.[54]

Averroes, in his commentary on Plato's *Republic*, writes:

The chiefs' lying to the multitude will be appropriate for them in the respect in which a drug is appropriate for a disease. . . . That is true because untrue stories are necessary for the teaching of the citizens. No bringer of a nomos [law] is to be found who does not make use of invented stories, for this is something necessary for the multitude to reach their happiness.[55]

In the early modern era, Erasmus states:

While it can never be lawful to go against the truth, it may sometimes be expedient to conceal it in the circumstances. . . . Theologians are agreed on some things among themselves which it is not expedient to publish to the common herd.[56]

Thomas Burnet writes on the subject at some length:

> What just or pious man ever scrupled to deceive children or lunaticks, when thereby they contributed to their safety and welfare? And why should not the rude and untractable multitude be dealt with after the same manner? . . . It is a crime to use dissimulation to the prejudice of another: but we innocently deceive, and are deceived, for the public good, and the supporting of the weak. There is something more sacred and inviolable in the nature of goodness, than in that of truth, and when it is impossible to join them together, the latter must give place to the former.[57]

Here is Rousseau, that apostle of the modern ideal of sincerity: the great founder of a nation, whose "sublime reason . . . rises above the grasp of common men," must place his wise commandments "in the mouth of the immortals in order to convince by divine authority those who cannot be moved by human prudence."[58] Again, in the *Encyclopedia* itself, there is an article by Diderot entitled "Mensonge officieux"—unofficial or salutary lie—which promotes the "wise maxim that the lie that procures good is worth more than the truth that causes harm."[59] And David Hume, pulling no punches, writes: "It is putting too great a Respect on the Vulgar, and on their Superstitions, to pique oneself on Sincerity with regard to them. Did ever one make it a point of honor to speak truth to Children or Madmen?"[60] Consider also Descartes's statement:

> I would not want to criticize those who allow that through the mouths of the prophets God can produce verbal untruths which, like the lies of doctors who deceive their patients in order to cure them, are free of any malicious intent to deceive.[61]

But let us cut straight to the hardest case. Most people would probably agree with Sissela Bok's assertion, in her classic work on lying, that of all the major thinkers of the Western tradition (with the possible exception of Kant), Augustine is the one who takes the strongest position against lying.[62] Yet since his position does not preclude concealment, here is Augustine's view of esoteric writing (which we have quoted once before): the pure stream of philosophy should be

> guided through shady and thorny thickets, for the possession of the few, rather than allowed to wander through open spaces where cattle [i.e., the

"common herd"] break through, and where it is impossible for it to be kept clear and pure. . . . I think that that method or art of concealing the truth is a useful invention.[63]

To say it again, we may find this view offensive, immoral, and even dangerous, especially in the contemporary world. But precisely if we value truthfulness, we must not allow our own moral sentiments or the new imperatives of our democratic and technological age to obscure the plain fact that, among philosophers of the past, the legitimacy of salutary lying or concealment was very widely accepted.[64]

In the preceding chapters, I have tried to rush into place—as quickly as intelligibility would allow—the key pieces of the big picture concerning esotericism: the testimonial evidence supporting it, the theoretical arguments explaining it, and the contemporary resistance obscuring it. For only in close conjunction with each other do these three pieces make full sense. For the sake of dispatch, I have abstracted from a host of details, above all the distinct forms into which esotericism is divided. But with this initial outline now in place, we may examine the phenomenon in a more leisurely and fine-grained manner, separating out the distinct kinds of and motives for esotericism—defensive, protective, pedagogical, and political.

PART TWO

The Four Forms of
Philosophical Esotericism

Fear of Persecution:
Defensive Esotericism

Censorship is the mother of metaphor.

—JORGE LUIS BORGES

Let us begin with the most readily understandable as well as most historically universal motive leading philosophers, as well as literary, political, and
religious writers, to practice esoteric communication: the pressing need to
evade censorship or avoid persecution. To properly appreciate the role and
influence of this need, however, its scope must not be construed too narrowly. The safety to be guaranteed is often that of the writer and his family.
But it may also extend to that of his writings or his philosophic movement
(if he has one) or even the philosophic way of life as such—and all of this,
not only in the present moment, but also with an eye to the reasonably fore-
seeable future.

The experience or fear of persecution thus understood routinely leads to
evasive methods of writing, as Lord Shaftesbury remarks with the matter-of-
factness of one who believes he is stating only what everyone knows.

If men are forbid to speak their minds seriously on certain subjects, they
will do it ironically. If they are forbid to speak at all upon such subjects, or if
they find it really dangerous to do so, they will then redouble their disguise,

involving themselves in mysteriousness, and talk so as hardly to be understood, or at least not plainly interpreted, by those who are disposed to do them a mischief.[1]

This widespread and obvious literary phenomenon is difficult to dismiss. Nobody denies, after all, that through most of history most thinkers and writers have been confronted with censorship of one sort or another. In the oft-quoted words of Tacitus: "Seldom are men blessed with times in which they may think what they like and say what they think."[2] The plain consequence of this plain fact is stated by Pierre Bayle: "Those who write with a view to publishing their thoughts accommodate themselves to the times and betray on a thousand occasions the judgment they form of things."[3] They are constrained to exclude from their works certain tenets they believe true and probably include others they believe false. They must consciously falsify their writings. This is already basic esotericism. It is but a small further step to add, as Shaftesbury does: many thinkers, chafing under this accommodation, have also ventured to leave hints as to what they did and did not really believe.

How there could be so much resistance to the recognition of this phenomenon is difficult to understand—or would be, if we had not just spent a chapter exploring the long list of cultural factors predisposing us against the general idea of esotericism. But turning now to a more detailed treatment of defensive esotericism in particular, we find a further twist. Contemporary culture also contains certain other, countervailing features that actually push *toward* a recognition of this practice—or ought to. These latter features restore to full strength the strangeness of our continuing resistance to defensive esotericism—while also giving hope that, with a bit more evidence and discussion, this resistance might be ready to crumble.

DEFENSIVE ESOTERICISM AND CONTEMPORARY CULTURE

Consider, for example, that contemporary society is exquisitely sensitive to the plight of minorities. We not only recognize the obvious dangers of persecution but, over time, have taught ourselves to understand all the complex, subtle, and sometimes hidden consequences of marginality. That is perhaps our greatest cultural forte. It is strange, then, that we have been so slow to apply this unique sensitivity and insight to the plight of the philosophical minority (albeit a plight faced, not in our time—but in most times).

What is more, something like defensive esotericism is precisely what would be predicted by prevailing literary theories, which highlight the relationship between writing and power. If everywhere there is a cultural "hegemon" asserting its power (although more obviously in nonliberal, "closed" societies), and if always the great refuge of those without force is fraud, then surely it *must be the case* that a large portion of the world's writers will have been systematically constrained to write between the lines.

To Fredric Jameson, for example, the literary world always and everywhere looks like this: "A ruling class ideology will explore various strategies of the legitimation of its own power position, while an oppositional culture of ideology will, *often in covert or disguised strategies*, seek to contest and undermine the dominant value system."[4] But somehow this crucial insight has not led Jameson or others to recognize the historical ubiquity of—indeed the almost structural necessity for—esoteric communication. The most notable exception is the distinguished literary critic Annabel Patterson, who has written a series of books showing with great ingenuity and detail the need to employ what she dubs a "hermeneutics of censorship" if one is properly to understand English literature from the sixteenth to the nineteenth centuries.[5]

To these two points, one must add one further aspect of our times that makes our resistance to defensive esotericism so perplexing and disturbing: for most of the previous century we had totalitarian regimes right before our eyes where dissident authors boldly registered their protest and sheltered their freedom between the lines. Here we are no longer in the land of abstract literary theory or of distant historical conjecture—one need only ask any ordinary citizen of these states. In conversations with people from this part of the world, I have repeatedly been told that a book on esotericism will not sell in Eastern Europe. "Everybody already knows all about it."

But we too might have known all about it, since lurid accounts of the experiences of major Russian and Eastern European writers have been available in the West for over sixty years. Vaclav Havel, for example, expressly tells us how, imprisoned in communist Czechoslovakia, he wrote his *Letters to Olga*:

> The letters, in fact, are endless spirals in which I've tried to enclose something. Very early on, I realized that comprehensible letters wouldn't get through, which is why the letters are full of long compound sentences and complicated ways of saying things. Instead of writing "regime," for instance, I would obviously have had to write "the socially apparent focus on the non-I," or some such nonsense.[6]

A related technique was also employed in the theater, according to Havel. In *Disturbing the Peace*, he states that censorship "has led the small theatres to adopt an increasingly sophisticated set of ciphers, suggestions, indirect references, and vague parallels."[7]

Similarly, regarding Romania, the celebrated poet and essayist Andrei Codrescu openly states:

> Against history, we developed community through the use of a subtle and ambiguous language that could be heard in one way by the oppressor, in another by your friends. Our weapons of sabotage were ambiguity, humor, paradox, mystery, poetry, song and magic.[8]

In *Censorship in Romania*, Lidia Vianu confirms this account:

> Creative minds found ways to outwit censorship. . . . A strong bond between writer and reader came into being, and the writer was eager to express what he was not allowed to say. The reader avidly waited for the least hint about how to read between the lines, an art perfected under communist censorship. Censored writers joined hands with censored readers in a dance of bitter frustration.[9]

Again, Czeslaw Milosz, the Polish poet and Nobel laureate, devotes an entire chapter (entitled "Ketman") in his celebrated work *The Captive Mind* (published in 1951) to an account of the ubiquitous dissimulation, acting, and secret communication practiced in the countries of the Soviet bloc.[10] His compatriot, the distinguished political philosopher Leszek Kolakowski, makes similar observations concerning the near universal practice of esotericism by the Polish intelligentsia. When interviewed in *Daedalus* by Danny Postel, who asked him point blank about the necessity "to resort to a certain kind of Delphic or esoteric idiom of writing under Stalinist rule," Kolakowski replied:

> When I was in Poland, *all of us who were intellectuals* were compelled to use a certain code language, a language that would be acceptable in the established framework. So we had an acute sense of the limits of what could be said, of censorship. . . . we tried to be intelligible without being transparent.[11]

Similarly, in the German context, J. M. Ritchie observes in his *German Literature under National Socialism*:

There was a tendency towards the veiled remark, the significant pause, the double or multiple meaning. It also involved reliance on the sensitivity of the reader to pick up a literary allusion, a biblical reference or a historical parallel with relevance to National Socialism. . . . No new forms, no new style emerged, only progressive refinement in techniques of making oblique statements.[12]

Thus, after the war, in an article on film censorship in communist East Germany, Daniela Berghahn states that "art was used to articulate issues that could not be publically discussed but which were, nonetheless, decoded by a public that was well versed in reading between the lines."[13]

One must look to the former Soviet Union, however, to see the greatest specimen of a living tradition of esoteric writing—or of "Aesopian language," as it has been known there for centuries. Russia, being the one part of the West that has never known a sustained period of liberal government or of freedom from censorship, is a kind of intellectual lost valley where the old practice and memory of esotericism, which died out everywhere else, still lingers on. Thus, the Soviet *Concise Literary Encyclopedia*, published in 1975, and even the American *Modern Encyclopedia of Russian and Soviet Literature*, published in 1978, contain long articles on "Aesopian language." As the article in the latter explains, this common practice, involving "the enciphering and deciphering of a subtext," was named for Aesop, the Phrygian slave who wrote fables because he lacked the power to speak openly. It was given this name by the writer M. E. Saltykov-Shchedrin (1826–89), who explained:

I am a Russian writer and therefore I have two slave's habits: first, to write allegorically and, second, to tremble. For the habit of allegorical writing I am indebted to the pre-reform Department of Censorship. It tormented Russian literature to such a degree, that it was as though it had vowed to wipe it off the face of the earth. But literature persisted in its desire to live and so pursued deceptive means. . . . On the one hand, allegories appeared; on the other, the art of comprehending these allegories, the art of reading between the lines. A special slave's manner of writing was created which can be called Aesopian, a manner which revealed a remarkable resourcefulness in the invention of reservations, innuendoes, allegories and other deceptive means.[14]

Thus, Lioudmila Savinitch of the Russian Academy of Sciences, writes: "The Aesopian manner of writing was the characteristic feature of Russian literature and journalism for centuries."[15] Or, as Roman Jakobson, the influential literary theorist, has put it, in reading Russian literature, it is essential that we understand "that the obtrusive and relentless censorship becomes *an essential co-factor in Russian literary history* . . . that a sense for reading between the lines becomes unusually keen in the reading public and that the poet indulges in allusions and omissions."[16] Even Lenin, in a prerevolutionary article, "The Party Organization and Party Literature," speaks of the "accursed days of Aesopian talk, literary bondage, slavish language, ideological serfdom!"[17]

The practice of Aesopianism—which extended to fiction as well as non-fiction, poetry as well as prose—was by no means limited to writing. In the first new study of the renowned Soviet film director Sergei Eisenstein written with access to his personal archives as well as the memoirs of his colleagues, Joan Neuberger has shown that his film *Ivan the Terrible*, which was commissioned by Stalin and awarded a Stalin Prize, was in fact an Aesopian work covertly communicating a "critique of tyranny and a brilliant challenge to the conventions of Socialist Realism."

> Eisenstein was well aware that a film with such a conception of Ivan would require a special strategy to evade the censors. "The most effective way of hiding something is to put it on display," he wrote. . . . In *Ivan the Terrible* Eisenstein used several forms of subterfuge. He put "on display" a surface narrative that was politically acceptable. Then he proceeded to undercut the surface narrative with editing, style, and narrative diversions.[18]

Aesopianism so suffused Russian and Soviet culture that, according to one art critic, we must also interpret the best painters of the socialist realist tradition with an eye to "how diabolically wily centuries of official culture have made Russian artists and writers": they too engaged in what he ventures to call "painting between the lines."[19] Again, in the realm of music, analogous claims on his own behalf were made by the ostensibly pro-Soviet composer Shostakovich in his posthumously published memoirs.[20]

It is not, of course, only in Eastern Europe and Russia that we have had ample opportunity to observe the consequences of censorship for literature. Such lessons are available from all corners of our present world. From Burma, for example. In an article in the *New York Times* entitled "Burmese Editor's Code: Winks and Little Hints," Seth Mydans, the *Times* Southeast Asia correspondent, describes the courageous writer and editor Tin Maung Than and his esoteric art form.

In Burma, as in other repressive states, writing under censorship is an art form in itself, for both the writer and the clever reader. Many of its rules are universal. "You cannot criticize," Mr. Tin Maung Than said. "You have to give hints that you are being critical, that you are talking about the current system. The hints are in your choice of words and your tones and your composition. You use words with double meanings."

This is, according to Than, "a game played *by all independent-minded writers* in the military dictatorship of Myanmar."[21]

In still another part of our world, South Africa under white minority rule, we hear from Nobel Prize-winning novelist and essayist J. M. Coetzee that, under conditions of censorship, "writing between the lines is of course a familiar strategy."[22] Again, in an article in *Critical Studies* by Michael Drewett entitled "Aesopian Strategies of Textual Resistance in the Struggle to Overcome the Censorship of Popular Music in Apartheid South Africa," we read:

Certainly, *specific forms of domination give rise to corresponding forms of resistance.* In particular there has been a long tradition of popular song writing using Aesopian strategies of masking lyrics and corresponding audience participation [in the act of interpretation].[23]

For one last example, we turn to Egypt under Hosni Mubarak. As poet and essayist Yahia Lababidi explains:

Literature under restrictive regimes has tended to develop a flair for allegory—confessing in code, or through the use of symbolism. As Borges shrewdly notes, "Censorship is the mother of metaphor." In repressive societies, means of indirect communication tend to thrive. Egyptians have a gift for this sort of thing. Past masters at innuendo, they deftly employ double meanings to get past the censors on stage and in life. Slyly they vent their sexual (and political) frustrations in jokes, songs and video clips that manage to hint at everything without really saying anything.[24]

Somehow without our noticing, the esoteric assertion of freedom has been going on all around us.

ESOTERICISM AT HOME

But it is actually not necessary to look to such foreign climes and repressive regimes to observe the practice of defensive esotericism. We can just observe ourselves. For don't we automatically revert to esoteric ways in the one domain still somewhat subject to censorship in liberal regimes: sexuality? This is most obvious where the sex is considered illicit, as for example with homosexuality. The phenomenon of "gaydar," the attunement through which gays understand the covert signals that others put out to indicate their sexual orientation and interest, is part of a conversational (as well as gestural, sartorial, and postural) esotericism. When transferred to print and electronic media, especially advertising, this kind of signaling is known as "gay vague." As explained on the website of the Commercial Closet Association, an organization promoting the interests of the GLBT community to the advertising industry,

> "Gay Vague" is a term coined by Michael Wilke at *Advertising Age* in 1997 for ads that covertly speak to gays or seem to imply gayness with a wink. . . . This can include ambiguous relationships, blurred gender distinctions, wayward same-sex glances or touching, camp/kitsch, or coded references to gay culture. . . . (An older term, "gay window," was also used before the 1990s.)[25]

But even where there is nothing illicit, sex is by nature a private matter that tends to be censored or restrained in the public realm. Thus, in conversation, popular music, TV sitcoms, and talk shows we automatically and almost unconsciously revert to a system of coy allusion and innuendo in sexual matters that everyone immediately knows how to detect and interpret. Similarly, most teenage listeners to rock 'n' roll in its earlier, more censored days knew of the practice of esotericism. As Peter, Paul, and Mary would sing even in the late sixties: "But if I really say it, the radio won't play it, unless I lay it between the lines."[26]

Of course, these examples from within a modern, liberal democratic society will seem somewhat trivial in comparison with those from more persecutory environments, but they are for that very reason particularly revealing. They demonstrate something that one might otherwise never suspect: how *very little* adversity it takes—certainly much less than systematic or violent persecution—to move sincere and high-minded people in the direction of esoteric behavior of some kind. A correspondent for the *New York Times* once confided to me that when he first heard of the theory of esotericism it struck him as highly implausible—until he reflected that he himself, when faced with resistance from his editor, would frequently (and often unthinkingly) resort to various more indirect ways of communicating his point.

A more far-reaching example concerns John Rawls, widely considered the most significant American moral philosopher of the last half-century. A new study of his thought has shown that when his *A Theory of Justice* (1971) is read in conjunction with his later *Lectures on the History of Moral Philosophy* (2000), as well as an unpublished manuscript containing notes for eighteen lectures on Kant and Hegel, it becomes clear that important elements of his theory derive from an elaborate and profound engagement with the thought of Hegel. But while Rawls's enormous debts to Kant are well-known because amply elaborated in *A Theory of Justice*, his similar debts to Hegel—who was something of a pariah in most analytic philosophy departments of that time—are virtually unknown, because completely suppressed. In the six-hundred-odd pages of the original edition of *A Theory of Justice*, there are only two fleeting mentions of his name. It would seem that, fearing the disapproval or at least the noncomprehension of his primary audience, Rawls remained silent about an intellectual relationship that is ultimately crucial for the full understanding of his thought.[27] Needless to say, this limited act of concealment does not rise to the level of full-blown esotericism. The point, however, is that this forceful and high-minded moral philosopher, who was already safely ensconced at Harvard, was nevertheless moved to take a real step in the direction of esotericism by conditions of "adversity" that fell very far short of genuine censorship or persecution. Once you open your eyes to it, in short, you discover that defensive esotericism is so natural a phenomenon that even in the extremely open and tolerant environments of modern liberal democracies you still come across traces of it with surprising frequency.

But esotericism arises not only with ease and frequency but also with surprising spontaneity. None of the writers who testify to the use of esotericism ever speak of it as some sudden invention or clever breakthrough that they made. They talk as if it just arose naturally from the pressure of the environment: there was censorship, so of course we had to resort to hints, riddles, and allusions. Esotericism did not require *inventing*, for it is somehow a tool already in our toolbox, ready for use when needed. After all, the whole realm of wit and humor makes use of irony, hints, and riddles. The whole realm of sexuality and flirtation makes use of coyness and innuendo. The whole realm of poetic expressiveness makes use of metaphor and allusion. In esoteric writing, these preexisting and well-practiced techniques are simply turned to a new use. Thus, no prior agreement or planning, no formal training or official code book is necessary—not even any general awareness of the phenomenon, of its history and its name. Indeed, the decision to use it need not even be conscious. As Hans Speier postulates (reflecting on the Nazi experience):

> There is much evidence to support the contention that whenever freedom of expression is suppressed, the sensitivity to allusion increases. A German writer reported about the Nazi regime that at the time "not only in reading but also in conversation the slightest allusion was understood." . . . Several other German authors with whom I talked after the war about their experiences in writing and talking between the lines during the Nazi period spontaneously testified in the same way to the heightened sensitivity of the listeners to critical allusions in times of extreme political stress and to the loss of such sensitivity when the stress relaxed.[28]

Indirect communication arises naturally, as if it were an adaptive strategy deeply rooted in the instincts of the speaking animal. Thus, one does not have to be Sigmund Freud to postulate here a kind of universal law of human behavior: wherever there is censorship or a threatening power differential, there will be coded messages of some kind.

As it turns out, this *was* the view of Freud. His *The Interpretation of Dreams* (1899) is a work parallel, in a sense, to the present one in that it aims to convince the skeptical reader of a related law of psychology: that our dreams have been composed with dissimulation and coded messages as a means of evading the internal censor. In order to render this controversial suggestion more plausible, he seeks an external analog, "a social parallel to this internal event in the mind":

> Where can we find a similar distortion of a psychical act in social life? Only where two persons are concerned, one of whom possesses a certain degree of power which the second is obliged to take into account. In such a case the second person will distort his psychical acts or, as we might put it, will dissimulate.

Freud goes on to give an example from his own writing: "When I interpret my dreams for my readers I am obliged to adopt similar distortions. The poet [Goethe] complains of the need for these distortions in the words: 'After all the best of what you know may not be told to boys.'" Then he offers a broader example:

> A similar difficulty confronts the political writer who has disagreeable truths to tell to those in authority. . . . A writer must beware of censorship, and on its account he must soften and distort the expression of his opinion. According to the strength and sensitiveness of the censorship, he finds himself compelled either merely to refrain from certain forms of attack, or to speak in allusions in place of direct references, or he must conceal his objectionable pronouncement beneath some apparently innocent disguise. . . . The stricter the censorship, the more far reaching will be the disguise and the more ingenious too may be the means employed for putting the reader on the scent of the true meaning.[29]

In sum, it is quite remarkable how effortlessly and universally people resort to esoteric ways as soon as they are faced with even fairly trivial-seeming obstacles to free expression. And, although no Freudian, I do think it just possible that all this comes so naturally to us partly because, as it were, we do it in our sleep.

At any rate, when we turn finally to the evidence of history, we find a great deal of testimony, stemming from every historical period, in support of this "law of psychology." In sixteenth-century France, Montaigne tells us that he lives in a time "when we cannot talk about the world except with danger or falsely." Therefore, he explains, they speak falsely: "dissimulation is among the most notable qualities of this century."[30] Likewise, in seventeenth-century Italy, Paolo Sarpi declares to a friend: "My character is such that, like a chameleon, I imitate the behavior of those amongst whom I find myself. . . . I am compelled to wear a mask. Perhaps there is nobody who can survive in Italy without one."[31] Again, in eighteenth-century England, John Toland states: "daily experience sufficiently evinces that there is no discovering, at least no declaring the truth in most places, but at the hazard of a man's reputation, employment, or life. These circumstances *cannot fail* to beget the woeful effects of insincerity [and] dissimulation." He describes these effects in terms that would be familiar to the contemporary authors quoted above: "men are become . . . reserved in opening their minds about most things, ambiguous in their expressions, supple in their conduct. . . . To what sneaking equivocations, to what wretched shifts and subterfuges, are men of excellent endowments forced to have recourse . . . merely to escape disgrace or starving?"[32] To conclude, "*in all ages*," Holbach laments, "one could not, without imminent danger, lay aside the prejudices which opinion had rendered sacred. . . . *All that the most enlightened men could do* was to speak with hidden meaning [*à mots couverts*]."[33]

Is it not reasonable to conclude, in short, that where freedom of thought is lacking—which is to say, in almost all times and places—writers will resort to defensive esotericism in one degree or another? This is exactly what our literary theories would predict (as well as common sense); it is precisely what we have seen with our own eyes in our own time; and it is abundantly acknowledged in the historical record. In every age, the powerless, the colonized, the endangered minorities, the captive minds have spoken in fables of one kind or another. Persecution begets dissimulation.

PHILOSOPHERS: THE "NATURAL" MINORITY

To understand the defensive esotericism of philosophers in particular, however, some further distinctions are needed concerning the kinds, motives, and subjects of persecution. One must distinguish, to begin with, between persecution that is historically contingent and that which is more enduring, perhaps even natural. In the long, turbulent course of history, chance has made now one group, now another into a persecuted minority—Christians, Jews, African Americans, kulaks, Gypsies, Kurds. But there has been one relative constant, with deep roots, it would seem, in the nature of things: the persecution of philosophers. To be sure, no one would argue that philosophers' sufferings have been the most severe: they are nothing as compared with those of slavery or the Holocaust. But they have arguably been the most constant. In the roughly two-thousand-year record of Western philosophy prior to, say, 1800, it is difficult to name a single major thinker who did not, at some point in his life, experience persecution or at least witness it close at hand.

It can be difficult for us, who live in a world where philosophy has become so narrowly technical, as well as so venerable and well-intentioned, to take fully seriously the idea of persecuting it. Little remains of the daring, transgressive, outlaw quality of the philosopher (unless one chances to read Nietzsche). But as we have seen, the earlier, especially the classical understanding of theory and praxis, assumed that the philosopher transcended ordinary practical life in a way that put him in tension with it and with the long-standing customs, myths, and prejudices of his society. He is fundamentally different, strange, suspect—like a follower of some alien god. And since the attainment and practice of this way of life require both rare genius and extraordinary strength of soul, the philosopher, where he exists at all, will necessarily form the smallest and most vulnerable of minorities. Almost by definition, then, the philosopher is alone in society, without party or clan, a stranger and misfit by nature and not merely by historical accident or convention.

That is why we find Montaigne speaking of "the *natural incompatibility* that exists between the common herd and people of rare and excellent judgment and knowledge, inasmuch as these two groups go entirely different ways."[34] And, as Voltaire adds: "Our miserable species is so constructed, that those who walk in the beaten path *always* throw stones at those who teach a new path. . . . *every* philosopher is treated as the prophets were among the Jews."[35] Similarly, Goethe's Faust remarks: "the few who understood something of the world and of men's heart and mind, who were foolish enough not to restrain their full heart [i.e., not to practice esotericism] but to reveal their feeling and their vision to the vulgar, have *ever been* crucified and burned."[36] In Plato's (or his Socrates's) even more extreme formulation, the philosopher in the city is "just like a human being who has fallen in with wild beasts."[37] The very powerful fears voiced here are not groundless. The human species surely has an amply documented proclivity for killing its sages and wise men.

So whereas the accidents of religious history in the West produced what is known as "the Jewish problem," and the contingencies of American history created "the race issue," something closer to the *nature* of things has produced what might be called "the philosopher problem." It is an inherently dangerous thing to be wise among so many who are foolish, to be adults in a world of overgrown children. Philosophers reside in society like alien and suspicious characters: wary, nervous, and with one eye always on the exit. As the *Encyclopedia* asserts, "the condition of the sage is very dangerous: there is hardly a nation that is not soiled with the blood of several of those who have professed it." And it continues: "What should one do then? Must one be senseless among the senseless? No; but one must *be wise in secret*."[38] One must wear a mask, play a role, employ a concealing rhetoric. As Pierre Charron puts it in his great work *On Wisdom*, the wise man is typically constrained

to act outwardly in one way, to judge inwardly in another, to play one role before the world, and another in his mind. The common saying *universus mundus exercet histrioniam* [all the world plays a role] should strictly and truly be understood of the wise man. . . . If he were on the outside what he is on the inside, people wouldn't know what to make of him, he would offend the world too much.[39]

This is a perennial problem with an equally perennial solution. Philosophy and secrecy naturally go together.

Thus we find that the general imperative "be wise in secret" has been something of a commonplace throughout the ages. When Descartes, for example, deeply shaken by the recent condemnation, imprisonment, and recantation of Galileo, expressed his desperate longing (in a letter to Mersenne) "to live in peace and to continue the life [of philosophy] I have begun," he added that he would do so by following Ovid's ancient dictum: *bene vixit, bene qui latuit* (he has lived well who has remained well hidden).[40] He looks upon his particular predicament, that is, as part of an old story with an old solution—just as Ovid himself was looking back three centuries to the famous motto of Epicurus and his followers: "live unseen."[41]

Such advice is found among the Stoics no less than the Epicureans. Seneca urges philosophy to conceal her differences with the world: "Let her not hold aloof from the customs of mankind, nor make it her business to condemn whatever she herself does not do. A man may be wise without parade and without arousing enmity."[42] The best way to live unseen, in other words, is to blend in, to speak and act like the people.

Alfarabi, the tenth-century Islamic Platonist, gives a similar admonition: the philosopher must strive to address the many "with arguments that are generally accepted among them, well known to them, and well received among them." Through this means "the philosopher associates with the public and becomes well protected so that he is not found burdensome or engaged in an objectionable business; for the public is in the habit of finding what is strange to them burdensome and what is out of their reach objectionable."[43]   *cf ⊥336*

Similarly, we read in Pascal: "We must keep our thought secret, and judge everything by it, while talking like the people."[44] Synesius of Cyrene speaks of the need "to love wisdom at home [and] to embrace fables abroad."[45] Again, Cesare Cremonini: "within, as you please; out of doors, as custom dictates."[46] Francis Bacon: "A man should speak like the vulgar and think like the wise."[47] Gracian: "Think with the few and speak with the many. He who would go counter to public opinion is as unlikely to establish truth as he is likely to fall into danger."[48] The Marquess of Halifax: "we should hearken to the fewest to learn what to think, and to the most, to learn what to speak."[49] Paolo Sarpi: "Your innermost thoughts should be guided by reason, but you should act and speak only as others do."[50] Montaigne: "the wise man should withdraw his soul within, out of the crowd, and keep it in freedom and power to judge things freely; but as for externals, he should wholly follow the accepted fashions and forms."[51] Erasmus: "As nothing is more foolish than wisdom out of place, so nothing is more imprudent than unseasonable prudence. And he is unseasonable who does not accommodate himself to things as they are, who is 'unwilling to follow the market.'"[52] Pierre Charron: "In all the external and common actions of life . . . one should agree and accommodate oneself to the common ways; for our rule does not extend to the outer and the action, but to the inner, the thought, and the secret, internal judgment."[53] And finally, Charles Blount: the philosophers "are too wise to hazard their own ruin for the instruction of foolish men. . . . Therefore, the wisest amongst the Heathens followed this rule in their Converse, *Loquendum cum vulgo, sentiendum cum sapientibus; & si mundus vult decipi, decipiatur* [Speak with the vulgar, think with the wise; and if the world wants to be deceived, let it be deceived]."[54] It would seem that the art of hiding one's wisdom has long been considered one of the most basic needs—and surest signs—of the philosopher.

When it has suited their purposes, however, philosophers have also openly reported on the caution and esotericism of their kind. Cicero stated (following Posidonius) that "Epicurus does not really believe in the gods at all, and that he said what he did about the immortal gods only for the sake of deprecating popular odium."[55] Condorcet, speaking of the ancient Greeks in general, asserts: "The philosophers thought to escape persecution by adopting, like the priests, the use of a double doctrine, whereby they confided only to tried and trusted disciples opinions that would too openly offend popular prejudice."[56] Similarly, Rousseau maintains:

Pythagoras was the first to make use of the esoteric doctrine. He did not reveal it to his disciples until after lengthy tests and with the greatest mystery. He gave them lessons in Atheism in secret and solemnly offered Hecatombs [sacrifices] to Jupiter. The philosophers were so comfortable with this method that it spread rapidly in Greece and from there to Rome, as may be seen in the works of Cicero, who along with his friends laughed at the immortal Gods to whom he so eloquently bore witness on the Rostrum. The esoteric doctrine was not carried from Europe to China, but it was born there too with Philosophy.[57]

Again, Locke states that Socrates

opposed and laughed at [the Athenians'] polytheisms and wrong opinions
of the Deity, and we see how they rewarded him for it. Whatsoever Plato,
and the soberest of the philosophers [Aristotle] thought of the nature and
being of the one God, they were fain, in their outward professions and worship, to go with the herd and keep to the religion established by law.[58]

This evidence notwithstanding, however, someone might still object that
the danger to the philosopher seems to be greatly overstated in the above
account. To be sure, many great thinkers were persecuted, but many others
were not. And when it is claimed that philosophers are alone in society,
without party or clan, that neglects the fact that many were protected by
powerful patrons or attained to high positions themselves. Is there not an
element of wounded vanity, not to say persecution complex, in this whole
melodrama of the lonely and endangered philosopher?

No doubt we are tempted to think so. But it would be strange to dismiss
so cavalierly the explicit, insistent, and repeated testimony of philosophers
themselves concerning the danger of their condition. Perhaps, then, there is
some bias or prejudice conditioning our own instincts in this matter.

Indeed, it is likely that the above objections seem powerful to us only because, for two centuries now, we have formed all our views of what the world
is like in ignorance of all the furious defensive maneuvering that was going
on behind the scenes. We see, for example, that Epicurus experienced no
persecution and naturally conclude that he faced no danger. The truth, however, is that he faced grave danger, which he successfully managed to avert
through the esoteric rhetoric described above by Cicero. Because we do not
see all of his effective defensive efforts, we assume, wrongly, that his safety
was effortless, that he was never in danger. We would seem to be in the position of people who look out into the world and conclude that it is a naturally
safe and peaceful place—because they do not see all of the vast defenses and
maneuverings that make it so. If the whole record of persecution were reexamined in full awareness of the elaborate and widespread use of esoteric
defenses, then what would emerge as truly noteworthy is not the few philosophers who managed to escape this danger, but the many who, despite
all their sophisticated defensive efforts, *still* fell prey to it. Ironically, our
ignorance of the practice of esotericism causes us systematically to underestimate the danger facing philosophers—and thus to discount the need for
esotericism. This is one of the ways in which the forgetfulness of esotericism,
once it has become established, becomes self-sustaining.

Similarly, it is true that philosophers often found safety through the patronage of those kings, tyrants, or aristocrats who happened to have intellectual interests and pretensions or, in later centuries, who sought the aid of philosophy in their struggle against the church. But again what has been forgotten is that philosophers were able to forge and maintain these crucial alliances only by virtue of their esoteric efforts. They did not speak openly or show themselves as they were, but had to serve—or, at the very least, refrain from contradicting—the ambitions, prejudices, or ideological interests of their nonphilosophic patrons. One has only to read some dedicatory letters to get a feel for this. By definition, philosophers do not cherish what other men cherish; their deepest interests are necessarily different from those of all others. They may indeed manage, by artfully disguising their true beliefs, to find patrons or form other kinds of alliances; but this proves nothing against the thesis that the philosopher *prior* to any mask or esoteric defense is the most isolated and vulnerable of men.

In sum, through most of history, philosophers believed themselves to be—and were—endangered beings. It is in the very nature of the philosopher to be radically exposed. To survive in such circumstances, they were forced to develop—as standard equipment for the philosophic way of life— a protective mask and an art of esoteric speech.

NOTES FOR A HISTORY OF PHILOSOPHICAL POLITICS

To appreciate the true spirit of philosophic esotericism, it is necessary to begin by emphasizing, as I have tried to, the natural and inherent vulnerability of the philosopher: what I have called "the philosopher problem." Once that is seen, however, it is equally necessary to emphasize that the danger confronting philosophers has varied greatly over time in its source, manifestation, and extent—and correspondingly, so has the rhetorical strategy for dealing with it.

Ultimately, it comes down to a question of politics. As naturally weak and isolated, the philosopher, more than any other type of human being, must be politic or political in order to preserve himself and his kind. Every philosophical rhetoric presupposes and serves a *philosophical politics*: an assessment of who, under prevailing political and religious conditions, are philosophy's enemies, who are its friends or protectors, and how each of them is to be managed. At different times and places, philosophers have sought to ally themselves with aristocratic patrons, with ancient tyrants, with the Catholic Church, with modern enlightened despots, with the bourgeois-liberal order. Philosophers are like hermit crabs: they are exposed by nature, but they can and do borrow shells from other creatures—whatever happens to be available under local conditions.

It would require a wonderfully learned and subtle work of history to describe all the myriad forms that changing times and circumstances have given to the relations between philosophers and the religio-political communities in which they have lived. Such a work—"A History of Philosophical Politics" or "A Comparative Sociology of Philosophy"—has never been undertaken. Yet such an analysis is essential if we are to gain an authentic understanding of the history of Western philosophy.[59]

Every minority is misunderstood. A special effort is required to see the world through its eyes and understand its particular plight. In recent years, in our multicultural age, many minority histories have been written. But not yet for this minority. We have, to be sure, no lack of "class analyses" of history, but the philosophic class is always arbitrarily assimilated to some larger social or economic class. All sense of its unique interests, needs, and dangers has been forgotten. Again, ever since Karl Mannheim, or perhaps Emile Durkheim, we have had the "sociology of knowledge," but it explores the function that thought performs for society, while ignoring the danger that society poses to philosophic thought. After two centuries of free speech, we take this curious cultural growth—philosophy—and the social status of the philosopher more or less for granted. We no longer have any feel for the questions that would drive a history of philosophical politics.

In the absence of such a work, let us consider a few illustrative, if very provisional, generalizations that might help awaken us to the issues at stake.[60] Censorship and persecution of thought have stemmed not only from political but also from religious authorities. Let us briefly compare, then, the situation of the philosopher in the premodern Christian world, the premodern Jewish and Muslim worlds, and the world of classical antiquity. (But given this focus on the religious dimension, it should be kept in mind that the following discussion is incomplete, leaving out, for the sake of simplicity, the sources of persecution deriving from the needs and interests of political authorities.)

Voltaire, expressing the common Enlightenment view, claims that "of all religions, the Christian should of course inspire the most toleration, but till now the Christians have been *the most intolerant* of all men."[61] Rousseau, while a bitter opponent of Voltaire's on many other issues, wholly agrees with this particular observation and tries to explain it in terms of three crucial doctrines that have made this religion of love uniquely persecutory.

First, Christianity (like Judaism and Islam) replaced the pluralism and

toleration inherent in pagan polytheism with monotheism—with the c
that there is one God, one moral and religious truth to be acknowledged by
all the world. Second, the extreme Christian emphasis on the afterlife with
eternal rewards and punishments raised the stakes of salvation to such an infinite height that it tempted men to employ even the most violent measures
to convert others or to protect the faith.

The third and most important doctrine in this context is that of salvation
by belief or faith. Greek and Roman paganism was a highly "political" religion in that the gods were seen as the source and supporters of the city and
its fundamental laws. This political element is also present in Judaism and
Islam, which are both religions of divine law: God has given His people the
Torah or the Sharia—an elaborate and minute code of behavior—and one's
primary religious obligation is to follow and study this law. But Christianity
broke with Judaism precisely by abolishing or transcending the old law as
well as the attachment to a particular political group or "chosen" people.
This extraordinary change, this separation of religion from the nation and
its law, is well described by Fustel de Coulanges:

> Among all ancient nations the law had been subject to, and had received
> all its rules from, religion. Among the Persians, the Hindus, the Jews, the
> Greeks, the Italians, and the Gauls, the law had been contained in the
> sacred books or in religious traditions. . . . *Christianity is the first religion that
> did not claim to be the source of law.* . . . Men saw it regulate neither the laws
> of property, nor the orders of succession, nor obligations, nor legal proceed-
> ings. It placed itself outside the law, and outside all things purely terrestrial.
> Law was independent; it could draw its rules from nature, from the human
> conscience, from the powerful idea of the just that is in men's minds. It
> could develop in complete liberty.[62]

Now, in taking the unparalleled step of abolishing or transcending the law
of the Torah, what did Christianity put in its place? A very inward and abstract injunction: to believe in and love God as well as to love one's neigh-
bor. Thus, as compared with paganism and even with the other monotheistic
religions, Christianity is above all a religion of inner faith or belief; and as the
official content of that belief became more elaborate over time, Christianity
became a doctrinal or dogmatic or theological religion that made salvation
contingent on the acceptance of certain often obscure or controversial dogmas (e.g., creation of the universe from nothing). And "who does not see,"
asks Rousseau, "that dogmatic and theological Christianity is, by the multi-

tude and obscurity of its dogmas, above all by the obligation to acknowledge them, a field of battle always open among men?" Again: "You must *think* as I do in order to be saved. This is the horrible dogma that desolates the world."[63] According to Rousseau, then, the combination of monotheism, eternal punishments and rewards, and the centrality of sacred dogma is what has made Christianity uniquely persecutory.

But there is another side to this familiar Enlightenment story. Under the reign of Christianity, philosophers were typically under very close scrutiny and were persecuted for specific doctrines deemed heretical—but not for *being philosophers* as such. Galileo, to take the most famous example, was tried and imprisoned by the church for embracing a proscribed doctrine, heliocentrism, but not for being a natural philosopher, that is, not simply for daring to "investigate the things under the earth and the heavenly things." But this, of course, is one of the crimes for which Socrates was tried and executed.[64] During the Christian Middle Ages, astronomy was part of the *quadrivium*, the established curriculum for the liberal arts, whereas in Periclean Athens, at the very height of the Greek Enlightenment, it was a capital crime.

Precisely because Christianity was a uniquely doctrinal or theological religion, it had *need* of philosophy to help elaborate and clarify its dogmas. So, far from being forbidden, philosophy became part of the official and required training for students of theology. Voltaire goes so far as to claim that "it was the philosophy of Plato that made Christianity." "When at last some Christians adopted the doctrines of Plato and mixed a little philosophy with their religion, they separated from the Jewish cult and gradually won some eminence."[65] Not only did Christianity need philosophy or metaphysics as a handmaid to theology, it also needed political philosophy. For the New Testament, in withdrawing the divine code from the realm of law and politics, freed these areas to be governed by man's natural lights. As Fustel states in the above passage, "law was independent; it could draw its rules from nature"—in the best case, from the public interest or natural law as discovered by philosophy.

Thus, Christianity's strong tendency to persecute certain heretical philosophical doctrines—so emphasized by the Enlightenment—is just the flip side of the emphatic Christian embrace and need of philosophy. Christianity is a uniquely philosophical religion. Yet, in a further twist, that embrace could be even more dangerous to philosophy than persecution, since it threatened to co-opt it. Christianity kept philosophy alive, but subdued and under house arrest.

In sum, the situation of the philosopher living under Christianity was complex. He faced the twin dangers of co-optation and of persecution for particular doctrines. But his way of life was not fundamentally suspect. The very idea of philosophy or rationalism was not anathema. "Philosopher" was, for the most part, a term of honor in the Christian world.[66] (Modern scholarship, which arose in a Christian world, has, partly for this reason, tended to understand the whole "philosopher problem" only in these less radical terms characteristic of the Christian world.)

The situation was quite different—to us more strange, but in itself perhaps more understandable—under (premodern) Judaism and Islam, where "philosopher" was typically a term of derogation. These are religions of divine law and not of sacred doctrine, and, as such, they hold jurisprudence—the minute study and interpretation of God's law—and not theology to be the highest human science and the proper approach to the divine. In such an environment, philosophy could not so easily establish its legitimacy. As George Hourani writes of the intellectual culture of the Islamic world:

> The right and the wrong for man were to be determined primarily by reference to the Koran supplemented by the Traditions; doubts about their interpretation were to be settled by the consensus of learned opinion; while *independent reasoning* by the lawyer was to be held as the last resort, and then only to be exercised in interpretation of Scripture, not in deducing the right or the wrong from the public interest, natural law, or any other standard independent of Scripture.[67]

The only legitimate use of independent reasoning is for the interpretation of Scripture—jurisprudence.

Similarly, Rashi, the most revered Jewish exegete of the Torah, in the very first line of his commentary on Genesis, poses a question that no Christian theologian (and no modern person) would ever think to ask: why has this account of God's creation of the universe been included at all? It is no proper concern of ours. The divine origin of the universe, so far from being a necessary dogma of the faith, as in Christianity, is something man has no clear business investigating. "The Torah, *which is the Law book of Israel*," writes Rashi, ought to have begun with the first verse of Exodus 12, for this is "the first commandment given to Israel."[68] Rashi's eventual answer to his question is that we need to know of God's creation of the earth in order to understand his legal right to transfer the promised land from the Canaanites to the people of Israel. The Jewish religion, as understood and represented by

Rashi, is so resolutely unmetaphysical or antiphilosophical that the pursuit of even the most basic speculative or cosmological knowledge is justifiable only to the extent that it has a direct bearing on the law.[69]

Thus, the great burden of Maimonides's *Guide of the Perplexed* is to show that the study of philosophy is, in fact, permitted by the law. Similarly, the contemporaneous *Decisive Treatise* of Averroes has the stated purpose "to examine, from the standpoint of the study of the Law, whether the study of philosophy and logic is allowed by the Law, or prohibited or commanded."[70] This is precisely the reverse of the situation in Thomas Aquinas's *Summa Theologica*—the Christian counterpart to these works—the very first article of which is: "Whether, besides philosophy, any further doctrine [i.e., divine revelation] is required." Thus, in the Jewish and, to a somewhat lesser extent, in the Islamic world, the danger to the philosopher was different in kind and usually greater in degree than in the Christian world: a danger directed not merely at particular doctrines or particular philosophers, but at the philosophic enterprise or way of life as such.[71] Here we see the "philosopher problem" in its fullest and most radical form.

If we turn to the world of Greek and Roman antiquity, we find the danger different still. There exists nothing like the extraordinary mixture of doctrinal persecution and official embrace that preserved and co-opted philosophy under Christianity, on the one hand, or the organized, orthodox hostility that endangered, invigorated, and finally destroyed philosophy under Judaism and Islam, on the other. Still, all things considered, the situation resembled the Jewish/Islamic one a good deal more than the Christian. But this suggestion—that philosophy faced fundamental danger in the ancient world—is resisted by modern classical scholarship, not only because the latter tends to take for granted the paradigm that existed within the Christian world, but also because it is heir to the Enlightenment and its "polemical" use of classical antiquity as a weapon with which to attack Christianity.

Since the Enlightenment, the image of ancient Greece as a lost Golden Age of philosophy, toleration, and freedom has played a crucial role in inspiring and arming the modern struggle for liberation. Most important was the assertion that there was little or no persecution of thought or belief in ancient Greece—a claim used to demonstrate that Christian persecution was both unprecedented and unnecessary. "Athens," proclaimed Voltaire, "allowed complete liberty not only to philosophy, but to all religions." The most obvious obstacle to this theory, the trial and execution of Socrates, Voltaire dismisses through the then novel (but now widespread) thesis that he was executed for partisan, political reasons and not at all on account of his opinions or alleged impiety.[72] This image of antiquity has maintained a firm hold on the imagination and scholarship of the West despite the impressive efforts of writers like Fustel de Coulanges, E. R. Dodds, and others to correct it.[73]

There is certainly an element of truth to it. In ancient Greece and Rome, there was no persecution for *heresy*—for deviations from an elaborate, obligatory, orthodox body of sacred doctrines—which came into being only under Christianity. (There was, however, much prosecution for *impiety*—for unholy actions or general atheistic beliefs.) Similarly, there was no religious sectarian conflict or holy war waged to convert the nonbelievers to the one true God. There also seems to have been no organized and systematic attempts at the censorship of thought: no public office for literary censorship, no licensing of publication, no prior restraint or preventive censorship, no index of proscribed books, no Inquisition.

But all of this did not add up to freedom or security for philosophy. Even if one grants all the Enlightenment arguments regarding the unique character of Christian intolerance, the persecutory tendencies of Greek polytheism must not be underestimated. The latter contained at least one powerful seed of persecution that Christianity, with its moral individualism, removed: fear that the gods would punish the whole city for the offenses of one individual. (Consider, for example, Sophocles's *Oedipus tyrannus* which depicts the ruinous plague afflicting Thebes owing to the past actions of Oedipus.)

Moreover, the ancient *polis*—small, unified, homogeneous, deeply, if fitfully, pious, with no separation or even distinction of church and state, and no principled recognition of individual rights, whether of thought or anything else—could be far more totalitarian and dangerous than the loose and disorganized states of Christendom (at least until the consolidation of the modern nation-state). The city could and did closely regulate not only public behavior and economic relations but also family life, education, public worship, and popular entertainments. True, these cities did not practice systematic review and censorship of individual works—our paradigm for intellectual persecution. But official censorship of individual writings is the flip side of official recognition of the general literary enterprise, of its necessity or legitimacy. In the ancient polis, the latter was often lacking along with the former. Thus, the very presence of a permanent theater in Rome was forbidden until the time of Augustus. On several occasions in Rome and even, for a short while, in Athens, all philosophers as such were summarily expelled.[74] Here and there, freedom of thought was relatively protected; but it was never secured in *principle*, as a permanent, constitutional right of the individual, but only *politically*. It came and went with the political fortunes of particular groups or individuals. Thus, despite—or rather because of—the fact that there was no official, institutionalized censorship in Athens, there was a great deal of ad hoc accusation, denunciation, and prosecution. Socrates, Anaxagoras, Damon, Euripides, Diagoras, and Protagoras—all were indicted in Athens, and all within the lifetime of Socrates. "It is a singular error," writes Fustel de Coulanges, "to believe that in the ancient cities men enjoyed [individual] liberty."[75]

But there is no need for modern, scholarly speculation concerning the security or vulnerability of the philosopher in the ancient world: we can consult the testimony of the philosophers themselves. This was an issue that clearly preoccupied them, although this is seldom observed today. If one examines Plato from this perspective, for example, one sees that the dialogues are concerned less to present a settled philosophical doctrine or system—the famous "Platonism"—than to investigate the foundations of the philosophic way of life in every sense: its goodness for our nature, its theoretical possibility, its moral legitimacy, and not least its precarious political situation in the city. One notices, for example, that everything in Plato, even the most abstruse, metaphysical discussion, is placed in a *political* context.[76] And in all the dialogues, there are constant echoes of and allusions to the trial and death of Socrates. The opening scene of the *Republic*, for example, depicts a playful arrest of Socrates by Polemarchus and his entourage—a scene also recapitulated at the beginning of book 5.

So what is the political situation of the philosopher, according to Plato? While a full and adequate analysis is beyond the scope of the present discussion, a general sketch can be drawn from a few explicit statements, mainly in *Republic* books 6 and 7. Plato's Socrates asserts there quite openly that "so hard is the condition suffered by the most decent men [the philosophers] with respect to the cities that there is no single other condition like it" (488a). And he likens the philosopher's situation to that of "a human being who has fallen in with wild beasts" (496d).

In all ordinary cities—as distinguished from the best regime, ruled by a philosopher-king—the philosopher grows up "spontaneously and *against the will* of the regime in each" (*Republic* 520b).[77] He is surrounded by enemies. The primary danger comes from the uneducated and superstitious multitude. For it is "part of the ordinary beliefs of mankind," according to Cicero in *De inventione*, that "philosophers are atheists."[78] Thus, as he states elsewhere: "philosophy is content with few judges, and of set purpose on her side avoids the multitude and is in her turn an object of suspicion and dislike to them, with the result that if anyone should be disposed to revile all philosophy, he could count on popular support."[79] The people hold strong beliefs, especially religious beliefs, and assert them vehemently, according to Plato's Socrates, and "they punish the man who is not persuaded with dishonor, fines and death" (*Republic* 492b–d).

The many also hate the philosophers for their detachment. The great majority, taking themselves and the particulars of their lives with infinite seriousness, are unable to achieve any detachment from their individuality and from the arbitrary particulars that they see with their senses, so as to perceive the universal, necessary, and suprasensible. Therefore "it is impossible . . . that a multitude be philosophic. . . . And so those who do philosophize are *necessarily blamed* by them . . . as well as by all those private men who consort with the mob and desire to please it" (*Republic* 494a; see *Timaeus* 28c). Neither can the many achieve detachment or acceptance in the face of death; so when Socrates asserts in the *Phaedo* that the philosopher studies "nothing but dying and being dead," his interlocutor replies: "I think the multitude . . . would say you were quite right, and our people at home would agree entirely with you that philosophers desire death, and they would add that they know very well that the philosophers deserve it" (64b; see 65a). In the allegory of the cave, therefore, when the philosopher, having seen the truth, returns to the cave, the people, "if they were somehow able to get their hands on and kill the man who attempts to release and lead up, wouldn't they kill him? No doubt about it, he [Glaucon] said" (*Republic* 517a).

There is danger not only from the multitude but also from the political class, especially those, mentioned above, "who consort with the mob and desire to please it." Such a man is Callicles in the *Gorgias*, a lover of the many (481d). He is plainly threatened and angered by the passive and unmanly posture of philosophic detachment, declaring ominously: "whenever I see an older man still philosophizing and not released from it, this man, Socrates, surely seems to me to need a beating" (485d). More generally, the ambitious political men in the city, who assert various claims to rule, while lacking the true claim—the art of ruling—insist that this art "isn't even teachable and are ready to *cut to pieces* the man who says it is teachable" (488b). In a similar vein, Plato has Protagoras declare, in the dialogue that bears his name, that the art of "sophistry"—using the term here in its original, nonpejorative, literal sense of education in "practical wisdom"—naturally arouses great hostility because it implicitly asserts that families and fathers lack the wisdom to educate their own children.

> Now I tell you that sophistry is an ancient art, and those men of ancient
> times who practiced it, *fearing the odium* it involved, disguised it in a decent
> dress, sometimes of poetry, as in the case of Homer, Hesiod, and Simonides;
> sometimes in mystic rites and soothsayings, as did Orpheus, Musaeus and
> their sects; and sometimes too, I have observed of athletics . . . ; and music
> was the disguise employed by your own Agathocles. . . . All these, as I say,
> from *fear of ill-will* made use of these arts as outer coverings.[80]

Finally, there was danger not only from the ignorant multitude and from
the politically ambitious and powerful, but also from the philosopher's rivals
in wisdom, the poets.

> There is an old quarrel between philosophy and poetry. For [the poets
> speak of] that "yelping bitch shrieking at her master," and "great in the
> empty eloquence of fools," "the mob of overwise men holding sway," and
> "the refined thinkers who are really poor" and countless others are signs
> of this old opposition. (*Republic* 607 b–c)[81]

In the *Apology* (18a–d), Socrates implies that the oldest and most dangerous
prejudice against him arose from the poet Aristophanes's attack on him in
the *Clouds*.[82]

It seems perfectly clear, then, that in the view of Plato—and who could
dare claim to know the situation better than Plato—the position of philosophers in fifth-century Greece was precarious. They were not the venerable
institution they have become for us. They lived dangerously.

As suggested above, philosophy's situation in Greece was most akin to
that within the Jewish and Islamic worlds, where thinkers were continually
forced to confront the most grave and radical challenges—both theoretical
and practical—to the whole philosophic way of life. And indeed, if one consults Plato's medieval Islamic commentators, one finds that they were very
much alive and attuned to the passages I have quoted above. Averroes, in his
epitome of the *Republic*, repeats even more forcefully than Plato: "If it happens that a true philosopher grows up in these cities, he is in the position of
a man who has come among perilous animals. . . . Hence he turns to isolation
and lives the life of a solitary." A few pages earlier, when summarizing a passage in which Plato likens the philosophers to physicians (489b–c), Averroes
goes beyond the text to add: "If the physicians tell [the multitude] that they
can be healed, they stone them to death."[83] Similarly, Alfarabi asserts in his
own name that, outside the best regime, the philosopher "is a stranger in the

present world and wretched in life." And he holds this also to be the view of Plato, who "stated that the perfect man, the man who investigates, and the virtuous man are in grave danger" from the multitude.[84]

This major and clearly stated Platonic theme, which was understood and emphasized by Plato's Islamic commentators, has gone virtually unnoticed by modern Western scholars. Modern commentaries on the *Republic*, for example, make little or no mention of the striking passages quoted above.[85] Stranger still, in contemporary interpretations of the trial of Socrates—the central symbol of this theme—the Voltairian view has won out almost completely: "it is the common view today," according to M. I. Finley, "that Socrates was tried and executed as an act of political vengeance by the restored democracy."[86] The inveterate fear and hatred of philosophy, so emphasized by Plato, had nothing to do with it. This extraordinary event that has reverberated down through the centuries was just a regrettable incident of local Athenian politics, nothing more. Modern thought in its harmonism has a kind of tone deafness to the conflictualist idea. Plato, at any rate, took precisely the opposite view. The trial and execution of Socrates was the local manifestation of a fundamental and permanent problem of the human condition, a problem, therefore, that Plato treats not only in the *Apology* but as a central theme throughout the dialogues: the principled resistance and natural hostility of the religio-political community to the life of reason.

Now that we have briefly indicated some differences in the situation of the philosopher in these three religio-political environments, it remains to discuss the consequences that these differences had for the defensive esotericism or the philosophical politics practiced by the philosophers so situated. Under Christianity, that uniquely philosophical religion, philosophers could often find safety merely by disguising certain particularly unorthodox opinions that they held. But under Judaism and Islam and in the ancient world, philosophers were often compelled to disguise the fact that they were philosophers at all or, alternatively, to disguise the true character and meaning of philosophy.

Some sense for this greater degree of imposture can be gotten from this remarkable account of Mullah Sadra Shirazi, a disciple of the philosopher Avicenna, who attempted a restoration of philosophy in seventeenth-century Iran. The account is given by Arthur Gobineau, who lived in Iran as a French diplomat for about six years in the middle of the nineteenth century. He describes here "the great and splendid expedient of *Ketman*," in Arabic, concealment, discretion.

He [Sadra] too was afraid of the mullahs. To incite their distrust was inevitable, but to provide a solid basis, furnish proof for their accusations, that
would have been to expose himself to endless persecutions, and to compromise at the same time the future of the philosophical restoration he medi-
tated. Therefore he conformed to the demands of his times and resorted to
the great and splendid expedient of *Ketman*. When he arrived in a city he
was careful to present himself humbly to all the moudjteheds or doctors of
the region. He sat in a corner of their salons, their talars, remained silent
usually, spoke modestly, approved each word that escaped their venerable
lips. He was questioned about his knowledge; he expressed only ideas borrowed from the strictest Shiite theology and in no way indicated that he
concerned himself with philosophy. After several days, seeing him so meek,
the moudjteheds themselves engaged him to give public lessons. He set to
work immediately, took as his text the doctrine of ablution or some similar
point, and split hairs over the prescriptions and inner doubts of the subtlest
theoreticians. This behavior delighted the mullahs. They lauded him to the
skies; they forgot to keep an eye on him. They themselves wanted to see him
lead their imaginations through less placid questions. He did not refuse.
From the doctrine of ablution he passed to that of prayer; from the doctrine
of prayer, to that of revelation; from revelation, to divine unity and there,
with marvels of ingenuity, reticence, confidences to the most advanced
pupils, self-contradiction, ambiguous propositions, fallacious syllogisms out
of which only the initiated could see their way, the whole heavily seasoned
with unimpeachable professions of faith, he succeeded in spreading Avicen-
nism throughout the entire lettered class; and when at last he believed he
could reveal himself completely, he drew aside the veils, repudiated Islam,
and showed himself the logician, the metaphysician that he really was.

It was above all necessary that the care he used to disguise his speech
he also use to disguise his books; that is what he did, and to read them one
forms the most imperfect idea of his teaching. I mean, to read them without
a master who possesses the tradition. Otherwise, one penetrates them without difficulty. From generation to generation, the students of Mullah Sadra
have been the heirs of his true teaching and they have the key to the terms
of which he makes use, not to express, but to indicate to them his thought.
It is with this oral corrective that the numerous treatises of the master are
today held in such great esteem and that, since his times, they have formed
the delight of a society drunk on dialectic, eager for religious opposition,
enamored of secret boldness, enraptured by artful imposture.

In reality, Mullah Sadra is not an inventor, nor a creator, he is only a re-

storer, but a restorer of the great asiatic philosophy, and his originality consists in having *clothed it* in such a way that it was acceptable and accepted in
the time in which he lived.[87]

In the ancient world, we find related forms of behavior. Indeed, certain
well-known but puzzling facts of classical thought take on new meaning
when interpreted in the context of this problematic. We find philosophers
sometimes hiding the fact that they are philosophers altogether, sometimes
acknowledging only part of their philosophical activity, and sometimes ad-
mitting they are philosophers but inventing a new "clothing" for philosophy
that makes it more acceptable.

In the passage quoted above from Plato's *Protagoras*, Protagoras claims
that in earlier times "sophists" (by which he means "wise men"), fearing
popular odium, disguised themselves as poets, soothsayers, mystics, and
teachers of athletics and music. Plutarch makes a similar claim: "Damon, it
is not unlikely, being a sophist, out of policy sheltered himself under the pro-
fession of music to conceal from people in general his skill in other things."[88]

Alternatively, Socrates, in the public account of his life depicted in Plato's
Apology, openly acknowledges that he is a philosopher, but categorically denies that he is a natural philosopher, claiming that in his mature period he
has always confined himself to the human things (ethics and politics) and
to the public-spirited effort to make his fellow citizens better. But from various passages in Plato and Xenophon, it seems clear that this is not the case.
While Socrates does grant a new importance to human or political philosophy, he by no means abandons natural philosophy. In Xenophon's words, "he
never ceased examining with his companions what each of the beings is."[89]
This is also obvious from Plato's *Republic* among other dialogues where Socrates is shown presenting a metaphysical account of the whole, involving the
theory of ideas and the idea of the good.[90]

What is new and daring in Plato is that he openly thematizes and celebrates the philosophic life without any such reservations. All of his dialogues, whatever their specific philosophical topic, are ultimately about
philosophy itself. His whole corpus seems to have the purpose of presenting a new and more effective "apology" to finally legitimize this marginal
and endangered activity. And among the primary ways he seeks to do this is
by dressing philosophy in religious clothing. According to Plutarch, it was
precisely through these efforts—this radical transformation in the public
appearance of philosophy—that Plato became the first to win some lasting
security for the philosophic way of life.

The first man to set down in writing the clearest and boldest argument of
all about the shining and shadowing of the moon [i.e., lunar eclipses] was
Anaxagoras. And neither was he ancient nor was the argument reputable,
but it was still secret and proceeded among a few and with a certain caution
or trust. For they [the many] did not abide the natural philosophers and
the praters about the heavens [*meteorolesches*], as they were called at that
time, because they reduced the divine to unreasoning causes, improvident
powers, and necessary properties. But even Protagoras went into exile, the
imprisoned Anaxagoras was barely saved by Pericles, and Socrates, who did
not concern himself with any of such things, nevertheless died on account
of philosophy. But later the reputation of Plato shone forth, on account of
the life of the man and because he placed the natural necessities under the
divine and more authoritative principles, and took away the slander against
these arguments and gave a path to these studies to all men.[91]

It is true that Plutarch, not wishing to undo what Plato did, implies but does
not state explicitly that this religious account of philosophy was a cloak fash-
ioned for the express purpose of protecting philosophy from society. But
here is how Montesquieu read this all-important passage:

See in Plutarch, *Life of Nicias*, how the physicists who explained the eclipses
of the moon by natural causes were suspect to the people. They called them
meteorolesches, persuaded that they reduced all divinity to natural and physical causes. . . . The doctrine of an intelligent [i.e., divine] being was found by
Plato *only as a preservative and a defensive arm against the calumnies of zealous
pagans.*[92]

One might object to this account that there is nothing new in Plato in
this regard since all pre-Socratic philosophers of whose writings we have any
knowledge presented themselves as believers in a god or gods. But this was
apparently a rather thin disguise; for in the *Laws* (967a–d), Plato's Athenian
Stranger openly states that most if not all of them were in fact atheists, that
they were eventually viewed as such even by the many, and that this is the
precise problem that led to the ancient attack upon philosophy by the poets.

Plato seems to have devoted himself to responding to this crucial problem. His writings are fairly steeped in religiosity—and of various kinds. Not
only are the dialogues full of references to the Olympic gods, of religious
stories and myths, and of semimystical metaphysical discussions, but philosophy is presented as a necessary precondition of genuine piety and in-

deed as itself an essentially religious activity. In the *Apology*, for example, Socrates is presented as having undertaken his philosophical activity in obedience to the command of the Delphic Oracle. It is a divine mission of sorts. Similarly, in the *Phaedo* (69c) and again in the *Symposium* (210a), the ascent to the philosophic truth is presented in terms borrowed from the Eleusinian Mysteries. And finally, as depicted in the *Phaedo* (118a7–8), Socrates's dying words—the final thoughts of this great philosopher—are to urge Crito to pay their debt to Asclepius by sacrificing a chicken. As John Toland, the eighteenth-century Deist, puts it in his essay on esoteric writing:

> Plato wisely providing for his own safety, after the poisonous draught was administered to Socrates . . . wrote rather poetically than philosophically . . . by epically transforming the nature of things, the elements, and the celestial globes . . . into Gods, Goddesses, Geniuses, and Demons.[93]

In sum, the great accomplishment of Plato was, through his uniquely poetic and religious portrait of philosophy, to have transformed it from a fringe activity that was viewed as unholy by the people—somewhat like vivisection or black magic—into something fairly respectable that would now become an abiding feature of Western culture. This great feat of transvaluation would seem to explain two other remarkable facts about Plato. His were the first ancient philosophical writings to be preserved in more than fragmentary form. And he was the first philosopher who was able, in broad daylight, to open a philosophic school or academy—a school that remained in existence uninterruptedly for the next eight centuries.

It should go without saying, however, that these various quotations do not begin to settle the whole immense question of Plato's religious thought, for it is certain, at a minimum, that he took the theological question extremely seriously. But what these passages do indicate is that, in the view of a long tradition adhered to by a wide variety of thinkers, *much* of what Plato and the other ancient philosophers asserted regarding the traditional gods of the city must be understood in terms of the perennial need to manage the mutual opposition of philosophy and society.

DEFENSIVE ESOTERICISM: ANCIENT AND MODERN

The most fundamental change, however, in the shifting history of defensive esotericism and philosophical politics occurred with the transition from premodern to modern thought in the period of the Enlightenment.

Above, we distinguished between persecution that is accidental or historically contingent and a kind that is more natural. This distinction needs to be reexamined in connection with the issue of theory and praxis and the divide between the ancient, conflictual view and the modern, harmonist one.

On the conflictual understanding of theory and praxis, all societies have a fundamental need for illusions of certain kinds, while philosophers have a fundamental need for freedom from illusion. Thus, what is a crucial good for the one is necessarily a great evil for the other. That is why they are in conflict—and why that conflict is not contingent, but "natural."

This conflictual view has three consequences for the premodern practice of defensive esotericism. First, it means that philosophical persecution is seen as a permanent problem: it can be controlled or managed in different ways in different times, but never completely uprooted and eliminated. On this understanding, then, the purpose of esotericism and philosophical politics is essentially passive or defensive: to hide from persecution or hold it at bay. There is no thought of going on the offensive—to confront and permanently abolish it.

Second, from the conflictual perspective, the persecution of philosophers is understood to stem not simply from ignorance and misunderstanding or from crude intolerance (although these play an important part), but also from an accurate intimation that philosophy is genuinely dangerous to society. This produces a somewhat different attitude toward intolerance and persecution than we are familiar with. While classical philosophers, no less than modern, have a life-and-death interest in combating and escaping persecution, they do not, for all that, regard it as pure viciousness and irrationality. They do not pronounce the very word "persecution" with the lip-curling rage and disgust that the Enlightenment thinkers feel. For in the end, they cannot altogether blame people for trying to protect themselves from something truly harmful to them.

On the contrary, they feel called upon to help society protect itself by shielding it from their subversive reflections. The third point, then, is that defensive esotericism, when thought through from the conflictual perspective, points to the need for protective esotericism. These esotericisms are two sides of the same coin. Philosophy and society being in conflict, esotericism is needed to protect each from the other. Thus, in turning now to explore protective esotericism—and in particular, the character of the danger that philosophy poses to society—we will also be continuing and deepening our exploration of defensive esotericism.

But as we have seen, a very different take on all of this emerged in modern philosophy with its commitment to the potential harmony of theory and praxis. On this view, the endangered condition of philosophy within society is not really a natural and necessary phenomenon, as the ancients believed, although it is not quite a historical accident either. All traditional societies did indeed incline to the persecution of philosophy, which tendency was, if you like, "natural" *to such societies.* But it is possible, the Enlightenment thinkers argued, to construct a radically new kind of society, one based on reason, in which the tension between society and philosophy would be permanently overcome and, with it, the deepest cause of persecution.

On this harmonist view, the three characteristics of defensive esotericism described above become transformed. First, modern thinkers go beyond the primarily passive, preservative stance of defensive esotericism to an activist, transformative rhetoric—what I am calling "political esotericism"—that aims to subvert and rebuild society in a way that, among other things, would finally eliminate persecution. Second, viewing intolerance and persecution as unnecessary and wholly irrational, they give themselves over unreservedly to vilifying them as *the* great evil, in a way that the ancient thinkers never did. And third, this whole subversive, activist project for the elimination of persecution becomes itself—temporarily—a new stimulus to persecution and thus a new source of the need for defensive esotericism.

[6]

Dangerous Truths:
Protective Esotericism

'Tis real Humanity and Kindness to hide strong truths from
tender eyes.
—SHAFTESBURY

Of the four forms of esotericism, protective esotericism is the one that raises
the profoundest issues and the profoundest resistance.

No one denies the reality of persecution—the threat to philosophy posed
by society. But almost everyone today denies the reality of "dangerous
truths"—the threat to society posed by philosophy. Thus, very few people
can be found who believe that philosophers of the past ever engaged in protective esotericism to any significant degree.[1]

But there is plenty of evidence to show that in the past, people saw this
phenomenon in a very different light. We must try to look through their eyes.

THE THREE PREMISES OF
PROTECTIVE ESOTERICISM

Jean d'Alembert, for example, in his *Analysis of the Spirit of the Laws* remarks
on what he calls Montesquieu's "voluntary obscurity" and "pretended lack of
method." He gives the following simple and approving explanation:

Montesquieu, having to present sometimes important truths whose absolute and direct enunciation might wound without bearing any fruit, has
had the prudence to envelope them, and by this innocent artifice, has veiled
them from those to whom they would be harmful, without letting them be
lost for the wise.[2]

This kind of literary prudence is described more generally by Montaigne:
"It is not new for the sages to preach things as they serve, not as they are.
Truth has its inconveniences, disadvantages, and incompatibilities."[3] It is
clear from this that he considers protective esotericism a well-founded as
well as long-standing practice. It may be said to rest on three premises, implied in this brief statement.

First, there are some important truths that are "inconvenient"—dangerous
to society or to ordinary life. Human rationality and human politicality are
often in conflict at the highest level.

Second, all human beings are not equal in their capacity to handle such
difficult truths: there are such things as "sages" for whom truth may be
simply good, indeed the greatest good; but for the vast majority truth can,
in one degree or another, be harmful.

Third, it is morally permissible for the former group to lie to the latter—
or at least to conceal or dilute the truth—for the latter's own benefit.

Should these three points be granted, it would follow that philosophers
may—perhaps they must—hide certain truths from those who would be
seriously harmed by them, just as we routinely protect children or the sick
from exposure to more than they can handle. Aquinas states the issue very
simply: "A teacher should measure his words that they help rather than hinder his hearer. . . . There are matters, however, that would be harmful to
those hearing them if they were openly presented." He concludes: "These
matters, therefore, ought to be concealed from those to whom they might
do harm."[4] This is how virtually all classical thinkers reasoned, according to
Bishop Warburton in his brief history of esotericism:

> that it was lawful and expedient to deceive for the public good. This *all
> the ancient philosophers* embraced: and Tully [Cicero], on the authority of
> Plato, thinks it so clear, that he calls the doing otherwise Nefas, a horrid
> wickedness.

Indeed, in Warburton's view, this desire to protect society from dangerous
truths—and not the avoidance of persecution—has historically been the

primary motive for the practice of philosophical esotericism. The *Encyclopedia* article "Exoteric and Esoteric," repeats the same claim: "the goal of these secret instructions was the public good."[5]

What seems so obvious, straightforward, and commonplace to a Shaftesbury, d'Alembert, Montaigne, Aquinas, or Warburton, however, appears to us in a very different light. As we have already seen, these premises strikes us as both implausible and repugnant. The first—the conflictual view of theory and praxis—violates our deep humanistic and Enlightenment faith in the harmony of reason and society. The second—the belief in "sages"—offends our democratic egalitarianism. The third—the permissibility of lying to someone for his own benefit—transgresses our moral attachment and scholarly commitment to honesty. So with the issue of protective esotericism, we are definitely heading into alien territory.

To ease the journey, it is important to remind ourselves that our purpose here is not to defend these earlier views (or to attack them). It is not to give *any* answer to the difficult philosophical question of whether these three premises grounding protective esotericism *are correct*. Our purpose is solely to answer the historical question of whether these premises were widely believed and acted upon by past thinkers, especially in the pre-Enlightenment period.

We have already investigated this question with respect to the latter two premises—concerning inequality and salutary lying—and answered strongly in the affirmative. In the present chapter, we will see still more evidence in support of these conclusions, especially signs of the inegalitarianism of most earlier philosophical thought.

It remains here to explore the first and crucial premise, that the truth can be harmful or dangerous. This is the deepest issue at stake in the matter of philosophical esotericism; it is the core of the conflictual view of theory and praxis; and it is also the deepest ground of the modern resistance to esotericism. Our goal is to try to relax the grip of that resistance and to achieve some genuine and sympathetic understanding of this premise. To succeed, we need to see not only *that* earlier thinkers embraced this alien view, but also something of the *why*. We need to gain some idea of its experiential basis and theoretical plausibility, some concrete sense of what this idea looks like from the inside. I will try to present it in as positive a light as possible. This view may well prove false in the end (or perhaps true regarding some societies, such as traditional ones, and false regarding others, like modern, liberal ones). But as a major philosophical alternative, it is unlikely to be wholly or uninterestingly false. It is a foreign country worth visiting.

THE BASIC IDEA OF DANGEROUS TRUTHS

To start from some very general reflections, it is clear that the idea of dangerous truths has, for a very long time, been commonplace, not to say a cliché. "A little bit of knowledge is a dangerous thing." "Curiosity killed the cat." "Ignorance is bliss." "What you don't know won't hurt you."

On a deeper level, one need only reflect on the story of the Tree of Knowledge and the Tower of Babel, or the myths of Prometheus, Daedalus, and Oedipus, or the story of the Sirens, or the argument for the "noble lie" in Plato's *Republic*, or the stories of Faust and Frankenstein to see that the notion of dangerous or forbidden knowledge has had a long and venerable history in the West. Indeed, of the two originary sources of Western culture, Socrates and the Bible, the one teaches that the idea of the good, the highest being and truth, is like the sun, which we can barely stand to look at directly, and the other teaches that if we should gaze upon the face of God, we would surely die.[6] Somehow the highest truths strain our human capacity not only to understand but to endure.

But why in the world should the truth be dangerous?, we persist in asking. If one is not unduly Pollyannaish or optimistic about how nicely the world fits together, couldn't one simply reply: Why *shouldn't* the truth be dangerous? Why would anyone expect the world to be all that we fervently wish or need it to be? Is there some reason why the truth must somehow always turn out to coincide with the fond hopes and comforting assumptions of ordinary life? Denial, wishful thinking, self-deceit, prejudice, delusion, myth—why do these phenomena play the central role that they do in human affairs if not because bare reality seldom conforms to the deepest demands of the human heart? Indeed, who among us is so bold as to claim to live without illusion? And where is the nation that is wholly able to justify its founding, its borders, its class structure, and its political legitimacy without recourse to myth of some kind?

Conversely, when we imagine to ourselves the serious pursuit of truth, we do not think of it as simply pleasant and untroubled. We revere truth, *Veritas*, as a great and noble ideal, precisely because we know and feel that it is something *difficult*, something that demands from us the greatest courage, firmness, and sacrifice, and therefore something necessarily threatening to those who lack the strength to recognize and adjust to it.

These very general considerations suggest that the idea of dangerous truths is not so outrageous as we incline to think, and that there may well be more basic common sense to the conflictual view than to the harmonist one. Indeed, perhaps the latter is just the product of Enlightenment hyper-rationalism, which is to say, precisely one form that illusion or superstition tends to adopt in the modern period.

TRUTHS THAT ARE TOO HIGH AND TOO LOW

If the truth, then, should sometimes fail to coincide with the presuppositions of ordinary life, it will do so, generally speaking, either because it falls too far beneath or rises too high above the latter. These two opposite possibilities give rise to a basic divide among esoteric writers: there are those who would hide the truth for fear that it is too harsh or disappointing for most people and those who would veil or dilute it for fear that it is too exalted and sublime.

In the first camp, for example, is Lucretius, who himself acknowledges that his austere materialism, undercutting all lofty human hopes and moral/political pieties, "seems rather too grim to those who have not dealt with it, and the multitude shrinks back away from it with a shudder." That is one reason why, as he explicitly states, he has chosen to present his brutally prosaic doctrine in an artfully sweetened poetical form.[7]

In the opposite camp are to be found the mystics as well as those religious and metaphysical thinkers who, seeing the truth as something exalted far above most men's capacity to comprehend, fear that if it were openly expressed, it would disorient or corrupt them because it would undercut the approximate truths and goods that are within their reach without putting anything else in their place.

This version of esotericism is of course a good deal more respectable than its subversive counterpart, and consequently it has, historically, been far more open in acknowledging its secretive ways. People are generally quite willing to accept the idea that there are exalted truths that are above their ability to comprehend. Thus, the long and influential tradition of Jewish mysticism known as Kabbalah made little secret of the fact that it engaged in esoteric writing and reading. Equally well known is that the Neoplatonists were—and explicitly declared themselves to be—esoteric writers and readers. These two sects were so open about their secretiveness that even scholars hostile to the whole idea of esotericism do not deny its existence in these two cases. But such scholars typically argue that the phenomenon was essentially confined to them (and to other, even less reputable practitioners of the occult), and they often mock those who suggest otherwise by calling them "Kabbalist" and "Neoplatonists."[8] But the fear that the highest truths may overwhelm or at least confuse most people is not so strange or unreasonable—so why should it be so rare? And, in fact, it is very easy to show that these sorts of concerns led to esoteric practices even in mainstream Judaism, Christianity, Islam, and other religions, as well as in mainstream philosophers.[9] (Indeed, esotericism is so far from being confined to the mystics that Gershom Scholem claims that the Kabbalists actually borrowed the practice from the Jewish and Islamic philosophers.)[10]

It is not, for example, in any mystical writing but in the Talmud itself, the primary text of Judaism after the Bible, that one reads these words:

> The Laws of incest may not be expounded to three persons, nor the Story of Creation before two persons, nor the subject of the Chariot before one person alone unless he be a Sage and comprehends of his own knowledge. Whoever puts his mind to these four matters it were better for him if he had not come into the World.[11]

Similarly, Maimonides, surely no Kabbalist, writes:

> The ancient sages enjoined us to discuss these subjects privately, with only one individual, and then only if he be wise and capable of independent reasoning. In this case, the chapter headings are communicated to him, and he is instructed in a minute portion of the subject. It is left to him to develop the conclusions for himself and to penetrate to the depths of the subject. These topics are exceedingly profound; and not every intellect is able to approach them.[12]

In Christianity, a similar tradition of protective esotericism—known as "the discipline of the secret" (*disciplina arcani*)—was once very widespread. An article devoted to it in the *Catholic Encyclopedia* describes it as "the custom which prevailed in the earliest ages of the Church [i.e., at least through the sixth century], by which the knowledge of the more intimate mysteries of the Christian religion was carefully kept from the heathen and even from those who were undergoing instruction in the Faith. The custom itself is *beyond dispute*."[13] This practice was modeled on the words and actions of Jesus himself, who told the apostles that he would speak to them plainly but to the people only in parables (Matt. 13:10–17).

Thus, even in the thirteenth century, when Aquinas in his commentary on Boethius addresses the article "Should Divine Realities Be Veiled by Obscure and Novel Words?," he responds unhesitatingly in the affirmative. For "when abstruse doctrines are taught to the uneducated they take an occasion of error from what they do not fully understand." He goes on to support his view first with the example of the Apostle Paul who told the Corinthians that he could not reveal to them the highest wisdom concerning God. It is only the truly spiritual man who is able to understand, "[b]ut I, brethren, could not address you as spiritual men, but as men of the flesh, as babes in Christ. I fed you with milk, not solid food; for you were not ready for it." Aquinas then adds the testimony of Saint Gregory. "Commenting on Exodus 21:33. . . . Gregory says: 'Anyone who now perceives the depths in the sacred words, should hide in silence their sublime meaning when in the presence of those who do not understand them, so that he will not hurt by interior scandal an immature believer or an unbeliever who might become a believer.'" Finally, appealing to the authority of Augustine, Aquinas writes:

> Certain things can be explained to the wise in private which we should keep silent about in public. Thus Augustine says: "There are some passages which are not understood in their proper force or are understood with difficulty, no matter how great, how comprehensive, or how clear the eloquence with which they are handled by the speaker. These should be spoken to a public audience only rarely, if there is some urgent reason, or never at all." In writing, however [as distinguished from speaking], this distinction does not hold because a written book can fall into the hands of anybody. Therefore, these matters should be concealed with obscure language, so that they will benefit the wise who understand them and be hidden from the uneducated who are unable to grasp them.[14]

In Islam, there is also a very strong tradition of protective esotericism, which is openly discussed by virtually all the major Islamic philosophers. Averroes, for example, explains that if one reveals the deeper interpretation of a Koranic passage, one that goes beyond the apparent meaning, to someone who is "unfit to receive" it, one will lead him into unbelief.

> The reason for this is that the interpretation comprises two things, rejection of the apparent meaning and affirmation of the interpretation; so that if the apparent meaning is rejected in the mind of someone who can only grasp apparent meanings, without the interpretation being affirmed in his mind, the result is unbelief.[15]

In sum, protective esotericism tends to veil the truth for two essentially opposite reasons, one as too subversive, the other as too sublime. The latter type, being more respectable, has typically been fairly open about its practices, the former, far more secretive.

But this rather neat distinction produces a further complexity: the existence of a lofty and publicly accepted esotericism provides the other sort with a natural way of disguising itself. Thus, it may be easy to distinguish the two forms of esotericism, but not so easy to say which thinker is of what sort. This difficulty may be illustrated by a statement of Maimonides. He asserts that the "true opinions [of the divine science]" have been "hidden, enclosed in riddles, and treated by all men of knowledge with all sorts of artifice through which they could teach them without expounding them explicitly." But why have they been hidden in this way? "Not because of something bad being hidden in them, or because they undermine the foundations of the Law, *as is thought by ignorant people* who deem that they have attained a rank suitable for speculation. Rather have they been hidden because at the outset the intellect is incapable of receiving them."[16] The "ignorant people" may be wrong in this particular case, but it is certainly reasonable and necessary to entertain the suspicion they hold: that the sublime sort of esotericism may sometimes be a front for the other kind.

The classic example would seem to be Averroes. Assimilating himself to a long tradition of Islamic religious esotericism, he wrote openly and at length about the concealment that he and other philosophers practiced. But a long tradition of interpretation suggests that what Averroes was in fact concealing was his rejection of most if not all of the claims of religion.

In this connection, consider one more time the passage from Plato's *Protagoras* (316d–e) where Protagoras claims that in ancient times the practitioners of skeptical philosophy or "sophistry"

> fearing the odium it involved, disguised it in a decent dress, sometimes of poetry, as in the case of Homer, Hesiod, and Simonides; sometimes *in mystic rites and soothsayings*, as did Orpheus, Musaeus and their sects.[17]

SOCIETY: TRADITIONAL AND MODERN

Now that we have seen this broad distinction and considered at some length the exalted or religious form of protective esotericism, it remains to examine more closely the other kind. For the idea of subversive truth has little plausibility today. We citizens of the enlightened, secular, liberal, pluralist, multicultural society have dared to open our doors to every idea and doctrine and have discovered, at length, that all the supposed dangers of doing so were greatly exaggerated. So we are inclined to ask with some skepticism, not to say condescension: exactly how is it that truth or philosophy is a threat to society?

To address this question in a clear and nonparochial manner, it is useful to spend a few moments considering some of the consequences of the fact that for nine-tenths of recorded history people lived not in enlightened, secular, liberal, pluralist, multicultural societies like our own but in what we loosely call "traditional societies." For whereas the former may be relatively impervious to the dangers of philosophic rationalism, the latter certainly were not. By examining the differences between traditional society and our own, we will see why, to the former, the conflictual view seemed so obviously right, while to us so obviously wrong.

SOCIETY: "CLOSED" AND "OPEN"

Human beings are political animals, everywhere united in societies. But for the sake of what do they unite? What do they share and hold in common in their communities? Wherever one looks in premodern history—whether at primitive tribes or ancient Greek city-states or medieval villages—the most prevalent way for human beings to unite was not on the minimal basis of the desire for life, liberty, and property (as in the limited, liberal state), but on the basis of shared traditions and mores: a communal conception of the right way to live, a shared view of the moral and the sacred. This would seem to be only natural, for a number of interrelated reasons. First, since the political community is, as Aristotle puts it, the most sovereign or authoritative community, the one that ultimately controls all the others, the one demanding our highest obedience and devotion, shouldn't it concern the highest and most important things in life, that is, the moral and the sacred? Second, if we, as social animals, seek to form a *community* in the fullest and deepest sense—seek to share one another's lives—then mustn't we be joined together at the level of our fullest and deepest concerns? Mustn't we hold in common the things that we hold most dear? And third, even aside from these higher things, even judging from the elemental standpoint of producing basic obedience, stability, and nonoppression, can these minimal ends ever be adequately secured through force alone, through the police? Don't they require the social pressure of a moral and religious consensus? Prior to the rise of the liberal state, all of this was basic political common sense. The very definition of a political community, as Augustine put it, is a group of people "bound together by a common agreement as to the objects of their love."[18]

That certainly does not mean, of course, that all or even most traditional societies were successful in producing this kind of moral and religious agreement, but this was what they aimed at and sought to build upon. And to the extent that societies fell short of it, they did indeed experience a loss of high purpose along with a loss of community and of basic stability. Traditional society, in sum, relied upon the moral and religious consensus of the community for the attainment of both its most basic necessities and its highest aspirations. It staked its all on that consensus, on "agreement as to the objects of their love."

Now, this traditional approach to communal life is profound, high-minded, and humanly comprehensive, but it is also extremely perilous, since such consensus is inherently fragile (at least in civilized states). Difference and disagreement, especially about such grand and uncertain issues of life, easily assert themselves. Therefore, an *essential* concomitant of the traditional approach to community is the need to protect the community's shared commitments or foundational beliefs. Hence we find that virtually all traditional societies were hostile, at least in principle, to the mixing of diverse religions, mores, and cultures in one society (just what we today celebrate). And we find that the censorship of ideas was, in one degree or another, practiced in all such societies. In a word, having staked everything on shared, settled, and authoritative answers to inherently uncertain fundamental questions, traditional society was and needed to be a *closed* society, that is, hostile, as a matter of structural necessity, to freedom of thought. And that is why traditional society *necessarily* looked upon the activity of philosophy—the most resolute and radical questioning of all established ideas—as its precise antithesis, as a direct threat to its very core.

Today, we scorn this fear of ideas as timid and benighted, because it does not apply to our own form of society. But this reaction of ours, obviously anachronistic, is also quite ironic. For, our modern society was largely founded by thinkers who were reacting to the wars of religion. They were primarily moved, that is, by this very fear concerning the fragility of moral and religious consensus. They felt it even *more* than earlier thinkers.

One could say that the simple, tragic flaw of political life is this. Whereas the lowest goods of life—food, shelter, clothing, safety—are self-evident to all, the higher goods, precisely in the degree to which they are more elevated and more important to us, are less clear and less available to general understanding. And this fact makes the higher things not only elusive but positively dangerous. For, given this obscurity, the discussion and pursuit of all the loftier goods of life are inherently prone to sectarian conflict, fanaticism, and obscurantism, as well as to skepticism, hypocrisy, and corruption. Therefore, traditional societies, which nobly attempt to unite men around some settled view regarding these highest questions, run a great risk of being infected, sooner or later, by these ills, especially since the rise in the West of philosophy, the Reformation, the printing press, and other historical circumstances that have weakened the hold of local certainties and rendered a stable moral-religious consensus almost impossible.

With these precise fears in mind, early modern thinkers such as Machiavelli, Hobbes, and Locke endeavored to find a form of politics that could do without such consensus. They deliberately set out to subvert traditional society and to replace it with a fundamentally new kind of social organization, one that would openly renounce the ever precarious attempt to define the truth about life's highest goods. Instead, it would unite men on the promise of preventing the most obvious and basic evils—the violation of elemental "rights," the loss of life, liberty, and property, the return to the "state of nature." For whereas the highest good, the *summum bonum*, is inextricably caught up in metaphysical and religious dispute, the *summum malum*—violent death—is a metaphysically and religiously neutral fact, a "self-evident truth" known to and felt by all human beings, regardless of their larger theoretical opinions. Thus, by standing traditional society on its head, by openly switching the purpose and moral basis of the state from our highest to our lowest end, they attempted to separate politics from the whole disputed sphere of morality and religion, to lift the state off its traditional foundations and to place it on its own self-evident ground, independent of and impervious to all larger theoretical issues.[19]

This does not mean, of course, that modern societies have completely succeeded in this effort. In practice, they continue to preserve many aspects of traditional society. Indeed, no state can truly be neutral with respect to every question of personal morals and way of life (and almost all liberal thinkers themselves have recognized this fact). Still, modern society represents a decisive shift away from political reliance on moral and religious consensus.

This radical innovation is what made it possible to establish, for the first time, an officially and intentionally "open society"—a tolerant, secularized, morally neutral, heterogeneous, pluralistic, modern state that was dedicated to freedom of thought as a matter of principle. In such a society, the flourishing of diversity of opinion, radical doubt, and philosophy, which in the past had existed only as by-products and symptoms of political decline—could be embraced for the first time as a form of social health. For the modern state is so structured that it is, as much as possible, a community of *interests* instead of *beliefs*—and therefore it no longer has the same vital stake in what its citizens believe. It can afford a certain intellectual permissiveness and easygoingness.

Again, traditional society—because it aimed at men's perfection or salvation more than their security, their duties more than their rights—often required its citizens to make strenuous exertions and painful sacrifices. And these are possible only on the basis of strong, intense beliefs, which society must therefore foster and protect. But modern society, with its more limited ambitions, asks much less of its citizens—don't steal, get a job, pay your taxes, support your children. Consequently, it can afford the luxury of a certain indifference to the content and pitch of its citizens' beliefs. Thus, it loses all real need to fear the freedom of thought—a fear that it soon comes to regard as simply foolish and cowardly.

One can go further: modern society, based on material interests, not only can *afford* openness, enlightenment, and freedom of thought, but positively requires them. For ultimately it is not quite true that the protection of life, liberty, and property is a metaphysically neutral and self-evident end, embraced equally by all worldviews. There are many views of life—medieval Christianity or contemporary Islamic fundamentalism, for example—that praise sacrifice, subservience, and asceticism and that condemn the sort of materialism prevailing in the modern Western state as sinful and decadent. In order to work as promised, then, the modern state requires the weakening of such beliefs. It requires a "rational" and "enlightened" citizenry that can be counted upon to follow its long-term material self-interests. For this reason, the modern state not only tolerates but actually requires philosophical skepticism—a polar reversal of the situation within traditional society. The natural antagonism between philosophy and society has been replaced by an artificial harmony.

Again, the modern state may be said to be built on an "agreement to disagree" regarding religion and the ultimate ends of life. But this agreement must constantly be protected against the resurgence of the longing for homogeneous community—protected through the ever-renewed demonstration of the impossibility of settling the larger questions of life in a way convincing to all. Thus, the modern state is not, after all, so indifferent to its citizens' state of belief. It requires a critical mass of citizens who cling to a skeptical, tolerant, "who's to say" worldview. It laughs at the traditional fear of philosophy and freedom of thought, but it fears traditional religion and the longing for consensus. In traditional society, it was common to ask, "Can an atheist be an honest man?"; in modern society, the question has become "Can a believer be a tolerant man?" Just as the former society demands unity and strength of belief, so the latter tends to demand pluralism and skepticism.

In sum, we are the offspring of modern society; and it has shaped all our instincts regarding the age-old conflict between philosophy and politics, theory and praxis. Specifically, we have a systematic tendency to misunderstand—or rather, to dismiss and forget—that conflict because the whole form of state in which we live was invented precisely in order to obscure or eliminate it. Modern, liberal society unites us, no longer on the basis of an ever-fragile agreement about morality and religion, but on the basis of a shared fear of our tendency to fight over these issues. Such a society is no longer in tension but in harmony with philosophic openness because it requires not the protection but the measured subversion of higher certainties. It thrives on popular enlightenment and the proliferation of intellectuals and artists whose perceived duty and social function is to *épater le bourgeois*, to shock society out of its "complacency," to be *iconoclastic*. Given this specific role, modern intellectuals are almost constitutionally incapable of appreciating the point being argued here: the legitimacy and necessity, within traditional society, of the fear of "dangerous truths."

But traditional society was fundamentally different. It had not yet invented the modern art of turning uncertainty and disagreement regarding the highest matters into a source of cooperation and obedience. It knew of no acceptable way to settle the basic political question—who has the right to rule—except by answering the largest moral and religious questions. Such a society, unable to separate political from intellectual stability, was necessarily a closed society—and therefore in essential tension with the radical openness of philosophy. To use a more contemporary term, traditional society was and had to be fundamentally "anti-intellectual."

There is, then, a crucial problem here that our present social environment has caused us to forget but that shaped all premodern philosophy. The realm of practice requires settled answers; the realm of theory, unsettling questions. There is both a closed and an open aspect to human nature—because we are both political animals and rational ones—and each is necessarily a danger to the other.

CUSTOM AS THE BASIS OF SOCIETY

If the idea of this fundamental tension has a certain plausibility, let us consider it in greater detail. We have seen that philosophy, which is a restless and irreverent quest for truth, is in conflict with traditional political community, which is an authoritative settlement regarding the fundamental questions of life. They are antithetical, as open is to closed. Now, obviously, reason is the source of the open, dynamic aspect of life, but what is it that produces and maintains the closing? What force or human faculty creates the authoritative settlement? What is the bond or foundation of society, and how does this bond relate to the faculty reason?

In traditional society, as the name implies, the authoritative settlement is rooted in *tradition*, in the weight and authority of custom. And tradition is a force not only different from reason but also — for a variety of reasons that we must now try to spell out — in fundamental tension with it. Thus, the conflict of philosophy and society stems, not only from the general opposition of *open and closed*, but also from the specific conflict of *reason and custom* — two rival sources of human guidance. Let us approach this dichotomy by beginning with some basic reflections on the human condition as it relates to practical wisdom, to the knowledge of how to live.

Human beings are rational animals. Part of what this ambiguous formula means is that we are not fundamentally guided by instinct. It would seem that as the power of reason evolved, the power of instinct receded to make way for it. Thus, unlike the other animals, whose basic "way of life" is determined by instinct, human beings possess very few true instincts and these leave the human way of life essentially undetermined. That is why, whereas the other animals are "unhistorical" — a lion today lives in pretty much the same manner as lions lived ten thousand years ago — the way of life of human beings varies dramatically from one time and place to another. Human beings are samurai warriors, American businessmen, Christian ascetics, aristocratic epicures, Buddhist monks, and classical philosophers. In short, the rational animal is the free, the uninstinctive, the historical or socially constructed animal.

Let me pause to emphasize, however, that from this famous variety of ways of life and this relative freedom from instinct, it does not necessarily follow that there is no human nature and no natural standard for human conduct (although it is common today to assume that it does). We are not led by instinct, for example, to any particular food or diet, as other animals are, and consequently the human diet has varied greatly over time and place.

But it nevertheless remains true that we have a natural constitution that is nourished by some foods and poisoned by others. It is even possible to speak of an optimal diet or of a diet most "in accordance with our nature," even though we are not *led to* this diet by nature, i.e., by instinct. So also in a larger sense we have a natural constitution—certain natural faculties of body and mind, along with certain natural needs, inclinations, and pleasures. Our natural constitution, for example, includes the capacity to walk upright, to reason, to speak and communicate our thoughts, to love, and to procreate. And it is reasonable to assume (until proven otherwise) that some ways of life develop, strengthen, enliven, and gratify our natural constitution while others stunt, weaken, shut down, and distress it. It is also possible that there is an optimal life that brings our various faculties and yearnings to their greatest harmony, flourishing, and satisfaction—what we mean by "happiness."

Properly understood, then, the unique freedom and indeterminacy characteristic of the rational animal consists in this: we are not *led by nature* to the life that is in *accordance with nature*, to the good and happy life. Indeed, we are not led by nature to any particular way of life at all. The human animal, "rational" and "free," is characterized above all by a radical *ignorance*, unknown to any other animal, an ignorance of itself and of what is good for it. Free of instinct's guidance, we are abandoned to ourselves to try to answer the most fundamental and inescapable question: What is the right way of life for us? What is our constitution and what will cause it to flourish?

Of course, the situation would not be so bad if this question were fairly easy to answer, but this turns out not to be the case. The human constitution is rather complex, and on top of that, it is always covered over and distorted by various kinds of prejudice and illusion. We have within us many different parts, faculties, and desires that compete to be regarded as highest or most important, as the true goal that should organize our lives, both individually and communally.

A quick survey. Is the good life the life of the hedonist, the lover of pleasure, on the theory that this good—pursued universally, even by infants and beasts—is the only real and truly natural good? Or perhaps we should rather be security lovers because our most fundamental need—and the object to which our natural pleasures and pains seem designed to steer us—is self-preservation. But there are things for which human beings will voluntarily risk pleasure and even life itself: Isn't the clearest test of what we should live for that for which we are willing to die? One such thing is love. Is love, then, the answer—or is it "blind," just a romantic illusion? And what exactly does it want? Among the various human ends, the other thing for which we are clearly willing to die is honor or the noble. But these two ends, almost always conjoined, need to be distinguished. Honor is just the external recognition and reward of nobility or moral excellence; and mustn't that *to which* men pay honor be of more value than the honor itself? Indeed, if we ask ourselves what we most admire—and not just, as above, what we desire—the life of moral excellence seems to come to light as the most attractive. This is what makes us rational, human, and superior to the animals. But moral actions— deeds of courage, moderation, justice, and prudence—must ultimately be in the service of some end beyond themselves. Courageous action must further some worthy purpose beyond merely acting courageously; otherwise it is simply foolhardiness. Yet what can this further purpose be? If the dignity of morality is to be preserved, it cannot be something lower than morality, like mere pleasure or security, but must be something higher. Is it the welfare of the community, the common good? But in what does this consist? If it is the mere security and prosperity of the community, this would again subordinate morality to something lower. But if it is the virtue or morality of the citizens, then this only returns us to the question of the ultimate end of moral excellence. Mustn't our ultimate end be found in the purest and fullest development of what we are, of our "humanness," that is, of the rational faculty that defines us? Mustn't the end be knowledge or philosophy or the detached contemplation of the cosmos? Yet how could the true fulfillment of human nature consist in something that very few human beings are ever seen to pursue? And is the human mind actually capable of understanding the cosmos? Is there even an unchanging cosmos out there for us to understand?

From this last step, we see that these questions about *human* nature and happiness cannot be fully answered without knowing the larger natural or supernatural whole of which human nature is a part and product. Certain metaphysical questions are unavoidable. Are we, like everything else, composed of mere matter, following its deterministic laws? Or does the world contain a second element—freedom or spirituality—that allows for moral responsibility and that explains the true yearnings of the human soul? And could this enable the soul to exist independently of the body? Do the dead, therefore, live on somewhere, unseen? And are there then other unseen beings—gods? Many serious people claim knowledge of a God and that he has revealed his will and wisdom to man and told him how to live, backed by divine rewards and punishments. Is this true? Yet there are many differing accounts of the divine; which is the true one—that of the Jews, the Christians, the Muslims, the Hindus, the Buddhists?

Difficult as they are, these issues cannot be dodged. They are not academic questions that the practical man, repelled by their abstractness and seeming futility, can simply walk away from. They must be addressed and—most of them—answered if we are to settle the urgent and inescapable human question: what way of life should I follow? Infinite things are at stake. But clearly, most people do not have the genius, the education, the experience, the energy, or the time to engage in such a vast philosophical and theological quest. It is an impossible burden. Thus, if the rational animal—in its lack of instinct, its radical freedom, its desperate ignorance—had only *reason* to guide it, it would have died out long ago, crippled by uncertainty, confusion, indecision, and disagreement, paralyzed before a world of questions that it cannot answer and cannot leave unanswered. In reality, what enables us to live—to find some kind of surety and agreement—is the existence of a second faculty within us, something more closed and blind than reason, but more open and searching than instinct: *custom* or tradition, social convention, culture, mores, law, *nomos*. It is custom that makes life possible—for the individual and the community—by authoritatively settling the question that (for all but a few philosophers) we cannot settle using our reason: the question of how to live.

Reason and custom—human life is largely a product of these two very different forces. To a considerable extent, of course, they work together: often what reason discovers becomes imbedded in custom, so that culture is preserved and transmitted, without having to be rediscovered by each individual. But in a deeper sense the two are opposite and antagonistic powers—a fundamental conflict within human souls and societies.

From the standpoint of reason and philosophy, custom is *the* great obstacle. Custom is the natural counterpoison to reason: it is what enables us to *stop* reasoning, to cease questioning, doubting, and searching. It does this by providing an alternative ground of belief—an alternative source of closure and decision, of certainty, confidence, and consensus—independent of reason.

What is more, it preemptively protects this alternative belief from being undermined by reason by putting the latter to sleep, as it were. Reason is set in motion by the awareness of arbitrariness or contingency. It is driven to wonder at and to question everything accidental or ungrounded—driven to seek the cause, the explanation, the underlying *necessity*. "Why this and not something else?" But custom is precisely the power to bestow upon the contingent the *appearance of necessity*. It makes us feel that what is and has been *must be*, that it simply *cannot* be otherwise. It thus settles all important questions invisibly, before they are raised, hiding the very possibility of alternatives that would have to be compared. By closing off the occasion for wonder or doubt, custom puts reason to sleep. There is nothing left to think about. Custom surely does not cure our radical ignorance; rather, it covers it over, seducing us to live unexamined lives. In the slumber world of customary society, it requires a great feat of defamiliarization—definitive of the philosophic effort—to wake up and recover knowledge of our ignorance.

Conversely, from the standpoint of custom or customary society, reason and philosophy necessarily pose a grave danger. They threaten to uncover the arbitrariness, the groundlessness, the false necessity of custom, of the whole belief system that grounds society and ordinary life. And what is more, they threaten to reveal that beneath the false floor of custom—covered over by it—lies, not a clear and obvious natural or instinctive ground, but a terrifying (if also bracing and alluring) abyss of ignorance regarding the most important things.

THE THREE ELEMENTS OF CUSTOMARY AUTHORITY

The radical opposition between reason and custom, which we have seen in a general way, can be made more concrete and vital if we stop to ask the question: How does custom work? What hold does it have over us? How does it get us to believe its claims and obey its strictures? The great power that custom exercises over human minds and hearts seems to stem from three distinct forces. And each of them will be seen to be in fundamental tension with reason.[20]

The force of custom is, in the first place, the force of habit. Free of instinct, the human animal is instead a creature of habit: we develop an inclination, fondness, and loyalty for that to which, over a long period of time, we have become "accustomed."

But this role of habituation leads to an essential tension between custom or customary law and reason, as Aristotle states in his classic reply to those who assert that the laws should be as open to change and reform as are the crafts or arts, the most elementary manifestation of reason.

> The argument from the example of the arts is false. Change in an art is not like change in law; for law has no strength with respect to obedience apart from habit, and this is not created except over a period of time. Hence the easy alteration of existing laws in favor of new and different ones weakens the power of law itself.[21]

Since custom works through habituation, which requires changelessness, a healthy traditional society is an essentially *static* society. It is sleepy and conservative. It stubbornly resists change—a fact much noted and deplored by modernizers—and by its nature it must do so. But this puts it in necessary conflict with reason, the arts, and philosophy, which are essentially dynamic phenomena, thriving on diversity, change, daring, innovation, and progress, and which naturally despise the arbitrary and stifling fixity of custom.

A custom is the habit not merely of an individual, however, but of a whole community. Customs are "our ways." Thus, the power of custom over our minds derives not merely from "force of habit" but also from "social pressure." It is reasonable that the near-unanimous judgment of society and especially of its oldest and most respected members should carry a great authority. But this rational deference to collective wisdom is further enforced by the unreasoning weight of public opinion, of honor and disgrace, which reward conformity and punish deviance. Custom, in other words, draws much of its power from a certain natural inclination within groups toward conformity, closed-mindedness, and intolerance. This is an inclination that modern culture deplores and fights against as senseless but that would seem to be essential (within measure) to the self-preservation of a traditional society, since its authority and worldview are supported, not by rational, objective demonstration, but only by the brute fact of long-standing agreement. "This is how it should be done, because . . . this is how we have always done it." Outside the communal consensus lies an abyss. Therefore, the very demonstration that it is *possible* to be different is deeply threatening. Hence people naturally fear the stranger and hate what is foreign. They rally to the defense of "our ways" with clannish, ethnocentric, xenophobic fervor. "Our ways are right and good because they are *ours*." Loyalty—the love of and belief in what is one's own simply because it is one's own—is the foundation of all wisdom.

But philosophy (as it was classically understood) is, by its nature, in conflict with this whole mode of thinking: it is fundamentally disloyal, a traitor in our midst, indifferent and even hostile to what is our own as merely our own. It looks beyond our own to the intrinsically good, beyond custom to nature. It gazes upon the foreign with wonder and delight, seeking to liberate itself from the familiar, from the shared commitments and unquestioned assumptions of the community. It hungers for de-immersion and defamiliarization. It seeks to stand outside the community, detached and objective, resting on the impartial ground of rational argument and empirical evidence. Nietzsche is particularly struck with this point and sees it clearly expressed in the writings of Plato:

Plato has given us a splendid description of how the philosophical thinker must within every existing society count as the paragon of all wickedness: for as critic of all customs he is the antithesis of the moral man, and if he does not succeed in becoming the lawgiver of new customs he remains in the memory of men as 'the evil principle.'[22]

But a habit that is shared by the whole community is still not all that is meant by a custom or tradition. It must also be very old—and more: ancestral. This is the third and greatest source of its power. Things that are very old, like those that are very large, naturally inspire awe, since they dwarf our own limited extension in time and space. The ancient customs come to us from the distant past—a haunting "beyond," forever inaccessible to us. We also revere such customs because they represent the consensus of long generations of men, as well as the product of a searching test of time.

But the key point here is that the customs are not merely old but *ancestral*: they are the "ways of our fathers and forefathers." The authority of the old is related to that of parents over children. The customs are not impersonal: they are the commands of our most ancient fathers—the highest authority in a traditional, patriarchal society.

Yet if this ancestral authority (and all these other factors) stood alone, without further support, it could not hold out against the debunking of ancient custom contained in the following reflection:

The first [human beings], whether they were earthborn or preserved from a cataclysm, are likely to have been similar to average or even simpleminded persons [today] . . . so it would be odd to abide by the opinions they hold. (Aristotle, *Politics* 1269a3–8)

Were not the ancestors ignorant primitives? Isn't the old actually inferior to the new, the past inferior to the present? The idea of progress threatens to subvert the hold of tradition. Thus, what ultimately vindicates the reverence for custom (and for patriarchal authority in general) is the traditional belief—essentially religious—that our ancestors were not primitives but somehow vastly superior to ourselves. We have not progressed beyond them; we are *fallen* from their elevated status.

There is a sort of logic to this view. Just as parents are stronger and wiser than children, so the ancestors are still greater than the parents. In general, what comes earlier must be superior to what comes later, since the former has created or begotten the latter. Indeed, thinking one's way back to the very beginning of the world, one realizes that the divine beings of the first age, who, without being the offspring of any earlier generation, generated the world itself, must have been absolutely the most powerful. In our own late and feeble age, this power has either diminished or withdrawn from the world since changes of such magnitude—the formation of great mountains and seas—no longer occur. But our earliest ancestors were close to this power, in the high-water mark of the world, a golden age when heroes strode the earth and men conversed with gods.

The ancient traditions, then, handed down by the ancestors to us poor, fallen epigones are to be cherished and revered as deriving from a divine source far greater and wiser than ourselves. Custom, then, in its fullest meaning, is not merely a parental or patriarchal idea, but a religious one: custom is the divine law. Customary society is in its essence a religious society, a sacred community. It is necessarily sacred, not only because the customs and laws, making strenuous demands upon the citizens, need to be enforced by divine rewards and punishments, but also and more fundamentally because the wisdom and superiority of the ancestral are ultimately intelligible only on a divine basis. The whole orientation of society by custom—the trust we place in it, the security we find in it—makes sense, in the end, only if it is sacred. That is why no premodern philosopher—no thinker before Pierre Bayle, to be exact—ever openly argued that society could be separated from religion. Traditional society is a religious phenomenon.

This foundational belief in the divine character of the past, of the customary law, and of the community founded upon it represents the third and greatest source of inescapable tension between philosophic rationalism and traditional society. Reason threatens not only the *fixity* needed for habituation and the *loyalty* needed for communal agreement, but also and above all the crucial attitude of *faith* in and *reverence* for the gods and the divine law.

In other words, what it means, on the deepest level, for a society to be "traditional" is not merely that its subjects happen to follow old habits and customs, but that, on some level, they understand themselves to be fallen from the originary fullness of the world, from the divine era; that they live in remembrance and repentance, in hunger for the past; that they cleave to tradition—to that which has been given them by their ancestors—with sacred awe as their sole, tenuous link to the ever-receding, life-giving, divine source. Conversely, they shrink in horror from everything that might cause them to forget or turn away from their ancestral ways. Novelty and innovation are essentially betrayal. The arts, while necessary, are deeply suspect— eternally gnawed upon by anxiety and guilt, as Prometheus would discover.

The proud claim to a knowledge of good and evil independent of the divine law is the fundamental sin. For all man's wisdom is fear of the Lord. And the pseudo-wisdom of the philosophers—which recklessly refuses to accept and revere the ancestral, to accept anything that cannot be made present here and now to our own unassisted human faculties—is altogether unholy and insane.

Owing to this third, religious dimension, the fundamental conflict between the philosophic way of life and traditional society was also known in classical times as the "old quarrel between philosophy and poetry," as Plato puts it (*Republic* 607b; see *Laws* 967c–d). For the poets were, if in a complex way, the spokesmen for and defenders of the sacred customs and the gods. Sophocles's classic tragedy *Oedipus tyrannus*, as well as Aristophanes's great comedy the *Clouds*, portray the destructive consequences of seeking forbidden knowledge, of allowing reason to venture beyond the bounds of sacred custom—consequences that culminate, in both plays, in the violation of the basic precondition of patriarchal authority and traditional society: the sacred taboos against father beating and incest. The danger of knowledge is extreme and ultimate. Euripides in the *Bacchae* states the moral: "The ancestral traditions, which have been ours time out of mind—no argument [*logos*] can cast these down: not even if invented by the cleverness of the most exalted minds." And therefore: "Moderation and reverence for that which pertains to the gods—this is best. And I think it the wisest practice in use by mortal men."[23] But this is the very opposite of what the philosophers practice.

Today, of course, the "old quarrel between philosophy and poetry" sounds as alien and opaque to our ears as does the conflict between reason and society, with which we are trying to reconnect. But the former does at least have a close analog of which we do have immediate understanding: the famous conflict of "reason vs. revelation." According to the latter, the philosophic life, constituted by the principled refusal to accept anything of importance on faith, stands in necessary conflict with—in violation of—the life based upon faith or revelation. The one seeks autonomy and self-reliance; the other, reverent devotion and obedience. The "reason vs. revelation" formula is useful for bringing out the essentially religious character of the conflict we have been discussing here, as well as for showing its absolute, unbridgeable character. It involves a fundamental either/or that does not allow of genuine escape or compromise.

Yet for all its usefulness in this context (and its inherent profundity), the Christian formula "reason vs. revelation" does also somewhat distort the original meaning of the "reason vs. society" conflict we are trying to clarify. For Christianity tends to sever or obscure the intimate connection between the new term it introduces, "revelation," and the term it replaces "society." "Reason vs. revelation" leaves out the political dimension of the original conflict, or, more precisely, it obscures the way in which the political dimension is inseparable from the religious, the way in which society is a religious phenomenon and religion a political one.

"Revelation," as understood within Christianity, is a remarkably apolitical phenomenon: it concerns certain abstract and ultimate truths or principles, but not the concrete social customs, mores, and usages and not the political regime that orders everyday social life. In striking contrast to Greek and Roman paganism and even to Judaism and Islam, Christianity does not claim to be the source of the *law*, of the local traditions and mores. Indeed, Jesus broke with Judaism precisely by abolishing or transcending the Mosaic law as well as the attachment to a particular people or nation. Christianity is a transcendent or universal religion of faith that, as such, has detached itself from the specific mores, customs, laws, and political constitutions existing within a particular society. Thus, in principle, it separates religion from politics, what is God's from what is Caesar's, the church from the state, and so divides—or rather complicates and obscures—the essential unity of what might properly be called the theologico-political realm. (This crucial separation of politics and religion was then later reinforced and deepened by the modern, liberal state.)

Pagan religion, by contrast, was highly political. In the classical city, according to Fustel de Coulanges, "all political institutions had been religious institutions, the festivals had been ceremonies of worship, the laws had been sacred formulas, and the kings and magistrates had been priests."[24] One might add that these institutions were also "moral" institutions. Our unique modern tendency to separate out the concepts and the realms of "morality," "politics," and "religion"—a product partly of Christianity and partly of modern philosophy—profoundly alters these phenomena and certainly is untrue to (pre-Christian) traditional society. The term "ancestral customs," for example, refers—as we are still able to sense—to something necessarily moral and religious at the same time, and also political. And it is doubtful whether these inner connections are ever fully broken: all moral ideas contain within themselves, however deeply buried, certain background beliefs about how the world works, about what should and does *rule*, both politically and cosmically.

Thus, the familiar formula "reason vs. revelation" is very helpful in giving us an immediate and intuitive grasp of what is ultimately at stake in the conflict between philosophy and traditional society—the religious aspect—but it does so at the price of obscuring the inner relation between the theological and the political dimensions of that conflict. (It turns out, in other words, that it is not only modern political thought or the liberal Enlightenment but also to some extent Christianity that is responsible for our modern estrangement from the issue we have been discussing.) The formula "reason vs. custom" is somewhat more revealing and comprehensive. For custom, in its full sense, is the ancestral and divine law—it is "revelation"—but, at the same time, it extends to the concrete mores, usages, and institutions that shape every aspect of daily social and political life.

Yet, to push the matter still further, one could say that the word "custom," which we have been using all along, like "revelation," is still too narrow and insufficiently political. In the vocabulary of classical political thought, the *polis* (city) is the name given to the comprehensive and indivisible whole we have been discussing: the moral-theological-political community. The classical *polis*—which is the fullest development of what I have been calling "traditional society"—is the complete association. It brings moral, political, and religious life to their peak. It is the natural home and chosen vehicle, as it were, of the sacred, the primary manifestation of the will and power of the gods on earth. With this in mind, the most philosophically adequate formulation of the conflict under discussion (which subsumes that between reason and revelation) is: "the philosopher vs. the city." By resolutely sticking to his own, autonomous reason as the sole ground of his beliefs, the philosopher immediately places himself outside and in subversive opposition to the sacred city—to the comprehensive customary world of religious reverence, political loyalty, and moral duty, to the moral-theological-political whole. In other words, philosophic rationalism stands in opposition not merely to "revelation"—if that means certain abstract, suprapolitical theological and moral principles—but to the whole sacred communal fabric of traditional life from top to bottom.

And just as philosophy necessarily threatens the city, so also conversely. Philosophy first arose out of traditional society through (among other factors) the subversive realization that different societies have different and even contradictory traditions, mores, and accounts of the origins. Struck by this conflict of views, the philosopher resolves to seek the one, true account. But he knows that his mind is not a blank slate, that he begins not from ignorance but from prejudice and ethnocentric illusion. To seek the truth, then, he must begin by freeing himself from that which blocks the truth, from the "cave." And he has seen that the primary source of illusion is the world of tradition—the customs, mores, and myths—sustaining and sustained by each culture or society. Therefore, in his pursuit of truth, he must struggle with all his might to free himself from the city, the cave, the community of sacred custom. Society along with its most essential beliefs are, in a sense, his greatest enemy. In other words, philosophy emerges as the pursuit of *phusis* or nature, which is understood in contradistinction to *nomos*—law, custom, convention. Therefore, there is something necessarily—and literally—antinomian and outlaw about the philosophic way of life.

REPUBLICAN VIRTUE

Thus far, we have discussed, in its multiple aspects, the systematic conflict between reason and custom as such (regardless of the particular content of that custom). We turn now to consider the concrete opposition between philosophy and certain specific customs, those relating to what used to be called "republican virtue."

In traditional society, a crucial element of the social bond is the moral commitment of the citizens to the welfare of the community. This is especially emphasized by the classical republican tradition, to which most premodern thinkers and many moderns subscribed. It held that the indispensable precondition of political liberty and social health is "republican virtue," an austere, strenuous, and selfless patriotism. (This, of course, is a claim foreign to the modern world of large, individualistic, commercial republics based on enlightened self-interest. Once again, a great effort is required to reconnect with the experiences and inner problematic of a vanished world.)

There was an ancient art of republican morals, now lost, and it taught that to cultivate and protect this ardent public-spiritedness, it is necessary to eliminate everything that softens and "privatizes" men—materialism, luxury, hedonism, inequality, idleness, sedentary ways—and to promote everything that hardens and mobilizes them: "Spartan" austerity and simplicity, discipline, continuous and vigorous activity, a martial spirit, and a healthy dose of xenophobia.

But the contemplative or philosophic life, if seen openly for what it is, is diametrically opposed to virtue understood in this activist and militantly patriotic way. By drawing the mind upward to the eternal cosmos, philosophy withdraws the heart from the city, which, from such a height, suddenly looks small, particular, imperfect, and ephemeral. As the quest for the universal and permanent, philosophy is necessarily at odds with the particular and transitory, with the here and now, with loyalty to one's own. Philosophy conflicts with the city as cosmopolitanism conflicts with patriotism.

Furthermore, it substitutes the contemplative for the active posture, undermining patriotic mobilization and promoting leisure and idleness. It legitimizes and even ennobles the private, sedentary life and self-indulgence — heretofore the most shameful things — by showing a private pleasure that can claim to be even loftier than public duty. It also encourages gentleness, understanding, and a contemplative passivity that sap the martial spirit. Nothing, in sum, could be more destructive of republican virtue and the outlook of the patriotic citizen. Sparta and philosophy do not go together.

Thus, Machiavelli, reflecting on the historical cycle of regimes, the law of the rise and fall of states, observes:

> Virtue gives birth to quiet, quiet to leisure, leisure to disorder, disorder to ruin; and similarly, from ruin, order is born; from order, virtue; and from virtue, glory and good fortune. . . . For as good and ordered armies give birth to victories and victories to quiet, the strength of well-armed spirits cannot be corrupted by a more honorable leisure than that of letters. . . . This was best understood by Cato when the philosophers Diogenes and Carneades, sent by Athens as spokesmen to the Senate, came to Rome. When he saw how the Roman youth was beginning to follow them about with admiration, and since he recognized the evil that could result to his fatherland from this honorable leisure, he saw to it that no philosopher could be accepted in Rome.[25]

Eventually, of course, Cato lost the struggle to keep philosophy out of Rome. The result is described by Rousseau in his famous *Discourse on the Sciences and Arts*, a radical restatement, from the heart of the Enlightenment, of the classical republican view:

> Rome was filled with philosophers and orators; military discipline was neglected, agriculture was scorned, [philosophic] sects were embraced and the fatherland forgotten. The sacred names of liberty, disinterestedness, obedience to laws were replaced by the names Epicurus, Zeno, Arcesilas.[26]

A similar argument was made in the Athenian context by Aristophanes, who attacked and ridiculed Socrates, Euripides, and the whole fifth-century Greek enlightenment for having corrupted the morals and sapped the political and military strength of Athens. Again, Montaigne reports:

When the Goths ravaged Greece, what saved all the libraries from being set afire was that one of the invaders spread the opinion that this item might well be left intact to the enemy, to divert them from military exercises and keep them busy in sedentary and idle occupations.[27]

All of this strikes modern ears as strange and overwrought. But to the traditional and especially the classical republican world, it was only moral common sense: contemplation and citizenship—the life of thought and the life of action—are fundamentally different and opposed. As Seneca testified, in a sentence quoted approvingly by Montaigne and again by Rousseau: "Since learned men have begun to appear among us, good men have disappeared."[28]

Some empirical support for this conflictual view of theory and praxis can also be found in certain basic facts of history. It is a common observation that the political peaks of nations and their intellectual peaks rarely coincide (particularly in premodern times). Where political health is at its height, especially as defined by the classical republican tradition—in the early Roman Republic, for instance, or in Sparta—philosophy is essentially excluded. Only as political health and republican virtue begin to decay do philosophers and other intellectuals begin to thrive. As W. E. H. Lecky writes in his classic *History of European Morals*:

> It is one of the plainest of facts that neither the individuals nor the ages most distinguished for intellectual achievements have been most distinguished for moral excellence, and that a high intellectual . . . civilization has often coexisted with much depravity.[29]

To be sure, this is a complicated issue with many special cases, but throughout most of history, the owl of Minerva, in Hegel's famous phrase, has spread its wings only at dusk.

To sum up, the conflict between philosophy and the city, as we have thus far examined it, consists not simply in the opposition of certain specific philosophical theses ("dangerous truths") to certain particular dogmas or laws of the city—although such oppositions do also exist, as we will see momentarily. Rather, it consists in a conflict between two incompatible ways of life. The city requires authoritative settlement and closure; philosophy demands openness and questioning. The city necessarily bases itself on custom, the philosopher seeks to base his life on reason—and these two foundations, custom and reason, are fundamentally opposed as fixity is opposed to innovation and dynamism, as loyalty to group belief is opposed to shameless, independent thinking, as humble and reverent obedience is opposed to autonomy and self-reliance, and as revelation is opposed to reason. Finally, the active, patriotic, self-sacrificing life of the classical, martial republic is contrary to the detached, cosmopolitan, gentle, and self-indulgent life of philosophic contemplation.

ON PIETY, PATRIOTISM, AND PLEASURE

In view of this systematic conflict, it would be surprising indeed if philosophers did not routinely make what efforts they could to manage and minimize its effects. Many of the maneuvers, described in the previous chapter, that philosophers undertook to escape persecution they undertook also to avoid harming society. In general, they sought to speak like the many, while thinking like the few. In their outward behavior, they endeavored to follow prevailing customs whatever these might be.

But to be more specific, foremost among these accommodations, as we have already seen at some length, was a certain level of religious imposture. As Augustine puts it, drawing upon writings of Seneca and Varro that we no longer possess:

> [W]ith respect to these sacred rites of the civil theology, Seneca preferred, as the best course to be followed by a wise man, to feign respect for them in act, but to have no real regard for them at heart. . . . [Seneca] worshipped what he censured, did what he condemned, adored what he reproached, because, forsooth, philosophy had taught him something great—namely, not to be superstitious in the world, but, on account of the laws of cities and customs of men, to be an actor, not on the stage, but in the temples.[30]

Similarly, Montaigne, speaking of the ancient philosophers in general, writes:

> Some things they wrote for the needs of society, like their religions; and on that account it was reasonable that they did not want to bare popular opinions to the skin, so as not to breed disorder in people's obedience to the laws and customs of their country.[31]

Even Epicurus, the ardent materialist and hedonist, respected prevailing mores in his outward behavior. As Diogenes Laertius asserts: "His piety towards the gods and his affection for his country no words can describe."[32]

Beyond the religious question, however, there are also certain other basic issues—pointed to in our analysis of the conflict of reason and society—that also typically called forth the philosopher's protective esotericism. I will briefly touch upon two here.

The most obvious is mentioned in Diogenes's statement about Epicurus, which emphasizes his "affection for his country," his patriotism. For within most traditional societies—but especially the martial republics—if the philosopher is to avoid doing and receiving harm, he must show himself a lover not only of God but of country. Certainly Plato makes great efforts to present Socrates as a citizen-philosopher who, if he has alienated his fellow countrymen, has done so only through an excess of zeal for their virtue and for the welfare of Athens. Yet in other places, he lets us see a Socrates who acknowledges that even in the very best regime, the philosopher would not be willing to rule unless compelled.[33] In the *Laws* (803b–804b), Plato's most political writing, the Athenian Stranger (the stand-in for Socrates) indicates his complex posture toward politics and human affairs as follows:

> Stranger: Of course, the affairs of human beings are not worthy of great seriousness; yet it is necessary to be serious about them. And this is not a fortunate thing. . . .
> Megillus: Stranger, you are belittling our human race in every respect!
> Stranger: Don't be amazed, Megillus, but forgive me! For I was looking away toward the god and speaking under the influence of that experience, when I said what I did just now. So let our race be something that is not lowly, then, if that is what you cherish, but worthy of a certain seriousness.

The philosopher takes politics and his city seriously, yet not because he cherishes it as a noble thing, inherently worthy of that seriousness, but merely as a practical necessity—especially as a concession to what nonphilosophers insistently cherish. This philosophical attitude toward politics was described by Pascal, who spoke of Plato and Aristotle as follows:

> [W]hen they diverted themselves with writing their *Laws* and *Politics*, they did it as an amusement; it was the least philosophic and least serious part of their lives. . . . If they wrote on politics, it was as if to bring order into a lunatic asylum; and if they presented the *appearance of speaking of a grand thing*, it is because they knew that the madmen to whom they spoke believed themselves kings and emperors. They entered into the latter's principles in order to make their madness as little harmful as possible.[34]

One sees an element of this dissimulation even in Cicero, the most politically active of ancient philosophers. In his *Laws* and *De finibus*, he defends the highly political and moralistic Stoic doctrine; indeed he personally plays the role of the Stoic in these dialogues. And in his *Republic*, he—or rather the character Laelius—argues for a version of Stoicism that goes so far in its patriotism as to defend Rome as the best regime possible and its far-flung empire as completely in accord with natural law. But it is clear from his *Tusculan Disputations* and other writings that in reality Cicero is not a Stoic at all but an Academic Skeptic—that is, a member of the highly skeptical New Academy, which wholly rejected Stoicism, which questioned the validity of natural law, and which had no illusions about the defects and depredations of Rome as indeed of all political regimes.[35]

This mask of citizenship—this exaggerated patriotism and republican virtue—worn by many of the ancient philosophers points, in turn, to the third very common item of protective esotericism: antihedonism or the extreme condemnation of pleasure. As we have seen, in traditional society and especially in the classical republics, the question of moral character was seen primarily in terms of the dichotomy "virtue vs. pleasure": either one lives the strenuous life of duty, virtue, and public-spirited devotion, as the healthy republic requires, or one gives in to sensuality, hedonism, and self-indulgence. And it was believed that the majority of men, the "many," are only too prone to the latter course, always ready, if one gives them so much as an inch of encouragement, to take a foot. Thus, many philosophers—knowing this tendency of the many and also fearing that the philosophic life, which itself involves a kind of higher self-indulgence, inevitably presented a dangerous and corrupting example—sought to counter this danger through an exaggerated, absolute condemnation of pleasure. In the *Nicomachean Ethics*, for example, Aristotle reports:

> For some say pleasure is the good, others that pleasure is, to the contrary, an altogether base thing—some of these latter perhaps because they have been persuaded that pleasure is such in fact, others because they suppose it to be better with a view to our life *to declare that pleasure is among the base things, even if it is not*. For the many, they suppose, tend toward it and are in fact enslaved to pleasure. Hence one ought to lead them toward its contrary, since in this way they might arrive at the middle.[36]

Aristotle goes on to say that he will not follow this practice, since it does not work in the long run, but he seems clearly to believe—from the critique of

Plato that follows—that the latter did. Certainly, it has long been noticed that the Platonic dialogues combine many strong condemnations of pleasure with some curiously favorable discussions of it.[37] More generally, according to Montaigne:

> In all the barracks of ancient philosophy you will find this, that the same workman publishes rules of temperance, and publishes at the same time amorous and licentious writings. . . . It is not that there is any miraculous conversion stirring them by fits and starts. Rather it is this: that Solon represents himself now as himself, now in the shape of a lawgiver; now he speaks for the crowd, now for himself. . . .
>
> For delicate stomachs we need strict and artificial diets. Good stomachs simply follow the prescriptions of their natural appetite. So do our doctors, who eat the melon and drink the new wine while they keep their patient tied down to syrups and slops.
>
> We must often be deceived that we may not deceive ourselves, and our eyes sealed, our understanding stunned, in order to redress and amend them. "For it is the ignorant who judge, and they must frequently be deceived, lest they err" [Quintilian]. When they [the sages] order us to love three, four, fifty degrees of things before ourselves, they imitate the technique of the archers who, to hit the mark, take aim a great distance above the target. To straighten a bent stick you bend it back the other way.[38]

Again, in Cicero's dialogue the *Laws*, we are surprised to see Atticus— Cicero's old friend and a lifelong Epicurean—agreeing here to the Stoic moral doctrine, with its condemnation of pleasure. Cicero seems clearly to suggest that whatever one's private views of pleasure (as of the gods), it is necessary to play the Stoic in public.[39]

Similarly, Averroes, in his commentary on Plato's *Republic*, emphasizes the political need for noble lies, and he connects this above all to the question of pleasure:

> The chiefs lying to the multitude will be appropriate for them. . . . Untrue stories are necessary for the teaching of the citizens. . . . Above all, they ought to reject statements that conduce to [preoccupation with the] pleasures. . . . They will listen to statements warning them to shun them.[40]

It is important to reemphasize, before concluding, that the few passages cited here cannot begin to settle the question of where Plato or Aristotle or anyone else finally stood on the complex issues of piety, patriotism, and pleasure. (And the clear examples of Xenophon and Cicero suffice to show that, whatever the theoretical basis, philosophers can be first-rate generals and statesmen.) But they do strongly suggest that a philosopher's surface assertions on these particular issues—issues vitally important to the health of the classical republic—may owe a lot to his dual effort to protect society and defend philosophy.

NOBLE LIES

Thus far, we have examined the general conflict between philosophy as a way of life and the way of life of traditional society, especially the classical republic. But beyond this, or rather as a part of it, one can also point to certain specific philosophical theses—certain "dangerous truths"—that are threatening to society. Or, to put it the other way around, there are certain salutary myths necessary to society.

The most obvious examples are quietly alluded to in Plato's infamous account of the "noble lie" in the *Republic* (414b–415d).[41] Here Plato, or his Socrates, is engaged in the effort to describe the best and most just society possible. It comes therefore as a great shock when Socrates declares that it is necessary to convince this society of a great myth or noble lie. That unjust regimes need to cover their crimes with lies comes as no great surprise. But the implication of Socrates's claim is that somehow political life itself is flawed in such a way that even the best possible regime will be radically defective, will need to lie to itself about itself, will need to hide from certain dangerous truths. The noble lie may be said to contain four crucial claims—four lies that every traditional society must tell itself.

The first element of the noble lie—an assertion common in early societies—is that of "autochthony": all of the citizens were originally born from the earth, which is their common mother. Traces of this primitive belief linger on even today when we find ourselves speaking of the motherland or fatherland. On the simplest level (and the one emphasized by Socrates), such a myth is obviously useful for motivating citizens to love and defend the motherland. But if that were the myth's only purpose, it is not clear why it would be so absolutely necessary. Is patriotism impossible without it? Do not the natural forces of habituation and of gratitude lead us to love our homeland, just as they lead us to love our homes?

But there is a further, deeper issue here: the citizens cannot wholeheartedly love and defend their homeland unless they feel that it is theirs by right.

But is it? While our maps have lines and boundaries on them, the earth does not. It has not been parceled up and distributed to the various peoples by nature or by any principle of deserving—but only by force and chance. Human beings are territorial land animals, and they possess the land they live on in the same way that other such animals—the lions of a given pride—possess their territory. Whatever may have been the case, say, fifty thousand years ago, before the earth was well populated, through all of *recorded* history there has scarcely been a people on earth that has acquired its land through any means other than forcibly displacing the previous inhabitants—who, however, had no just complaint since they, in turn, displaced the inhabitants before them. In short, virtually all existing societies are founded in conquest, though for some fortunate peoples, these events may be lost in the mists of time. This is the harsh reality that must be covered over by a myth of just origins: we were born from this land—or it is the Promised Land given to us by God, or we are owed it by Manifest Destiny.

To appreciate this issue, we must keep in mind that the originary violence at the beginning of society posed a much more obvious and powerful problem for traditional societies than for our own. The former, rooted in custom, are based on the belief in the superiority of the past to the present, on reverence for the ancestors or founders and for the traditions they bequeathed us. The fact of originary crime or usurpation therefore constitutes a direct challenge to the whole orientation by tradition. Thus, just as a supernatural event is needed, as we have seen, to account for or vindicate the wisdom of the ancient customs or laws, so also one is needed to explain and ground the rightful possession of the motherland.

Modern states, by contrast, are based, not on reverence for the sacred, ancestral order, but on fear of our original disorder, fear of return to the savage "state of nature," and pride in our human conquest of this defective natural condition. They rest, in a word, on the faith in *progress*, not belief in *tradition*—on myths of the future, not of the past. That is why modern thinkers like Machiavelli and Hobbes go out of their way to emphasize and even exaggerate the originary violence, while ancient thinkers like Plato and Aristotle do their best to hide it (while pointing to it between the lines).[42]

The second tenet of the noble lie, following directly from the first, is that the citizens, born of the common motherland, are all brothers—as, again, citizens even today will often rhetorically assert. And again, the purpose is not merely to express or heighten patriotism but, more important, to cover over another politically troublesome truth of the human condition: just as the earth has no natural boundary lines, so the human species is not divided up by nature into specific political groups—although we must live as if it were. Humanity is one, justice is universal—but states are particular. Human life is political life, which consists in arbitrarily separating off some portion of the human species and uniting it, largely through opposition to other such arbitrary units. Our moral and political existences are essentially organized around the distinction between insiders and outsiders, citizens and foreigners, although this distinction is ultimately arbitrary and false. Nature has not made Athenians and Spartans. The state would be truly just and rational only if it were universal, a world-state, but that is impossible (especially in premodern times). Reason demands cosmopolitanism; political life demands patriotism.

To be sure, we feel this problem less acutely in our modern, polyglot, globalizing society, where the distinction between citizens and foreigners daily becomes less significant (at least, during peacetime). Indeed, the modern social-contract state openly acknowledges its artificiality. Yet even today, we feel that if some people are starving or oppressed in, say, San Diego, that is terribly wrong, a great injustice, a scandal, and a moral reflection on all of us. We say: these are *Americans*! But should these very same people chance to live just a few miles to the south, in Tijuana, we think: well, it's unfortunate, but it's not *our* problem; that's just the way the world is. The event has a fundamentally different moral status. The one is a matter of justice; the other, at most, of generosity or compassion.

This phenomenon—the connection between morals and borders—was far more pronounced through most of history, and especially in the classical republics. The operative morality was necessarily "citizen morality": do good to friends and harm to enemies. And this moral orientation is fundamentally in tension with the fact that it is only by chance that this particular person is a fellow citizen to whose rights and welfare I dedicate my life, instead of a foreigner to whose interests I am indifferent or hostile. As Pascal writes in the *Pensées*:

> Why do you kill me?—What! do you not live on the other side of the water? My friend, if you lived on this side, I should be an assassin, and it would be unjust to slay you in this way; but since you live on the other side, I am a hero, and it is just. (No. 293)

Outside the world-state, political life can never wholly escape this need to transmute certain accidental differences into morally essential distinctions. In the *Republic*, this problem is indicated also in the following manner. In book 1 (331e–335e), when Polemarchus defines justice as helping friends and harming enemies, Socrates, through a somewhat playful and ultimately aporetic argument, brings him momentarily to admit that true justice consists in helping all human beings and harming no one. Yet later, in book 2 (375a–e), when Socrates is engaged in constructing the best possible regime, he is compelled to reinstate the citizen morality that he earlier rejected: the ruling "guardians" must be like "noble dogs" who are friendly to citizens as such and hostile to foreigners as such. Political life requires a myth that hides the cosmopolitan truth, the fact of our common humanity, and justifies the arbitrary exclusivity of the political community: we citizens are a race apart, we are all brothers born from this land—or a single family, the seed of Abraham, or a distinct "nationality" with its own *Volksgeist* or "general will," or a unique "culture" with group rights.

What we have seen so far is that political life unites by dividing: it cuts off a piece of the earth and a piece of humanity and then uses a noble lie to give this arbitrary cut the appearance of a moral unit and a natural whole. But a political community also requires an internal "cut": the distinction of rulers and ruled. Perfect unanimity, the rule of all, is not possible; and therefore, within every society, some part of the whole—one, few, or many—must rule over the rest. The choice of rulers, then, is in need of justification, and that is the purpose of the third tenet of the noble lie. When the citizens were formed beneath the earth, Socrates's tale continues, the god mixed iron and bronze into those naturally destined for the farmer and artisan class, silver into those naturally fit for the auxiliary or military class, and gold into those individuals who were naturally meant to rule.

Yet one may ask why a myth is needed to justify this hierarchy. At least on Plato's principles and those of most classical thinkers, it is *true* that certain individuals have a natural right to rule. Human beings are not all the same, not all equal, not all fit for the same jobs. Some are far more wise and virtuous than others, and these most admirable individuals, they argued, are the natural rulers, for they alone can rule well, that is, justly and wisely. Rational rule is rule of the rational. So if there is a natural, rational basis for the ruler/ruled division, what need is there of a myth?

The need arises from still another basic defect of the human condition that undermines the political power and relevance of the true "natural rulers." Although wisdom and virtue are indeed essential for the proper exercise of rule, and although they are genuine, objective qualities, they are not externally obvious, they are not readily *visible* to others, especially to those who, lacking them, most need to recognize and defer to them. Owing to this crucial *problem of invisibility*, the truly natural or rational principle of rule—"The wise and virtuous should rule the foolish and vicious"—will, in practice, almost always result in a chaotic free-for-all, as various possessors and pretenders to excellence advance their claims. If only nature were better arranged, if only the internal excellence of the mind and character were unfailingly correlated with some clear and easily measured external expression—say, height—then the rights of wisdom and virtue would have effect in the world, then political authority could be directly based on reason and truth. But as it is, the only fully rational ground for rule is politically unusable, and therefore all actual rule must legitimize itself through some recourse to convention and myth: the rulers are a golden race, or of superior blood, or descendants of the gods, or anointed by divine right. In virtually all traditional societies, the government's claim to legitimate authority was based in one way or another on myth.

The fourth part of the noble lie addresses and justifies a fourth necessary but highly problematic division among the inhabitants of every developed society. The rise of civilization—of an economic surplus, leisure, and the higher development of reason and the arts—is made possible only by the division of labor. But, as we have already seen, this leads to the grave problem that certain jobs that are necessary to society are harmful to the individuals who must do them. The rise of civilization is purchased at the price of social justice. This crucial, "civilizing" institution can be justified only if traced to nature or the gods. Thus, according to the noble lie, the citizens, when born from the earth, emerged together with the tools of their particular trade. Human beings, like bees, are born and naturally suited for all the particular jobs that society needs and in just the right numbers. There are natural garbage men and natural coal miners.

Also natural slaves. The problem of the division of labor taken in its most extreme and obvious form is the problem of slavery. The economic precondition for the high level of freedom and civilization of the ancient Greek and Roman republics was an enormous slave class. Prior to the industrial revolution, in fact, highly civilized societies were unavoidably built on the existence of serfs, slaves, or some other form of economic exploitation. That is why, when Aristotle, at the beginning of the *Politics* (1253b15–1255b40), makes his classic argument for the naturalness of the *polis*, he is under the plain necessity of arguing—as his version of Plato's noble lie—that of course we human beings come in two kinds: natural masters and natural slaves.[43] The plain fact is, all developed traditional societies were built on massive, manifest, and unavoidable oppression, and they required myths to justify this.

THE MYTHS OF ORDINARY LIFE

The above discussion has emphasized the conflict between rationalism and politics strictly understood. But many other aspects of practical life involve a similar conflict with reason. Consider a few obvious examples.

The passion of romantic love is famous for its rootedness in illusion. It calls upon us to embrace an exaggerated view of the virtues of our beloved, of the power of love, and of the indissolubility, even the eternity, of the romantic bond.

The institution of the family, especially the traditional, aristocratic family, rests on certain necessary illusions such as the heritability of worth or nobility (the belief in "blood") and such as the inherent superiority of the ancestors to the present generation, of old to young, of the oldest son to the rest of the children, and of men to women. It also rests on the hope that when we are dead, we somehow truly live on in our progeny.

The passion for fame or glory rests on the illusion that our name can live eternally and that, if it did, this could somehow matter to us when we are dead.

The limitless desire for money grows from the illusion that there are limitless pleasures or that there is some amount of wealth that can bring us absolute security.

We also embrace illusion in our opinions of ourselves—our estimate of our worth and rank within society and ultimately within the universe.

Ordinary life is suffused with "noble lies." As Lessing, in an early comedy, has one of his characters state: "We are meant to live happily in the world.... Whenever the truth is a hindrance to this great final purpose, one is bound to set it aside, for only a few spirits can find their happiness in the truth itself."[44] Indeed, where is the person who lives without illusion, whose life could withstand the scrutiny of Socratic examination? This question, in fact, forms the core of the Platonic defense of philosophy: the philosophic life is better than others not simply because more satisfying, but because it is the only truly honest, self-consistent, and "disillusioned" life. In one manner or another, all others embrace "the lie within the soul."

What is it in human nature that shrinks from the truth and courts illusion? Perhaps only a true philosopher in the above sense could be in a position to address this question fully and conclusively. But it seems fairly clear that an important part of the answer concerns the problem of mortality. On this telling, the stubborn dualism within human life ultimately derives from the fact that every instinct and longing of our nature pushes us toward preservation and life, but our unique faculty of reason shows us that we and everything that we love must die. This is why every subphilosophic soul is in some way at war with itself and with the truth. We live in denial of death.

Presumably for this reason, Plato's Socrates, in the *Phaedo* (64a), does not define philosophy as knowledge of the ideas or of the metaphysical truth: "Those who pursue philosophy aright study nothing but dying and being dead." Psychologically, this is the hardest thing for a human being to do. As La Rochefoucauld remarks: "Neither the sun nor death can be looked at fixedly."[45] Again, Montaigne states:

> It is only for first-class men to dwell purely on the thing itself [death], consider it, and judge it. It belongs to the one and only Socrates to become acquainted with death with an ordinary countenance, to become familiar with it, and play with it. He seeks no consolation outside the thing itself; dying seems to him a natural and indifferent incident. He fixes his gaze precisely on it, and makes up his mind to it, without looking elsewhere.[46]

But very few are able to fix their gaze in this way, staring reality in the face. In the Platonic metaphor, which has become a standard trope, the light of truth is too strong for most eyes.

Whatever the full reason for this fact, the natural response to it, to say it one last time, is clear: protective esotericism. As Synesius of Cyrene puts it:

> Philosophic intelligence, though an observer of truth, acquiesces in *the use of falsehood*. Just consider this analogy: light is to the truth as the eye is to the intellect. Just as it would be harmful for the eye to feast on unlimited light and just as darkness is more helpful to diseased eyes, so, I assert, *falsehood is of advantage to the demos* and the truth would be harmful to those not strong enough to peer steadfastly on the clear revelation of that which truly is.[47]

Similarly, Shaftesbury writes:

> 'Tis the same with Understandings as with Eyes: To such a certain Size and Make just so much light is necessary, and no more. Whatever is beyond, brings Darkness and Confusion. 'Tis real Humanity and Kindness to hide strong truths from tender eyes.[48]

Finally, consider Emily Dickinson:

Tell all the Truth but tell it slant—
Success in Circuit lies
Too bright for our infirm Delight
The Truth's superb surprise

As Lightning to the Children eased
With explanation kind
The Truth must dazzle gradually
Or every man be blind—[49]

DO "SUBVERSIVE IDEAS" REALLY SUBVERT?

I have been laboring to give some inner plausibility to the classical view that an inherent tension between reason and ordinary life makes protective esotericism necessary. It could be argued, however, that even if one acknowledged the reality of this tension, the need for such esotericism would still not necessarily follow.

People today will incline to make the following objection. The whole theory of protective esotericism exaggerates the power of reason or truth. Precisely if the classical thinkers are right in stressing the great psychological force and social necessity of illusion, these illusions are likely to have the strength and staying power to withstand the contrary opinions of a few philosophers. Our illusions are not brittle like glass, ready to shatter at the mere touch of truth. No nihilistic abyss will open up beneath our feet. People will not run wild in the streets. Given the psychological weakness of reason, "dangerous truths," in practice, are not truly dangerous, and thus esoteric protection is not really necessary.

It is very true, as this objection suggests, that the manner in which illusion and truth interact within the human mind and within society is a question demanding some delicacy. There is no precise science of human irrationality, no accurate sociology of false beliefs. It can sometimes happen in certain individuals that illusion does indeed shatter like glass, that the scales fall from one's eyes. But that is rare. Particularly within societies, beliefs tend to change gradually and one must track their mutations in terms of generations.

Still, there is nothing implausible in the classical supposition that if philosophers, the most impressive minds of their times, always spoke openly about their rejection of prevailing beliefs, then over time these beliefs would, not indeed shatter, but weaken or decay or be distorted in some important manner. In different historical conditions, of course, this weakening of fundamental beliefs will involve very different consequences. It can certainly lead to the weakening of restraints—moral and social—upon our baser impulses and thus to an increase in lawlessness or antisocial behavior. But even where it does not unleash our worst impulses, it can lead to the weakening of our best ones; that is, to the decline of idealism, commitment, and striving and thus to listlessness and apathy or to a degraded concentration on narrow self-indulgence.

Again, the undermining of fundamental beliefs can lead to uncertainty and anxiety, which in turn produce depression, withdrawal, and hopelessness. Or this same uncertainty can produce the fanatical embrace of new, more dogmatic certainties that are more hardened against the questioning power of reason. Under very favorable circumstances, the undermining of existing beliefs can lead to the formation of new ones that are healthier. There is no general rule. It is a matter of political judgment. Therefore, just as philosophers, in their strategies to protect themselves from society, had to assess the unique dangers and resources existing in their particular time and place, so also in their efforts to protect society from their philosophic activity they had to determine which of the prevailing myths and prejudices could be openly questioned without long-term ill effects and which could not.

Even in the face of this more nuanced statement, however, contemporary thinkers are still likely to remain skeptical. People today, shaped by the unique intellectual conditions prevailing within modern liberal democracies, are strongly inclined to doubt that protective esotericism was ever really necessary in any historical circumstances. For our constant experience is this: we see that opinions long considered outrageous and subversive eventually get openly expressed and yet the nation prospers. It seems an empirical fact: so-called harmful truths simply do no harm.

The clearest and most extreme example of this phenomenon concerns the now widespread doctrine of historicism or cultural relativism—the view that moral values and social norms have no objective or universal validity but derive from the arbitrary commitments of one's culture, which are not intrinsically superior to the different or opposite commitments of other cultures. As this doctrine was developing over the last two hundred years, it was accompanied by dire warnings that, if accepted, it would produce a condition of nihilistic angst and paralysis and destroy all firm sense of right and wrong. But today in America a large proportion of the population has come to embrace some version of historical relativism, and yet life goes on pretty much as before. We have become a nation of cheerful nihilists and moralistic relativists.

Thus, our very experience of ourselves—and of the most radical doctrines—has taught us firsthand that somehow subversive ideas do not subvert. Reason is superficial; talk is cheap; ideas hardly matter. That is ultimately why we find it so hard to take seriously the argument for protective esotericism. In the end, we actually *agree* with the classical view that all social life is based on illusion or myth or commitments without foundation. We disagree—strangely—only by asserting that this momentous fact does not really matter.

That is how we are given to see things today. Thus, in order to judge accurately of the attitudes and esoteric practices of *past* ages concerning "dangerous ideas," we need to appreciate just how historically atypical is our whole experience of the role of ideas. Unfortunately, an adequate analysis of this phenomenon would require more space and a better sociology of beliefs than are available. Some brief suggestions will have to suffice.

I have already argued that, from the beginning, the modern liberal state was invented with the express purpose of transforming our posture toward ideas, of making large moral and religious beliefs—the great source of instability and conflict—as politically irrelevant as possible. The state was placed on a new foundation. Liberal citizens would unite, no longer on the basis of moral and religious agreement, but on the basis of a shared fear of disagreement. The community of beliefs would be replaced by a community of interests. A new world of practice was thus created that was remarkably "ideologically neutral" and impervious to large ideas. And over time, such a world naturally tended to generate citizens who were similarly impervious, whose every observation and experience taught them that ideas mattered less, did less work in the world, than earlier ages had for some reason supposed.

To be sure, this world suffered a major shock in the twentieth century with the rise of fascism and communism and the deadly serious battle of ideas that ensued. But these battles over, we soon settled back into "the end of ideology" if not "the end of history." (It is still too soon to tell how the struggle with Islamic fundamentalism may alter this situation.) The rapid spread of postmodernism in the post-cold-war period can be said to represent the ultimate fulfillment (if by different means) of the original early modern intention to drain all "grand narratives" of their seriousness and weight.

This attitude toward ideas has been further reinforced by the effect on people of the extreme openness and freedom of speech that the new ideologically neutral state made possible. When people grow up in an environment where everything is openly disputed and questioned, with shocking and contrarian opinions on constant display, a common result is that they eventually throw up their hands in despair and adopt a "who's to say" posture toward all fundamental questions. As I hear all the time from my students: "Some people think this, others think that. It's all a matter of opinion. You can believe whatever you like. It's all good. Whatever." As Marcuse put it in a famous essay, we suffer from "repressive tolerance": amid all the constant chatter, everything gets talked to death, all edges are blunted, opposites are neutralized, and the mind anaesthetized.[50] At a certain point, a degree of mental numbness is reached where nothing sinks in, where ideas simply lose their power to shock or move us.

It is not that people today have no real or heartfelt beliefs, but under the pressure of an environment of great skepticism and dispute, they shelter these beliefs by pushing them underground. This too is a way to protect oneself from dangerous ideas. Thus, a gulf has opened up between what we think and what, deep down, we really believe. Our true beliefs have become increasingly unreachable, while our thinking has become increasingly insincere. As many observers of our condition have maintained, ours is the great "age of inauthenticity." We no longer reason with our whole souls. We don't connect. Some such account would seem to be necessary to explain the most remarkable intellectual phenomenon of our time: the proliferation of cheerful relativists and smiley-face nihilists who, as such, do not really believe what they think or think what they believe.

I have been arguing—very loosely, to be sure—that if our world has scorned and abandoned protective esotericism with no apparent ill effects, that is primarily because it has found new forms of protection against threatening ideas in the combination of political liberalism and personal inauthenticity. In our ideologically neutral and intellectually insincere world, subversive ideas have lost the power to subvert. We can no longer be shocked. So protective esotericism has become largely superfluous for us.

But if we understand how anomalous this state of affairs is, then we will not allow it to mislead us into the anachronistic conclusion that the situation was the same in the past and that people have always been as impervious to dangerous ideas as we are. The long history of persecution, if nothing else, testifies to the fact that past ages felt and feared the power of ideas. And thus philosophers of the past felt a powerful impulsion to embrace protective esotericism.

INAUTHENTICITY VS. ESOTERICISM

One further conclusion follows from the suggestion I have been making that, in the strange intellectual climate of late modernity, inauthenticity has largely replaced esotericism as our main intellectual defense mechanism. It powerfully illustrates the importance of the third motive for esoteric writing to which we now turn: the pedagogical motive.

We must keep in mind that while philosophers seek to protect people in general from the loss of their illusions, they also seek to help potential philosophers to escape theirs. That is indeed their primary task—philosophical education. Now, if illusion tended to shatter like glass at the touch of truth, the latter task at least—intellectual liberation—would be easy. But this is not the case. On the contrary, as we have just seen, when people are constantly confronted with more questions or more troubling ideas than they can handle at the moment, they will protect themselves in various ways, including a kind of intellectual withdrawal and numbness that prevents them from really feeling their thoughts. It may well be the case that, in our time, this condition of inauthenticity serves just as well as esotericism to protect society from subversion. But what it can never do is serve the needs of philosophical education. One might argue that inauthenticity, arising from the great openness and neutrality of liberal society, poses a far more elusive and stubborn obstacle to genuine philosophical liberation than the earnest provincialism characteristic of more closed societies.

For the sake of the liberation from illusion, then, even more than for the maintenance of it, some restraint in the communication of truth is necessary. That, at any rate, is the thought behind pedagogical esotericism.

The Educational Benefits of Obscurity:
Pedagogical Esotericism

The words of the wise and their riddles.

—PROVERBS 1:6

Of the four motives for philosophical esotericism, the pedagogical is the most genuinely philosophical. The other forms seek the avoidance of persecution, the prevention of subversion, and the promotion of political change. These are all worthy things that philosophers may pursue, but they are not philosophy. The purpose of pedagogical esotericism, by contrast, more directly concerns philosophy itself: the transmission of philosophical understanding. In this sense, it is esotericism's purest form.

Its essential premise is this: one must embrace obscurity (of the right kind) as something essential to effective philosophical communication. Naturally, this seems counterintuitive, not to say twisted and perverse. In addition, it involves the celebration of obscurity as a positive good—unlike the other forms that merely embrace it as a necessary evil.

For these reasons, pedagogical esotericism, while the purest form, is also the strangest. It is the one we find the most difficult to understand—and to stomach. But it is possible, if we reflect for a moment, to view it in an opposite manner.

If it is indeed the case that the practice of esoteric writing is a genuine and widespread historical phenomenon, that is largely bad news for scholars. It means a lot more work. It would be easier to accept this vexing fact, however, if there were also something good and attractive about this practice. And that is precisely what pedagogical esotericism—and it alone—promises. It claims that esoteric obscurity is not just an ugly obstacle to understanding, as we have been assuming up until now, but rather something engaging, even charming, and at any rate good for us—an important aid to our philosophical development. Thus, with its strange, positive promises (if borne out), pedagogical esotericism can make it easier for us to come to terms with the fact of esotericism and—who knows—perhaps even come to like it.

Stranger things have happened. Take the case of Alexander Herzen, the great nineteenth-century Russian writer and revolutionary. He knew at first hand the evils of czarist censorship, having been arrested several times, and he knew the difficult constraints of "Aesopian language." He dedicated his life to the struggle for liberty in every form, above all freedom of the press. Still, as a writer, he also had a fine sensitivity to matters of rhetoric and persuasion, which led him to the following observations *in praise* of esoteric writing:

> censorship is highly conducive to progress in the mastery of style and in the ability to restrain one's words. . . . In allegorical discourse there is perceptible excitement and struggle: this discourse is more impassioned than any straight exposition. The word implied has greater force beneath its veil and is always transparent to those who care to understand. A thought which is checked has greater meaning concentrated in it—it has a sharper edge; to speak in such a way that the thought is plain yet remains to be put into words by the reader himself is the best persuasion. Implication increases the power of language.[1]

Make no mistake, Herzen—who eventually emigrated to London where he founded the Free Russian Press—hated censorship with a passion fueled by bitter experience. But, impressively, he did not allow his hatred and personal suffering to prevent him from also recognizing—indeed, even coming to like—the many literary and rhetorical advantages of an esoteric style. He emphatically saw the positive side of obscurity.[2] We must strive, in the face of our own loathings, to approach the phenomenon in a similar spirit.

In the end, however, should we still incline to doubt the purported benefits of pedagogical esotericism, it is important to remind ourselves once again that the decisive issue for present purposes is not whether we ourselves find the pedagogical argument persuasive, or even whether it is true, but only whether the writers of previous ages believed it and acted upon it. And about that, as I hope to show, there can be little doubt.

THE MODERN ETHIC OF LITERALNESS AND CLARITY

In view of the strangeness of this older view and our deep resistance to it, let us begin by stating openly our current instincts on this subject. That is easily done: we find obscurity hateful. To be sure, there are fields so inherently difficult and counterintuitive that a fair amount of obscurity is unavoidable—as in contemporary physics. The thing we hate is *voluntary* obscurity. In almost all such cases, the source of unclarity is a desire to appear wiser than one is, to surround oneself with a cultish air of mystery or profundity, and to shelter oneself from criticism. Voluntary obscurity arises from vanity or insecurity at best, charlatanry at worst. Obviously, then, all decent and serious thinkers will strive to speak as precisely, openly, and directly as possible. They will say exactly what they mean. There is simply no valid argument for anything else.

That is what we want to say, especially we in the Anglo-American world, where philosophy is viewed as something that is—or at least ought to be—an exact and rigorous matter that should not stoop to "rhetoric," ambiguity, or multivocal speech of any kind. We proudly stand by an ethic of literalness and clarity.

Yet as obvious and normal as this attitude may seem to us, historically speaking it is quite rare. As soon as one ventures beyond the narrow shores of our modern world—whether one looks to the ancient Greeks and Romans or to the Bible and the Koran or to the traditional societies of the East, of Africa, and of Native America—virtually everywhere one finds the same thing: "The words of the wise and their riddles." It is the characteristic way of the wise to speak indirectly, to talk in figures, proverbs, and puzzles. All the sages of premodern cultures seem to share a belief in the ineffectiveness of open statements, the superficiality of direct communication. Wisdom, it seems, would not be so rare and difficult a thing if it could simply be "told" by one person to another.

We are aware of this view, of course, but dismiss it as primitive, irrational, or superstitious. But is it? Even the philosophers of the past rarely attempted to write in the precise and methodical way that, to us, seems so obviously necessary. They seem to have held to a more complex view of education and communication than we do, granting a crucial role to the full range of human modes of expression, including the more suggestive and concealed ones, such as allusion, metaphor, parable, epigram, allegory, and riddle. For the same reason, they also employed a greater range of compositional forms: not just treatises, as today, but poems, aphorisms, dialogues, essays, commentaries, dictionaries, and epistles.

Indeed, classical rationalism at its peak (as distinguished from Enlightenment rationalism) regarded the issue of whether wisdom is teachable at all as a grave and open question. In Plato's *Protagoras* (319a–320c), we see Socrates arguing that wisdom and virtue cannot be taught (although they can be learned). There are profound limits, this great teacher held, to what one human being can explain to another. Somehow, philosophical education is inherently problematic.

Compounding this difficulty, classical thinkers were also very much preoccupied with the problem of writing. Can books ever be useful for such education, or must all genuinely philosophical instruction be oral and personal? In Plato's *Phaedrus*, this question was answered firmly in the negative by Socrates, who, like Pythagoras before him, eschewed philosophical writing altogether. And even Plato himself expressed serious doubts on this score in his Seventh Letter (341c–e, 343a, 344c–345a). Again, Thomas Aquinas in explaining the fact that Jesus—the other great teacher of the West— also did not write, argued that the most excellent teachers must follow the practice of Pythagoras and Socrates, for "Christ's doctrine . . . cannot be expressed in writing."[3] In short, classical and medieval rationalism endorsed and explored the profound intuition—found everywhere outside the modern West—that the whole enterprise of using books for the transmission of philosophic wisdom is an extraordinarily difficult (and possibly futile) undertaking that, when pursued, requires rhetorical techniques extending well beyond the contemporary ethic of literalness and clarity.

It is manifest, then, that this ethic is anything but obvious and historically universal. It is, in fact, the creation of a very particular culture—the modern Enlightenment. As Donald Levine, the distinguished sociologist, writes in his important study *The Flight from Ambiguity*:

> The movement against ambiguity led by Western intellectuals since the seventeenth century figures as a unique development in world history. There is nothing like it in any premodern culture known to me.[4]

Levine's book explores the great but—as we will no longer be surprised to learn—almost entirely unstudied transformation of our rhetorical and communicative culture that took place beginning in the early modern period.

This transformation may be attributed to a number of different factors. The whole reorientation of philosophy that one sees in Bacon, Descartes, and Hobbes, especially the harmonist effort to give philosophic reason a new level of power and control within the world of practice, gave new and fundamental importance to certainty and exactness. For in intellectual matters, rigor is power. Thus, modern epistemology in both its rationalist and its empiricist branches mistrusted the natural workings of the human mind and proclaimed the need for "method," for the adoption of artificially redesigned ways of thinking and speaking.

Later, the striking success of the modern scientific paradigm encouraged the view that, in all fields, intellectual progress required the reform of language, replacing ordinary parlance with a rigorous, technical vocabulary. Again, in the economic sphere, the increasing "rationalization" of the world—the rise of bureaucracy, technology, commerce, specialization, and legal regulation—made clear and distinct communication a practical necessity.[5] Similarly, in the sphere of religion, ascetic Puritanism, with its ideal of sincerity, its dislike of adornment, and its suspicion of arcane, priestly doctrine led to a call for plain, simple, and direct speaking—a kind of semantic prudishness.

Last but surely not least, on the political level, Bacon, Spinoza, Hobbes, and the Enlightenment thinkers emphasized that prejudice and superstition—and the oppressive political and religious powers they support—draw much of their strength from the human tendency to be fooled by obscure speech, by metaphors, rhetoric, poetry, and the other nonrational aspects of human discourse. Thus, for the sake of justice and the triumph over oppression, public discourse generally must become as literal and precise as possible.[6]

Through the sustained pressure of these factors and others, modern Western discourse has become forcibly purged and "rationalized." Whether in scholarship, pedagogy, the workplace, or ordinary conversation, we believe in a controlled, no-nonsense, utilitarian kind of talk: unambiguous, literal, unadorned, frank, and to the point. Everything else strikes us as pompous, unctuous, or childish. This transformation is so pervasive that we have lost all awareness of it, but as we have seen, it is quite visible to non-Westerners and clearly described, over and over again, in the voluminous literature on intercultural communication. And of course this "flight from ambiguity" is also visible, as I have been suggesting, in the historical uniqueness of our noncomprehension of esotericism.

It seems obvious to us that philosophy should be a pure matter of propositions and arguments, rigorously laid out, as in a contemporary journal of analytic philosophy. But this attitude rests on a premise: the hyperrationalist assumption, inherited from the Enlightenment, that human beings can be addressed from the start as rationalists seeking the truth.

But as the tradition of classical rationalism emphasized, we may be "rational animals" in that we possess the faculty of reason, but we are hardly born rationalists. Rather, we are born in "the cave." Illusion has very powerful roots within us, both social and psychological. We are moved by a host of passions, most of which are in tension with the love of truth. Thus, the primary aim of philosophic education must be less to instruct than to convert, less to elaborate a philosophical system than to produce that "turning around of the soul" that brings individuals to love and live for the truth. But precisely if the primary *end* of education is to foster the love of truth, this love cannot be presupposed in the *means*. The means must rather be based on a resourceful pedagogical rhetoric that, knowing how initially resistant or impervious we all are to philosophic truth, necessarily makes use of motives other than love of truth and of techniques other than "saying exactly what you mean." In sum, the modern ethic of literalness and clarity—at least in the view of most earlier ages—is plainly too narrow and dogmatic. To be sure, the bad use of obscurity and concealment—which is ninety percent of it—remains hateful. But there really is a good use. The good use—pedagogical esotericism—is made necessary by two sets of problems: the natural difficulties of philosophic education and the inherent shortcomings of writing.

What, then, are these difficulties? A brief examination of the obstacles to a philosophical education that is conveyed through books will put us in a position to see why esoteric concealment has often been embraced as the solution.

THREE DANGERS OF READING

The invention of writing brought epochal changes to human civilization—most of them good. But books also made possible a whole host of intellectual vices and distortions unknown to preliterate, oral societies. With respect to philosophy, there is a real danger that, in the words of Voltaire, "the multitude of books is making us ignorant." In a variety of ways, "book knowledge" is the death of philosophy—so much so that a "philosophy book" is almost a contradiction in terms.

In chapter 3 we briefly discussed the contradiction that exists between the univocity of writing and the duality of lives. The problem there was the potential harm done by a philosophic book when it falls into the hands of a nonphilosophic reader. This problem leads to the need for defensive and protective esotericism. Here we examine the harm such books can do precisely to the philosophic reader—which is the root of pedagogical esotericism.

A book is a strange and unseemly thing. It delivers into one person's hands the distilled essence of another's thinking. It gives one things one has not earned. That is the core difficulty from which all the more specific problems flow, as we will see. And that is why the solution to all of these problems will involve some form of esotericism: some effort to give away less and to make the reader work more for what he or she is getting.

The first danger of reading books is that it allows you to skip too many stages, shortcutting the proper intellectual development. Especially harmful is that it prevents the humble confrontation with your own ignorance. Reading makes you prematurely wise. Before you have had a chance to face the questions and live with them a while, you have seen the answers. Books give a false sense of knowledge and sophistication based on borrowed wisdom, on the belief that you know what you have only read. Thus, they rob you of the proper state of mind for true education. As Socrates argues in the *Phaedrus*—putting these words in the mouth of an Egyptian god, Thamus, who is rebuking the inventor of writing—through writing "you offer your pupils the appearance of wisdom, not true wisdom, for they will read many things without instruction, and will therefore seem to know many things, when they are for the most part ignorant" (275a–b). As we have seen, Plato himself gives this same explanation when he asserts, in the Seventh Letter, that he has not and would not ever commit to writing an open statement of his deepest thoughts. Reading such an account, he explains, would not help people but rather fill them with a "lofty and empty hope as if they had learned awesome matters" (341e). The false presumption of wisdom, which is generated by books, presents the greatest obstacle to the acquisition of the real thing. Whence the inner logic of Milton's description: "Deep versed in books and shallow in himself."[7]

This same problem is elaborated very powerfully in *Emile*, Rousseau's book on education: "I hate books. They only teach one to talk about what one does not know." And again: "Too much reading only serves to produce presumptuous ignoramuses." The key point is that bookish presumptuousness is what makes people ignoramuses. "The abuse of books kills science. Believing that we know what we have read, we believe that we can dispense with learning it."[8] Intellectual humility and the keen sense of our ignorance are the necessary starting points for genuine philosophical development;

therefore, books—even as they transmit brilliant philosophical insights—undercut philosophy at its root.

The most obvious way for an author to counteract this danger is to scrupulously avoid handing the reader any clear and readymade answers. One might also go further: make a point of including in one's books enough difficulty and obscurity to humble the reader and force him to confront his ignorance. Friedrich Schleiermacher, the nineteenth-century German philosopher, theologian, and classical scholar, attributes precisely such a rhetorical strategy to Plato. In his dialogues, the latter sought to "bring the still ignorant reader nearer to a state of knowledge"; but Plato also clearly recognized the very great necessity "of being cautious with regard to him not to give rise to an empty and conceited notion of his own knowledge in his mind."

> [Therefore, it] must have been the philosopher's chief object to conduct every investigation in such a manner from the beginning onwards, as that he might reckon upon the reader's either being driven to an inward and self-originated creation of the thought in view, or submitting to surrender himself most decisively to the feeling of not having discovered or understood anything. To this end, then, it is requisite that the final object of the investigation be not directly enunciated and laid down in words, a process which might very easily serve to entangle many persons who are glad to rest content, provided only they are in possession of the final result, but that the mind be reduced to the necessity of seeking, and put into the way by which it may find it. The first is done by the mind's being brought to so distinct a consciousness of its own state of ignorance, that it is impossible it should willingly continue therein. The other is effected either by an enigma being woven out of contradictions, to which the only possible solution is to be found in the thought in view, and often several hints thrown out in a way apparently utterly foreign and accidental which can only be found and understood by one who does really investigate with an activity of his own. Or the real investigation is overdrawn with another, not like a veil, but, as it were, an adhesive skin, which conceals from the inattentive reader, and from him alone, the matter which is to be properly considered or discovered, while it only sharpens and clears the mind of an attentive one to perceive the inward connection.[9]

This kind of esoteric artfulness is essential, according to Schleiermacher, to avoid what I am calling the first danger of reading.

But book learning thwarts philosophic education by fostering not only a false presumption of wisdom but also an enfeebling passivity. "Much reading is an oppression of the mind," remarks William Penn, "and extinguishes the natural candle, which is the reason of so many senseless scholars in the world."[10] As Montaigne puts it: "We let ourselves lean so heavily on the arms of others that we annihilate our own powers."[11] The same point is made by Schopenhauer:

> When we read, another person thinks for us: we merely repeat his mental process. . . . So it comes about that if anyone spends almost the whole day in reading . . . he gradually loses the capacity for thinking; just as the man who always rides, at last forgets how to walk. This is the case with many learned persons: they have read themselves stupid.[12]

The solution to this problem is to be found, once again, in employing a salutary obscurity that does not allow the readers passively to rely on the writer's thinking, but forces them to think for themselves. Thus, Thomas Aquinas, in considering the question of why the Bible often uses veiled, metaphorical language, remarks: "The very hiding of truth in figures is useful for the exercise of thoughtful minds."[13] Augustine makes the same point: the disciples "have spoken with a helpful and healthy obscurity in order to exercise and somehow refine their readers' minds."[14] Similarly, Sallustius, the fourth-century Neoplatonist, in discussing why the Greeks shrouded their religious teachings in myth, remarks:

> There is this first benefit from myths, that we have to search and do not have our minds idle. . . . To wish to teach the whole truth about the Gods to all produces contempt in the foolish, because they cannot understand, and lack of zeal in the good; whereas to conceal the truth by myths prevents the contempt of the foolish, and compels the good to practice philosophy.[15]

Somewhat similar is Rousseau's description of his writing style in the preface to the *Letter to M. d'Alembert*. In this book—which he identifies as a popular work as distinguished from his other, philosophical writings, addressed to the few—he states: "I do not speak here to the few but to the public, nor do I attempt to make others think but rather to explain my thought clearly. Hence, I had to change my style."[16] In a striking reversal of our own attitudes toward writing, Rousseau sets up here a strict disjunction between "making others think," the task of his philosophical books, and "explaining my thought clearly," the job of his merely popular writings. To get others to think, one must carefully avoid doing everything for them. A famous statement by Montesquieu—which may have been in the back of Rousseau's mind—expresses the same idea: "One must not always so exhaust a subject that one leaves nothing for the reader to do. It is not a question of making him read but of making him think."[17]

Still another danger of reading, closely related to that of mental passivity, is the development of an excessive trust and dependence on the author. Books—with their steadfast endurance over time, their unwavering repetition of the identical words and thoughts, and even (since Guttenberg) the more-than-human regularity of their type—inspire a kind of reverence. Writing has a tendency to become "scripture." We undergo a curious distortion of the mind whereby we come to look for truth in books, not in the world. We replace thinking with reading. This is especially true when studying the great philosophers. To quote Montaigne:

> We know how to say: "Cicero says thus; such are the morals of Plato; these are the very words of Aristotle." But what do we say ourselves? What do we judge? What do we do? A parrot could well say as much.[18]

Cicero clearly describes the problem—as well as his particular solution:

> Those who seek to learn my personal opinion on the various questions [of philosophy] show an unreasonable degree of curiosity. In discussion it is not so much weight of authority as force of argument that should be demanded. Indeed, the authority of those who profess to teach is often a positive hindrance to those who desire to learn; they cease to employ their own judgment, and take what they perceive to be the verdict of their chosen master as settling the question.[19]

As he goes on to describe here, Cicero's solution was to frustrate the reader's "unreasonable degree of curiosity" by ensuring that his own final position remained unclear. He did so by composing his philosophical writings in the form of dialogues or of treatises that merely surveyed the arguments both for and against the various schools.

In sum, there is an inherent tension between philosophy and books. The philosophical writer stands in danger of harming his readers in the very act of trying to help them, by fostering an unhealthy presumption, passivity, and dependence.

THE PARADOX OF PHILOSOPHICAL EDUCATION

But this characterization of the problem of writing—along with the general solution: refraining from a full and open statement of one's thought—does not quite get at its deepest level. For philosophical education requires not merely that one avoid discouraging the reader in these three ways from employing his own mind, but that one positively motivate him to think and, above all, to think authentically and for himself. One must somehow induce in him a new level of awakeness, inner-directedness, and self-ownership. But how can a book or even a live teacher do that? The central paradox of philosophical education, whether in writing or in person, is this: how can one transmit to others something that can never genuinely be given from without, but only generated from within? For that is of the essence of philosophy: it can never be done for you. It is our "ownmost" activity: you must do it all for yourself or you haven't done it at all.

This is the case for a number of related reasons. By definition, philosophy aims, not at "right opinion," but "knowledge": not simply at possessing correct answers but at knowing how and why they are correct. It aims at truths the origin and grounding of which one completely understands. Thus, it does not help—it is often a hindrance—to be given the answers from the outside, when the truly essential thing is to begin at the beginning and re-enact their discovery by and for oneself.

But this rediscovery, furthermore, is not simply a matter of retracing the logical sequence of arguments. For the "knowledge" at which philosophy aims is not purely intellectual or academic—like book knowledge. One must feel these truths from the inside, make them one's own, and live them. The rediscovery, then, must start from one's own personal perplexity, draw upon one's own lived experience, and make use of the inner activity of one's own powers of reasoning and realization. Amid all the far-ranging ventures of one's thinking, one must maintain the concrete and vital connection of thought to life. In other words, "thinking for oneself" means not only that it is oneself that does the thinking but that one thinks for one's own case, thinks from out of one's own care, future, and fate.

Finally, it is only thinking for oneself in this deeply personal sense that produces a real and transformative effect upon the soul. It is only in this way that one undergoes what Plato speaks of as definitive of the truly philosophic life: a "turning around of the soul," a fundamental reorientation of the objects of one's longing and the manner of one's being.

If this is the character of genuine philosophy, then it really *is* an open question whether it is teachable. Wisdom cannot be told. The central paradox of philosophical pedagogy, to say it again, is: how can one transmit from the outside what can only grow from within? Is there something that one can do for a person that will somehow make him do everything for himself?

This is the problem that the "Socratic method" (as we have come to call it) is intended to address. It has at least four elements, all of them making use of "esotericism" in one sense or another. The first, which we have now seen over and over again, is the negative imperative: Do not give away the answers. The Socratic teacher leaves the most important things unsaid or at least unclear. Yet, second, there is also something positive that the teacher or writer can do: he can stimulate the student to think for himself—while subtly guiding that thinking—by making artful use of questions, hints, and puzzles of the right kind.

But, third, for this thinking and questioning to maintain an authentic connection to the student's life, it must be *dialectical*. This means (among many other things) that it must take its start from where the student is, from what he believes right now, and proceed through an internal critique. One cannot begin abstractly—from first principles or from a general statement of the big questions—if the student is truly to think for himself, with his own life on the line. For he does not begin as a blank slate. Whatever may be the situation at birth, by the time a student is old enough to be thinking about philosophical questions, he is already fully immersed in a world of beliefs and answers. He is trapped in a cave of illusions. Thus, his education must begin by lighting up and then questioning the things that he already believes, the foundations of the life that he is already living. He cannot jump out of his skin and make a new beginning: he must start from the inside and slowly, painstakingly work his way out.

But people draw their initial beliefs primarily from the worldview of their particular society. It follows, then, that a writer who seeks to educate philosophically through Socratic dialectics must make a special effort to enter sympathetically into the received opinions of his time and place—though he may consider them false—while pointing quietly to certain puzzles or contradictions within those opinions. This means that the demands of philosophical pedagogy largely parallel those of the defensive and protective motives for esotericism. On the surface of his writings, a philosophical author will embrace the views prevailing in his time, not only to defend himself from persecution and to protect society from harm, but also to help the student to begin his philosophical reflections from what, for him, is the necessary beginning point.

This idea is well expressed by Kierkegaard, who goes so far as to call it "the secret of the art of helping others." In *The Point of View for My Work as an Author*, an autobiographical essay devoted to explaining his technique of writing, he states:

> One can deceive a person for the truth's sake, and (to recall old Socrates) one can deceive a person into the truth. Indeed it is only by this means, i.e., by deceiving him, that it is possible to bring into the truth one who is in an illusion. Whoever rejects this opinion betrays the fact that he is not over-well versed in dialectics, and that is precisely what is especially needed when operating in this field. . . . Direct communication presupposes that the receiver's ability to receive is undisturbed. But here such is not the case; an illusion stands in the way. . . . What then does it mean 'to deceive'? It means that one does not begin directly with the matter one wants to communicate, but begins by accepting the other man's illusion as good money.[20]

This is necessary because "if real success is to attend the effort to bring a man to a definite position, one must first of all take pains to find him where he is and begin there. This is the secret of the art of helping others."[21]

A fourth element of the Socratic method—actually, just a further aspect of its dialectical character—is that a proper philosophical education must proceed in *stages*. Just as education must begin by addressing the student where he is, so, as he learns and changes, it must stay with him. The internal or dialectical critique of received opinion takes place not in a single stroke but in a series of successive approximations to the truth, each of which will seem in its time to be the final one. The student must not be encouraged to race through these stages to the end, but on the contrary made to settle down and live with each for a while, so that he has the time to truly take it in and absorb it—and to allow it to transform him. Our lives do not change as quickly as our thoughts. If the student tries to move too fast, he leaves his life behind, and his thinking becomes purely intellectual. He ceases to believe what he thinks and think what he believes. Tempo is everything. Prematurity—showing the student more than he is ready to understand or digest at the moment—is the great wrecker of educations. As Rousseau remarks in *Emile*, "never show the child anything he cannot see." Again: the child "must remain in absolute ignorance of ideas . . . which are not within his reach. My whole book is only a constant proof of this principle of education."[22]

This principle—the need for proper tempo and stages, adjusted to the individual characteristics of the student, so that his thinking remains firmly

rooted in his own experience and life—is why a perfect education would require what is depicted in *Emile*: a philosopher devoting himself full-time to
the raising and education of a single student from birth. While this is hardly
to be expected in practice, it highlights what is so terribly problematic about
books: they are impersonal and fixed, saying the same thing to all regardless of their state of readiness. That indeed is Socrates's primary objection to
writing as stated in the *Phaedrus* (275d–e)—the *univocity* of writing. To the
extent that there is a solution to this problem, it lies, once again, in esotericism—in writing on two or even more levels—so that the same book will say
different things to different people, or to the same person at different times,
depending on their stage of understanding.

To promote a genuinely philosophical education, in sum, it is necessary to
write esoterically in at least four ways—to withhold the answers, to begin by
embracing received opinion, to guide the reader by way of hints and riddles,
and to address the different stages of understanding by writing on multiple
levels.

THE RHETORICAL EFFECT OF OBSCURITY

In order to clarify and extend some of the preceding points—especially the
core assumption that obscurity can and should be used as a stimulus to genuine thought—let us take up an obvious objection. Even if it is true that one
hinders philosophic education in various ways by telling a student too much,
still doesn't one hinder it even more by saying too little? A writer who hides
what he knows and fills his book with stumbling blocks will only frustrate
and discourage the reader. Nobody denies that a pedagogically effective
writing must above all stimulate the mind to its own efforts, but nothing is
more deadening than obscurity.

When it is pointless and impenetrable, obscurity is indeed deadening.
But the right kind of obscurity—the kind that, with the proper effort, can
be deciphered and penetrated—turns out, in fact, to be the greatest stimulus to thought. Everyone loves a secret. Mystery is alluring. Hide something
and we will seek it. This simple fact is the first premise of all pedagogical
esotericism.

It is a fact that has been noticed throughout the ages. Jesus—who hides
his thought in parables—gives this famous literary advice: "Do not give dogs
what is holy; and do not throw your pearls before swine" (Matt. 7:6). The
medieval *Glossa Ordinaria* on this passage elaborates: "What is hidden is

more eagerly sought after; what is concealed appears more worthy of reverence; what is searched for longer is more dearly prized."[23] Similarly, Augustine remarks: "Lest the obvious should cause disgust, the hidden truths arouse longing; longing brings on certain renewal; renewal brings sweet inner knowledge."[24] Again, according to Nietzsche:

> The misfortune suffered by clear-minded and easily understood writers is that they are taken for shallow and thus little effort is expended on reading them: and the good fortune that attends the obscure is that the reader toils at them and ascribes to them the pleasure he has in fact gained from his own zeal.[25]

Clement of Alexandria, in a chapter of his *Stromata* entitled "Reasons for Veiling the Truth in Symbols," observes that "all things that shine through a veil show the truth grander and more imposing; as fruits shining through water, and figures through veils."[26] In short, the objection stated above has the rhetorical situation exactly backward: the right kind of obscurity is far more intellectually stimulating than is a plain and explicit statement. As Augustine puts it:

> All those truths which are presented to us in figures tend, in some manner, to nourish and arouse the flame of love . . . and they stir and enkindle love better than if they were set before us unadorned, without any symbolism of mystery. It is hard to explain the reason for this; nevertheless, it is true that any doctrine suggested under an allegorical form affects and pleases us more, and is more esteemed, than one set forth explicitly in plain words.[27]

It may indeed be unfortunate, but surely that is how it is.

Yet once it is conceded that hiddenness and obscurity of the right kind do indeed have this stimulating power, one may go on to raise an opposite objection to their use in philosophical pedagogy. For if it should turn out that this stimulating power ultimately stems from irrational or immature impulses, one would hardly want to encourage it in serious writing. This would seem to be the real objection of those who hate the idea of pedagogical obscurity: not that such writing is too deadening but that it is too exciting in the wrong way, that it appeals to people's primitive, childish, and easily abused enchantment with secrets and mysteries. A proper education should endeavor to make people mature, sober, and clear-minded. Are we really to believe that the best means that the greatest minds of the past could find to educate people to rationality was to exploit their adolescent fantasies about buried treasure?

The question thus becomes: What is the true source of obscurity's rhetorical power? Is it simply childish? How does it work? And is there a legitimate role for it in a literature of philosophic rationality? Without aspiring to an exhaustive treatment of this complex subject, let us focus on three elements of obscurity's appeal.

Obscurity and Reader Involvement

The first and least controversial of these is that by withholding the answers and speaking in hints and riddles the esoteric text constrains the reader to think for himself. We have already seen that thinking for oneself is philosophically essential; the further point here is that it is a strong stimulant, a powerful source of motivation and encouragement for the reader. As Nietzsche has just put it, "the reader toils at [obscure writings] and ascribes to them the pleasure he has in fact gained from his own zeal."

This is not true, of course, for every reader or perhaps even for most— not for those who would rather be told the answers. But "if you have to be told everything, do not read me," Rousseau declares (for "if you have to be told, how will you understand it?").[28] That is the unstated maxim of all esoteric texts. As Jean d'Alembert, in his *Analysis of the Spirit of the Laws*, states regarding the famous obscurity of Montesquieu's work: "We will say of the obscurity that can be permitted in such a work, the same thing we said about the lack of order; what would be obscure for vulgar readers is not for those whom the author had in view."[29] To understand the workings of esoteric rhetoric, one must appreciate that it is a frankly elitist practice. It is narrowly designed for a specific and relatively rare kind of reader: those who love to think, those who, from an early age, could always be heard to say "now wait . . . don't tell me." In a variety of ways, such readers will be stimulated by the puzzles the text poses: they will feel energized by the exercise of their faculties, feel pride in the progress of their understanding, and joy in the powerful sense of insight that accompanies a discovery one has made for oneself.

If this is a correct description, then it seems fair to say that there is nothing immature or irrational in the power of obscurity to generate philosophical motivations such as these. Indeed, it is a power that has been noted, praised, and employed by a long line of thinkers. Nietzsche, that master of the coy and aphoristic style, speaks of

The effectiveness of the incomplete.—Just as figures in relief produce so strong an impression on the imagination because they are as it were on the point of stepping out of the wall but have suddenly been brought to a halt, so the relief-like, incomplete presentation of an idea, of a whole philosophy, is sometimes more effective than its exhaustive realization: more is left for the beholder to do, he is impelled to continue working on that which appears before him so strongly etched in light and shadow, to think it through to the end.[30]

Montesquieu alluded to this same "effectiveness of the incomplete" in his famous remark quoted above: "One must not always so exhaust a subject that one leaves nothing for the reader to do. It is not a question of making him read but of making him think." Indeed, Montesquieu's artful incompleteness was finely calculated to tantalize and please the acute reader, as was beautifully described in Hippolyte Taine's account of the *Spirit of the Laws*:

He seems to be always addressing a select circle of people with acute minds, and in such a way as to render them at every moment conscious of their acuteness. No flattery could be more delicate; we feel grateful to him for making us satisfied with our intelligence. We must possess some intelligence to be able to read him, for he deliberately curtails developments and omits transitions; we are required to supply these and to comprehend his hidden meanings. He is rigorously systematic but the system is concealed, his concise completed sentences succeeding each other separately, like so many precious coffers. . . . He thinks in summaries; . . . the summary itself often bears the air of an enigma, of which the charm is twofold; we have the pleasure of comprehension accompanying the satisfaction of divining.[31]

This statement is strikingly similar to the view of Theophrastus as approvingly described in *On Style*, a work on rhetoric attributed to the fourth-century BC orator Demetrius of Phaleron:

These, then, are the main essentials of persuasiveness; to which may be added that indicated by Theophrastus when he says that all possible points should not be punctiliously and tediously elaborated, but some should be left to the comprehension and inference of the hearer who when he perceives what you have omitted becomes not only your hearer but your witness, and a very friendly witness too. For he thinks himself intelligent because you have afforded him the means of showing his intelligence. It seems like a slur on your hearer to tell him everything as though he were a simpleton.[32]

Again, Rousseau in his pedagogical work *Emile* emphasizes that, for the sake of heightening the student's interest and motivation, it is vital to leave things unsaid. He criticizes modern writers like La Fontaine who place an explicit statement of the "moral" at the end of their stories.

> Nothing is so vain or ill conceived as the moral with which most fables end — as if this moral were not or should not be understood in the fable itself. . . . Why, then, by adding this moral at the end, take from [the reader] the pleasure of finding it on his own? Talent at instruction consists in making the disciple enjoy the instruction. But in order for him to enjoy it, his mind must not remain so passive at everything you tell him that he has absolutely nothing to do in order to understand you. The master's *amour-propre* [pride] must always leave some hold for the disciple's; he must be able to say to himself, "I conceive, I discern, I act, I learn." . . . One must always make oneself understood, but one must not always say everything.[33]

A page later, Rousseau indicates that he has followed this pedagogical strategy himself in the composition of *Emile*, declaring: "I also do not want to say everything."[34]

The ancient writers are the true masters of this technique of energizing incompleteness, as Rousseau emphasizes. He particularly admires Thucydides's pedagogical style: "He reports the facts without judging them, but he omits none of the circumstances proper to make us judge them ourselves."[35]

The other ancient historian most famous for his brevity and obscurity is Tacitus. The specific pleasure and encouragement produced by his rhetoric are nicely described by Sir Richard Baker (1568–1645), the English historian and writer. And his point is essentially the same as that made by Nietzsche, Montesquieu, Taine, Theophrastus, Demetrius, and Rousseau: Tacitus's obscurity

> is pleasing to whosoever by laboring about it, findes out the true meaning; for then he counts it an issue of his owne braine, and taking occasion from these sentences to goe further than the thing he reads, and that without being deceived, he takes the like pleasure as men are wont to take from hearing metaphors, finding the meaning of him that useth them.[36]

Still another statement of the same point is made by Thomas Gordon, Tacitus's eighteenth-century English translator. Tacitus

> is remarkable for a surpassing brevity. . . . He starts the Idea and leaves the Imagination to pursue it. The sample he gives you is so fine, that you are presently curious to see the whole piece, and then you have your share in the merit of the discovery; a compliment which some able Writers have forgot to pay their readers.[37]

Again, the Roman rhetorician Quintilian recommends that when arguing in court, one speak elliptically and just let the facts silently point to your claim, because then

> [t]his ensures that the judge himself searches for something which perhaps he would not believe if he heard it, and then believes what he thinks he has found out for himself.[38]

And later, he adds that with such speeches, "the hearer enjoys understanding it, thinks well of his own cleverness, and praises himself for someone else's speech."[39]

Boccaccio, in his *Life of Dante*, declares: "Whatever has been gained by hard work has a certain pleasure. . . . Therefore, in order that [the truth] should be more appreciated by being gained through labor and for that reason better preserved, poets hid it under many details which seem contrary to it."[40] And Samuel Butler, in his esoteric interpretation of the French naturalist Buffon, speculates that Buffon "intended his reader to draw his inferences for himself, and perhaps to value them all the more highly on that account."[41]

In sum, the right kind of obscurity energizes and pleases the right kind of reader by making him active and responsible. That is a forgotten piece of "reader response theory" with an extremely long history.

Love of the Hidden and Reverence for the Obscure

A second general aspect of obscurity's appeal is the well-known phenomenon that whatever is veiled strikes us as more alluring and desirable. As Emily Dickinson writes:

> A Charm invests a face
> Imperfectly beheld —

> The Lady dare not lift her Veil
> For fear it be dispelled[42]

There are at least two reasons for this phenomenon. If something is completely present, available, and open to view, it gives no scope to imagination or longing. It is what it is. What you see is what you get. But whatever is partly hidden holds out a promise for more—an open promise onto which imagination is free to project all our hopes and longings. That is why it is absence that makes the heart grow fonder. Presence can be a bit dispiriting.

In addition, we have a natural tendency to value things by what they cost us. We despise what is too available. Obstacles arouse us and strengthen desire. Difficulty ennobles. We pursue most eagerly what is hard to get. Thus an esoteric text—suggestive and challenging, full of promises and obstacles—arouses the mind and charges it with strong hopes and vigorous striving.

Finally, obscurity motivates and inspires the reader in still a third way when it derives not merely from an intentional coyness but from an inherent loftiness that seems to surpass our understanding. Then it overawes us and makes us feel that we are in the presence of something greater than ourselves. Thus, as the *Glossa Ordinaria* quoted above states: "what is concealed appears more worthy of reverence." The natural rhetorical effect of this kind of obscurity is to call us to attention and inspire us with reverence, awe, and wonder.

So are either of these latter two rhetorical effects—love of the hidden and reverence for the obscure—childish and irrational? They could not fairly be called "childish," but they could be charged with appealing to our "irrational tendencies," depending on one's understanding of ultimate reality. If the "true world" is of a beauty and perfection that far transcends the sensory world, then the curious tendency of our imaginations to idealize what is hidden will come to light as a crucial divination of the truth. Similarly, if there is a God, then the reverence-inspiring tendency of scriptural obscurity is an appropriate and accurate effect that helps to put us onto the path of truth and righteousness. A more materialist or at least more skeptical thinker, on the other hand, will deny the rationality of these rhetorical effects.

But even such thinkers as find the rhetorical power of obscurity irrational may still judge that it is a legitimate and useful tool in the difficult task of philosophical pedagogy. After all, that task—the conversion to philosophy—would not be so difficult if one's readers were already fully rational beings who could be motivated and instructed by purely rational means.

In reality, one must often make artful use of the student's irrational motives until one has succeeded in strengthening the rational ones—just as we use grades to motivate students until the hoped-for time when they come to see the inherent interest or utility of the subject matter.

Furthermore, if obscurity has so strong and irrational an effect on us, that can only be because we ourselves remain irrational. Obscurity has a way of tapping into the groundless hopes and fears that we continue to harbor within us. And the best way to purge ourselves of these may well be, not to ignore them or bury them in disdain, but precisely to stimulate them, bring them out in the open, and truly work them through. Only a person fully in touch with the irrational temptations buried within him has a chance of becoming genuinely rational. For this reason too, an effective philosophical pedagogy will not necessarily shrink from—indeed, it may positively require—an esoteric rhetoric that makes initial appeal to our irrational tendencies.

THE RHETORICAL EFFECT OF THE PROSAIC

One last point in reply to those who would reject the pedagogical use of obscurity or indeed of any kind of rhetoric as unphilosophical: Is there really an alternative? Is it *ever* possible to avoid rhetoric and its irrational effects? In practice, it seems the only real choice is between helpful and unhelpful rhetoric. The modern rationalist, the believer in literalness and clarity, holds that by writing in a dry, neutral, and rigorous manner one appeals directly to the rational faculties, without any involvement of rhetorical bias. The problem is that such a style is not really neutral, for the *prosaic too* has a powerful rhetorical effect and not a simply rational or salutary one.

The flip side of our irrational idealization of the hidden is our irrational devaluation of the open, public, and familiar. That is the reason for what Nietzsche called above "the misfortune suffered by clear-minded and easily understood writers;" namely, that "they are taken for shallow and thus little effort is expended on reading them." We have a curious tendency—regrettable but very powerful—to close our minds to what is open and available. It would seem that if the truth does not somehow hide from or abandon us, then we abandon it. With us, obviousness is insulting; clarity is a sign of superficiality; and familiarity breeds contempt. That is the powerful rhetorical distortion produced by the seeming avoidance of rhetoric. The open and prosaic is intellectually clear but existentially stunting: it conveys the right information but the wrong attitude; it puts the deeper reaches of the soul to sleep. It is fine for engineering, bad for philosophy. Profound ideas somehow evaporate when laid out openly for every passing eye. They become overexposed, discharged, profaned. They lose their power to move us. To maintain their potency, they need to be husbanded. "Silence is a fence around wisdom," states Maimonides.[43] Indeed, Pythagoras was famous for imposing a lengthy period of silence on his students to prepare their souls for philosophy.

Many earlier thinkers were moved by this spirit of husbanding. They embraced the rhetoric of hiddenness, notwithstanding its involvement with certain irrational effects, as a necessary counterpoison to the still more irrational effects of the prosaic and open. For example, Diogenes Laertius, in his account of the notoriously obscure writings of Heraclitus, remarks: "according to some, he deliberately made it the more obscure in order that none but adepts should approach it, and lest familiarity should breed contempt."[44] We have already seen a similar remark by Augustine: "Lest the obvious should cause disgust, the hidden truths arouse longing."

Today, we have lost this instinct for husbanding. The open society is highly sensitive to the dangers of obscurity but blind to those of plainness and clarity. Ultimate reality, we seem to presuppose, is what exists in broad daylight and is accessible to everyone in his everyday mood. But many earlier thinkers saw the greatest obstacle to philosophic insight precisely in the deadening effect that the prosaic has on the soul: a kind of trivializing everydayness arising from our dispersal in the world, from our excessive garrulousness, from the grip of stale custom and convention, and from the loss of mystery, wonder, and awe.

In a number of ways, the rhetoric of hiddenness is helpful in counteracting these harmful effects of the rhetoric of clarity. It trains the spirit in the right attitude toward thought and the world. Terse and indirect communication concentrates the mind. It teaches caution, patience, delicacy, and respect. It makes every word count. At the same time, it awakens us from our sleepy everydayness, our casual contempt for the world, by showing, through its own example, that beneath the familiar and superficial there lies something mysterious and intriguing.

Finally, such writing both issues from and engenders a reverence for one's own soul and its rarer states, a sense of reserve and inwardness, a delicacy that shelters one's higher and more fragile experiences from the coarsening glare of the public as well as from the clumsiness of words and propositions. "Every choice human being," writes Nietzsche, "strives instinctively for a citadel and a secrecy where he is saved from the crowd." Again: "Whatever is profound loves masks. . . . There are occurrences of such a delicate nature that one does well to cover them up with some rudeness to conceal them."[45] One cannot philosophize in public any more than one can make love there. Irwin Straus, the phenomenological psychologist, makes a distinction between two kinds of shame: concealing and protective. The former is the familiar impulse to conceal what is base, but the latter is the less frequently noted instinct to hide what is precious and vulnerable.[46] Cast not your pearls before swine. Pedagogical esotericism is, among other things, a very natural manifestation of protective shame, an instinctive taste for concealing, sheltering, and husbanding our higher spiritual states. And writing that exhibits this shame also inspires it in the reader.

While it is true, then, that pedagogical obscurity often makes appeal to our irrational inclinations, a plausible case can be made that the same is true of any alternative style of exposition and that, for the right kind of reader, it is in fact the best means for promoting philosophic rationality.

THE BURDEN OF ESOTERIC INTERPRETATION

One further dimension of pedagogical esotericism—and of the contemporary mind's instinctive resistance to it—will emerge from the consideration of one final objection. All the foregoing arguments notwithstanding, most people today will still find it implausible—because so plainly counterproductive—that the great philosophic writers of the past would have written esoterically for pedagogical reasons. This practice seems just too inconsistent with the practical requirements of philosophical learning. If past thinkers deliberately wrote their books in the manner suggested, they would impose on the reader the enormous burden of navigating artificial labyrinths, solving elaborate puzzles, and cracking obscure codes—and all of this effort would be needed just in order to arrive at an understanding of what the book's real argument is. The reader will then scarcely have time or energy left to do the real business of philosophy: to examine the argument, compare it with those of other writers (who must also be interpreted esoterically), and finally decide what he himself thinks of it. The task of interpretation will squeeze out that of philosophical reflection. Even under the best of circumstances, philosophy is almost impossibly difficult. Why would anyone choose to compound the difficulty by adding to it the endless and uncertain task of esoteric interpretation? Whatever the advantages might be of esoteric pedagogy considered in the abstract, in reality it makes no sense— there is simply no *time* for it. It is believable that past thinkers were sometimes forced to write esoterically in order to avoid persecution, but that they would have also done so voluntarily in an effort to *enhance* the transmission of philosophical understanding is implausible in the extreme.

There is no doubt that we feel this objection very powerfully. But, once again, we must remind ourselves that the issue is not whether we ourselves approve of and incline to practice pedagogical esotericism, but whether thinkers in the past did so. And by now we have seen a large number of explicit statements by past thinkers acknowledging and praising the use of esoteric writing for pedagogical purposes. What is perhaps even more striking in this context is that I have been unable to find *any* statements, prior to the nineteenth century, *criticizing* esotericism for the aforementioned problem. It would seem that earlier ages were, for some reason or other, much less troubled by this problem than we are.

LEISURE AND ESOTERIC LITERACY

One likely reason for this difference is a change of historical conditions. Today we labor under the great burden of a philosophic tradition that now stretches back 2,500 years. There are hundreds of major philosophical works to master and—since the rise of modern scholarship about 150 years ago— there are also hundreds of secondary writings devoted to each one of these primary works. Indeed, in our time, it is hardly possible to walk through the stacks of a major research library and not feel, among other things, oppressed by the crushing weight of so many books. The fact is that modern scholars find themselves in an impossible intellectual situation, which, though it is seldom thematically discussed, conditions all of their hermeneutical instincts. It strongly inclines us to dismiss as implausible—because simply unbearable—any suggestion that would increase our already overwhelming scholarly burden.

But of course this condition of overload did not always exist. In classical times, the heyday of pedagogical esotericism, intellectual life breathed a very different air. There were many fewer thinkers and books. Nor were books written for busy scholars and university professors who were constantly driven by the pressure to publish. Free from these burdens, intellectual life had a far more leisurely and focused character. And this greatly affected the whole manner in which books were written and read. Historians Rolf Engelsing and David Hall among others have spoken of a "reading revolution" that occurred in the mid-eighteenth century through which the traditional, "intensive" practice of reading a few books over and over again was replaced with the modern, "extensive" practice of reading a book once and moving on to the next.[47] Thus, a hundred years later, John Stuart Mill remarks:

> It must be remembered that they [the Greeks and Romans] had more time, and they wrote chiefly for a select class, possessed of leisure. To us who write in a hurry for people who read in a hurry, the attempt to give an equal degree of finish would be a loss of time.[48]

We find a similar observation in Tocqueville:

> One ought to remark, furthermore, that in all of antiquity books were rare and expensive, and great difficulty was experienced in reproducing them and having them circulate. These circumstances came to concentrate the taste for and use of letters in a few men, who formed almost a small literary aristocracy of the elite of a great political aristocracy.[49]

In such intellectual circumstances, Tocqueville continues, where the writer could count upon the patient, sustained, and repeated attention of a highly cultivated reader, nothing is "done in haste or haphazardly; everything there is written for connoisseurs."[50] Books were written with extreme care to be read with extreme care. Therefore, there was no ingrained resistance—such as we feel very strongly today—to the very idea that a book should deliberately impose on the reader a significant interpretive burden.

On the contrary, that was precisely their taste and preference. The whole tendency of classical culture, in Winckelmann's famous expression, was one of noble simplicity and quiet grandeur. This manifested itself in a literary style of urbane understatement and lapidary concision. As Mill puts it: "The ancients were *concise*, because of the extreme pains they took with their compositions; almost all moderns are prolix because they do not." Modern prose tends to be wordy and overstated, he continues, "for want of time and patience, and from the necessity we are in of addressing almost all writings to a busy and imperfectly prepared public."[51] By contrast, the primary addressees of classical writing—a small, refined, exclusive, and homogeneous literary aristocracy with a dense background of shared taste and understanding—naturally delighted in nuance and economy of expression, taking joy in seeing just how much could be conveyed by the smallest of indications. This cultural ideal expressed itself in their conversation no less than their writing. In his "Life of Lycurgus," Plutarch describes how Spartan children were educated to "comprehend much matter of thought in few words." Therefore, "as their swords were short and sharp, so, it seems to me, were their sayings. They reach the point and arrest the attention of the hearers better than any."[52] Yet not just the Spartans in Laconia, but the classics in general, were famously laconic. Thus, even apart from the issue of leisure, the marked classical taste for refined understatement would have made classical audiences naturally receptive to the idea of pedagogical esotericism in a way that modern readers—lacking this taste—clearly are not.

Furthermore, having a taste for literary subtlety and having grown up with a literature that practiced it, ancient readers would have learned the rudiments of esoteric reading almost along with the art of reading itself. They were socialized into a laconic culture. Thus, the burden imposed by esoteric interpretation would have impressed them as less onerous as well as less distasteful than it does contemporary readers, who have grown up, as it were, esoteric illiterates.

ESOTERICISM VS. THE MODERN IDEAS OF PROGRESS AND PUBLICATION

But it is not only the pressure of unread books, the disappearance of a leisured culture of aristocratic understatement, and the want of socialization in esoteric ways that make us view pedagogical esotericism as so burdensome and thus improbable. Crucially important is also the central role played by the idea of progress in the shaping of modern intellectual life.

The idea of progress, which today seems almost too obvious to explain, holds that human knowledge tends continually to advance because each generation can build on the achievements of the preceding one. Yet there is an unstated presupposition here regarding the matter of transmission. Faith in progress is based on the (very un-Socratic) assumption that wisdom or knowledge can be not only taught but "published" in the modern sense: written down in books in such a way as to be easily and genuinely appropriated, so that the next generation, after a brief period of learning, can begin where the previous one left off.

A second, related assumption of modern progress-philosophy is that intellectual production functions in essentially the same way as economic production: the progress of both results from "teamwork," from the division of labor or specialization within a group. And just as the essential precondition of the economic division of labor is exchange, so the precondition of intellectual specialization is the efficient exchange of knowledge—through publication.

In the modern period, the whole enterprise of philosophy and science has been organized around this idea of progress. The pursuit of knowledge has become uniquely "socialized," become a team effort, a collective undertaking, both across generations and across individuals within a single generation. This has affected our whole experience of the intellectual life. The modern scholar or scientist ultimately does not—and cannot—live to think for himself in the quiet of his study. He lives to "make a contribution" to an ongoing, public enterprise, to what "we know." He has externalized his intellectual life. His thinking has become a means to his writing. He lives to publish. Thus, the living core of this effort at collective knowing is the modern institution of publication, through which each can make his contribution and readily appropriate the contributions of the others. Writing and publication have a unique meaning for modern thought; they play a special role that was unknown to earlier thinkers, even though they too of course wrote books.

It is no surprise, then, that the modern intellect instinctively recoils at the very idea of voluntary obscurity and pedagogical esotericism: this practice and its premises run directly counter to core modern assumptions about the easy transmission of knowledge through publication and thus to the whole collective organization of modern intellectual life. It inevitably appears to us not only as destructive but transgressive, a violation of the sacred ethics of publication that is the lifeblood of modern knowing.

But this reaction was wholly alien to the premodern world, which inclined to reject the basic assumptions behind the idea of progress. Whatever may be the case for certain limited, technical aspects of philosophy, genuine philosophical depth and insight cannot simply be written down and transmitted from one generation to another. Wisdom cannot be told. So each generation by no means starts where the previous one left off. The classics had no faith in progress because they had no faith in publication in the modern sense. Indeed, they were skeptical of books of every kind, as we have seen.

They also rejected the second pillar of progress-philosophy, the division of labor. The philosophic life—the radically personal effort to see life whole—can never be genuinely pursued as a collective enterprise of specialists who read each other's articles. This whole system makes sense only when philosophy has been externalized, when the original meaning of philosophy as a unique way of life and the achievement of some kind of internal clarity or enlightenment has been replaced by a collective, public enterprise, in which each individual's personal thoughts have become only a means to his external contribution. From the classical standpoint, progress-philosophy is self-refuting, as it were, since it itself constitutes a great decline.

To be sure, something like the division of labor has always existed. In every age people are strongly tempted to rely upon the thinking and find-ings of others. And this can often seem like a useful shortcut. But if phi-losophy is to remain internal and authentic and not degenerate into a "tra-dition," then above all it must resist this dangerous temptation—the very temptation upon which modern progress-philosophy seeks to build. It was precisely to counteract this temptation that, as we have seen, classical thought turned to the use of pedagogical esotericism: by hiding the truth in the right way, it hoped to force others to rediscover it by and for themselves, without the excessive reliance upon others. But this means that the objec-tion stated above—through which we moderns tend to dismiss the practice of pedagogical esotericism as implausible because such a great hindrance to the ready transmission of knowledge—is precisely what led the classics to embrace that practice: it is a great obstacle to the easy appropriation of others' ideas.

THE ESOTERIC BOOK AS AN IMITATION OF NATURE

But even granting this huge difference in perspective, we might still try to reformulate, using classical premises, our modern objection to pedagogical esotericism. Let us assume with the ancients that the primary aim of philo-sophical writing is to promote, not the progress over time of a collective intellectual enterprise, but the philosophical authenticity of the rare indi-vidual. Still, is increasing the interpretive difficulty of a book really the best way to get the reader to think for himself? Granted, it may prevent him from adopting the author's views unthinkingly. But, as argued above, it will also burden him with a difficult interpretive task that will stand in the way of his main job of philosophizing. The author's artificial literary puzzles will serve only to mire the reader in textual minutiae and distract him from the great puzzle of the world. The most likely effect of this kind of writing, then, is to make the reader not authentically philosophical, but rather bookish and pedantic.

We have already seen a large part of the reply to this objection. Clas-sical philosophical texts were written not primarily for scholars and other workers in a collective enterprise but for the "rare individual," the person of extraordinary philosophical and interpretive gifts, who, as such, would not be excessively burdened by its interpretive challenges. And, as we have just seen, both the taste for and the art of close reading were more highly developed in past ages.

But there is a deeper reply to this objection that also points to a crucial dimension of pedagogical esotericism that we have so far neglected. The objection assumes that the deciphering of an esoteric text is a task altogether different from—and therefore obstructive of—philosophizing. It assumes that the puzzles contained in the esoteric book are purely "artificial" and unrelated to the puzzles in reality that occupy the philosopher. But this is not necessarily the case. Indeed, one of the primary purposes of pedagogical concealment is precisely to train the reader for the kind of thinking needed to philosophize. But whether and how it is able to serve this purpose depend on how one understands the true character of philosophy and of the reality it seeks to penetrate.

If, for example, philosophy is able to know the world through a deductive system of some kind, then presumably "philosophizing" would have nothing in common with the practice of esoteric reading. But if, on the other hand, reality is hidden from us by a cave of opinion or convention, as Plato maintains, and if philosophy largely consists, not in a science of geometric deduction, but in the delicate art of freeing oneself from received opinion by detecting its subtle flaws and contradictions, then the art of esoteric interpretation might well be the best possible training for philosophy. In learning how to read the text, you learn how to read the world. More generally, if the world is composed of appearance and reality, of a surface and a depth, then a book that consciously imitates that structure might best prepare one for comprehending the world.

Again, if true philosophy is dogmatic, system-philosophy that would banish all mystery from the world, then the human activity or posture of "questioning" would not be truly central to the philosophic life, and the open-endedness of an esoteric text would have no essential relation to philosophy. But if true philosophy is some form of skepticism—not the modern, Cartesian kind that is only a prelude to dogmatism, but classical, zetetic or erotic skepticism that puts the human stance of questioning, wondering, and longing permanently at the center of the philosophic life—then the elusive question-world of an esoteric book might be the most suitable training ground for philosophy.

Socrates, for example, who claimed to know only that he knew nothing, was a skeptic in this sense—to adopt here the interpretation of Leo Strauss.

For Socrates, philosophy is knowledge of ignorance. But one cannot *know* that one is fundamentally ignorant without knowing that the world poses fundamental questions to which one does not have the definitive answer. Knowledge of ignorance, then, is not ignorance; it is knowledge. It is knowledge of the permanent problems, the fundamental perplexities that stimulate and structure our thinking. For the skeptic Socrates, then, these questions (and not the eternal Ideas) are the most fundamental and permanent beings that he knows, beings that continually summon him to thought. He experiences the whole as neither perfectly transparent nor perfectly opaque, but elusive and alluring. And this experience derives not simply from the limitations of human reason but from the character of the world: hiddenness is a property of being itself. Nature is esoteric. Now, if this is the case, then the puzzle-quality of an esoteric text would not be artificial and obstructive of philosophy but rather natural and necessary, being an accurate imitation of reality. Thus, according to Strauss, Plato wrote his dialogues so as to "supply us not so much with an answer to the riddle of being as with a most articulate 'imitation' of that riddle."[53] Similarly, Thucydides's history "imitates the enigmatic character of reality."[54] A rhetoric of concealment would be most useful, perhaps even necessary, to disclose reality as it is in its hiddenness.[55]

Rationalizing the World:
Political Esotericism

No experiment can be more interesting than that we are now
trying, and which we trust will end in establishing the fact,
that man may be governed by reason and truth.
—THOMAS JEFFERSON to John Tyler

[Esotericism is] practiced not by the Ancients alone; for to declare the Truth, it is more in Use among the Moderns.
—JOHN TOLAND, *Pantheisticon*

We turn, finally, to the fourth and last form of esoteric writing, political esotericism, which stands apart from the other three as, among other things,
a uniquely modern form. The three types of esotericism discussed thus far,
while all obviously different, do not, for all that, exclude or stand opposed
to one another. On the contrary, they clearly fit together: most premodern
writers practiced all three. That is because, to a large extent, they are only
three distinct consequences of a single underlying principle: the conflictual
view of theory and praxis. If philosophical rationalism is in serious and inescapable tension with ordinary social life, then each must be shielded from
the other—whence the twin necessity of defensive and protective esotericism. And on the same premise, the gifted individual's conversion from the

ordinary to the philosophic life—from one side of a fundamental opposition to the other—will involve a difficult rupture that needs to be prepared and eased by an artful pedagogical rhetoric.

Political esotericism is a case apart. Although it may seem to overlap with and strongly resemble the other three forms in a variety of ways, it is ultimately not only different from them but largely opposed to and defined against them. For it is an outgrowth of the opposite premise: the potential harmony of theory and praxis.

At first glance, of course, this new premise might be expected to produce the *disappearance* of esotericism and not the rise of some still new form of it. If reason and society are truly harmonious, then what need is there to hide anything? The answer turns on the crucial role played by the word "potential" in this premise. The early modern philosophers who first embraced this premise did not disagree with earlier thinkers that, within all present and hitherto existing societies—within "traditional society"—there was indeed a deep chasm between the world of philosophy, reason, and truth and that of politics, custom, and myth. Their break with earlier thought consisted not in denying the existence of this tragic rift, but in denying that it was natural or necessary: in a fundamentally new kind of society, it might be healed. If philosophy would first radically reform itself—embracing a less utopian, more realistic approach, a more scientific or exact method, a more activist stance toward the realm of politics, and a more conquering posture toward the realm of nature—then it could, in consequence, radically reform the political world, abolishing traditional society and refounding the political community on an essentially rational basis. In short, this new premise—the unity of theory and praxis—was originally embraced, not as a fact, and not merely as a possibility, but as a *project*, one that gave modern philosophy a wholly new orientation and purpose.

But ironically, this very project to create a rational society and, correlatively, an end to all social hostility toward and censorship of philosophy required at first a rigorous new esotericism—one that, in general, would aid philosophical writings in their new quest to become instruments of political power and, more specifically, would help them manage, in a safe and prudent manner, the gradual subversion of traditional society and its replacement with a philosophically grounded politics. Thus arose what I am calling "political esotericism," which may be defined as esotericism in the service of the newly political goal of philosophy: to actualize the potential harmony of reason and social life through the progressive rationalization of the political world.

With this definition in mind, one can understand the surface resemblances and essential differences between political esotericism and the other three forms.[1] What political esotericism has in common with the pedagogical form, to begin with, is that both are outgrowths of the *positive objective* of philosophical publication. Whereas defensive and protective esotericism are responses to the unintended consequences, the negative by-products of writing—persecution and subversion—both political and pedagogical esotericism grow directly from the positive purpose of writing in the first place. But on the grounds of this similarity, one sees most clearly the difference.

The main positive purpose of most classical philosophical writings was philosophical. Without doubt, they also pursued practical aims, largely along the lines of what I have called "philosophical politics." Nevertheless, their most fundamental purpose, I would argue, was philosophizing and philosophical education. But in the modern period, as we have just seen, the purpose of philosophical writing (and the whole understanding of the public role of the philosopher or intellectual) underwent a radical change. To a much greater extent, philosophical texts came to be written for (although not necessarily written to) society at large for the purpose of enlightening and transforming the political and religious world. Yet this historical shift in the main positive motive for philosophical publication—from pedagogy to politics—led not to a decline in esotericism, but only to a shift in kind. For the need to speak artfully is hardly less pressing in political matters than in pedagogical ones. Thus, philosophers' positive motive for writing continued to compel them to write esoterically—only no longer as educators addressing the philosophic few, but as political actors addressing the political class or society in general. From the standpoint of the positive aim of philosophical writing, then, political esotericism may be described as the modern counterpart to and replacement for pedagogical esotericism (although it did not completely replace it).[2]

As a result of this difference in positive purpose, there arises a characteristic difference in esoteric form or technique: as compared with the other three modes, political esotericism tends to be more transparent or easily deciphered. For it aims at being understood not merely by the philosophic few but by more general readers. It seeks to produce political change and, what is more, general "enlightenment," the gradual transformation of public consciousness. Unlike classical esotericism, which primarily aims at concealing philosophy (if sometimes behind a very public mask), it intends to be publicly provocative, even subversive, but in a measured, insinuating, and conspiratorial way.

But in being thus more open—as well as more frankly political and de-signedly subversive—it inevitably arouses a greater amount of suspicion and opposition. It follows that it must strongly resemble or overlap with defensive esotericism: it must be centrally concerned with the problem of persecution and the hostility of society to philosophy. Yet here too there is a crucial difference. Classical defensive esotericism—which assumes the naturalness and inevitability of society's hostility—is essentially resigned to that hostility and seeks only to help the philosopher hide from it or tame it in some limited way. Political esotericism—premised on the harmony of philosophy and politics in a better world—seeks not merely to escape persecution but, over the long term, to abolish it.

Finally, political esotericism is strongly akin to protective esotericism in that both are centrally concerned with the welfare of society. But ultimately the former constitutes a reversal of the latter. For protective esotericism seeks to help society by insulating it from what it takes to be the inevitably corrosive effects of reason. Political esotericism has exactly the opposite purpose: to help society by inducing it—albeit, cautiously and gradually—to open itself up to reason and embrace political rationalization. Political esotericism seeks to promote precisely what protective esotericism exists to prevent: the widespread social influence of philosophical rationalism.

In the end, political esotericism ultimately reverses or overcomes even itself: it strives to abolish the whole need for esotericism. It thus helps to create the world and the mindset in which we now live—where the whole phenomenon of esotericism has slowly been outlived, forgotten, and, at last, insistently denied.

In simplest terms, political esotericism is philosophical dissimulation in the service of a political as distinguished from a philosophical or pedagogical project. Thus, its character can be fleshed out in two steps: by examining, first, how political activity leads to esoteric speech, and, then, how philosophy turned, in the modern period, to political activity.

THE ESOTERIC CHARACTER OF POLITICAL SPEECH

This final category of esotericism, involving as it does the political use of dissimulation, is in some respects the one most familiar and plausible to us, partly because it is characteristically modern, but especially because it is political. For although we are deeply resistant to the idea that a true philosopher would lie, we quite cheerfully affirm that most politicians are liars. Indeed, a simple google search for the precise phrase "all politicians lie" retrieves over twenty-thousand hits. "All philosophers lie" (at the present moment) retrieves only one. An op-ed piece in the *Washington Post* by Michael Kinsley begins with the matter-of-fact observation: "All successful politicians must have at least some talent for telling lies about what's in their hearts and convincing people that it is the truth." Or, in his more pointed formulation: "A gaffe is when a politician tells the truth."[3] Similarly, a biography of I. F. Stone is entitled *All Governments Lie*, after a famous declaration of the renowned journalist.[4] George Orwell, in his famous essay "Politics and the English Language," explains: "Political language—and with variations this is true of all political parties, from Conservatives to Anarchists—is designed to makes lies sound truthful."[5] Again, Hannah Arendt, in her essay "Truth and Politics," flatly asserts:

> No one has ever doubted that truth and politics are on rather bad terms with each other, and no one, as far as I know, has ever counted truthfulness among the political virtues. Lies have always been regarded as necessary and justifiable tools not only of the politician's or the demagogue's but also of the statesman's trade.[6]

In short, everyone knows that the realm of politics is inseparable from spin, rhetoric, and propaganda. No one is so naive as to assume that the speech of political actors always represents their heartfelt beliefs. Their speech is always what we call "politic" and "diplomatic," these very words expressing the strong inner connection between politics and artful speech.

Thus, when it comes to the political realm, virtually everyone adheres to an esoteric theory of communication—without ever calling it that. After hearing an important public address, we turn to the indispensable "political commentators," who help us cut through the spin, read between the lines, and figure out what the speaker is really saying. He has used this expression because it is code for this view; he has made that concession in order to mollify that element of his constituency; he has been silent on this subject—so prominent in his earlier speeches—in order to give himself this new look, and so forth. During the 2008 presidential primary season, the *New York Times* website ran a regular feature entitled "Decoding the Candidates," which carried this explanatory blurb: "You've heard what the presidential candidates are saying, but what exactly do they mean? And what are the real ideas beneath the buzz and spin?" Esoteric speech and esoteric interpretation of that speech are universal features of political life. This is an ugly fact, to be sure, but one that we tend to acknowledge, not to say exaggerate. (Indeed, it may be that our disgust at the pervasive dishonesty of the political sphere is partly at the root of our deep reluctance to acknowledge any form of dishonesty in the intellectual world.) Putting philosophers aside for the moment, then, let us think a bit about politicians and their need to "speak politically."

What is the nature of political speech? It is not theoretical but practical. Its purpose is not the communication of truth for its own sake but rather persuasion and the production of some practical effect. Political speech serves not knowledge but action; and thus the measure of its success is not truth but efficacy. Often, to be sure, the most effective way of producing the desired action will be the truthful explication of its purpose and advantages. But this presupposes general agreement on the ultimate goals of action. Where this does not obtain—where interests or beliefs strongly conflict, as they most often do in politics—persuasive speech may require the use of something other than the truth.

To start with the most cynical case, sometimes the advantages sought by the political actor are primarily his own aggrandizement (or that of his class, sect, party, or clan), so he must lie in order to give his selfish ends the appearance of the common good. It is primarily with an eye to such cases, for example, that Machiavelli asserts that the ambitious prince will "know well how to color his nature, and to be a great pretender and dissembler; and men are so simple and so obedient to present necessities that he who deceives will always find someone who will let himself be deceived."[7]

But there are also opposite cases where the political actor intends the common good but is faced with a political or religious establishment that does not. In such circumstances, it is his good intentions that he must conceal. He must find a way to communicate his salutary designs while hiding them from the powers that rule and oppress his society.

In still other cases, however, the problem may be with society itself. A well-intentioned political actor may find that society is divided among discordant parties or interest groups. In order to succeed, he must put together an uneasy coalition that may require him to "speak out of both sides of his mouth" so that each party can find in his statement what it wants. The classic account is Macaulay's description of the famous settlement of 1689 in England through which a host of rival parties were brought to agree to the proposition that James II had legally forfeited his crown. Strictly speaking, the agreed-upon resolution was both ambiguous and contradictory. In its defense Macaulay explains:

Such words are to be considered, not as words, but as deeds. If they effect that which they are intended to effect, they are rational, though they may be contradictory. If they fail of attaining their end, they are absurd, though they carry demonstration with them. Logic admits of no compromise. The essence of politics is compromise. It is therefore not strange that some of the most important and most useful political instruments in the world should be among the most illogical compositions that ever were penned. . . . [The framers of the settlement] cared little whether their major [premise] agreed with their conclusion, if the major secured two hundred votes, and the conclusion two hundred more. In fact the one beauty of the resolution is its inconsistency. There was a phrase for every subdivision of the majority.[8]

Finally, the problem with society may run deeper than mere partisanship. A well-intentioned political actor or party may be obstructed by the ignorance or irrationality of people who do not understand abstract principles or see their own long-term good. To win their allegiance, it may be necessary to appeal to nonrational factors. Quoting Macaulay again:

Every political sect has its esoteric and its exoteric school, its abstract doctrines for the initiated, its visible symbols, its imposing forms, its mythological fables for the vulgar. It assists the devotion of those who are unable to raise themselves to the contemplation of pure truth by all the devices of Pagan or Papal superstition. It has its altars and its deified heroes, its relics and pilgrimages, its canonized martyrs and confessors, its festivals and its legendary miracles.[9]

The most extreme and thus clearest case of this general phenomenon is that of the great founder who seeks revolutionary changes that will lead his society far beyond its accustomed ways. Thus, the very novelty and magnitude of the public good he seeks to produce put it outside the understanding of most of those he would benefit. He will therefore resort to myths of some kind to persuade the people of what they are unable to grasp rationally. As Machiavelli puts it:

And truly there was never any orderer of extraordinary laws for a people who did not have recourse to God, because otherwise they would not have been accepted. For a prudent individual knows many goods that do not have in themselves evident reasons with which one can persuade others. Thus wise men who wish to take away this difficulty have recourse to God. So did Lycurgus; so did Solon; so did many others who have had the same end as they.

We have already seen the identical point made by Rousseau: the great founder of a nation, whose "sublime reason . . . rises above the grasp of common men," must place his commandments "in the mouth of the immortals in order to convince by divine authority those who cannot be moved by human prudence."[10]

For all of these reasons—some higher, some lower—those who seek to act within society are often constrained to speak "politically." But while this is true of politicians, what has it to do with philosophers and philosophical speech?

PHILOSOPHY'S "POLITICAL TURN" IN THE MODERN PERIOD

Pure thought is an entirely private matter. But as soon as a philosopher publishes his thoughts, he has engaged in a public action—though not yet necessarily a political one. His act of publication may possibly result in harm to society or to himself, and to manage these twin dangers, he may need to practice protective and defensive esotericism. But to the extent that he does so simply by concealing his most dangerous or provocative ideas—by withdrawing them from the public sphere—he does not, and does not need to, engage in political action. He controls the situation simply by changing his own behavior, not by trying to change that of others.

But this purely self-restraining and apolitical esoteric strategy may not be the most effective in all circumstances. Sometimes, a thinker will judge that the best way to protect his society from subversion by philosophic ideas is to alter its beliefs somewhat, if he can, to make them relatively less fragile or less grossly in contradiction with the truth. Again, sometimes a philosopher may conclude that the most effective way to protect himself from persecution is not simply to hide himself away but to actively court the patronage of some element within society, while also doing what he can to strengthen the political power and influence of that element. Through these more active esoteric strategies, the philosopher becomes engaged in politics in some degree—in what I have called "philosophical politics"—and, like other political actors, he may then find himself constrained to "speak politically." In this way, the practice of protective and defensive esotericism can shade into something that might also be termed "political esotericism."

But, as suggested above, it is more useful to reserve the term "political esotericism" for a distinct and more radical phenomenon: philosophical writings that, under the influence of the new faith in the harmony of reason and society in a reformed world, have shifted from pedagogy to politics as their primary purpose. Moreover, the politics to which they have shifted is not of the ordinary kind but a revolutionary politics seeking the rational reconstruction of social life. Finally, this transformative political project is also unique because it seeks to accomplish its (secular) goals, to an unprecedented degree, by the force of philosophical writing as such, by books.

This crucial turn of philosophy to politics, motivated by the harmonistic view of theory and praxis, can be redescribed in more familiar terms. There is a consensus among scholars of almost all persuasions that, starting in the Renaissance, with the emergence of "humanism," philosophers began to abandon their ivory towers, their Epicurean gardens, or their monasteries. They rejected the Olympian, withdrawn, or otherworldly stance of classical and Christian thought, the view that the contemplative life, being above practical affairs as well as powerless to fundamentally change them, must stand in calm aloofness from the world. They began to argue that theory can be a direct guide to practical life, if only it will abandon the fruitless utopianism of earlier thought. They started speaking less of the theoretical or contemplative ideal and more about matters of practical and bodily urgency, less about the rarified ends of the philosophic few and more about the common welfare of humanity, less about the joys of knowledge as an end in itself and more about knowledge as a means to political, economic, and technological progress. In Marx's famous formula, they came to believe that the true task of philosophy was not to understand the world but to change it. Theory took on practical aims, philosophy became "engaged" and politicized, and philosophical treatises, while not completely abandoning their pedagogical mission, began more and more to take on the character of political pamphlets and "tracts for the times."

Thus, Burke reports a novel phenomenon particularly visible in his time: the rise of "a new description of men. . . . I mean the political Men of Letters."[11] Along with these new, activist philosophers also arose still another new description of men: what would now be called intellectuals. According to Condorcet:

Soon there was formed in Europe a class of men less occupied to discover
or deepen the truth than to spread it.... [They] placed their glory in de-
stroying popular errors rather than in extending the boundaries of human
knowledge.[12]

And this new, multipartite "political turn" by theory produced a correlative
novelty, the "theoretical turn" by politics: the well-known rise, in modern
times, of ideological or doctrinal politics.

It is true, of course, that books like Plato's *Republic* and *Laws* or Aristotle's
Politics and *Ethics* had—and were intended to have—a general political
effect, as an offshoot of their primary, pedagogical mission. But they were not
political tracts, not politically "engaged." They did not take the form of promoting a particular party or endorsing some one single form of government
as the only legitimate one. Rather, looking down from an Olympian height,
they explored the multiform merits and demerits of all the various parties
and regimes. They expressed general preferences, to be sure, but these were
utopian and impractical. They gave no specific advice or commands ready
for immediate application, proclaimed no legalistic doctrine, declared no
universal principles. Instead, they endeavored to give their readers a general
education in statesmanship, elevating, broadening, and above all moderating their political views.

And as the very last stage of this political moderation, they showed the
ultimate superiority of the detached, theoretical life to the life of political
action altogether. The Platonic dialogues and Aristotle's writings *begin from*
immersion in the most urgent and practical questions—"what is justice,"
"what is courage"—but in a brilliant yet predictable dialectic they always
work their way around to the same answer: *philosophy*! It would seem that
they begin from politics less for political than for pedagogical reasons: because that is where most of their readers begin. Their initial engagement
with politics—as, in other writings, their engagement with romantic love
or the love of gain—proves to be only the entering step on a long dialectical
ladder, the top rung of which is the contemplative life. Thus, even their most
political books prove, in the end, to be transpolitical. The *Republic* is no more
a serious blueprint for political reform than the *Symposium* is a love manual.
Both books end up very far from where they begin.

In marked contrast stand Hobbes's *Leviathan*, Locke's *Second Treatise* and
Rousseau's *Social Contract*, which are not pedagogical but genuinely political
books. They are works of natural constitutional law describing the specific
form of government demanded by the universal principles of right or legiti-

macy. Such books are not designed to point to the contemplative life, which they do not so much as mention. On the contrary, they speak exclusively of politics—and do more than *speak*: they actively *engage* in politics. Publishing them is itself a political act, through which the authors seek to become participants in the world they are describing. Like Marx's *Communist Manifesto*, these books are calls to action. They became—and were meant to become—powerful agents of political and cultural change. They transformed the world, and continue to do so, in ways that no premodern philosophical writing ever dreamed of doing.

Admittedly, it is difficult to find two modern thinkers who actually agree regarding the precise ends to be pursued through this new stance of political activism. Yet beneath all these noisy disagreements, there remains a broad, fundamental consensus about their shared "Enlightenment project": to overturn traditional society—rooted in authority, custom, and revelation—and to replace it with a historically unprecedented kind of social organization, one more or less based on reason. Their common enemy was "the kingdom of darkness" (in Hobbes's phrase): the medieval world of superstition and priestly power that also went hand in hand with political regimes that were by turns too weak and too despotic.[13]

The distinctiveness of these modern thinkers and their writings, then, is not adequately indicated simply by saying that they were more engaged in politics—which might seem truer of Cicero than of Hobbes. Crucial were two additional factors. First, as just mentioned, the politics in which they were engaged was not normal politics, not ordinary statesmanship (like Cicero's), but a philosophically grounded "great politics" of revolutionary historical transformation.

Second, the daring pursuers of this project were precisely not (typically) men of political authority (like Cicero) or of military power, or even of wealth and position. They were philosophers and intellectuals. They undertook, that is, to fight this ambitious and dangerous battle with a wholly new form of power: that of ideas and books. This is something that Cicero never imagined. He was a philosopher who happened to engage in politics (or, to his detractors, a politician who happened to engage in philosophy). But the Enlightenment thinkers engaged in politics precisely in their capacity as philosophers. In other words, their new optimism about the possibility of historically unprecedented political transformation went hand in hand with a new optimism about what could be accomplished through a book (in the new age of printing) and through the coordinated efforts of philosophers and intellectuals newly united in the "republic of letters," the "party of reason." In the words of one scholar: the thinkers of this period developed "an awareness that cumulatively they were a force in the world, and this birth of a self-conscious sense of power among the literati proved to be one of the revolutionary events of modern times."[14] They discovered, as Burke would put it, that "[w]riters, especially when they act in a body, and with one direction, have great influence on the publick mind."[15] Their new politics, in sum, was not only revolutionary but ideological: they aspired to radically transform the world, not with the sword but with the pen.

It follows that, like ordinary politicians, they were under a great compulsion to "speak politically"—only far more so, since speaking was, for them, *their whole mode of action.* This is what gives rise to political esotericism in the strict sense, a historically unique phenomenon.

Philosophical writings now become finely crafted weapons in an ongoing war of ideas. In this capacity, they develop a new rhetoric: sometimes subversive and destructive, sometimes inspiring and constructive, but always artful and manipulative. In short, political esotericism, as it developed in the Renaissance and Enlightenment, is the forerunner of such distinctive modern phenomena as "ideology" and "propaganda."

Political esotericism, then, arises as part of a fundamentally new stage in the relation of thought and action, philosophy and political life. In a sense, it is the stage familiar to us, the modern stage of ideologized politics and politicized philosophy. It is the stage of the modern intellectual, that new kind of truth lover who, as Condorcet describes, lives less for the discovery of truth than the spreading of it. For he follows a historically unique calling: to unify theory and praxis.

We belong, however, to the late period of this stage, when this unification has largely been accomplished and the powerful initial need for esotericism has overcome itself and been forgotten. We need to reacquaint ourselves, then, with the early, esoteric period of our own stage of history.

THE MODERN PHILOSOPHICAL CONSPIRACY: SOME EXTERNAL INDICATIONS

There are two kinds of secrecy. If one had to pick a single word that best conveyed the essential characteristic of premodern philosophical secrecy, it would be *cloister*—the effort to create a permanently hidden and protected garden of knowledge, available only to the few who understand. But for modern, political esotericism, the term would be *conspiracy*, which is initial concealment for the sake of future disclosure. Unlike a cloister, a conspiracy embraces secrecy not as the final end but as a momentary tactic. It hides something not in order to *keep it hidden*, but as a means for eventually bringing it more powerfully into the open. In a letter to Voltaire describing the kind of esoteric restraint that he and Diderot impose as editors of the *Encyclopedia*, d'Alembert uses the familiar French expression *reculer pour mieux sauter*: fall back the better to jump forward.[16] In the face of a world currently given over to prejudice and unreason, political esotericism serves a posture not of settled withdrawal (as in premodern esotericism) but of *strategic withdrawal* for the sake of future advance.

There is a great deal of historical evidence for this politically conspiratorial character of early modern philosophical writing. One of the clearest indications is the dramatic growth and importance in this period of a literary underground where subversive manuscripts were passed secretly from hand to hand, much like *samizdat* in the former Soviet Union. This phenomenon has been widely documented.[17] According to Jonathan Israel:

> The diffusion of forbidden philosophical literature in manuscript, for the most part in French, immeasurably furthered the spread of radical thought in late seventeenth- and early eighteenth-century Europe. Clandestine philosophy circulating in manuscript was not, of course, in itself new. As a European cultural phenomenon, it reaches back at least to the era of Bodin [1530–96] and Giordano Bruno [1548–1600], and possibly earlier. Yet there was a decisive broadening and intensification of such activity from around 1680, after which it fulfilled a crucial function in the advance of forbidden ideas for over half a century.[18]

To be more specific, almost *all* of the major philosophical works produced in this period belonged to the "forbidden sector" of manuscripts and books. As Robert Darnton, who has made a lifelong study of this phenomenon, states in *The Forbidden Best-Sellers of Pre-Revolutionary France*, the literary underground was "enormous."

> In fact, it contained almost the entire Enlightenment and everything that Mornet was later to identify with the intellectual origins of the French Revolution. To French readers in the eighteenth century, *illegal literature was virtually the same as modern literature*.[19]

Similar observations can be found in other works such as Ira O. Wade's seminal *The Clandestine Organization and Diffusion of Philosophic Ideas in France,*

1700–1750 and Miguel Benitez's *The Hidden Face of the Enlightenment: Research on the Clandestine Philosophical Manuscripts of the Classical Age.*[20]

Another phenomenon indicating the highly secretive character of modern philosophy is the widespread use of pseudonyms and other methods of maintaining anonymity. Speaking of the love of glory, Cicero famously remarked: "those very philosophers even in the books which they write about despising glory, put their own names on the title-page."[21] That was almost universally true in antiquity, but in a striking reversal, early modern writers, pressed by the danger of their subversive political projects, almost universally avoided putting their names on the title page. Descartes's *Discourse on Method*, Spinoza's *Theological-Political Treatise*, Locke's *Two Treatises of Government*, Hume's *Treatise of Human Nature*, Montesquieu's *Spirit of the Laws* and *Persian Letters*, as well as the major writings of Voltaire, Diderot, and Holbach—all were originally published anonymously.[22] Voltaire, in particular, a master strategist in the Enlightenment culture wars, ceaselessly entreated his disciples and compatriots that "one must never give anything under one's name."[23] He openly favored a kind of intellectual guerrilla warfare. His motto was "strike and conceal your hand."[24]

Still another well-documented historical phenomenon that attests to the central importance of secretiveness and conspiracy in the diffusion of modern philosophical ideas is the surprising role played in this period by the enigmatic movement of Freemasonry. This fraternal organization, with its mysterious initiation rituals and secret doctrines, fills us today with considerable suspicion, not to say scorn. It represents the very opposite of everything the Enlightenment stood for, with its resolute campaign of demystification. Surely, whatever may be the case for plainer folk, philosophers do not join Masonic lodges. It therefore comes as a great shock to learn how many major figures of the Enlightenment period were personally involved in the Masonic movement. Although the evidence is sometimes imperfect given the secrecy surrounding membership, individuals strongly associated with the Masons include Newton, Toland, Burke, Montesquieu, Voltaire, Helvétius, Condorcet, d'Alembert, Lessing, Mozart, Washington, Jefferson, and Franklin. Lessing even wrote a dialogue on the subject—*Ernst and Falk: Dialogues for Freemasons*—which explicitly links Freemasonry to philosophical esotericism.[25]

To be sure, Freemasonry was a complex, even contradictory phenomenon that stood for different things in different places. But it does seem that many serious thinkers of this period nourished the hope to use this secretive movement as one further means to advance progressive ideas and more:

as an organization that might in some degree imitate and counterbalance the institutional power of the church and the universities. And their hopes were by no means unreasonable. As Margaret Jacob and other scholars have shown, beginning in the eighteenth century, Freemasonry did become an important vehicle in certain places for the covert spread of Enlightenment ideas and especially for the development of social organizations and movements dedicated to the creation of a new order built around these ideas.[26] In the United States, it is well known, if underappreciated, that many of the Founders were Masons. Similarly, "on the Continent there were two social structures that left a decisive imprint on the Age of Enlightenment," writes Reinhart Koselleck, "the Republic of Letters and the Masonic lodges."[27]

These three well-attested phenomena—the vast literary underground, the widespread use of pseudonyms and anonymity, and the important role of Freemasonry—all illuminate different aspects of the markedly clandestine character of early modern philosophy. It may strike us as contradictory that a movement cherishing enlightenment, openness, and intellectual freedom should proceed by means of concealment, deception, and cabals. But the creation of our open society, we need to remind ourselves, required a revolution—and revolutions require conspiratorial secrecy.

THE PHILOSOPHICAL CONSPIRATORS

With all this as introduction, we are in a better position to understand and take seriously some of the more specific descriptions to be found in the historical record of the originators of modern philosophy and their later followers. These descriptions—of such thinkers as Machiavelli, Bacon, Descartes, and Spinoza—point to and illustrate many of the features of political esotericism described above.

Let us begin not with the earliest but with the most surprising and illuminating case, with what might be called the flagship of the modern Enlightenment and its project of political rationalization: the great *Encyclopedia*. This famous work is what one thinks of when, recoiling from the above evidence, one still wants to insist that the Enlightenment stood for nothing if not the courageous unmasking of myth and falsehood and the resolute dedication to public honesty, openness, and the dissemination of truth. Thus, if one can find esotericism in the *Encyclopedia* of all places, it would seem that one no longer has a right to be surprised at finding it anywhere.

We have already seen that the *Encyclopedia* in fact makes explicit and approving reference to the practice of esotericism in over two dozen different articles, by many different authors, including one bearing the title "Exoteric and Esoteric." There is also an article entitled "Mensonge officieux" (Unofficial or Salutary Lie), which champions the "wise maxim that the lie that procures good is worth more than the truth that causes harm."[28] A similar conclusion is also defended in the immediately preceding article, "Mensonge" (Lie), by Louis de Jaucourt.

But there is more: according to explicit statements by both of its primary editors, d'Alembert and Diderot, the *Encyclopedia* not only speaks about esoteric writing and not only praises it, but also *systematically engages in it*. As d'Alembert remarks in the letter to Voltaire already quoted above:

> No doubt we have some bad articles in theology and metaphysics, but with theologians as censors . . . I defy you to make them better. There are other articles, less open to the light, where all is repaired. Time will enable people to distinguish *what we have thought from what we have said*.[29]

Precisely how this doubletalk is to work, Diderot explains more fully within the *Encyclopedia* itself, in his long article entitled "Encyclopedia," a kind of unadvertised instruction manual for the proper use of the work as a whole. There he claims, surprisingly, that the single most important feature of the *Encyclopedia*'s composition is the *renvois*, the cross-references, the innocuous-seeming little "see xxx" appended to the articles. Cross-references, he explains, are useful in two opposite ways. Most obviously, they link articles to others on related topics, helping to connect ideas and form a larger system of thought. But sometimes they will be used to do the very reverse, employing one article to *undermine* another—just as d'Alembert suggests in his letter. Diderot explains:

> When it is necessary, [the cross-references] will also produce a completely opposite effect: they will counter notions; they will bring principles into contrast; they will *secretly attack, unsettle, overturn certain ridiculous opinions which one would not dare to insult openly*. . . . There would be a great art and an infinite advantage in these latter cross-references. The entire work would receive from them an internal force and a secret utility, the silent effects of which would necessarily be perceptible over time. Every time, for example, that a national prejudice would merit some respect, its particular article ought to set it forth respectfully, and with its whole retinue of plausibility and charm; but it also ought to overturn this edifice of muck, disperse a vain pile of dust, by cross-referencing articles in which solid principles serve as

the basis for the contrary truths. This means of undeceiving men operates very promptly on good minds, and it operates infallibly and without any detrimental consequence—secretly and without scandal—on all minds. It is the art of deducing tacitly the boldest consequences. If these confirming and refuting cross-references are planned well in advance, and prepared skillfully, they will give an encyclopedia the character which a good dictionary ought to possess: this character is that of changing the common manner of thinking.[30]

Here in the *Encyclopedia*—*the* great symbol of enlightenment, the work most resolutely dedicated to the overturning of prejudice and the spread of truth—precisely here we see an explicit, open, unmistakable embrace of esotericism. But note that it is esotericism of the modern, political kind: *conspiratorial* secrecy, hiding ideas today not in order to keep them hidden but to enhance their future dissemination. The encyclopedists practiced "the art of deducing *tacitly* the boldest consequences," firm in the conviction that, if not immediately, then over time this devious art will "operate infallibly," not only on "good minds" but "all minds" so as to change "the common manner of thinking."

There is good reason to believe that what is manifestly true of the *Encyclopedia* was also true of the earlier, founding figures of modern philosophy: because they sought to enlighten the world, they too needed to use this new form of esotericism. For example, Diderot, in his *Encyclopedia* article "Machiavellianism," attributes to the famous Florentine an esoteric technique that will become a favorite among modern writers: slyly undermining a political or religious institution by defending it in an unconvincing way. He argues that *The Prince*, that most famous handbook for monarchs and tyrants, was secretly an effort to discredit absolute monarchy under the pretense of recommending and explaining it.

> It is as if he said to his fellow citizens, read well this work. If you ever accept a master, he will be such as I paint him: here is the ferocious beast to whom you will abandon yourselves. . . . Chancellor Bacon was not fooled [by *The Prince*] when he said: this man teaches nothing to tyrants; they know only too well what they have to do, but he instructs the peoples about what they have to fear.[31]

This esoteric reading of Machiavelli is to be found not only in Diderot and Bacon but also in Spinoza and Rousseau. The former speculates that, in *The Prince*, Machiavelli's true intention was "to show how cautious a free multitude should be of entrusting its welfare absolutely to one man."[32] And in the *Social Contract*, Rousseau states:

> [B]eing attached to the Medici household, [Machiavelli] was forced, during the oppression of his homeland, to disguise his love of freedom. The choice of his execrable hero [Cesare Borgia] is in itself enough to make manifest his hidden intention.

His "hidden intention" was this: "While pretending to give lessons to kings, he gave great ones to the people. Machiavelli's *The Prince* is the book of republicans." But Machiavelli's target was not only the throne but also the altar. Rousseau continues: "The court of Rome has severely forbidden this book. I can well believe it; it is the court that he most clearly depicts."[33]

Similarly, the account of Francis Bacon given by Antoine de La Salle, his eighteenth-century French translator, also speaks of an esoteric attack on throne and altar. Imagining what Bacon himself would have said to explain the true character and purpose of his writings if for one moment he had been free to speak openly, La Salle writes:

> Speaking to a king who is a bigoted theologian, before tyrannical and suspicious priests, I will not be able to display my opinions fully; they would shock dominant prejudices too much. Often obliged to envelop myself in general, vague, and even obscure expressions, I will not be understood at first, but I will take care to pose the principles of truths that will, I dare say, have long term consequences, and sooner or later the consequences will be drawn. . . . . Thus without directly attacking throne and altar, which today support one another, both resting on the triple base of long-standing ignorance, terror, and habit and appearing unshakeable to me, all the while respecting them verbally, I will undermine both by my principles.[34]

Even more striking is d'Alembert's assertion, in his brief history of modern philosophy in the *Preliminary Discourse* for the *Encyclopedia*, that Descartes—whom we tend to read as a detached, apolitical thinker, like a contemporary philosophy professor—should rather be viewed as "a leader of conspirators." D'Alembert praises Descartes, who had the courage to be the first to "rise against a despotic and arbitrary power and who, in preparing a resounding revolution, laid the foundations of a more just and happier government, which he himself was not able to see established."[35] The "despotic and arbitrary power" was the church (and its intellectual base in scholastic Aristotelianism), which, in 1633, had just arrested Galileo and compelled him to recant his Copernicanism or heliocentrism. Struck by this event, Descartes suppressed the publication of *The World*, his just-completed exposition of his own mechanistic and pro-Copernican physics. Instead, eight years later, he published his *Meditations*, a work ostensibly confined to metaphysics and theology. But in a letter to Marin Mersenne, he reveals:

> there are many other things in them; and I tell you, between ourselves, that these six Meditations contain all the foundations of my physics. But that must not be spread abroad, if you please; for those who follow Aristotle will find it more difficult to approve them. I hope that [my readers] will accustom themselves insensibly to my principles, and will come to recognize their truth, before perceiving that they destroy those of Aristotle.[36]

Speaking from the other side of the barricades, George Berkeley makes comparable claims about the conspiratorial role of Spinoza:

> Spinoza [is] the great leader of our modern infidels, in whom are to be found many schemes and notions much admired and followed of late years:—such as undermining religion under the pretence of vindicating and explaining it.[37]

Bayle conveys a similar idea in the definition he gives of a "Spinozist": "One calls Spinozist all those who hardly have any religion, and who do not hide this fact very much."[38] What is definitive in this definition is not that the Spinozists have little religion or that they hide this fact—which was common enough among premodern thinkers—but that they do not hide it *very much*. As political esotericists, the Spinozists sought to spread what they were hiding as widely as they dared in furtherance of a political agenda. This aspect of modern thought and writing—and its marked departure from premodern ways—is also indicated by Edmund Burke:

> Boldness formerly was not the character of atheists as such. They were even of a character nearly the reverse; they were formerly like the old Epicureans, rather an unenterprising race. But of late they are grown active, designing, turbulent, and seditious. They are sworn enemies to kings, nobility, and priesthood.[39]

Condorcet also gives a vivid description of how modern thinkers—here, from the late seventeenth century and early eighteenth—consciously deployed a cunning and multiform political esotericism to carry forward the philosophic cabal against throne and altar.

> In England, Collins and Bolingbroke; in France Bayle, Fontenelle, Voltaire, Montesquieu and the schools formed by these celebrated men, fought on the side of reason, employing by turns all the arms that erudition, philosophy, wit, and literary talent can furnish to reason; using every tone, employing every form from humor to pathos, from the most learned and vast compilation to the novel or pamphlet of the day; *covering the truth with a veil to spare eyes too weak, and leaving others the pleasure of divining it*; sometimes skillfully caressing prejudices, the more effectively to attack them; almost never threatening them, and then never several at one time, nor ever one in its entirety; sometimes consoling the enemies of reason in seeming not to want more than a semi-tolerance in religion and a semi-liberty in politics; sparing despotism when it combated the absurdities of religion and religion when it rose against tyranny; attacking these two scourges in their principles, even when they seemed merely to oppose their more revolting or ridiculous abuses, and striking these deadly trees at their roots, when they seemed to limit themselves to pruning away a few stray branches; sometimes teaching the friends of liberty that superstition, which covers despotism with an impenetrable shield, is the first victim that they must burn, the first chain that they must break; sometimes, to the contrary, denouncing religion to the despots as the true enemy of their power, and frightening them with a picture of its hypocritical plots and its sanguinary furies; but always united in order to vindicate the independence of reason and the freedom of the press as the right and the salvation of the human race; rising up with indefatigable energy against all the crimes of fanaticism and of tyranny.[40]

As this remarkable statement testifies—in perfect agreement with the preceding ones—the early modern philosophers saw themselves as fellow conspirators in a great war of ideas. And with this war in mind, they rethought, from a highly political and strategic point of view, all the old questions of rhetoric and literary form. Some found it useful to write philosophic treatises, others novels, pamphlets, dictionaries, plays, and encyclopedias. But virtually all found it necessary—in the very pursuit of popular enlightenment and freedom of speech—to employ a tactical esotericism. Being opposed in principle to virtually all existing authorities both political and religious, they were not strong enough—or reckless enough—to declare their true beliefs openly and all at once. They had to pick their fights carefully. They had to forge temporary alliances with one enemy to undermine the other. They needed to hide the full extent of their aims, speaking often of reform while secretly pursuing radical change. And they had to manage the truth, releasing it into the world in measured doses, so that it would be useful and not dangerous to themselves and others.

Some indication of how widespread esotericism was during the modern period can be gleaned from the letter—quoted once before—from Diderot to François Hemsterhuis concerning the latter's somewhat clumsy use of the technique: "You are one example among many others where intolerance has constrained the truth and dressed philosophy in a clown suit. . . . I know *only one modern author* who spoke clearly and without detours; but he is hardly known."[41] The statement of Rousseau is also worth repeating. Notwithstanding his famous outspokenness and his romantic sanctification of sincerity, he explicitly affirms that his own philosophical project demanded artful caution and esoteric insinuation:

> Having so many interests to contest, so many prejudices to conquer, and
> so many harsh things to state, in the very interest of my readers, I believed
> I ought to be careful of their pusillanimity in some way and let them per-
> ceive only gradually what I had to say to them. . . . Some precautions were
> thus at first necessary for me, and it is in order to be able to make every-
> thing understood that I did not wish to say everything. It was only *gradually*
> and always *for few readers* that I developed my ideas. It is not myself that I
> treated carefully, but the truth, so as to get it across more surely and make
> it more useful. I have often taken great pains to try to put into a sentence,
> a line, a word tossed off as if by chance the result of a long sequence of re-
> flections. Often, most of my readers must have found my discourses badly
> connected and almost entirely rambling, for lack of perceiving the trunk of
> which I showed them only the branches. But that was enough for those who
> know how to understand, and I have never wanted to speak to the others.[42]

This is a classic confession of political esotericism, above all in Rousseau's assertion that he hid the truth as a means to "get it across more surely and make it more useful."

In this connection, consider also a letter written in 1770 to a friend by the abbé Galiani, the Italian diplomat and political economist, on the subject of his principal work, *Dialogues on the Grain Trade*.

> You tell me first, that after the reading of my book, you are hardly any further along concerning the heart of the question. How by the devil! You who are of Diderot's sect and mine, do you not read the white [spaces] of works? Certainly, those who read only the black of a writing will not have seen anything decisive in my book; but you, read the white, read *what I did not write and what is there nonetheless*; and then you will find it.[43]

Galiani is clearly surprised and indignant that his correspondent could be so witless as not to understand the necessity of reading him esoterically. He takes for granted that this is something that an intelligent person of the time should understand.

Helvétius affords still another example. Diderot, in his late essay *Refutation of the work of Helvétius entitled Of Man*, describes Helvétius's esoteric caution. While Diderot is, as we have seen, certainly in favor of such restraint, he finds Helvétius's caution excessive and cowardly.

> Everywhere where the author speaks of religion he substitutes the word popery [*papisme*] for Christianity. Thanks to this pusillanimous circumspection, posterity, not knowing what his true sentiments were, will say: "What? This man who was so cruelly persecuted for his freedom of thought, believed in the trinity, Adam's sin, and the incarnation!" For these dogmas are in all Christian sects. . . . It is thus that the fear one has of priests has ruined, ruins, and will ruin all works of philosophy . . . and has introduced into modern works a mixture of unbelief and superstition that disgusts.[44]

In this account, Diderot corroborates the claim made by Condorcet in the long passage quoted above that one esoteric technique frequently used by modern writers is to put forward a daring, reformist agenda to conceal an even more radical agenda. Helvétius pretends to be an intrepid religious reformer who, accepting the central dogmas of Christianity, opposes only the corrupt institution of papal authority—when in fact he opposes Christianity as such. Indeed, according to Diderot, modern philosophical works are generally characterized by an esoteric mixture of unbelief and insincere "superstition."

As a last illustration, let us consider the striking case of Fra Paolo Sarpi (1552–1623), the Italian statesman, Servite friar, close friend of Galileo, and one of the greatest historians of the early modern period. Once a major figure, known and read throughout Europe, Sarpi has since fallen into obscurity. During his lifetime and long after, there was a great deal of uncertainty regarding the principles or purposes underlying his actions and writings. At times, he seemed an orthodox Catholic, serving as the state theologian of the Republic of Venice and twice recommended for a bishopric. Yet in other respects, he appeared to be a Catholic reformer, part of the Counter-Reformation, as, for example, in his major writing, *History of the Council of Trent*, which is essentially an attack on papal absolutism. Yet there were also persistent rumors that he was a secret Protestant, rumors fed by the fact that, in various ways, he sought to aid the establishment of a Protestant church in Venice and even to encourage the Protestant powers to invade Italy.

The solution to the puzzle of Sarpi's motives might have gone to the grave with him were it not for the fact that his secret diaries or notebooks, his *Pensieri*, somehow found their way into the Venetian archives where they were preserved, although they were not published in a complete edition until 1969. In these notebooks, one discovers that if Sarpi's true beliefs and motives always seemed somehow hidden, that was no accident. He writes:

> Never lightly let slip a word against common opinion, but keep "verba in tua potestate" [words in your power], to which end "minimum cum aliis loqui, plurimum secum" [speak as little as possible with others; as much as possible with oneself]; and if you can stay masked in this way with all, *do not let anyone see your face.*[45]

His true face was eventually espied by Lord Acton, who seems to have been the only historian to have found and read the complete *Pensieri* in the Venetian archives prior to their publication a century later. In an essay on Sarpi written in 1867, Acton reports:

> Judaism and Christianity, Catholicism and Protestantism, are forms of speculation which he tries to explain by human causes . . . studying them as phenomena with less interest than Schelling or Comte — without passion, but without approbation or any degree of assent. . . . It is now certain he despised the doctrines which he taught, and scoffed at the mysteries

which it was his office to celebrate. Therefore, his writings must have been composed in order to injure, not to improve, the religion he professed to serve.[46]

Acton's judgment has been confirmed and elaborated by David Wootton, author of the definitive study of Sarpi and his *Pensieri*. The secret notebooks disclose, according to Wootton, that Sarpi was not only a nonbeliever, and not only a firm critic of the baneful political consequences of Christianity, but an adherent of the view—almost one hundred years before Bayle first made a public statement of it—that a well-ordered polity could be secular, that society could dispense altogether with religious support. This belief gave to Sarpi's atheism and to his secrecy the telltale conspiratorial character of modern political esotericism. As Wootton puts it:

> Like other unbelievers of his day Sarpi had to confine knowledge of his unbelief to a small circle of personal intimates, but unlike most of them Sarpi sought to employ his public avowal of faith not merely as a passive defense against persecution but also as a shield behind which he could advance the cause of irreligion.[47]

His secrecy was not only defensive but conspiratorial.

From the *Pensieri*, Wootton is also able to reconstruct the basic strategy that Sarpi followed in seeking to further this cause. In that writing, Sarpi explores what Wootton calls a "theory of propaganda": systematic reflections on how to go about weakening prevailing beliefs and introducing new ones. We have already seen the crucial first step: "do not let anyone see your face." A frontal attack on prevailing errors along with a plain statement of the truth will rarely succeed, Sarpi maintains. Prejudices and superstitions are rooted in needs and weaknesses that cannot be cured overnight. Thus, a more oblique approach is preferable.

First, one should attack the fundamental principles that underlie prevailing views, without spelling out what would follow from these attacks. Slowly, over time, this will have its desired effect—a thought common to many of the thinkers quoted above.

Second, one can weaken prevailing errors by using the force of other, popular but countervailing errors. To illustrate this second point, Wootton instances the most puzzling aspect of Sarpi's career, his strange but unmistakable campaign to increase the presence and power of Protestantism in

Italy and Venice. From the *Pensieri*, it is perfectly clear that this did not stem from a genuine commitment to the Protestant faith. Rather, Wootton argues, it must be understood as a scheme "to see Catholic power counterbalanced by Protestant power." Sarpi "became convinced of the need to employ the same weapons as the enemy, to fight religion with religion."[48] Specifically:

> The religious conflicts in France had led, after all, to the growth of the *politique* movement [which sought a more secular society to eliminate religious strife] and, it was generally held, to the spread of moral atheism. Might not religious conflict of this sort be a necessary precondition for the establishment of a secular society?[49]

This indeed is the very argument most often advanced by present-day historians to explain the evolution of liberal or secular regimes in the West: the rise of religious conflict in the wake of the Reformation created the political necessity for a religiously neutral politics. But almost all historians regard this concatenation of events as an accidental one, unintended by the actors involved. It now appears, however, that Sarpi at least embraced this historical dynamic as a conscious strategy.

The case of Paolo Sarpi, then, is particularly revealing on a number of counts. Thanks to his *Pensieri*, we have a direct personal confession that not only acknowledges his practice of political esotericism, but also justifies this practice as an evident strategic necessity. What is more, with Sarpi, we are able to view some of the concrete content of that esotericism. Specifically, we see an illustration of the claim, made above by Condorcet, that modern philosophic writers were not merely reserved, but manipulative and conspiratorial, full of political calculation—for example, forging temporary alliances with one enemy to counter another. They not only hid their genuine beliefs and goals, but often gave intellectual support to existing movements or forces with which they disagreed as part of a long-term strategy for promoting their true aims.

There is much evidence, in sum, for the explicit claims of Toland, Diderot, and others that a vigorous esotericism was practiced by virtually all the early modern philosophers and that this esotericism was uniquely "political"—not only in its ultimate motives or ends, but in the conspiratorial and manipulative character of its means.

THE EARLY MODERN ATTITUDE TOWARD ESOTERICISM: INCREASING OPENNESS—AND HOSTILITY

Now that we have seen the basic details of political esotericism, it would be interesting as well as useful to follow the story at some greater length. This would make possible a fuller contrast with classical esotericism, further clarifying both. But also, in the unfolding story of political esotericism, we will find a convergence of the two basic topics of this book: the "existence question" concerning the historical reality of esotericism and the "reception question" concerning the denial of this reality in late modernity. In exploring the history of this new form of esotericism we will see that it necessarily brings with it fundamental changes in attitude toward the older forms and indeed toward esotericism as such, culminating in our own state of forgetting.

The first change in attitude toward esotericism that one detects in early modernity is a general increase in openness. Philosophers in this period not only continue to write and read esoterically but also now begin to *write about* esotericism with a new frequency and candor. There is the extensive treatment of the subject in the *Encyclopedia*, for example, as well as the treatise-length discussions in Toland's and Warburton's influential writings—and all of these appeared within a thirty-year period (1720–51).[50] To be sure, here and there in the classical and medieval worlds, there is a protracted discussion of it—in Maimonides, for example, and especially Clement of Alexandria. But in this modern period, esotericism now becomes a relatively sustained theme of public discussion. We need to ask what it is about political esotericism that should lead to this new openness.

But this first change also enables us to glimpse a second one. Peering through the window that this new, freer discussion opens up, one is able to discern a second, strangely countervailing shift in attitude: a more negative assessment of esotericism. This applies, initially, to premodern esotericism, both defensive and especially protective. But also, one detects in many of the practitioners of the new, political esotericism a considerable ambivalence toward their own esotericism. Thus, somehow the rise of political esotericism also contributed to the unique hostility toward all forms of esotericism that developed in later modernity.

When we put these two changes in attitude together, the issue that it remains for us to explore is this: how is it that the modern period embraces a sudden new public openness concerning esotericism and yet, shortly thereafter, it displays an increased hostility toward it as well, culminating, in our own time, with the angry denial that it has ever existed?

THE INCREASED OPENNESS REGARDING
ESOTERICISM IN EARLY MODERNITY

Thus far we have focused more or less exclusively in this work on the question: what motives led philosophers to write esoterically? But the issue of openness falls under the heading of a different question: what motives have led them to write about esotericism, to openly discuss the phenomenon and not just quietly to practice it? So let us first explore these latter motives in a general way before turning to our specific question: why, in the early modern period, did these motives suddenly lead philosophers to a much greater openness about esotericism?

Why Write about Esotericism:
Practical and Theoretical Motives

Not surprisingly, there are a number of different reasons for speaking about esotericism, but they all may be placed into the two broad categories of "practical" and "theoretical." Esoteric writers who speak with some openness about the practice of esotericism do so for practical reasons when they hope thereby to make their own esoteric communication more practically effective, that is, more successful in the delicate esoteric effort to convey a teaching while also concealing it. By contrast, they speak openly for theoretical reasons when they emphasize the historical practice of esotericism in order to make a theoretical point about the history of philosophy. The practical motive is found, in one degree or another, at all times; whereas the theoretical motive seems to be unique to the modern period.

For examples of the practical motive, consider first Lucretius, who openly explains, in *On the Nature of Things*, that he has covered his true doctrine, so bitter at first tasting, with a sweet poetic surface; or consider Montesquieu, who declares in the front matter to *The Persian Letters* that his seemingly rambling, epistolary novel is bound together "by a chain that is secret and, in some manner, unknown." Presumably, these authors engage in these "open discussions" of esotericism (very limited as they may be) motivated by the practical desire to alert intelligent readers that it is necessary here to read between the lines and to give these readers some very general hint about how to do so.[51] They use such discussions, in other words, as one means to make needed adjustments—fine tuning—to achieve just the right level of concealment and disclosure in their writings.

In Maimonides, as is well known, one finds perhaps the most extensive and elaborate discussion by an author of his own esotericism. In the general introduction to the *Guide of the Perplexed* and the introduction to the third part, he proclaims loudly and in unmistakable terms that his book—as well as the Bible, which it is an effort to interpret—is a highly esoteric text. He also explains some of the reasons for this manner of writing and even goes so far as to give the reader some lessons on how to read esoterically—all without openly revealing, of course, the secret teaching itself.

Maimonides is perfectly—indeed painfully—aware that his great openness regarding esotericism is new and potentially harmful (because too revealing), and he endeavors to justify it by stating his motives. These turn out, again, to be what I am calling "practical"—indeed, essentially a more extreme version of the motive just seen in Lucretius and Montesquieu. He was faced by a crisis situation, he explains, in which the true esoteric teaching and manner of reading were in danger of being completely lost. The exile of the Jewish people and their subjection to alien ways and doctrines over many centuries had finally produced a condition in which "the knowledge of the matter has ceased to exist in the entire religious community, so that nothing great or small remains of it."[52] He believed that under these particular historical circumstances, it became a practical necessity to restore, through an unusually explicit discussion, the lost awareness of esotericism.[53]

For a last example, consider the *Nicomachean Ethics*, where Aristotle, in his lengthy discussion of hedonism (previously quoted), not only reveals that certain earlier writers on the subject wrote esoterically but even openly discloses their secret. Without naming names, he asserts that some of the philosophers who argue that pleasure is altogether base do not really believe their claims but speak this way because

> they suppose it to be better with a view to our life to declare that pleasure is among the base things, even if it is not. For the many, they suppose, tend toward it and are in fact enslaved to pleasure. Hence one ought to lead them toward its contrary, since in this way they might arrive at the middle.[54]

Aristotle's reason for engaging in this open, indeed unmasking, discussion seems clear: he believes that this particular esoteric strategy is counterproductive, and so he wants to discourage others from following it (as well, perhaps, as to justify his decision not to do so himself). As he goes on to explain, people who, in their writings, overstate their opposition to pleasure are soon refuted by their deeds; and this hypocrisy, once exposed, has the effect of discrediting in the public's eyes all arguments, even the good ones, for moderating one's pursuit of pleasure. In this case, then, the motive for discussing esotericism remains practical, but its aim is not to inform or educate readers about how to read, but to tell other writers about how to write.

But not all open discussions of esotericism have the purpose of conveying such practical advice to readers and writers. They can also have, as I have said, a *theoretical* purpose: to use the fact of this practice in order to prove some thesis regarding the history of philosophical thought. What this means we will see momentarily. But since it is a motive and form of argument that is confined to modernity, I will elaborate it in the course of returning to the question with which we began: why did a new openness regarding esotericism suddenly emerge in the early modern period? We will see that this historical shift derives from certain changes within both of these types of motives—theoretical and practical.

The New Openness: The Theoretical Motive Stemming from the Philosophical Turn to History

On the theoretical level, the change regarding esotericism derives from still another, larger change: the rise, in early modernity, of what may be called a philosophical interest in history. The theoretical motive for discussing the historical practice esotericism, I am arguing, is one aspect of this larger philosophical interest in history.

Just as philosophy in this period made a stark "political turn," as argued above, so also and closely related, it made a "historical turn." Consider the simple fact, for example, that with the exception of Xenophon, no major classical or medieval philosopher wrote a work of history. But many, indeed most, early modern philosophers did: Machiavelli, Bodin, Bacon, Hobbes, Voltaire, Montesquieu, Hume, and others. This new phenomenon of *philosophical historiography* has a number of causes and meanings, but very generally there seems to have been a new effort to derive or ground philosophical truth, not merely on abstract, theoretical argument, but also on the concrete evidence of history and (somewhat later) the immanent logic and trajectory of the historical process. The full-blown philosophies of history that emerged in Hegel, Marx, and other mid-nineteenth-century thinkers, as well as the "historicism" that emerged in the wake of their demise, are only the distant culmination of various tendencies already discernible in the earliest modern thinkers.[55]

As Ernst Cassirer among others has argued, the historical turn of early modern philosophy emerged first and most profoundly in the context of the issue of reason vs. revelation.[56] It seems that, finding this central philosophical issue insoluble on the level of pure philosophy — of speculative metaphysics and theology — modern thinkers were driven to seek other ways to address it and turned to history with the hope that this realm of phenomena might, in one way or another, be brought to bear on the question. It is in this spirit, for example, that Spinoza took the enormously influential step of originating the historical criticism of the Bible. By situating the Holy Scriptures in historical time and context, disaggregating their various books and authors, and raising difficult questions of transmission, interpretation, and authenticity, this new turn to history did much to weaken the authority of biblical revelation and to strengthen the claims of reason.

History also moved to the center of the reason-revelation debate in a somewhat different way (more relevant to the issue of esotericism) through the central argument of Enlightenment Deism: the claim that unaided human reason is able, on its own, to derive the essential tenets of religion — a single and beneficent creator-God and an afterlife of divine rewards and punishments. Thus, according to the Deists, God made himself and his commandments sufficiently known to all human beings when he gave them reason. It follows that revelation is something demonstrably unnecessary, redundant, and so very unlikely to have its origin in divine action. Thus, its origin is to be traced, with far greater plausibility, to the actions of ambitious priests or legislators who invented it to gain power over the credulous masses, perverting in the process the pure and natural religion of reason and filling the world with irrational ceremonies, superstitions, mysteries, and the persecution and strife to which they inevitably give rise.

But the Deist thesis faces a crucial difficulty: how does one *prove* that the normal exercise of human reason does in fact point to this pure theism, how does one show that so-called natural religion is really natural? It is not sufficient to demonstrate that you can make rational-sounding arguments in support of God and the afterlife, for how can you be sure that in your methodology, your assumptions, your categories, and other aspects of your use of reason you have not been unconsciously guided by what you have actually come to know only through revelation? Steeped in almost two millennia of Christian civilization, how can you be sure of what you owe purely to "unaided human reason"? The difficulty is stated clearly by Bishop War-burton, the great opponent of Deism and defender of Christian revelation.

> Having of late seen several excellent systems of Morals, delivered as the
> *Principles of natural Religion*, which disclaim, or at least do not own, the aid
> of Revelation, we are apt to think them, in good earnest, the discoveries of
> natural Reason; and so to regard the extent of [reason's] powers as an objec-
> tion to the necessity of any further light [revelation]. The objection is plau-
> sible; but sure, there must be some mistake at bottom; and the great differ-
> ence in point of excellence, between these *supposed* productions of mere
> Reason, and those *real* ones of the most learned Ancients, will increase our
> suspicion. The truth is, these modern system-makers had aids, which as they
> do not acknowledge, so, I will believe, they did not perceive. These aids
> were the true principles of Religion, delivered by *Revelation*: principles so
> early imbibed, and so clearly and evidently deduced, that they are now mis-
> taken to be amongst our first and most natural ideas: But those who have
> studied Antiquity know the matter to be far otherwise.[57]

Warburton's point is that to form a true assessment of the natural tendencies of human reason when unaided and uncorrected by revelation, it is neces-sary to turn to *history* to see what reason *actually produced* prior to the arrival of Christian revelation, especially in the age of classical rationalism, where reason reached its pre-Christian peak. Through this argument, a purely *his-torical* question—what did the ancient Greek and Roman philosophers be-lieve—becomes central for the accurate philosophical evaluation of what human reason can and cannot do when unaided.

If we take up this historical question, then, the results seem initially to go against the Deists' bold claims regarding reason and the existence of a universal religion of nature—just as Warburton suggests. For starters, the Greeks and Romans were polytheists who, it would seem, never managed to reason their way to the idea of a single and beneficent creator-God. What an extraordinary demonstration of the inadequacy and waywardness of human reason when not set on the right path by divine revelation! Even the greatest of the ancient philosophers endorsed this childish polytheism.

If, that is, you read them literally. But here is where the issue of esoteri-cism enters the story. John Toland, perhaps the most influential and cer-tainly the most prolific of the Deists, published his elaborately titled work *Clidophorus, or, of the Exoteric and Esoteric Philosophy; that is, Of the External and Internal Doctrine of the Ancients: The one open and public, accommodated to popular prejudices and the Religions established by Law; the other private and secret, wherein, to the few capable and discrete, was taught the real Truth stripped of all disguises.* Toland wrote this explicit and detailed treatise on esotericism in order to demonstrate that the history of human reason—which has now become a central philosophical issue—is not at all what it appears to be. Owing to fear of persecution, all the ancient philosophers embraced the prevailing polytheism on the surface of their writings, but beneath that surface, he implied, they rejected it in favor of a more monotheistic conception. The existence of a natural religion of reason, and thus the sufficiency of unaided human reason, can be vindicated only on the basis of a proper awareness of the practice of esoteric writing.

It is this argument that Bishop Warburton then attempts to refute in his attack on Toland and the other Deists—but not by denying the existence of esotericism, a phenomenon he takes to be beyond dispute. On the contrary, he proceeds to publish his own explicit and detailed treatise on esotericism, as part of his principle work, the *Divine Legation of Moses Demonstrated on the Principles of a Religious Deist.* In this treatise, he contrives to turn the Deist argument against itself: the ancient philosophers, with their unaided human reason, did indeed secretly go beyond the primitive polytheism of the established religions. So much to their and reason's credit. But they also secretly rejected all belief in an afterlife of divine rewards and punishments (the second essential element in the supposed natural religion). Thus, according to Warburton, when their full esoteric position is seen, it is clear that the ancient philosophers, the greatest representatives of unaided human reason, all rejected essential elements of the universal religion of reason posited by the Deists.

Yet the ancient philosophers, Warburton goes on to argue, wrote esoterically, concealing this universal rejection of the afterlife, not primarily from fear of persecution, as Toland had maintained, but rather from fear of harming society. For they all saw that belief in an afterlife of divine rewards and punishments was absolutely essential for the maintenance of human society. Thus, for Warburton, the historical institution of esotericism—this universally felt need to conceal the results of philosophical reason—constitutes a kind of official admission of bankruptcy, a standing acknowledgment that human reason, unaided, cannot provide human life (or, at least, human society) with its needed basis. Thus, revelation, so far from being unnecessary or harmful for humans, as the Deists contend, is rather the one thing needful.

This brief discussion is not meant as a comprehensive account of the quarrel between Toland and Warburton, still less of the larger Deist controversy. It seeks only to provide one example of the new, *theoretical* motive for discussing esotericism that emerged in early modernity and that led to the considerably greater openness on this subject that is our topic here.

To summarize this somewhat convoluted argument, starting in the Renaissance, modern philosophy embarked on a complex "historical turn." One eventual consequence of this is that the historical record of the actual behavior and achievements of the human mind—especially the record of what unaided reason actually produced before the Christian era—becomes a crucial datum for the understanding of human reason, especially in its contest with revelation. But obviously, the more the historical record of human thinking becomes philosophically crucial, the more the open acknowledgment of esotericism—which is needed to avoid the *systematic misreading and misconstruction* of that record—also becomes philosophically crucial. The understanding of esotericism, that is, now becomes essential, not merely (as it always was before) for gaining access to the authentic beliefs and arguments of particular thinkers about particular issues, but also as part of a fundamentally new approach to understanding the character of human reason as such. It becomes part of the uniquely modern effort at what might be called "historical epistemology": the effort to use the actual historical record of two thousand years of human thinking and writing as a clue to how reason works, as empirical evidence for what the unaided human mind can and cannot do. As a result, then, of philosophy's turn to history, the phenomenon of esotericism acquires a new *theoretical* importance that it did not possess for earlier ages. And this, in turn, leads to a great increase in the open and thematic discussion of esotericism, as we have just seen in the notable examples of Toland and Warburton.[58]

The New Openness: Three Practical Motives

But the new modern openness regarding esoteric writing also stemmed from another source: changes that occurred on the level of the first, *practical* motives for speaking about esotericism that we began by discussing. These motives involve the attempt to adjust the writing of esoteric works so that they will function better, so that they will be more likely to succeed in their particular communicative purpose.

Now, the new political esotericism that emerged in the modern period differed from earlier forms precisely in its primary communicative purpose: no longer the education of the philosophical few but the gradual enlightenment of the broad population. Given its wider audience, it no longer needed or desired to maintain such a high level of concealment as did earlier forms. Thus we see Diderot, for example, in the above-quoted passage from the *Encyclopedia*, openly proclaiming the esotericism of that work and even explaining the primary esoteric technique employed—the use of cross-references. Modern esotericism's new political purpose is clearly better served if esoteric writing is more freely discussed, more of an open secret, so that a wider range of readers will know to go searching between the lines.

There is also a second way—still on the practical level—in which the new esotericism led to greater openness, indeed to spirited, public debate about its practices. Because of its uniquely political character, this esotericism sought not only to address a wider range of readers, but also to involve a larger body of writers—and in a coordinated way. Political esotericism was political not only in its goals but in its means: it was a *collective* activity. This new mode of writing was the undertaking not simply of individual philosophers, as in premodern esotericism, but of the clique of philosophers acting in concert—a philosophical cabal, a republic of letters, a party of reason, a "movement."

But as the inevitable consequence of this new effort at coordinated action, every thinker's practice of esotericism suddenly became the proper business—the legitimate subject of criticism—of every other thinker. As is well known, efforts to form a tightly unified party with a common course of action very often produce the very opposite result: an increase in conflict over what that common action should be. The danger is all the greater when the party is composed of philosophers and intellectuals. Thus, the uniquely political or collective character of the new esotericism naturally led to a great increase in open debate and public criticism among its practitioners.

This tendency to generate open debate—inherent within the new esotericism—was then further magnified by a third circumstance: there was so much to debate about, because the esotericism was so new. Political esotericism resulted, after all, from a great revolution in thought, concerning both what reforms society was capable of receiving and what political effects philosophy was capable of producing. It represented the momentous transition from the conflictual to the harmonist view of theory and praxis. So naturally there was a great deal that needed to be sorted out and debated. The whole purpose and strategy of esotericism was up for grabs in a way that it had not been in all previous ages. This too, then, produced a great increase in the open discussion of esotericism.

The Three Primary Debates over Esotericism

While a substantive and comprehensive account of these complex debates is well beyond the scope of this work, a few details will at least give us some inner sense of this important new stage in the history of esotericism.

What the particular issues were in this debate can be deduced, as it were, from the very definition of political esotericism. The latter is the effort to write in a style both cautious and subversive, gradually spreading philosophical ideas to the larger population, with the ultimate aim of establishing a new political order free of gross superstition and based more or less on rational foundations. The major elements of this description point to the three major issues around which the esotericism debates of the period primarily raged. First, what does "both cautious and subversive" mean in practice? What is the proper mix of boldness and prudence? Second, in seeking to spread enlightenment to "the larger population," who exactly should be included and addressed: everyone or some more restricted subset of the population? Third and most fundamental, how complete could the elimination of religious superstition and the reliance on purely rational foundations ever be? How fully harmonized, that is, could reason and society ever become?

Regarding the first issue, daring vs. caution, the extreme position on the side of caution was famously represented by the French writer Fontenelle (1657–1757), who, though himself a great popularizer and often called the first of the philosophes, nevertheless declared in a Parisian salon one evening that if his hand were full of truths, he would not open it to release them to the public, because it is not worth the effort or risk. This simple statement struck a chord that reverberated through French society and literature for the better part of a century, triggering constant debate. But in the end, it seems to have represented for most, even for Fontenelle himself, not so much a settled rejection of the Enlightenment project as a forceful venting of the fears and frustrations that everyone must have felt in one degree or another in the face of an undertaking so full of dangers and setbacks.[59]

Fontenelle's declaration reappears, for example, in the extensive exchange of letters on this subject—one of the great documents of the esotericism debate—between d'Alembert and Frederick the Great of Prussia, the famous "enlightened despot." In his most despairing moment, Frederick wrote emphasizing the unconquerable ignorance of the people and endorsing the statement of Fontenelle. D'Alembert replies:

> It seems to me that one should not, like Fontenelle, keep one's hand closed
> when one is sure of having the truth in it; it is only necessary to open *with*
> *wisdom and caution* the fingers of the hand one after another, and little by
> little the hand is opened entirely.... Philosophers who open the hand too
> abruptly are fools.[60]

As a general statement, d'Alembert's sober reply would seem to represent
the almost unanimous consensus among early modern thinkers. Unsurpris-
ingly, very few appear to have held consistently to the anti-enlightenment
statement of Fontenelle. But even more clearly, there was no "Fontenelle" on
the other side: no one who openly rejected the need for "wisdom and caution," for esoteric restraint, in revealing the truth. (Perhaps Holbach came
closest, as Diderot suggests.) Virtually everyone agreed that "philosophers
who open the hand too abruptly are fools." But this general agreement still
left undetermined the particular question of what constituted, in each individual case, the right degree of caution and daring. And this question, a difficult judgment call, became a source of constant discussion and dispute.

The clearest example of an accusation of incaution, indeed of reckless-
ness, comes from an earlier period: Erasmus's reaction to Luther's writings.
While he supports the latter's ends, the radical reform of Christianity, he is
appalled by the incaution of Luther's means. As he explains in a letter:

> For seeing that truth of itself has a bitter taste for most people, and that it
> is of itself a subversive thing to uproot what has long been commonly ac-
> cepted, it would have been wiser to soften a naturally painful subject by
> the courtesy of one's handling than to pile one cause of hatred on another.
> ... *A prudent steward will husband the truth*—bring it out, I mean, when the
> business requires it and bring it out so much as is requisite and bring out
> for every man what is appropriate for him—[but] Luther in this torrent of
> pamphlets has poured it all out at once, making everything public.[61]

In a similar but less extreme example, Bayle rebukes Descartes, or rather
his followers, for being too bold, with the result that they generated a lot
of opposition that needlessly retarded the progress of their ideas. Bayle's
position here remains distinctly modern, since its ultimate end is the gradual public dissemination of Descartes's ideas; but he argues that the proper
means to this end involve sticking somewhat closer to the more concealed,
ancient style of esotericism. Thus, in the article on Aristotle in his *Histori-*

cal Dictionary, in the context of describing why Aristotelianism has been so readily accepted by theologians, Bayle appends the following remark:

> If all those who have embraced the philosophy of Monsieur Descartes had had this wise reserve, which makes one stop when one reaches a certain point; if they had known how to discern what must be said and what must not be said, they would not have caused such an outcry against the sect in general. The method of the ancient masters was founded on good reasons. They had dogmas for the general public and dogmas for the disciples initiated into the mysteries. At any rate, the application that one has tried to make of the principles of Monsieur Descartes to the dogmas of religion has brought great prejudice against his sect and has arrested its progress.[62]

Writing after the Revolution, L.-S. Mercier expresses a similar criticism—with a similar longing for a more ancient and concealing esotericism—in his widely read *Tableaux de Paris*:

> It might perhaps have been desirable if the idea of the double doctrine, which the ancient philosophers taught according to whether they believed they should reveal or not reveal their true ideas, fell into the heads of the first writers of the nation. They would not have exposed philosophy to the furious and offensive rantings of the fools, the ignorant, and the wicked; they would not have incurred the hatred and vengeance of the priests and sovereigns. . . . The public good, or what represents it, the public repose, sometimes demands that one hide certain truths. When they fall without preparation in the midst of a people, they cause an explosion that does not redound to the profit of the truth, and only irritates the numerous enemies of all enlightenment.[63]

These examples notwithstanding, however, most of the time, the philosophes tended to find that each other's writings erred on the side of too much caution and concealment. And perhaps inevitably, this particular shortcoming was blamed not simply on an error of judgment but on a failing of character—on cowardice. Voltaire, for instance, repeatedly attacks Fontenelle's famous declaration by calling him a coward.[64] We have already quoted, in the previous section, from the *Refutation of the work of Helvétius entitled Of Man*, where Diderot expresses considerable disgust at Helvétius's caution—which he labels "pusillanimous circumspection"—for attacking only "popery" when his true target was Christianity as such. But in an earlier work, *Of Mind*, we find Helvétius himself leveling the very same criticism at Montesquieu. He quotes approvingly from a letter of Lord Chesterfield:

> It is a shame that Monsieur Montesquieu, held back, no doubt, by fear of the ministry, did not have the courage to say everything. One senses in general what he thinks on certain subjects; but he does not express himself clearly and strongly enough.[65]

In light of these ongoing accusations, we are better able to understand a sentence of Rousseau's that was quoted above. In the course of describing his own use of esoteric concealment, he hastens to add: "It is not myself that I treated carefully, but the truth, so as to get it across more surely and make it more useful." He is defending himself here—preemptively—against the possible accusation of cowardice.

Indeed, while Rousseau was cautious enough to write esoterically, he made up for it through an action regarded at the time as recklessly bold: he put his name on the front page of all his writings. He bravely and ostentatiously broke with the practice of authorial anonymity (or pseudonymity) followed by virtually all the other philosophes and championed by Voltaire. This in fact was one major source of the considerable hostility toward Rousseau felt by all the others: his very title pages implicitly accused them of cowardice.[66]

Again, the sober d'Alembert, who is constantly defending himself in his letters to Voltaire against the latter's accusations that he has been too timid in his editing of the *Encyclopedia*,[67] in his *Preliminary Discourse* to that work himself accuses Francis Bacon of "having perhaps been too timid." For, while Bacon boldly desired to overturn the whole scholastic system that had distorted all the sciences, "nonetheless, he seems to have shown a little too much caution or deference to the dominant taste of his century in his frequent use of the terms of the scholastics, sometimes even of scholastic principles." Thus, although d'Alembert seems to regard the substance of Bacon's thought as ultimately superior to Descartes's, it is the latter whom he praises as a man of "great courage" and as the true "leader of conspirators" because he "dared at least to show intelligent minds how to throw off the yoke of scholasticism, of opinion, of authority."[68]

It has often been observed that the relations among philosophers during the Enlightenment were unusually rancorous. This was no mere accident of personality or national character (as Francophobes have urged) but an inevitable consequence of the rise of political esotericism and its concomitants: the desperate struggle to maintain a united philosophical front while also facing heightened danger arising from political activism. Under these new conditions, political courage became a crucial philosophical virtue, and for the first time in history contemplative men began routinely accusing each other of cowardice.

This first topic of debate that raged among the political esotericists—daring vs. caution—primarily concerned a matter of means or tactics. As we move now through the next two issues, however, the debate will become increasingly more fundamental.

The goal of the Enlightenment philosophers, as everyone knows, was the overturning of prejudice and superstition. When stated in this familiar and abstract way—as if these evils were self-subsistent entities—it was indeed a goal that everyone could share. But as soon as the goal was made concrete, disagreements arose: Precisely *whose* mind is going to be liberated from prejudice and superstition? Are the ignorant peasants, who make up the great majority of the population, to be included?

While concern for "humanity" was a constant trope on the lips of philosophers in this period, many and perhaps most of them actually expected that only a small part of the species could truly be liberated from prejudice and superstition. Voltaire is the clearest example:

> I understand by "people" the populace which has only its hands to live by. I doubt that this order of citizens will ever have the time or capacity to educate itself; they would die of hunger before becoming philosophers. It seems to me essential that there be ignorant wretches. . . . It is not the day laborer who must be educated, it is the good bourgeois, it is the inhabitant of the cities, this enterprise is difficult and great enough.[69]

Living prior to the industrial revolution and not envisioning the eventual eradication of dire poverty or the advent of universal education, Voltaire and many others did not think it possible that genuine enlightenment could ever extend to all classes of society. The poor will always be with us. But this seemingly economic argument is ultimately based on a psychological presupposition: the primary source of prejudice is in the human soul itself, in the illusions of the passions and the senses. That is why a very extensive and rigorous education is needed to root it out, an education that, requiring leisure, is unavailable to those without wealth.

This view was attacked, often bitterly, by the more radical thinkers like

Rousseau, Diderot, Helvétius, and especially Holbach and Condorcet, on the basis of three claims. On the psychological level, the sources of prejudice are not internal (we are "naturally good" as Rousseau proclaimed), but primarily external, foisted upon us by our political and religious oppressors. On the philosophical level, the analytic method, which called for the breaking down of every question and idea into its elemental components (which, as such, would be easily understood), implied that rare intelligence or genius was not required for clear understanding. Method could replace genius. And on the epistemological level, the empiricist claim that we are all blank slates at birth implied that differences of intelligence, too, were externally caused. Thus, in Helvétius's famous formula, "education can do everything." From these claims it followed that prejudice and error might be eradicable for all in a new, nonoppressive social order that provided minimal education to everyone. But even these thinkers (with the exception of Holbach and Condorcet) were ultimately pessimistic about the chances of ever realizing this possibility, and in practice they too confined their enlightening efforts to the middle and upper classes.[70]

This second issue points straight to the third. To what extent can the ultimate goal of the movement be the construction of a society built on purely rational foundations? If genuine enlightenment will remain the preserve of a small segment of the population, then, for this reason and others, won't society continue to require political, moral, and religious beliefs that go beyond what reason can support? Won't noble lies, pious frauds, respectable prejudices—and the ancient-style protective esotericism that supports them—remain necessary in some degree? In short, how complete could the promised harmonization of truth and politics, theory and praxis ever really become?

This issue, which concerns the central presupposition of the Enlightenment and of political esotericism, was vigorously debated in letters, treatises, and academic essay contests in the eighteenth century (although, remarkably, the debate is virtually absent from present scholarly accounts of the period). We are all aware, of course, that Rousseau criticized the whole Enlightenment project in his *Discourse on the Sciences and Arts* for its excessively broad dissemination of knowledge. He condemns the philosophic popularizers, who, lacking the proper degree of esoteric restraint,

> have removed the difficulties that blocked access to the Temple of the
> Muses and that nature put there as a test of strength for those who might
> be tempted to learn. . . . [They] have indiscreetly broken down the door of

the sciences and let into their sanctuary a populace unworthy of approaching it.[71]

But we tend to dismiss this early essay of Rousseau's—his entry for the competition of the Academy of Dijon—as the idiosyncratic and perhaps insincere outburst of a young contrarian, an isolated incident without serious historical antecedent or consequence. But in addition to the fact that Rousseau's essay was awarded the prize and indeed made him famous throughout Europe, it was preceded by the parallel and equally famous episode concerning Fontenelle. Together, these two incidents suggest that the precise relation between truth and society remained very much an open question, hotly debated even among the most enlightened elements of society at this time.

To get a sense of this debate, consider a quick list of relevant events occurring during a small slice of the eighteenth century. After Rousseau's essay won the prize in 1750, it gave rise to a long series of critiques and refutations (including one by King Stanislaus of Poland) and corresponding replies by Rousseau, which stretched on for three years (and eight times as many pages as the original essay). Also, in 1751, the article on esotericism in the *Encyclopedia* was published. Then, in 1762, the Economic Society of Berne proposed its own essay contest on a related question: "Are there respectable prejudices that a good citizen should hesitate to combat publicly?" In 1763, Voltaire published the *Treatise on Toleration*, which included a chapter entitled "Whether It Is Useful to Maintain the People in Superstition." A year later, his *Philosophical Dictionary* appeared, which contained many entries also bearing on this issue, especially the famous article "Fraud: Should Pious Frauds Be Practiced on the Common People?" This led, in 1765–66, to a long exchange of letters between Voltaire and Mme du Deffand debating this question. In 1769–70, there was a similar epistolary debate between d'Alembert and Frederick the Great of Prussia. In 1770, Holbach laid out a radical and impassioned analysis of the matter in his *Essay on Prejudices*. To this, Frederick replied, in the same year, in his *Examination of the Essay on Prejudices*. This, in turn, caused Diderot to step into the fray with his *Letter on the Examination of the Essay on Prejudices*. In 1776–77, Lessing wrote *Ernst and Falk: Dialogues for Freemasons*, his discussion of philosophical esotericism. In 1777, Samuel Formey—author of the *Encyclopedia* article on esotericism—published his *Examination of the Question: Are All Truths Good to State?* In 1780, yet another essay contest was proposed, this one by the Academy of Berlin (at the urging of Frederick, who had been spurred on by d'Alembert), on the question "Is It Useful to Deceive the People?" Such competitions played a very important role in the intellectual life of the eighteenth century; and this one was uniquely successful, drawing more participants than any previous contest. Roughly a third of the entries argued in the affirmative (in favor of deception), two-thirds in the negative. Condorcet composed an essay for this competition but ultimately published it separately under the title "Critical Reflections on This Question: Is It Useful to Men to Be Deceived?" Four years later, in 1784, Kant produced his famous essay *What Is Enlightenment?* touching on these same questions.

And all of this literary activity took place in the space of thirty-four years. That is what I am calling a new openness. In the long history of philosophical esotericism stretching back two millennia, there has never been (so far as we know) anything approaching this period of intense open discussion of the central question: the social utility of falsehood and truth.

As to the substance of this debate, the main issue, although certainly not the only one, was religion. On the radical side stood thinkers like Bayle, Diderot, Holbach, and Condorcet whose ultimate goal was a fully secular or atheist society and therefore (by their lights) a fully rational one. On the more moderate side were thinkers such as Voltaire, Montesquieu, Rousseau, Frederick the Great, and even Helvétius who, arguing that all societies required some sort of religious support, sought to promote a very basic, deistic civil or moral religion.

To summarize, there were both theoretical and practical motives behind the rise of an extraordinary new openness and intense debate on the subject of esotericism in the eighteenth century. On the theoretical level, the modern "historical turn" meant that the history of philosophy itself now became a crucial datum within philosophical argumentation. In particular, the content and trajectory of past thought were seen as vital empirical evidence for what the human mind, unassisted by revelation, could and could not do. This in turn gave a new theoretical significance, unknown within premodern thought, to the phenomenon and history of esoteric writing, since only if the latter were correctly understood could the history of philosophy and therewith human reason be correctly understood. This naturally led to a great increase in open debate on the subject.

At the same time, on the practical level, the new esotericism, being political, necessarily led to greater openness, since it needed to address an audience far wider than that of classical esotericism. Moreover, it was also political in its means of action: it was (or sought to be) *collective* esotericism, a coordinated activity by the unified body of philosophers. The pursuit of this ever-elusive coordination necessitated much discussion and debate. Finally, the radical newness of the whole philosophico-political project added to the need for this debate. As political esotericists, modern philosophers needed to settle whom they were trying to enlighten, how completely they could hope to enlighten them, and how bold or cautious they ought to be in the pursuit of these and other ends.

Before concluding, one final observation on this topic needs to be made. There is a stunning contrast between this noisy eighteenth-century debate about esotericism and the almost total silence about this debate in contemporary scholarship on the Enlightenment. The best and almost the only discussion of it I have found is Lester Crocker's "The Problem of Truth and Falsehood in the Age of Enlightenment" (1953), which begins with the following observation:

> The new critical rationalism of the Age of Enlightenment conceived as its mission the task of freeing the world from a morass of falsehood. The errors and prejudices that the eighteenth century attacked, and its own explanation of things, have been intensively studied. But the controversy over the premise itself, that errors and prejudices should be destroyed, has been neglected. And yet on no question did the rationalists assemble greater concentration of interest.[72]

When Roland Mortier produced a study of this same subject in 1969 under the title "Esotérisme et Lumières," he had the same reaction. Sixteen years later, he could only refer back to Crocker's article as "the only profound study that touches on this question."[73]

In this way, we are reminded once again of the curious obtuseness from which we suffer on this subject. Indeed, it is amazing that a phenomenon that had been debated so openly and intensely could fade from awareness so quickly and completely even among scholars dedicated to that precise period.

This reminder is also timely. In turning now to the second change of attitude that accompanied the rise of political esotericism—a growing hostility to the whole phenomenon—we will also find some of the distant roots of our present blindness.

THE INCREASING AMBIVALENCE AND HOSTILITY TOWARD ESOTERICISM IN MODERNITY

The new political esotericism brought with it, not only heightened openness and debate, but also an increasing level of disapproval or hostility towards esotericism. At first this hostility was simply directed toward the esotericism of the past, both defensive and especially protective. But eventually the adherents of the new, political form also came to feel uneasy regarding their own esoteric practices.

The Rejection of the Old Esotericism

The first half of this change—the turn against the older forms—is easy to understand. After all, the new esotericism is based on the opposite, harmonist premise regarding theory and praxis. Thus, hostility to protective esotericism is the very essence of political esotericism: precisely what the former existed to protect—the irrational traditions and myths of society—the latter arose to undermine and replace. Conversely, the very thing the former endeavored to prevent—the transformation of society through the corrosive power of rationalism—the latter existed to promote.

This new hostility to protective esotericism is on display, for example, in the following statement of Diderot's from his article "Divination" in the *Encyclopedia*.

But if the universality of a prejudice [i.e., the practice of divination in the ancient world] can prevent the timid philosopher from defying it, it cannot prevent him from finding it ridiculous; and if he were courageous enough to sacrifice his repose and expose his life in order to disabuse his fellow citizens regarding a system of errors which makes them miserable and wicked, he would only be the more estimable, at least in the eyes of posterity which judges the opinions of past times without partiality. Does it not today consider the books that Cicero wrote on the nature of the gods and on divination as his best writings, even though they must naturally have brought down upon him, from the pagan priests, the injurious titles of impiety, and from those moderate men who hold that one must respect popular prejudices, the epithets of "dangerous and turbulent spirit"? From which it follows that in whatever time and among whatever people it may be, virtue and truth alone merit our respect. Is there not today, in the middle of the

eighteenth century, in Paris, still a great deal of courage and merit to cast-
ing underfoot the extravagances of paganism? It was under Nero that it
was beautiful to denounce Jupiter and that is what the first heroes of Christianity dared to do, and what they would not have done if they had been
among these cramped geniuses and these pusillanimous souls that keep
truth captive whenever there is some danger in declaring it.[74]

Clearly, Diderot is attacking the practice of protective esotericism that holds
that "one must respect popular prejudices" and "keep truth captive" when
it might subvert prevailing beliefs. Wherever one is, "truth alone merit[s]
our respect." There are many similar statements to be found in the *Encyclopedia*—in the articles "Polytheism" and "Greeks," for example—that criticize
the Greek and Roman philosophers for not having been more open in their
opposition to the prejudices and superstitions of their day. Let me try to
spell out more systematically the argument implicit in Diderot's somewhat
disjointed statement.

The basic claim of ancient protective esotericism is that when philosophers discover the falseness of the basic myths and prejudices of their society, they should keep that discovery mostly to themselves for the good of
society. For certain beliefs are essential for the good order of society, above
all the religious and superstitious ideas that ground reverence and obedience to the laws. To be sure, these beliefs will also involve superstitions that
are irrational, cruel, or offensive. When possible, philosophers may help to
selectively trim away the worst of these. But their essential posture will be
one of silence and accommodation rather than crusading reform, because
it is dangerous to overturn long-standing traditions that are deeply rooted
in society. Furthermore, since many of these beliefs stem from the strong
superstitious tendencies of the people, they cannot easily be eradicated, and
when they are, they are soon replaced by new beliefs, often equally bad or
worse. Protective esotericism, then, constitutes the wisest and most socially
responsible public posture on the part of the philosophers.

To this, the practitioners of the new political esotericism make essentially the following reply. Society does not in fact require religious support
(according to the more radical early moderns) or at least the support of anything more than a minimalist, deistic religion, purged of all the traditional
accretions of fable, superstition, and ritual. And while it is agreed that one
must proceed very cautiously and gradually in overturning deeply rooted
beliefs, it is definitely possible to do so and without great fear of ending up

with beliefs that are still worse, because the people are not incurably superstitious. The people are taught their superstitions by the priests and rulers, who invent them as a means for control and oppression. And if the people are also seen to display some spontaneous inclinations to superstition, that too is largely a consequence of this oppression. So the beliefs and myths that are said to be necessary for the good of society are not. They are necessary only for the good of society's exploiters. Thus, the existence of prejudice and illusion is a condition that both can be changed and must be changed—by opening the fingers of one's hand slowly one by one.

This reasoning culminates in a complete revaluation of protective esotericism. So far from being the wisest policy, it is based on a fundamental mistake regarding society's need for religious support. And so far from being the most socially responsible or public-spirited practice, it gives powerful if unwitting aid to society's oppressors. The philosophers retire to their gardens and abandon the world to its madness. And worse, by their silence or exoteric support, they lend the weight of their authority to that madness, thus stunting progress and reform. In short, *protective* esotericism just protected *prejudice*—when it should have fought against it. Thus, it prolonged the age of superstition and helped to keep the world ignorant and enslaved.

The source of protective esotericism, on this telling, is a mistake concerning society's needs—but is it simply an intellectual mistake? In the passage above, Diderot speaks of "the timid philosopher," "cramped geniuses," and "pusillanimous souls," implying that a lack of courage or at least the retiring inclination to live a contemplative life disinclines the philosopher to see the opportunities available for social reform. And this "timidity" he seems to trace in turn to an insufficient love of glory. The philosopher would not only see the opportunities for social progress but find the courage to seize them if only he fully valued the admiration that this would win for him in the eyes of posterity. In other words, not only a revised understanding of society, but a revised understanding of philosophy—a critique of the purely contemplative ideal—is an important element in the new critique of protective esotericism.[75] Such was the character and basis of the attack by the early modern philosophers on the old form of esotericism.

The Self-Loathing of the New Esotericism

But powerful as it was, this attack led modern philosophers not to the wholesale rejection of esotericism as such but rather, as we have seen, to the development of a new, political form, necessary for their new project of enlightenment. And this new esotericism became very widely and vigorously practiced.

Yet, for all that, the new esotericism never became, like the premodern forms, a stable phenomenon with an untroubled conscience. In many thinkers of this period one detects an ambivalence bordering on distaste toward their own esoteric practice. This ambivalence is no accident, but results from the fact that political esotericism is in inherent tension with itself. The fundamental basis and goal of the new esotericism is the eventual harmony of politics and truth, social order and freedom of thought. Thus, it is embraced for the precise purpose of creating a world in which it will no longer be necessary. It is merely a means, a necessary evil. But more, it is a means that works by (temporarily) violating the end that it seeks. It is a conspiracy to create openness. A lie designed to end all lying. Political esotericists censor themselves out of a longing for freedom of thought and speech. How could they not chafe at the employment of such means? If they do not hate these means, how could they love the ends for which they use them? Disliking this new esotericism is the very motive for adopting it.

In comparison with this anguished self-contradiction, premodern esotericism—defensive, protective, and pedagogical—comes to light as remarkably self-consistent, stable, and harmonious. All three of the classical philosopher's fundamental aims—defending himself, protecting society, and educating the potential philosophers—are served by the same policy of concealing his thought. Thus, for example, the great "cowardice problem" that so plagues early modern philosophers scarcely arises, because if a thinker is unusually cautious and concealed, he cannot be accused of timidly selling out the cause of society, since that same policy of caution is also seen as the most socially beneficial (although it might hinder his would-be students and disciples).

Again, the premodern esotericists give no sign of resenting the esoteric restraint they need to exercise. They see it as something to be proud of. No particular disgrace or humiliation attaches to the cautious behavior needed to mollify the censors (except under extreme circumstances) because this same caution would be exercised for other reasons, even in the absence of censorship. Nor do they think that proper censorship is itself an unreasonable thing: they do not live in outrage at a world without free speech. In sum, esoteric restraint is in no way associated, in their eyes, either with the vice of cowardice or with the humiliation of yielding to brute force. Quite the opposite, it strikes them as a genuine virtue of character, indeed *the* great classical virtue: moderation. Esotericism is precisely *the virtue of moderation in the sphere of speech*: to be a "safe speaker," to keep a civil tongue that stays within the narrow limits of what is best for all concerned. The wise are properly men of few words.

Many of the modern, political esotericists, by contrast, tended to very much resent the need for esoteric restraint, even as they acknowledged the temporary (but protracted) necessity for it. *It was a policy not a virtue*—and a policy premised on the view that the concealment of truth was ultimately a great misfortune for all concerned. Thus John Toland, in his treatise on esotericism, acknowledges and describes the necessity for esoteric restraint in a world without free speech—but, as we have seen, he also rails against it:

> To what sneaking equivocations, to what wretched shifts and subterfuges, are men of excellent endowments forced to have recourse . . . merely to escape disgrace or starving?[76]

Similarly, Diderot, to quote once again his letter to Hemsterhuis, frankly confesses his use of esotericism, but still betrays real bitterness in describing how "intolerance has constrained the truth and dressed philosophy in a clown suit, so that posterity, struck by their contradictions, of which they don't know the cause, will not know how to discern their true sentiments."[77] And therefore he declares elsewhere: "I love a philosophy clear, clean and frank, such as in the *System of Nature* and even more in *Good Sense* [by Holbach]."[78]

One other aspect of the modern discomfort with esotericism is also indicated here when Diderot complains that posterity will misread present esoteric authors and not know how to "discern their true sentiments." In a letter to Mme d'Epinay, the abbé Galiani expresses a related concern about the common practice of publishing books pseudonymically by attributing them to deceased authors.

> I do not like very much that the practice of attributing new works to the dead is spreading; that will be furiously puzzling to posterity. At least there ought to be a secret archive that restores works to their true authors when the latter pass away in their turn.[79]

The point of these latter objections is this. We have seen in the long passage of Diderot's quoted above that, in his view, what pushes the modern philosopher beyond the ancient posture of contemplative withdrawal and inspirits him to risk his life to rid the world of prejudice is primarily the love of glory. But if that is the case, then the modern philosopher must chafe at the necessity to remain concealed. He wishes to be fully seen and understood, especially by posterity. So once again, we find a dislike of political esotericism on the part of its very practitioners—a dislike that grows inevitably out of the tension existing between this practice and the motives for employing it.

In sum, the new political esotericism, by its very definition and inner logic, gives rise to two fundamental shifts in philosophic attitudes toward esotericism: an increase in openness—and in hostility. The latter, in turn, takes two forms: a hostility to protective esotericism for protecting what it should have subverted, and a hostility to political esotericism itself for embracing dissimulation and self-censorship for the sake of truthfulness and free speech.

OUR RESISTANCE AND BLINDNESS TO ESOTERICISM

The later modern abandonment of the practice of esotericism in all its forms is a direct consequence of political esotericism's new double hostility, which first sweeps away the classical forms and then, in a final act of self-overcoming, sweeps itself away too.

But the primary issue of interest to us is not that people eventually stopped practicing esotericism, which is easy enough to understand, but that after a certain point they stopped believing that anyone else had ever practiced it either. This is the strange forgetting that we have been laboring to understand.

In each of the previous chapters, we have explored how the various principles and commitments of our world—our humanistic, harmonistic, enlightening, scientific, egalitarian, homogeneous, liberal, authenticity-loving, progress-oriented world—have generated a combination of wishful and anachronistic thinking that powerfully undermines in our eyes the whole plausibility of esoteric behavior. The present chapter furthers the discussion in two ways.

First, regarding political esotericism, we have seen that, on the one hand, it is perhaps the easiest of the four forms to understand and credit and, furthermore, that its own inner logic led it to an unusual degree of public openness. Nevertheless, we still find it hard to believe that philosophers in any number ever engaged in it—and for the same reason that its practitioners themselves eventually came to feel uneasy about it: it is internally contradictory. It employs secrecy to promote openness. Thus, we find it incredible that the *Encyclopedia*, for example, could have been written esoterically. To us, the idea of "Enlightenment esotericism" seems a plain contradiction in terms. What we have forgotten here or not sufficiently appreciated is that during this period philosophy, having hurled itself into the realm of political action, was indeed forced to accept the contradictions between ends and means that commonly afflict that realm.

At the same time, the plausibility of the classical forms of esotericism was also undermined by the long-term success of political esotericism. As the Enlightenment experiment moved forward, overturning old prejudices and superstitions, and (in most places) without dire consequences or social collapse, the whole premise of protective esotericism—that a healthy society absolutely requires prejudices and illusions—came to seem less and less plausible. The slow march of progress—the improvement of the world through the public dissemination of truth—slowly buried the conflictual perspective, until people forgot that it had ever been there. It came to seem that classical rationalism was always nothing but a nascent form of eighteenth-century rationalism—harmonist, enlightening, and progressive. The Enlightenment image of the philosopher—the public-spirited rationalist bringing light to the world—came to seem the only one. And therefore esotericism was never anything but the practice of mystics and astrologers.

PART THREE

The Consequences of the Recovery of Esotericism

[9]

A Beginner's Guide to Esoteric Reading

You tell me . . . that after the reading of my book, you are hardly any further along concerning the heart of the question. How by the devil! . . . do you not read the white [spaces] of works? Certainly, those who read only the black of a writing will not have seen anything decisive in my book; but you, *read the white, read what I did not write and what is there nonetheless; and then you will find it.*

—ABBÉ GALIANI to a friend

THE LONELINESS OF MODERN READERS

If it is really true that most philosophers prior to the nineteenth century wrote esoterically, then we had better read them esoterically. Otherwise, we risk finding ourselves in the uncomfortable position of Galiani's friend.

In fact, doesn't the experience that his friend reports have some real ring of familiarity? We start out, many of us do, as enthusiastic undergraduates, eagerly hoping to learn from the great and wise thinkers of the past about whom people speak with such reverence. But after some time spent reading their books, we often find that we are "hardly any further along concerning the heart of the question." While these books contain many interesting ideas and sentiments, they also seem full of contradictions, illogic, and leaps of faith. From an early age, a quiet sense of disappointment hovers over our experience of such reading.

And yet we know that people in the past report having been greatly moved and formed by these classic works. Somehow these books spoke to them in a way that they do not to us. Isn't it reasonable to wonder whether our unique alienation from the writers of the past might not be due, at least in part, to our ignorance of their manner of writing? If we were to recover the art of esoteric reading, perhaps we might also restore something of this lost connection to the past.

Still, to say that "we" must learn to read esoterically does not necessarily mean that every one of us must. Some amount of division of labor is both possible and necessary in scholarship. Cautious analytic minds will do close analyses; bold, synthetic ones will provide sweeping syntheses. Those able to assimilate vast amounts of material in multiple languages from alien times will discover and detail the historical context. So also, those with a gift and taste for close textual analysis and reading between the lines will pursue the esoteric dimension.

All of us do not have to specialize in every one of these jobs, but we all have to appreciate the necessity of each. We also need to be well enough versed in each of the jobs to be able to understand, judge, and assimilate their particular contributions. In short, *some* of us need to devote ourselves to esoteric reading, and the rest need to be willing and able to give this work an intelligent hearing.

YOU CAN LEARN ESOTERIC INTERPRETATION

For those seeking to learn to read esoterically, the first thing that needs to be understood is that there is not and cannot be a science of esoteric reading. It is an art, and even a particularly delicate one. Therefore, it is also not something easily taught.

There could be a science of esoteric reading, of course, if esoteric writing consisted of employing an exact "secret code," where the enciphered message can, in a rigorous, mechanical way, be deciphered. But such a code, useful in wartime and on other occasions, would clearly fail the purposes of esoteric writing. For if the writer is trying to avoid persecution and especially prosecution, the last thing he or she would want to do is hide a secret message in such a way that it could be demonstrably and scientifically decoded. Again, if the writer is esoteric for pedagogical reasons—to compel readers to think and discover for themselves—a mechanically decipherable message would again be completely useless. Given the long, variegated history of esoteric philosophical writing, one hesitates to assert categorically that no one has ever employed a strict code of this kind, but in general I agree with the formulation of Paul Cantor: "a demonstrably esoteric text is a contradiction in terms."[1] Thus, esoteric writing cannot be a science, in the first instance, because its very purpose compels it to avoid being so.

Even without such compulsion, however, esoteric reading could never be a science because there is too much individual variation in it: no two esoteric writers are the same. Thinkers have different beliefs, different mixtures of motives for writing esoterically, and they face different external conditions regarding censorship, the reigning political and religious ideas of their times, the degree of social health and corruption, and so forth. And even where all these factors are essentially the same—as with Plato and Xenophon, who were of the same age, born and raised in the same city, and both disciples of Socrates—one still sees a very considerable difference in general styles of composition as well as in esoteric technique.

But most fundamentally, there is no science of esoteric interpretation for the same reason that there is none for reading a poem or figuring out a joke. These are not rule-based activities—and, by their nature, they cannot be. Both a poem and a joke are ruined the moment they become obvious or predictable. The same is clearly true of esoteric writing. And there cannot be a science of the unpredictable—of indirection, allusion, and suggestion. To be sure, these are modes of communication that human beings are fully capable of understanding—there cannot be any serious doubt about that. But people understand them not by following a small number of general and stateable rules, but by the appreciation and combination of a thousand small rules and particular observations that, taken together, constitute what we mean by such things as intuition, tact, delicacy, sensibility, taste, and art.

So if esoteric reading is an art, how then does one acquire it? Approaching this question in Aristotelian fashion, one might say that, if it were a science, following fixed rational principles, it would be fully teachable. If, at the other extreme, it were a natural gift, like say perfect pitch, it would be neither teachable nor even learnable, but innate. But as an art, it is in the middle: it cannot be strictly taught, but it can be learned. So how, then, does one learn it? And the good Aristotelian answer is: by doing it.

No one teaches you, for example, how to understand jokes –but you do learn it (although here, as with poetic and esoteric reading as well, there is also probably an element of "gift"). There are no *rules* of humor that one person can or does convey to another, but only a *sense* of humor that each must, by his own efforts, exercise and develop within himself. You do so simply by listening to jokes and trying to figure them out, with others helping only by telling you if you got it right or not (or occasionally by explaining this or that particular joke, without conveying anything of a more general nature). Through this process the sense of humor—the particular intuitions and sensibilities involved—gets awakened, exercised, and honed.

The case of interpreting poetry, like that of esoteric reading, is similar, only more complicated. In the end, both are also learned and perfected by doing. But here there is a relatively larger role for teaching.

The first and most important thing for reading well is simply to *connect* with the text in the right way. If you do that, all the rest will tend to follow of its own. And to connect well, one needs certain attitudes and practices with respect to the text that can be described, explained, and conveyed by a teacher. To a beginning student of poetry, for example, one might first explain that to activate the full power of a poem, it is important to read it slowly and also to read it out loud. Similarly, one must give oneself over fully to the sounds and rhythms of the words, letting them work their effect on you, in a way that one commonly avoids doing in reading prose.

Beyond this, there are also certain general techniques, tips, and rules of thumb that can be very useful, even if they do not quite take one (as in a science) to the true heart of the matter. And these too are fully teachable. Thus, one can explain to our beginning reader of poetry the character and uses of the different meters and rhyme schemes, as well as rhetorical effects like metaphor, synecdoche, onomatopoeia, and so forth.

Last, it is very useful for stimulating and training one's interpretive abilities to have models for emulation, to observe the masters—either live or in print—in the exercise of their art. The masters cannot teach their art, but they can perform it, display it, and from this the students are able somehow or other to "catch on."

Generally speaking, these are the three categories of things that one can try to provide for the guidance of readers of poetry—and of esoteric texts: connection or attitude, common techniques and rules of thumb, and models for emulation. After that, it is pretty much up to them.

"ONLY CONNECT": THE RIGHT ATTITUDE
TOWARD THE TEXT AND READING

The most essential thing for becoming a good reader of any kind, but especially an esoteric one, is simply coming from the right place with respect to the text—connecting with it. That is what awakens the requisite intuitive faculties and, before long, shows us that we are capable of far greater delicacy and insight than we previously imagined. This can be illustrated by a simple example.

Imagine you have received a letter in the mail from your beloved, from whom you have been separated for many long months. (An old-fashioned tale, where there are still beloveds—and letters.) You fear that her feelings toward you may have suffered some alteration. As you hold her letter in your unsteady hands, you are instantly in the place that makes one a good reader. You are responsive to her every word. You are exquisitely alive to every shade and nuance of what she has said—and not said.

"Dearest John." You know that she always uses "dearest" in letters to you, so the word here means nothing in particular; but her "with love" ending is the weakest of the three variations that she typically uses. The letter is quite cheerful, describing in detail all the things she has been doing. One of them reminds her of something the two of you once did together. "That was a lot of fun," she exclaims. "Fun"—a resolutely friendly word, not a romantic one. You find yourself weighing every word in a relative scale: it represents not only itself but the negation of every other word that might have been used in its place. Somewhere buried in the middle of the letter, thrown in with an offhandedness that seems too studied, she briefly answers the question you asked her: yes, as it turns out, she has run into Bill Smith—your main rival for her affection. Then it's back to chatty and cheerful descriptions until the end.

It is clear to you what the letter means. She is letting you down easy, preparing an eventual break. The message is partly in what she has said—the Bill Smith remark, and that lukewarm ending—but primarily in what she has not said. The letter is full of her activities, but not a word of her feelings. There is no moment of intimacy. It is engaging and cheerful but cold. And her cheerfulness is the coldest thing: how could she be so happy if she were missing you? Which points to the most crucial fact: she has said not one word about missing you. That silence fairly screams in your ear.

The example of this letter and your reading of it, while fanciful, is meant to be realistic: if you really had been in this situation, you really would have read the letter in something like this manner; that is to say, with a degree of sensitivity and insight—moving almost *effortlessly* from the lines to what lies between them—that far exceeds your experience with other texts. If this is granted, what it demonstrates is the primacy of connection over technique: if only one is situated in the right place with respect to a text, one can suddenly become, without prior training, a passable esoteric reader. It just comes naturally, because, from that particular place, our faculty of "communicative intuition," so to speak, which lies dormant or rather underutilized within most of us, suddenly gets activated and exquisitely sensitized.

The first task in teaching esoteric reading, then, is to teach how to achieve something loosely resembling this kind of connection with a book. But this means that the crucial beginning point is to choose the right book to read in the first place. For reading is not a mechanical skill that can be applied indifferently to any text. How one reads is inseparable from why and what one reads.

Thus, one must choose a book that one is capable of feeling passionately and personally about based on the hope of learning things of the greatest importance. If one reads with only a dry, academic interest, one is likely to achieve only a dry, academic reading. Real passion is necessary, first, to motivate the great effort and intensity that good reading requires. As Thoreau remarks in *Walden*:

> To read well, that is, to read true books in a true spirit, is a noble exercise, and one that will task the reader more than any exercise which the customs of the day esteem. It requires a training such as the athletes underwent, the steady intention almost of the whole life to this object. *Books must be read as deliberately and reservedly as they were written.*[2]

We must feel passionately also to awaken and energize our deeper intuitions and concerns—to make full contact, read with our whole souls. Finally, passion is necessary to establish a real connection with the author of the book, who presumably shares with you this passion for its subject.[3]

But to actualize this connection, one must also approach the book with the right "tempo." Esoteric reading, being very difficult, requires one to slow down and spend much more time with a book than one may be used to. One must read it very slowly, and as a whole, and over and over again. It will probably be necessary to adjust downward your whole idea of how many books you can expect to read in your lifetime.

The issue here is not just the *amount* of time devoted to going through a book but also the *kind*—as in the difference between driving and hiking as ways of going through the world. When you journey by foot you are no longer in that automotive state of "on-the-way." There is a spirit of tarrying and engagement that lets you enter fully into the life of each place as you reach it. This is how you must travel through a book. Nietzsche describes this very beautifully in the final paragraph of his preface to *Daybreak*, a passage that could well stand as the preface to every profound book.

> A book like this, a problem like this, is in no hurry; we both, I just as much as my book, are friends of *lento* [slowly]. It is not for nothing that I have been a philologist, perhaps I am a philologist still, that is to say, a teacher of slow reading:—in the end I also write slowly. Nowadays it is not only my habit, it is also to my taste—a malicious taste, perhaps?—no longer to write anything which does not reduce to despair every sort of man who is 'in a hurry.' For philology is that venerable art which demands of its votaries one thing above all: to go aside, to take time, to become still, to become slow— it is a goldsmith's art and connoisseurship of the word which has nothing but delicate, cautious work to do and achieves nothing if it does not achieve it *lento*. But precisely for this reason it is more necessary than ever today, by precisely this means does it entice and enchant us the most, in the midst of an age of 'work,' that is to say, of hurry, of indecent and perspiring haste, which wants to 'get everything done' at once, including every old or new book:—this art does not so easily get anything done, it teaches to read *well*, that is to say, to read slowly, deeply, looking cautiously before and aft, with reservations, with doors left open, with delicate eyes and fingers. . . . My patient friends, this book desires for itself only perfect readers and philologists: *learn* to read me well![4]

A teacher of esotericism is necessarily, like Nietzsche, a teacher of slow reading in this sense.

At this lower speed, new sorts of experiences and connections start to become possible. You begin to live with the book. It becomes your companion and friend. Your interactions with it become more unhurried, and so more wide-ranging, bold, and experimental, and at the same time more delicate, nuanced, and intimate.

And what is especially important for the esoteric reader, at this lower speed the "particularity" of the text starts to emerge. For when you first read one of these books, say Plato's *Republic*, you are simply overwhelmed. Three

hundred pages of claims, arguments, observations, images, stories. All you
can hope to grasp are the most gross features of the book. You inevitably experience most of the rest through a kind of haze—it's just one thing after
another. Only after a long time and many slow readings can you start to see
all of it in its detail.

And then more than its detail: its particularity. That is, you begin to wonder—as you did with your beloved's letter—why use this word here instead of these other words? Why broach this topic now and not a different
one? Before this, you didn't feel such questions because you were too overwhelmed and also because the text was covered in a false sense of necessity.
The book is a classic, part of the canon. And the printed words sit there
on the page in all their mechanical perfection—timeless, flawless, and universal—the same words that are there in countless other copies sitting on
library shelves throughout the world. The book in all its details seems as necessary and immutable as a Platonic idea.

But when, through many slow readings, you gradually settle in to the
book, this sense of false inevitability lifts, and you begin to feel how every
topic, every argument, every word is the product of a *choice*. That, indeed, is
what a writing *is*: not a fixed, necessitated thing, but a vast, delicate web of
human decisions. As this thought fully dawns on you, you become truly alive
to the text and full of wonder at its every decision and detail. These now cry
out for interrogation and understanding. It is from this place—this connection—that you start to become a good reader.

But with books, unlike personal letters, it is very difficult to get to—and
to stay in—this place. It often helps, as you read, to remind yourself of another story, this one true. One fine day in ancient Greece, Plato, a man of
flesh and bone, sat down at his table before a clean sheet of papyrus. And
after a few moments' reflection, he chose to write a word, then another and
still another, and these words became the *Republic*. A book is a sequence of
choices.

Next, in order to make sense of these choices, one must strive to get close,
to acquaint oneself as fully as possible with the text. That, to repeat, is why
one must read slowly. But, in addition, one must read the book in its original language when at all possible. Many of the text's linguistic subtleties,
which can take on particular importance in esoteric interpretation, may be
lost in translation. But one cannot learn every language, so where this is not
possible, one should at least seek out the most literal translation available.
The last thing one wants is a translation that, in its eagerness to win over the

modern reader, papers over the difficulties, irregularities, and strangenesses of the text, which may turn out to be necessary parts of the author's design.

Since no text exists in a vacuum, it is also important to familiarize yourself with the history surrounding it—both political and philosophical. The political history is of importance at all times, since writers are always addressing audiences that have been conditioned by existing political arrangements, but it will be especially important in those (typically modern) authors who are writing for the purpose of having a major political effect. Such writers are political actors, who, as such, cannot be understood without a close acquaintance with prevailing political circumstances.

Studying the *philosophical* history surrounding the text will also be important in helping one to figure out the author's vocabulary of terms, concepts, and questions. Often in a certain passage, a writer will be debating someone without openly acknowledging it, especially if the other is a contemporary. One needs to know the surrounding scene well enough to figure these things out.[5] But it should also be kept in mind, of course, that the thinkers who had the greatest influence on the author or those whom he is truly responding to will not necessarily be those closest in time or place. If I were studying Thomas Aquinas's *Summa Theologica*, for example, I would surely spend far more of my background time reading Aristotle, whom Thomas calls "the philosopher," and Averroes, whom he calls "the commentator," than Brother John of Vercelli.

It is not enough, however, to form this vital connection to the text: one must also be able, as it were, to protect and sustain that connection against the powerful forces that oppose it. For notwithstanding the passionate desire to learn that may connect us to some classic work, when we actually get close to the book, inevitably a secondary force emerges that pushes us away. This force of resistance is composite, made up primarily of vanity, laziness, and ethnocentrism, in varying proportions. Thus, in our reading, when we come across a claim by the author that strikes us as incorrect, we puzzle over it for a while, but soon lazily dismiss it as a bit of weak reasoning on the author's part that we are clever enough to have seen through or else as a prejudice of the author's time. "That's just what people thought back then." We dismiss the author's claim, rupturing our connection, rather than doing what it is our true desire and interest to do: to strain every fiber to see if there is not after all some superior wisdom to his claim, and to search our own souls to see if it is not rather we who are prejudiced by our times.

Similarly, when we come across a passage that is textually incongruous—

that makes no clear sense or contradicts earlier statements or departs from the author's declared plan, and so forth—we are quickly inclined to discount the problem as due to negligence on the author's part, or an unannounced change of mind, or the effect of competing influences, later editors, and so forth. We give in to our lazy dismissiveness instead of vigorously exploring all the other possibilities, including especially that the textual irregularity is part of the author's well-controlled effort to communicate esoterically.

These are the resistances that slowly wear us down. It is imperative, then, to find some systematic way to *sustain* our connection in all its original earnestness and energy.

The best way of doing so—although this suggestion will be met with great resistance—is to provisionally adopt, as a working hypothesis or heuristic device, the assumption that the author is essentially omniscient: correct in all the major aspects of his thinking and also in perfect control of all the major aspects of his writing. Since humans are never omniscient, this assumption obviously involves a considerable exaggeration (a point to be discussed at greater length below). Nevertheless, embracing it—*provisionally*, as I say—is a useful heuristic device and indeed a rational expedient because necessary to counteract the even more harmful and distorting tendency within most of us to believe the opposite. It is a question of self-management. We *need* an exaggerated faith in authorial omniscience to save us from the debilitating influence of our laziness, vanity, and prejudice, and to empower us to maintain the energetic level of open-mindedness that we truly intend.

A similar piece of advice is given by Montesquieu, who, in his *Pensées*, presents his own brief account of how one ought to read a book.

> When one reads a book, it is *necessary* to be *in a disposition to believe* that the author has seen the contradictions that one imagines, at the first glance, one is meeting. Thus it is necessary to begin by *distrusting one's own prompt judgments*, to look again at the passages one claims are contradictory, to compare them one with another, then to compare them again with those passages that precede and those that follow to see if they follow the same hypothesis, to see if the contradiction is in the things or only in one's own manner of conceiving. When one has done all that, one can pronounce as a master, "there is a contradiction."
>
> This is, however, not always enough. When a work is systematic, one must also be sure that one understands the whole system. You see a great machine made in order to produce an effect. You see wheels that turn in opposite directions; you would think, at first glance, that the machine was

going to destroy itself, that all the turning was going to arrest itself. . . . It keeps going: these pieces, which seem at first to destroy one another unite together for the proposed object.[6]

But, to repeat, this whole posture, which is very much out of step with our times, will raise hackles and suspicions. People will rush to object that the assumption of authorial omniscience can easily be taken too far, leading to abuses. That is obvious enough. There have been whole periods in history, like the Middle Ages, when the reigning religious and philosophical dogmas pushed people toward an excessive deference for thinkers of the past, and this had the effect of greatly stifling thought. In such times, a very different, exaggeratedly *skeptical* heuristic device would be needed to stimulate thought.

But we do not live in the Middle Ages. We live in the digital age of breezy irreverence and short attention spans where excessive authorial deference is, to say the least, not our major problem. What is more, the reigning philosophical doctrines of our day, with their celebration of "the death of the author" (in Roland Barthes's famous phrase), all push powerfully in the other direction—almost as if they were expressly designed to flatter the forces of resistance and dismissal. So the assumption of authorial omniscience, although always dangerous, is nevertheless necessary today and precisely because it runs strongly counter to the tendency of our times.

There is also another big advantage to this provisional assumption: it is self-correcting, whereas its opposite is self-confirming. By giving the author every benefit of the doubt, every opportunity to prove himself right, one still leaves open the very real possibility that he will fail and so prove himself wrong. The provisional assumption of infallibility will eventually correct itself if it does not pay off. But the opposite assumption that prevails today—call it "authorial hyperfallibility"—tends to confirm itself. By flattering our inclination to dismiss the author after relatively little effort when he disagrees with us, this assumption works to close off the possibility of discovering that the author was right after all. If you assume there is not much to find, you will likely not find much. Thus, although both assumptions involve an exaggeration, the former is manifestly preferable as a heuristic device—as an aid to genuine connection and discovery.

But in order to maintain and properly develop one's connection to the book, one further working hypothesis is required—this one in tension, not with our times, but with the central thesis of this work. One must proceed— at least at the beginning and for a good long time—on the assumption that the book is *not* written esoterically. In *Persecution and the Art of Writing*, Strauss presents a number of rules for the responsible conduct of esoteric reading. The first two are these:

> Reading between the lines is strictly prohibited in all cases where it would be less exact than not doing so. Only such reading between the lines as starts from an exact consideration of the explicit statements of the author is legitimate.[7]

In other words, one must always *begin by reading literally*, taking the surface text, the "explicit statements," at face value. And if one is able to understand and explain the text adequately in this manner, then one has no warrant to go searching beneath the surface. But if the text contains significant problems that, despite one's very best efforts, resist resolution on the literal level, then and only then does it become legitimate to investigate whether they can be successfully resolved through a nonliteral, esoteric interpretation (especially if the author hints at this possibility, for example by speaking of the esoteric practices of some other writer). But even then, of course, not any esoteric interpretation is warranted, but only one that, as it were, grows out of the surface text and out of an exact understanding of its particular problems and puzzles.

These rules suggested by Strauss are reasonable and necessary, but in practice they give rise to the following grave difficulty. One's awareness of the possibility or even likelihood that the text is esoteric—an awareness promoted by his writings and mine—can easily undermine one's ability to take the surface seriously and to exert these needed efforts. One sees this problem especially in graduate students (but not only there). Once they learn about esotericism, they feel they have achieved a privileged perspective. They don't want to undertake the long and challenging work of studying the surface argument. The surface is for dupes. They want to cut to the chase. What's the secret? Whenever they encounter a seeming contradiction or puzzle in the text, they quickly decide that the author does not really mean it, he's being esoteric here, when some further hard thinking or historical research might reveal that there is a perfectly good explanation on the literal level. In other words, the awareness of esotericism itself becomes yet another factor contributing to the aforementioned forces of resistance and dismissal: it hinders people from thinking with the requisite energy and seriousness about the surface argument of the text.

This is a real problem and there is no simple solution to it. Certainly, it helps to be aware of it. One further thing to try is another working hypothesis or heuristic posture: one must emphasize to oneself the uncertainty as to whether the author is really esoteric, or at least very esoteric, or, at a minimum, whether this particular puzzle in the text is due to esotericism. And one must continually stress one's scholarly duty to always give the literal level its full due. One might even make some sort of rule for oneself: no esoteric interpreting allowed until after the completion of three careful, literal readings, including a full engagement with the secondary literature.

One's attitude to the secondary literature is a large part of the problem being addressed here. When students hear of esotericism, their first impulse is to turn their backs on the nonesoteric scholarly literature. They need to be shown that precisely the opposite attitude is what they especially need. For given the absolute necessity of beginning from a thoughtful nonesoteric and literal reading of the text, and given the peculiar disadvantage that they themselves labor under in this area as believers in esotericism, they are the ones in greatest need of the secondary literature that has devoted itself to this task.

In short, an important part of learning to read esoterically is becoming aware of and cautious about the dangerous temptations to which this interpretive approach itself inevitably gives rise.

SOME COMMON ESOTERIC TECHNIQUES

If one truly connects with a book, I have been arguing, one will spontaneously begin to read it with delicacy, tact, and, where appropriate, esoteric sensitivity. This is possible because many esoteric techniques—like poetic ones and comic ones—are intuitively obvious and do not need to be studied. One of the ways this intuition works is that when you suspect an author of hiding something, you start to think about how you would go about hiding that thing if you were in his place. Like every good detective, you start to think like a criminal. Continuing in this vein, I will try to describe, explain, and historically confirm some of the more common techniques of esoteric writing.

It is necessary to emphasize once again, however, that every esoteric writer is different. Thus, a more precise account would treat each individual thinker separately. Since lack of space, to say nothing of other shortcomings, prevents me from doing so, all I can hope to provide here is a basic "starter kit," which the reader will have to supplement in turning to any particular writer.

Let us begin where we left off: esoteric interpretation must start from a literal reading, taking the surface text at face value. It acquires the right as well as the means for venturing beyond the surface only if it encounters problems there—contradictions, ambiguities, surprises, puzzles—that *compel* it to go beyond. The *surface itself* must point you beyond it.

If most people do not see these pointers on the surface, that is, paradoxically, because they do not read literally enough. Consider very simply what we do when we read. We do not plod along like second-graders, reading one word after another. We skim along the words and sentences, taking a representative sample, and then we essentially *form a guess* of—conjecturally reconstruct—the meaning from that partial information. Certain speed-reading techniques even teach you to read a line left to right and then, to save time on the return, the next line right to left—or several lines at once. Surprisingly, we are able to do this—precisely because in reading we are not passive but active. Since we are conjecturally putting the meaning together for ourselves, it is not necessarily a problem that we encounter the parts in the wrong order.

This fairly commonplace observation about the constructive character of reading has an important further consequence. Part of the difficulty of this inferential process is that, not only are some of the words missing, but others, which are present, do not easily fit into the meaning that we have conjecturally constructed for ourselves. So an inseparable part of this process is the ability to ignore or wave off the pieces that do not fit our meaning-hypothesis (unless the lack of fit becomes too glaring and we have to go back and start over). In other words, normal, "literal" reading is not only a *constructive* process, but also—what necessarily goes along with this—a *suppressive* one, shutting our eyes to things that do not seem to fit.

And this filtering process is a large part of what makes esoteric writing possible. It turns out that you can plant all kinds of "pointers"—problems and contradictions—right there on the surface of the text and they won't be noticed. You can hide things in plain sight. Either the reader, busy constructing the meaning for himself, eager to make sense of it all, will not notice them at all, or if he does, he will just dismiss them as part of the standard level of meaningless noise to be encountered in every text. The point is: *shrugging off textual problems* is an essential aspect of the normal, constructive process of reading. Without being aware of it, we are always cleaning up the text, eagerly making it more coherent than it is. That is why this kind of reading does not typically become aware of the irregularities and puzzles through which, in an esoteric work, the surface points beyond itself.

Thus, in saying that the first step in esoteric interpretation is a literal reading, what I mean is a *genuinely* literal reading. This is not normal reading but something that becomes possible only through a conscious break with normal reading. One has to stop one's mind from grabbing a few words and running off to construct a meaning. One has to stay glued to the text, slowly reading every word, but above all one has to stop filtering out the things that don't fit. One has to see the text in its messiness. It is only through a literal reading in this precise sense that one can encounter the textual problems that legitimate and guide an esoteric interpretation.

Once one has become aware, through this process, of the problems in the text, the next step is to interpret or make esoteric sense of them. But how does one do that? John Toland, in his treatise on esotericism, suggests that one should look for a key in the text itself: "It is to be, for the most part, borrowed by the skillful from the writers themselves."[8] Since the author certainly desires that the intelligent reader be able to penetrate his veils, it makes sense that he might endeavor to provide him some subtle guidance. Thus, it is very important to be on the lookout for such clues, especially whenever the author speaks about writing in general or his own writings in particular. Rousseau, for example, places a "Notice on the Notes" at the beginning of his *Second Discourse*, where he declares:

> These notes sometimes stray so far from the subject that they are not good to read with the text. . . . Those who have the courage to begin again will be able to amuse themselves the second time in beating the bushes, and try to go through the notes. There will be little harm if others do not read them at all.

It is reasonable to take this as a clue that his deeper thoughts, intended for "those who know how to understand," are to be found especially in the notes; and if there are any contradictions between the notes and the main text (which there are), these should be resolved in favor of the former.

Similarly, Francis Bacon has included in his *Advancement of Learning*—albeit in widely scattered places—an extensive discussion of writing that is very useful for the interpretation of his own works.[9] Other thinkers give hints about how they should be read by showing us how they read other writers. Thus, Strauss, in his interpretations of Maimonides, Spinoza, and Machiavelli, draws primary guidance from how the first two read the Bible and the latter, Livy.[10]

Beyond this, there is also a certain logic inherent in the situation of trying to communicate esoterically, a logic that makes it possible to deduce certain elemental strategies. If the thought to be conveyed has the structure "I claim X about Y," then there are essentially three possible ways to dissemble in communicating it. One can dissemble regarding the "I," the person who is making the claim, or regarding "Y," the object of the claim, or regarding "X," the content of the claim itself. One could of course also combine several of these strategies.

In the first case, one openly states the objectionable idea but manages to put it in somebody else's mouth. In the broadest sense, you do that by publishing the whole book anonymously or pseudonymously—and no one denies that this was done all the time, especially in the early modern period. So it stands to reason that a writer might also pursue the same strategy in a more targeted fashion by arranging to have a certain specific view expressed by some character, real or fictional, from whom the writer can conspicuously distance himself. One possibility is to put it in the mouth of a child, a madman, a drunkard, or a fool, speakers who enjoy a certain immunity because they are presumed not to know what they are saying. For example, Diderot explains in a letter to Sophie Volland regarding his work *D'Alembert's Dream*:

> It is of the greatest extravagance and at the same time, the most profound philosophy; there is some cleverness in having put my ideas in the mouth of a man who is dreaming: it is often necessary to give to wisdom the appearance of folly to obtain admission for it.[11]

Appropriately, in *In Praise of Folly*, Erasmus has Folly herself explain this idea:

> From [fools] not only true things, but even sharp reproaches, will be listened to; so that a statement which, if it came from a wise man's mouth, might be a capital offense, coming from a fool gives rise to incredible delight. Veracity, you know, has a certain authentic power of giving pleasure, if nothing offensive goes with it: but this the gods have granted only to fools.[12]

Alternatively, one might put the offending claim in the mouth of a villain, again real or fictional. The English Deists, for example, would often quote some irreligious passage from the villainous works of Hobbes or Holbach, suitably surrounded with words of high disdain and refutation. But they would also make sure that the refutation came off as bland and weak in comparison with the power of the quoted passage. In this way, they sought, in the already quoted remark of Bishop Berkeley, to "undermin[e] religion under the pretence of vindicating and explaining it."[13] A like strategy was commonly practiced—and similarly attacked—in Renaissance Italy by such thinkers as Tommaso Campanella, Giulio Cesare Vanini, and Cesare Cremonini.[14] In both czarist and Soviet Russia this technique was also very common. According to Lev Loseff, a Soviet dissident writer who wrote a book about the use of Aesopian language in Russia,

> In political journalism quotations have been Aesopically manipulated since the nineteenth century by one favored and still widely used method: the stated opinions of the regime's ideological opponents, when quoted, are framed by what from the standpoint of the Russian censorship are ideologically correct counter-claims; these latter arguments, however, take such a deliberately banal form that they are given no credence by the reader and are merely screens.[15]

As Strauss points out, the broad popularity of this general strategy helps to explain an otherwise puzzling fact about the great literature of the past, that it contains "so many interesting devils, madmen, beggars, sophists, drunkards, epicureans, and buffoons."[16]

The second strategy consists in expressing a criticism openly and in one's own name, but dissembling the true target of it. In the *Discourses*, Machiavelli explicitly discusses this strategy in speaking, not indeed of himself, but of Roman writers under the empire. They were forbidden to criticize Caesar, who was the source of all the subsequent emperors' authority. Silenced in this way, they expressed their views covertly by criticizing Catiline, who had tried and failed to do just what Caesar had done, and also by praising Brutus: "unable to blame Caesar because of his power, they celebrate his enemy."[17]

But in describing this strategy of speaking about Z when you mean Y, Machiavelli is at the same time employing it, for this open description of the Roman writers is also meant, covertly, to be about himself—to teach us how to read him. This becomes clear, as Strauss points out, in the very next chapter, where Machiavelli celebrates the great virtues of pagan Roman religion—an indirect way of criticizing its enemy Christianity.[18]

Another example, which many scholars have pointed out, is Montaigne's very explicit critique of Mohammed's and especially Plato's doctrine's of the afterlife: his true target was something else. As one critic put it: "Montaigne stabs the Christian teaching . . . through the body of Plato."[19] It was indeed a very common practice, especially among early modern thinkers, to go on at length about the ancients, the Chinese, the Amerindians, the Hindus—

either in extravagant praise or blame—as an indirect means of criticizing their own government and religion.

The same strategy is just as apparent in more contemporary authors. According to J. M. Ritchie, writers in Nazi Germany could count on "the sensitivity of the reader to pick up a literary allusion, a biblical reference or a historical parallel with relevance to National Socialism."[20] Similarly, an article in the *New York Times* about the covert practices of Tin Maung Than, a dissident writer and newspaper editor in Myanmar (Burma), reports:

> "You cannot criticize," Mr. Tin Maung Than said. "You have to give hints that you are being critical, that you are talking about the current system." . . . He wrote about repression in the education system under British colonial rule. Readers were nudged to draw their own conclusions about the education system of today. He wrote about flag burning in the United States, ostensibly to criticize it but, between the lines, to give a glimpse of freedom. "If we want to talk about fear, we cannot talk about fear in the political context," he said. "So we talk about children's fear and its impact on society. The key is that you have to give little hints that you are not really talking about children."[21]

Again, the article "Aesopian Language" in *The Modern Encyclopedia of Russian and Soviet Literature* reports:

> Writers tended to employ a number of stock situations, comparisons and contrasts as well as techniques. These included narration about life in foreign countries with implicit application to the writer's own society, such as Saltykov-Shchedrin's 1863 article "Parasite Dramatists in France" . . . [and] narration about current events in the guise of an account about the past.[22]

Lev Loseff agrees and emphasizes the particular popularity of this technique:

> In literary writing, and in Russian literature particularly since the latter half of the eighteenth century, one of the most widely proliferated types of Aesopian plot has been the exotic variety, its infallibility ironically sworn to by Nekrasov:
>
> > When the action is shifted to Pisa
> > Endless volumes of fiction are spared.[23]

The two strategies we have discussed so far are relatively concrete and uncomplicated, since the main issue — the *content* of the claim or thought involved — is stated openly, and all that is dissembled is the very narrow question of the source or the target of that claim. And it is not as if there is a wide range of possible answers in play. In each case, the esoteric reader is really faced with a simple, yes-or-no question: contrary to appearances, is the claim being advanced secretly embraced by the author himself and is it really meant to target the author's own time and place? To be sure, the answers may still be difficult to arrive at, but at least the questions themselves are very obvious and determinate, and thus the reader can know exactly what he or she is looking for.

The situation becomes much more complex and open-ended when we turn to the third strategy, which involves dissembling the very content of the thought or claim. Here, at least in principle, the hidden thought of the author could be anything at all. The esoteric reader is much more at sea. There are some thinkers, to be sure, regarding whom the possible alternatives are, in practice, very narrow. Most Hobbes scholars would agree, for example, that if there is any issue of esotericism here at all, it is confined to the very specific question: atheist or unorthodox believer? (But even here, it is not so clear that the issue of religious belief can be completely separated from other elements of Hobbes's thought such as the status of natural law, the meaning of obligation, and the source of the binding power of consent and social contract.) At any rate, with many other thinkers, with Plato, for example, the possibilities in play are far broader. To judge simply by the history of the interpretation of Plato and the "Academic school" beginning in antiquity, his esoteric teaching could be anything from mysticism to Epicureanism, extreme dogmatism to extreme skepticism — and everything in between.

Further contributing to the complexity and open-endedness of the third strategy is the fact that there is a very wide range of possible methods and techniques that can be used when one seeks to cover over, but subtly indicate, the content of one's thought. In what follows, I will describe some of the most important of these, without aspiring to anything approaching exhaustiveness.

The most obvious way to express a thought while not making it too clear is simply to state it unclearly. In one degree or another, every esoteric writer employs this basic expedient. We have already seen Thomas Aquinas openly recommend it:

> Certain things can be explained to the wise in private which we should keep
> silent about in public. . . . Therefore, these matters should be concealed with
> obscure language, so that they will benefit the wise who understand them
> and be hidden from the uneducated who are unable to grasp them.[24]

There are, however, a number of different ways of speaking unclearly, most
of which are listed by Diderot in a previously quoted letter where he explains
how he avoided the censors: "Me, I saved myself by the most agile irony that
I could find, by generalities, by terseness, and by obscurity."[25] One can avoid
clarity, he suggests, by speaking in very general and unspecific terms (generality), or by compressing one's thinking into very few words (terseness), or
by expressing oneself in terms that seem to mean either nothing at all (obscurity), or the opposite of what one means (irony), or—I would add—more
than one thing (ambiguity).

Since these forms of unclarity are all fairly obvious, let me just briefly
illustrate two. An example of obscurity is provided by Vaclav Havel, who
describes, in a passage previously quoted, how he wrote his *Letters to Olga*
while under the eyes of his prison guards in communist Czechoslovakia:

> Very early on, I realized that comprehensible letters wouldn't get through,
> which is why the letters are full of long compound sentences and com-
> plicated ways of saying things. Instead of writing "regime," for instance,
> I would obviously have had to write "the socially apparent focus on the
> non-I," or some such nonsense.[26]

Terseness or brevity is another form of unclarity with a particularly long history. We have seen, for example, Rousseau's statement about how he wrote
the *First Discourse*:

> I have often taken great pains to try to put into a sentence, a line, a word
> tossed off as if by chance the result of a long sequence of reflections. Often,
> most of my readers must have found my discourses badly connected and
> almost entirely rambling, for lack of perceiving the trunk of which I showed
> them only the branches. But that was enough for those who know how to
> understand, and I have never wanted to speak to the others."[27]

In his thinking, he engages in a long sequence of reflections (the "trunk") but
then shows the reader only his conclusions (the "branches") which therefore

appear disconnected and rambling. He shows us some dots and challenges us to connect them. A similar form of terseness is used by Montesquieu according to the account of Hippolyte Taine (quoted earlier):

> We must possess some intelligence to be able to read him, for he deliberately curtails developments and omits transitions; we are required to supply these and to comprehend his hidden meanings. . . . He thinks in summaries.[28]

Similarly, Maimonides declares in his introduction that one way in which he has hidden his teaching in the *Guide for the Perplexed* is by extreme brevity, conveying only "the chapter headings." And in using this technique (and this phrase) he is only following the explicit injunction of the Talmud:

> The Account of the Chariot [i.e., of Divine Science] ought not to be taught even to one man, except if he be wise and able to understand by himself, in which case only the chapter headings may be transmitted to him.[29]

A means of avoiding clarity that is very different from those just considered—generality, terseness, obscurity, irony, and ambiguity—and one that can also be elaborately suggestive, is the use of stories, allegories, myths, fables, parables, and so forth. The very fact that, in Russia, the practice of esotericism was known as "Aesopian language" testifies to the popularity of this technique. Francis Bacon, in his list of the various forms and uses of poetry in the *Advancement of Learning*, states that a poetic style can be used to help demonstrate and illustrate a body of thought, but it can also be used for the opposite purpose: "to retire and obscure it: that is, when the secrets and mysteries of religion, policy, or philosophy are involved in fables or parables."[30] Similarly, Hobbes speaks of the ancients who "rather chose to have the science of justice wrapped up in fables, than openly exposed to disputations."[31] This technique is obviously a great favorite with Plato. In all his analogizing, dramatizing, storytelling, and mythmaking, he isn't just being poetic, but esoteric. As we have heard Alfarabi report in his commentary on the *Laws*:

> The wise Plato did not feel free to reveal and uncover the sciences for all men. Therefore, he followed the practice of using symbols, riddles, obscurity, and difficulty.[32]

Toland makes the same point in saying that Plato wrote "rather poetically than philosophically" as a means of concealment.[33] For readers to whom this still seems unlikely, consider that Plato himself makes exactly the same point about an even more unlikely subject: he claims that Homer, Hesiod, and some other early poets were covertly presenting Heraclitean ideas about nature when they gave their genealogies of the gods and other mythical accounts. As Socrates states in the *Theaetetus*:

> Have we not here a tradition from the ancients who hid their meaning from the common herd in poetical figures, that Ocean and [his wife, the river goddess] Tethys, the source of all things, are flowing streams and nothing is at rest? (180c–d)[34]

Similarly, Montaigne, a writer notable for his frequent use of stories and quotations, acknowledges at one point that he often uses these forms to suggest things that he is not willing to state openly:

> And how many stories have I spread around which say nothing of themselves, but from which anyone who troubles to pluck them with a little ingenuity will produce numberless essays. Neither these stories nor my quotations serve always simply for example, authority, or ornament. I do not esteem them solely for the use I derive from them. They often bear, outside my subject, the seeds of a richer and bolder material, and sound obliquely a subtler note, both for myself, who do not wish to express anything more, and for those who get my drift.[35]

As we have seen, even Jesus makes it explicit that he employs his famous parables for the express purpose of obscuring his meaning:

> Then the disciples came and said to him, "Why do you speak to [the people] in parables?" And he answered them, "To you it has been given to know the secrets of the kingdom of heaven, but to them it has not been given." (Matt. 13:10–12)

Another method, distantly related to what Plato attributes to Homer and Hesiod, is to state one's views, but to conceal their novelty and heterodoxy by clothing them as much as possible in the terminology and categories of the reigning philosophical and religious orthodoxy. This tactic is clearly described—indeed resolutely insisted upon—by Descartes in a letter to one of his more imprudent disciples:

> Do not propose new opinions as new, but retain all the old terminology for supporting new reasons; that way no one can find fault with you, and those who grasp your reasons will by themselves conclude to what they ought to understand. Why is it necessary for you to reject so openly the [Aristotelian doctrine of] substantial forms? Do you not recall that in the *Treatise on Meteors* I expressly denied that I rejected or denied them, but declared only that they were not necessary for the explication of my reasons?[36]

In the *Advancement of Learning*, Bacon, another enemy of Aristotelity and scholasticism, indicates that he follows this same practice, without of course openly revealing why. "Wheresoever my conception and notion may differ from the ancient, yet I am studious to keep the ancient terms."[37] D'Alembert sees very clearly that Bacon practices this esoteric technique and even criticizes him, as we have seen, for taking it too far, timidly hiding his novelty too much. Bacon "seems to have shown a little too much caution or deference to the dominant taste of his century in his frequent use of the terms of the scholastics."[38]

Because many esoteric writers employ this practice in one degree or another, it is an important rule of esoteric reading to carefully follow the usage and potentially changing meaning of key terms and concepts in the text. It is essential, for example, to closely monitor Machiavelli's every use of the word "virtue," in order to see how he gradually brings this crucial, traditional term around to a radically new meaning.

There is another very common esoteric strategy that enables a writer, should he so desire, to state a novel or dangerous thought even quite clearly—just so long as he takes it all back by contradiction. More specifically, he must make the dangerous statement in a muted and unobtrusive way and surround it with more explicit and more emphatic and far more numerous statements to the contrary. He will soon discover that most readers will find a hundred reasons to discount and ignore the first statement. For in reading a book, as in reading the world, we all start with a profound and powerful tendency to believe that what we see repeated everywhere must be true. The beginning of wisdom in both realms is to recognize this as a fundamental illusion. The most important truths tend, on the contrary, to be rare and secret, covered over by what is repeated everywhere. Thus, in esoteric reading, we must resolutely reverse valuations and give more weight and credence to the quiet, isolated statement than to the ones noisily repeated everywhere else in the book.

The esoteric reader, then, must be especially on the lookout for those unique places where the mask of conformity momentarily slips and the heterodox truth is allowed to be glimpsed. At those moments, to be sure, the internal voice of conventionality, imperfectly conquered, may reassert itself. One thinks: "Can it *really be* that the author spent all that time and all that effort asserting and even thoughtfully elaborating and arguing for the orthodox view when he didn't really believe in it?" To which one must firmly reply: it is much easier to see why a heterodox thinker would frequently say the orthodox thing than why an orthodox thinker would ever say the heterodox thing. For this reason, John Toland asserts as a fairly reliable rule of esoteric reading:

> When a man maintains what's commonly believ'd, or professes what's publicly injoin'd, it is not always a sure rule that he speaks what he thinks: but when he seriously maintains the contrary of what's by law establish'd, and openly declares for what most others oppose, then there's a strong presumption that he utters his mind.[39]

A strikingly similar claim is made by Malebranche—and later quoted approvingly by Bayle:

> It is a rule of good sense that when someone speaks in the language of the people and following common prejudices, we should not take literally everything said even if it is repeated often in the same terms; but if someone says only one single time something contrary to prejudice we must take it with great strictness. Should a philosopher say only one or two times in his life that animals do not consciously perceive, I believe him a Cartesian on that ground and I have reason to believe it: but even if he says one hundred times a day that his dog knows him and loves him, I do not know what to think of his sentiments, because when one speaks as the others do and following common ideas one does not always say what one thinks.[40]

Sometimes, of course, an author will contradict the conventional or orthodox view not openly and frontally but only indirectly through the denial of one of its essential premises or consequences. Thus, we find this somewhat modified formulation of the rule in Strauss:

If an able writer who has a clear mind and a perfect knowledge of the ortho-dox view and all its ramifications, contradicts surreptitiously and as it were in passing one of its necessary presuppositions or consequences which he explicitly recognizes and maintains everywhere else, we can reasonably sus-pect that he was opposed to the orthodox system as such and—we must study his whole book all over again, with much greater care and much less naiveté than ever before.[41]

At this point, however, a very common counterargument—call it the "fal-libility objection"—will be raised. At the risk of a brief digression, it will be useful to confront it at some length. The rule for reading just recommended proceeds on the assumption that the contradictions (and other blunders) one comes across in the text are intentional, part of the author's exquisitely controlled esoteric design. But how can one ever be sure of this? People make mistakes and contradict themselves in their writings all the time. Thus, isn't this particular kind of esoteric interpretation that works by seizing upon the author's supposedly intentional blunders based on some kind of old-fashioned idealization of human nature? Doesn't it ignore what our more realistic or honest age is able to see more clearly: the simple phenomenon of *human fallibility*—the random lapses, the meaningless errors, the inevitable irregularity to be found in every writing? There is just too much "human static" on the line to permit of the kind of esoteric interpretation that draws large consequences from tiny irregularities.[42]

This important objection (which continues the discussion of "authorial omniscience" begun in the previous section) is one manifestation of the her-meneutical pessimism that is a leading characteristic of our time. But does this marked tendency of our age represent a unique insight or a local preju-dice? That is what is unclear.

In reply to this specific objection, one must start from a distinction that has been neglected. It is certainly true—and has always been known—that *most* books are filled with all kinds of unintentional errors and shortcomings. But the particular procedures for esoteric reading being proposed here are not intended to apply to most books: they do not aim to supply any kind of "universal hermeneutical theory." They are expressly designed for a tiny subset of books, primarily the great masterpieces and works of rare genius. And while rare geniuses too are fallible—if "even Homer nods," as Horace says—still they are sometimes capable of feats of concentration, control, and perfection that are in a class entirely by themselves. We would all like to in-sist on our ordinary sense of plausibility, but in truth there is nothing at all plausible about the *Divine Comedy*, or the B Minor Mass or the *Pietà*. If we did not know such things existed, we might well be tempted to say they are not possible. To pick a simpler example, most people cannot even imagine being able to play an entire game of chess blindfold, but there are people who can play twenty such games simultaneously. The current world record is forty-six.[43] There is a great danger in claiming to know what human beings are and are not capable of.

What is clear is that we today feel very powerfully that past ages naively entertained too exalted a view of the great thinkers and writers; but we must concede, if we are honest, that it is possible that, on the contrary, it is we who somehow take too jaundiced a view. To judge of the latter possibility, it would help if we could step outside of our own perspective and see ourselves from the standpoint of an earlier observer.

Enter Tocqueville, who is ready with some apt observations on just this issue. We have already heard him describe the familiar leveling tendency of democratic cultures: "the general idea of the intellectual superiority that any man whatsoever can acquire over all the others is not slow to be obscured."[44] Beyond this, he emphasizes that in our informal, mobile, and dynamic commercial society, we have grown dangerously accustomed to writing that is hasty, prolix, artless, and inexact—in a word, peculiarly "fallible." He dedicates an entire chapter of *Democracy in America* to the claim that, for an antidote, we desperately need to immerse ourselves in the literature of classical antiquity, lest we altogether forget what exquisite care and refinement, what jewels of delicacy and precision, great writers are really capable of.[45] In short, he predicts something like our coming hermeneutical pessimism and "fallibilism" and regards it as a culture-bound distortion.

To Tocqueville's observations one could add the closely related fact that earlier ages seem to have taken the whole question of rhetoric and composition far more seriously than we do. The greatest ancient philosophers—Plato, Aristotle, Cicero—all dedicated major works to rhetoric, as did certain medieval and early modern philosophers like Augustine, Thomas Aquinas, Erasmus, and Hobbes. More generally, from antiquity through the late nineteenth century, rhetoric—being one-third of the "trivium"—constituted an essential part of the established curriculum of higher, liberal education. Today, it is so utterly neglected that most people are completely unaware that it was ever considered so important. Something like rhetoric and composition, on a very rudimentary level, are taught in our primary schools, but rarely in college, except on a remedial basis, and not at all in graduate school.[46] Somehow, nobody today finds it the least bit strange that graduate students, future academics, who will be spending the rest of their lives reading, writing, and lecturing, study not one word of rhetoric. Our actions and institutions speak loudly, betraying a deep and unquestioned assumption that there is nothing too terribly serious to be learned here.

This remarkable neglect seems to represent the ultimate expression of the cultural transformation that Tocqueville feared: conditioned by modern society, we have essentially come to forget that prose composition is or ever was a high art that could be studied and practiced and—with great and sustained effort—polished to a high degree of perfection. Thus, we approach writing with a combination of artistic inexperience and literary easygoingness, which makes it more or less inevitable that when we read masterful writers of the past, we often fail to appreciate their well-honed art of composition or even to recognize that such an art exists and that they are practicing it. Thus, we systematically underestimate the degree of control and precision that these great past writers of prose aspired to and were in fact able to achieve, their general human fallibility notwithstanding.

Our experience of past writers has been still further distorted by one additional factor: our ignorance of esotericism. This has caused us to assume that all the many contradictions and other blunders we find in the text are unintentional, whereas many and especially the most egregious are probably part of the author's esoteric design. As a result, we systematically overestimate the frequency of genuine errors and contradictions to be found in the greatest writers. In this way, ignorance of esotericism inevitably leads to the exaggeration of fallibility. This in turn leads us to conclude that close esoteric reading is impossible. In this way the long-standing denial of esotericism comes to be self-confirming.

While these arguments do not come close to settling the matter, there is at least good reason to suspect that our dominant literary instincts of pessimism and hyperfallibilism are culture-bound, deriving from certain limitations imposed by our particular historical circumstances and experiences. With this suspicion in mind, let us return to the point from which we began this digression, the question of whether major contradictions (and other blunders) in the text should be regarded as intentional. Let us try to evaluate the dominant paradigm of our culture by examining the views on this issue of readers from a variety of other historical periods. Consulting the views of earlier readers is particularly important here because in earlier periods, prior to the age of forgetfulness, people had vastly more concrete, hands-on experience of esoteric reading than we do, so their reactions are likely to be far more educated and empirically based than our own. They speak from experience, we from a combination of gut feelings and abstract theory.

We certainly find an attitude starkly different from our own in Maimonides, who, in his lengthy introduction to the *Guide of the Perplexed*, takes up the very question of what to make of the contradictions that one finds in various kinds of texts. He is speaking here primarily in his capacity as a *reader* of texts, including esoteric ones. It is clear from his finely observed account—he explores no fewer than seven different causes of contradictions—that he is no less "realistic" and hardheaded than we and fully acquainted with the fallible, sloppy, random side of human nature. Thus, one cause of contradictions, he reports, is when the author changes his mind but leaves both views in his book, and another is when the author is simply unaware of the contradiction. But at the same time, Maimonides emphasizes the great inequalities that exist among human minds; and he does not hesitate to assert that he is particularly experienced in the higher levels of thought and literary artistry. It is this direct experience that gives him the confidence to assert that in the greatest writings we possess (as also in his own), major contradictions are almost certainly intentional, produced by one form or another of esoteric design.[47] That is what his own experience of reading and interpreting—as well as his experience of writing esoterically—tells him.

A similar conclusion is reached by Toland. He begins by endorsing an observation of Cicero about the great prevalence of contradiction in philosophical writing: "[Cicero] rightly concludes that the same philosophers do not always seem to say the same thing, though they continu'd of the same opinion." Toland adds that this ancient claim regarding contradiction is also "as true as Truth itself, of many writers in our own time." What then is the cause of this striking phenomenon? He answers:

> Nor are we to wonder any longer, that the same men do not always seem to say the same things on the same subjects, which problem can only be solv'd by the distinction of the External and Internal Doctrine.[48]

Again, we have already seen Machiavelli's admonition—"When one sees a great error made by an enemy, one ought to believe that there is deception underneath"—as well as the similar statement by Pope: "Those oft are stratagems which errors seem / Nor is it Homer nods, but we that dream."[49] Even in the thoroughly modernist James Joyce, one reads:

—The world believes that Shakespeare made a mistake, he said, and got out of it as quickly and as best he could.

—Bosh! Stephen said rudely. A man of genius makes no mistakes. His errors are volitional and are the portals of discovery.[50]

In contrast to the reigning opinion of today, these various thinkers, representing vastly different times and places, all agree that, notwithstanding our great human fallibility, the significant contradictions to be found in the works of the greatest writers should be—and, with some care, *can* be—interpreted as part of their intentional esoteric design.

What is also apparent from these diverse statements is that over the last two thousand years, the strategy of deliberate contradiction has been very widely practiced. And from this simple fact, this long-running popularity, it is perhaps possible to draw further support for our conclusion. For it would seem to indicate that this esoteric technique has also met with reasonable success, that it has tended to be recognized by its intended audience.

After all, esoteric philosophical writers typically start off as *readers* of earlier philosophers—indeed *esoteric readers*. And it is very likely that this initial hermeneutic experience is very important in helping them determine what strategies to use in their own esoteric writing. If they had commonly found, in their own personal efforts at esoteric interpretation, that the technique of contradiction and of other intentional blunders was too difficult to decipher owing to the frequency of unintentional blunders (as predicted by the fallibility objection), they surely would not have continued to use that technique in their own writing. They do, after all, want to be understood. Therefore, when a thinker makes significant use of a given esoteric technique, he is at the same time asserting, through that deed, his considered opinion—probably based on long, personal experience of esoteric reading—that that technique is indeed decipherable by a careful reader. Thus, when we encounter a widely popular esoteric technique, like deliberate contradiction, that *popularity* must also be seen as wide *testimony* to its decipherability—testimony that is, in this case, very broadly distributed over time and place and that represents the considered reflection of some of the greatest minds applied to a great range of firsthand hermeneutic experience. By contrast, the skeptical and pessimistic objections of our contemporaries are based on little if any hands-on experience of esoteric interpretation. In view of all this, it seems reasonable to conclude that the interpretive pessimism uniquely characteristic of our time should be viewed with considerable skepticism, and that the rules for interpreting contradictions in the text as stated above by Toland and Strauss are likely to prove both sound and practicable for the careful reader.

In the same vein, it is also important to be on the lookout for other intentional blunders. One common practice, for example, is the use of altered quotations. We have already seen a classic example of this in the second chapter: Machiavelli quotes a phrase from the New Testament as part of his description and criticism of David's tyrannical behavior—but in the Bible, the phrase refers to the actions not of David but of God.[51]

Another very common esoteric strategy that is, in a way, the opposite of contradiction is dispersal. With contradiction, you state the dangerous idea whole, but then negate it by placing an opposite whole on top of it. With dispersal, you divide the idea into parts, presenting one in one place, another in a different place, so that the whole idea is present in the book, but hidden because dismembered and dispersed.[52]

As we have seen, Maimonides declares in the introduction to the *Guide* that the truths he means to convey are

> not set down in order or arranged in coherent fashion in this Treatise, but rather are scattered and entangled with other subjects that are to be clarified. For my purpose is that the truths be glimpsed and then again be concealed.[53]

Similarly, Clement of Alexandria, the Platonizing second-century church father, indicates in the very title of one of his books—*Stromata* or "Miscellanies"—his intention to use this esoteric technique, "since the composition aims at concealment." As he explains in a chapter entitled "The Meaning of the Name Stromata":

> Let these notes of ours . . . be of varied character—and as the name itself indicates, patched together—passing constantly from one thing to another, and in the series of discussions hinting at one thing and demonstrating another.

As he continues in a later chapter, his book has

> here and there interspersed the dogmas which are the germs of true knowledge, so that the discovery of the sacred traditions may not be easy to any one of the uninitiated.[54]

Montesquieu is another writer who employs this strategy, although he is less willing to announce it openly in the way that Maimonides and Clement do. The obvious drawback, however, of following this strategy without announcing it is that then your book will tend to be dismissed as rambling and disordered—a fate certainly suffered by the *Spirit of the Laws*, especially in more recent times. It is only in a private letter defending his book against this particular charge that Montesquieu states more openly how he has written it:

> That which renders certain articles of the book in question obscure and ambiguous is that they are often at a distance from the others which explain them and that the links of the chain which you have noted are very often at a distance the ones from the others.[55]

In a similar way, d'Alembert, in his admiring analysis of the book, feels the need to respond to "the pretended lack of method of which some readers have accused Montesquieu." It is necessary, he claims, to "distinguish apparent disorder from real disorder."

> The disorder is merely apparent when the author puts in their proper places the ideas he uses and leaves to the readers to supply the connecting ideas: and it is thus that Montesquieu thought he could and should proceed in a book destined for men who think, whose genius ought to supply the voluntary and reasoned omissions.[56]

Montesquieu encountered the problem that he did largely because, for a variety of reasons, he sought to combine the strategy of dispersal with a book that took the outward form of a systematic treatise, so that the lack of order, deriving from his strategy, made his book seem fundamentally defective.

Other literary forms—dialogues, essays, dictionaries, and encyclopedias—being inherently more disjoint and promising less in the way of order and system, go together more naturally with the dispersal strategy. By writing dialogues, for example, Plato is able to move from one very partial account of things to another without producing an appearance of defect or failure. One of the keys to understanding Plato, according to Strauss, is to see that each dialogue is intentionally partial or one-sided, abstracting from something important relating to its subject matter. In the *Republic*, the dialogue on justice, for example, the whole erotic side of life is both downplayed and denigrated—think of the collectivization (i.e., abolition) of family life or the identification of the tyrant with *eros*—in a way that is reversed in the *Symposium*.[57]

Montaigne is another classic practitioner of dispersal. His *Essays*, with its repeated claims of spontaneity and the deliberate avoidance of order, is a perfect vehicle for this strategy. While pretending to allow his mind simply to wander where it will, he carefully plants the disassembled pieces of his systematic view. As he acknowledges at one point:

> My ideas follow one another, but sometimes it is from a distance, and look at each other, but with a sidelong glance. . . . It is the inattentive reader who loses my subject, not I. Some word about it will always be found off in a corner, which will not fail to be sufficient, though it takes little room.[58]

Seeing how this particular game is played, one might turn one's suspicions next to Pierre Bayle, who happens to have been a great admirer of both Maimonides and Montaigne, and who does appear to be employing a version of their dispersal strategy in his sprawling *Historical and Critical Dictionary*, with its rambling essays and byzantine notes inside of notes. In the "Clarifications" that he appended to the second edition in reply to some criticisms by religious authorities, he more or less openly admits this. Speaking of some of the heterodox opinions that he reports in his *Dictionary*, he states:

> If a man . . . should relate, among vast historical and literary collections, some error about religion or morality, one should not be disturbed at all about it. . . . No one takes as a guide in that matter an author who only speaks about it in passing and incidentally, and who, by the very fact that he acts as if he were tossing off his views like a pin in a field, makes it well enough known that he does not care to have followers at all. . . . This is how the faculties of theology in France behaved with regard to the book of Michel de Montaigne. They allowed all this author's maxims to pass, he who without following any system, any method, any order, heaped up and stirred together all that came into his mind. But when Pierre Charron [Montaigne's friend and disciple] . . . bethought himself to relate some of the views of Montaigne in a methodical and systematic treatise on morality, the theologians did not remain tranquil.[59]

Bayle explicitly acknowledges that in composing his *Dictionary* as he did, he was seeking to give it the same immunity and appearance of harmlessness that Montaigne had given to his *Essays*, and by the same means—intentional disorder, offhandedness, and dispersal.

Still further testimony to the popularity of this technique can be found in Condorcet's lengthy description, examined above, of the wily literary campaign waged against throne and altar by the philosophers of the early modern period. He describes these writers as

> employing every form from humor to pathos, from the most learned and vast compilation to the novel or pamphlet of the day; covering the truth with a veil to spare eyes too weak, and leaving others the pleasure of divining it; sometimes skillfully caressing prejudices, the more effectively to attack them; almost never threatening them, and then *never several at one time, nor ever one in its entirety.*[60]

These last items point to the strategy of dispersal: one never shows all of one's cards or presents the whole of one's critique in any one place.

This turns out to be exactly what Strauss reports finding in his studies of Spinoza and also of Hobbes:

> To exaggerate for purposes of clarification, we may say that each chapter of [Spinoza's] *Treatise* serves the function of refuting one particular orthodox dogma while leaving untouched all other orthodox dogmas. . . . Fundamentally the same procedure is followed by Hobbes in the Third Part of his *Leviathan*.[61]

Let me cite one last report of the technique of dispersal—this one by another careful reader, John Locke. The first, if much less well-known, of Locke's *Two Treatises of Government* is a close interpretation and refutation of Filmer's treatise *Patriarcha*—which Locke reads esoterically. As he explains, Filmer feared to put off his readers by too precise and complete an account of his doctrine of authority, so "clear distinct speaking not serving everywhere to his purpose, you must not expect it in him." Instead, Filmer intentionally "scattered" his teaching "in the several parts of his writings" or "up and down in his writings." Filmer acted

> like a wary physician, when he would have his patient swallow some harsh or corrosive liquor, he mingles it with a large quantity of that which may dilute it that the scattered parts may go down with less feeling and cause less aversion.[62]

One may of course wonder whether Locke himself did not also make use of this technique that he attributes to Filmer.[63]

In all of the esoteric strategies discussed so far, the dangerous thought is indeed stated, but hidden in some way—by being obscured, contradicted, or dispersed. But the purest or most classic esoteric technique is to communicate a thought precisely by *not* saying it—by meaningful silence or conspicuous omission. This may sound particularly arcane, but it is actually a fairly common and intuitive form of communication. For example, according to communications scholars Ge Gao and Stella Ting-Toomey, it is characteristic of the indirect style of conversation found in contemporary China, which "emphasizes what is implied or not said, rather than what is said. . . . That is, focusing on *how* something is said, and on what is *not* said, is equally, if not more important, than what is said."[64]

In this context, it is also well to recall your beloved's letter: almost all the important thoughts were conveyed by significant omissions, especially by her failure to mention that she missed you. In normal communication, every positive statement derives much of its meaning through reference to a silent background of expectations—expectations produced by the situation, by shared understandings, and by the preceding statements. This is what makes it possible to convey ideas by *not* saying certain things, that is, by the conspicuous violation of those expectations.

Thus, in the first chapter of Xenophon's *Constitution of the Lacedaemonians*, where he proposes to examine the uniqueness and wisdom of the famous Spartan regime, he sets up a certain structure or rhythm: first he describes how certain things are done in the other Greek cities and then he explains the very different, almost opposite practices of Sparta. But, as Strauss points out, in one case he omits the parallel. He tells us that in the other Greek cities young maidens are kept on a very austere diet with respect to food and wine, but he neglects to say a word about the Spartan practice in this matter. This is a loud silence, since it breaks the rhythm, violating the expectation the author has just created. It spurs us to supply the missing thought ourselves, and, following the established pattern, we are led to conclude that Spartan maidens must be immoderate with respect to food and wine. This thought, furthermore, is clearly meant to play into a widely held opinion that Spartan women were rather licentious, not only with respect to food and wine, but—perhaps in consequence of the latter indulgence—with respect to sex. This proves to be the first of many passages in which Xenophon's artful and playful silences turn this grave encomium of Sparta into a very subtle satire.[65]

Another, particularly striking example of the esoteric use of omission occurs in Alfarabi's *The Philosophy of Plato, Its Parts, and the Grades of Dignity of Its Parts, From Its Beginning to Its End*. In this summary of Plato's thought, the very title of which creates the expectation of comprehensiveness, there turns out to be not a single reference to the afterlife or the immortality of the soul. Even the summary of the *Phaedo* is completely silent on the subject. This striking omission, Strauss argues, is Alfarabi's esoteric way of indicating that Plato's genuine beliefs did not include his famous teaching regarding the soul's immortality.[66]

A further esoteric strategy, not unrelated to that of omission, involves the arrangement or plan of a writing. For you can convey information not only by what you say (or don't say) but also by where you say it. For example, if you arrange the topics of your discourse in a discernible pattern, say, from less to more important, then you can communicate your view of the relative importance of various issues or phenomena without having to say anything explicitly—just by where you place the discussions. Again, Plato presents an extensive account of theology in the tenth book of his *Laws*, but on closer examination one notices that he has placed it in the context of a discussion of penal legislation. That conveys something about his views of religion's role in political life. Obviously there are a hundred ways in which the placement or context of a discussion can silently communicate something important about its content. Conversely, one can also present a hint or puzzle to the reader by the violation of one's plan, either by the introduction of a brief digression or of a wholly unannounced or ill-fitting topic, or by a surprising omission. For this reason, one of the first things that the esoteric reader should do in approaching a text is to construct a careful outline, paying particular attention to deviations and anomalies.

Still another esoteric technique concerning order is repetition. An author can make a claim or argument and then, somewhat later, "repeat" it—only with some significant (but perhaps barely visible) change. In this way, the writer signals the careful reader that the first statement was not his final or genuine view and points him in the direction of his true understanding.[67]

Finally, concerning order or arrangement in general, it is possible to formulate a basic rule. Common sense tells us—as does Cicero in his writings on rhetoric—that in the construction of a speech or writing, one should put the most important points at the beginning and at the end. The weaker or less important ones should go in the middle. This is because the listener's or reader's attention is typically greatest at the beginning, wandering off toward the middle, and picking up again at the end—at the sound of "and finally . . ." Consequently, if a writer has a heterodox idea that he seeks to communicate, not with maximum clarity and power but rather quietly and surreptitiously, he will carefully follow the opposite of this basic rhetorical rule and bury the dangerous idea somewhere toward the middle, while filling the beginning and ending with earnest protestations of the orthodox view. Indeed, through a somewhat stylized extension of this common practice, many writers will often signal what thought is really on their minds by placing it (or some hint of it) in the exact center of a list or sequence that they have constructed.[68]

This list of esoteric techniques is far from exhaustive. I have simply tried to include those that are most common while also being most immediately intelligible and plausible by virtue of either their internal logic or their external testimony or both.

SOME EXAMPLES OF ESOTERIC INTERPRETATION

In addition to establishing a genuine connection with the text and possessing a basic understanding of common esoteric techniques, budding esoteric readers should also study some examples of esoteric interpretation—to see it done. Unfortunately, there is no single book that, in my view, combines all of the qualities that one would want in such a model for instruction and emulation. What follows is a short list of imperfect models.

But in using this list, readers must select works on writers that genuinely interest them. To appreciate a performance of esoteric interpretation and to learn from it, you must be a participant and not a spectator. You must begin by reading the text carefully on your own and struggling to interpret it. Only then will you be ready to understand and appreciate what the interpreter has found. If you sit back with arms folded, like a king who commands his wise man to say something wise, it will all fall flat.

From my own experience, I do believe that Strauss's interpretations are generally the best from the standpoint of esoteric penetration and especially philosophical profundity. They also seem to me quite sober and accurate—not at all prone to "perverse ingenuity." But their drawback for current purposes is that they are themselves quite difficult to understand. By taste as well as conviction, Strauss is averse to making things easy for the reader. He prefers to state his conclusions in a fairly compressed manner and challenge his readers to figure out for themselves how he arrived at them. He also likes to speak in the original vocabulary of the thinker he is interpreting without repackaging him in the terms and concepts of today, and this too can give his writings an initially antique and forbidding quality. I will recommend certain of his works below, but they are not the best place to begin.

To begin, we need an author who, in his interpretations, is willing to follow the very un-Straussian injunction—often found on mathematics exams—"show all work." We need to see, once or twice, how the sausage is made. The best writing for this purpose that I am familiar with comes from an appropriately un-Straussian source: Stanley Fish. His "Georgics of the Mind: The Experience of Bacon's *Essays*" is a brilliant and nuanced exercise in close textual analysis that openly displays, at every stage of Fish's encounter with the text, what he thinks and why he thinks it.[69] He shows us what it feels like to truly take a text seriously, to engage its every word with patience and delicacy, to actually *trust* the author one has chosen to read, and to undergo, while striving to understand, the complex experience that the author, in his artfulness, has prepared for the careful reader.

Another excellent and highly communicative reader who, like Fish, is associated with the reader-response school of criticism is Robert Connor. His *Thucydides* is a very sensitive reading of Thucydides's great history, a reading openly arrived at and clearly conveyed.[70] In conjunction with this, one should also read Clifford Orwin's superb *The Humanity of Thucydides*.[71] After that, one could try Strauss's chapter on Thucydides in *The City and Man*, a brilliant essay, although not an easy one.[72] This trio of works strikes me as perhaps the single best initial training course in close and esoteric reading, but it would involve a very serious commitment of time, especially when several readings of Thucydides himself must be included.

For shorter and easier fare, I would recommend—again, starting with non-Straussians—David Wootton's closely argued "Narrative, Irony, and Faith in Gibbon's *Decline and Fall*,"[73] and David Berman's "Deism, Immortality, and the Art of Theological Lying."[74] Then, for some Straussians: Wayne Ambler's esoteric reading of Aristotle's defense of natural slavery in the *Politics*, "Aristotle on Nature and Politics: The Case of Slavery."[75] Also, Clifford Orwin's careful reading of chapter 17 of the *Prince*: "Machiavelli's Unchristian Charity."[76] And Strauss's dense but clear "On the Intention of Rousseau."[77]

Another particularly clear piece by Strauss is the posthumously published book *Leo Strauss on Plato's Symposium*.[78] This is essentially the transcript of a course that Strauss gave at the University of Chicago (edited and polished a bit by Seth Benardete). A more difficult but more finished work that was intended by Strauss precisely as a demonstration of how to read an esoteric text is *On Tyranny*. This work includes a detailed interpretation of

Xenophon's short dialogue *Hiero or Tyrannicus* as well as a debate on it with Alexandre Kojève.

Other especially helpful writings on Plato are David Leibowitz, *The Ironic Defense of Socrates: Plato's Apology*; Allan Bloom, *The Republic of Plato*;[79] and Christopher Bruell, *On the Socratic Education: An Introduction to the Shorter Platonic Dialogues*.[80]

Two other works to be recommended are Thomas Pangle's *Montesquieu's Philosophy of Liberalism: A Commentary on the Spirit of the Laws*, and Harry Jaffa's *Thomism and Aristotelianism: A Study of the Commentary by Thomas Aquinas on the Nicomachean Ethics*.

Finally, I would mention two last examples of esoteric reading, these more interesting for their source perhaps than for their content: both are by earlier philosophers. Augustine in *The City of God* gives an extended esoteric interpretation of the religious writings of the Roman philosopher Varro (and to a lesser extent of Seneca).[81] It seems a clear and thoughtful interpretation, following many of the principles described above. In the end its utility for us is somewhat limited by the fact that Varro's writings have been lost in the intervening centuries.

Another, particularly charming example is provided by Samuel Butler (1835–1902), author of *The Way of All Flesh*, who was something of a philosopher as well as novelist. In 1879, he published a book on evolution entitled *Evolution Old and New: Or the Theories of Buffon, Dr. Erasmus Darwin and Lamarck as Compared with That of Charles Darwin*. Chapters 9 and 10 on the French naturalist and philosopher Buffon give an esoteric reading of his famous work *Histoire naturelle, générale et particulière*. Butler tries to show, among other things, that Buffon, while adhering to the biblical view on the surface, embraces an evolutionary view between the lines. Butler writes with wit and displays a particularly good feel for the motives, techniques, and pleasures of esoteric writing and interpretation. His work shows, better than most, how one could actually enjoy reading esoterically. Unfortunately, there is a drawback here too: whereas Buffon's book has not been lost, it does run to over thirty volumes.

Defending Reason:
Esotericism and the Critique of Historicism

The genuine, sole, and most profound theme of all world and human history—a theme to which all others are subordinate—remains the conflict between belief and unbelief.
—GOETHE

The relation of history to reason remains constitutive for the discourse of modernity—for better or worse.
—JÜRGEN HABERMAS

Supposing that the claims made here regarding the widespread practice of esoteric writing are true, what then? Exactly what follows? The most obvious and solid consequence is the *practical* one drawn in the previous chapter: we should be prepared to recognize esoteric writings when we encounter them and to read them appropriately.

But the stakes are potentially higher still. There may also be profound *theoretical* repercussions—consequences relating to the whole character of human reason and the legitimacy of rationalism. The rediscovery of esotericism opens up wholly new paths of argument in the ongoing struggle to ground philosophical rationalism and to defend it against the powerful forces arrayed against it today. This further, philosophical reach of the esotericism issue should not come altogether as a surprise since, as we have seen, esotericism was from the start a direct outgrowth of a central problem of reason: the theory/praxis dualism—that is, the problem that arises from the fact that we are not pure minds, the problem of how reason stands in relation to its nonrational context and preconditions. We turn in conclusion to this potentially larger, philosophical dimension of the recovery of esotericism.

The simplest and best way of doing this, I believe, is by examining the thought of Leo Strauss. Whatever may be the case with the whole foregoing account of esotericism, we have finally reached a point where we clearly need him. For Strauss is literally the only thinker who has explored this crucial issue at any length. It is his great and unique contribution. Indeed, this (and not any imagined political scheme) constitutes the true core of his thought, the focus of his lifelong intellectual project. For this reason, Strauss is the best introduction to this issue—and this issue forms the best entrée into Strauss.

Of course, after this lengthy survey of this complex issue many readers will remain unpersuaded. It is therefore important to emphasize, one last time, that the historical reality of esoteric philosophical writing, and the great practical importance of that historical fact, will continue to stand, unscathed, even if one completely rejects the following interpretation regarding its larger philosophical significance.

LEO STRAUSS AND THE
CONTEMPORARY CRISIS OF REASON

As we late moderns have moved through the twentieth and into the twenty-first century, we find ourselves in very strange intellectual territory. We face an unprecedented double attack on reason. The legitimacy of Western science, philosophy, and rationalism is being radically challenged by two opposite but mutually reinforcing movements: the ancient force of religious orthodoxy and the "postmodern" one of historicism or cultural relativism. Reason is under serious assault—in a kind of spontaneous pincer movement—from both the faith-based thinkers and the cutting-edge, secular intellectuals, from the "church" as well as the "university." This is the great philosophical predicament of our time, what Strauss called the "crisis of modernity." The whole of his thought is an effort to respond to it.

It is very difficult today to have a fruitful discussion of this issue, however, because, largely as a consequence of this crisis of reason, ours is a period of extreme intellectual dislocation in which we constantly talk past one another. Not only are the answers up for grabs, but the questions are as well—along with the proper concepts, categories, and principles of justification. What some people regard as the main philosophical issues of our time, others consider tiresome pseudoproblems that dissolve when the proper perspective is attained. The consequence of all this is that one must spend a good deal of time defending the legitimacy of one's question—as I will try to do here—before developing an answer. This is especially the case with the questions of historicism, relativism, and rationalism that Strauss is centrally concerned with. In many circles today, this weighty concern over the fate of reason, indeed this whole mode of grave "crisis consciousness" that has largely characterized Western thought since Nietzsche, is very much out of fashion.

Let us try to find some neutral ground. In 1995, a conference specifically devoted to clarifying "the present state of philosophy" was convened by the Polish Academy of Sciences in Warsaw, and Jürgen Habermas, Richard Rorty, and Leszek Kolakowski were invited to debate their differing perspectives on this central issue. With Habermas being arguably the premier contemporary defender of some form of Enlightenment rationalism and Rorty arguably the premier representative of the postmodernist position, and Kolakowski one of the finest minds intimately acquainted with both sides, the debate was particularly well constructed. This is especially the case because Habermas and Rorty also stand out for the efforts they have consistently made to acquaint themselves with and debate rival positions, both Continental and Anglo-American. Habermas's paper was entitled "Coping with Contingencies—The Return of Historicism"; Rorty's, "Relativism—Finding and Making"; and Kolakowski's, "A Remark on Our Relative Relativism." As Jozef Niznik, an organizer of the conference and the editor of its proceedings, accurately remarked in his preface:

> What is especially interesting is that, without exception, the dominant concepts and problems that appeared in the texts of all three main participants were those of relativism and rationality. . . . The debate shows—in a fascinating way—that these problems create what are probably the most important philosophical issues of contemporary human life and constitute the core of contemporary intellectual anxieties.[1]

This is precisely Strauss's view as well.

But let us see if we can derive the same view in a more concrete and, as it were, bottom-up manner. A great many observers today, popular no less than scholarly, speak about a growing weakness in the basic respect for reason and in the role that it plays in our lives. To begin on the popular level, there has been a spate of books, of varying quality, devoted to this precise phenomenon, including two best-sellers, Susan Jacoby's *The Age of American Unreason* and former vice president Al Gore's *The Assault on Reason*. All argue that if you look at the various debates and conflicts that we have been having in this country, you see that in recent years it has become far more acceptable to ignore or dismiss the concern for reasoning, logic, empirical evidence, and science. The point is not that people are reasoning badly but that the prestige and authority of reason itself—and especially the respect for science—seem to be in decline.[2]

What is the source of this change? These works point to a number of different causes: political factors such as the growing use of manipulation and fear-mongering in our increasingly partisan world, as well as various sociological factors such as the overstimulation of the emotions by the entertainment industry, advertising, and the twenty-four-hour news cycle and the shortening of attention spans by television-induced passivity or internet-induced hyperactivity. But these are potentially passing trends, and at any rate not fundamental.

As most of these works ultimately conclude, what makes possible the truly serious "assault on reason" or "war on science" is the appeal to a source of authority outside and above reason—the appeal to revelation. The key to the serious undermining of reason in our time is the dramatic rise of religious feeling and fundamentalist belief in this country (to say nothing of Islamic fundamentalism, Hindu fundamentalism, and like phenomena around the world). This, and not any of the other factors mentioned, is what makes possible the trumping of scientific evidence in the grand debates over creationism, abortion, stem cell research, and so forth. This is why, ninety years after the Scopes monkey trial, creationism is increasingly powerful and only 39 percent of the U.S. population reports believing in the theory of evolution.[3] The essential phenomenon, to repeat, is the surprising late modern resurgence of religion, of the ancient conflict of reason and revelation. Somehow, two and a half centuries after the rise and triumph of the Enlightenment, with its rationalizing and secularizing mission, we are experiencing a powerful revival of the oldest and most fundamental challenge to rationalism.

Still, this religious revival itself would not necessarily be anything lasting and fundamental if it were merely a matter of popular movements, which come and go. (In Strauss's time in particular, this popular-level revival had not yet really appeared.) What is more crucial, then, is that the religious resurgence had also been taking place on the highest planes of philosophical reflection for well over a century in the radical religious turn of thinkers like Kierkegaard and William James, the mystical turn of Bergson and Wittgenstein, and the religious murmurings of Heidegger, as well as of recent postmodernists like Gianni Vattimo, Jacques Derrida, and Jean-François Lyotard. Thus, the current religious revival would seem to be not merely a popular, sociological phenomenon but a philosophical one, a shift in the reason-revelation balance occurring at the profoundest level of Western thought. That indeed is how Strauss found the situation in his own personal grapplings with the religious question.

Yet this first, religious challenge to reason, as powerful as it is, is still only half the story. Strangely, what tends to be forgotten by Gore, Jacoby, and most others who earnestly deplore the irrational effects of the religious critique of reason is that there is, in our times, a second and no less powerful source of the assault on reason, one that primarily resides on their own side of the intellectual or ideological spectrum. I am referring to the very widespread but amorphous intellectual movement most commonly known today as postmodernism. This is largely the same as what Strauss, using an older vocabulary, called historicism.

Now, it is notoriously difficult to define postmodernism or historicism in a way that includes all of its many variants and practitioners. But it is also not necessary for current purposes. Suffice it to say here (I will say a bit more momentarily) that philosophical postmodernism in most of its forms is a questioning and subversion of "modernism," understood primarily as the Enlightenment project with its universalistic understanding of reason and its hegemonic design for world rationalization, as epitomized by Descartes (at the origins) and Hegel (at the peak). Postmodernism is, in Jean-Francois Lyotard's famous definition, an "incredulity towards meta-narratives," that is, a chastening effort to particularize, localize, and temporalize—in a word, historicize—rationality.[4] As such, it involves a wide-ranging critique of reason—a humbling of Enlightenment rationalism, a debunking of the idea of universal, objective, and eternal Truth. Among postmodernism's various proponents, this critique involves such things as a rejection of foundationalism, essentialism, subject/object dualism, binary oppositions, and a leveling of the distinctions between literature and philosophy and between rhetoric and logic. For most, the key element of this critique of reason is the claim that all thought is necessarily based on or conditioned by something unthought, something given by language, politics, or history and therefore particular, contingent, and transitory. This widespread postmodernist disempowering of reason, in which modern philosophy seems to have culminated, constitutes the second powerful source of the contemporary attack on reason.

This crisis of reason is what formed the beginning point for Strauss's path of thought and the focus of his philosophical project. Beginning in the 1930s, Strauss was among the first clearly to identify and to confront this precise double challenge and also the first to explain it—that is, to explain the inner connection between these two opposite antirational forces, such that both of them should be surging at the same time. He argued that the strange, late modern resurgence of religion, the shift in the reason-revelation balance, has largely been caused by the triumph of postmodernism or historicism, because postmodernism has undermined the Enlightenment rationalism that had been undermining religion. The postmodernist critique holds that reason is unable to attain to anything like universal, timeless truth and furthermore that such truth is a thing that our culture can easily learn to do without. We can get by with our local "narrative." But this critique of reason deprives it of the firmest grounds upon which to oppose revelation. You can do many things with a "narrative," but you cannot refute God. Thus, the ancient force of religion has gained a surprising new lease on life at the end of modernity— and not for sociological reasons but for powerful philosophical ones: through the rise of postmodernism, corrosive modern reason has at length turned on itself, undermining its own capacity to contest the claims of revelation.

But then why did historicism or postmodernism itself arise? According to Strauss, modern, Enlightenment rationalism eventually produced postmodernism—that is, its own self-destruction—largely because of the peculiar defects present within that rationalism from its very foundations, laid by such thinkers as Machiavelli, Descartes, and Hobbes: its dogmatic demand for certainty, for presuppositionless "foundations," for political realism and practical efficacy, for historical progress, and, above all, for the harmony of theory and praxis, rationality and politicality. Yet this fateful weakness of modern philosophy, he continues, was itself no accident: it arose from the peculiar demands of the fierce battle it was fighting—both political and philosophical—against religion. Modern "rationalism" had become deformed by its particularly bruising struggle with revelation—an inevitable and fundamental struggle that was somehow handled in a less distorting way by classical and even medieval rationalism.

In Strauss's view, then, it is no accident that modern thought has culminated in the unique double assault on rationalism that confronts us today, which he describes as "the victory of orthodoxy through the self-destruction of rational philosophy [i.e., historicism]."[5] Strauss's philosophical project, then, was to see if it was possible, in the face of the twin challenge of revelation and relativism, to mount a defense of rationalism in some form, especially by moving back, prior to the defective beginnings of modern rationalism, back to classical rationalism properly understood, that is, to a minimalist, skeptical, Socratic rationalism. All of Strauss's varied writings and far-flung research serve the single aim of "philosophic apologetics": he is less concerned to elaborate a philosophical system than to see if the whole enterprise of rationalism can be rationally justified by replying to these two most fundamental challenges.

One must immediately add, however, that Strauss did not undertake this reply in a spirit of either certainty or indignation. He was not a rationalist crusader. He was a seeker. Strongly attracted both to historicism and to religion (Judaism), he felt their power and appeal, while being struck by the narrowness and superficiality of most of the existing attacks upon them. In his view, there were no simple, airtight proofs on any side of this issue. It had to be approached with constantly renewed openness, delicacy, and appreciation for complexity.

In what follows, to keep things manageable, I will leave aside the religious question and confine my account to a basic outline of Strauss's reply to historicism or postmodernism. Although the religious question is clearly the more fundamental one in Strauss's eyes, it is less relevant to the present inquiry since it is not connected to the phenomenon of esotericism in as intimate and complex a way.[6]

Strauss's critique of historicism, I will argue, is perhaps the most powerful of those that have been put forward. This is partly due to the fact that Strauss, having been steeped in the thought of Nietzsche and Husserl and having been educated in and around the Heideggerian circle, begins from an inner understanding and appreciation of the three thinkers most important in bringing the historicist perspective to its highest development. These three thinkers remain fundamental for all the later manifestations of postmodernism.

But the unique power of Strauss's critique is above all due to that aspect of his thought that at first seems least relevant: his theory of esoteric writing. In multiple ways—in six distinct lines of argument, as I will try to show—Strauss's theory of esotericism contributes to a highly original, multifaceted, and powerful attack on historicism. Those six arguments, then, constitute Strauss's answer to the question of the larger *philosophical* significance of esotericism—which is what we are seeking. Taken together, these arguments show that the rediscovery of esotericism may possibly open the path to a "posthistoricist" or "post-postmodernist" relegitimation of reason through a new return to authentic Socratic rationalism.

THE "CRISIS OF HISTORICISM"

Let us begin by trying to make somewhat clearer what it is that Strauss is endeavoring to combat. What is meant by "historicism"– to revert to this older, although still current, terminology—and why must it be combated?

"Always historicize!" proclaims Fredric Jameson at the beginning of *The Political Unconscious.*[7] That indeed would seem to be the underlying imperative of contemporary thought. Over the last two centuries—arguably since the Renaissance—modern thinkers have labored under an ever-increasing pressure to understand texts, doctrines, and indeed every expression of human reason as manifestations of their times. To be sure, there has been much dispute regarding what it is that actually constitutes or determines "the times." Major contenders in this ongoing struggle include the Hegelian zeitgeist understood as a stage in the dialectical unfolding of the Idea, Marx's forces and relations of production, linguistic and grammatical conventions, political relations of domination and subjugation, Wittgenstein's "forms of life," Thomas Kuhn's "paradigms of normal science," and Heidegger's epochal destinings of Being. All of this striking disagreement, however, renders only more amazing the underlying agreement: everyone agrees in feeling that there is *something* in the times that rules and structures human thought. Strangely, we are more certain *that* we are products of our times than *how*. The profound philosophic aspiration to view things from the standpoint of eternity or in terms of our common humanity has slowly lost credibility. All our belief and delight lies in the act of reducing thought to its external conditions. This driving impulse to radically "immanentize," and "contextualize" reason—this tendency not only to remove the human mind from its unconditioned, transcendental perch but to fully submerge it in the soil of practical needs and local contingencies so that the mind can never be more than a fruit of its times—is what is meant by "historicism."

Clearly, it is a rebellion against so-called Platonism: the ideal of the "God's-eye-view," of the pure mind, unconditioned by praxis, in touch with the pure, unchanging truth. But while Platonist rationalism sought merely to "transcend" the contingent world of praxis, it was Enlightenment rationalism that sought to conquer and reform it. The latter pursued the radically un-Platonic project to unify theory and praxis through the rationalization of the political world. Thus, historicism is above all a specific revolt against this modern, universalizing form of reason. It might even be described as the revenge of the long repressed and devalued world of praxis against the colonialism of Enlightenment rationality. In other words, historicism is less anti-Platonist than counter-Enlightenment (or postmodern). But, at the same time, for all its rebellion against the imperialist Enlightenment, it does not return to Platonist withdrawal: it still shares the Enlightenment's activist aim to mend the world, to unify theory and praxis—only in the opposite manner, by fully subordinating reason to the demands of practical life rather than the reverse.

Over the last two centuries, this tendency has become increasingly widespread and powerful. In his famous 1924 essay "Historicism," Karl Mannheim wrote:

> Historicism has developed into an intellectual force of extraordinary significance; it epitomizes our *Weltanschauung*. The historicist principle not only organizes, like an invisible hand, the work of the social and cultural sciences, but also permeates everyday thinking.[8]

What was true in 1924 has become truer still in the antifoundational, multiculturalist world of contemporary postmodernism. Thus, Hans-Georg Gadamer emphasizes the pervasive and profound influence of this heightened sense of historicity:

> The appearance of historical self-consciousness is very likely the most important revolution among those we have undergone since the beginning of the modern epoch. . . . We understand historical consciousness to be the privilege of modern man to have a full awareness of the historicity of everything present and the relativity of all opinions.[9]

Similarly, Habermas states in the above-mentioned debate:

> One way to deal with the rather unspecific topic of the "present state of philosophy" is to focus on an obvious feature of contemporary debates—the *contextualist mood* that prevails in most of the debates, whether in moral and political philosophy, the philosophy of language, or the philosophy of science.

He identifies this contextualism with historicism and describes Derrida and Rorty, in particular, as representing "the most sophisticated version of present historicism."[10]

As both Mannheim and Habermas imply here, historicism is more of a general tendency than a specific doctrine or school, and one finds manifestations of it across almost all the social sciences and humanities, although with different names, formulations, and heroes. In philosophy, one could point to neopragmatism, poststructuralism, antihumanism, deconstructionism, anti-essentialism, and epistemological pluralism; in history and philosophy of science, to the Kuhnian school and Paul Feyerabend's epistemological anarchism; in sociology, to the sociology of knowledge, social epistemology, and social constructionism; in psychology, to linguistic relativity or the Sapir-Whorf hypothesis; in anthropology, to the Boasian school of American anthropology, poststructuralism, and Geertzian symbolic anthropology; in law, to critical legal studies; and in various cultural and literary disciplines, to postcolonialism, queer theory, and cultural studies. Although involving widely different methods, vocabularies, and audiences, each of these movements consciously undertakes to fulfill the modern imperative: always historicize.

At the same time, however, the growth of this historicist imperative over the last few centuries has also been accompanied by a growing sense of its dangers. Ever since Nietzsche's *On the Advantage and Disadvantage of History for Life* (1874), the "crisis of historicism"—as it was later named in Ernst Troeltsch's influential *Der Historismus und seine Probleme* (1922)—has been a major preoccupation of modern thought. Historicism—especially the radical historicism of Heidegger—would seem to entail what a host of books in the last several decades have loudly proclaimed: "the end of philosophy." Indeed, it would seem to lead to the relativizing of all moral, scientific, and philosophical thinking. For if there are an indefinite number of conflicting cultures, metanarratives, or *Weltanschauungen*—comprehensive views of God, the universe, and humanity—and if no standpoint outside them is possible from which to judge one truer than the others, it is hard to see how one set of fundamental beliefs and values could be said to be superior to any number of alternative sets.

RELATIVISM: CRISIS OR PANACEA?

It is at this point, however, that the radical disconnectedness of our intellectual life, alluded to above, becomes most apparent and problematic. For as many have pointed out, while the first, "existentialist" wave of Heidegger's influence filled the cafes and universities with grave talk of nihilism, meaninglessness, angst, and the abyss, the second, "postmodernist" wave privileged a diametrically opposite stance: a lighthearted posture of irony, playfulness, and free-spirited delight in the liberation from God and metaphysics. Suddenly all that high-Nietzschean seriousness has come to seem benighted and passé. Whether this remarkable shift represents a deepening of understanding and a growing postmetaphysical maturity or a form of spiritual exhaustion and denial cannot be explored here. Let us simply confine ourselves to evaluating the moral/political argument that forms one important strand behind the later, positive attitude that sees not a crisis but an opportunity, even a panacea, in historicist relativism.

Surveying the French historicist/postmodernist scene in *On Human Diversity*, Tzvetan Todorov speaks of "relativism, which is presented as a miraculous solution to our problems."[11] Similarly, within the Anglo-American tradition, Hilary Putnam speaks of the "fashionable panacea of relativism."[12] Todorov summarizes this now familiar view—the moralistic demand for relativism—as follows:

> The universalist pretension has turned out, over the centuries, to be nothing but a mask worn by ethnocentrism. Thus, the universalist ideology is responsible for events that number among the most unfortunate in recent European history—namely, the colonial conquests.... Universalism is imperialism.... Even within states, heterogeneity has been stifled in the name of these same (pseudo)-universal ideals. That is why it is time to leave claims to universalism behind, and to recognize that all judgments are relative: relative to a time, to a place, to a context. This relativism need not be confused with nihilism or with cynicism (the rejection of all values); from this standpoint, values are recognized, but their extension is limited.[13]

Rorty, for example, in his brief autobiography, speaks of the much-needed tolerance that will result from "realizing how many synoptic visions there have been, and how little argument can do to help you choose among them."[14]

Part of this view—its understanding of the *problem*—makes a good deal of sense. For the fear expressed here of the grave political evils—intolerance, persecution, imperialism—that can arise from reason's triumphant grasp of "universal truth" is in fact nothing but a restatement of (one version of) the conflictual view of theory and praxis that we have been exploring. Theoretical truth can be dangerous to practical life.

What is new and problematic in this view, however, is its solution, its turn to relativism as the universal antidote to intolerance and related evils. (The discovery of this solution also returns its adherents to the harmonist fold with a vengeance, since it means that the *real* theoretical truth is not some dangerous moral universal but rather relativism itself—which is a doctrine that, in their view, harmonizes perfectly with the most urgent needs of the practical world.)

The basic argument for this view holds that relativism will lead to toleration for two reasons: it decreases the temptations to intolerance while also increasing the appreciation of tolerance. Relativism weakens the inclination to intolerance because, by undermining the belief in truth with a capital T, a single, objective, universal, and permanent truth, it attenuates people's beliefs or their sense of certainty and thus disinclines them to the zealous and intolerant effort to impose their views on others. At the same time relativism strengthens the positive appreciation of tolerance as a virtue because, by showing that there are no true and absolute values, it demonstrates—or could seem to demonstrate—that the only rational moral posture left is one of tolerance toward all value positions. Since all are equally ungrounded, all should be equally respected.

These two arguments are fairly sensible, and there is no doubt that, under the right circumstances, relativism can lead to an increase in toleration and a decrease in persecution, sexism, racism, homophobia, imperialism, colonialism, and other forms of moralistic intolerance. The only problem with this project is that relativism is a complex phenomenon, pregnant with other possibilities. Ironically, the proponents of relativism, so proudly anti-universalistic in every other respect, seem naively universalistic when they describe the moral and sociological effects of relativism. Let me quickly describe five alternative paths that lead out from relativism straight to intolerance.

It was argued above that relativism logically leads to toleration as the only value consistent with the realization that there are no universal values. This argument can be questioned, and will be below, but let us take it at face value for the moment. If it is simply thought through completely, it itself opens a broad new path to intolerance. For it does not merely support the value of tolerance: it produces an unparalleled exaltation of it. On this argument, tolerance becomes the sole value left standing, everything else having been undercut by relativism, per hypothesis. It is no longer one virtue among many, but the only virtue, the sole source of moral worth. Likewise, intolerance becomes the single root of all evil. Now, as the proponents

of relativism themselves will especially understand, this kind of moral intensification and especially this unification of evil into one thing—this demon-
ization of a single trait—can be highly dangerous (no less than the nonrelativist claims to universal truth). Inevitably, it will lead certain moralistically
inclined individuals to denounce the "universalists," "absolutists," or "non-
relativists" as uniquely wicked, the one group never to be tolerated. In this
way the relativist argument easily and (more or less) logically comes around
to its own unique strain of intolerance: persecution in the name of toleration. This is essentially what is meant by "political correctness," a phenomenon that we do commonly see around us today.

At the same time, among other sorts of people, relativism can lead to intolerance in a completely opposite way. Relativism may—as advertised—
initially lead to toleration by attenuating the dogmatic confidence and zeal
of people's value commitments. But eventually this "attenuation effect" may,
in certain individuals, extend to the value of toleration itself (a more strictly
logical consequence than the heightening of that value just described).
When that point is reached, things reverse course: people become more accepting of intolerance. This means that they become too morally easygoing
to stand up to the intolerance of others and, more important, to overcome
within themselves the crude or intolerant impulses that form, for many
people, an essential part of feeling good about themselves. To be sure, these
mellow relativists will engage less in the crusading, moralistic kind of intolerance, but they will engage more in the thoughtless and heartless kind—a
swaggering, in-crowd arrogance or at least a complacent, easygoing loutish-
ness. And this too is something that we see on the rise all around us.

There is yet a third obvious way in which relativism works to undermine
the belief in toleration. The value of toleration gets its psychological force primarily from a kind of empathy: the belief that despite our surface differences
we are all fundamentally the same, we share a common humanity, a single
nature, a universal dignity. But this belief in human nature—essentialist
and universalist—is emphatically rejected by most forms of historicist relativism, which typically hold that we are socially constructed all the way
down. There are Germans, Chinese, and Nigerians—but no such thing in
the world as "humans." Todorov points to the possible consequences:

The consistent relativist writes off the unity of the human species. Now this
is an even more dangerous position than the naive ethnocentrism of certain
colonialists. The absence of unity allows exclusion, which can lead to exter-
mination.[15]

In short, relativism undercuts all good explanations for why I should tolerate strange and annoying people who violate my values.

Still another path—the profoundest—from relativism to intolerance runs as follows. Historicist relativism is antifoundationalist. It holds that the true sources of human thought are to be found not in universal, self-evident truths available to human reason everywhere and always, but in the unique practices, traditions, and conventions of one's particular cultural community. This implies that the deepest thinking is achieved, not by detaching oneself from one's community and adopting a neutral, objective, cosmopolitan, and thus tolerant posture, but rather by cleaving as closely as possible to one's own tradition, to our "shared commitments," and seeking out what is genuinely native and homegrown. In this way, relativism leads to the replacement of the ideal of detachment with that of commitment, and the ideal of objectivity with that of solidarity (as Rorty explicitly demands). This shift not only subverts the dignity of the neutral stance of toleration but can easily lead to a heightened fear of foreign pollution, an intellectual nationalism, a philosophically motivated xenophobia that has far more in common with intolerance and fascism than with tolerance and the open society.

The fifth and final point builds on the previous one. If, on the relativist view, all meaning, truth, and value grow from the soil of local traditions and conventions, then one needs to ask where, in turn, do these conventions come from and what sustains them? In answering this question, people today like to use the passive, neutral term "socially constructed." But precisely how does this process work? Who does the constructing when something is socially constructed—and how do they do it? It is surely not all of us. It is those with power, the hegemons. And they do not do it by consensus. Why does all of present-day South and Central America (excluding Brazil) speak Spanish and worship Jesus? It is not the result of a spontaneous philo-Iberian movement welling up from the masses. It is the work of the conquistadores. Cultures and conventions come primarily from conquests, great founders, ruling elites—from force and will. It's all political: truth is subordinate to power. That is—and must be—the relativist view.

The nonrelativist, while acknowledging the role of power, could add that an important role is also played by the objective truth of things, the inherent principles of justice, which—permanent and unmoved by human force and "construction"—make themselves known to humans over time and shape their beliefs and values. But for the relativist, there is no objective truth of things standing above the imposed creations of men. Everything is humanly constructed—by the hegemons. And of course, there is no prior, objective justice to help determine who the hegemons will or should be. All there is is a naked struggle for domination, at the end of which the victors not only write the history, but create the values and the truths. In this way, relativism, which at first seems a moderating, anticolonial influence — since it removes the temptation to conquer in the name of universal values — easily becomes an incitement to conquest since it generates new and far grander temptations: to become oneself the creator of new values and worldviews. There is a direct connection, in other words, between Nietzsche's two great themes: relativism and the will to power.

For this reason, no one should be surprised to hear the insightful words of praise for relativism famously spoken by Benito Mussolini:

> In Italy, relativism is simply a fact. . . . Everything I have said and done in these last years is relativism by intuition. . . . If relativism signifies contempt for fixed categories and for men who claim to be the bearers of an objective immortal truth . . . then there is nothing more relativistic than Fascist attitudes and activity. . . . From the fact that all ideologies are of equal value, that all ideologies are mere fictions, the modern relativist infers that everybody has the right to create for himself his own ideology and to attempt to enforce it with all the energy of which he is capable.[16]

Indeed, given that the most profound sources of contemporary relativism are Nietzsche and Heidegger, and that neither of them — to say the least — understood it as either an argument or a force for liberal toleration, it is hard to understand how intelligent people today can be so blithely confident of this connection. Relativism is full of contradictory inner possibilities, some of them quite horrific, and no one can say which will triumph in the long run.

Looking beyond the issue of toleration, moreover, we find many other reasons to fear historicist relativism. It may not lead to the triumph of our basest impulses — as some people fear — but it can easily attenuate our highest ones, as the relativists themselves emphasize. This can sap our capacity for idealism and energetic striving, miring us in apathy and anomie.[17] Most directly, it would seem to threaten the way of life built around the longing for truth. For that reason, in Kolakowski's contribution to the Warsaw debate, he describes "the present state of philosophy" as follows:

> Husserl's unflagging pleas for Truth — spelled with upper case — in the face of the relativist corruption of European civilization went largely un-

heeded, and this was not so because his arguments were necessarily faulty, but rather because the *prevailing cultural trends* were going in another direction and eradicated, step by step, the belief in perennially valid standards of intellectual work, [the belief] in the regulative ideal of *episteme*, and finally [the belief] in the very usefulness of the concept of truth. These trends have reached their climax in our time.[18]

This is the "crisis of historicism."

In his own contribution to the Warsaw debate, Habermas situates contemporary historicism and postmodernism in the context of the long struggle between "Platonists" and "anti-Platonists" that, in one form or another, has been going on since Plato's time. As for himself, he states that while he feels a political sympathy with the "anti-Platonist iconoclasts," his philosophical sympathy is fully on the side of what he calls "the custodians of reason" in those periods when the justified critique of reason starts to put in danger the very possibility of rationality.[19]

Strauss's philosophical sympathy may be described in the same way. He is precisely a "custodian of reason." While full of skepticism for excessive "Platonism" (indeed, even doubtful that Plato was ever a "Platonist"), he is intent on saving the cause of rationality from the excesses of historicism.

HOW TO CONFRONT HISTORICISM

If one is convinced of the need to combat historicism, however, one quickly encounters the next great obstacle: it is very difficult to arrange a clear confrontation with so amorphous a movement. As Strauss remarks, echoing the above statement of Mannheim, historicism is "not just one philosophical school among many, but a most powerful agent that affects more or less all present-day thought."[20] Thus, "historicism appears in the most varied guises and on the most different levels. Tenets and arguments that are the boast of one type of historicism, provoke the smile of adherents of others."[21] In short, there are many historicisms, displaying varying degrees of sophistication and rigor. One must begin by reconstructing what the serious case for historicism is before trying to respond to it.

Strauss suggests that the historicist position does not rest on any single line of argument but derives from the combined effect of at least three different kinds of evidence—let us call them the historical, the theoretical, and the experiential. First, there is the purely *historical* evidence, such as the dispiriting spectacle of the great variety of philosophical systems. But by itself this kind of evidence proves little: disagreement is not disproof.

It needs to be supplemented by the second, "theoretical" kind of evidence: a philosophical analysis, a "critique of reason" that, extending the line of argument of Hume and Kant, shows the impossibility of rational ethics and of theoretical metaphysics while also showing the inescapable dependence of the positive sciences on moral and metaphysical presuppositions. But a critique of reason of this kind, Strauss argues, takes us only as far as skepticism, which, unlike historicism, is still compatible with philosophy. (Indeed, Strauss holds that it is precisely skepticism rightly understood, Socratic or zetetic skepticism, that is the most defensible philosophic position.) Furthermore, a *theoretical* critique of reason could not culminate in historicism without contradicting itself, without relativizing its own claims.[22]

Thus, Strauss argues, the complete historicist position—the radical or existentialist historicism of Heidegger—emerges from and rests upon a critique of thought that is no longer theoretical, but "committed": it addresses itself to and attempts to articulate a particular experience, the so-called "experience of history" or of "historicity." This is the third, "experiential" ground for historicism. To be sure, this inner experience is excited by the sorts of historical observations mentioned above—the meaningless flux of historical conditions and beliefs—but it extends beyond them. It claims to represent a unique awareness or divination that has been given to recent generations almost like a special revelation. It is a feeling of anguish or angst, which when confronted honestly and spelled out discloses an awareness that all meaning, all horizons of intelligibility, have no other ground than the dispensation of fate. "The fundamental experience, i.e., an experience more fundamental than every science, is the experience of the objective groundlessness of all principles of thought and action, the experience of nothingness."[23]

But Strauss suggests that appeal to this irreducible experience (much like the appeal to revelation) must confront the problem of the seeming multiplicity of such experiences or revelations. We have many experiences that claim to put everything in its proper perspective—moral experiences, for example, or the experience of humble awe and wonder. How do we know, then, that the anguished experience of historicity is the basic experience that reveals the fundamental situation of man as man? Furthermore, upon careful examination such experiences in fact turn out to have subtle presuppositions that can and must be brought to light and tested by reason. Thus, the crucial appeal to revelatory experience cannot completely escape or trump the authority of rational argument.[24]

Since Strauss sees historicism as resting on such a complex combination of different kinds of evidence, his response to it is equally complex. His writings are fairly brimming with observations and arguments that are meant as replies to one or another of the strands of the historicist case. But Strauss does have a basic overarching strategy that is clearly enunciated and pursued in *Natural Right and History* and indeed in his scholarly corpus as a whole. Near the end of the first chapter of that work, Strauss declares that to judge historicism,

> [w]e need, in the first place, a nonhistoricist understanding of nonhistoricist philosophy. But we need no less urgently a nonhistoricist understanding of historicism, that is, an understanding of the genesis of historicism that does not take for granted the soundness of historicism.[25]

Strauss announces here a two-pronged approach.

First, in order to assess the overall plausibility of historicism, it is not sufficient to contest an argument here or an observation there. We need a clear view of the alternative. But historicism is not a specific or isolated thesis; it is or rests upon a comprehensive interpretation of human experience. Thus, historicism as a whole must be confronted by an alternative whole. Now, historicist thought is something that we are privileged to see at its peak in the thought of Heidegger, a (then) living philosopher of towering genius who tended to dazzle and silence all of his contemporaries. In order to free our minds from dazzlement and to consider what an alternative interpretation of the phenomena and experiences emphasized by historicism might look like, we need to see nonhistoricist thought at its peak—which is to be found, Strauss believed, in classical thought. The problem is that the contemporary interpretation of classical thought is itself based on the presuppositions and historiographical methods of historicism. To avoid circularity, we need a new, "nonhistoricist understanding of nonhistoricist philosophy." That is what Strauss attempts to provide or prepare in the new interpretation of classical political philosophy or Socratic rationalism presented in the third and fourth chapters of *Natural Right and History* and in many of his other writings. In light of this newly revived alternative, we may begin to seriously entertain the possibility that historicism has been a colossal mistake.

But, second, to help confirm this suspicion, we also need a history of historicism, one that explains how that mistake could have arisen, how historicism could have seemed so right to so many great minds and yet be wrong. In his various studies of early modern thought, of Machiavelli, Hobbes, and Spinoza, Strauss attempts to uncover the forgotten—and problematic—foundations of modern philosophy and to explain, in these terms, its relentless downward spiral into historicism.

THE SELF-OVERCOMING OF HISTORICISM OR THE RISE OF "POSTHISTORICISM"

These two particular lines of investigation, it is important to add, not only make good sense in their own right but are required, as it were, by the consistent adherence to historicism itself. Sooner or later, Strauss suggests, they must bring about the self-overcoming of historicism.

This point is clearest with reference to Strauss's second line of investigation, his effort to give a historical analysis of historicism itself. A truly consistent historicism, he points out, "must be applied to itself."

> Precisely the historicist approach would compel us then to raise the question of the essential relation of historicism to modern man, or, more exactly, the question as to what specific need, characteristic of modern man, as distinguished from pre-modern man, underlies his passionate turn to history.[26]

Strauss seeks to give a historical explanation for the modern mind's strange and unique inclination to historicism. He historicizes historicism.

Similarly, Strauss's first line of attack, his effort to recover an authentic understanding of nonhistoricist or classical thought, is also the necessary result of a consistent historicism. For genuine historicism, he argues, compels one to seek a less provincial, more sympathetic understanding of past thought, to uncover its hidden roots, so as more fully to overcome it. Strauss is thinking here of Heidegger's famous efforts at a "destruction of the tradition."[27] For example, Heidegger's "intention was to uproot Aristotle: he thus was compelled to disinter the roots, to bring them to light, to look at them with wonder." More generally, "by uprooting and not simply rejecting the tradition of philosophy, [Heidegger] made it possible for the first time after many centuries—one hesitates to say how many—to see the roots of the tradition as they are."[28] But this earlier thought, toward which a consistent historicist must strain to move ever closer, is all nonhistoricist in character. Therefore:

The historian who started out with the conviction that true understanding of human thought is understanding of every teaching in terms of its particular time or as an expression of its particular time, necessarily familiarizes himself with the view, constantly urged upon him by his subject matter, that his initial conviction is unsound.[29]

He comes at length to "understand the possibility which Heidegger had opened without intending it: the possibility of a genuine return to classical philosophy."[30] This end result is what Strauss explicitly calls the "self-destruction of historicism."[31]

Strauss's acknowledged debt to Heidegger means that it is precisely historicism at its peak that eventually, if unintentionally, produced the radical new openness to and reinvigoration of nonhistoricist thought at its peak. Thus, in both of his lines of attack, Strauss sees his own path of thought as not simply sui generis but representing the self-overcoming of historicism. This is perhaps the ground of the confidence Strauss seems to have harbored that the future would bring a settled return to nonhistoricist modes of thought.[32]

To put this point in a more contemporary vocabulary, many people assert that we have entered a postmodern era characterized by the final break with modern thought and the triumph of some version of historicism. Yet Strauss would argue (as we will see) that historicism is not truly postmodern because, while rejecting important modern elements, it is ultimately the fullest expression of the underlying tendency of modern thought. But he further argues that this modernist historicism is internally unstable and that, worked through, it points beyond itself, back to classical philosophy. One might call this condition—in which historicism, in overcoming itself, opens the path to the recovery of Socratic rationalism—"posthistoricism." In these terms (which are not used by Strauss himself), what Strauss stands for is *authentic* postmodernism—which is posthistoricism.

ESOTERICISM AND THE CRITIQUE OF HISTORICISM

We are finally in a position to examine Strauss's specific arguments against historicism. In what follows, I will pick out six strands of Strauss's complex argument against historicism and show the crucial role played in each by the doctrine or the phenomenon of esotericism.

Very briefly, the first two strands concern Strauss's reply to the historical evidence for historicism, while the remaining ones involve his response to the theoretical and experiential grounds. Of these, the second two strands are part of Strauss's effort to recover a genuine understanding of nonhistoricist thought at its peak, that is, of Socratic rationalism, whereas the final two strands concern his attempt to explain the rise of historicism historically.

1. Historical Evidence

The simplest and most common strand of the historicist argument involves the appeal to historical evidence. The argument holds, as Strauss puts it, that human history presents "the depressing spectacle of a disgraceful variety of thoughts and beliefs and, above all, of the passing-away of every thought and belief ever held by men." There have been almost as many distinct philosophies as there have been philosophers. "Why are philosophers" asks Rorty, "now as in Cicero's day, still arguing inconclusively, tramping round and round the same dialectical circles, never convincing each other?"[33] This experience of centuries of disagreement and failure seems finally to have exposed the grand delusion of nonhistoricist thinking: there is no final, transhistorical, universal truth.[34]

This is a weak argument on a number of counts. The spectacle of sectarian disagreement, Strauss points out, has been well known since ancient times without leading to this historicist conclusion. Why, then, does it have that effect on us? Indeed, it is an obvious fallacy to argue from the fact that people disagree to the conclusion that no one of them has the truth—or, worse, that there is no truth. Why, then, are we so tempted by this faulty reasoning?

Strauss's answer is that, from the start, modern thought aspired to "realism": to have an effect, to overcome the gulf between theory and praxis. It sought not merely to understand the world but to change it.[35] Thus, it tended to identify the rational with the real or the powerful—with what works or what wins. More crudely stated, it tended to worship success. We moderns lack the Olympian detachment from the world and from history that was the hallmark of classical thought. Consequently, all our thinking is shaped by an unspoken epistemological premise: if there is a truth, it will show itself in the world, it will win out in the marketplace of ideas, it will be proved by history. It is because of this very questionable premise that we have become inordinately dispirited by the familiar, age-old spectacle of sectarian disagreement and that we have drawn the unwarranted conclusion from it that there is no transhistorical truth.

But in addition to this reply, Strauss also argues that there is in fact much

less disagreement among the major philosophers than a conventional reading of their works would lead one to think. As we have seen, prior to the
nineteenth century, all philosophers, in one degree or another, adjusted
the presentation of their thought to the particular conventions prevailing
in their time and place. This esoteric practice had the effect of systematically exaggerating the appearance of philosophical disagreement. At the
same time, philosophers have inclined to hide their deepest thoughts and
experiences, especially those at the root of the philosophic life. This has had
the effect of systematically obscuring their points of agreement—what one
might call the unity of philosophic experience.

For example, it is axiomatic in modern classical scholarship that there
are fundamental disagreements between Plato and Aristotle. But Strauss,
reading esoterically, rejoined a long tradition of ancient Greek and medieval
Arabic commentators on Plato and Aristotle that regarded them as in essential agreement on the most important questions.[36] Similarly, Strauss argues
that an appreciation of esotericism is necessary in order to see the hidden
unity of early modern thought:

> We no longer understand that in spite of great disagreements among those
> thinkers, they were united by the fact that they all fought one and the same
> power—the kingdom of darkness, as Hobbes called it. . . . This will become
> clearer to us the more we learn again to understand those thinkers as they
> understood themselves and the more familiar we become with the *art of
> allusive and elusive writing* which all of them employ, although to different
> degrees. The series of those thinkers will then come to sight as a line of war-
> riors who occasionally interrupt their fight against their common enemy to
> engage in a more or less heated but never hostile disputation among them-
> selves.[37]

This is not to deny, of course, that there exist real disagreements among philosophers. Still, ignorance of the phenomenon of esoteric writing has led to a
systematic misreading of the history of philosophy, portraying it as far more
diverse and chaotic than in fact it has been.

2. Historical Evidence II

The historicist would reply that even if this were so, the mere issue of diversity does not get at the main lesson to be drawn from the historical evidence.
As Strauss writes, "*most* historicists *consider decisive* the fact, which can be

established by historical studies, that a close relation exists between each political philosophy and the historical situation in which it emerged."[38] For example, R. G. Collingwood, in his *The Idea of History*, writes:

> The *Republic* of Plato is an account, not of the unchanging ideal of political life, but of the Greek ideal as Plato received it and reinterpreted it. The *Ethics* of Aristotle describes not an eternal morality but the morality of the Greek gentleman. Hobbes' *Leviathan* expounds the political ideas of seventeenth century absolutism in their English form. Kant's ethical theory expresses the moral convictions of German pietism.[39]

There is by now a vast store of historical evidence, compiled over the past two centuries by philosophers and intellectual historians, demonstrating that even the greatest thinkers of the past were merely mouthpieces for the assumptions of their times, which they naively mistook for timeless Truth. As Karl Marx puts it in a famous passage, "What else does the *history of ideas* prove than that intellectual production changes its character in proportion as material production is changed? The ruling ideas of each age have ever been the ideas of its ruling class."[40] Marx considers this historical finding to be not merely true but perfectly obvious.

Marx is not wrong. The historical evidence for this view is indeed massive. But Strauss's rediscovery of esotericism makes possible the following reply: *of course* the great thinkers of the past *appear* to be prisoners of their times, hawkers of prevailing conventions, but that is because they deliberately hid their true thoughts behind a veil of conventionality. Through most of history, the price of real intellectual freedom was precisely the well-cultivated appearance of being a bound prisoner of one's time. Thus, to address two of Collingwood's examples above, if one reads carefully and between the lines in Plato's *Republic* and Aristotle's *Ethics*, one easily sees that the former ultimately had grave reservations about the Greek ideal of political life as did the latter about the morality of the Greek gentleman.[41] In this way, the doctrine of esoteric writing—*and it alone*—can explain away the otherwise massive historical evidence in favor of historicism.[42]

This doctrine also explains a related puzzle. Precisely if the evidence for historicism is as obvious as the historicist insists, then why was it not noticed by earlier centuries? Why are modern thinkers alone in drawing the historicist conclusion? Again the solution is provided by esotericism. Unlike earlier readers, we alone naively take the pious and conventional surface of past writings for their true teaching. We take our blindness for insight. In short, it is the modern forgetfulness of esotericism that is largely responsible for the strange and unique susceptibility of the modern mind to historicism.

Thus, on the historical level, when the evidence is read properly—that is, in light of the phenomenon of esotericism—it by no means points clearly to historicism. Indeed, as Strauss goes on to argue, it actually points away from it.

> Far from legitimizing the historicist inference, history seems rather to prove that all human thought, and certainly all philosophic thought, is concerned with the same fundamental themes or the same fundamental problems, and therefore that there exists an unchanging framework which persists in all changes of human knowledge of both facts and principles.[43]

At a minimum, even if permanent answers elude us, the fundamental questions of life are within our grasp, and this crucial "knowledge of ignorance" is all that is needed for a Socratic life of erotic skepticism and passionate questing.

3. Ancients and Moderns

The most serious case for historicism, according to Strauss, derives not from this first category of evidence—these purely historical arguments—but rather from the second and third categories: what I have called the theoretical and experiential grounds. Historicists offer elaborate theoretical analyses that purport to show the inherent limitations of human knowledge. Furthermore, this theoretical "critique of reason," when properly interpreted, also helps to articulate the fundamental "experience of history" or of 'historicity" that is somehow the deepest experience of the modern mind. This combination of philosophical critique and inner experience reveals that, from its very origins in Greece some twenty-five hundred years ago, Western rationalism was fundamentally deluded and nihilistic—based on presuppositions that it could not defend or even fully articulate—and that the whole subsequent history of philosophy has been the inevitable, step-by-step self-destruction of this overreaching, rationalist enterprise. Both Nietzsche and Heidegger, as Strauss reports, "regard as decisive the nihilism which according to them began in Plato (or before) . . . and whose ultimate consequence is the present decay."[44]

While Strauss has considerable sympathy for this line of argument, he has one basic objection: "I began . . . to wonder whether the self-destruction of reason was not the inevitable outcome of modern rationalism as distinguished from pre-modern rationalism."[45] This led to Strauss's central intellectual project: first, to uncover the fundamental gulf between ancient and modern rationalism and, then, to demonstrate that, unlike the latter, the former—which is nonhistoricist thought at its peak—was genuinely self-knowing and able to give an adequate justification of itself. Both parts of this project rely decisively on the rediscovery of esotericism.

To begin with, there is the central question—which depends decisively on how we *read*—of whether such a fundamental divide actually exists: is modern thought essentially different from classical (and Christian) thought? Such a view seems to have been the self-understanding of the Enlightenment, which boasted of its novelty and was much preoccupied with the famous "quarrel between the ancients and the moderns." But somehow this crucial perspective was lost. It is certainly not the view prevailing today.

A revisionist view took over in the nineteenth century when the romantic reaction against the Enlightenment and the turn away from reason to tradition inclined a new generation of historians—especially the "historical school" of Friedrich Carl von Savigny and Otto von Gierke—to downplay the radicalness of this break and to emphasize the essential continuity of the tradition reaching back from modern times to ancient Greek and Roman thought.

Moreover, the counter-Enlightenment reaction also involved a return to Christianity and an effort to reinterpret the Enlightenment in Christian terms. As Strauss puts it, "from this [Christian] *reaction* to the Enlightenment, the Enlightenment itself [became] interpreted as Christianly *motivated*." He adds, referring to esotericism: "and this [reinterpretation] succeeds because the Enlightenment had *always accommodated* itself, for *political* reasons, to Christianity. The thus created *fable convenue* is the basis of the view ruling today."[46] One example of "the view ruling today" is the widespread claim—found in different forms in Hegel, Wilhelm Dilthey, Max Weber, and others—that the Enlightenment represents, not a radical break with the premodern, but merely a "secularization" of Christian and especially of Protestant thought.

Subsequent scholarship on the history of Western philosophy has been largely shaped by these two revisionist views, which one may call the "continuity thesis" and the "secularization thesis." Nietzsche and Heidegger, who see the whole of Western rationalism, notwithstanding its inner mutations, as more or less of a piece, would also seem to be heirs of this later tradition of historiography.[47]

Strauss seeks to revive the earlier idea of a radical rift. But once lost, this view is extremely difficult to recover in anything more than a superficial way. For the early modern thinkers, precisely because they were conscious of making a radical and subversive break with the past, took considerable pains to obscure that break, at least in its full range and meaning. For example, "Locke makes it particularly difficult for us to recognize . . . how much he deviates from the natural right tradition. He was an eminently prudent man. . . . We are then apparently confronted with an unbroken tradition of perfect respectability that stretches from Socrates to Locke."[48] Scholars recognize that there is clearly something new in the early modern thinkers, but they are understandably dubious of the claims to fundamental originality that these thinkers occasionally make, primarily because these claims are surrounded by longer and more emphatic statements on religion and related matters that clearly indicate—at least, to nonesoteric readers—a continuing dependence on the Christian tradition.[49]

Strauss's rediscovery of esotericism, then, was the crucial precondition for his famous "ancients-moderns" theme: his rejection of the historiography of "continuity" and "secularization" and his recovery of the radical but partly hidden break in Western thought that makes it possible to decouple classical philosophy from the relentless downward spiral and self-destruction of modern philosophy.

4. The New Interpretation of Classical Philosophy

This decoupling of ancient thought from modern was just a first step. Strauss then needed to demonstrate that classical rationalism, unlike modern, was actually able to defend itself against the historicist critique of reason, both "theoretical" and "experiential."

He believed, however, that it was manifestly *not* able to defend itself, so long as it was understood in the traditional way, a way decisively shaped by methods of interpretation that presuppose the truth of historicism. To escape this circle, Strauss saw the need, as we have seen, for a new, nonhistoricist interpretation of classical thought. His recovery of the art of esoteric interpretation—which shows that the classical philosophers were not so much reflecting their times as hiding from them—opened the way to a comprehensive, new understanding of classical thought that was not only more genuine, in his view, but more able to fend off the historicist critique.

Obviously, it is not possible here to elaborate in any detail Strauss's interpretation of ancient thought. But let me briefly touch on three central as-

pects of that interpretation that are both crucial to the reply to historicism
and that depend on esoteric reading.

Classical Skepticism

The first aspect is the minimalism or extreme skepticism of classical rationalism. Strauss returned to classical thought via medieval thought, especially
via Maimonides and, on the latter's express recommendation, Alfarabi. It is
with the help of these thinkers, who speak explicitly of their own esotericism
and that of the classical writers, that Strauss was led to his own rediscovery of the phenomenon. And guided by Alfarabi's esoteric reading of Plato,
Strauss came to the view that the true Platonic philosopher—who does not
differ essentially from the Socratic or Aristotelian philosopher—was not the
"Platonist," the dogmatic metaphysician who knows the ideas, but rather
the zetetic skeptic who knows his own ignorance and who lives in wonder and questioning. Strauss found crucial confirmation for this unorthodox reading of Plato in another long-neglected source, Xenophon, a writer
who, since the end of the eighteenth century, had been largely dismissed as
philosophically superficial for the good reason that if one does not see the
esoteric depths of his Socratic writings, one sees only the sometimes charming, sometimes boring recollections of a retired general.

   In Strauss's new, skeptical interpretation of classical rationalism, derived
from Alfarabi, Plato, and Xenophon,

> Socrates was so far from being committed to a specific cosmology that
> his knowledge was knowledge of ignorance. Knowledge of ignorance is
> not ignorance. It is knowledge of the elusive character of the truth, of the
> whole. Socrates, then, viewed man in the light of the mysterious character
> of the whole. He held therefore that we are more familiar with the situation
> of man as man than with the ultimate causes of that situation. We may also
> say that he viewed man in the light of the unchangeable ideas, i.e., of the
> fundamental and permanent problems.[50]

Understood in this minimalist and skeptical way, classical philosophy
presents a much smaller target for attack. On this basis, classical rationalism remains relatively unscathed by such things as the refutation of teleology, the rise of modern science—and by the "theoretical" critique of reason
that forms the second ground of historicism. On this interpretation, for example, classical rationalism escapes the central Heideggerian charge that

it dogmatically identifies "being" with "intelligible" or "object."[51] Similarly, it is only on this interpretation that the above-mentioned historical evidence—the persistence, amid the flux of answers, of the same fundamental questions—may be taken as a decisive vindication of philosophy against the claims of historicism. "No more [than the permanence of the problems] is needed to legitimize philosophy in the original Socratic sense."[52]

The Double Challenge of Religion and Poetry

Related to this emphasis on skepticism is the second key aspect of Strauss's reinterpretation of classical thought: the centrality of the confrontation with religion and poetry. For if it is true that the philosopher "in the original Socratic sense" possesses no completed metaphysical system but lives "in the light of the mysterious character of the whole," through what means can he defend his rationalism in the face of the sacred claims of the city and the poets? Similarly, if we have no certain theoretical knowledge of the larger whole, if we must fall back on our direct human experience of the human—well, isn't the philosopher very clumsy and ill equipped for this, as is classically argued by Aristophanes in the *Clouds*? For the philosophers are typically detached from and contemptuous of the human things, the merely mortal realm; they are rationalists seeking the universal, the necessary, and the eternal. It follows that true wisdom is the preserve not of the philosophers but of the poets who immerse themselves in human life, who know it from the inside, and who are able to imitate and articulate the unique experience of the human in all its inescapable particularity, contingency, and changeableness. In Strauss's new interpretation, meeting this fundamental difficulty—the inevitable challenge to skeptical rationalism posed by divine and poetic wisdom—is the defining task of classical political philosophy and the core meaning of the Socratic revolution.

But this is not at all the teaching of the surface of the Platonic dialogues—or of the conventional scholarship based upon it—which rather hold, in Strauss's words, that "the opposite, or the opponent, of classical political philosophy is sophistry, the teaching and the practice of the Greek sophists." Socrates is the citizen-philosopher, the great defender of virtue and justice against the sophists. But in Strauss's esoteric reading, it is not the sophists but the poets who are truly central. "The great alternative to classical political philosophy is poetry." Again: "I limit myself to the question concerning the character and claim of classical political philosophy, to the question concerning the problem which it tried to solve, concerning the obstacle it tried to overcome. That problem and that obstacle appeared clearly in Aristophanes' presentation of Socrates."[53] For "Aristophanes' presentation of Socrates is the most important document available to us on the ancient disagreement and opposition between poetry and philosophy as such."[54]

The crucial significance of this second interpretive claim is this: beneath the surface, the real problem that Socrates—and classical political philosophy generally—faced was something quite similar to the great problem that confronts philosophy in Strauss's and our own time: the double challenge of religion and not of course historicism, but poetry—for poetry appeals to many of the same phenomena and experiences as does historicism. Indeed, the Nietzschean attack on Socrates was in many respects a restatement of the ancient poetic attack as epitomized by Aristophanes.[55] Thus, the main purpose of the dialogues of Plato and Xenophon, on Strauss's esoteric reading, is to show how Socrates, by virtue of his unique turn to political philosophy, was able to defend the philosophic life successfully against this double challenge to its legitimacy, the religious and the poetic (or "historicist").

Indeed, Socratic political rationalism is able not only to defend itself, in Strauss's view, but also to form the basis of a counterattack against historicism and against its third, "experiential" basis. Radical historicism understands itself to rest ultimately on a unique inner experience of historicity that has been granted to the late modern mind like a revelation. But Strauss suggests that this unique "discovery of History" may in fact be "an arbitrary interpretation of phenomena which had always been known and which had been interpreted much more adequately prior to the emergence of 'the historical consciousness' than afterward."[56] That more adequate interpretation, Strauss tries to show, can be found in Socrates's sympathetic understanding of and response to the challenge of poetic wisdom. To put it differently, through his esoteric interpretations of Plato, Xenophon, and Aristophanes, Strauss brings out the striking resemblance of the Socratic turn to the historicist turn—and the fundamental superiority of the former to the latter.

The Theory of Esotericism: The Conflict of Theory and Praxis

The third theme of Strauss's esoteric reading of classical thought is the necessary tension between the philosopher and the city, theory and praxis. This theme follows from the first two, from Socratic skepticism and the critique of poetry and religion. For cities cannot be skeptics: they have and need their certainties. And because these certainties cannot be grounded in reason, they require divine and poetic support. Therefore, there is an inescapable tension between rationalism and social existence, between the philosopher's way of life and the citizen's, between theory and praxis.

Once again, this is a theme almost wholly absent from the traditional scholarship on classical thought. But here we have a theme that not only derives from esoteric reading but also points to the derivation of esoteric writing. It is largely because philosophy and the city are inherently opposed, are dangerous to one another, that philosophers must write esoterically.

Now, this fact, in turn, points to a still more direct and essential relation between esotericism and historicism, a point elaborated in chapter 3. What classical esotericism and historicism *are*, are two opposing answers to the same fundamental question; namely, what is the relation between theory and praxis? As we have seen, generally speaking, two answers are possible: they are either in harmony or in opposition.

The belief in a harmony of theory and praxis—which, Strauss will argue, is the defining characteristic of modern thought—itself logically divides into two opposite forms, depending on which of the two forces is seen as dominant. The Enlightenment view holds that theory is in harmony with praxis because it is able to rule practice, to bring society into accord with reason. The opposite—but still harmonist—view is the historicist thesis, according to which theory is in harmony with practice because it ultimately serves practice, being an outgrowth or expression of existing social life.[57]

We are in the habit of regarding this famous opposition—Enlightenment rationalism vs. romanticism and historicism—as exhaustive, a habit that stems from and hides the basic presupposition of modern thought. But standing opposed to both of these harmonist views is the classical understanding, which denies that practice rules theory or theory, practice. Rather there is an unbridgeable gulf, a fundamental opposition or incompatibility between the two, which must therefore be mediated by esotericism, to protect each from the other.

Thus, the third element of Strauss's new understanding of classical thought—the theory of esotericism—constitutes a direct attack on historicism (as well as on the modern harmonist view generally). It holds that the philosopher's deepest knowledge—the knowledge that makes him a philosopher—is not an expression of his society's beliefs for the simple reason that this socially destructive knowledge could never form the basis of a society. His truths are not the expression of his historical actuality because such truths could not be embodied in any historical actuality. The theory of esotericism argues that historicism is based on a fundamentally incorrect understanding of the relation of reason and history.[58]

THE GROWTH OF HISTORICISM FROM THE
ABANDONMENT OF ESOTERICISM

The connection between historicism and esotericism is even more complex and more intimate than I have indicated, as will be seen if we turn now to the question of the historical causes of historicism.

Recall that Strauss follows a two-part strategy in confronting historicism. The first part, which we have now discussed, is the effort to revive nonhistoricist thought at its peak—Socratic skeptical rationalism—by distinguishing it from narrow and dogmatic modern rationalism (the "ancients-moderns" distinction), and then by producing a new interpretation of it that is untainted by historicist assumptions and historiographical methods, and finally by showing that, properly understood, it is capable of defending itself against the *theoretical* historicist critique of reason and, what is more, that it constitutes a superior interpretation of the fundamental *experiences* at the root of historicism. It also leads to a superior understanding of the relation of theory and praxis that contradicts the historicist view.

The second part of Strauss's response is to apply historicism to itself, as a consistent historicism requires: to give a historical explanation of the modern mind's strange compulsion to "always historicize." Strauss's causal account of historicism is naturally quite complex, but one particularly important strand of it is this: "the rise of modern historical consciousness came simultaneously with the interruption of the tradition of esotericism."[59] Somehow, there is a crucial causal connection between the decline in the practice of esoteric writing and the rise of historicism. This is the case, in fact, for three distinct reasons.

The first we have already seen. Over the last two centuries, the forgetfulness of esotericism has led modern readers to identify the true thought of past writers with the merely exoteric and conventional surface of their writings. This crucial interpretive error has led to the systematic overestimation of philosophic disagreement and has also produced the false appearance that all human thought is merely the reflection of prevailing conventions.

But the rise of historicism, Strauss will argue, derives not only from the decline of esoteric reading but also and more fundamentally from the decline of esoteric writing. If the classics were right regarding the essential incompatibility of theory and praxis, then the reduction or removal of the esoteric shield that protects society and philosophy from each other must eventually do harm to both. Historicism has arisen, Strauss suggests, as a reaction against or consequence of each of these two harms.

5. Historicism as a Reaction against the Harm Done to Society by the Decline of Esoteric Writing

To find the historical origins of historicism, a uniquely modern phenomenon, one must look to the origins of modernity itself. On Strauss's reading, we have seen, the philosophic initiators of modernity were primarily moved by opposition to the kingdom of darkness or what he calls "anti-theological ire."[60] On the deepest level, this means they sought to assure themselves of the falsity of the claims of revelation.[61] Believing that a theoretical refutation of revelation—one based on a completed metaphysical system—was not possible, they were forced into the realm of practice. Revelation could be refuted "experimentally," refuted by history, as it were, if philosophers would abandon their contemplative detachment and actively conspire to create a new world of justice and prosperity, a world in which men could be wholly "at home," attached, and satisfied, and thus a world in which the phenomenon of religion and religious experience could be observed to wither away.[62]

To this end, the modern thinkers demanded that theory abandon the utopian form of classical thought and become "realistic"—that it root itself in the actual and the practical—so that, on one hand, it would be powerful and effective in transforming the world, and so that, on the other, it would avoid erecting standards that permanently transcend and so devalue historical reality. They set themselves against all transcendent standards, all notions of a "beyond," both religious and philosophical. They demanded, in other words, the harmonization or unification of theory and praxis: of the ideal and the historically actual, of the ought and the is, of the rational and the real. By overcoming these classical dualisms, they hoped to eliminate every source of alienation or dissatisfaction, to remove every ground of appeal beyond the actual, to seal off the human sphere from everything claiming to be higher, and so to produce an absolute attachment, loyalty, and rootedness, an unqualified this-worldliness, and thus a secularization that would demonstrate its own legitimacy.[63]

This great modern effort to eliminate all transcendence, to unify theory and praxis, initially took the form of Enlightenment rationalism. In such thinkers as Descartes, Hobbes, Locke, and Diderot, the traditional attempt of classical esotericism to keep theory and praxis apart, to shelter political life from the corrosive effects of philosophic reason, was discarded. It was replaced by its opposite: the Enlightenment project to disseminate philosophic or scientific knowledge in the hope of progressively bringing the world of practice into conformity with reason. Of course, as we have seen, this enlightening project itself still required a kind of esotericism to manage the process of measured subversion. But this temporary "political esotericism" was far more limited than classical esotericism in its degree of concealment as well as its duration.

But as history teaches (along with the contemporary experience of modernization in third-world countries), this unleashing of theoretical reason on the world of practice, whatever its benefits, produced a host of problems. It led to a dangerous universalism, political doctrinairism, and ideological imperialism epitomized by the French Revolution (and, later, the Communist Revolution); it uprooted peoples from their ancient traditions and local customs; it fostered alienation, skepticism, materialism, and the decay of traditional mores. The great Enlightenment effort to make men more rooted and at home on earth was, in many respects, having precisely the opposite of its intended effect.

These political dangers were first pointed out by the great romantics and conservatives who rose up in reaction against the Enlightenment, starting with Rousseau and Burke. It is these thinkers—and especially the "historical school"—who took the crucial turn to history. Of course, having rediscovered the classical insight concerning the danger that undiluted rationalism poses to politics, they might simply have accepted that conflict and returned to the classical solution of esotericism. Instead, they moved forward toward historicism because, for all their passionate and seemingly total opposition to modernity, they remained modern thinkers in the decisive respect: they were still at war with the "kingdom of darkness" and still clung to the underlying, modern strategy to unify theory and praxis that also motivated their Enlightenment opponents. They merely saw the necessity of pursuing that strategy of unification in an opposite way by subordinating thought to social reality. They endeavored to prevent or combat the harms done by theory to practice by imbedding theory within practice, by making thought ground itself in local tradition, in short, by *historicizing* reason.[64]

In Strauss's telling, the long, tortured history of modern philosophy is largely the story of the conflict between reason and social life unleashed by the gradual abandonment of esoteric writing. The more that philosophic rationalism, liberated by the Enlightenment, moved aggressively into the open, the more it posed dangers to healthy moral and political life and thus the more it generated a hostility toward reason. This led to persecution from the nonphilosophers but to something far worse from the philosophers—to *la trahison des clercs*, the flight from reason, the politicization of philosophy, the rise of *philosophic antirationalism*.

For the modern philosophers, increasingly impressed by the social dangers of reason, but unwilling to abandon the great humanistic hope to eliminate all transcendence by harmonizing reason and political life, were compelled to engage in ever more extreme efforts to reinterpret and tame reason, to force it into the service of practical life.[65] Thus arose the great modern imperative to "always historicize"—the visceral suspicion of rationalism and the eagerness to humble it—that continues to move us to this day. As we have seen, a somewhat simplified version of this political critique of reason—"rational universalism leads to intolerance and imperialism"—remains at the heart of most contemporary historicism and postmodernism. This is how the decline in esotericism—the abandonment of the classical effort to insulate practice from theory and to hide philosophy from politics—has powerfully contributed to the rise of historicism.[66]

6. Historicism as an Effect of the Harm to Philosophy Resulting from the Decline of Esoteric Writing

Strauss's history of historicism also involves a second and still more direct way in which the rise of historicism was caused by the decline of esotericism. The above discussion treats the development of historicism in terms of the growth of the imperative to—the profound need and desire for—such a view. The political dangers of Enlightenment rationalism and more ultimately the theological problem created a need within modern thought to deny all transcendence, a need to see theoretical reason as subordinate to practice and incapable of transcending its historical situation. But it still remains to ask: how did the modern thinkers come to be not only so *eager* but also so *able* to embrace the historicist thesis? Historicism is not one of those perennial philosophical positions, always available if desired. Almost all past ages seem to have found it a rather unlikely thesis. What is it, then, about the modern mind that causes it to find historicism so immediately plausible?

Historicism Is True—of Modern Thought

Part of the answer we have seen. Our ignorance of esotericism causes us to mistake the conventional and historically parochial surface for the true teaching in the writings of past philosophers.

But Strauss also provides another, deeper answer. For a variety of reasons, he suggests, the modern mind has worked itself into a very unusual and unnatural condition—what he occasionally calls, playing on the famous Platonic metaphor, the "cave beneath the cave."[67] "The cave" is Plato's term for the imbeddedness of the human mind in its historical situation. For Plato, we naturally grow up in a cave of prejudice and illusion, deriving from the limitations of the human senses and the arbitrary conventions of social life. But at the same time, these elemental illusions tend to be crude and riddled with contradictions, so that there is a relatively clear dialectical path, for those willing to follow it, leading beyond these illusions and into the light of reality. In speaking of the cave beneath the cave, Strauss suggests that modern thought has created for itself a second, artificial layer of prejudice and historical entrapment—and one that, being a product of philosophical thought, is much more difficult to see through and escape. The modern mind is uniquely imprisoned in its historical situation.

With this strange-seeming claim, Strauss is just giving his own elaboration to the observation of a long line of thinkers—Schiller, Hegel, Husserl, and Heidegger among them—to the effect that modern thought, especially as compared with ancient thought, is peculiarly abstract and derivative: it lacks direct connection to pretheoretical, commonsense experience. It is out of touch with the sources of its own premises, concepts, and questions.[68] Because of this, when we moderns study the thought of some earlier modern philosopher or even when we consider our own thought in an honest and reflective way, we almost always have the same experience: we are struck by the fact that this thought is based on presuppositions that remain unproved and even unexamined, that it is based on ideas and attitudes that were inherited from some time in the past and never radically questioned. In short, our repeated experience is of the historical imbeddedness, the historicity, of our own minds. That is why we moderns naturally gravitate to historicism and find it so immediately plausible: it corresponds to our own inner experience.

According to Strauss, then, there is a relative truth to historicism: it is true of modern thought. Somehow the modern mind, for all its proud claims to liberation, is actually more enslaved to its history and traditions, more trapped in a cave, than was the case in earlier ages. And then modern thinkers compound this problem by naively generalizing their particular situation—the historicity of their own minds—attributing it to all human thought as such.

The Idea of Progress as the Source of the Historicity of Modern Thought

To account for the rise of historicism in modern times, as Strauss is attempting to do, it remains to explain why modern thought is so abstract and self-ignorant, so out of touch with its own foundations, and thus so trapped in its historical cave. Strauss cites a number of different factors. First, modern thought rests upon a long tradition of philosophy stretching back two thousand years, and it is in the nature of tradition to cause many things to be taken for granted and forgotten. Second, this philosophical tradition was for a very long time intertwined, in ways now difficult to disentangle, with a tradition of revelation, that is, of intellectual acceptance and unquestioning obedience.

Third, modern philosophy emerged through an indignant revolt against medieval and classical thought. This polemical character of modernity has had two consequences. It has made it particularly difficult for modern thinkers to recognize, beneath all their noisy opposition, the degree and character of their continued dependence on earlier thought. And it has given modern philosophy a reactive and academic character, because it means that modern philosophy arose not "naturally" from a direct confrontation with the phenomena or from wonder at the permanent riddles of life, but from a reaction against an already existing body of philosophical ideas. In other words, classical philosophy was defined against nonphilosophic life and the realm of commonsense "opinion" out of which it emerged. Modern philosophy, by contrast, is defined against an existing false philosophy, against scholasticism, and so has a far more academic and historically contingent character.[69]

But the feature of modern thought that is most responsible for its self-ignorance and historicity, according to Strauss, is its famous reliance on the idea of progress. In its commitment to being practical and politically effective—and in its resulting need to overcome skepticism and arrive at settled, certain answers—modern rationalism embraces a kind of hyperfoundationalism: it hopes once and for all to lay down solid, even indubitable, foundations and on this basis to build up a great and ever-increasing edifice of reliable knowledge. In a word, it seeks to make philosophy *progressive*, like the technical arts.

> This idea [of progress] implies that the most elementary questions can be settled once and for all so that future generations can dispense with their further discussion, but can erect on the foundations once laid an ever-growing structure. In this way, the foundations are covered up.[70]

This progressive attitude is clearest in the field of natural science, but also characterizes modern philosophy as a whole. The basic foundations were laid by Machiavelli, Bacon, Hobbes, and Descartes—for example, a negative or conquering posture toward nature or a demand for the unity of theory and praxis—and subsequent generations took this as their starting point. To be sure, modern thought is characterized by great turbulence and disagreement, but mainly because each successive generation has gone further in the same direction. Locke reworks Hobbes; Rousseau reworks Locke; Kant reworks Rousseau; Hegel reworks Kant; and so forth. Everyone senses that to study any modern philosopher, one has to study the history of philosophy up to his time, because modern philosophy is a historical sequence: every thinker is picking up the ball where the preceding generation left it. As Strauss often asserts, there is a "modern project," a common enterprise. Modern philosophers are never sui generis. They never make a truly new beginning.

Now, if modern thought as a whole rests on the idea of progress, what does this methodological posture do to philosophy? The idea of progress means that the premises are laid by one thinker, the conclusions are drawn at a later date by others. Thus, progress has the effect of spreading philosophy out over time. It separates the philosopher temporally from his own foundations and thus makes his thought historical. The more that philosophy makes progress, the more its basic presuppositions—what they are, how they are to be justified, and what the real alternatives to them are—become lost in the past and unavailable to it. In other words, from the beginning, modern thought—enlightened and progressive—prided itself especially in its freedom from tradition and its willingness to question everything anew. But the great irony is that the belief in progress necessarily creates a new, more inescapable kind of tradition. Under the sway of this idea, not just religion or custom, but philosophy itself prompts one to accept the teachings of the past without serious examination and move on. All modern thinkers stand on the shoulders of giants—that is why their thought is so ungrounded.

In sum, the growth in modern times of historicism—meaning now the development, not of the will to such a view, but of the inner sense of its plausibility—is largely due to the rise of the idea of progress. For this latter idea is what caused modern philosophy to be so dependent on its own history and traditions, trapped in a cave beneath the cave. And eventually the modern mind, judging of things from its own inner experience, came to its unique "insight," which all earlier ages had found implausible: the historical imprisonment of *all* human thought.

The Rise of Progress and the Decline of Esotericism

If the idea of progress was crucial in this way to the rise of historicism, then what does all this have to do with esotericism and its decline in the modern period? The answer is that the idea of esotericism and the idea of progress are opposites—opposite conceptions of how philosophy should relate to its own roots or foundations. (Above, we saw that esotericism is, in a different sense, the opposite of both historicism and Enlightenment rationalism— opposite concerning how philosophy should relate to political practice.) Because of this essential opposition, the decline of esotericism was the crucial precondition for the rise in modernity of the idea of progress and therewith of historicism.

The point here is this. We have seen that the methodology of progress tends to historicize philosophical thinking by putting a thinker out of touch with his foundations or presuppositions. But the practice of esotericism— considering it now in its *pedagogical* meaning and use—is designed to have the precise opposite effect: when successful, it permits, indeed forces, a thinker to examine and fully appropriate his foundations. There are at least two distinct ways in which esotericism exercises this self-appropriating function.

First, the esoteric writer, by hiding his true thoughts, refuses to give the philosophic reader anything that he can take on authority or take for granted. By limiting himself to hints and puzzles, he forces the reader to rediscover everything for himself. Such compulsion is necessary because philosophy has a natural tendency to decay over time—to turn into a tradition, to "historicize"—because people tend to accept too passively and unquestioningly the conclusions of the great philosophers of the past. This tendency is deadly to genuine philosophy, which requires that one always think everything through from the beginning and for oneself. In the modern period, this dangerous natural tendency to rely on the findings of others was artificially strengthened by the idea of progress, which turns this very tendency into a virtue, into a philosophical method. For whereas such dependence is harmful to clarity and self-knowledge, it is very useful for system building.

But premodern rationalism, which seeks not to build systems but to see clearly, is exquisitely aware of just this danger to philosophy. It puzzles over the question: how do you transmit to others something that can never genuinely be given from without, but only generated from within? The answer it found is esotericism: by hiding the truth in the right way, one entices others to discover it for themselves. Esotericism is the literary counterpart of the

Socratic method. A properly esoteric text does not allow the philosophic reader to form a dependence on the writer or on foundations laid in the past; rather it artfully compels him to develop and rely on his own inner powers. In precise opposition to the method of progress, esotericism is a device for forcing thinkers to be self-reliant, for constraining them to stand, not on the shoulders of others and thus within history, but on their own two feet.

Esotericism as Preserving the Possibility of Return

There also seems to be a second way in which esotericism — in opposition to the methodology of progress — is crucial in enabling the philosophic mind to appropriate its own foundations, although I am less certain that I understand Strauss correctly on this point. It concerns a second natural danger to the genuinely philosophic life. Even if a thinker remains free of excessive reliance upon others, his thought may still rest on certain fundamental presuppositions of which he is insufficiently aware. That, of course, is the core of the historicist critique. If philosophy is to hope to escape dependence on such unexamined presuppositions, then the primary task of philosophy must become, not moving progressively forward to elaborate its principles, but moving backward to search its origins and foundations. In a word, philosophy must embrace, not progress, but return.

The philosophical need for return to the ordinary and pretheoretical is an imperative Strauss shares with many late modern thinkers, such as Husserl, Heidegger, and Wittgenstein. In Strauss's view, however, the truest fulfillment of this need is to be found in the famous Socratic turn, that is, his return to the human things. No matter how high philosophy, with divine madness, soars toward the sun, it must always recollect its origin in and continued dependence upon the cave, the world of opinion, the average-everyday, the commonsense surface of things. It must continually test itself by returning to the phenomena as they present themselves to the ordinary, prephilosophic consciousness.

But here is the great problem that confronts a philosophy of return: once one leaves the cave, it is very difficult genuinely to return to it. As Socrates remarks, one's eyes can no longer see in the dark (*Republic* 516e–517a). Few things are more difficult than trying to regain lost innocence or to become naive again. Moreover, this loss of access or awareness is not confined to the philosophers themselves, but afflicts to some extent the society around them. Even where there is no deliberate cultivation of popular enlightenment, the very existence of philosophy or science within a culture tends to modify or distort its natural, prephilosophic consciousness. The second danger to philosophy, then, is this: philosophy is to a certain extent a self-undermining activity because, to remain healthy, it needs to maintain awareness of its origins in the world of pretheoretical experience and yet it inevitably tends to obscure or transform that world, to render it inaccessible.

Now, in the modern period, this second natural danger to philosophy has been, once again, artificially strengthened by the ideas of progress and enlightenment. The great but obstructed task for philosophy is return. But the idea of progress proclaims that the proper task of philosophy is rather to move ever forward, without looking back. It teaches that the origin, the prescientific, commonsense world, is a realm of mere superstition and folklore that should be transcended and forgotten. Similarly, the related idea of enlightenment involves modern philosophy in the deliberate attempt to transform popular awareness, to abolish traditional society and the old world of prescientific common sense, and to replace it with a new form of consciousness, a secularized, disenchanted, scientific culture. In these ways, modern philosophy aggressively tears up its own roots and closes off every access to the pretheoretical world. It climbs up a ladder and then throws it away. That is why modern thought is so un-Socratic, so lacking in the self-awareness that comes only from continually returning to and grounding oneself in the experiences of ordinary life.

Classical thought avoids these evils—it remains remarkably concrete, self-aware, and rooted in ordinary experience—because it is a philosophy not of progress and enlightenment but of return. And though there are formidable natural obstacles to return, as we have just seen, classical thought possesses a device for dealing with these: through esotericism, the philosophers protect and preserve the commonsense, pretheoretical awareness of the city. They do not allow it to be corrupted or degraded by their own theoretical pursuits. In other words, Strauss often emphasizes that Socrates practiced protective esotericism because he became fully aware of his dependence on the city. But this dependence is not limited to his bodily needs—of which, presumably, earlier thinkers were not unaware. It is also and especially an intellectual dependence on the city as the natural repository of prephilosophical experience. It is this he seeks to protect. Esotericism is, then, the necessary supplement for a philosophy of return: it helps to preserve that to which philosophy needs to return—preserve it from the effects of philosophy. It is the natural corrective for the inherently self-undermining character of philosophy: it makes it possible for philosophic activity to live safely side by side with the prephilosophic awareness that it needs.

This preservative aspect of esotericism has also a second dimension. Esoteric writings help to secure the philosophers' access to the pretheoretical perspective not only by protecting that perspective within living society but also by presenting and preserving it in books. As Strauss frequently emphasizes, the writings of classical political philosophy have a unique directness, freshness, and concreteness that are not to be found in modern writings because—on their surface as distinguished from their depth—they deliberately adopt and elaborate the ordinary citizen's perspective on political things. They do not look down on the political world from some scientific standpoint outside and above, but rather take on the internal, practical, prephilosophical point of view. These writings are forever the great corrective to every kind of excessive sophistication. They are agents of Socratic simplicity and return, helping one to recall and to get back in touch with elemental, pretheoretical common sense.

Thus, in two ways, the classical philosophers wrote in a manner that preserved their access to the prephilosophical. By writing esoterically—that is, by hiding the truth—they sheltered society and its pretheoretical perspective from corruption. And by writing exoterically—that is, by presenting an alternative, salutary doctrine on the surface of their writings—they described and preserved in literary form a version of the prephilosophical view.

I am not claiming, of course, that preserving the prephilosophical perspective of the city is the only or even the primary purpose of classical esotericism. Preserving philosophy itself is obviously a more urgent and fundamental aim, and it is one that is in some tension with the first. It seems clear, for example, that Plato seeks not simply to protect existing Greek ideas about the gods but to reform them in such a way as to make philosophy appear to be a pious and thus respectable activity. But within the bounds set by this latter concern, Plato does also seek to preserve, if not heighten, the moral and religious hopes, longings, and beliefs of the pretheoretical world.

To summarize the second half of Strauss's overall argument, having revived the great alternative to historicism—Socratic skeptical rationalism—he seeks to give a historical account of the unique modern susceptibility to historicism. He traces the historicist *imperative*—the *need* to see reason as imbedded in history—largely to a reaction against the political dangers that resulted when philosophers abandoned esoteric restraint in favor of crusading Enlightenment rationalism. More ultimately, he traces it to the defining modern concern to combat "the kingdom of darkness" through the denial of all transcendence, including that of theory over praxis.

But Strauss also tries to explain the genesis of the unique inner experience of the modern mind that causes it to find historicism not only desirable but immediately plausible. Modern thought, he argues, is fundamentally different from classical thought in that the former attempts to ground philosophy through progress and the latter through return. Classical philosophy endeavored to legitimize itself, to illuminate and test its basic presuppositions, through the constant return to and confrontation with the world of prephilosophic experience (relying on esotericism to preserve that world from transformation in the face of this confrontation).

Modern thought is built on the opposite hope that by its success in transforming, enlightening, and disenchanting the world and by its continual progress in explaining the kinds of things that it can explain, it will cause all testimony to or experience of the kinds of things that it cannot explain to simply wither away. The world of traditional society, with its spirits, gods, and poets, will simply disappear, refuted by history. In short, modern thought hopes to legitimize itself precisely through the *obliteration* of pretheoretical experience.

But having thus systematically cut itself off from its own roots and foundations, modern "progress philosophy" eventually discovers to its surprise that it rests upon choices and presuppositions of which it has lost awareness. And that is why historicism carries an immediate plausibility for modern thinkers that it simply did not possess for earlier generations: our recurring inner experience, whenever we honestly introspect, is of the historicity of our own thought.

But eventually, as we have seen, historicism facilitates the restoration of our lost awareness of esotericism. And this can—if something like Strauss's readings and arguments are correct—restore to view the lost path of skeptical Socratic rationalism while also uncovering the hidden history of the rise of historicism as the characteristic modern prejudice. This might, in turn, lead to a *genuinely postmodernist*, because posthistoricist, relegitimation of reason.

Although Strauss argues, as I have tried to show, that the decline in the practice of esoteric writing greatly contributed to the rise of historicism, he did not hold (and it does not follow) that this practice must therefore be universally restored and the Enlightenment somehow be undone—a change that he hardly envisioned—in order for historicism to be overturned. Modern thinkers can liberate themselves from historicism so long as they recover the art of esoteric reading and engage in patient historical studies that will free them from modern prejudices while acquainting them with the genuine Socratic alternative.

[NOTES]

PREFACE

1. Goethe to Passow, 20 October 1811, in Goethes Briefe und Briefe an Goethe, ed. Karl Robert Mandelkow (Munich: Beck, 1988), 3:168. Translated by Werner J. Dannhauser.

2. Alexandre Kojève, "The Emperor Julian and His Art of Writing," in Ancients and Moderns: Essays on the Tradition of Political Philosophy in Honor of Leo Strauss, ed. Joseph Cropsey, trans. James H. Nichols Jr. (New York: Basic Books, 1964), 95.

3. This whole identification of individual freedom with secrecy will initially strike us as counterintuitive, since we associate it rather with openness and transparency. Certainly it is true that secrecy practiced by the government is a threat to freedom. But when we think about the actions of the individual, don't we rather cherish the "rights of privacy"—which is to say, of secrecy? We feel that our freedom is endangered if we are totally transparent, if others can easily read our letters, access our email, and tap our phones. Individual freedom is inseparable from some capacity to hide from the government and the public at large.

4. See James C. Scott, Domination and the Arts of Resistance: Hidden Transcripts (New Haven: Yale University Press, 1990), which takes for its epigraph and theme the Ethiopian Proverb quoted above. This brilliant and inspiriting study of the myriad ways in which subordinate groups secretly assert their independence points inevitably—as the author is well, if somewhat uneasily, aware—to the Straussian thesis concerning philosophical esotericism. "The political environment in which Western political philosophy was written, seldom permits a transparency in meaning" (183n).

5. For a powerful illustration of the point from a somewhat unexpected quarter, see the most recent work on Shakespeare by the distinguished literary critic Stephen Greenblatt. As few would deny, Greenblatt yields to no one in his appreciation of the constraints of every kind laid upon an author by his times. As he emphasizes on page 1, Shakespeare "lived his life as the bound subject of a monarch in a strictly hierarchical society that policed expression in

speech and in print." Yet, in the aptly named Shakespeare's Freedom (Chicago: University of Chicago Press, 2010), Greenblatt writes to demonstrate that, when read with some appreciation for his irony and peasant cunning, Shakespeare reveals himself to be the very "embodiment of human freedom" (1). This work is a brilliant delineation and celebration, by the very founder of the New Historicist School, of Shakespeare's remarkable freedom from his times.

INTRODUCTION

1. Leo Strauss, *Persecution and the Art of Writing* (Glencoe, IL: Free Press, 1952), 111n46.

2. The awareness today—indeed, the open and willing recognition—of the *mystical part* of the esoteric tradition may to some extent be credited with helping to keep some memory of the phenomenon alive during its long period of forgetfulness. But at the same time, this recognition has also contributed to the contemporary *resistance* to esotericism in the fuller sense. For by closely identifying esotericism with the occult, it has made it seem, in the eyes of most scholars, a superstitious and childish practice that no serious philosopher would engage in. It has marginalized and stigmatized the phenomenon.

Partly because of this situation, perhaps, Strauss actually prefers to speak of "exotericism" rather than "esotericism." In his usage, a book that contains an external, "exoteric" teaching and, hidden beneath it, a secret, "esoteric" teaching should be called an "exoteric book." An "esoteric book" would be one that presents the secret teaching relatively (although never completely) openly (see Strauss, *Persecution*, 111, 111n45, and *What Is Political Philosophy? And Other Studies* [Glencoe, IL: Free Press, 1959, 273). Since this is a bit confusing, I have reverted to the more common usage and call a book with both a surface and hidden teaching an "esoteric" work.

While we are on the subject of terminology, it should also be said that there is nothing essential or universal about the terms "esoteric" and "exoteric." Many different expressions have been used in different times and places to refer to esoteric writing, including Aesopian literature, acroatic or acroamatic writings, double doctrine, twofold doctrine, twofold philosophy, pious frauds, noble lies, medicinal lies, economy of truth, *disciplina arcani*, discipline of the secret, enigmatical writing, defensive raillery, and others.

3. For some discussion of these different possibilities, see Miriam Galston, *Politics and Excellence: The Political Philosophy of Alfarabi* (Princeton, NJ: Princeton University Press, 1990), 22–43; Frederick J. Crosson, "Esoteric versus Latent Teaching," *Review of Metaphysics* 59, no. 1 (September 2005): 73–94; and Paul J. Bagley, "On the Practice of Esotericism," *Journal of the History of Ideas* 53, no. 2 (April–June 1992): 231–47. One could quarrel with my usage and reserve the term "esotericism" for just one of these forms, say, multilevel writing. The question is not settled for us by history, since there is no precise widely accepted definition of the term. Thus, we are free to define our terms in whatever way is most useful to our purposes, so long as we are clear. I have defined esotericism very broadly—to include *every form of secretiveness in the communication of thought*—because that seemed to me most useful from the standpoint of our needs as readers. After all, the most fundamental thing we need to know in taking up the works of earlier philosophers is this: should we approach these writings with an essentially literal cast of mind, assuming that their authors, like contemporary philosophers, express their thought as clearly as they can? Or do we need a fundamentally different mindset with such thinkers, a hermeneutics of suspicion, as it were, through which we remain constantly alive to the possibility that—for one reason or another and by means of one technique or another—they do not openly say all that they think or perhaps think all that they say? From the standpoint of this basic practical question, it seemed most useful to place the line between the esoteric and the nonesoteric where I have.

But, as I have been emphasizing, one must also remain aware of the different forms that esotericism can take. Furthermore, these forms are not only different but unequally esoteric.

For example, Enlightenment political esotericism—being less secretive, more temporary or transitional, and narrower in its motives—is less completely esoteric, one may say, than classical esotericism, which was more secretive, more permanently or essentially linked to philosophy, and broader in its purpose, combining the defensive, protective, and pedagogical motives. Therefore, while defining esotericism very broadly, I would also say that classical esotericism is esotericism in the most complete sense.

4. See the last section of chapter 9 for some suggested reading along these lines.

5. It is also possible, of course, to follow an intermediate course between these two approaches and focus on the history of esotericism within a limited historical period. Such work is also going on. For a particularly good example, see Moshe Halbertal, *Concealment and Revelation: Esotericism in Jewish Thought and Its Philosophical Implications*, trans. Jackie Feldman (Princeton, NJ: Princeton University Press, 2007). See also Edward Muir, *The Culture Wars of the Late Renaissance: Skeptics, Libertines, and Opera* (Cambridge, MA: Harvard University Press, 2007), and Perez Zagorin, *Ways of Lying: Dissimulation, Persecution, and Conformity in Early Modern Europe* (Cambridge, MA: Harvard University Press, 1990).

CHAPTER ONE

1. Samuel Formey, "Exoterique & Esoterique," in *Encyclopédie, ou dictionnaire raisonné des sciences, des arts et des métiers, etc.*, ed. Denis Diderot and Jean le Rond d'Alembert, University of Chicago ARTFL Encyclopédie Project (Spring 2013 edition), ed. Robert Morrissey, http://encyclopedie.uchicago.edu, translation mine (emphasis in the original). Use or mention of this distinction is also made in the articles "Aius-Locutius, god of speech," "Ame," "Aristotelisme," "Asiatiques," "Augures," "Cabale," "Casuiste," "Celtes," "Divination," "Egyptiens," "Eléatiques," "Encyclopédie," "Grecs," "Hébraique," "Idole, idolâtre, idolâtrie," "Indiens," "Ioniques," "Japonais," "Juifs," "Lettrés," "Philosophie," "Platonisme," "Pythagorisme," "Samanéen," and "Xenxus."

2. William Warburton, *The Divine Legation of Moses Demonstrated, in Nine Books*, in vol. 2 of *The Works of the Right Reverend William Warburton, Lord Bishop of Gloucester, in Seven Volumes* (London: Nichols & Cadell, 1788), 3.2.14.

3. Edward Gibbon, who was greatly influenced by Warburton, asserted that "he reined the dictator and the tyrant of literature." Quoted by A. W. Evans in *Warburton and the Warburtonians: A Study in Some Eighteenth-Century Controversies* (London: Oxford University Press, H. Milford, 1932), 1.

4. John Toland, *Clidophorus* (London: J. Brotherton & W. Meadows, 1720), 69.

5. G. W. Leibniz, *New Essays on Human Understanding*, trans. Peter Remnant and Jonathan Bennett (Cambridge: Cambridge University Press, 1981), 260.

6. Pierre Bayle, "Aristote," in *Dictionnaire historique et critique*, 5th ed. (Amsterdam: P. Brunel, 1740), 1:329.

7. Thomas Burnet, *Archæologiæ Philosophicæ or, the Ancient Doctrine Concerning the Originals of Things. Written in Latin by Thomas Burnet, L.L.D., Master of the Charter-House. To which is added, Dr Burnet's Theory of the Visible World, by way of Commentary on his own Theory of the Earth; being the second Part of his Archiologiæ* [sic] *Philosophicæ. Faithfully translated into English, with Remarks thereon* (London: J. Fisher, 1736), 67 (emphasis added). First published 1692 by Gualt. Kettilby, London.

8. Francis Bacon, *The Advancement of Learning*, ed. G. W. Kitchin (Philadelphia: Paul Dry Books, 2001), 132–33 (2.17.5).

9. Toland, *Clidophorus*, 94; John Toland, *Pantheisticon* (London: Sam Patterson, 1751), 99 (emphasis added).

10. G. W. Leibniz, *Sämtliche Schriften und Briefe*, ed. Preussische Akademie der Wissenschaften, (Darmstadt and Leipzig, 1923–54), 2.1:506, quoted and translated by Richard Ken-

nington, *On Modern Origins: Essays in Early Modern Philosophy*, ed. Pamela Kraus and Frank Hunt (Lanham, MD: Lexington Books, 2004), 197.

11. Denis Diderot to François Hemsterhuis, summer 1773, in vol. 13 of *Correspondance*, ed. George Roth (Paris: Editions de Minuit, 1955–70), 25–27. Translation mine (emphasis added).

12. Antoine-Nicolas de Condorcet, *Sketch for a Historical Picture of the Progress of the Human Mind*, trans. June Barraclough (New York: Noonday Press, 1955), 46, 64, 90, 108–9, 136–38; Rousseau, "Observations by Jean-Jacques Rousseau of Geneva On the Reply Made to his Discourse," in *The Collected Writings of Rousseau*, ed. and trans. Judith Bush, Roger Masters, and Christopher Kelly (Hanover, NH: University Press of New England, 1992), 2:45n (emphasis added); see also "Preface to Second Letter to Bordes," in ibid., 2:184–85.

13. Erasmus to Luigi Marliano, March 25, 1521, and Erasmus to Justus Jonas, May 10, 1521, in *The Correspondence of Erasmus: Letters 1122 to 1251*, ed. P. G. Bientenholz, trans. R. A. B. Mynors (Toronto: University of Toronto Press, 1988), 8:173, 203.

14. Giovanni Boccaccio, *The Life of Dante (Tratatello in laude di Dante)*, trans. Vincenzo Zin Bollettino (New York: Garland, 1990), 40. We regard Boccaccio and the great writers he is talking about as poets, as distinguished from philosophers. But Boccaccio's own view is that poets of the first rank must be seen as philosophers too. After quoting some lines of poetry, for example, he asks: "Is there any reader so muddled as not to see clearly that Vergil was a philosopher? . . . Or can anyone believe that he wrote such lines without some meaning or intention hidden behind the superficial veil of myth?" *Boccaccio on Poetry: Being the Preface and the Fourteenth and Fifteenth Books of Boccaccio's Genealogia Deorum Gentilium*, ed. and trans. Charles G. Osgood (Princeton: Princeton University Press, 1930), 52–53.

15. Thomas Aquinas, *Faith, Reason and Theology: Questions I–IV of His Commentary on the De Trinitate of Boethius*, trans. Armand Maurer (Toronto: Pontifical Institute of Medieval Studies, 1987), 53–54.

16. Moses Maimonides, *The Guide of the Perplexed*, ed. and trans. Shlomo Pines (Chicago: University of Chicago Press, 1963), 79 (1.34), 6 (1.Introduction).

17. *Plato's Laws*, trans. Muhsin Mahdi, in *Medieval Political Philosophy: A Sourcebook*, ed. Ralph Lerner and Muhsin Mahdi (New York: Free Press, 1963), 84–85 (emphasis added).

18. Augustine, *Letters*, ed. Ludwig Schopp and Roy Joseph Deferrari, trans. Sister Wilfrid Parsons, vol. 1 (New York: Fathers of the Church, 1951), 3 (letter no. 1).

19. Cicero, *De natura deorum*, trans. H. Rackham, Loeb Classical Library 268 (Cambridge: Harvard University Press, 1933), 11–15 (1.4.9–1.5.11); *Tusculan Disputations*, trans. J. E. King, Loeb Classical Library 18 (Cambridge: Harvard University Press, 1927), 435 (5.4.11).

20. Augustine, *The City of God*, trans. Marcus Dods (New York: Modern Library, 1950), 152–53.

21. Denis Diderot, "Aius Locutius," in *The Encyclopedia of Diderot and d'Alembert Collaborative Translation Project*, trans. Stephen J. Gendzier (Ann Arbor: MPublishing, University of Michigan Library, 2009), http://hdl.handle.net/2027/spo.did2222.0001.297 (accessed October 7, 2011). See Rousseau, *Collected Writings*, 2:45–46n.

22. Edward Gibbon, *The History of the Decline and Fall of the Roman Empire in 7 Volumes* (London: George Bell & Sons, 1891), 1:38, 36, 39.

23. Schleiermacher, in his very influential critique of the idea of Platonic esotericism, tries to evade this difficulty by claiming that Plato made it clear right on the surface that he rejected "polytheism and the vulgar religion." *Schleiermacher's Introductions to the Dialogues of Plato*, trans. William Dobson (Cambridge: J. & J. J. Deighton, 1836), 11. But this is hardly the case, as many contemporary scholars acknowledge. See, for example, W. R. Connor, "The Other 399: Religion and the Trial of Socrates," *Bulletin of the Institute of Classical Studies* 37 (January 1991): 49–56. To be sure, here and there, Socrates speaks in passing of "the god"—as he does also of Zeus, Chronos, and many other gods of the Greek pantheon. If we seek a more weighty statement, consider the *Apology* where Socrates attributes the whole origin of his

philosophic quest to a pronouncement of the Oracle of Apollo at Delphi. And in the *Phaedo*, the philosopher is depicted as devoting his dying words to an appeal to Crito to sacrifice a chicken to Asclepius. The most one could say is that the dialogues present a jumble of different religious ideas, references, stories, myths, and arguments with no views being consistently preferred. In short, Schleiermacher's own reading of Plato on this issue is precisely an *esoteric* reading, if a likely one.

24. *The Republic of Plato*, trans. Allan Bloom (New York: Basic Books, 1968), 14 (337a).

25. Augustine, *City of God*, 248. Strictly speaking neither Plato nor Xenophon invented the Socratic dialogue, an honor that belongs to certain older members of the Socratic circle like Antisthenes and Aischines. But they perfected it. See Diskin Clay, *Platonic Questions: Dialogues with the Silent Philosopher* (University Park: Pennsylvania State University Press, 2000), 3–13.

26. Friedrich Nietzsche, *Beyond Good and Evil: Prelude to a Philosophy of the Future*, trans. Walter Kaufmann (New York: Vintage Books, 1966), 41.

27. *The Complete Essays of Montaigne*, trans. Donald M. Frame (Stanford, CA: Stanford University Press, 1958), 377 (2.12).

28. Plato, Seventh Letter 341d–e (emphasis added); see also 344c, d–e; and Second Letter 312e–314c. Unpublished translation by Jenny Strauss Clay. On the reading of this passage suggested here, see Leo Strauss, "On a New Interpretation of Plato's Political Philosophy," *Social Research* 13 (September 1946): 326–67. For arguments against the Seventh Letter's authenticity, see especially Ludwig Edelstein, *Plato's Seventh Letter* (Leiden: E. J. Brill, 1966). On the other side, see Kurt von Fritz, "The Philosophical Passage in the Seventh Platonic Letter and the Problem of Plato's 'Esoteric' Philosophy," in *Essays in Ancient Greek Philosophy*, ed. John P. Anton and George L. Kustas (Albany: State University of New York Press, 1971), 408–47; and Glenn Morrow, *Plato's Epistles* (Indianapolis: Bobbs-Merrill, 1962).

29. This approach is suggested in the excellent article by Kenneth M. Sayre, "Plato's Dialogues in Light of the Seventh Letter," in *Platonic Writings, Platonic Readings*, ed. Charles L. Griswold (New York: Routledge, 1988), 93–109.

30. See also *Parmenides* 136d–e.

31. Alfarabi, *The Harmonization of the Two Opinions of the Two Sages*, in *Alfarabi: The Political Writings: Selected Aphorisms and Other Texts*, trans. Charles E. Butterworth (Ithaca, NY: Cornell University Press, 2001), section 12:131.

32. Diogenes Laertius, *Lives of Eminent Philosophers*, trans. R. D. Hicks (Cambridge, MA: Harvard University Press, 1966), 1:333.

33. See, for example, George Boas, "Ancient Testimony to Secret Doctrines," *Philosophical Review* 62, no. 1 (1953): 90–91.

34. *Plato's Theaetetus*, trans. Francis M. Cornford (Indianapolis: Bobbs-Merrill, 1959), 180c–d; see 152e. See also *Protagoras* 316d–e; *Cratylus* 402a–c; *Euthyphro* 3c; *Phaedo* 62b, 69c–d; and *Republic* 378d.

35. *Plato's Theaetetus* 152c, 155e.

36. For the purposes of the present argument it does not really matter if Plato (or his Socrates) is wrong in these attributions of esotericism to earlier thinkers—as someone will want to object. One might possibly go further. Scholars skeptical of esotericism typically argue that such attributions—for example, Neoplatonist attributions of esotericism to Plato and Aristotle—should be rejected as reflecting only the over-eager esotericism of the testimony's *source* rather than anything about its *subject*. But if this reasoning were applied to the present case, it would follow that if Plato is indeed wrong in his attributions of esotericism to earlier thinkers—over-eagerly seeing it where it is not—that can be taken as a sign of his own esotericism.

37. This points to a general problem of circularity that tends to afflict much of the scholarly discussion of this issue. Scholars rightly demand to see the documentary evidence for esotericism, but at the same time they use the acknowledgment of esotericism as a strong indicator

of the inauthenticity or bias of the source document. On the other hand, it should be acknowledged in this particular case that the Seventh Letter ranges over a number of different topics, and it is not just the esotericism discussion that some scholars have judged implausible.

38. Alexander Grant, "On the Exoterikoi Logoi," appendix B in *The Ethics of Aristotle, Illustrated with Essays and Notes* (London: Longmans, 1885), 399.

39. Boas, "Ancient Testimony," 92; see also George Boas, *Dominant Themes of Modern Philosophy: a History* (New York: Ronald Press, 1957), 59.

40. The great exception is Schleiermacher, who gives a very powerful description of Plato's pedagogical esotericism. See Schleiermacher, *Introductions*, 17–18.

41. Eduard Zeller, *Aristotle and the Earlier Peripatetics* (New York: Russell & Russell, 1962), 120–21.

42. Grant, "On the Exoterikoi Logoi," 400.

43. Ingemar During, *Aristotle in the Ancient Biographical Tradition* (Göteborg, 1957; distributed by Almqvist & Wiksell, Stockholm), 436.

44. Adam Smith, *The History of the Ancient Logics and Metaphysics*, in *Essays on Philosophical Subjects*, ed. W. P. D. Wightman and J. C. Bryce (Indianapolis: Liberty Classics, 1982), 122n. In an ironic reversal, Smith's twentieth-century editor, Wightman, takes it upon himself to correct what he sees as an obvious historical misrepresentation in a footnote to this passage: "The coexistence of esoteric and exoteric writings is pretty well attested among men far from being 'out of their senses.' There are plausible grounds for believing that Plato in his later years may have been among them" (ibid., 122n9).

45. There are strong indications that, at least in his later thought, Smith did recognize the existence of certain forms of esotericism (and may even have practiced them). In his later *Lectures on Rhetoric and Belles Lettres*, ed. J. C. Bryce (Indianapolis: Liberty Fund, 2007), for example, he claims that both Hobbes and Lord Shaftsbury were "against every scheme of revealed religion" and indeed in their writings "sought to overturn the old systems of religion" (37, 38). But Smith surely knew that he was attributing to them motives and views that were at variance with the surface claims of their writings. And he probably also knew that Shaftesbury, in his major writing, spoke explicitly about the need to employ "irony" and "disguise" when writing about forbidden ideas (see Lord Shaftesbury, *Characteristics of Men, Manners, Opinions, Times*, ed. Lawrence E. Klein [Cambridge: Cambridge University Press, 2004], 34).

Similarly, Smith's very close friend David Hume was widely known then, and even now, as a (thinly) disguised atheist. And Hume too spoke openly in his writings and letters about the need to employ caution and dissimulation in writing. See David Hume, *An Enquiry concerning the Principles of Morals*, in *Hume: Moral and Political Philosophy*, ed. Henry D. Aiken (Darien, CT: Hafner, 1970), 257–58; and Hume to Col. James Edmonstoune, April 1764, in *New Letters of David Hume*, ed. Raymond Klibansky and Ernest C. Mossner (Oxford: Clarendon Press, 1954), 82–84. Indeed, Hume wrote a letter to Smith about his *Dialogues concerning Natural Religion*, confiding that "nothing can be more cautiously and more artfully written." And Smith seems to have wholeheartedly *agreed* about the necessity for Hume's caution and art—finding it, in fact, insufficiently carried out, since he strongly opposed publication of the work, even posthumously. As Smith asserts to William Strahan, the publisher, "Tho' finely written I could have wished [it] had remained in Manuscript to be communicated only to a few people." Smith to William Strahan, September 5, 1776, and Hume to Smith, August 15, 1776, in *The Correspondence of Adam Smith*, ed. Ernest Campbell Mossner and Ian Simpson Ross (Oxford: Clarendon Press, 1977), 211, 205.

In fact, there is ample reason to suspect that Smith himself employed a good deal of caution and art in his own discussions of religion. See the excellent discussion of this—and of all the points above—in Peter Minowitz, *Profits, Priests, and Princes: Adam Smith's Emancipation of Economics from Politics and Religion* (Stanford, CA: Stanford University Press, 1993), 5–9.

Finally, there is the striking fact, also discussed by Minowitz, that Karl Marx in *Capi-*

tal explicitly treats Smith as an esoteric writer and reads *The Wealth of Nations*—not without reason—as oscillating between an esoteric doctrine, which presents his descriptive, scientific analysis of the economic world, and a somewhat different exoteric doctrine, which supports a bourgeois ideology designed to promote the good functioning of that world. See Karl Marx, *Capital: A Critique of Political Economy*, trans. David Fernback (New York: Random House, 1981), 2:276, 290, 297, 448, 454, 465.

46. There are a few works by minor authors that could, at first blush, seem to be efforts to disprove the existence of esotericism. On more narrow inspection, these authors all turn out to acknowledge the reality (and even the propriety) of certain forms of esoteric writing, just not the forms favored or emphasized by the particular thinker they are attacking. See for example the critique of Warburton and his disciple John Towne by Arthur Ashley Sykes (1684–1756), an English religious controversialist, in his *A Vindication of the Account of the Double Doctrine of the Ancients. In answer to A Critical Enquiry into the Practices of the Antient Philosophers* (London: Printed for John and Paul Knapton, at the Crown in Ludgate-Street, 1747); see especially p. 30. See also the attack on both Toland and Warburton by the French historian Jean Philippe René de La Bléterie (1696–1772) in his *The Life of Julian the Apostate: Translated from the French of F. La Bletterie. And Improved with Dissertations on Several Points Relating to Julian's Character, and to the History of the Fourth Century. By V. Desvoeux* (Dublin: S. Powell, for Peter Wilson, 1746), 258–311.

47. That is why the temptation to interpret Plato esoterically has never been completely uprooted. It lingers on even in the twentieth century, where there are a number of major scholars who, independently of Strauss and of each other, have developed powerful esoteric interpretations. See J. N. Findlay, *Plato: The Written and Unwritten Doctrines* (New York: Humanities Press, 1974). Also, the so-called Tubingen School, especially the writings of Hans Joachim Kramer and Konrad Gaiser. For Aristotle, by contrast, the issue of esotericism is now completely dead (outside of the Straussian circle).

48. In his theoretical studies of rhetoric, Aristotle also is known for placing strong emphasis on the importance of clarity; see *Rhetoric* 1400b23ff, 1404b2, 1407a33, *Poetics* 1458a18, and *On Sophistical Refutations* 165b23 ff.

49. The most thorough and influential discussions of Aristotelian (and Platonic) esotericism are Friedrich Schleiermacher's "General Introduction" in *Introductions*, 8–19; Zeller, *Aristotle*, 105–36; Alexander Grant, "On the Exoterikoi Logoi"; Boas, "Ancient Testimony," 79–92; and During, *Aristotle in the Ancient Biographical Tradition*.

I would argue that among the other difficulties to be discussed below, all five accounts share this basic defect: they tend to identify the whole phenomenon of esotericism with the mystical version of it. Thus, they approach the question very narrowly, without an appreciation of the broad history of esotericism and of the very different forms and motives that it can have. By "secret" or "esoteric" doctrines they primarily mean doctrines that are literally unpublished (i.e., not simply published between the lines) and mystical in content. With this very strict and narrow definition of esotericism, they examine the relevant texts with great learning and show, convincingly, that there is scant evidence for it. But in fact these same texts are full of evidence—which they ignore—for esotericism more comprehensively understood.

50. "Philosophies for Sale" [The Sale of Lives], in *Lucian*, trans. A. M. Harmon (London: William Heinemann, 1929), 2:503. This is the first known use of the word "esoteric" in ancient Greek, and it is thought that Lucian may actually have coined the term in this very play on words.

51. See *Politics* 1254a34, 1278b31, 1323a22; *Nicomachean Ethics* 1102a26, 1140a1 (consider also 1096a4); *Physics* 217b31; *Eudemian Ethics* 1217b20, 1218b32; and *Metaphysics* 1076a28.

52. *Aristotle's Nicomachean Ethics*, ed. Robert C. Bartlett and Susan D. Collins (Chicago: University of Chicago Press, 2011), 23.

53. Translated by Grant in "On the Exoterikoi Logoi," 402.

54. Ibid., 407–8. Even this generalization is really too broad. "Exoteric" may refer, as Grant is claiming, to an external, in the sense of superficial, treatment of a subject (or relatedly and perhaps more originally, a treatment addressed to an external audience, in the sense of uninitiated outsiders), but it may also simply mean an account that is external because outside the present topic or field of study. Thus Thomas Aquinas, in his *Commentary on Aristotle's Nicomachean Ethics*, trans. C. I. Litzinger (Notre Dame, IN: Dumb Ox Books, 1993), interprets the first example given in the text in this manner. The "exoteric arguments" to which Aristotle refers the reader are labeled such because, Thomas conjectures, they are to be found in *De anima* which is a work "outside the scope of the immediate science [i.e., ethics]" (ibid., 76). Also consider Aristotle, *Politics* 1254a33, 1264b39.

55. In the writings we possess, the use of the name "exoteric" for this particular purpose first occurs in Cicero (*De finibus* 5.5.12; *Letters to Atticus* 4.16 [letter 89]), who seems to be relying on Antiochus of Ascalon (130–68 BC). But Cicero claims that this term was Aristotle's own. While we possess no Aristotelian text expressly applying this (or any) name to the whole first category of his writings, this appellation is at any rate consistent with the usage that he does make of this term, as we have just seen. The first extant use of "acroamatic" (or "acroatic") to name the second category of writings occurs, not in Cicero who mentions no name for it, but in Plutarch and shortly after in Aulus Gellius, both of whom are relying on Andronicus of Rhodes (c. 60 BC). They also indicate that the usage is Aristotle's, but this word does not appear in any Aristotelian text that we possess (with the possible exception of the letter to be considered below).

56. For testimonial evidence for this distinction, consider Cicero (*De finibus* 5.5.12), who states that it is Aristotle's works on the human good, as distinguished from those on nature and logic, that were of these two distinct kinds, the exoteric and (in his terms) those in "notebooks" (*commentarii*). In the other fields, he implies, there were no exoteric works. Regarding the acroamatic works, Plutarch in one place seems to restrict them to writings on nature and logic—but perhaps he is speaking here of what I am calling the "more acroamatic" ("Life of Alexander" 7.3–5). For in another place (*Reply to Colotes* 1115b–c) he distinguishes the "exoteric dialogues" not only from the writings on physics but also from the "ethical notebooks" (using *upomnema*, the Greek equivalent of Cicero's *commentarii*)—thus acknowledging that there were acroamatic works of some sort also concerning the human good.

57. There is an earlier statement by Cicero (106–43 BC) that some scholars emphasize, but, as I will argue below, it does not really address the questions before us.

58. Plutarch, *Alexander* 7.3–5. Translated by Jenny Strauss Clay.

59. *Attic Nights* 20.5.12. Translated by Lorraine Pangle in *Aristotle and the Philosophy of Friendship* (Cambridge: Cambridge University Press, 2003), 9.

60. Plutarch, *Alexander* 7.3–5, in *The Lives of the Noble Grecians and Romans*, trans. John Dryden (New York: Modern Library, 1932), 805.

61. What remains unaddressed by Plutarch and Gellius is the second part of the second question: whether the exoteric works were also multilevel writings. While it would be nice to know the answer, it is of no great practical importance given that we do not possess these writings.

62. See Paul Moraux, *Les listes anciennes des ouvrages d'Aristote* (Louvain: Université de Louvain, 1951), 169–70; and Grant, "On the Exoterikoi Logoi," 400. For possible evidence of such influence, see Plutarch, *Isis and Osiris*, in *Moralia*, trans. Frank Cole Babbitt (Cambridge, MA: Harvard University Press, 1936), 5:182–83 (382e). For a good account of Plutarch's many discussions of Aristotle that concludes that the former had a deep and accurate understanding of the latter, see G. Verbeke, "Plutarch and the Development of Aristotle," in *Aristotle and Plato in the Mid-Fourth Century: Papers of the Symposium Aristotelicum Held at Oxford in August, 1957*, ed. Ingemar During (Göteborg: Elanders, 1960), 236–47.

63. Grant, "On the Exoterikoi Logoi," 400. See also Zeller, *Aristotle*, 120, for a similar view.

64. George Boas's influential article "Ancient Testimony to Secret Doctrines" aims to settle once and for all the question of ancient esotericism by attempting to carefully and exhaustively "list and analyze exactly what the ancients said concerning this matter" (79). He claims to find that, in reality, there is no such testimony. He triumphantly declares in his conclusion: "We have seen, I hope, that not even the Peripatetic commentators attributed any secrecy to any of Aristotle's doctrines" (92). His readers have indeed seen this, but only because all of the crucial testimony—the explicit statement from Lucian that we have just seen and those from Simplicius, Themistius, Ammonius, Alfarabi, Olympiodorus, Elias, and Philoponus to be presented below—are missing from Boas's list. He does include the famous statement of Plutarch with which we began and does acknowledge that it "indicates that the theoretical sciences were secret," but he goes on to dismiss this claim on the grounds that "the secrecy of the . . . sciences is not accentuated" (81).

65. Simplicius, *In Aristotelis Physicorum Libros Quattuor Priores Commentaria*, ed. H. Diels, in *Commentaria in Aristotelem Graeca* (Berlin: Reimer, 1882), 9:8, quoted and translated by David Bolotin in *An Approach to Aristotle's Physics* (Albany: State University of New York Press, 1998), 6.

66. Themistius, *Analyticorum Posteriorum Paraphrasis*, ed. M. Wallies, in *Commentaria in Aristotelem Graeca* (Berlin: Reimer, 1900), 5.1:1. Quoted and translated by Bolotin in *Approach to Aristotle's Physics*, 5.

67. Ammonius, *On Aristotle's Categories*, trans. S. Marc Cohen and Gareth B. Matthews (Ithaca, NY: Cornell University Press, 1991), 9 (1.10).

68. Ibid., 15 (7.7).

69. Alfarabi, *Harmonization of the Two Opinions of the Two Sages*. Unpublished translation by Miriam Galston, quoted by Bolotin in *Approach to Aristotle's Physics*, 6.

70. On Alfarabi's understanding of Aristotelian and Platonic esotericism, see the excellent discussion in Muhsin Mahdi, "Man and His Universe in Medieval Arabic Philosophy," in *L'homme et son univers au Moyen Age*, ed. Christian Wenin (Louvain-La-Neuve: Editions de L'Institut Supérior de Philosophie, 1986), 102–13. As Mahdi explains, Alfarabi sees the two thinkers as adopting opposite approaches to esotericism. "The secret of Plato's books consists in concealing his occasional clear statements by means of habitual ambiguity, that of Aristotle's consists in concealing his occasional ambiguous statements by means of habitual clarity" (110).

71. Olympiodorus *in Meteor* 4, 16–18. Cited and translated by Richard Sorabji in *The Philosophy of the Commentators, 200–600 AD*, vol. 3: *Logic and Metaphysics* (London: Gerald Duckworth, 2004), 46.

72. See Charles B. Schmitt, "Aristotle as Cuttlefish: The Origin and Development of a Renaissance Image," *Studies in the Renaissance* 12 (1965): 60–72.

73. While all these very different thinkers agree in finding unmistakable signs of intentional obscurity in Aristotle, they of course disagree as to what lies behind that obscurity. At one extreme are certain Neoplatonists who find a mystical teaching. At the other is Montaigne, who finds a concealed skepticism: "We see him [Aristotle] often deliberately covering himself with such thick and inextricable obscurity that we cannot pick out anything of his opinion. It is in fact a Pyrrhonism in an affirmative form" (Montaigne, *Complete Essays*, 376 [2.12]; for elaboration, see pp. 408, 414).

74. Elias, *Aristotelis Categorias Commentaria*, ed. A. Busse, in *Commentaria in Aristotelem Graeca* (Berlin: Reimer, 1900), 18.1:115.3–4. Unpublished translation by Jenny Strauss Clay. There is some uncertainty as to whether this commentary is to be attributed to Elias or David.

75. Moraux, *Les listes anciennes*, 171n91. A.-H. Chroust, "Eudemus, or On the Soul: A Lost Dialogue of Aristotle on the Immortality of the Soul," *Mnemosyne* 19 (1966): 22–23.

76. There is a passing reference in Moraux, *Les listes anciennes*, 168, and Zeller, *Aristotle*, 113n2.

77. During, *Aristotle in the Biographical Tradition*, 437–39.

78. See Ammonius, *Aristotelis Categorias Commentarius*, ed. A. Busse, in *Commentaria in Aristotelem Graeca* (Berlin: Reimer, 1895), 4.4:4.18; and Olympiodorus, *Prolegomena et in Categorias Commentarium*, ed. A. Busse, in *Commentaria in Aristotelem Graeca* (Berlin: Reimer, 1902), 12.1:7.5.

79. Olympiodorus, *Prolegomena*, 12.1:7.5. Unpublished translation by Jenny Strauss Clay.

80. Elias, *Aristotelis Categorias Commentaria*, 18.1:125.

81. The same is also true of Philoponus (490–570), a Christian thinker, largely critical of Neoplatonism. He is in some ways the hero of During's story, since he too strongly embraces the single-doctrine view defended by the three other commentators (see Philoponus, *Aristotelis Categorias Commentarium*, ed. A. Busse, in *Commentaria in Aristotelem Graeca* [Berlin: Reimer, 1898], 13.1:3.16, 4.12), but he is untarnished by their grossly mistaken interpretation (in During's view) of Alexander. But even Philoponus agrees that Aristotle was a multilevel esotericist:

> Now, he practiced obscurity on account of his readers, so as to make those who were naturally suited eager to hear the argument, but to turn those who were uninterested away right from the beginning. For the genuine listeners, to the degree that the arguments are obscure, by so much are they eager to struggle and to arrive at the depth. (6.22–26. Unpublished translation by Jenny Strauss Clay)

82. Elias, in responding to Alexander's embrace of the opposite view, states: "Alexander, this is not appropriate for a philosopher; for to choose the false, but to hide the truth is not lawful." And then he quotes Achilles from the *Iliad* 9.312–13:

> Hateful to me as the gates of Hades is that man
> Who hides one thing in his heart, but says another.
> (Elias, *Aristotelis Categorias Commentaria*, 18.1:115.3–4)

83. More generally, as E. N. Tigerstedt remarks: "The neo-Platonists properly speaking— Plotinus, Porphyry, Iamblichus, and their disciples—do not distinguish between an exoteric and esoteric Platonism. To them, there is only an esoteric one." *Interpreting Plato* (Stockholm: Almqvist & Wiksell, 1977), 65. The Neoplatonist view of Aristotle is similar. They affirm that his exoteric and acroamatic writings both teach the same doctrine—just as most modern scholars do. But by this affirmation, the latter mean that Aristotle has no distinct esoteric teaching. The Neoplatonists mean that he has no distinct exoteric teaching, that *all* his writings ultimately convey the same secret, esoteric teaching.

84. Some scholars attach great importance to a statement by Cicero that they read as affirming that the two categories of writings contain no differences of doctrine (see Moraux, *Les listes anciennes*, 168; Boas, "Ancient Testimony," 83–84; Grant, "On the Exoterikoi Logoi," 399). In Cicero's dialogue *De finibus* 5.5.12, the character Marcus Piso is giving a brief account of the peripatetic school, speaking first of their writings on nature, then on logic, and finally—in the passage at issue—on the human good. In each of these three discussions he makes a point of clarifying any differences that might exist between Aristotle and Theophrastus, his immediate successor at the Lyceum.

> Concerning the highest good, because there are two kinds of books, the one written in a popular style, which they call exoteric, and the other, written more carefully, which they left in notebooks, they don't always seem to say the same thing. However, in the very chief thing, there is no difference, between those [people] whom I have named, nor any disagreement between themselves. But on the subject of the good life . . . they do sometimes seem to differ. (Unpublished translation by Jenny Strauss Clay)

This somewhat ambiguous passage can be read in a number of different ways, but none of them yield the interpretation given by these scholars. When Piso says, in the first sentence, that "they don't always seem to say the same thing," and then, in the second, that in fact "there is no difference, between those [people] whom I have named," he is in both cases clearly referring not to the books—exoteric and "in notebooks" (acroamatic)—but to the men, Aristotle and Theophrastus.

What is unclear is the meaning of the further phrase "nor any disagreement between themselves." This could be a further statement about the relation between the two men (which would be a bit repetitious), or it could refer to the relation of each man to himself: each is being consistent and not contradicting himself. If it means the latter, there are two ways this could be the case. Either, for each thinker, there is no difference between what he says in his exoteric books and what he says in his acroamatic books (as the scholars argue), or there *are* differences but there is no real contradiction because the exoteric statement is merely popular or provisional, whereas the "more careful" acroamatic statement is the final truth.

But even if this unclarity were resolved in favor of the scholars' view, that still would not justify their interpretation. For what is undeniable is that the whole discussion in this passage concerns only one specific issue, "the highest good" and "the very chief thing," that is, the *summum bonum*, which is wisdom. But as the passage and its sequel go on to plainly emphasize, regarding *other* issues—the "subject of the good life" and whether good fortune is needed in addition to wisdom—the situation is quite different. Here there are genuine differences. So on no reading can this passage be taken to assert that on all important issues there are no differences between the teachings of the exoteric and the acroamatic works.

It should also be remarked that Cicero's authority on this whole subject is, at any rate, not great considering that he does not seem to have had access to most of the acroamatic works including the *Nicomachean Ethics*. See Zeller, *Aristotle*, 107n1, and Rackham in Marcus Tullius Cicero, *De finibus bonorum et malorum*, trans. H. Rackham (London: W. Heinemann, 1914), 404n.

85. This fact itself, however, may possibly have some bearing on our question. The writings of Aristotle that we possess all derive from the authoritative edition of Andronicus. If we lack the exoteric works, that is because Andronicus made the fateful decision not to include them. Had a Neoplatonist done the editing, one feels confident he would have behaved very differently. While we do not know why Andronicus made the choice that he did, it is certainly one that harmonizes more with Alexander's whole view of things.

86. Elias, *Aristotelis Categorias Commentaria*, 18.1:114.15–115.13. See Chroust, "Eudemus," 22.

87. This observation also bears on our earlier discussion of Aristotle's artful obscurity. There is no doubt that much of the time, especially on uncontroversial issues, Aristotle is extremely—one might even say ostentatiously—clear and methodical. But here we have one of the biggest of the big questions of life—what will happen to me when I die—and suddenly we see a very different Aristotle. He surrounds the whole issue with a mixture of silence, evasion, and obscurity. This is the cuttlefish in action. This is a clear and simple example of what that very large consensus of commentators and philosophers had in mind in attributing to Aristotle an obvious and intentional obscurity.

88. The argument is open to two major lines of criticism. The ancient commentator Themistius (in *Libros Aristotelis de Anima Paraphrasis*, ed. R. Heinze, in *Commentaria in Aristotelem Graeca* [Berlin: Reimer, 1899], 5.3:106), argues that there is no ultimate discrepancy between *De anima*, on the one hand, and the *Eudemus* and also Plato's several discussions of this issue, on the other, because, despite appearances, the latter works, just like the former, actually attribute immortality only to part of the soul, to the *nous*. But this argument requires an esoteric reading of the latter works (which on the surface clearly endorse a stronger concept of personal immortality) and thus concedes the main point in dispute—that Aristotle (and Plato) occasionally affirm doctrines that they do not really believe. (But, see Chroust, "Eudemus," 24–25, for a discussion of contemporary scholars who attempt to prove the same thesis

in a nonesoteric manner. See also Lloyd P. Gerson, *Aristotle and Other Platonists* [Ithaca, NY: Cornell University Press, 2005], 51–59).

Werner Jaeger, however, in his classic work *Aristotle: Fundamentals of the History of His Development* (Oxford: Clarendon Press, 1948), rejects Themistius's argument (49–51), and in general argues powerfully for the stark differences between the *Eudemus* and the other exoteric dialogues, on the one hand, and the acroamatic works, on the other. But he explains these differences as reflecting, not esotericism, but Aristotle's honest changes of mind as he evolved from a young disciple of Plato into a mature and independent thinker. Jaeger's famous developmental thesis would not account, however, for the other indications of esotericism, the evasion and obscurity, that we have found. Furthermore, as I will argue below, this same embrace of conflicting doctrines can also be found within works all written in Aristotle's mature period.

89. Such statements are not simply confined to the ethical and political writings. Consider *Topics* 105a5: "People who are puzzled to know whether one ought to honor the gods or love one's parents or not need punishment." *The Basic Works of Aristotle*, ed. Richard McKeon (New York: Random House, 1941), 198.

90. Sir David Ross, *Aristotle* (London: Methuen, 1965), 5, 179; Grant, "On the Exoterikoi Logoi," 292.

91. One must indeed wonder what changes of thought or circumstances led Aristotle, who felt compelled to speak exoterically about the gods in the acroamatic *Ethics* and *Politics*, to speak so openly in the *Metaphysics* (which, for that reason, I have labeled "more acroamatic"). But whatever the reason, the existence of this difference is extremely useful in rendering plainly visible to us how willing Aristotle is to affirm views that he does not believe. (Of course, one must also wonder whether even the doctrine of the *Metaphysics* is Aristotle's true and final view of the matter.)

92. Ross, *Aristotle*, 186. Again, "the expression 'God and nature' seems to be a concession to ordinary ways of thinking" (126).

93. Ibid., 126. For similar accounts, see Abraham Edel, *Aristotle and His Philosophy* (Chapel Hill: University of North Carolina Press, 1982), 66; Mariska Leunissen, *Explanation and Teleology in Aristotle's Science of Nature* (Cambridge: Cambridge University Press, 2010), 40–42. See also Abram Shulsky, "The 'Infrastructure' of Aristotle's *Politics*: Aristotle on Economics and Politics," in *Essays on the Foundation of Aristotelian Political Science*, ed. Carnes Lord and David O'Connor (Berkeley: University of California Press, 1991), 89.

94. Once again, Ross duly points out the surprising contradiction between the claims made in the *Politics* and the teleological theory elaborated in the scientific writings. But in the case of this central Aristotelian doctrine, in contrast with the religious issues discussed above, Ross seems unwilling to entertain the idea that Aristotle might again be engaging in some kind of "accommodation" or salutary falsification. Concerning the extrinsic and anthropocentric teleology endorsed in the *Politics*, he can only bring himself to observe: "but there he is not writing biology" (*Aristotle*, 126n2), as if that could begin to explain why he has openly contradicted his settled view.

95. Consider also Plato, *Republic* 499b, where Socrates asserts that the best regime, the rule of philosopher-kings, may exist at the present time "in some barbaric place."

96. For some examples of esoteric readings of Aristotle's works, see Thomas L. Pangle, *Aristotle's Teaching in the Politics* (Chicago: University of Chicago Press, 2013); Harry Jaffa, *Thomism and Aristotelianism: A Study of the Commentary by Thomas Aquinas on the Nicomachean Ethics* (Chicago: University of Chicago Press, 1952); Ronna Burger, *Aristotle's Dialogue with Socrates: On the Nicomachean Ethics* (Chicago: University of Chicago Press, 2008); and David Bolotin, *An Approach to Aristotle's Physics*.

97. See Edward T. Hall, *Beyond Culture* (New York: Doubleday, 1976).

98. Peace Corps, *Culture Matters: The Peace Corps Cross-Cultural Workbook* (Washington DC: Peace Corps Information Collection and Exchange T0087, 1997), 81.

99. George Kennedy, *Comparative Rhetoric: An Historical and Cross-Cultural Introduction* (Oxford: Oxford University Press, 1998), 71.

100. Joy Hendry and C. W. Watson, *An Anthropology of Indirect Communication* (London: Routledge, 2001), 5–8.

101. Ibid., 2.

102. Ge Gao and Stella Ting-Toomey, *Communicating Effectively with the Chinese* (Thousand Oaks, CA: Sage Publications, 1998), 37, 36, 38.

103. Henry Kissinger and Clare B. Luce, *The White House Years* (Boston: Little Brown, 1979), 1247.

104. R. S. Zaharna, "Understanding Cultural Preferences of Arab Communication Patterns," *Public Relations Review* 21, no. 3 (1995): 249, 251.

105. Milton J. Bennett, "Intercultural Communication: A Current Perspective," in *Basic Concepts of Intercultural Communication: Selected Readings*, ed. Bennett (Yarmouth, ME: Intercultural Press, 1998), 17.

106. Sheila J. Ramsey, "Interactions between North Americans and Japanese: Considerations of Communication Style," in Bennett, *Basic Concepts of Intercultural Communication*, 124.

107. Michael Slackman, "Iranian 101: A Lesson for Americans—The Fine Art of Hiding What You Mean to Say," *New York Times*, August 6, 2006.

108. It would be more accurate to say that direct speech has been the cultural norm in the *liberal* West. Those parts of Europe that lived under Nazi or communist totalitarianism became well acquainted with the uses and ways of indirect speech, as will be seen in chapter 5 on defensive esotericism.

109. See, for example, Zaharna, "Understanding Cultural Preferences," 249; Gao and Ting-Toomey, *Communicating Effectively*, 35, 75; and Ramsey, "Interactions," 113, 121.

CHAPTER TWO

1. Diderot, "Machiavelisme," in *Encyclopédie*, ed. Diderot and d'Alembert, University of Chicago ARTFL Encyclopédie Project, http://encyclopedie.uchicago.edu; Spinoza, *A Political Treatise*, in *The Chief Works of Benedict Spinoza*, trans. R. H. M. Elwes (New York: Dover Publications, 1951), 315; Rousseau, *Social Contract*, in *On the Social Contract, with Geneva Manuscript and Political Economy*, ed. Roger D. Masters, trans. Judith R. Masters (New York: St. Martin's Press, 1978), 88 and 88n.

2. Machiavelli to Guicciardini, May 17, 1521. Quoted by Leo Strauss in *Thoughts on Machiavelli* (Chicago: University of Chicago Press, 1978), 36.

3. Machiavelli, *Discourses on Livy*, trans. Harvey C. Mansfield and Nathan Tarcov (Chicago: University of Chicago Press, 1996), 307 (3.48).

4. Alexander Pope, *An Essay on Criticism*, in *Pope: Poetical Works*, ed. Herbert Davis (Oxford: Oxford University Press, 1978), 69 (lines 175–80) (emphasis added).

5. Machiavelli, *Discourses*, 61–62 (1.26).

6. See Strauss, *Thoughts*, 35–36, 48–49.

7. Machiavelli, *The Prince*, trans. Harvey C. Mansfield (Chicago: University of Chicago Press, 1985), 56.

8. 1 Samuel 17:50 (RSV).

9. 1 Samuel 17:45–47.

10. See Machiavelli, *Discourses* 2.2. For a remarkably open expression of these "Machiavellian" views, see Rousseau, *Social Contract* 4.8, "On Civil Religion." On this interpretation of the *Prince*, see Harvey Mansfield's introduction in Machiavelli, *Prince*, xxi–xxii.

11. Plato, *Republic* 368b; see 362d.

12. Karl Marx, "Manifesto of the Communist Party," in *The Marx-Engels Reader*, ed. Robert C. Tucker, 2nd ed. (New York: Norton, 1978), 491.

CHAPTER THREE

1. Since I am no philosopher in the sense to be elaborated below (nor do I believe I have ever met anyone who is), it is hard to know whether this radically different way of life is actually possible. Perhaps the noble ideal of the classical philosopher is the product of illusory hopes (see, for example, Augustine's famous argument to this effect in book 19 of the *City of God*). This is a crucial and extremely difficult question. But it is one — the first of many, as we will see — that present purposes allow us, fortunately, to leave unsettled. It suffices to know that, rightly or wrongly, some such ideal was broadly subscribed to in premodern times and that it radically impacts the issue of how philosophers should act and speak in the world.

2. Although Heidegger, in his own unique way, sought to restore something like the classical sense of radical dualism, his postmodernist progeny, especially in the United States, have become even more insistently monist. Thus, Richard Rorty claims that American pragmatists have become very dubious of "the idea of a distinctive, autonomous, cultural activity called 'philosophy.'" "When Platonic dualisms go, the distinction between philosophy and the rest of culture is in danger" (Jürgen Habermas, Richard Rorty, and Leszek Kolakowski, *Debating the State of Philosophy*, ed. Jozef Niznik [Westport, CT: Praeger, 1996], 35; see 36, 40).

3. Plato, *Republic* 518c–e; Aristotle, *Nicomachean Ethics* 1177b27–1178a8. It should be said, however, that in Plato there seem to be two quite different accounts of the philosopher's distinctness. In the *Republic*, the philosopher is said to live in the true world of ideas or universals — or what Aristotle calls the realm of the necessary and eternal (1139a6–18) — while others live in the world of particularity and change. In the more skeptical account of the *Apology*, however, the philosopher (or Socrates) is said only to have freed himself from the illusions and false certainties of ordinary life and thus to have achieved knowledge of ignorance.

4. While emphasizing the stark dualism of these two ideal types, the theoretical life and the practical life, classical thought was also abundantly aware that in practice all kinds of mixes and in-between positions were possible.

5. Plato, *Phaedrus* 275d–e, in *Gorgias and Phaedrus*, trans. James H. Nichols Jr. (Ithaca, NY: Cornell University Press, 1998), 212. I have slightly altered the translation.

6. Xenophon, *Memorabilia* 4.6.15.

7. Diogenes Laertius, *Lives of Eminent Philosophers*, trans. Hicks, 109 (1.105).

8. Aristotle, *Nicomachean Ethics* 1141a22.

9. See *Nicomachean Ethics* 1102a25–1103a10, 1166a15–25, 1178a5–8; *Metaphysics* 980a22–30.

10. See *Politics* 1252a25–1253a40; *Nicomachean Ethics* 1169b17, 1155a5.

11. Richard Rorty, "Solidarity or Objectivity," in *Objectivity, Relativism, and Truth: Philosophical Papers*, vol. 1 (Cambridge: Cambridge University Press, 1991), 21 (emphasis added).

12. If we take this question back to the evolutionary level, we come across the "social brain hypothesis" (best known from the work of British anthropologist Robin Dunbar), which holds that human reason evolved not primarily to meet the challenges of the natural world but to help us manage the complexities of tightly knit social groups. Intelligence evolved as social intelligence. A thought akin to this is present in germ in the Greek word *logos*, which means both reason and speech (i.e., social connection).

13. Of course, there were also some nonsecular figures in the counter-Enlightenment, such as Kierkegaard, Franz Rosenzweig, and Karl Schmitt.

14. For a discussion of Burke from this point of view, see Leo Strauss, "The Crisis of Modern Natural Right: Burke," chap. 6b in *Natural Right and History*, 294–323.

15. As Strauss put it: "I must make one observation in order to protect myself against gross misunderstanding. A modern phenomenon is not characterized by the fact that it is located,

say, between 1600 and 1952, because premodern traditions of course survived and survive. And more than that, throughout the modern period, there has been a constant movement against this modern trend, from the very beginning." "Progress or Return?," in Leo Strauss, *The Rebirth of Classical Rationalism*: *An Introduction to the Thought of Leo Strauss*, ed. Thomas Pangle (Chicago: University of Chicago Press, 1989) 242–43.

16. Rorty, *Objectivity, Relativism, and Truth*, 13.

17. It may be objected that while Rorty fits the harmonist paradigm quite neatly, other post-modernists do not, especially Foucault with his searing emphasis on conflict and oppression and the never-ending need for resistance. It must be kept in mind, however, that a "harmonist," as I use the term, is one who expects the end not of every form of conflict and oppression (military, economic, etc.), but only of the fundamental conflict between the two elements of our nature, sociality and rationality. On this score, like all Enlightenment and counter-Enlightenment thinkers, Foucault begins by denouncing the existing disharmony between the two, and, like a counter-Enlightenment thinker, he puts the primary blame on reason through his historical unmaskings of our distorting and oppressive sciences. But he engages in all this denouncing and unmasking precisely because he, unlike a conflictualist, does not see this problem as inescapable. Specifically, he does not consider the new thinking that he himself engages in to be dangerous to society. On the contrary, he expects his new insights and unmaskings—if he has found the right means to express and disseminate them—to eventually make the world a better place (no matter how pessimistically he, like many Enlightenment philosophes before him, may occasionally express himself). And (in a complex way) he finds the key to this reconciliation between science and social well-being in his central insight into the reducibility of truth to power or at least the ultimate unity of the two. But this is an emphatically harmonist view.

18. To briefly adumbrate the main points, the harmonist view holds that while heretofore philosophy and society have been at odds wherever philosophy has existed, the two can in fact be brought into unity in a new, more rational kind of society. The new political activism characteristic of modern philosophy aims at bringing that rational society into being. It is thus distinguished from the philosophical politics of premodern philosophy in at least four crucial respects. First, philosophical politics aims specifically at the class interests of philosophers, which, on the conflictual view, are understood to often differ from those of other classes or of the rest of society as a whole. Modern philosophical activism, by contrast, is more public-spirited or humanitarian (as it constantly proclaims), because activated by the belief that these conflicts of interest can be overcome. Second, philosophical politics is very limited in its goals, seeking only to manage an ill that can never be truly cured. Modern philosophical activism, by contrast, is engaged not in limited or ordinary politics, but in a "great politics" of revolutionary historical transformation. It seeks a permanent and (eventually) universal change in the relation of politics and rationality—an age of reason. Third, it seeks to bring about this change, not primarily through political or military action, but through books, through the power of publication (in the new age of printing), through universal enlightenment—a mode of action and a goal not imagined by premodern philosophers. Finally, this new activism in political philosophy goes along with a new activism in natural philosophy— the turn away from a contemplative posture toward nature to one of technological mastery.

19. Even on harmonist premises, however, pedagogical esotericism continues to be useful, if less strictly necessary. Virtually all philosophers, to one extent or another, agree regarding the utility of the "Socratic method" that withholds answers in order to force students to think for themselves.

CHAPTER FOUR

1. See Kojève, "Emperor Julian and His Art of Writing"; Leo Strauss, *On Tyranny*: *Including the Strauss-Kojève Correspondence* (New York: Free Press, 1991); Arnaldo Momigliano, "Her-

meneutics and Classical Political Thought in Leo Strauss" and "In Memoriam: Leo Strauss,"
in *Essays on Ancient and Modern Judaism*, ed. Silvia Berti (Chicago: University of Chicago
Press, 1994); Gershom Scholem, *On the Kabbalah and Its Symbolism*, trans. Ralph Mannheim
(New York: Schocken Books, 1965), 51; Hans-Georg Gadamer, "Philosophizing in Opposi-
tion: Strauss and Voegelin on Communication and Science," in *Faith and Political Philosophy: The Correspondence between Leo Strauss and Eric Voegelin, 1934–1964*, trans. and ed. Peter
Emberley and Barry Cooper (College Park: Pennsylvania State University Press, 1993); also see
Hans-Georg Gadamer, *Truth and Method*, 2nd rev. ed., trans. Joel Weinsheimer and Donald G.
Marshall, 2nd rev. ed. (New York: Continuum, 1989), 532–41; and Strauss and Gadamer, "Correspondence concerning *Wahrheit und Methode*," *Independent Journal of Philosophy* 2, no. 10
(1978): 5–12.

2. Stephen Holmes, *The Anatomy of Antiliberalism* (Cambridge, MA: Harvard University
Press, 1993), 86.

3. Gregory Vlastos, "Further Lessons of Leo Strauss: An Exchange," *New York Review of
Books*, April 24, 1986.

4. George H. Sabine, Review of *Persecution and the Art of Writing*, *Ethics* 63, no. 3 (April
1953): 220.

5. For a more extreme account that employs Lacanian analysis to argue that Strauss's
theory of esotericism is fundamentally perverted, see Sean Noah Walsh, *Perversion and the Art
of Persecution: Esotericism and Fear in the Political Philosophy of Leo Strauss* (New York: Lexington Books, 2012). For a perceptive discussion of the resistance to Strauss's work, see G. R. F.
Ferrari, "Strauss's Plato," in *Arion* 5, no. 2 (Fall 1997): 36–65.

6. Mark 4:34 (ESV).

7. Thomas Aquinas, *Summa Theologica*, trans. Fathers of the English Dominican Province,
vol. 3 (Westminster, MD: Christian Classics, 1981), III qu 42, a 3.

8. John Calvin, *Commentary on a Harmony of the Evangelists, Matthew, Mark, and Luke*,
trans. Rev. William Pringle (Grand Rapids: W. B. Eerdmans, 1949), 2: commentary on
Matthew 13:1–17. See commentary on Mark 4:1–12, 4:24–25; Luke 8:1–10, 8:18, 10:23–24, section 11.

9. Hugo Grotius, *De jure belli ac pacis libri tres*, trans. Francis W. Kelsey (Oxford: Clarendon
Press, 1925), 612.

10. Augustine, *Quaestiones XVII in Matthaeum*, question 14. Quoted by Thomas Aquinas
in *Catena Aurea, Commentary on the Four Gospels: Collected out of the Works of the Fathers by St.
Thomas Aquinas*, trans. Mark Pattison, J. D. Dalgairns, and T. D. Ryder (Oxford: John Henry
Parker, 1841–45), 1:488 (emphasis added).

11. John Locke, *The Reasonableness of Christianity: As Delivered in the Scriptures*, ed.
George W. Ewing (Washington, DC: Regnery, 1965), 70 (§108).

12. Frank Kermode, *The Genesis of Secrecy: On the Interpretation of Narrative* (Cambridge,
MA: Harvard University Press, 1979), 25 (emphasis added).

13. On this great "expense of learning" employed to deny Jesus' esotericism, see ibid.,
149n4; see also John Drury, "The Sower, the Vineyard, and the Place of Allegory in the Interpretation of Mark's Parables," *Journal of Theological Studies* 24, no. 2 (1973): 367–79; and
C. F. D. Moule, "Mark 4:1–20 Yet Once More," in *Neotestamentica et Semitica: Studies in Honour
of Principal Matthew Black*, ed. E. Earle Ellis and Max Wilcox (Edinburgh: T. & T. Clark, 1969).

14. For the sake of simplicity and initial clarity, I am using the term "tragedy" in a somewhat loose way in labeling the classical conflictual view "tragic." In a more precise sense, the
classical philosophers, while not actively resistant to the tragic view as modern thought is,
did not simply embrace it either. They were unflinchingly open to the many permanent tensions and contradictions of life—above all, that between truth and political community. They
saw this conflict as posing grave problems for the stability of the political community and
the psychic integrity and tranquility of the citizen. But in the end, they did also believe that

there was a solution—for those rare individuals able to rise to the philosophic life. To be sure, on the practical level, the philosophic individual will actually experience increased danger owing to the heightened conflict between his way of living and thinking and that of the city. But these dangers, while grave, are still manageable in most circumstances. The decisive consideration is that, within his own soul, he will overcome the theory-praxis conflict through a wholehearted devotion to truth. He will achieve a human happiness. Thus, human life, with its grave inner contradictions, is tragic for most human beings—but not for the highest individuals. It is in this sense that the classical philosophers may be said to have rejected the tragic view of life.

15. "Mankind always sets itself only such tasks as it can solve." Karl Marx, preface to *A Contribution to the Critique of Political Economy*, in Karl Marx and Friedrich Engels, *The Marx-Engels Reader*, ed. Robert C. Tucker, 2nd ed. (New York: Norton, 1978), 5.

16. This powerful humanist-harmonist tendency was then reinforced by two further factors, discussed in the previous chapter. Modern philosophy, in its embrace of the harmonist view, became so caught up in the epic internecine battle between the two opposite versions into which that view logically divides—the crusading rationalism of the Enlightenment vs. the historicism of the counter-Enlightenment—that it effectively lost sight of the excluded conflictual alternative.

The fact of this exclusion, moreover, became hidden—and so perpetuated—by the tendency of the two fundamental alternatives to appear as their own opposites. The harmonist view, by inspiring political activism, temporarily heightens the tension between philosophy and society, and so looks like the very embodiment of conflictualism; whereas, the genuine conflictualist view, which renounces all hope for major improvement, seeks merely to cover over the problem, and so looks like the harmonist view.

17. P. N. Furbank, "A No-Code Zone," *Times Literary Supplement*, June 4, 1999.

18. The standard critical account of Strauss's thought is still Shadia B. Drury's *The Political Ideas of Leo Strauss* (New York: St. Martin's Press, 1988). See also her *Leo Strauss and the American Right* (New York: St. Martin's Press, 1997). For a more extreme account, see Nicholas Xenos, *Cloaked in Virtue: Unveiling Leo Strauss and the Rhetoric of American Foreign Policy* (New York: Routledge, 2008). There are a number of excellent works offering replies. See, for example, Peter Minowitz, *Straussophobia: Defending Leo Strauss and Straussians against Shadia Drury and Other Accusers* (Lanham, MD: Lexington Books, 2009); Catherine H. Zuckert and Michael P. Zuckert, *The Truth about Leo Strauss: Political Philosophy and American Democracy* (Chicago: University of Chicago Press, 2006); Thomas L. Pangle, *Leo Strauss: An Introduction to His Thought and Intellectual Legacy* (Baltimore: Johns Hopkins University Press, 2006); and Steven B. Smith, *Reading Leo Strauss: Politics, Philosophy, Judaism* (Chicago: University of Chicago Press, 2006).

19. The central issue of the conflictual vs. harmonist view of theory and praxis will be addressed in chapter 6 on protective esotericism. The more "literary" issues of obscurity and of childishness or playfulness will be taken up in chapter 7 on pedagogical esotericism. The issue of prudence or cowardice and that of cloistering vs. disseminating knowledge will be treated in the discussion of the Enlightenment in chapter 8 on political esotericism. And the issue of the hidden liberation of the philosopher from his times vs. historicist contextualism will be discussed in chapter 10, "Esotericism and the Critique of Historicism."

20. See, for example, the work of Annabel Patterson, Perez Zagorin, Lev Loseff, David Berman, David Wootton, and Moshe Halbertal.

21. Leo Strauss, "On Classical Political Philosophy," in *What Is Political Philosophy?*, 91.

22. Strauss, "New Interpretation," 351.

23. From 1958 until his death in 1973, almost all of Strauss's classes were taped and then transcribed. These transcripts—about forty in all—as well as the original audio recordings (where they have survived) are being made available online by the Leo Strauss Center at the

University of Chicago (http://leostrausscenter.uchicago.edu). From the fifteen or so transcripts that I have read, two facts stand out about Strauss's classes. First, unlike many of his published writings, they are extremely clear, displaying a kind of piercing Socratic simplicity. Second, they are remarkably unpolitical. All his courses are devoted to the close reading of some earlier thinker or thinkers: not one is organized around a contemporary political question, movement, or regime. (The closest he comes is a class on historicism or historical relativism.)

Furthermore, most other political theorists (myself included), when teaching earlier thinkers, tend to bring in a lot of contemporary political examples to make the discussion more concrete and relevant. It is amazing how rarely Strauss does even that. For example, of all classic political writings, perhaps Thucydides's history of the great war between the rival empires of Athens and Sparta is the one that most cries out for the use of contemporary political parallels, most obviously the rivalry between the United States and the Soviet Union. At the University of Chicago, Strauss devoted an entire graduate seminar to Thucydides's history in the winter quarter of 1962 — at the height of the Cold War, a little more than a month after the end of the Cuban missile crisis. But in the course of the whole semester, in a transcript that runs to four hundred single-spaced typed pages, he made only six trivial references to the Soviet Union (three of them in response to questions) and one passing mention of President Kennedy, and he spoke not a single word about the Cuban missile crisis. It would be extremely difficult, I think, for someone to read through all these transcripts and continue to believe that Leo Strauss's intellectual activity was primarily moved by some fervent political project (especially, as some have recently maintained, a project for "American empire").

24. Much of the suspicion directed at Strauss derives from the fact that he not only discusses esotericism but also seems to practice it. When discussing it, he addresses not only the historical question of whether earlier philosophers wrote esoterically (to which I limit myself here) but also the much harder, philosophical question of whether it was necessary and right for them to do so. He answers both questions in the affirmative. It is not surprising, then, that he would write esoterically himself, and virtually all of his followers, as best I can tell, agree that he does so. But there the agreement ends. There is much debate concerning why he does so and what his true teaching is. Catherine and Michael Zuckert, in their excellent work *The Truth about Leo Strauss* (115–54), present a good overview. They themselves argue that Strauss's esotericism is simply of the pedagogical kind. For criticism of this claim see the review by Steven J. Lenzner, "Guide for the Perplexed" (*Claremont Review of Books* 7, no. 2 [Spring 2007]: 53–57), as well as the debate in the letters in subsequent issues. (For a very interesting elaboration of an alternative view — with which I ultimately disagree — see Laurence Lampert, *The Enduring Importance of Leo Strauss* [Chicago: University of Chicago Press, 2013]). I would argue that Strauss believed in and practiced protective esotericism — for the kinds of reasons elaborated in chapter 6 — as well as pedagogical and perhaps defensive esotericism. But what is most noteworthy for our purposes here is that, amid all this disagreement, none of his followers argues that he practiced *political* esotericism, that he was esoteric on behalf of a secret scheme for political transformation.

25. Among the theories that are not named here and that I would largely exempt from this generalization are the "reader response" and Cambridge schools. Both impose genuine interpretive discipline, the former (at least in its less subjectivist, more uniformist variants represented by critics like Wolfgang Iser and Stanley Fish) through meticulous attention to the text, the latter through scrupulous study of historical sources.

Furthermore, as it turns out, both theories open up a clear pathway to the recognition of esoteric writing (albeit without particularly intending to). For one way of describing the theory of esotericism is that texts can communicate more than they openly state, that what they say is not the whole of what they do, that these texts are not complete in and by themselves but rather start a process that must be completed by the reflections of the reader him or herself. But this idea, rejected as implausible by so many, is the core idea of reader response theory, which finds it at work, in one degree or another, in all texts. The theory of esotericism would simply add this further step—hardly implausible once you take the first one—that there are certain authors who, acutely aware of this phenomenon, deliberately employ it in order to convey something to one set of readers (one "interpretive community") while excluding others.

Quentin Skinner and the Cambridge school actually begin from the same essential idea as the reader response school, albeit via the thought of John L. Austin. "In saying something we are doing something," as Austin liked to put it (*How to Do Things with Words* [Cambridge, MA: Harvard University Press, 1962], 12). Our words have an "illocutionary force" (in Austin's infelicitous phrase) that conveys things not contained within the simple meaning of the words, but filled in by the knowing reader. This insight naturally leads Skinner to the possibility of esoteric communication. Thus, he explicitly discusses "the various oblique strategies which a writer may always decide to adopt in order to set out and at the same time disguise what he means by what he says about some given doctrine" ("Meaning and Understanding in the History of Ideas," *History and Theory* 8, no. 1 (1969): 32). He suggests, for example, that Hobbes's *Leviathan* is "replete with rhetorical codes," especially in its discussion of religion (*Reason and Rhetoric in the Philosophy of Hobbes* [Cambridge: Cambridge University Press, 1996], 13).

But to Austin's theory of illocutionary force, Skinner adds the further step that the text is able to communicate its unstated message primarily by drawing upon certain background conventions that are highly localized in place and time. This is what causes him to be critical of the strong textual emphasis of the Straussian and reader response schools, and leads him to the highly contextual and historical emphasis of the Cambridge school. Thus, in *Reason and Rhetoric*, Skinner uses the meticulous historical study of the theory and practice of rhetoric in Renaissance England as a means for unlocking the esoteric level of Hobbes's writings.

26. See the excellent study by Paul Cantor, "Leo Strauss and Contemporary Hermeneutics," in *Leo Strauss's Thought: Toward a Critical Engagement*, ed. Alan Udoff (Boulder, CO: Lynne Rienner, 1991), 267–314.

27. Rousseau, "Preface to Second Letter to Bordes," in *Discourse on the Sciences and Arts, and Polemics*, vol. 2 of *The Collected Writings of Rousseau*, ed. Roger D. Masters and Christopher Kelly (Hanover, NH: University Press of New England, 1992), 184–85 (emphasis added).

28. Alexis de Tocqueville, *Democracy in America*, trans. Harvey C. Mansfield and Delba Winthrop (Chicago: University of Chicago Press, 2000), 613 (2.3.21).

29. Ibid., 479–82 (2.2.1).

30. Ibid., 535 (2.3.1).

31. Pierre Charron, *De la sagesse: Trois livres*, new ed. (Paris: Lefèvre, 1836), 287 (bk. 2, chap. 2, section 2). Translation mine.

32. Francesco Guicciardini, *Maxims and Reflections of a Renaissance Statesman*, trans. Mario Domandi (New York: Harper & Row, 1965), 76 (§140).

33. Livy, *History of Rome* 31.34, quoted by George Boas, *Vox Populi: Essays in the History of an Idea* (Baltimore: Johns Hopkins University Press, 1969), 47.

34. Benedict de Spinoza. *Theologico-Political Treatise*. In *The Chief Works of Benedict Spinoza*, trans. R. H. M. Elwes (New York: Dover Publications, 1951),78.

35. *De natura deorum* 3.27.

36. Montaigne, *Complete Essays*, trans. Frame, 104 (1.25).

37. Quoted by George Hourani (from a medieval Arabic commentary on Galen) in *Averroes: On the Harmony of Religion and Philosophy*, trans. Hourani (London: Gibb Memorial Trust, 1961), 106.

38. Maimonides, *Guide*, ed. Pines, 16.

39. Horace, *Odes* 3.1, in *The Complete Works of Horace*, trans. Charles E. Passage (New York: Frederick Ungar, 1983), 209.

40. Epistle 105, quoted and translated by Paul Rahe in *Republics Ancient and Modern: Classical Republicanism and the American Revolution* (Chapel Hill: University of North Carolina Press, 1992), 226.

41. Lucius Annaeus Seneca, *Ad Lucilium Epistulae morales*, trans. Richard Gummere (Cambridge, MA: Harvard University Press, 1917), 1:209 (24.11). For the Epicurus quotation, see Hermann Usener, *Epicurea* frag. 187 (Cambridge: Cambridge University Press, 2010), 157.

42. Julien Offray de La Mettrie, "Preliminary Discourse," in *Machine Man and Other Writings*, trans. and ed. Ann Thomson (Cambridge: Cambridge University Press, 1996), 162.

43. Friedrich Nietzsche, *The Gay Science; with a Prelude in Rhymes and an Appendix of Songs*, trans. Walter Kaufmann (New York: Random House, 1974), 343 (§381).

44. Nietzsche, *Beyond Good and Evil*, 42 (§30; emphasis added).

45. Elizabeth A. Brandt, "On Secrecy and the Control of Knowledge: Taos Pueblo," in *Secrecy: A Cross-Cultural Perspective*, ed. Stanton K. Teft (New York: Human Sciences Press, 1980), 131. See also Numa Denis Fustel de Coulanges, *The Ancient City* (Garden City, NY: Doubleday, 1956), 194.

46. *The Geography of Strabo* (Cambridge, MA.: Harvard University Press, 1969), 10.3.9.

47. Generally speaking, the phenomenon of religious esotericism has been more widely acknowledged and documented than that of philosophical esotericism. See, for example, Hans G. Kippenberg and Guy G. Stroumsa, eds., *Secrecy and Concealment: Studies in the History of Mediterranean and Near Eastern Religions* (Leiden: E. J. Brill, 1995); Kees W. Bolle, ed., *Secrecy in Religions* (Leiden, E. J. Brill, 1987); Mary H. Nooter, "Secrecy: African Art That Conceals and Reveals," *African Arts* 26, no. 1 (January 1993): 55–70; Scholem, *On the Kabbalah*; Jean Danielou, "Les traditions secrètes des Apôtres," *Eranos-Jahrbuch* 31 (1962): 199–215; Guy G. Stroumsa, *Hidden Wisdom: Esoteric Traditions and the Roots of Christian Mysticism* (Leiden: E. J. Brill, 1996); Alex Wayman, *The Buddhist Tantras: Light on Indo-Tibetan Esotericism* (New York: S. Weiser, 1973); Mohammad Ali Amir Moezzi, *The Divine Guide in Early Shiism: The Sources of Esotericism in Islam* (Albany: State University of New York Press, 1994).

48. On the general subject of secrecy, see Simmel's classic discussion "The Secret and the Secret Society," in *The Sociology of Georg Simmel*, trans. Kurt H. Wolff (New York: Free Press, 1950); see also H. Webster, *Primitive Secret Societies: A Study of Early Politics and Religion* (New York: Macmillan, 1908). See also Hans Speier, "The Communication of Hidden Meaning," chap. 9 in *The Truth in Hell and Other Essays on Politics and Culture, 1935–1987* (Oxford: Oxford University Press, 1989), 206.

49. W. E. H. Lecky, *History of European Morals from Augustus to Charlemagne* (New York: D. Appleton, 1879), 1:138; cf. 155. See also "The Wisdom of Life," in *The Essays of Arthur Schopenhauer*, trans. T. Bailey Saunders (New York: Willey Books, 1935), 70–73. And see Francis Fukuyama, *Trust: The Social Virtues and the Creation of Prosperity* (New York: Free Press, 1995).

50. Hannah Arendt, *Between Past and Future: Eight Exercises in Political Thought* (New York: Penguin Books, 1977), 232.

51. Dio Chrysostom, "On the Cultivation of Letters," *Discourses* (18.16–17), quoted and translated by Robert Bartlett in *Xenophon: The Shorter Socratic Writings* (Ithaca, NY: Cornell University Press, 1996), 4.

52. Plutarch, *On Stoic Self-Contradictions* 1055e–56a, quoted and translated by Thomas L. Pangle and Peter J. Ahrensdorf, *Justice among Nations: On the Moral Basis of Power and Peace* (Lawrence: University Press of Kansas, 1999), 275n7.

53. Grotius, *De jure belli ac pacis libri tres*, trans. Kelsey et al., 610 (3.1.9.3).

54. Maimonides, *Guide*, ed. Pines, 79 (1.34).

55. *Averroes on Plato's Republic*, trans. Ralph Lerner (Ithaca, NY: Cornell University Press, 1974), 24.

56. Erasmus to Lorenzo Campeggi, December 6, 1520, in Erasmus, *Correspondence*, 8:113.

57. Burnet, *Archæologiæ Philosophicæ*, 53–54.

58. Rousseau, *Social Contract*, ed. Masters, 69–70 (2.7).

59. *Encyclopédie*, ed. Diderot and d'Alembert, University of Chicago ARTFL Encyclopédie Project, http://encyclopedie.uchicago.edu, translation mine. A similar conclusion can be found in the preceding article, "Mensonge," by Louis de Jaucourt.

60. Hume to Col. James Edmonstoune, April 1764, quoted in Rahe, *Republics*, 242.

61. René Descartes, *Meditations, Second Replies*, in *Œuvres de Descartes*, ed. Charles Adam and Paul Tannery (Paris: J. Vrin, 1964–69), 8:143, quoted by Abraham Anderson in *The Treatise of the Three Impostors and the Problem of Enlightenment: A New Translation of the Traité des Trois Imposteurs (1777 edition) with Three Essays in Commentary* (Lanham, MD: Rowman & Littlefield, 1997), 150n22.

62. Sissela Bok, *Lying: Moral Choice in Public and Private Life* (New York: Vintage Books, 1989), 32–39.

63. Augustine, *Letters*, 1:3.

64. See Grotius, *De jure belli ac pacis libri tres*, trans. Kelsey et al., 607–22 (3.1).

CHAPTER FIVE

1. Shaftesbury, *Characteristics*, ed. Klein, 34.

2. Fifteen hundred years later, David Hume, still struck by the abiding truth of this statement, selected it as the epigraph for his first major philosophical writing. Tacitus, *The Histories* 1.1, quoted and translated by David Hume, *A Treatise of Human Nature*, ed. Ernest C. Mossner (Harmondsworth, UK: Penguin, 1969), 32, and cited by Paul Russell, "Epigram, Pantheists, and Freethought in Hume's Treatise: A Study in Esoteric Communication," *Journal of the History of Ideas* 54, no. 4 (October 1993): 659–60.

3. Pierre Bayle, *Various Thoughts on the Occasion of a Comet*, trans. Robert C. Bartlett (Albany: State University of New York Press, 2000), 8.

4. Fredric Jameson, *The Political Unconscious* (Ithaca, NY: Cornell University Press, 1981), 84 (emphasis added), quoted by Annabel Patterson in *Censorship and Interpretation: The Conditions of Writing and Reading in Early Modern England* (Madison: University of Wisconsin Press, 1984), 119.

5. Patterson, *Censorship and Interpretation*; *Fables of Power: Aesopian Writing and Political History* (Durham, NC: Duke University Press, 1991); *Reading between the Lines* (Madison: University of Wisconsin Press, 1993). At Patterson's instigation, an entire issue of *PMLA* (January 1994) was devoted to the question of literature and censorship. See also Sue Curry Jansen, *Censorship: The Knot That Binds Power and Knowledge* (Oxford: Oxford University Press, 1988).

6. Vaclav Havel, *Letters to Olga*, trans. Paul Wilson (New York: Henry Holt, 1989), 8, quoted by Patterson, *Censorship*, 11. See also the excellent discussion of East European dissidence by the Hungarian dissident G. M. Tamas in "The Legacy of Dissent: Irony, Ambiguity, Duplicity," *Uncaptive Minds* 7, no. 2 (Summer 1994): 19–34. Tamas makes explicit use of Strauss's theory.

7. Vaclav Havel, *Disturbing the Peace: A Conversation with Karel Hvizdala*, trans. Paul Wilson (New York: Alfred A. Knopf, 1990), 55.

8. Andrei Codrescu, *The Disappearance of the Outside: A Manifesto for Escape* (New York: Addison-Wesley, 1990), 38–39.

9. Lidia Vianu, *Censorship in Romania* (Budapest, Hungary: Central European University Press, 1998), ix–x.

10. Czeslaw Milosz, *The Captive Mind*, trans. Jane Zielonko (New York: Alfred A. Knopf, 1953). Milosz compares the habits of speech and action in Eastern Europe to the esoteric practices or "Ketman" (in Arabic: concealment, discretion) traditionally used by the Shiites of Persia, as described by Gobineau in *Les religions et les philosophies dans l'Asie Centrale*, in *Œuvres*, ed. Jean Gaulmier, vol. 2 (Paris: Gallimard, 1983).

11. Leszek Kolakowski, "Dialogue between Leszek Kolakowski and Danny Postel: On Exile, Philosophy and Tottering Insecurely on the Edge of an Unknown Abyss," *Daedalus* 134, no. 3 (Summer 2005): 85 (emphasis added).

12. J. M. Ritchie, *German Literature under National Socialism* (Totowa, NJ: Barnes & Noble, 1983), 119. For other discussions of esoteric communication in the Third Reich, see: R. Schnell, "Innere Emigration und kulturelle Dissidenz," in *Widerstand und Verweigerung in Deutschland 1933 bis 1945*, ed. R. Löwenthal and P. von zur Muhlen (Bonn: Dietz, 1982), 211–25; Jerry Muller, "Enttäuschung und Zweideutigkeit: Zur Geschichte rechter Sozialwissenschaftler im Dritten Reich," *Geschichte und Gesellschaft* 3 (1986): 289–316, and *The Other God That Failed: Hans Freyer and the Deradicalization of German Conservatism* (Princeton: Princeton University Press, 1987).

13. Daniela Berghahn, "Film Censorship in a 'Clean State': the Case of Klein and Kohlhaase's *Berlin um die Ecke*," in *Censorship and Cultural Regulation in the Modern Age*, ed. Beate Muller (Amsterdam: Rodopi, 2004), 134.

14. Quoted by Ray J. Parrott Jr., "Aesopian Language," in *Modern Encyclopedia of Russian and Soviet Literature*, ed. Harry B. Weber (Gulf Breeze, FL: Academic International Press, 1977), 41. For other examples and discussions of Aesopian language, see Katerina Clark and Michael Holquist, *Mikhail Bakhtin* (Cambridge, MA: Harvard University Press, 1984); Lauren G. Leighton, *The Esoteric Tradition in Russian Romantic Literature: Decembrism and Freemasonry* (University Park: Pennsylvania State University Press, 1994); Lev Loseff, *On the Beneficence of Censorship: Aesopian Language in Modern Russian Literature*, trans. Jane Bobko (Munich: Sagner, 1984); Martin Dewhirst and Robert Farrell, eds., *The Soviet Censorship* (Metuchen, NJ: Scarecrow Press, 1973); Daniel Balmuth, *Censorship in Russia, 1865–1905* (Washington, DC: University Press of America, 1979); Roman Jakobson, *Pushkin and His Sculptural Myth*, trans. John Burbank (The Hague: Mouton, 1975), 50; Joseph Frank, *Dostoevsky: The Seeds of Revolt, 1821–1849* (Princeton, NJ: Princeton University Press, 1976), 220; G. A. Svirsky, *A History of Post-War Soviet Writing: The Literature of Moral Opposition*, trans. Robert Dessaix and Michael Ulman (Ann Arbor, MI: Ardis, 1981); Thomas Venclova, "The Game of the Soviet Censor," *New York Review of Books*, March 31, 1983, 34–35; Hedrick Smith, *The Russians* (New York: Ballantine, 1977), 508–9; and Alexander Herzen, *My Past and Thoughts: The Memoirs of Alexander Herzen*, trans. Constance Garnett (New York: Alfred A. Knopf, 1968), 2:407.

This view of Aesop as a classic of defensive esotericism is not unique to Russian writers. Julian the Apostate, writing in mid-fourth-century Rome, observes: "For since the law did not allow him freedom of speech, [Aesop] had no resource but to shadow forth his wise counsels and trick them out with charms and graces and so serve them up to his hearers." *To the Cynic Heracleios* 207c, in vol. 2 of *The Works of the Emperor Julian*, trans. Wilmer Cave Wright (London: William Heinemann, 1913), 81.

15. Lioudmila Savinitch, "Pragmatic Goals and Communicative Strategies in Journalistic Discourse under Censorship," in *Power without Domination: Dialogism and the Empowering Property of Communication*, ed. Eric Grillo (Philadelphia: John Benjamins, 2005), 107.

16. Jakobson, *Pushkin*, 50 (emphasis added).

17. "The Party Organization and Party Literature," in *Vladimir Lenin: The Collected Works* (Moscow: Progress, 1972), 10:44, quoted by Loseff, *On the Beneficence*, 7. So firmly entrenched were the Aesopian habits of the Bolshevik revolutionaries, habits formed during their struggle with the czar, that they continued them even after their victory. This produced the great historical anomaly of a ruling elite that communicated esoterically with itself and with the people. (This situation also grew out of the unique needs of a mass party that employed democratic centralism and claimed a monopoly on ideological truth.) Loseff gives a clear example: "a [newspaper] article may refer at considerable length and in glowing terms to agricultural advances, but make only passing mention in its next to last paragraph of the poorly

organized procurement of cattle feed 'in certain areas'; for an experienced reader, the content of the article amounts to a forewarning of immanent meat shortages" (*On the Beneficence*, 56). On state esotericism, see Myron Rush, "Esoteric Communication in Soviet Politics," *World Politics* 11, no. 4 (July 1959): 614–20, and *The Rise of Khrushchev* (Washington, DC: Public Affairs Press, 1958), 88–94; and Nathan Leites and Elsa Bernaut, *Ritual of Liquidation* (Glencoe, IL: Free Press, 1954). See also Alexander George, *Propaganda Analysis: A Study of Inferences Made from Nazi Propaganda in World War II* (Evanston, IL: Row, Peterson, 1959).

18. Joan Neuberger, *Ivan the Terrible: The Film Companion* (London: I. B. Tauris, 2003), 32, 30. Eisenstein completed the second part of his projected trilogy on Ivan shortly after the release of the first part, but this time the censors were on to him and it was never displayed in his lifetime.

19. Lee Siegel, "Persecution and the Art of Painting," *New Republic* 219, no. 9 (August 31, 1998): 41, 39. The same suggestion is made by Milosz, *Captive Mind*, 80.

20. See *Testimony: The Memoirs of Dmitri Shostakovich*, as related to and edited by Solomon Volkov, trans. Antonina W. Bouis (New York: Harper & Row, 1979). Questions have been raised, however, about the authenticity of this book. See Edward Rothstein, "Sly Dissident or Soviet Tool? A Musical War," *New York Times*, October 17, 1998; and Terry Teachout "The Composer and the Commissars," *Commentary*, October 1999, 53–56.

21. Seth Mydans, "Burmese Editor's Code: Winks and Little Hints," *New York Times*, June 24, 2001 (emphasis added).

22. J. M. Coetzee, *Giving Offense: Essays on Censorship* (Chicago: University of Chicago Press, 1996), 152.

23. Michael Drewett, "Aesopian Strategies of Textual Resistance in the Struggle to Overcome the Censorship of Popular Music in Apartheid South Africa," *Critical Studies* 22 (2004): 193 (emphasis added).

24. Yahia Lababidi, "Empire of the Senses," *New Internationalist*, May 1, 2010.

25. http://www.commercialcloset.org/cgi-bin/iowa/portrayals.html?mode=4 (accessed 05/06/2018, no longer available), the website of the Commercial Closet Association (since renamed AdRespect). On this general theme, see A. J. Frantzen, "Between the Lines: Queer Theory, the History of Homosexuality, and Anglo-Saxon Penitentials," *Journal of Medieval and Early Modern Studies* 26, no. 2 (1996): 255–96.

26. Peter, Paul, and Mary, "I Dig Rock and Roll Music," from *Album 1700* (Stookey/Mason/ Dixon-Neworld Media Music-ASCAP, 1967).

27. See Margaret Meek Lange, "Defending a Liberalism of Freedom: John Rawls's Use of Hegel" (PhD diss., Columbia University, 2009). For similar conclusions, see Jörg Schaub, *Gerechtigkeit als Versöhnung: John Rawls' politischer Liberalismus* (Frankfurt: Campus Verlag, 2009).

28. Speier, *Truth in Hell*, 202. He quotes Werner Bergengruen, foreword to Rudolf Pechel, *Zwischen den Zeilen: Der Kampf einer Zeitschrift für Freiheit und Recht* (Wiesentheid: Droemersche Verlagsanstalt, 1948), 8–9. See also Milosz, *Captive Mind*, 78.

29. Sigmund Freud, *The Interpretation of Dreams*, ed. and trans. James Strachey (New York: Penguin Books, 1976), 223–24. The Goethe quotation is from *Faust*, Part I, Scene 4, lines 1840–41.

30. Montaigne, *Complete Essays*, ed. Frame, 623 (3.3), 505 (2.18).

31. Sarpi to Gillot, May 12, 1609, in *Lettere ai Gallicani*, ed. Boris Ulianich (Wiesbaden: F. Steiner, 1961), 133, quoted and translated by David Wootton, *Paolo Sarpi: Between Renaissance and Enlightenment* (Cambridge: Cambridge University Press, 1983), 119.

32. Toland, *Clidophorus*, 67–68, vii, emphasis added.

33. Paul Henri Thiry, Baron d'Holbach, *Le bon sens puisé dans la nature; ou, Idées naturelles opposées aux idées surnaturelles* (Rome, 1792). Translation mine (emphasis added).

34. Montaigne, *Complete Essays*, ed. Frame, 97 (1.25; emphasis added).

35. Voltaire, "Letters, Men of Letters, or Literati," in *Philosophical Dictionary*, trans. Peter Gay (New York: Basic Books, 1962), 349 (emphasis added).

36. *Faust* 1.588–93, quoted and translated by Leo Strauss in *Thoughts on Machiavelli*, 174 (emphasis added).

37. *Republic* 496d; see also *Phaedo* 64b; *Gorgias* 185d–186d. For similar views of the philosopher's danger see Isocrates, *Antidosis* 243, 271–73, 304–5; Cicero, *Tusculan Disputations* 2.4; Alfarabi, *The Philosophy of Plato* 22.15; Averroes, *On Plato's Republic* 63.20–25, 64.23–28; Maimonides, *Guide of the Perplexed* 2.36; Boethius, *The Consolation of Philosophy* 1.3.

38. "Pythagorisme ou Philosophie de Pythagore," in *Encyclopédie*, ed. Diderot and d'Alembert, University of Chicago ARTFL Encyclopédie Project, http://encyclopedie.uchicago.edu (emphasis added). Translation mine. A more extensive and concrete account of the reasons for philosopher-hating will be given in chapter 6, which discusses protective esotericism and the necessary tension between philosophy and society.

39. Charron, *De la sagesse*, 289 (2.2). Translation mine.

40. Descartes to Mersenne, April 1634, in *Œuvres de Descartes*, 1:284–91; Ovid, *Tristia* 3.4.25.

41. Epicurus, *Extant Remains: With Short Critical Apparatus*, trans. Cyril Bailey (Oxford: Clarendon Press, 1926), 138 (frag. 86). This dictum, of course, contains multiple layers of meaning. Often it is interpreted simply to mean that honor, fame, and political position are empty pursuits. But, for Epicurus, they are empty above all because they are really deluded attempts to achieve "protection from men," which can be achieved successfully only through withdrawal. "The most unalloyed source of protection from men . . . is in fact the immunity which results from a quiet life and the avoidance of the many" (98 [frag. 14, "Principle Doctrines"]). I have altered the translation. See also frags. 6, 7, 13, and 39; and Lucretius, *De rerum natura* 5.1127–28).

42. Seneca, *Ad Lucilium Epistulae morales*, trans. Gummere, 3:189 (103.5).

43. Alfarabi, *Paraphrase of Aristotle's Topics*, MS, Bratislava, no. 231, TE 40, fol. 203, quoted and translated by Muhsin Mahdi in "Man and His Universe," 113.

44. *Pascal's Pensées*, trans. William Finlayson Trotter (New York: E. P. Dutton, 1958), 94 (aph. 336).

45. Epistle 105, quoted and translated by Rahe, *Republics*, 226.

46. As reported by Gabriel Naudé et al., in *Naudaeana et Patiniana, ou, Singularitez remarquables* (Amsterdam: F. vander Plaats, 1703), 53–57, quoted and translated by Rahe, *Republics*, 237.

47. Bacon, *Advancement of Learning*, ed. Kitchin, 126 (2.14.11).

48. Baltasar Gracian y Morales, *The Science of Success and the Art of Prudence*, trans. Lawrence C. Lockley (San Jose, CA: University of Santa Clara Press, 1967), 43 (aph. 13).

49. George Savile, *Miscellanys*, in *The Works of George Savile, Marquis of Halifax: In Three Volumes*, ed. Mark N. Brown (Oxford: Clarendon Press, 1989), 3:281.30–31, quoted by Rahe, *Republics*, 241.

50. Paolo Sarpi, *Opere*, ed. Gaetano Cozzi and Luisa Cozzi (Milan: R. Ricciardi, 1969), 92, quoted and translated by Wootton, *Paolo Sarpi*, 128.

51. Montaigne, *Complete Essays*, ed. Frame, 86 (1.23).

52. Erasmus, *The Praise of Folly*, trans. Hoyt Hopewell Hudson (Princeton: Princeton University Press, 1941), 38.

53. Charron, *De la sagesse*, 286 (2.2). Translation mine.

54. Charles Blount, *Great Is Diana of the Ephesians, or, the Original of Idolatry* (London, 1695), 22.

55. Cicero, *De natura deorum* 1.123. My point in quoting this interpretation, as others throughout, is that it is *esoteric*—not that it is necessarily *correct*, which it is not my purpose to

investigate here. It is in the nature of things that there will be far more testimony and agreement about the existence than about the precise content of any given philosopher's esotericism. That being said, the same interpretation of Epicurus may be found in Sextus Empiricus, *Against the Physicists* 1.58; Pierre Bayle, *Various Thoughts on the Occasion of a Comet*, para. 178; Condorcet, *Sketch*, 64; and Ralph Cudworth, *The True Intellectual System of the Universe* (London: Thomas Tegg, 1845), 104–5.

56. Condorcet, *Sketch*, 46.

57. Rousseau, "Observations," in *Collected Writings*, ed. Masters and Kelly, 2:45–46n.

58. Locke, *Reasonableness*, ed. Ewing, 166 (§238).

59. In the introduction to *Persecution and the Art of Writing*, however, Strauss writes: "The following essays may be said to supply material useful for a future sociology of philosophy" (7).

60. In what follows, I rely heavily on Strauss's argument in the introduction to *Persecution and the Art of Writing* as well as the introduction to Ralph Lerner and Muhsin Mahdi, eds., *Medieval Political Philosophy: A Sourcebook* (New York: Free Press, 1963). Also see Paul Rahe, *Republics*, 219–32. See Hourani, introduction to *Averroes*.

61. Voltaire, "Toleration," in *Philosophical Dictionary*, 485 (emphasis added).

62. Fustel de Coulanges, *Ancient City*, 186–93 (emphasis added).

63. Jean-Jacques Rousseau, *Lettres écrites de la montagne*, vol. 3 of *Œuvres Complètes*, ed. Bernard Gagnebin and Marcel Raymond, 4 vols. (Paris: Gallimard, Bibliothèque de la Pléïade, 1959–69), 705, translation mine; *Geneva Manuscript*, in *On the Social Contract, with Geneva Manuscript and Political Economy*, ed. Roger D. Masters, trans. Judith R. Masters (New York: St. Martin's Press, 1978), 199, emphasis added. See also *Geneva Manuscript*, 199, 160–61; *Social Contract*, ed. Masters, 124–31; *Emile: or, On education*, trans. Allan Bloom (New York: Basic Books, 1979), 257; Voltaire, "Religion," *Philosophical Dictionary*; Locke, "Error," "Sacerdos," in Lord Peter King, *The Life and Letters of John Locke with Extracts from his Journals and Common-place Books* (New York: Burt Franklin, 1972), 282–83, 288–90; "Essay on Toleration," in H. R. Fox Bourne, *The Life of John Locke* (London: Henry S. King, 1876), 194; Holbach, "Le Christianisme dévoilé," in *Premières œuvres* (Paris: Editions Sociales, 1971), 118–22. And see the section "The Political Problem of Christianity" (345–50), in Arthur M. Melzer, "The Origin of the Counter-Enlightenment: Rousseau and the New Religion of Sincerity," *American Political Science Review* 90, no. 2 (June 1996): 344–60.

64. Plato, *Apology* 19a. See Plutarch, *Pericles*, in *Lives*, trans. Dryden, 206 (sec. 32). Consider Thomas Aquinas: "all knowledge is good and even honourable," *Commentary on Aristotle's De Anima*, trans. Kenelm Foster, O.P., and Sylvester Humphries, O.P. (New Haven: Yale University Press, 1951, http://dhspriory.org/thomas/english/DeAnima.htm#11L, html edition by Joseph Kenny, O.P.), I-1:3. See Stanley L. Jaki, *The Savior of Science* (Washington, DC: Regnery Gateway, 1988), for a vigorous defense of the view that natural science, which was "still-born" everywhere else, ultimately succeeded in the West only because of Christianity.

65. Voltaire, *Histoire de l'établissement du Christianisme*, in vol. 3 of *Œuvres Completes*, ed. Louis Moland (Paris: Garnier, 1877–83), 72; "Toleration," *Philosophical Dictionary*, 486. For a similar view, see Rousseau, *Observations*, in *Collected Writings*, 44–46. One is reminded of Nietzsche's famous formula: "Christianity is Platonism for 'the people'" (*Beyond Good and Evil*, 3). On these themes, see Allan Arkush, "Voltaire on Judaism and Christianity," *AJS Review* 18, no. 2 (1993): 223–43.

66. There were of course many and important exceptions to this rule, the most famous being Tertullian (160–230). "Off with those who have put forward a Stoic, Platonic, and dialectical Christianity. After Jesus Christ, we have no need for curiosity; nor do we need inquiry after the Gospel" (Tertullian, *De Praescriptione Haereticorum*, 7, quoted and translated by Rahe, *Republics*, 221).

67. Hourani, *Averroes*, 2.

68. Rashi [Rabbi Shlomo Itzhaki], *Chumash with Targum Onkelos, Haphtaroth and Rashi's Commentary*, trans. Rabbi A. M. Silbermann (Jerusalem: Routledge & Kegan Paul, 1934), 1:2.

69. See also Rousseau: "The People chosen by God never cultivated the sciences, and it was never advised to study them. . . . Its leaders always made efforts to keep it as separate as possible from the idolatrous and learned Nations surrounding it. . . . After frequent dispersions among the Egyptians and the Greeks, Science still had a thousand difficulties developing in the heads of the Hebrews." *Observations*, in *Collected Writings*, 2:44). And Spinoza: "None of the Apostles philosophized more than did Paul, who was called to preach to the Gentiles; other Apostles preaching to the Jews, who despised philosophy, similarly adapted themselves to the temper of their hearers, and preached a religion free from all philosophical speculations." *Theologico-Political Treatise*, trans. Elwes, 1:164.

70. Hourani, *Averroes*, 44.

71. This is not to deny that in certain times and places—in tenth- and eleventh-century Iraq, Syria, and Persia, and in twelfth-century Spain—philosophy managed to flourish in these communities (and eventually to have a radical, liberating influence, especially in the form of Latin Averroism, on the more "protected" and co-opted philosophy of the Christian West). But *in principle*, it was always a more suspect phenomenon, it always had to struggle more to defend its very right to exist—and eventually it lost that struggle. Philosophical inquiry was more or less extinguished in the Islamic world by the end of the twelfth century and in the Jewish world by the end of the fifteenth. See Richard Walzer, *Greek into Arabic: Essays on Islamic Philosophy* (Cambridge, MA: Harvard University Press, 1962), 1–28.

72. Voltaire, *Essai sur les moeurs* (Paris: Garnier, 1963), 1:94.

73. See Fustel de Coulanges, *Ancient City*; E. R. Dodds, *The Greeks and the Irrational* (Berkeley: University of California Press, 1951). For the denial or minimizing of persecution in antiquity, see also John Milton, who simply ignores the case of Socrates (see *Areopagitica*, in *John Milton: Selected Prose*, ed. C. A. Patrides [Columbia: University of Missouri Press, 1985], 201–3). J. B. Bury, in his classic *A History of Freedom of Thought* (New York: Henry Holt, 1913), 50, asserts that in "classical antiquity as a whole, we may almost say that freedom of thought was like the air men breathed. It was taken for granted and nobody thought about it." On this whole issue see also Jansen, *Censorship*; Peter J. Ahrensdorf, *The Death of Socrates and the Life of Philosophy: An Interpretation of Plato's Phaedo* (Albany: State University of New York Press, 1995); Connor, "Other 399"; Eudore Derenne. *Les procès d'impiété intentés aux philosophes à Athènes au Vme et au IVme siècles avant J.-C.* (Liège: Vaillant-Carmanne, 1930).

74. See Aulus Gellius, *The Attic Nights* 15.11; Diogenes Laertius, "Theophrastus," in *Lives* 5.38–39; Xenophon, *Memorabilia* 1.2.31.

75. Fustel de Coulanges, *Ancient City*, 223.

76. Alfarabi, in his summary of the philosophy of Plato, and Averroes, in his epitome of the *Republic*, goes so far as to leave out all mention of the theory of ideas. See Strauss, "Farabi's Plato," in *Louis Ginzberg Jubilee Volume on the Occasion of His Seventieth Birthday* (New York: American Academy for Jewish Research, 1945), 357–93; and Joshua Parens, *Metaphysics as Rhetoric: Alfarabi's Summary of Plato's* "Laws" (Albany: State University of New York Press, 1995).

77. Emphasis added, here and below.

78. Cicero, *De inventione, De optimo genere oratorum, Topica*, trans. H. M. Hubbell (Cambridge, MA: Harvard University Press, 1949), 85–87 (1.29.46).

79. Cicero, *Tusculan Disputations*, trans. King, 149 (2.5). See Plutarch, *Nicias*.

80. Plato, *Protagoras and Meno*, trans. Robert C. Bartlett (Ithaca, NY: Cornell University Press, 2004), 316d–e (emphasis added). See Plato, *Euthyphro* 3c.

81. The passages in quotation marks are all from lost plays or poems.

82. For other discussions of the philosopher's danger see Isocrates, *Antidosis* 243, 271–73, 304–5; Boethius, *The Consolation of Philosophy* 1.3; Plutarch, *Nicias*.

83. Averroes, *Averroes on Plato's Republic*, 78, 76.

84. Alfarabi, *Aphorisms of the Statesman*, trans. D. M. Dunlop (Cambridge: Cambridge University Press, 1961), 72; *The Philosophy of Plato and Aristotle*, trans. Muhsin Mahdi (Ithaca, NY: Cornell University Press, 1962), 67. The notion of the philosopher as "stranger," "weed," "solitary," and "human being living among beasts" is a recurrent theme in Islamic thought. See especially Avempace's *Governance of the Solitary* and Ibn Tufayl's *Hayy the Son of Yaqzan*. Among Jewish writers, see Maimonides, *Guide*, ed. Pines, 372 (2.36): the philosopher should "regard all people according to their various states, with respect to which they are indubitably either like domestic animals or like beasts of prey. If the perfect man who lives in solitude thinks of them at all, he does so only with a view to saving himself from the harm that may be caused by those among them who are harmful . . . or to obtaining an advantage that may be obtained from them if he is forced to it by some of his needs."

85. To take three standard works, there is no reference to the passages at *Republic* 488a, 492b, 496d, and 517a (or more generally, to the theme of misology and philosopher-hating) in Nicholas P. White's *A Companion to Plato's Republic* (Indianapolis: Hackett, 1979); C. D. C. Reeve's *Philosopher-Kings: The Argument of Plato's Republic* (Princeton, NJ: Princeton University Press, 1988); or Terrence Irwin's *Plato's Ethics* (New York: Oxford University Press, 1995).

86. M. I. Finley, *Aspects of Antiquity*, 2nd ed. (Middlesex: Penguin Books, 1977), 64. Again: "It was Politics, not Religion, that cost Socrates his life." Arnold Toynbee, *A Study of History* (London: Oxford University Press, 1939), 7:472. I. F. Stone, in *The Trial of Socrates* (Boston: Little Brown, 1988), takes the same view. For a good overview of the contemporary debate, see Connor, "Other 399." Although Connor returns to the view that the impiety charge was serious and not a mask for political concerns, he continues to approach the event as a historical contingency, without larger significance.

87. Quoted and translated by Milosz, *Captive Mind*, 59–60 (except for the last two paragraphs, which are my translation). Gobineau, *Les religions*, 465–67 (emphasis added). Milosz quotes this passage because "[t]he similarities between *Ketman* and the customs cultivated in the countries of the New Faith [i.e., the communist bloc] are so striking that I shall permit myself to quote at length" (57).

88. Plutarch, *Pericles*, in *Lives*, trans. Dryden, 184. On Damon, see Isocrates, *Antidosis* 235–36: "Pericles studied under two of the sophists, Anaxagoras of Clazomenae and Damon, the latter in his day reputed to be the wisest among the Athenians" (in *Isocrates*, vol. 2: *On the Peace, Areopagiticus, Against the Sophists, Antidosis, Panathenaicus*, trans. George Norlin, Loeb Classical Library 229 [Cambridge, MA: Harvard University Press, 1929], 317).

89. Xenophon, *Memorabilia* 4.6.1; Plato, *Apology* 19c, 26d. See *Phaedo* 96a6–99d2; Xenophon, *Oeconomicus* 6.13–17, 11.1–6; *Symposium* 6.6–8; and Diogenes Laertius, "Socrates" 2.45, in *Lives*. For an excellent discussion of the ambiguity of the original claims in the *Apology*, see David Leibowitz, *The Ironic Defense of Socrates: Plato's Apology* (Cambridge: Cambridge University Press, 2010), 50–52. On the other side, consider Aristotle, *Metaphysics* 1.6.2 and 12.4.3–5, and the quotation from Plutarch below.

90. This has not gone unnoticed by Plato scholars, of course. But unwilling to entertain the possibility that Socrates (or Plato) was lying about his avoidance of natural philosophy, they have been forced to the conclusion that Plato somehow decided, in writing his later dialogues, to attribute his own physical and metaphysical doctrines to Socrates. As Alexander Grant, for example, puts it, "The sublime developments of philosophy made by the disciple are with a sort of pious reverence put into the mouth of the master" (*The Ethics of Aristotle, Illustrated with Essays and Notes* [London: Longmans, 1885], 1:158). In general, it would be an odd thing for one philosopher to attribute his own greatest discoveries to another. But it would be an extremely odd form of "pious reverence," if that indeed was the motive, to falsely attribute one's metaphysical theories to a thinker who solemnly swore before the whole city that he had no such theories and completely avoided such studies. At any rate, whichever way

this puzzle is solved, it supplies strong evidence of esotericism. Either Socrates was telling the truth in his claim to confine himself to the human things, in which case Plato was for some reason consciously falsifying his account of the Socratic life in the later dialogues. Or Plato was giving an accurate account and it is Socrates who was lying about his way of life.

91. Plutarch, *Nicias* 23, quoted and translated by Peter Ahrensdorf in *The Death of Socrates*, 12.

92. Montesquieu, *Mes pensées* 2097, in *Œuvres complètes* (Paris: Librairie Gallimard, 1949), 1:1546–47, translation mine (emphasis added). Hobbes makes a similar suggestion regarding Aristotle, at the end of a discussion of the latter's doctrine of separated essences. "And this shall suffice for an example of the errors which are brought into the Church from the *entities* and *essences* of Aristotle (which it may be he knew to be false philosophy, but writ it as a thing consonant to, and corroborative of, their Religion—and fearing the fate of Socrates)." Thomas Hobbes, *Leviathan: With Selected Variants from the Latin Edition of 1668*, ed. E. M. Curley (Indianapolis: Hackett, 1994), 460 (46.18). See also Diderot: "The fear that one has of priests has ruined, ruins, and will ruin all philosophical works; [it] has made Aristotle alternately an attacker and defender of final causes." *Refutation d'Helvétius*, in *Œuvres complètes* (Paris: Garnier, 1875), 2:398, translation mine. For a powerful presentation of the view that Aristotle's doctrine of teleology—at least in the extreme and quasi-religious form in which Aristotle typically presents it—is merely exoteric, see Bolotin, *Approach to Aristotle's Physics*.

93. Toland, *Clidophorus*, 75.

CHAPTER SIX

1. The strong contrast in the contemporary reception of these two forms is most clearly illustrated by Annabel Patterson, who wrote several very fine books on the practice of defensive esotericism in English literature, but who, in the introduction to the revised edition of her first book on the topic, *Censorship and Interpretation* (24–28), fiercely attacks the whole idea of protective esotericism (and Leo Strauss for describing and emphasizing it).

2. Montesquieu, *Œuvres complètes* (Paris: A. Belin, 1822), 3:450–51, quoted and translated by Pangle, *Montesquieu's Philosophy of Liberalism: A Commentary on The Spirit of the Laws* (Chicago: University of Chicago Press, 1973), 12.

3. Montaigne, *Complete Essays*, ed. Frame, 769 (3.10).

4. Aquinas, *Faith, Reason and Theology*, 53 (art. 4).

5. Warburton, *Divine Legation*, 13 (emphasis added); Formey, "Exoterique & Esoterique," in *Encyclopédie*, ed. Diderot and d'Alembert, University of Chicago ARTFL Encyclopédie Project, http://encyclopedie.uchicago.edu.

6. Plato, *Republic* 515e–516a; Exod. 33:20, 20:19, 24:1–2; Deut. 18:15–18; Isa. 6:5; 1 Tim. 6:16. See Eccles. 1:18 (AKJV): "for in much wisdom is much grief; and he that increaseth knowledge increaseth sorrow."

7. Lucretius, *On the Nature of Things* 1.943–50 (see 4.10 ff.), quoted from James H. Nichols Jr., *Epicurean Political Philosophy: The De rerum natura of Lucretius* (Ithaca, NY: Cornell University Press, 1972), 34. The poetic "sweetening" serves the double purpose of attracting the potentially philosophic readers while shielding or comforting "the multitude."

8. Actually, it is only recently and against much resistance that Kabbalism has again been recognized as a serious Jewish tradition. As Gershom Scholem, the foremost scholar of Jewish mysticism, writes: "For centuries the Kabbalah had been vital to the Jews' understanding of themselves." But "this world had been lost to European Jewry. Down to our own generation, students of Jewish history showed little understanding for the documents of the Kabbalah and ignored them almost completely." *On the Kabbalah*, 1–2.

9. See Kippenberg and Stroumsa, *Secrecy and Concealment*; Bolle, *Secrecy in Religions*; and Wayman, *Buddhist Tantras*.

10. Scholem, *On the Kabbalah*, 50–51.

11. Mishnah Hagigah 2.1, quoted by Roger Shattuck, *Forbidden Knowledge: From Prometheus to Pornography* (New York: St. Martin's, 1996), 341. See Babylonian Talmud Hagigah 11b, 13a 14b.

12. Maimonides, *Mishnah Torah*, bk. 1, chap. 2, section 12, in *A Maimonides Reader*, ed. Isadore Twersky (New York: Behrman House, 1972), 47.

13. Charles G. Herbermann et al., eds., *The Catholic Encyclopedia*, vol. 5 (New York: Gilmary Society, 1909), 32 (emphasis added). See also F. L. Cross, ed., *The Oxford Dictionary of the Christian Church* (London: Oxford University Press, 1957), 405.

14. Aquinas, *Faith, Reason*, 53–54 (art. 4). In this passage, Thomas is quoting 1 Corinthians 3:1–2, Saint Gregory, *Moralia* 17.26.38, and Augustine, *De doctrina christiana* 9.23. On esotericism in Christianity, see also Stroumsa, *Hidden Wisdom*.

15. Averroes, *The Decisive Treatise*, trans. George F. Hourani, in *Medieval Political Philosophy: A Sourcebook*, ed. Ralph Lerner and Muhsin Mahdi (New York: Free Press, 1963), 181. See Moezzi, *Divine Guide*.

16. Maimonides, *Guide*, ed. Pines, 71.

17. Emphasis added. While scholars like Grant, Boas and other proponents of the "legend" theory attempt to dismiss the historical testimony to philosophical esotericism by attributing it to the influence of Neoplatonist and other mystical forms of thinking, here we see evidence that actually events sometimes ran the other way. Sometimes it is the legend of mysticism that must be dismissed as an esoteric mask worn by secular philosophers. See also Kojève's argument that the Emperor Julian, Sallustius, and Damascius, who have been taken to be Neoplatonists—because they present themselves as such—are in fact highly skeptical, "Voltairian" philosophers hiding under the cloak of mysticism. Kojève, "Emperor Julian," 95–113; and Strauss, *On Tyranny*, 269–75. Also consider the point made by Gershom Scholem above that the (genuine) Jewish mystics borrowed the practice of esotericism from the preexisting esoteric tradition of the philosophers.

18. Augustine, *City of God*, trans. Dods, 706 (19.24).

19. On this interpretation of the modern revolution, see Robert P. Kraynak *History and Modernity in the Thought of Thomas Hobbes* (Ithaca, NY: Cornell University Press, 1990).

20. The general argument of this section has been inspired by Mircea Eliade, *Cosmos and History: The Myth of the Eternal Return*, trans. Willard Trask (New York: Harper and Row, 1959), and *Myth and Reality*, trans. Willard Trask (New York: Harper and Row, 1963); Strauss, "Progress or Return?" and *Natural Right and History*; and Edward Shils, *Tradition* (Chicago: University of Chicago Press, 1981). See also Daniel Lerner, *The Passing of Traditional Society: Modernizing the Middle East* (Glencoe, IL: Free Press, 1958).

21. Aristotle, *The Politics*, trans. Carnes Lord (Chicago: University of Chicago Press, 1984), 1269a19–24. We do not tend to feel the power of this argument because the dynamic modern state is based on a strong distinction between constitutional law and regular law, which was introduced precisely in order to make it easier and less problematic to change or reform the latter. When we think about the Constitution, however, we instinctively revert to the Aristotelian argument for the necessity of relative changelessness.

22. Friedrich Nietzsche, *Daybreak: Thoughts on the Prejudices of Morality*, trans. R. J. Hollingdale (Cambridge: Cambridge University Press, 1997), 202 (aph. 496).

23. Euripides, *Bacchae* 200–204, 1150–53, quoted and translated by Rahe, *Republics*, 215, 216.

24. Fustel de Coulanges, *Ancient City*, 352.

25. Machiavelli, *Florentine Histories*, trans. Laura F. Banfield and Harvey C. Mansfield (Princeton, NJ: Princeton University Press, 1988), 185 (5.1).

26. Rousseau, *The First and Second Discourses*, trans. Roger D. Masters and Judith R. Masters (New York: St. Martin's Press, 1964), 45.

27. Montaigne, *Complete Essays*, trans. Frame, 106 (1.25).

28. Seneca, *Ad Lucilium* 95.13; Montaigne, *Complete Essays*, trans. Frame, 103 (1.25); Rousseau, *First and Second Discourses*, trans. Masters and Masters, 45.

29. Lecky, *History of European Morals*, 1:149–50.

30. Augustine, *City of God*, trans. Dods, 203 (6.10).

31. Montaigne, *Complete Essays*, trans. Frame, 379 (2.12).

32. Diogenes Laertius, *Lives* 10.10.

33. *Republic* 520a; see 347c–d; and Aristotle, *Nicomachean Ethics* 1134b4–7.

34. Pascal, *Pascal's Pensées*, trans. Trotter, 93 (aph. 331). I have slightly altered the translation (emphasis added).

35. See Cicero *Tusculan Disputations* 2.4, 4.47, 5.11.

36. Aristotle, *Aristotle's Nicomachean Ethics*, ed. and trans. Robert C. Bartlett and Susan D. Collins (Chicago: University of Chicago Press, 2011), 1172a27. Also see Aristide Tessitore, "A Political Reading of Aristotle's Treatment of Pleasure in the *Nicomachean Ethics*," *Political Theory* 17, no. 2 (1989): 247–65.

37. Plato, *Phaedo* 64c–65c.

38. Montaigne, *Complete Essays*, trans. Frame, 757 (3.9), 769 (3.10). The quotation from Quintilian comes from *Institutes* 2.17.28.

39. Cicero, *Laws* 1.21–39, 3.26.

40. Averroes, *Averroes on Plato's Republic*, 24.

41. See the excellent discussion, on which I have relied, in Bloom's interpretive essay in Plato, *Republic*, 365–69.

42. See Plato, *Laws* 3; Aristotle, *Politics* 1.2.

43. For a careful esoteric reading of Aristotle's discussion of natural slavery, see Wayne Ambler, "Aristotle on Nature and Politics: The Case of Slavery," *Political Theory* 15, no. 3 (August 1987): 390–410; and Thomas Pangle, *Aristotle's Teaching in the Politics* (Chicago: University of Chicago Press, 2013), 42–51.

44. Gotthold Lessing, *The Freethinker*, in *Lessing's Theological Writing*, trans. Henry Chadwick (London: Adam and Charles Black, 1965), 42–43, quoted by Hans Blumenberg. *The Legitimacy of the Modern Age* (Cambridge, MA: MIT Press, 1983), 421.

45. François de La Rochefoucauld, *Collected Maxims and Other Reflections*, ed. and trans. E. H. Blackmore, A. M. Blackmore, and Francine Giguère (Oxford: Oxford University Press, 2007), maxim 26.

46. Montaigne, *Complete Essays*, trans. Frame, 632 (3.4).

47. Epistle 105, quoted and translated by Rahe, *Republics*, 226 (emphasis added).

48. Shaftesbury, *Characteristics*, ed. Klein, 30.

49. "Tell all the Truth but tell it slant," in *The Complete Poems of Emily Dickinson*, ed. Thomas H Johnson (Boston: Little, Brown, 1960), poem 1129.

50. Herbert Marcuse, "Repressive Tolerance," in Robert Paul Wolff, Barrington Moore Jr., and Herbert Marcuse, *A Critique of Pure Tolerance* (Boston: Beacon Press, 1965), 81–123.

CHAPTER SEVEN

1. Quoted by Loseff, *On the Beneficence*, 11. Consider also this account by Lidia Vianu in her *Censorship in Romania*:

Censorship brought one good thing to literature: as Paul Valéry used to say, any obstacle in front of creation is a true sun. Not being able to say what you think was an excellent school of poetic indirectness, creating its devious writers and its eager readers who were always ready to probe between the lines. The conspiracy of writer-reader was a marvel of obliqueness and dissent at the same time. (x)

2. This is not to deny that he also celebrated the advantages of press freedom. As he remarks in his memoirs:

Two or three months later, Ogarev passed through Novgorod. He brought me Feuerbach's *Essence Of Christianity* [an openly atheist and secularizing work]; after reading the first pages I leapt up with joy. Down with the trappings of masquerade; away with the stammering allegory! We are free men and not the slaves of Xanthos [Aesop's master]; there is no need for us to wrap the truth in myth. (*My Past and Thoughts*, 2:407)

3. Thomas Aquinas, *Summa Theologica*, vol. 3, pt. 3, ques. 42, art. 4, p. 2243.

4. Donald Levine, *The Flight from Ambiguity: Essays in Social and Cultural Theory* (Chicago: University of Chicago Press, 1985), 21.

5. See ibid., 2–8, 37–38.

6. See Gordon Wood, "Conspiracy and the Paranoid Style: Causality and Deceit in the Eighteenth Century," *William and Mary Quarterly* 39 (1982): 403–41. See also Bryan Garsten, *Saving Persuasion: A Defense of Rhetoric and Judgment* (Cambridge, MA: Harvard University Press, 2006).

7. John Milton, *Paradise Lost and Paradise Regained*, ed. Christopher Ricks (New York: New American Library, 1968), 389 (bk. 4, line 327).

8. Rousseau, *Emile*, trans. Bloom, 184, 450.

9. Schleiermacher, *Introductions to the Dialogues of Plato*, 17–18.

10. William Penn, *Fruits of a Father's Love: Being the Advice of William Penn to his Children Relating to their Civil and Religious Conduct* (Dover, NH: James K. Remich, 1808), chap. 2, para. 19.

11. Montaigne, *Complete Essays*, trans. Frame, 101 (1.25).

12. Arthur Schopenhauer, "On Books and Reading," in *Religion: A Dialogue, and Other Essays*, trans. T. Bailey Saunders (New York: Macmillan, 1899), 51.

13. Aquinas, *Summa*, vol. 1, pt. 1, ques. 1, art. 9, p. 6.

14. Augustine, *De Doctrina Christiana*, ed. and trans. R. P. H. Green (Oxford: Clarendon Press, 1995), 223 (4.61).

15. Sallustius, *On the Gods and the World*, in pt. 3 of *Five Stages of Greek Religion*, trans. Gilbert Murray (New York: Columbia University Press, 1925), 242–43.

16. Jean-Jacques Rousseau, *Politics and the Arts, Letter to M. d'Alembert on the Theatre*, trans. Allan Bloom (Glencoe, IL: Free Press, 1960), 6.

17. Montesquieu, *The Spirit of the Laws*, trans. Anne Cohler, Basia Miller, and Harold Stone (Cambridge: Cambridge University Press, 1989), 186 (11.20).

18. Montaigne, *Complete Essays*, trans. Frame, 100 (1.25).

19. Cicero, *De natura deorum*, trans. Rackham, 13 (1.5).

20. Søren Kierkegaard, *The Point of View for My Work as an Author; A Report to History, and Related Writings*, trans. Walter Lowrie (New York: Harper & Row, 1962), 39–40.

21. Ibid., 27. Kierkegaard also adds here a related but different argument for the necessity of concealment and indirection:

No, an illusion can never be destroyed directly, and only by indirect means can it be radically removed. . . . A direct attack only strengthens a person in his illusion, and at the same time embitters him. There is nothing that requires such gentle handling as an illusion, if one wishes to dispel it. If anything prompts the prospective captive to set his will in opposition, all is lost. And this is what a direct attack achieves, and it implies moreover the presumption of requiring a man to make to another person, or in his presence, an admission which he can make most profitably to himself in private. This is what is achieved by the indirect method, which, loving and serving the truth, arranges everything dialectically for the prospective captive, and then shyly withdraws (for love is always shy), so as not to witness the admission which he makes to himself alone before God—that he has lived hitherto in an illusion. (24–26)

The point Kierkegaard makes here—that a refined and delicate modesty is often what stands behind the practice of esotericism—is extremely important for us since it helps to counteract our strong tendency to recoil from esotericism as something inevitably rooted in exclusiveness and arrogance.

22. Rousseau, *Emile*, trans. Bloom, 183, 178.

23. Quoted by Aquinas in *Faith, Reason*, 52 (art. 4).

24. Augustine, *Letters*, ed. Ludwig Schopp and Roy Joseph Deferrari, trans. Wilfrid Parsons, vol. 3 (New York: Fathers of the Church, 1953), 34 (letter 137).

25. Friedrich Nietzsche, *Human All Too Human*, trans. R. J. Hollingdale (Cambridge: Cambridge University Press, 1986), 92 (vol. 1, chap. 4, aph. 181).

26. *Stromata*, in *The Writings of Clement of Alexandria*, trans. Rev. William Wilson (Edinburgh: T. & T. Clark, 1869), 254–55 (vol. 2, bk. 5, chap. 9).

27. Augustine, *Letters*, 1:277 (letter 55).

28. Rousseau, *Emile*, trans. Bloom, 137, 111.

29. Jean d'Alembert, *Œuvres complètes* (Paris: A. Belin, 1822), 3:450–51, quoted and translated by Pangle, *Montesquieu's Philosophy*, 12.

30. Nietzsche, *Human All Too Human*, 92 (vol. 1, chap. 4, aph. 178).

31. Hippolyte Taine, *The Ancient Regime*, trans. John Durand (New York: Henry Holt, 1876), 4:260.

32. Demetrius of Phaleron, *On Style*, trans. W. Rhys Roberts (Cambridge: Cambridge University Press, 1902), 222.

33. Rousseau, *Emile*, trans. Bloom, 248.

34. Ibid., 249.

35. Ibid., 239.

36. Translator's preface to Vergilio Malvezzi, *Discourses upon Cornelius Tacitus*, trans. Richard Baker (London: R. Whitaker and Tho. Whitaker, 1642), quoted by Alfred Alvarez in *The School of Donne* (London: Chatto and Windus, 1961), 40.

37. Thomas Gordon, *Discourses upon Tacitus: The Works of Tacitus, With Political Discourses Upon that Author* (London: T. Woodward & J. Peele, 1770), 4:149–50, quoted by Rahe, *Republics*, 246.

38. Quintilian, *Institutes* 9.2.72.

39. Ibid., 9.2.79.

40. Boccaccio, *Life of Dante*, trans. Bollettino, 40.

41. Samuel Butler, *Evolution Old and New: Or, the Theories of Buffon, Dr. Erasmus Darwin and Lamarck as Compared with That of Charles Darwin* (New York: E. P. Dutton, 1911), 87.

42. "A Charm," poem 421 in *The Complete Poems of Emily Dickinson*, quoted by Roger Shattuck, *Forbidden Knowledge*, 125.

43. Moses Maimonides, *Laws concerning Character Traits*, in *Ethical Writings of Maimonides*, trans. Raymond Weiss with Charles Butterworth (New York: Dover Publications, 1975), 33 (2.5).

44. Diogenes Laertius, *Lives of Eminent Philosophers*, trans. Hicks, 413 (9.6).

45. Nietzsche, *Beyond Good and Evil*, trans. Kaufmann, 37 (aph. 26), 50 (aph. 40).

46. Irwin Straus, *Phenomenological Psychology*, trans. Erling Eng (New York: Basic Books, 1966), 217–24.

47. See Rolf Engelsing, "Die Perioden der Lesergeschichte in der Neuzeit: Das statische Ausmass und die soziokulturelle Bedeutung der Lektüre," *Archiv für Geschichte des Buchwesens* 10 (1969), cols. 944–1002, and *Der Bürger als Leser: Lesergeschichte in Deutschland, 1500–1800* (Stuttgart, 1974); David Hall, "The Uses of Literacy in New England, 1600–1850," in *Printing and Society in Early America*, ed. W. L. Joyce, 2nd ed. (Worcester, MA: American Antiquarian Society, 1983), 1–47. See Dorinda Outram, *The Enlightenment* (Cambridge: Cambridge University Press, 2005), 16–18.

48. John Stuart Mill, *Inaugural Address Delivered to the University of St. Andrews* (London: Longmans, Green, Reader, & Dyer, 1867), 34.

49. Tocqueville, *Democracy in America*, trans. Mansfield and Winthrop, 451 (vol. 2, pt. 1, chap. 15).

50. Ibid., 451 (vol. 2, pt. 1, chap. 15).

51. Mill, *Inaugural Address*, 37–38 (emphasis added).

52. Plutarch, *Lycurgus*, in *Lives*, trans Dryden, 64–65.

53. Strauss, "New Interpretation," 351.

54. Leo Strauss, "Thucydides: The Meaning of Political History," in *Rebirth*, 94.

55. For a discussion of these claims, see Strauss, "What Is Political Philosophy?" in *What Is Political Philosophy?*, 38–40. See also his "An Introduction to Heideggerian Existentialism" (in *Rebirth*, 43), where Strauss seems to follow Heidegger in maintaining that "*to be* means to be elusive or to be a mystery." See Leo Strauss, *The City and Man* (Chicago: Rand McNally, 1964), 61–62. And see Benardete who, on this basis, attributes to the ancients what he calls "metaphysical esotericism." Seth Benardete, "Strauss on Plato," in *The Argument of the Action* (Chicago: University of Chicago Press, 2000), 409.

CHAPTER EIGHT

1. In the remainder of this section, for the sake of theoretical clarity, I try to draw the distinction between political esotericism and the other three forms as precisely and starkly as possible. In practice, however, thinkers can adopt compromise positions on theory and praxis—conflictual in some respects, harmonist in others—that blur these distinctions. This fact will become increasingly obvious and important below when we explore political esotericism in its concrete, historical manifestations.

2. Pedagogical esotericism remains because, whatever their projects for political transformation, philosophers always remain vitally interested in philosophical education as well. And while this pedagogical concern does not necessarily lead to esotericism, it often does. For philosophers of virtually every era and persuasion share the general goal of inducing their students to think for themselves, and a Socratic esotericism—presenting riddles instead of answers—is often the best means of doing so. That is why, in the previous chapter on pedagogical esotericism, much of the testimony presented was actually drawn from modern thinkers.

Still we have seen two reasons why this kind of esotericism is less fully at home, so to speak, in modern times. First, on the premodern, conflictual view of theory and praxis, the philosophic life represents a radical and initially painful break with ordinary life. On this view, philosophical education has a more difficult and personal task to perform than on the modern, harmonist premise. It requires not just intellectual training but something more like a conversion. It is concerned less to teach a philosophical doctrine than to change one's life. This is a delicate undertaking, far more in need of dialectical, esoteric management. Second, modern "progress philosophy" is largely oriented by the idea that each generation should quickly accept and assimilate the progress that came before it, in order to move forward to new discoveries. And this, in turn, requires that philosophical writing be clear and precise—not esoteric and riddling—for the sake of quick and easy transmissibility. Premodern thought was not oriented in this way by the needs of philosophy understood as a collective and progressive enterprise. It was focused on the inner state of the philosophic individual and on his personal need to think everything through for himself—radically and back to the beginning—without accepting anything merely handed down. Pedagogical esotericism is well suited to this need, precisely because it prevents the too-easy assimilation of earlier thought.

3. Michael Kinsley, "McCain and the Base Truth," *Washington Post*, May 19, 2006; "Political gaffe," Wikipedia, http://en.wikipedia.org/wiki/Political_gaffe (accessed September 24, 2013).

4. Myra MacPherson, *All Governments Lie: The Life and Times of Rebel Journalist I. F. Stone*, (New York: Scribner, 2006).

5. George Orwell, "Politics and the English Language," in *All Art Is Propaganda: Critical Essays* (New York: Houghton Mifflin Harcourt, 2008), 286.

6. Arendt, *Between Past and Future*, 227. Regarding international relations, see John Mearsheimer, *Why Leaders Lie: The Truth about Lying in International Politics* (New York: Oxford University Press, 2011).

7. Machiavelli, *Prince*, trans. Mansfield, 70. Almost all leaders must sometimes behave this way in foreign policy, where there often is no common good.

8. Thomas Babington Macaulay, *The History of England from the Accession of James II* (eBookMall Inc., 2000), 674–75.

9. Macaulay, *Critical and Historical Essays Contributed to the Edinburgh Review*, 6th ed. (London: Longman, Brown, Green, and Longmans, 1849), 1:116.

10. Machiavelli, *Discourses*, trans. Mansfield and Tarcov, 35 (1.11); Rousseau, *Social Contract*, ed. Masters, 69–70 (2.7).

11. Edmund Burke, *Reflections on the Revolution in France*, in *Select Works of Edmund Burke: A New Imprint of the Payne Edition* (Indianapolis: Liberty Fund, 1999), 2:88.

12. Condorcet, *Esquisse d'un tableau historique des progrès de l'esprit humain*, ed. Monique Hincker and François Hincker (Paris: Editions Sociales, 1971), 215. Translation mine.

13. It bears repeating that not every chronologically modern thinker was "a modern" in the sense of participating in this project. What is more, there were important disagreements about the project among thinkers thought to be archetypal representatives of it, as will be discussed at length below.

14. Richard N. Schwab, introduction to *Preliminary Discourse to the Encyclopedia of Diderot*, trans. Richard N. Schwab and Walter E. Rex (New York: Bobbs-Merrill, 1963), xii.

15. Burke, *Reflections*, 2:89.

16. D'Alembert to Voltaire, July 21, 1757, in *Œuvres et correspondances inédites de d'Alembert*, ed. Charles Henry (Geneva: Slatkine, 1967), 5:51.

17. "Clandestine philosophical literature has been a recognized field of research since 1912, when Gustave Lanson discovered a number of manuscript copies of 'philosophical' or anti-Christian texts in municipal libraries throughout the French provinces." Antony McKenna, "Clandestine Literature," in *Encyclopedia of the Enlightenment*, ed. Alan Charles Kors (Oxford: Oxford University Press, 2005).

18. Jonathan Israel, *Radical Enlightenment: Philosophy and the Making of Modernity, 1650–1750* (Oxford: Oxford University Press, 2001), 684.

19. Robert Darnton, *The Forbidden Best-Sellers of Pre-Revolutionary France* (New York: W. W. Norton, 1995), xix (emphasis added). See also Robert Darnton, *The Literary Underground of the Old Regime* (Cambridge, MA: Harvard University Press, 1982).

20. Ira O. Wade, *The Clandestine Organization and Diffusion of Philosophic Ideas in France, 1700–1750* (Princeton, NJ: Princeton University Press, 1938); Miguel Benitez, *La face cachée des Lumières: recherches sur les manuscrits philosophiques clandestins de l'âge classique* (Paris: Universitas, 1996). See also Guido Canziani, ed., *Filosofia e religione nella letteratura clandestina: secoli XVII e XVIII* (Milan: FrancoAngeli, 1994).

21. Cicero, *For Archias*, in vol. 2 of *The Orations of Marcus Tullius Cicero*, trans. C. D. Yonge (London: G. Bell & Sons, 1874–97), 11.26.

22. On this phenomenon, see Christopher Kelly, *Rousseau as Author: Consecrating One's Life to the Truth* (Chicago: University of Chicago Press, 2003), 12–13.

23. Quoted by Christopher Kelly in "Rousseau's Critique of the Public Intellectual in the Age of the Enlightenment," in *Between Philosophy and Politics: The Public Intellectual*, ed. Arthur Melzer, Jerry Weinberger, and Richard Zinman (New York: Rowman & Littlefield, 2003), 56.

24. Quoted in P. N. Furbank, *Diderot: A Critical Biography* (New York: Alfred A. Knopf, 1992), 167.

25. See Chaninah Machler, "Lessing's *Ernst and Falk: Dialogues for Freemasons*, a Translation

with Notes," *Interpretation* 14, no. 1 (January 1986): 1–49. And for an interpretation, see Leo Strauss, "Exoteric Teaching," in *Rebirth*, 63–71.

26. See Margaret Jacob, *The Radical Enlightenment: Pantheists, Freemasons and Republicans* (Boston: G. Allen & Unwin, 1981), and *Living the Enlightenment: Freemasonry and Politics in Eighteenth-Century Europe* (Oxford: Oxford University Press, 1991); Richard Weisberger, *Speculative Freemasonry and the Enlightenment: A Study of the Craft in London, Paris, Prague, and Vienna* (Boulder, CO: East European Monographs, 1993); Bernard Fay, *Revolution and Freemasonry: 1689–1800* (Boston: Little, Brown, 1935).

27. Reinhart Koselleck, *Critique and Crisis: Enlightenment and the Pathogenesis of Modern Society* (Oxford: Berg, 1988), 62.

28. *Encyclopédie*, ed. Diderot and d'Alembert, University of Chicago ARTFL Encyclopédie Project, http://encyclopedie.uchicago.edu. Translation mine.

29. D'Alembert to Voltaire, July 21, 1757, in d'Alembert, *Œuvres et correspondances*, 5:51 (emphasis added).

30. *Encyclopédie*, ed. Diderot and d'Alembert, University of Chicago ARTFL Encyclopédie Project, http://encyclopedie.uchicago.edu. Translation mine (emphasis added).

31. Ibid.

32. Spinoza, *Political Treatise*, trans. Elwes, 315 (5.7).

33. Rousseau, *Social Contract*, ed. Masters, 88, 88n. For Spinoza's similar reading of *The Prince*, see Spinoza, *Political Treatise* 5.7.

34. Antoine de La Salle, *Preface générale*, in *Œuvres de Fr. Bacon*, trans. Antoine de La Salle (Dijon: L. N. Frantin, 1799–1800), 1:xlii–xliv.

35. D'Alembert, *Preliminary Discourse to the Encyclopedia of Diderot*, trans. Richard Schwab and Walter Rex (New York: Bobbs-Merrill, 1963), 80.

36. *Œuvres de Descartes*, 3:297–98, quoted and translated by Hiram Caton, *The Origin of Subjectivity: An Essay on Descartes* (New Haven: Yale University Press, 1973), 17.

37. George Berkeley, *Alciphron, or the Minute Philosopher*, ed. David Berman (New York: Routledge, 1993), 155–56.

38. Pierre Bayle, quoted by Jonathan Israel in *Radical Enlightenment*, 13n39, who cites Georg Bohrmann, *Spinozas Stellung zur Religion* (Giessen: A. Töpelmann, 1914), 76.

39. Edmund Burke, *Thoughts on French Affairs*, in *The Works of Edmund Burke* (London: George Bell & Sons, 1909), 377.

40. Condorcet, *Esquisse*, 216–17, translation mine (emphasis added).

41. Diderot to Hemsterhuis, summer 1773, in Diderot, *Correspondance*, 13:25–27, translation mine (emphasis added).

42. Rousseau, "Preface," 184–85 (emphasis added).

43. Abbé Galiani, *Correspondance* (Paris: Calmann Lévy, 1881), 1:245. Translation mine (emphasis added).

44. *Œuvres complètes de Diderot*, ed. J. Assézat (Paris: Garnier, 1875–77), 2:398.

45. Sarpi, *Opere*, 92. Unpublished translation by Christopher Nadon and John Alcorn (emphasis added). The two Latin quotations are from Seneca, *Epistles* 59.4 and 105.6. Unpublished translation by Jenny Strauss Clay.

46. Lord Acton, *Essays on Church and State*, ed. Douglas Woodruff (London: Hollis & Carter, 1952), 255.

47. Wootton, *Paolo Sarpi*, 3. See 2–3, 19, 27.

48. Ibid., 38, 127.

49. Ibid., 38; see 127–35.

50. As these examples suggest, the move to greater openness appears, not in the sixteenth century at the very birth of modernity, but in its maturity during the Enlightenment.

51. Lucretius, *On the Nature of Things* 1.943–950; Montesquieu, *Lettres persanes* (Paris: Garnier, 1960), 4.

52. Maimonides, *Guide*, ed. Pines, 415 (introduction to part 3). See 175 (1.71). And see Moshe Halbertal's brilliant study of the long sequence of actions and reactions within Jewish thought set off by Maimonides's open discussion of esotericism: *Concealment and Revelation: Esotericism in Jewish Thought and its Philosophical Implications*.

53. I believe that Strauss would make a similar argument about the loss of the awareness of esotericism in our time in partial explanation of why he himself wrote so openly about it.

54. Aristotle, *Nicomachean Ethics* 1172a27.

55. On this theme, see Leo Strauss, *The Political Philosophy of Hobbes: Its Basis and Its Genesis* trans. Elsa M. Sinclair (Chicago: University of Chicago Press, 1952), 79–107.

56. Ernst Cassirer, *The Philosophy of the Enlightenment*, trans. Fritz Koelln and James P. Pettegrove (Boston: Beacon Press, 1951), 182–96.

57. Warburton, *Divine Legation of Moses*, 144–45 (3.5).

58. Strauss too, in speaking openly and thematically about esotericism, had a "theoretical" motive of this kind, in addition to the practical, "Maimonidean" one mentioned above. The modern "historical turn" eventually culminated, in our time, in the widespread movement of "historicism" or historical relativism—the view that reason is unable to ascend to any kind of universal, transhistorical truth, but remains always imbedded in the fundamental presuppositions of a particular time and place. It was Strauss's defining project to attempt to defend reason against the challenge of historicism, as well as of revelation. But the case for historicism, far more even than that for revelation, is rooted in the data of history, the long record of failed philosophical systems, for example, and the seemingly clear evidence linking each philosopher's highest truths to the established beliefs and practices of his time. But this all-important historical record takes on a wholly new meaning—no longer so favorable to the historicist thesis—when interpreted in light of the practice of esoteric writing, which caused philosophers to systematically *pretend* to mirror their times precisely because they were so radically opposed to them. In the context of the central challenge of historicism, then, the phenomenon of esotericism becomes of fundamental philosophical importance. This (together with the practical motive) is what led Strauss to speak of it so thematically, a point that will be elaborated at length in chapter 10.

59. Regarding the puzzling tension between Fontenelle's actions and his words on this issue, see Steven F. Rendall, "Fontenelle and His Public," *Modern Language Notes* 86, no. 4 (May 1971): 496–508.

60. D'Alembert, in *Œuvres de Frédéric le Grand* (Berlin: R. Decker, 1846–57), 24:470–76, translation mine (emphasis added).

61. Erasmus to Justus Jonas, May 10, 1521, in Erasmus, *Correspondence*, 8:203.

62. Bayle, "Aristote," 328–29 (remark 10).

63. L.-S. Mercier, *Tableau de Paris* (Amsterdam, 1783–89), 204–5.

64. See Voltaire to Helvétius, June 26, 1765, September 15, 1763; Voltaire to d'Argental, June 22, 1766, in Voltaire. *Les œuvres complètes de Voltaire*, ed. Theodore Besterman et al. (Geneva: Voltaire Foundation, 1968), vol. 110.

65. Helvétius, *De l'esprit* (Paris: Durand, 1758), 518 (discourse 4, chap. 4). Helvétius makes the same accusation in a letter to Montesquieu and in another to Saurin: see Montesquieu, *Œuvres complètes*, ed. Roger Caillois (Paris: Librairie Gallimard, 1949–51), 6:313–22.

66. On this issue see the excellent study by Christopher Kelly, *Rousseau as Author*, 8–28. There was one big exception to Rousseau's antipseudonymity posture: his long set piece on religion in the fourth book of *Emile* is attributed to a "Savoyard vicar."

67. See d'Alembert, *Œuvres et correspondances*, 5:48–60.

68. D'Alembert, *Preliminary Discourse*, 76, 80.

69. Voltaire to Damilaville, April 1, 1766, in *Œuvres complètes de Voltaire*, vol. 110.

70. On these themes, see Lester Crocker, "The Problem of Truth and Falsehood in the Age of Enlightenment," in *Journal of the History of Ideas* 14, no. 4 (October 1953): 575–603;

Harry C. Payne, *The Philosophes and the People* (New Haven: Yale University Press, 1976), 94–116; D. W. Smith, "The 'Useful Lie' in Helvétius and Diderot," in vol. 14 of *Diderot Studies* (Geneva: Librairie Droz, 1971), 190–92; and Peter Gay, *Voltaire's Politics: The Poet as Realist* (Princeton, NJ: Princeton University Press, 1959), 220–27.

71. Rousseau, *Discourse on the Sciences and Arts*, in *Collected Writings*, 2:21. See also *Final Reply*, in ibid., 2:115.

72. Crocker, "Problem," 575.

73. Roland Mortier, "Esotérisme et lumières," in *Clartés et ombres du siècle des lumières: Etudes sur le 18e siècle littéraire* (Geneva: Droz, 1969), 60.

74. Diderot, "Divination," in *Encyclopédie*, ARTFL Encyclopédie Projet, http://encyclopedie .uchicago.edu.proxy2.cl.msu.edu/. Translation mine.

75. On these themes, see Christopher Kelly, *Rousseau as Author*, 147.

76. Toland, *Clidophorus*, vii.

77. Diderot to Hemsterhuis, summer 1773, in *Correspondance*, 13:25–27. Translation mine.

78. Diderot, *Refutation d'Helvétius*, 2:398.

79. Abbé Galiani to Mme d'Epinay, September 19, 1772, quoted by Mortier, "Esotérisme at lumières," 60–103, 92.

CHAPTER NINE

1. Cantor, "Leo Strauss," 277. Throughout this chapter I rely on this superb essay which the reader is urged to consult directly.

2. Henry David Thoreau, *Walden*, ed. Stephen Fender (Oxford: Oxford University Press, 1997), 92 (emphasis added).

3. This kind of passion and connection cannot, of course, simply be willed. One can feel them only on the basis of certain presuppositions that are increasingly uncommon. One must be a real, old-fashioned believer in books and especially in old books (old enough to have been written esoterically). One must harbor, that is, the lively hope that some of these old classics can teach one things of the first importance for one's life that cannot so easily be found in more modern books. But if instead one is a firm believer in progress (so that later books inevitably contain all the solid wisdom of earlier ones) or, alternatively, in historicism (so that old classics are inevitably time-bound, expressing only the unquestioned assumptions of their society), then one will lack all reasonable basis for this kind of passion. With the best of intentions, one will be psychologically incapable of anything but an academic interest in these old books—which, given their difficulty, is too weak a motive and connection to enable one to unlock and truly understand them. In this way, the doctrines of progress and historicism—with their implicit but unavoidable dismissiveness toward the thought and writings of the past—become self-confirming: we expect that there is nothing truly important there, and that is what we find.

4. Friedrich Nietzsche, *Daybreak: Thoughts on the Prejudices of Morality*, trans. R. J. Hollingdale (Cambridge: Cambridge University Press, 1997), 5 (emphasis in the original). My attention was drawn to this passage by the website of Lance Fletcher, who also has an interesting discussion of it there, from which I have borrowed freely. See http://www.freelance-academy .org.

5. See Quentin Skinner's *Reason and Rhetoric in the Philosophy of Hobbes*, which gives a powerful demonstration of how the careful historical study of the rhetorical practices of Hobbes's age aid us in understanding his art of esoteric writing.

6. Montesquieu, *Œuvres complètes*, ed. Caillois, 1:1228, quoted and translated by Pangle, *Montesquieu's Philosophy*, 13 (emphasis mine).

7. Strauss, *Persecution*, 30.

8. Toland, *Clidophorus*, 76.

9. For both of these examples, see the excellent discussion by Cantor, "Leo Strauss."

10. See "The Literary Character of the *Guide for the Perplexed*," in Strauss, *Persecution*, 55–78; "How to Study Spinoza's *Theologico-Political Treatise*," in ibid., 142–201; and Strauss, *Thoughts*, 29–53.

11. Quoted and translated by Lester G. Crocker in *Diderot: The Embattled Philosopher* (New York: Free Press, 1954), 311.

12. Erasmus, *Praise of Folly*, trans. Hudson, 50.

13. For an excellent account, see David Berman, "Deism, Immortality and the Art of Theological Lying," in *Deism, Masonry, and the Enlightenment: Essays Honoring Alfred Owen Aldridge*, ed. J. A. Leo Lemay (Newark, NJ: Associated University Presses, 1987), 61–78; and *A History of Atheism in Britain: From Hobbes to Russell* (New York: Croom Helm, 1988).

14. See Zagorin, *Ways of Lying*, 305–16; and Don Cameron Allen, *Doubt's Boundless Sea; Skepticism and Faith in the Renaissance* (Baltimore: Johns Hopkins University Press, 1964).

15. Loseff, *On the Beneficence*, 109.

16. Strauss, *Persecution*, 36.

17. Machiavelli, *Discourses*, trans. Mansfield and Tarcov, 32 (1.10).

18. Strauss, *Thoughts*, 33.

19. Montaigne, *The Essays of Michel de Montaigne*, ed. and trans. Jacob Zeitlin (New York: A. A. Knopf, 1934), 2:500–501, quoted by David Schaefer, *The Political Philosophy of Montaigne* (Ithaca, NY: Cornell University Press, 1990), 94.

20. Ritchie, *German Literature*, 119.

21. Seth Mydans, "Burmese Editor's Code: Winks and Little Hints," *New York Times*, June 24, 2001.

22. Parrott, "Aesopian Language," 43.

23. Loseff, *On the Beneficence*, 65.

24. Aquinas, *Faith, Reason*, 53–54 (art. 4).

25. Diderot to François Hemsterhuis, summer 1773, in Diderot, *Correspondance*, 13:25–27. Translation mine.

26. Havel, *Letters to Olga*, 8, quoted by Patterson, *Censorship and Interpretation*, 11.

27. Rousseau, "Preface," 2:184–85.

28. Taine, *Ancient Regime*, trans. Durand, 260 (4.1.4), quoted and translated by Pangle, *Montesquieu's Philosophy*, 17–18.

29. Maimonides, *Guide* 6, quoting from Babylonian Talmud, Hagigah 11b, 13a.

30. Bacon, *Advancement of Learning*, ed. Kitchin, 81 (2.4.4).

31. Preface to *De Cive*, in *Thomas Hobbes: Man and Citizen*, ed. Bernard Gert (Indianapolis: Hackett, 1991), 103.

32. Alfarabi, *Plato's Laws*, 84–85.

33. Toland, *Clidophorus*, 75.

34. See also 152e; and *Cratylus* 402a–c. For a similar view, see Sextus Empiricus, *Against the Physicists* 1.4–9; and Aristotle, *Metaphysics* 1.984b15–30.

35. Montaigne, *Essays*, 185 (1.40).

36. *Œuvres de Descartes*, 3:491–92, quoted and translated by Hiram Caton, "The Problem of Descartes' Sincerity," *Philosophical Forum* 2, no. 1 (Fall 1970): 363.

37. Bacon, *Advancement of Learning*, ed. Kitchen, 88 (2.7.2); see 89.

38. D'Alembert, *Preliminary Discourse*, 76.

39. Toland, *Clidophorus*, 96.

40. Nicolas de Malebranche, *Réponse à une dissertation de Mr Arnaud contre un éclaircissement du traité de la nature et de la grace* (Rotterdam: Reinier Leers, 1685). Quoted by Pierre Bayle in Bayle, Daniel de Larocque, Jean Barrin, and Jacques Bernard, *Nouvelles de la république des lettres* (Amsterdam: H. Desbordes, May 1685), 794–95 (art. 8).

41. Strauss, *Persecution*, 32; see 169–70, 177–81, 186.

42. For a good example of this argument, see John Dunn, "Justice and the Interpretation of Locke's Political Theory," *Philosophy* 16, no. 1 (1968): 68–87.

43. Eliot Hearst and John Knott, *Blindfold Chess* (Jefferson, NC: McFarland, 2009).

44. Tocqueville, *Democracy in America*, trans. Mansfield and Winthrop, 613 (2.3.21).

45. Tocqueville, *Democracy in America* 2.1.15: "Why the Study of Greek and Latin Literature Is Particularly Useful in Democratic Societies"; see also 2.1.11–14, 2.1.16–21.

46. To be sure, many scholars today write *about* rhetoric as a theoretical topic, but that makes all the more striking their neglect of it as a *practice*—as something that could teach them and others how to write.

47. Maimonides, *Guide*, ed. Pines, 17–20.

48. Toland, *Clidophorus*, 77, 85.

49. Machiavelli, *Discourses*, trans. Mansfield and Tarcov, 307 (3.48); Pope, *Essay on Criticism*, 69 (lines 175–80).

50. James Joyce, *Ulysses: An Unabridged Republication of the Original Shakespeare and Company Edition, Published in Paris by Sylvia Beach, 1922* (Mineola, NY: Dover, 2009), 182. Although Stephen Dedalus is clearly Joyce's alter ego, one cannot assume that the view expressed here is Joyce's settled opinion.

51. Machiavelli, *Discourses* 61–62 (1.26).

52. On this technique, see the superb discussions by Ralph Lerner, from which I have profited, in "Dispersal by Design: The Author's Choice," in *Reason, Faith, and Politics: Essays in Honor of Werner J. Dannhauser*, ed. Arthur Melzer and Robert Kraynak (Lanham, MD: Lexington Books, 2008), 29–41, and in *Playing the Fool: Subversive Laughter in Troubled Times* (Chicago: University of Chicago Press, 2009).

53. Maimonides, *Guide*, ed. Pines, 6–7 (introduction).

54. *Stromata*, in *The Writings of Clement of Alexandria*, trans. Rev. William Wilson (Edinburgh: T. & T. Clark, 1869), 140–41 (bk. 4, chap. 2), 489 (bk. 7, chap 18).

55. Montesquieu to Pierre-Jean Grosley, April 8, 1750, quoted and translated by Paul Rahe, *Montesquieu and the Logic of Liberty* (New Haven: Yale University Press, 2009), 87.

56. D'Alembert, *Œuvres complètes* (Paris: A. Belin, 1822), 3:450–51, quoted and translated by Pangle, *Montesquieu's Philosophy*, 11–12.

57. See Strauss, *City and Man*, 62, 69, 110–11; and Strauss, *Rebirth*, 154–55.

58. Montaigne, *Complete Essays*, trans. Frame, 761 (3.9).

59. Pierre Bayle, *Historical and Critical Dictionary: Selections*, trans. Richard H. Popkin (Indianapolis: Hackett, 1991), 396–97.

60. Condorcet, *Esquisse*, 216–17. Translation mine (emphasis added).

61. Strauss, *Persecution*, 184 and n82.

62. Locke, *First Treatise*, in *Two Treatises of Government*, ed. Peter Laslett (New York: New American Library, 1965), sections 23, 8, 9, 7.

63. See the discussion of Locke's reading and writing in Richard Cox, *Locke on War and Peace* (Oxford: Clarendon Press, 1960), 1–44; and Michael Zuckert, *Launching Liberalism: On Lockean Political Philosophy* (Lawrence: University Press of Kansas, 2002), 33–43.

64. Gao and Ting-Toomey, *Communicating Effectively*, 38.

65. See Leo Strauss, "The Spirit of Sparta or the Taste of Xenophon," *Social Research* 6, no. 4 (1939): 502–36. On the notorious licentiousness of Spartan women, see 504n3.

66. See Strauss, *Persecution*, 9–16. For further discussion of the technique of omission, see Strauss, *Thoughts*, 30–32.

67. See Strauss, *Persecution*, 62–64; and Strauss, *Thoughts*, 42–45.

68. See Cicero, *Orator* 15.50; *De oratore* 2.313–15; Strauss, *Persecution*, 185; and Cantor, "Leo Strauss," 273–74.

69. Stanley Fish, "Georgics of the Mind: The Experience of Bacon's *Essays*," in *Self-Consuming Artifacts: The Experience of Seventeenth-Century Literature* (Berkeley: University of California Press, 1974), 78–156.

70. W. Robert Connor, *Thucydides* (Princeton, NJ: Princeton University Press, 1984). Reader response is the contemporary method that has most in common with the approach to reading being proposed here. For a brief comparison of the two, see Cantor, "Leo Strauss," 271–72.

71. Clifford Orwin, *The Humanity of Thucydides* (Princeton, NJ: Princeton University Press, 1994).

72. Strauss, *City and Man*, chap. 3.

73. David Wootton, "Narrative, Irony, and Faith in Gibbon's Decline and Fall," in *History and Theory* 33, no. 4 (December 1994): 77–105.

74. Berman, "Deism, Immortality," 61–78.

75. Ambler, "Aristotle," 390–410.

76. Clifford Orwin, "Machiavelli's Unchristian Charity," in *American Political Science Review* 72, no. 4 (December 1978): 1217–28.

77. Leo Strauss, "On the Intention of Rousseau," in *Hobbes and Rousseau: A Collection of Critical Essays*, ed. Maurice Cranston and R. S. Peters (Garden City, NY: Anchor Books, 1972), 254–90.

78. Leo Strauss and Seth Benardete, *Leo Strauss on Plato's Symposium* (Chicago: University of Chicago Press, 2001).

79. Allan Bloom, "Interpretive Essay," in *The Republic of Plato*, 305–436.

80. Christopher Bruell, *On the Socratic Education: An Introduction to the Shorter Platonic Dialogues* (Lanham, MD: Rowman & Littlefield, 1999).

81. Augustine, *City of God*, trans. Dods, 138–40 (4.31–32), 185–201 (6.2–9).

CHAPTER TEN

1. Habermas, Rorty, and Kolakowski, *Debating the State of Philosophy*, ix.

2. Susan Jacoby, *The Age of American Unreason* (New York: Pantheon Books, 2008); Albert Gore, *The Assault on Reason* (New York: Penguin, 2007). See also Todd Gitlin, "The Renaissance of Anti-intellectualism," *Chronicle of Higher Education*, December 8, 2000; Charles P. Pierce, *Idiot America: How Stupidity Became a Virtue in the Land of the Free* (New York: Doubleday, 2009); Chris Mooney, *The Republican War on Science* (New York: Basic Books, 2005); Alex B. Berezow and Hank Campbell, *Science Left Behind: Feel-Good Fallacies and the Rise of the Anti-Scientific Left* (New York: Public Affairs, 2012); Maggie Jackson, *Distracted: The Erosion of Attention and the Coming Dark Age* (Amherst, NY: Prometheus Books, 2008); Richard Shenkman, *Just How Stupid Are We?: Facing the Truth about the American Voter* (New York: Basic Books, 2008); Mark Bauerlein, *The Dumbest Generation: How the Digital Age Stupefies Young Americans and Jeopardizes Our Future (or, Don't Trust Anyone under 30)* (New York: Jeremy P. Tarcher/Penguin, 2008); Nicholas G. Carr, *The Shallows: What the Internet Is Doing to Our Brains* (New York: W. W. Norton, 2010).

3. See the Gallup poll taken in 2009, on the occasion of the two hundredth anniversary of Darwin's birth: http://www.gallup.com/poll/114544/darwin-birthday-believe-evolution.aspx.

4. Jean-François Lyotard, *The Postmodern Condition: A Report on Knowledge* (Minneapolis: University of Minnesota Press, 1984), xiv.

5. Strauss, *Spinoza's Critique of Religion*, 30; see Strauss, "Giving of Accounts," 460; and Strauss, "Preface to Hobbes Politische Wissenschaft," 453.

6. For the omitted, religious side of Strauss's thought, see Kenneth Hart Green, *Jew and Philosopher: The Return to Maimonides in the Jewish Thought of Leo Strauss* (Albany: State University of New York Press, 1993); Leora Batnitzky, *Leo Strauss and Emmanuel Levinas: Philoso-*

phy and the Politics of Revelation (Cambridge: Cambridge University Press, 2006); and above all, Heinrich Meier's superb *Leo Strauss and the Theological-Political Problem* (Cambridge: Cambridge University Press, 2006).

7. Jameson, *Political Unconscious*, 9, quoted in Peter C. Herman, *Historicizing Theory* (Albany: State University of New York Press, 2004), 1.

8. Karl Mannheim, "Historicism," in *Essays on the Sociology of Knowledge*, ed. Paul Kecskemeti (London: Routledge and Kegan Paul, 1952), 84.

9. Hans-Georg Gadamer, "The Problem of Historical Consciousness," trans. Jeff L. Close, *Graduate Faculty Philosophy Journal* 5 (Fall 1975): 8.

10. Habermas, Rorty, and Kolakowski, *Debating the State of Philosophy*, 1–2 (emphasis added); see 8.

11. Tzvetan Todorov, *On Human Diversity: Nationalism, Racism, and Exoticism in French Thought* (Cambridge, MA: Harvard University Press, 1993), 389.

12. Hilary Putnam and James Conant, *Realism with a Human Face* (Cambridge, MA: Harvard University Press, 1990), 18.

13. Todorov, *On Human Diversity*, 387–88.

14. Richard Rorty, *Philosophy and Social Hope* (New York: Penguin Books, 1999), 20.

15. Todorov, *On Human Diversity*, 389.

16. Benito Mussolini, *Diuturna* (Milan: Imperia, 1924), 374–77, quoted by Helmut Kuhn, *Freedom Forgotten and Remembered* (Chapel Hill: University of North Carolina Press, 1943), 17–18. Strauss also argues that relativism has a strong inner tendency to lead to intolerance, "fanatical obscurantism," and fascism; see Strauss, *Natural Right and History*, 5–6.

17. See the brief discussion of these themes in chapter 6, the section "Do 'Subversive Ideas' Really Subvert?"

18. Habermas, Rorty, and Kolakowski, *Debating the State of Philosophy*, 69 (emphasis added).

19. Ibid., 6.

20. Strauss, "Political Philosophy and History," in *What Is Political Philosophy?*, 57.

21. Ibid., 59.

22. See Strauss, *Natural Right and History*, 20, 24–27.

23. Leo Strauss, "Relativism," in *Relativism and the Study of Man*, ed. Helmut Schoeck and J. W. Wiggins (Princeton, NJ: Van Nostrand, 1961), 155; see Strauss, *Natural Right and History*, 19–28; and "Introduction to Heideggerian," 32, 35–36.

24. See Strauss, *Natural Right and History*, 18, 22; "Introduction to Heideggerian," 32; Strauss, "How to Begin to Study Medieval Philosophy," in *Rebirth*, 215; "Progress or Return?," 255; Strauss, "Kurt Riezler," in *What Is Political Philosophy?*, 260.

25. Strauss, *Natural Right and History*, 33; see Strauss, "On Collingwood's Philosophy of History," *Review of Metaphysics* 5, no. 4 (June 1952): 559–86, 585–86.

26. Strauss, "Political Philosophy and History," 73.

27. For an excellent discussion of Strauss's relation to Heidegger, see Richard Velkley, *Heidegger, Strauss, and the Premises of Philosophy: On Original Forgetting* (Chicago: University of Chicago Press, 2011).

28. Strauss, "An Unspoken Prologue," in Green, *Jewish Philosophy and the Crisis of Modernity*, 450; see Strauss, "Giving of Accounts," 458, 462–63; *City and Man*, 9.

29. Strauss, *Persecution*, 158.

30. Strauss, "Unspoken Prologue," 450.

31. Strauss, *Persecution*, 158.

32. See Strauss, "On a New Interpretation," 326; "Political Philosophy and History," 77.

33. Habermas, Rorty, and Kolakowski, *Debating the State of Philosophy*, 36.

34. Strauss, *Natural Right and History*, 18–19; see Strauss, "Political Philosophy and History," 62–63.

35. Strauss, "What Is Political Philosophy?," 40–55.

36. The classic work here is Alfarabi's *The Harmonization of the Two Opinions of the Two Sages, Plato the Divine and Aristotle.* See Strauss's discussion in his "Farabi's *Plato.*" See also Strauss, "On a New Interpretation," 345–49, 354–55. And see Carol Poster, "Aristotle's *Rhetoric* against Rhetoric: Unitarian Reading and Esoteric Hermeneutics," *American Journal of Philology* 118 (Summer 1997): 221: "In the 15,000 extant pages of the *Greek Commentaries on Aristotle,* the fundamental unity of Plato and Aristotle is almost universally acknowledged." This is also the view of Antiochus, Cicero's teacher, as presented in the latter's *De finibus* 5.3 and *Academica* 1.17.

37. Strauss, *Thoughts on Machiavelli,* 231 (emphasis added).

38. Strauss, "Political Philosophy and History," 63 (emphasis added).

39. R. G. Collingwood, *The Idea of History* (Oxford: Clarendon Press, 1946), 229, quoted by Strauss in "On Collingwood's Philosophy of History," 575.

40. Marx, "Manifesto," 489 (emphasis added).

41. See Strauss, *City and Man,* 50–138; Jaffa, *Thomism and Aristotelianism.*

42. Strauss, "Political Philosophy and History," 63–64; *Natural Right and History,* 199n43; Strauss, "On a Forgotten Kind of Writing," in *What Is Political Philosophy?,* 227; and "Persecution and the Art of Writing," *Social Research* 8 (November 1941): 503n21.

43. Strauss, *Natural Right and History,* 23; see 32; "Political Philosophy and History," 59–60, 69–72.

44. Strauss, "Philosophy as Rigorous Science and Political Philosophy," in *Studies in Platonic Political Philosophy* (Chicago: University of Chicago Press, 1983), 33.

45. Strauss, *Spinoza's Critique,* 31.

46. Strauss, "Correspondence concerning Modernity: Karl Löwith and Leo Strauss," *Independent Journal of Philosophy* 4 (1983): 112 (emphasis in the original).

47. See the excellent discussion of the continuity thesis and the secularization thesis in Daniel Tanguay, *Leo Strauss: An Intellectual Biography* (New Haven: Yale University Press, 2007). On Heidegger's reliance on Savigny and the historical school, see Richard Velkley, *Heidegger, Strauss,* 183–84n16, 185n40. For Strauss's highly critical evaluation of the most famous version of the secularization thesis, Weber's theory of the origin of modern capitalism from decayed Calvinism, see *Natural Right and History,* 60n22. On Hegel and secularization, see Strauss, *On Tyranny,* 191–92. See also "Three Waves of Modernity," in *An Introduction to Political Philosophy: Ten Essays by Leo Strauss,* ed. Hilail Gildin (Detroit: Wayne State University Press, 1989), 82–83, 95. For a very interesting defense of the continuity and secularization theses, see Michael Allen Gillespie, *The Theological Origins of Modernity* (Chicago: University of Chicago Press, 2008).

48. Strauss, *Natural Right and History,* 165.

49. Strauss, *Political Philosophy of Hobbes,* 1–5.

50. Strauss, "What Is Political Philosophy?," 38–39; see Strauss, "Progress or Return?," 262.

51. Strauss, *Natural Right and History,* 30; Strauss, "Progress or Return?," 262.

52. Strauss, *Natural Right and History,* 32.

53. Strauss, "The Problem of Socrates: Five Lectures," in *Rebirth,* 169, 171, 168–69.

54. Leo Strauss, *Socrates and Aristophanes* (New York: Basic Books, 1966), 311. Consider Nietzsche: "there is nothing that has caused me to meditate more on Plato's secrecy and sphinx nature than the happily preserved *petit fait* that under the pillow of his deathbed there was found no 'Bible,' nor anything Egyptian, Pythagorean, or Platonic—but a volume of Aristophanes." *Beyond Good and Evil,* trans. Kaufmann, 41.

55. See Strauss, "Problem of Socrates," 103; *Socrates and Aristophanes,* 3–8.

56. Strauss, *Natural Right and History,* 32, 33.

57. See Leo Strauss, *Faith and Political Philosophy: The Correspondence between Leo Strauss*

and Eric Voegelin, 1934–1964, trans. and ed. Peter Emberley and Barry Cooper (University Park: Pennsylvania State University Press, 1993), 65–66, 71, 75.

58. See ibid., 66, 75–76; *Persecution*, 7–8, 21.

59. Strauss, *Persecution*, 58.

60. Strauss, "What Is Political Philosophy?," 44; see Leo Strauss, "Marsilius of Padua," in *The History of Political Philosophy*, ed. Leo Strauss and Joseph Cropsey, 3rd ed. (Chicago: University of Chicago Press, 1987), 294.

61. Strauss, *Thoughts on Machiavelli*, 231; Leo Strauss, "Niccolo Machiavelli," in Strauss and Cropsey, *History of Political Philosophy*, 296–97.

62. Leo Strauss, *Philosophy and Law*, trans. Fred Baumann (New York: Jewish Publication Society, 1987), 12–13.

63. Strauss, *Natural Right and History*, 13–16, 33, 178; "What Is Political Philosophy?," 40–41, 51; "Three Waves of Modernity," 83–89; *On Tyranny*, 106n5, 210–12; "Progress or Return?," 242–45.

64. Strauss, *Natural Right and History*, 13–16; "On the Intention of Rousseau," 285.

65. Strauss, *Natural Right and History*, 13–16, 26, 252, 256–63, 302–23.

66. Not that this was the only root of the will to historicism. More fundamental was the original, underlying project of modernity: the effort to make man absolutely at home in his time and place and therefore manifestly indifferent to a religious beyond. Historicism is the ultimate expression of this original, antitranscendent modern impulse. But this impulse arrived all the quicker at its final, historicist destination because its first incarnation, Enlightenment rationalism, produced political evils that generated their own, more immediately practical motives for subordinating reason to history. Still, this latter concern does not stand on its own, because philosophers would not have been so vitally concerned with these merely political problems if the primary modern project had not first given them a fundamental stake in — a theoretical concern with — the course of political and religious history.

67. Strauss, *Philosophy and Law*, 112n2, 37–38; *Persecution*, 155; see Heinrich Meier, *Leo Strauss*, 56–57, 57n2.

68. Friedrich Schiller, *On Naive and Sentimental Poetry*, trans. Julius A. Elias (New York: F. Ungar, 1966); G. W. F. Hegel, *The Phenomenology of Mind*, trans. J. B. Baillie (New York: Harper and Row, 1967), 94; Edmund Husserl, *The Crisis of European Sciences and Transcendental Phenomenology*, trans. D. Carr (Evanston, IL: Northwestern University Press, 1970), 366–67, 373–75; Strauss, "Political Philosophy and History," 75; "Philosophy as Rigorous Science," 31; Jacob Klein, *Greek Mathematical Thought and the Origin of Algebra*, trans. Eva Brann (Cambridge, MA: MIT Press, 1968), 117–25; *Jacob Klein: Lectures and Essays*, ed. Robert Williamson and Elliot Zuckerman (Annapolis, MD: St. John's College Press, 1985), 65–84.

69. Strauss, "On Classical Political Philosophy," 49–50; "What Is Political Philosophy?," 27–29; "Political Philosophy and History," 73–77; *Philosophy and Law*, 37–38, 112n2; *Persecution*, 154–58; see Klein, *Greek Mathematical Thought*, 117–25.

70. Strauss, "Political Philosophy and History," 76.

Acton, Lord [Sir John Dalberg-Acton]. *Essays on Church and State*. Edited by Douglas Wood-
    ruff. London: Hollis & Carter, 1952.
Ahrensdorf, Peter J. *The Death of Socrates and the Life of Philosophy: An Interpretation of Plato's
    Phaedo*. Albany: State University of New York Press, 1995.
Alfarabi, Abū Naṣr Muḥammad ibn Muḥammad. *Aphorisms of the Statesman*. Translated by
    D. M. Dunlop. Cambridge: Cambridge University Press, 1961.
————. *The Harmonization of the Two Opinions of the Two Sages*. In *Alfarabi: The Political Writ-
    ings: Selected Aphorisms and Other Texts*, translated by Charles E. Butterworth, 115–68.
    Ithaca, NY: Cornell University Press, 2001.
————. *The Philosophy of Plato and Aristotle*. Trans. Muhsin Mahdi. Ithaca, NY: Cornell Univer-
    sity Press, 1962.
————. *Plato's* Laws. Translated by Muhsin Mahdi. In *Medieval Political Philosophy: A Source-
    book*, edited by Ralph Lerner and Muhsin Mahdi, 83–94. New York: Free Press, 1963.
Allen, Don Cameron. *Doubt's Boundless Sea: Skepticism and Faith in the Renaissance*. Baltimore,
    MD: Johns Hopkins University Press, 1964.
Alvarez, Alfred. *The School of Donne*. London: Chatto and Windus, 1961.
Ambler, Wayne. "Aristotle on Nature and Politics: The Case of Slavery." *Political Theory* 15,
    no. 3 (August 1987): 390–410.
Ammonius. *Aristotelis Categorias Commentarius*. Edited by A. Busse. In vol. 4.4 of *Commentaria
    in Aristotelem Graeca*. Berlin: Reimer, 1895.
————. *On Aristotle's* Categories. Translated by S. Marc Cohen and Gareth B. Matthews.
    Ithaca, NY: Cornell University Press, 1991.
Anderson, Abraham. *The Treatise of the Three Impostors and the Problem of Enlightenment: A New
    Translation of the Traité des Trois Imposteurs (1777 edition) with Three Essays in Commentary*.
    Lanham, MD: Rowman & Littlefield, 1997.

Aquinas, Thomas. *Catena Aurea, Commentary on the Four Gospels: Collected out of the Works of the Fathers by St. Thomas Aquinas*. Vol. 1. Translated by Mark Pattison, J. D. Dalgairns, and T. D. Ryder. Oxford: John Henry Parker, 1841–45.

———. *Commentary on Aristotle's De anima*. Translated by Kenelm Foster, OP, and Sylvester Humphries, OP New Haven: Yale University Press, 1951. http://dhspriory.org/thomas /english/DeAnima.htm#11L.

———. *Commentary on Aristotle's Nicomachean Ethics*. Translated by C. I. Litzinger. Notre Dame, IN: Dumb Ox Books, 1993.

———. *Faith, Reason and Theology: Questions I–IV of His Commentary on the De Trinitate of Boethius*. Translated by Armand Maurer. Toronto: Pontifical Institute of Medieval Studies, 1987.

———. *Summa Theologica*. Translated by Fathers of the English Dominican Province. Vol. 3. Westminster, MD: Christian Classics, 1981.

Arendt, Hannah. *Between Past and Future: Eight Exercises in Political Thought*. New York: Penguin Books, 1977.

Aristotle. *Aristotle's Nicomachean Ethics*. Translated and edited by Robert C. Bartlett and Susan D. Collins. Chicago: University of Chicago Press, 2011.

———. *The Basic Works of Aristotle*. Edited by Richard McKeon. New York: Random House, 1941.

———. *The Politics*. Translated by Carnes Lord. Chicago: University of Chicago Press, 1984.

Arkush, Allan. "Voltaire on Judaism and Christianity." *AJS Review* 18, no. 2 (1993): 223–43.

Augustine, Saint. *The City of God*. Translated by Marcus Dods. New York: Modern Library, 1950.

———. *De Doctrina Christiana*. Edited and Translated by R. P. H. Green. Oxford: Clarendon Press, 1995.

———. *Letters*. Edited by Ludwig Schopp and Roy Joseph Deferrari. Translated by Sister Wilfrid Parsons. Vol. 1. New York: Fathers of the Church, 1951.

———. *Letters*. Edited by Ludwig Schopp and Roy Joseph Deferrari. Translated by Sister Wilfrid Parsons. Vol. 3. New York: Fathers of the Church, 1953.

Austin, John L. *How to Do Things with Words*. Cambridge, MA: Harvard University Press, 1962.

Averroes. *Averroes on Plato's Republic*. Translated by Ralph Lerner. Ithaca, NY: Cornell University Press, 1974.

———. *The Decisive Treatise*. Translated by George F. Hourani. In *Medieval Political Philosophy: A Sourcebook*, edited by Ralph Lerner and Muhsin Mahdi, 163–86. New York: Free Press, 1963.

———. *On the Harmony of Religion and Philosophy*. Translated and edited by George Hourani. London: Gibb Memorial Trust, 1961.

Bacon, Francis. *The Advancement of Learning*. Edited by G. W. Kitchin. Philadelphia: Paul Dry Books, 2001.

Bagley, Paul J. "On the Practice of Esotericism." *Journal of the History of Ideas* 53, no. 2 (April–June 1992): 231–47.

Baker, Richard. Translator's preface to Vergilio Malvezzi, *Discourses upon Cornelius Tacitus*, translated by Richard Baker. London: R. Whitaker and Tho. Whitaker, 1642.

Balmuth, Daniel. *Censorship in Russia, 1865–1905*. Washington, DC: University Press of America, 1979.

Batnitzky, Leora. *Leo Strauss and Emmanuel Levinas: Philosophy and the Politics of Revelation*. Cambridge: Cambridge University Press, 2006.

Bauerlein, Mark. *The Dumbest Generation: How the Digital Age Stupefies Young Americans and Jeopardizes Our Future (or, Don't Trust Anyone under 30*. New York: Jeremy P. Tarcher/Penguin, 2008.

Bayle, Pierre. "Aristote." In *Dictionnaire historique et critique*. 5th ed. Vol. 1. Amsterdam: P. Brunel, 1740.

————. *Historical and Critical Dictionary: Selections.* Translated by Richard H. Popkin. Indianapolis: Hackett, 1991.

————. *Various Thoughts on the Occasion of a Comet.* Translated by Robert C. Bartlett. Albany: State University of New York Press, 2000.

Bayle, Pierre, Daniel de Larocque, Jean Barrin, and Jacques Bernard. *Nouvelles de la république des letters.* Amsterdam: H. Desbordes, 1685.

Benardete, Seth. "Strauss on Plato." In *The Argument of the Action,* 407–17. Chicago: University of Chicago Press, 2000.

Benitez, Miguel. *La face cachée des Lumières: recherches sur les manuscrits philosophiques clandestins de l'âge classique.* Paris: Universitas, 1996.

Bennett, Milton J. "Intercultural Communication: A Current Perspective." In *Basic Concepts of Intercultural Communication: Selected Readings,* edited by Milton J. Bennett, 1–34. Yarmouth, ME: Intercultural Press, 1998.

Berezow, Alex B., and Hank Campbell. *Science Left Behind: Feel-Good Fallacies and the Rise of the Anti-scientific Left.* New York: Public Affairs, 2012.

Bergengruen, Werner. Foreword to Rudolf Pechel, *Zwischen den Zeilen: Der Kampf einer Zeitschrift für Freiheit und Recht.* Wiesentheid, Germany: Droemersche Verlagsanstalt, 1948.

Berghahn, Daniela. "Film Censorship in a 'Clean State': The Case of Klein and Kohlhaase's *Berlin um die Ecke.*" In *Censorship and Cultural Regulation in the Modern Age,* edited by Beate Muller, 111–38. Amsterdam: Rodopi, 2004.

Berkeley, George. *Alciphron, or the Minute Philosopher.* Edited by David Berman. New York: Routledge, 1993.

Berman, David. "Deism, Immortality and the Art of Theological Lying." In *Deism, Masonry, and the Enlightenment: Essays Honoring Alfred Owen Aldridge,* edited by J. A. Leo Lemay, 61–78. Newark, NJ: Associated University Presses, 1987.

————. *A History of Atheism in Britain: From Hobbes to Russell.* New York: Croom Helm, 1988.

Bloom, Allan. "Interpretive Essay." In *The Republic of Plato,* translated by Allan Bloom, 305–436. New York: Basic Books, 1968.

Blount, Charles. *Great Is Diana of the Ephesians, or, the Original of Idolatry.* London, 1695.

Blumenberg, Hans. *The Legitimacy of the Modern Age.* Cambridge, MA: MIT Press, 1983.

Boas, George. "Ancient Testimony to Secret Doctrines." *Philosophical Review* 62, no. 1 (1953): 79–92.

————. *Dominant Themes of Modern Philosophy: A History.* New York: Ronald Press, 1957.

————. *Vox Populi: Essays in the History of an Idea.* Baltimore: Johns Hopkins University Press, 1969.

Boccaccio, Giovanni. *Boccaccio on Poetry: Being the Preface and the Fourteenth and Fifteenth Books of Boccaccio's Genealogia Deorum Gentilium.* Edited and translated by Charles G. Osgood. Princeton, NJ: Princeton University Press, 1930.

————. *The Life of Dante (Tratatello in laude di Dante).* Translated by Vincenzo Zin Bollettino. New York: Garland, 1990.

Bohrmann, Georg. *Spinozas Stellung zur Religion.* Giessen: A. Töpelmann, 1914.

Bok, Sissela. *Lying: Moral Choice in Public and Private Life.* New York: Vintage Books, 1989.

Bolle, Kees W., ed. *Secrecy in Religions.* Leiden: E. J. Brill, 1987.

Bolotin, David. *An Approach to Aristotle's Physics.* Albany: State University of New York Press, 1998.

Brandt, Elizabeth A. "On Secrecy and the Control of Knowledge: Taos Pueblo." In *Secrecy: A Cross-Cultural Perspective,* edited by Stanton K. Teft, 123–47. New York: Human Sciences Press, 1980.

Bruell, Christopher. *On the Socratic Education: An Introduction to the Shorter Platonic Dialogues.* Lanham, MD: Rowman & Littlefield, 1999.

Burger, Ronna. *Aristotle's Dialogue with Socrates: On the Nicomachean Ethics*. Chicago: University of Chicago Press, 2008.

Burke, Edmund. *Reflections on the Revolution in France*. In vol. 2 of *Select Works of Edmund Burke: A New Imprint of the Payne Edition*. Indianapolis: Liberty Fund, 1999.

———. *Thoughts on French Affairs*. In *The Works of Edmund Burke*. London: George Bell & Sons, 1909.

Burnet, Thomas. *Archæologiæ Philosophicæ or, the Ancient Doctrine Concerning the Originals of Things. Written in Latin by Thomas Burnet, L.L.D., Master of the Charter-House. To which is added, Dr Burnet's Theory of the Visible World, by way of Commentary on his own Theory of the Earth; being the second Part of his Archiologiæ* [sic] *Philosophicæ. Faithfully translated into English, with Remarks thereon*. London: J. Fisher, 1736. First published London: Gualt. Kettilby, 1692.

Bury, J. B. *A History of Freedom of Thought*. New York: Henry Holt, 1913.

Butler, Samuel. *Evolution Old and New: Or, the Theories of Buffon, Dr. Erasmus Darwin and Lamarck as Compared with That of Charles Darwin*. New York: E. P. Dutton, 1911.

Calvin, John. *Commentary on a Harmony of the Evangelists, Matthew, Mark, and Luke*. Translated by Rev. William Pringle. Vol. 2. Grand Rapids, MI: W. B. Eerdmans, 1949.

Cantor, Paul. "Leo Strauss and Contemporary Hermeneutics." In *Leo Strauss's Thought: Toward a Critical Engagement*, edited by Alan Udoff, 267–314. Boulder, CO: Lynne Rienner, 1991.

Canziani, Guido, ed. *Filosofia e religione nella letteratura clandestina: secoli XVII e XVIII*. Milan: FrancoAngeli, 1994.

Carr, Nicholas G. *The Shallows: What the Internet Is Doing to Our Brains*. New York: W. W. Norton, 2010.

Cassirer, Ernst. *The Philosophy of the Enlightenment*. Translated by Fritz Koelln and James P. Pettegrove. Boston: Beacon Press, 1951.

Caton, Hiram. *The Origin of Subjectivity: An Essay on Descartes*. New Haven: Yale University Press, 1973.

———. "The Problem of Descartes' Sincerity." *Philosophical Forum* 2, no. 1 (Fall 1970): 355–70.

Charron, Pierre. *De la sagesse: Trois livres*. New ed. Paris: Lefèvre, 1836.

Chroust, Anton-Hermann. "Eudemus, or On the Soul: A Lost Dialogue of Aristotle on the Immortality of the Soul." *Mnemosyne* 19 (1966): 17–30.

Cicero, Marcus Tullius. *De finibus bonorum et malorum*. Translated by H. Rackham. London: W. Heinemann, 1914.

———. *De inventione. De optimo genere oratorum. Topica*. Translated by H. M. Hubbell. Cambridge, MA: Harvard University Press, 1949.

———. *De natura deorum*. Translated by H. Rackham. Loeb Classical Library 268. Cambridge, MA: Harvard University Press, 1933.

———. *For Archias*. In vol. 2 of *The Orations of Marcus Tullius Cicero*, translated by C. D. Yonge. London: G. Bell & Sons, 1874–97.

———. *Tusculan Disputations*. Translated by J. E. King. Loeb Classical Library 18. Cambridge, MA: Harvard University Press, 1927.

Clark, Katerina, and Michael Holquist. *Mikhail Bakhtin*. Cambridge, MA: Harvard University Press, 1984.

Clay, Diskin. *Platonic Questions: Dialogues with the Silent Philosopher*. University Park: Pennsylvania State University Press, 2000.

Clement of Alexandria. *Stromata, or Miscellanies*. In vol. 2 of *The Writings of Clement of Alexandria*, translated by Rev. William Wilson. Edinburgh: T. & T. Clark, 1869.

Codrescu, Andrei. *The Disappearance of the Outside: A Manifesto for Escape*. New York: Addison-Wesley, 1990.

Coetzee, J. M. *Giving Offense: Essays on Censorship*. Chicago: University of Chicago Press, 1996.

Collingwood, R. G. *The Idea of History*. Oxford: Clarendon Press, 1946.

Condorcet, Antoine-Nicolas de. *Esquisse d'un tableau historique des progrès de l'esprit humain.* Edited by Monique Hincker and François Hincker. Paris: Editions Sociales, 1971.

———. *Sketch for a Historical Picture of the Progress of the Human Mind.* Translated by June Barraclough. New York: Noonday Press, 1955.

Connor, W. Robert. "The Other 399: Religion and the Trial of Socrates." *Bulletin of the Institute of Classical Studies* 37 (January 1991): 49–56.

———. *Thucydides.* Princeton, NJ: Princeton University Press, 1984.

Cox, Richard. *Locke on War and Peace.* Oxford: Clarendon Press, 1960.

Crocker, Lester G. *Diderot: The Embattled Philosopher.* New York: Free Press, 1954.

———. "The Problem of Truth and Falsehood in the Age of Enlightenment." *Journal of the History of Ideas* 14, no. 4 (October 1953): 575–603.

Cross, F. L., ed. *The Oxford Dictionary of the Christian Church.* London: Oxford University Press, 1957.

Crosson, Frederick J. "Esoteric versus Latent Teaching." *Review of Metaphysics* 59, no. 1 (September 2005): 73–94.

Cudworth, Ralph. *The True Intellectual System of the Universe.* London: Thomas Tegg, 1845.

D'Alembert, Jean-Baptiste le Rond. *Œuvres complètes.* Vol. 3. Paris: A. Belin, 1822.

———. *Œuvres et correspondances inédites de d'Alembert.* Edited by Charles Henry. Vol. 5. Geneva: Slatkine, 1967.

———. *Preliminary Discourse to the Encyclopedia of Diderot.* Translated by Richard Schwab and Walter Rex. New York: Bobbs-Merrill, 1963.

Danielou, Jean. "Les traditions secrètes des Apôtres." *Eranos-Jahrbuch* 31 (1962): 199–215.

Darnton, Robert. *The Forbidden Best-Sellers of Pre-Revolutionary France.* New York: W. W. Norton, 1995.

———. *The Literary Underground of the Old Regime.* Cambridge, MA: Harvard University Press, 1982.

Davidson, Donald. "On the Very Idea of a Conceptual Scheme." In *Inquiries into Truth and Interpretation,* 183–98. Oxford: Oxford University Press, 1984.

Demetrius of Phaleron. *On Style.* Translated by W. Rhys Roberts. Cambridge: Cambridge University Press, 1902.

Derenne, Eudore. *Les procès d'impiété intentés aux philosophes à Athènes au Vme et au IVme siècles avant J.-C.* Liège: Vaillant-Carmanne, 1930.

Descartes, René. *Œuvres de Descartes.* Edited by Charles Adam and Paul Tannery. 11 vols. Paris: J. Vrin, 1964–69.

Dewhirst, Martin, and Robert Farrell, eds. *The Soviet Censorship.* Metuchen, NJ: Scarecrow Press, 1973.

Dickinson, Emily. "Tell all the Truth but tell it slant." *The Complete Poems of Emily Dickinson,* edited by Thomas H Johnson. Boston: Little, Brown, 1960.

Diderot, Denis. "Aius Locutius." In *The Encyclopedia of Diderot and d'Alembert Collaborative Translation Project,* translated by Stephen J. Gendzier. Ann Arbor: MPublishing, University of Michigan Library, 2009. http://hdl.handle.net/2027/spo.did2222.0001.297 (accessed October 7, 2011).

———. *Correspondance.* Edited by George Roth. Vol. 13. Paris: Editions de Minuit, 1955–70.

———. "Divination." "Encyclopédie." "Machiavelisme." "Mensonge officieux." "Pythagorisme ou Philosophie de Pythagore." In *Encyclopédie, ou dictionnaire raisonné des sciences, des arts et des métiers,* edited by Denis Diderot and Jean le Rond d'Alembert. University of Chicago ARTFL Encyclopédie Projet (Winter 2008 edition), ed. Robert Morrissey. http://encyclopedie.uchicago.edu.

———. *Œuvres complètes.* Edited by J. Assézat. Vol. 2. Paris: Garnier, 1875–77.

———. *Refutation d'Helvétius.* In vol. 2 of *Œuvres complètes.* Paris: Garnier, 1875.

Diderot, Denis, and Jean le Rond d'Alembert, eds. *Encyclopédie, ou dictionnaire raisonné des sci-*

ences, des arts et des métiers. Ed. Robert Morrissey. University of Chicago: ARTFL Encyclopédie Projet (Winter 2008 edition), http://encyclopedie.uchicago.edu.

Diogenes Laertius. *Lives of Eminent Philosophers.* Translated by Robert Drew Hicks. Cambridge, MA: Harvard University Press, 1966.

Dodds, E. R. *The Greeks and the Irrational.* Berkeley: University of California Press, 1951.

Drewett, Michael. "Aesopian Strategies of Textual Resistance in the Struggle to Overcome the Censorship of Popular Music in Apartheid South Africa." *Critical Studies* 22 (2004): 189–207.

Drury, John. "The Sower, the Vineyard, and the Place of Allegory in the Interpretation of Mark's Parables." *Journal of Theological Studies* 24, no. 2 (1973): 367–79.

Drury, Shadia B. *Leo Strauss and the American Right.* New York: St. Martin's Press, 1997.

———. *The Political Ideas of Leo Strauss.* New York: St. Martin's Press, 1988.

Dunn, John. "Justice and the Interpretation of Locke's Political Theory." *Philosophy* 16, no. 1 (1968): 68–87.

During, Ingemar. *Aristotle in the Ancient Biographical Tradition.* Göteborg, 1957. Distributed by Almqvist & Wiksell, Stockholm.

Edel, Abraham. *Aristotle and His Philosophy.* Chapel Hill: University of North Carolina Press, 1982.

Edelstein, Ludwig. *Plato's Seventh Letter.* Leiden: E. J. Brill, 1966.

Eliade, Mircea. *Cosmos and History: The Myth of the Eternal Return.* Translated by Willard Trask. New York: Harper and Row, 1959.

———. *Myth and Reality.* Translated by Willard Trask. New York: Harper and Row, 1963.

Elias. *Aristotelis Categorias Commentaria.* Edited by A. Busse. In vol. 18.1 of *Commentaria in Aristotelem Graeca.* Berlin: Reimer, 1900.

Engelsing, Rolf. *Der Bürger als Leser: Lesergeschichte in Deutschland, 1500–1800.* Stuttgart, 1974.

———. "Die Perioden der Lesergeschichte in der Neuzeit: Das statische Ausmass und die soziokulturelle Bedeutung der Lektüre." *Archiv für Geschichte des Buchwesens* 10 (1969): cols. 944–1002.

Epicurus. *Extant Remains: With Short Critical Apparatus.* Translated by Cyril Bailey. Oxford: Clarendon Press, 1926.

Erasmus, Desiderius. *The Correspondence of Erasmus: Letters 1122 to 1251.* Edited by P. G. Bientenholz. Translated by R. A. B. Mynors. Vol. 8 of *The Collected Works of Erasmus.* Toronto: University of Toronto Press, 1988.

———. *The Praise of Folly.* Translated by Hoyt Hopewell Hudson. Princeton, NJ: Princeton University Press, 1941.

Evans, A. W. *Warburton and the Warburtonians; A Study in Some Eighteenth-Century Controversies.* London: Oxford University Press, H. Milford, 1932.

Fay, Bernard. *Revolution and Freemasonry,: 1689–1800.* Boston: Little, Brown, 1935.

Ferrari, G. R. F. "Strauss's Plato." *Arion* 5, no. 2 (Fall 1997): 36–65.

Findlay, J. N. *Plato: The Written and Unwritten Doctrines.* New York: Humanities Press, 1974.

Finley, M. I. *Aspects of Antiquity.* 2nd ed. Harmondsworth, UK: Penguin Books, 1977.

Fish, Stanley. "Georgics of the Mind: The Experience of Bacon's *Essays.*" In *Self-Consuming Artifacts: The Experience of Seventeenth-Century Literature,* 78–156. Berkeley: University of California Press, 1974.

Formey, Samuel. "Exoterique & Esoterique." In *Encyclopédie, ou dictionnaire raisonné des sciences, des arts et des métiers, etc.,* ed. Denis Diderot and Jean le Rond d'Alembert. University of Chicago ARTFL Encyclopédie Project (Spring 2013 edition), ed. Robert Morrissey, http://encyclopedie.uchicago.edu.

Frank, Joseph. *Dostoevsky: The Seeds of Revolt, 1821–1849.* Princeton, NJ: Princeton University Press, 1976.

Frantzen, A. J. "Between the Lines: Queer Theory, the History of Homosexuality, and Anglo-Saxon Penitentials." *Journal of Medieval and Early Modern Studies* 26, no. 2 (1996): 255–96.

Frederick the Great. *Œuvres de Frédéric le Grand*. Berlin: R. Decker, 1846–57.

Freud, Sigmund. *The Interpretation of Dreams*. Edited and translated by James Strachey. New York: Penguin Books, 1976.

Fritz, Kurt von. "The Philosophical Passage in the Seventh Platonic Letter and the Problem of Plato's 'Esoteric' Philosophy." In *Essays in Ancient Greek Philosophy*, edited by John P. Anton and George L. Kustas. Albany: State University of New York Press, 1971.

Fukuyama, Francis. *Trust: The Social Virtues and the Creation of Prosperity*. New York: Free Press, 1995.

Furbank, P. N. *Diderot: A Critical Biography*. New York: Alfred A. Knopf, 1992.

———. "A No-Code Zone," *Times Literary Supplement*, June 4, 1999.

Fustel de Coulanges, Numa Denis. *The Ancient City*. Garden City, NY: Doubleday, 1956.

Gadamer, Hans-Georg. "Philosophizing in Opposition: Strauss and Voegelin on Communication and Science." In *Faith and Political Philosophy: The Correspondence between Leo Strauss and Eric Voegelin, 1934–1964*, translated and edited by Peter Emberley and Barry Cooper, 249–61. College Park: Pennsylvania State University Press, 1993.

———. "The Problem of Historical Consciousness." Translated by Jeff L. Close. *Graduate Faculty Philosophy Journal* 5 (Fall 1975): 1–52.

———. *Truth and Method*. Translated by Joel Weinsheimer and Donald G. Marshall. 2nd rev. ed. New York: Continuum, 1989.

Gadamer, Hans-Georg, and Leo Strauss. "Correspondence concerning *Wahrheit und Methode*." *Independent Journal of Philosophy* 2 (1978): 5–13.

Galiani, abbé. *Correspondance*. Vol. 1. Paris: Calmann Lévy, 1881.

Galston, Miriam. *Politics and Excellence: The Political Philosophy of Alfarabi*. Princeton, NJ: Princeton University Press, 1990.

Gao, Ge, and Stella Ting-Toomey. *Communicating Effectively with the Chinese*. Thousand Oaks, CA: Sage Publications, 1998.

Garsten, Bryan. *Saving Persuasion: A Defense of Rhetoric and Judgment*. Cambridge, MA: Harvard University Press, 2006.

Gay, Peter. *Voltaire's Politics: The Poet as Realist*. Princeton, NJ: Princeton University Press, 1959.

George, Alexander. *Propaganda Analysis: A Study of Inferences Made from Nazi Propaganda in World War II*. Evanston, IL: Row, Peterson, 1959.

Gerson, Lloyd P. *Aristotle and Other Platonists*. Ithaca, NY: Cornell University Press, 2005.

Gibbon, Edward. *The History of the Decline and Fall of the Roman Empire in 7 Volumes*. London: George Bell & Sons, 1891.

Gillespie, Michael Allen. *The Theological Origins of Modernity*. Chicago: University of Chicago Press, 2008.

Gobineau, Joseph Arthur. *Les religions et les philosophies dans l'Asie Centrale*. In vol. 2 of *Œuvres*, edited by Jean Gaulmier. Paris: Gallimard, 1983.

Goethe, J. W. von. *Goethes Briefe und Briefe an Goethe*. Edited by Karl Robert Mandelkow. Munich: Beck, 1988.

Gordon, Thomas. *Discourses upon Tacitus: The Works of Tacitus, With Political Discourses Upon that Author*. Vol. 4. London: T. Woodward & J. Peele, 1770.

Gore, Albert. *The Assault on Reason*. New York: Penguin, 2007.

Gracian y Morales, Baltasar Jeronimo. *The Science of Success and the Art of Prudence*. Translated by Lawrence C. Lockley. San Jose, CA: University of Santa Clara Press, 1967.

Grant, Alexander. *The Ethics of Aristotle, Illustrated with Essays and Notes*. London: Longmans, 1885.

———. "On the Exoterikoi Logoi." Appendix B in *The Ethics of Aristotle, Illustrated with Essays and Notes*. London: Longmans, 1885.

Green, Kenneth Hart. *Jew and Philosopher: The Return to Maimonides in the Jewish Thought of Leo Strauss*. Albany: State University of New York Press, 1993.

Greenblatt, Stephen. *Shakespeare's Freedom*. Chicago: University of Chicago Press, 2010.

Grotius, Hugo. *De jure belli ac pacis libri tres*. Translated by Francis W. Kelsey. Oxford: Clarendon Press, 1925.

Guicciardini, Francesco. *Maxims and Reflections of a Renaissance Statesman*. Translated by Mario Domandi. New York: Harper & Row, 1965.

Habermas, Jürgen, Richard Rorty, and Leszek Kolakowski. *Debating the State of Philosophy*. Edited by Jozef Niznik, Westport, CT: Praeger, 1996.

Halbertal, Moshe. *Concealment and Revelation: Esotericism in Jewish Thought and Its Philosophical Implications*. Translated by Jackie Feldman. Princeton, NJ: Princeton University Press, 2007.

Hall, David. "The Uses of Literacy in New England, 1600–1850." In *Printing and Society in Early America*, edited by W. L. Joyce, 1–47. 2nd ed. Worcester, MA.: American Antiquarian Society, 1983.

Hall, Edward T. *Beyond Culture*. New York: Doubleday, 1976.

Havel, Vaclav. *Disturbing the Peace: A Conversation with Karel Hvizdala*. Translated by Paul Wilson. New York: Alfred A. Knopf, 1990.

———. *Letters to Olga*. Translated by Paul Wilson. New York: Henry Holt, 1989.

Hearst, Eliot, and John Knott. *Blindfold Chess*. Jefferson, NC: McFarland, 2009.

Hegel, G. W. F. *The Phenomenology of Mind*. Translated by J. B. Baillie. New York: Harper and Row, 1967.

Helvétius, Claude Adrien. *De l'esprit*. Paris: Durand, 1758.

Hendry, Joy, and C. W. Watson, eds. *An Anthropology of Indirect Communication*. London: Routledge, 2001.

Herbermann, Charles G., Edward A. Pace, Conde B. Pallen, Thomas J. Shahan, and John J. Wynne, eds. *The Catholic Encyclopedia*. Vol. 5. New York: Gilmary Society, 1909.

Herman, Peter C. *Historicizing Theory*. Albany: State University of New York Press, 2004.

Herzen, Alexander. *My Past and Thoughts: The Memoirs of Alexander Herzen*. Translated by Constance Garnett. Vol. 2. New York: Alfred A. Knopf, 1968.

Hobbes, Thomas. *Leviathan: With Selected Variants from the Latin Edition of 1668*. Edited by E. M. Curley. Indianapolis: Hackett, 1994.

———. *Thomas Hobbes: Man and Citizen*. Edited by Bernard Gert. Indianapolis: Hackett, 1991.

Holbach, Paul Henri Thiry, Baron d'. *Le bon sens puisé dans la nature; ou, Idées naturelles opposées aux idées surnaturelles*. Rome, 1792.

———. "Le Christianisme dévoilé." In *Premières œuvres*. Paris: Editions Sociales, 1971.

Holmes, Stephen. *The Anatomy of Antiliberalism*. Cambridge, MA: Harvard University Press, 1993.

Horace. *Odes*. In *The Complete Works of Horace*, translated by Charles E. Passage. New York: Frederick Ungar, 1983.

Hourani, George. Introduction to *Averroes: On the Harmony of Religion and Philosophy [The Decisive Treatise]*. London: Luzac, 1961.

Hume, David. *An Enquiry concerning the Principles of Morals*. In *Hume: Moral and Political Philosophy*, edited by Henry D. Aiken. Darien, CT: Hafner, 1970.

———. *New Letters of David Hume*. Edited by Raymond Klibansky and Ernest C. Mossner. Oxford: Clarendon Press, 1954.

———. *A Treatise of Human Nature*. Edited by Ernest C. Mossner. Harmondsworth, UK: Penguin, 1969.

Husserl, Edmund. *The Crisis of European Sciences and Transcendental Phenomenology*. Translated by D. Carr. Evanston, IL: Northwestern University Press, 1970.

Irwin, Terrence. *Plato's Ethics*. New York: Oxford University Press, 1995.

Isocrates. *Antidosis.* In *Isocrates*, vol. 2: *On the Peace, Areopagiticus, Against the Sophists. Antidosis, Panathenaicus*, translated by George Norlin. Loeb Classical Library 229. Cambridge, MA: Harvard University Press, 1929.

Israel, Jonathan. *Radical Enlightenment: Philosophy and the Making of Modernity, 1650–1750.* Oxford: Oxford University Press, 2001.

Jackson, Maggie. *Distracted: The Erosion of Attention and the Coming Dark Age.* Amherst, NY: Prometheus Books, 2008.

Jacob, Margaret. *Living the Enlightenment: Freemasonry and Politics in Eighteenth-Century Europe.* Oxford: Oxford University Press, 1991.

———. *The Radical Enlightenment: Pantheists, Freemasons and Republicans.* Boston: G. Allen & Unwin, 1981.

Jacoby, Susan. *The Age of American Unreason.* New York: Pantheon Books, 2008.

Jaeger, Werner. *Aristotle: Fundamentals of the History of His Development.* Oxford: Clarendon Press, 1948.

Jaffa, Harry. *Thomism and Aristotelianism: A Study of the Commentary by Thomas Aquinas on the Nicomachean Ethics.* Chicago: University of Chicago Press, 1952.

Jaki, Stanley L. *The Savior of Science.* Washington, DC: Regnery Gateway, 1988.

Jakobson, Roman. *Pushkin and His Sculptural Myth.* Translated by John Burbank. The Hague: Mouton, 1975.

Jameson, Fredric. *The Political Unconscious.* Ithaca, NY: Cornell University Press, 1981.

Jansen, Sue Curry. *Censorship: The Knot That Binds Power and Knowledge.* Oxford: Oxford University Press, 1988.

Jaucourt, Louis de. "Mensonge." In *Encyclopédie, ou dictionnaire raisonné des sciences, des arts et des métiers*, edited by Denis Diderot and Jean le Rond d'Alembert. University of Chicago: ARTFL Encyclopédie Projet (Winter 2008 edition), ed. Robert Morrissey. http://encyclopedie.uchicago.edu.

Jefferson, Thomas. *The Writings of Thomas Jefferson.* Edited by Andrew A. Lipscomb, Albert Ellery Bergh, and Richard Holland Johnston. Vol. 11. Washington, DC: Thomas Jefferson Memorial Association of the United States, 1905.

Joyce, James. *Ulysses: An Unabridged Republication of the Original Shakespeare and Company Edition, Published in Paris by Sylvia Beach, 1922.* Mineola, NY: Dover, 2009.

Julian [Julianus], Flavius Claudius. *To the Cynic Heracleios.* In *The Works of the Emperor Julian*, translated by Wilmer Cave Wright. Vol. 2. London: William Heinemann, 1913.

Kelly, Christopher. *Rousseau as Author: Consecrating One's Life to the Truth.* Chicago: University of Chicago Press, 2003.

———. "Rousseau's Critique of the Public Intellectual in the Age of the Enlightenment." In *Between Philosophy and Politics: The Public Intellectual*, edited by Arthur Melzer, Jerry Weinberger, and Richard Zinman. New York: Rowman & Littlefield, 2003.

Kennedy, George. *Comparative Rhetoric: An Historical and Cross-Cultural Introduction.* Oxford: Oxford University Press, 1998.

Kennington, Richard. *On Modern Origins: Essays in Early Modern Philosophy.* Edited by Pamela Kraus and Frank Hunt. Lanham, MD: Lexington Books, 2004.

Kermode, Frank. *The Genesis of Secrecy: On the Interpretation of Narrative.* Cambridge, MA: Harvard University Press, 1979.

Kierkegaard, Søren. *The Point of View for My Work as an Author; A Report to History, and Related Writings.* Translated by Walter Lowrie. New York: Harper & Row, 1962.

Kippenberg, Hans G., and Guy G. Stroumsa, eds. *Secrecy and Concealment: Studies in the History of Mediterranean and Near Eastern Religions.* Leiden: E. J. Brill, 1995.

Kissinger, Henry, and Clare B. Luce. *The White House Years.* Boston: Little Brown, 1979.

Klein, Jacob. *Greek Mathematical Thought and the Origin of Algebra.* Translated by Eva Brann. Cambridge, MA: MIT Press, 1968.

———. *Jacob Klein: Lectures and Essays*. Edited by Robert Williamson and Elliot Zuckerman. Annapolis, MD: St. John's College Press, 1985.

Kojève, Alexandre. "The Emperor Julian and His Art of Writing." In *Ancients and Moderns: Essays on the Tradition of Political Philosophy in Honor of Leo Strauss*, edited by Joseph Cropsey, 95–114. New York: Basic Books, 1964.

Kolakowski, Leszek. "Dialogue between Leszek Kolakowski and Danny Postel: On Exile, Philosophy and Tottering Insecurely on the Edge of an Unknown Abyss." *Daedalus* 134, no. 3 (Summer 2005): 82–88.

Koselleck, Reinhart. *Critique and Crisis: Enlightenment and the Pathogenesis of Modern Society*. Oxford: Berg, 1988.

Kraynak, Robert P. *History and Modernity in the Thought of Thomas Hobbes*. Ithaca, NY: Cornell University Press, 1990.

Kuhn, Helmut. *Freedom Forgotten and Remembered*. Chapel Hill: University of North Carolina Press, 1943.

La Bléterie, Jean Philippe René de. *The Life of Julian the Apostate: Translated from the French of F. La Bletterie. And Improved with Dissertations on Several Points Relating to Julian's Character, and to the History of the Fourth Century. By V. Desvoeux*. Dublin: S. Powell, for Peter Wilson, 1746.

La Mettrie, Julien Offray de. "Preliminary Discourse." In *Machine Man and Other Writings*, translated and edited by Ann Thomson. Cambridge: Cambridge University Press, 1996.

Lampert, Laurence. *The Enduring Importance of Leo Strauss*. Chicago: University of Chicago Press, 2013.

Lange, Margaret Meek. "Defending a Liberalism of Freedom: John Rawls's Use of Hegel." PhD diss., Columbia University, 2009.

La Rochefoucauld, François. *Collected Maxims and Other Reflections*. Edited and translated by E. H. Blackmore, A. M. Blackmore, and Francine Giguère. Oxford: Oxford University Press, 2007.

La Salle, Antoine de. *Préface générale*. In vol. 1 of *Œuvres de Fr. Bacon*, translated by Antoine de La Salle. Dijon: L. N. Frantin, 1799–1800.

Lecky, W. E. H. *History of European Morals from Augustus to Charlemagne*. 2 vols. New York: D. Appleton, 1879.

Leibniz, G. W. *New Essays on Human Understanding*. Translated by Peter Remnant and Jonathan Bennett. Cambridge: Cambridge University Press, 1981.

———. *Sämtliche Schriften und Briefe*. Edited by Preussische Akademie der Wissenschaften. Vol. 2. Darmstadt and Leipzig, 1923–54.

Leibowitz, David. *The Ironic Defense of Socrates: Plato's Apology*. Cambridge: Cambridge University Press, 2010.

Leighton, Lauren G. *The Esoteric Tradition in Russian Romantic Literature: Decembrism and Freemasonry*. University Park: Pennsylvania State University Press, 1994.

Leites, Nathan, and Elsa Bernaut. *Ritual of Liquidation*. Glencoe, IL: Free Press, 1954.

Lenin, Vladimir. *The Collected Works*. Vol. 10. Moscow: Progress, 1972.

Lenzner, Steven J. "Guide for the Perplexed." *Claremont Review of Books* 7, no. 2 (Spring 2007): 53–57.

Lerner, Daniel. *The Passing of Traditional Society: Modernizing the Middle East*. Glencoe, IL: Free Press, 1958.

Lerner, Ralph. "Dispersal by Design: The Author's Choice." In *Reason, Faith, and Politics: Essays in Honor of Werner J. Dannhauser*, edited by Arthur Melzer and Robert Kraynak, 29–41. Lanham, MD: Lexington Books, 2008.

———. *Playing the Fool: Subversive Laughter in Troubled Times*. Chicago: University of Chicago Press, 2009.

Lerner, Ralph, and Muhsin Mahdi, eds. *Medieval Political Philosophy: A Sourcebook*. New York: Free Press, 1963.

Leunissen, Mariska. *Explanation and Teleology in Aristotle's Science of Nature*. Cambridge: Cambridge University Press, 2010.

Levine, Donald. *The Flight from Ambiguity: Essays in Social and Cultural Theory*. Chicago: University of Chicago Press, 1985.

Locke, John. "Error," "Sacerdos," "Defence of Nonconformity" in Lord Peter King, *The Life and Letters of John Locke with extracts from his Journals and Common-place books*. New York: Burt Franklin, 1954.

———. "An Essay on Toleration." In H. R. Fox Bourne, *The Life of John Locke*. London: Henry S. King, 1876.

———. *The Reasonableness of Christianity: As Delivered in the Scriptures*. Edited by George W. Ewing. Washington, DC: Regnery, 1965.

———. *Some Thoughts concerning Education; and, Of the Conduct of the Understanding*. Edited by Ruth Grant and Nathan Tarcov. Indianapolis: Hackett, 1996.

———. *Two Treatises of Government*. Edited by Peter Laslett. New York: New American Library, 1965.

Loseff, Lev. *On the Beneficence of Censorship: Aesopian Language in Modern Russian Literature*. Translated by Jane Bobko. Munich: Sagner, 1984.

Lucian. "Philosophies for Sale" [The Sale of Lives]. In vol. 2 of *Lucian*, translated by A. M. Harmon. London: William Heinemann, 1929.

Lyotard, Jean-François. *The Postmodern Condition: A Report on Knowledge*. Minneapolis: University of Minnesota Press, 1984.

Macaulay, Thomas Babington. *Critical and Historical Essays Contributed to the Edinburgh Review*. 6th ed. Vol. 1. London: Longman, Brown, Green, and Longmans, 1849.

———. *The History of England from the Accession of James II*. eBookMall Inc., 2000.

Machiavelli, Niccolo. *Discourses on Livy*. Translated by Harvey C. Mansfield and Nathan Tarcov. Chicago: University of Chicago Press, 1996.

———. *Florentine Histories*. Translated by Laura F. Banfield and Harvey C. Mansfield. Princeton, NJ: Princeton University Press, 1988.

———. *The Prince*. Translated by Harvey C. Mansfield. Chicago: University of Chicago Press, 1985.

Machler, Chaninah. "Lessing's *Ernst and Falk: Dialogues for Freemasons*, a Translation with Notes." *Interpretation* 14, no. 1 (January 1986): 1–49.

MacPherson, Myra. *All Governments Lie: The Life and Times of Rebel Journalist I. F. Stone*. New York: Scribner, 2006.

Mahdi, Muhsin. "Man and His Universe in Medieval Arabic Philosophy." In *L'homme et son univers au Moyen Age*, edited by Christian Wenin, 102–13. Louvain-La-Neuve: L'Institut Supérior de Philosophie, 1986.

———, trans. *The Philosophy of Plato and Aristotle*. Ithaca, NY: Cornell University Press, 1962.

Maimonides, Moses. *The Guide of the Perplexed*. Edited and translated by Shlomo Pines. Chicago: University of Chicago Press, 1963.

———. *Laws concerning Character Traits*. In *Ethical Writings of Maimonides*, translated by Raymond Weiss with Charles Butterworth. New York: Dover Publications, 1975.

———. *A Maimonides Reader*. Edited by Isadore Twersky. New York: Behrman House, 1972.

Malebranche, Nicolas de. *Réponse à une dissertation de Mr Arnaud contre un éclaircissement du traité de la nature et de la grace*. Rotterdam: Reinier Leers, 1685.

Mannheim, Karl. "Historicism." In *Essays on the Sociology of Knowledge*, edited by Paul Kecskemeti, 84–133. London: Routledge and Kegan Paul, 1952.

Marcuse, Herbert. "Repressive Tolerance." In Robert Paul Wolff, Barrington Moore Jr., and Herbert Marcuse, *A Critique of Pure Tolerance*, 81–123. Boston: Beacon Press, 1965.

Marx, Karl. *Capital*. Vol. 2 of *Capital: A Critique of Political Economy*. Translated by David Fern-
    back. New York: Random House, 1981.
————. "Manifesto of the Communist Party." In *The Marx-Engels Reader*, edited by Robert C.
    Tucker, 469–501. 2nd ed. New York: Norton, 1978.
————. Preface to *A Contribution to the Critique of Political Economy*. In *The Marx-Engels
    Reader*, edited by Robert C. Tucker, 3–7. 2nd ed. New York: Norton, 1978.
McKenna, Antony. "Clandestine Literature." In *Encyclopedia of the Enlightenment*, edited by
    Alan Charles Kors. Oxford: Oxford University Press, 2005.
Mearsheimer, John. *Why Leaders Lie: The Truth about Lying in International Politics*. New York:
    Oxford University Press, 2011.
Meier, Heinrich. *Leo Strauss and the Theological-Political Problem*. Cambridge: Cambridge Uni-
    versity Press, 2006.
Melzer, Arthur M. "The Origin of the Counter-Enlightenment: Rousseau and the New Reli-
    gion of Sincerity," *American Political Science Review* 90, no. 2 (June 1996): 344–60.
Mercier, Louis Sebastien. *Tableau de Paris*. Amsterdam, 1783–89.
Mill, John Stuart. *Inaugural Address Delivered to the University of St. Andrews*. London: Long-
    mans, Green, Reader, & Dyer, 1867.
Milosz, Czeslaw. *The Captive Mind*. Translated by Jane Zielonko. New York: Alfred A. Knopf,
    1953.
Milton, John. *Areopagitica*. In *John Milton: Selected Prose*, edited by C. A. Patrides, 196–249.
    Columbia: University of Missouri Press, 1985.
————. *Paradise Lost and Paradise Regained*. Edited by Christopher Ricks. New York: New
    American Library, 1968.
Minowitz, Peter. *Profits, Priests, and Princes: Adam Smith's Emancipation of Economics from Poli-
    tics and Religion*. Stanford, CA: Stanford University Press, 1993.
————. *Straussophobia: Defending Leo Strauss and Straussians against Shadia Drury and Other Ac-
    cusers*. Lanham, MD: Lexington Books, 2009.
Moezzi, Mohammad Ali Amir. *The Divine Guide in Early Shiism: The Sources of Esotericism in
    Islam*. Albany: State University of New York Press, 1994.
Momigliano, Arnaldo. "Hermeneutics and Classical Political Thought in Leo Strauss." In
    Essays on Ancient and Modern Judaism, edited by Silvia Berti, 178–90. Chicago: University
    of Chicago Press, 1994.
————. "In Memoriam: Leo Strauss." In *Essays on Ancient and Modern Judaism*, edited by Silvia
    Berti. Chicago: University of Chicago Press, 1994.
Montaigne, Michel de. *The Complete Essays of Montaigne*. Translated by Donald M. Frame.
    Stanford, CA: Stanford University Press, 1958.
Montesquieu, Charles de Secondat, Baron de. *Lettres persanes*. Paris: Garnier, 1960.
————. *Œuvres complètes*. Paris: A. Belin, 1822.
————. *Œuvres complètes*. Edited by Roger Caillois. Paris: Librairie Gallimard, 1949–51.
————. *The Spirit of the Laws*. Translated by Anne Cohler, Basia Miller, and Harold Stone.
    Cambridge: Cambridge University Press, 1989.
Mooney, Chris. *The Republican War on Science*. New York: Basic Books, 2005.
Moraux, Paul. *Les listes anciennes des ouvrages d'Aristote*. Louvain: Université de Louvain, 1951.
Morrow, Glenn. *Plato's Epistles*. Indianapolis: Bobbs-Merrill, 1962.
Mortier, Roland. "Esotérisme et lumières." In *Clartés et ombres du siècle des lumières: Etudes sur
    le 18e siècle littéraire*. Geneva: Droz, 1969.
Moule, C. F. D. "Mark 4:1–20 Yet Once More." In *Neotestamentica et Semitica: Studies in Hon-
    our of Principal Matthew Black*, edited by E. Earle Ellis and Max Wilcox. Edinburgh: T. &
    T. Clark, 1969.
Muir, Edward. *The Culture Wars of the Late Renaissance: Skeptics, Libertines, and Opera*. Cam-
    bridge, MA: Harvard University Press, 2007.

Muller, Jerry. "Enttäuschung und Zweideutigkeit: Zur Geschichte rechter Sozialwissen-schaftler im Dritten Reich." *Geschichte und Gesellschaft* 3 (1986): 289–316.

———. *The Other God That Failed: Hans Freyer and the Deradicalization of German Conserva-tism*. Princeton: Princeton University Press, 1987.

Mussolini, Benito. *Diuturna*. Milan: Imperia, 1924.

Naudé, Gabriel, Guy Patin, Claude Lancelot, Louis Cousin, Pierre Bayle, and Jean-Aimar Piganiol de La Force. *Naudaeana et Patiniana, ou, Singularitez remarquables*. Amsterdam: F. vander Plaats, 1703.

Neuberger, Joan. *Ivan the Terrible: The Film Companion*. London: I. B. Tauris, 2003.

Nichols, James H., Jr. *Epicurean Political Philosophy: The De rerum natura of Lucretius*. Ithaca, NY: Cornell University Press, 1972.

Nietzsche, Friedrich Wilhelm. *Beyond Good and Evil: Prelude to a Philosophy of the Future*. Translated by Walter Kaufmann. New York: Vintage Books, 1966.

———. *Daybreak: Thoughts on the Prejudices of Morality*. Translated by R. J. Hollingdale. Cambridge: Cambridge University Press, 1997.

———. *The Gay Science; with a Prelude in Rhymes and an Appendix of Songs*. Translated by Walter Kaufmann. New York: Random House, 1974.

———. *Human All Too Human*. Translated by R. J. Hollingdale. Vol. 1. Cambridge: Cambridge University Press, 1986.

Nooter, Mary H. "Secrecy: African Art That Conceals and Reveals." *African Arts* 26, no. 1 (January 1993): 55–70.

Olympiodorus. *Prolegomena et in Categorias Commentarium*. Edited by A. Busse. In vol. 12.1 of *Commentaria in Aristotelem Graeca*. Berlin: Reimer, 1902.

Orwell, George. "Politics and the English Language." In *All Art Is Propaganda: Critical Essays*. New York: Houghton Mifflin Harcourt, 2008.

Orwin, Clifford. *The Humanity of Thucydides*. Princeton, NJ: Princeton University Press, 1994.

———. "Machiavelli's Unchristian Charity." *American Political Science Review* 72, no. 4 (December 1978): 1217–28.

Outram, Dorinda. *The Enlightenment*. Cambridge: Cambridge University Press, 2005.

Pangle, Lorraine. *Aristotle and the Philosophy of Friendship*. Cambridge: Cambridge University Press, 2003.

Pangle, Thomas L. *Aristotle's Teaching in the Politics*. Chicago: University of Chicago Press, 2013.

———. *Leo Strauss: An Introduction to His Thought and Intellectual Legacy*. Baltimore: Johns Hopkins University Press, 2006.

———. *Montesquieu's Philosophy of Liberalism: A Commentary on The Spirit of the Laws*. Chicago: University of Chicago Press, 1973.

Pangle, Thomas L., and Peter J. Ahrensdorf. *Justice among Nations: On the Moral Basis of Power and Peace*. Lawrence: University Press of Kansas, 1999.

Parens, Joshua. *Metaphysics as Rhetoric: Alfarabi's Summary of Plato's Laws*. Albany: State University of New York Press, 1995.

Parrott, Ray J., Jr. "Aesopian Language." In *Modern Encyclopedia of Russian and Soviet Literature*, edited by Harry B. Weber. Gulf Breeze, FL: Academic International Press, 1977.

Pascal, Blaise. *Pascal's Pensées*. Translated by W. F. Trotter. New York: E. P. Dutton, 1958.

Patterson, Annabel. *Censorship and Interpretation: The Conditions of Writing and Reading in Early Modern England*. Madison: University of Wisconsin Press, 1984.

———. *Fables of Power: Aesopian Writing and Political History*. Durham, NC: Duke University Press, 1991.

———. *Reading between the Lines*. Madison: University of Wisconsin Press, 1993.

Payne, Harry C. *The Philosophes and the People*. New Haven: Yale University Press, 1976.

Peace Corps. *Culture Matters: The Peace Corps Cross-Cultural Workbook*. Washington, DC: Peace Corps Information Collection and Exchange T0087, 1997.

Penn, William. *Fruits of a Father's Love: Being the Advice of William Penn to his Children Relating to their Civil and Religious Conduct*. Dover, NH: James K. Remich, 1808.

Philoponus. *Aristotelis Categorias Commentarium*. Edited by A. Busse. In *Commentaria in Aristotelem Graeca*. Berlin: Reimer, 1898.

Pierce, Charles P. *Idiot America: How Stupidity Became a Virtue in the Land of the Free*. New York: Doubleday, 2009.

Plato. *Gorgias and Phaedrus*. Translated by James H. Nichols Jr. Ithaca, NY: Cornell University Press, 1998.

———. *The Laws of Plato*. Translated by Thomas L. Pangle. New York: Basic Books, 1980.

———. *Phaedo*. Translated by Harold North Fowler. London: William Heinemann, 1914.

———. *Protagoras and Meno*. Translated by Robert C. Bartlett. Ithaca, NY: Cornell University Press, 2004.

———. *Plato's Theaetetus*. Translated by Francis M. Cornford. Indianapolis: Bobbs-Merrill, 1959.

———. *The Republic of Plato*. Translated by Allan Bloom. New York: Basic Books, 1968.

———. *Timaeus*. Translated by R. G. Bury. London: William Heinemann, 1929.

Plutarch. *Isis and Osiris*. In vol. 5 of *Moralia*, translated by Frank Cole Babbitt. Cambridge, MA: Harvard University Press, 1936.

———. *The Lives of the Noble Grecians and Romans*, translated by John Dryden. New York: Modern Library, 1932.

Pope, Alexander. *An Essay on Criticism*. In *Pope: Poetical Works*, edited by Herbert Davis. Oxford: Oxford University Press, 1978.

Poster, Carol. "Aristotle's *Rhetoric* against Rhetoric: Unitarian Reading and Esoteric Hermeneutics." *American Journal of Philology* 118 (Summer 1997): 219–49.

Putnam, Hilary, and James Conant. *Realism with a Human Face*. Cambridge, MA: Harvard University Press, 1990.

Rahe, Paul. *Montesquieu and the Logic of Liberty*. New Haven: Yale University Press, 2009.

———. *Republics Ancient and Modern: Classical Republicanism and the American Revolution*. Chapel Hill: University of North Carolina Press, 1992.

Ramsey, Sheila J. "Interactions between North Americans and Japanese: Considerations of Communication Style." In *Basic Concepts of Intercultural Communication: Selected Readings*, edited by Milton J. Bennett. Yarmouth, ME: Intercultural Press, 1998.

Rashi [Rabbi Shlomo Itzhaki]. *Chumash with Targum Onkelos, Haphtaroth and Rashi's Commentary*. Translated by Rabbi A. M. Silbermann. Jerusalem: Routledge & Kegan Paul, 1934.

Reeve, C. D. C. *Philosopher-Kings: The Argument of Plato's Republic*. Princeton, NJ: Princeton University Press, 1988.

Rendall, Steven F. "Fontenelle and His Public." *Modern Language Notes* 86, no. 4 (May 1971): 496–508.

Ritchie, J. M. *German Literature under National Socialism*. Totowa, NJ: Barnes & Noble, 1983.

Rorty, Richard. *Philosophy and Social Hope*. New York: Penguin Books, 1999.

———. "Pragmatism, Relativism, and Irrationalism." In *Consequences of Pragmatism: Essays, 1972–1980*, 160–75. Minneapolis: University of Minnesota Press, 1982.

———. "Solidarity or Objectivity." In *Objectivity, Relativism, and Truth: Philosophical Papers*, vol. 1, 21–34. Cambridge: Cambridge University Press, 1991.

Ross, Sir David. *Aristotle*. London: Methuen, 1965.

Rousseau, Jean-Jacques. *Discourse on the Sciences and Arts, and Polemics*. Vol. 2 of *The Collected Writings of Rousseau*, edited and translated by Judith Bush, Roger Masters, and Christopher Kelly. Hanover, NH: University Press of New England, 1992.

———. *Emile: Or, On education*. Translated by Allan Bloom. New York: Basic Books, 1979.

———. *The First and Second Discourses*. Translated by Roger D. Masters and Judith R. Masters. New York: St. Martin's Press, 1964.

———. *Lettres écrites de la montagne.* Vol. 3 of *Œuvres complètes*, edited by Bernard Gagnebin and Marcel Raymond. 4 vols. Paris: Gallimard, Bibliothèque de la Pléïade, 1959–69.

———. "Observations by Jean-Jacques Rousseau of Geneva On the Reply Made to his Discourse." In *Discourse on the Sciences and Arts, and Polemics.* Vol. 2 of *The Collected Writings of Rousseau*, edited by Roger D. Masters and Christopher Kelly, 23–25. Hanover, NH: University Press of New England, 1992.

———. *On the Social Contract, with Geneva Manuscript and Political Economy.* Edited by Roger D. Masters. Translated by Judith R. Masters. New York: St. Martin's Press, 1978.

———. *Politics and the Arts, Letter to M. d'Alembert on the Theatre.* Translated by Allan Bloom. Glencoe, IL: Free Press, 1960.

———. "Preface to Second Letter to Bordes." In *Discourse on the Sciences and Arts, and Polemics.* Vol. 2 of *The Collected Writings of Rousseau*, edited by Roger D. Masters and Christopher Kelly, 182–86. Hanover, NH: University Press of New England, 1992.

Rush, Myron. "Esoteric Communication in Soviet Politics." *World Politics* 11, no. 4 (July 1959): 614–20.

———. *The Rise of Khrushchev.* Washington, DC: Public Affairs Press, 1958.

Russell, Paul. "Epigram, Pantheists, and Freethought in Hume's Treatise: A Study in Esoteric Communication." *Journal of the History of Ideas* 54, no. 4 (October 1993): 659–73.

Sabine, George H. Review of *Persecution and the Art of Writing. Ethics* 63 no. 3 (April 1953): 220–22.

Sallustius. *On the Gods and the World.* In *Five Stages of Greek Religion*, translated by Gilbert Murray, 191–212. New York: Columbia University Press, 1925.

Sarpi, Paolo. *Lettere ai Gallicani.* Edited by Boris Ulianich. Wiesbaden: F. Steiner, 1961.

———. *Opere.* Edited by Gaetano Cozzi and Luisa Cozzi. Milan: R. Ricciardi, 1969.

Savile, George. *The Works of George Savile, Marquis of Halifax: In Three Volumes.* Edited by Mark N. Brown. Vol. 3. Oxford: Clarendon Press, 1989.

Savinitch, Lioudmila. "Pragmatic Goals and Communicative Strategies in Journalistic Discourse under Censorship." In *Power without Domination: Dialogism and the Empowering Property of Communication*, edited by Eric Grillo, 107–37. Philadelphia: John Benjamins, 2005.

Sayre, Kenneth M. "Plato's Dialogues in Light of the Seventh Letter." In *Platonic Writings, Platonic Readings*, edited by Charles L. Griswold. New York: Routledge, 1988.

Schaefer, David. *The Political Philosophy of Montaigne.* Ithaca, NY: Cornell University Press, 1990.

Schaub, Jörg. *Gerechtigkeit als Versöhnung: John Rawls' politischer Liberalismus.* Frankfurt: Campus Verlag, 2009.

Schiller, Friedrich. *On Naive and Sentimental Poetry.* Translated by Julius A. Elias. New York: F. Ungar, 1966.

Schleiermacher, Friedrich. *Introductions to the Dialogues of Plato.* Translated by William Dobson. Cambridge: J. & J. J. Deighton, 1836.

Schmitt, Charles B. "Aristotle as Cuttlefish: The Origin and Development of a Renaissance Image." *Studies in the Renaissance* 12 (1965): 60–72.

Schnell, R. "Innere Emigration und kulturelle Dissidenz." In *Widerstand und Verweigerung in Deutschland 1933 bis 1945*, edited by R. Löwenthal and P. von zur Muhlen. Bonn: Dietz, 1982.

Scholem, Gershom. *On the Kabbalah and Its Symbolism.* Translated by Ralph Mannheim. New York: Schocken Books, 1965.

Schopenhauer, Arthur. *The Essays of Arthur Schopenhauer.* Translated by T. Bailey Saunders. New York: Willey Books, 1935.

———. *Religion: A Dialogue, and Other Essays.* Translated by T. Bailey Saunders. New York: Macmillan, 1899.

Schwab, Richard N. Introduction. In *Preliminary Discourse to the Encyclopedia of Diderot*, translated by Richard N. Schwab and Walter E. Rex, ix–l. New York: Bobbs-Merrill, 1963.

Scott, James C. *Domination and the Arts of Resistance: Hidden Transcripts*. New Haven: Yale University Press, 1990.

Seneca, Lucius Annaeus. *Ad Lucilium Epistulae morales*. Translated by Richard Gummere. 3 vols. Cambridge, MA: Harvard University Press, 1917.

Shaftesbury, Antony Ashley Cooper, Earl of. *Characteristics of Men, Manners, Opinions, Times*. Edited by Lawrence E. Klein. Cambridge: Cambridge University Press, 2004.

Shattuck, Roger. *Forbidden Knowledge: From Prometheus to Pornography*. New York: St. Martin's, 1996.

Shenkman, Richard. *Just How Stupid Are We?: Facing the Truth about the American Voter*. New York: Basic Books, 2008.

Shils, Edward. *Tradition*. Chicago: University of Chicago Press, 1981.

Shulsky, Abram. "The 'Infrastructure' of Aristotle's *Politics*: Aristotle on Economics and Politics." In *Essays on the Foundation of Aristotelian Political Science*, edited by Carnes Lord and David O'Connor, 74–112. Berkeley: University of California Press, 1991.

Simmel, Georg. "The Secret and the Secret Society." In *The Sociology of Georg Simmel*, trans. Kurt H. Wolff, 307–79. New York: Free Press, 1950.

Simplicius. *In Aristotelis Physicorum Libros Quattuor Priores Commentaria*. Edited by H. Diels. In vol. 9 of *Commentaria in Aristotelem Graeca*. Berlin: Reimer, 1882.

Skinner, Quentin. "Meaning and Understanding in the History of Ideas." *History and Theory* 8, no. 1 (1969): 3–53.

———. *Reason and Rhetoric in the Philosophy of Hobbes*. Cambridge: Cambridge University Press, 1996.

Smith, Adam. *The Correspondence of Adam Smith*. Edited by Ernest Campbell Mossner and Ian Simpson Ross. Oxford: Clarendon Press, 1977.

———. *The History of the Ancient Logics and Metaphysics*. In *Essays on Philosophical Subjects*, edited by W. P. D. Wightman and J. C. Bryce, 118–33. Indianapolis: Liberty Classics, 1982.

———. *Lectures on Rhetoric and Belles Lettres*. Edited by J. C. Bryce. Indianapolis: Liberty Fund, 2007.

Smith, D. W. "The 'Useful Lie' in Helvétius and Diderot." In vol. 14 of *Diderot Studies*. Geneva: Librairie Droz, 1971.

Smith, Hedrick. *The Russians*. New York: Ballantine, 1977.

Smith, Steven B. *Reading Leo Strauss: Politics, Philosophy, Judaism*. Chicago: University of Chicago Press, 2006.

Speier, Hans. *The Truth in Hell and Other Essays on Politics and Culture, 1935–1987*. Oxford: Oxford University Press, 1989.

Spinoza, Benedict de. *A Political Treatise*. In *The Chief Works of Benedict Spinoza*, trans. R. H. M. Elwes, 267–387. New York: Dover Publications, 1951.

———. *Theologico-Political Treatise*. In *The Chief Works of Benedict Spinoza*, trans. R. H. M. Elwes, 3–266. New York: Dover Publications, 1951.

Stone, I. F. *The Trial of Socrates*. Boston: Little Brown, 1988.

Strabo. *The Geography of Strabo*. Cambridge, MA.: Harvard University Press, 1969.

Straus, Irwin. *Phenomenological Psychology*. Translated by Erling Eng. New York: Basic Books, 1966.

Strauss, Leo. *The City and Man*. Chicago: Rand McNally, 1964.

———. "Correspondence concerning Modernity: Karl Löwith and Leo Strauss." *Independent Journal of Philosophy* 4 (1983): 105–19.

———. "Exoteric Teaching." In *The Rebirth of Classical Rationalism: An Introduction to the Thought of Leo Strauss*, edited by Thomas Pangle, 63–71. Chicago: University of Chicago Press, 1989.

———. *Faith and Political Philosophy: The Correspondence between Leo Strauss and Eric Voegelin, 1934-1964*. Translated and edited by Peter Emberley and Barry Cooper. University Park: Pennsylvania State University Press, 1993.

———. "Farabi's Plato." In *Louis Ginzberg Jubilee Volume on the Occasion of His Seventieth Birthday*, 357–93. New York: American Academy for Jewish Research, 1945.

———. "A Giving of Accounts: Jacob Klein and Leo Strauss." In *Jewish Philosophy and the Crisis of Modernity*, edited by Kenneth Hart Green, 457–66. Albany: State University of New York Press, 1997.

———. "How to Begin to Study Medieval Philosophy." In *The Rebirth of Classical Rationalism: An Introduction to the Thought of Leo Strauss*, edited by Thomas Pangle, 207–26. Chicago: University of Chicago Press, 1989.

———. "An Introduction to Heideggerian Existentialism." In *The Rebirth of Classical Rationalism: An Introduction to the Thought of Leo Strauss*, edited by Thomas Pangle, 27–48. Chicago: University of Chicago Press, 1989.

———. *Jewish Philosophy and the Crisis of Modernity*. Edited by Kenneth Hart Green. Albany: State University of New York Press, 1997.

———. "Kurt Riezler." In *What Is Political Philosophy? And Other Studies*, 233–60. New York: Free Press, 1959.

———. "Marsilius of Padua." In *The History of Political Philosophy*, edited by Leo Strauss and Joseph Cropsey, 276–95. 3rd ed. Chicago: University of Chicago Press, 1987.

———. *Natural Right and History*. Chicago: University of Chicago Press, 1953.

———. "Niccolo Machiavelli." In *The History of Political Philosophy*, edited by Leo Strauss and Joseph Cropsey, 296–317. 3rd ed. Chicago: University of Chicago Press, 1987.

———. "On a Forgotten Kind of Writing." In *What Is Political Philosophy? And Other Studies*, 221–32. New York: Free Press, 1959.

———. "On a New Interpretation of Plato's Political Philosophy." *Social Research* 13 (September 1946): 326–67.

———. "On Classical Political Philosophy." In *What Is Political Philosophy? And Other Studies*, 49–62. New York: Free Press, 1959.

———. "On Collingwood's Philosophy of History." *Review of Metaphysics* 5, no. 4 (June 1952): 559–86.

———. "On the Intention of Rousseau." In *Hobbes and Rousseau: A Collection of Critical Essays*, edited by Maurice Cranston and R. S. Peters, 254–90. Garden City, NY: Anchor Books, 1972.

———. *On Tyranny: Including the Strauss-Kojève Correspondence*, edited by Victor Gourevitch and Michael S. Roth. New York: Free Press, 1991.

———. "Persecution and the Art of Writing." *Social Research* 8 (November 1941): 488–504.

———. *Persecution and the Art of Writing*. Glencoe, IL: Free Press, 1952.

———. *Philosophy and Law*. Translated by Fred Baumann. New York: Jewish Publication Society, 1987.

———. "Philosophy as Rigorous Science and Political Philosophy." In *Studies in Platonic Political Philosophy*. Chicago: University of Chicago Press, 1983.

———. "Political Philosophy and History." In *What Is Political Philosophy? And Other Studies*, 56–77. New York: Free Press, 1959.

———. *The Political Philosophy of Hobbes: Its Basis and Its Genesis*. Translated by Elsa M. Sinclair. Chicago: University of Chicago Press, 1952.

———. "Preface to Hobbes Politische Wissenschaft." In *Jewish Philosophy and the Crisis of Modernity*, edited by Kenneth Hart Green, 453–56. Albany: State University of New York Press, 1997.

———. "The Problem of Socrates: Five Lectures." In *The Rebirth of Classical Rationalism: An Introduction to the Thought of Leo Strauss*, edited by Thomas Pangle, 103–86. Chicago: University of Chicago Press, 1989.

———. "Progress or Return?" In *The Rebirth of Classical Rationalism: An Introduction to the Thought of Leo Strauss*, edited by Thomas Pangle, 227–70. Chicago: University of Chicago Press, 1989.

———. *The Rebirth of Classical Rationalism: An Introduction to the Thought of Leo Strauss*, edited by Thomas Pangle. Chicago: University of Chicago Press, 1989.

———. "Relativism." In *Relativism and the Study of Man*, edited by Helmut Schoeck and J. W. Wiggins, 135–57. Princeton, NJ: Van Nostrand, 1961.

———. *Socrates and Aristophanes*. New York: Basic Books, 1966.

———. *Spinoza's Critique of Religion*. Translated by E. M. Sinclair. New York: Schocken Books, 1965.

———. "The Spirit of Sparta or the Taste of Xenophon." *Social Research* 6, no. 4 (1939): 502–36.

———. *Thoughts on Machiavelli*. Chicago: University of Chicago Press, 1978.

———. "Three Waves of Modernity." In *An Introduction to Political Philosophy: Ten Essays by Leo Strauss*, edited by Hilail Gildin. 81–98. Detroit: Wayne State University Press, 1989.

———. "Thucydides: The Meaning of Political History." In *The Rebirth of Classical Political Rationalism*, edited by Thomas L. Pangle, 72–102. Chicago: University of Chicago Press, 1989.

———. "An Unspoken Prologue." In *Jewish Philosophy and the Crisis of Modernity*, edited by Kenneth Hart Green, 449–52. Albany: State University of New York Press, 1997.

———. "What Is Political Philosophy?" In *What Is Political Philosophy? And Other Studies*. Glencoe, IL: Free Press, 1959.

———. *What Is Political Philosophy? And Other Studies*. Glencoe, IL: Free Press, 1959.

Strauss, Leo, and Seth Benardete. *Leo Strauss on Plato's Symposium*. Chicago: University of Chicago Press, 2001.

Strauss, Leo, and Hans-Georg Gadamer. "Correspondence concerning *Wahrheit und Methode*." *Independent Journal of Philosophy* 2 (1978): 5–12.

Stroumsa, Guy G. *Hidden Wisdom: Esoteric Traditions and the Roots of Christian Mysticism*. Leiden: E. J. Brill, 1996.

Svirsky, G. A. *A History of Post-War Soviet Writing: The Literature of Moral Opposition*. Translated by Robert Dessaix and Michael Ulman. Ann Arbor, MI: Ardis, 1981.

Sykes, Arthur Ashley. *A Vindication of the Account of the Double Doctrine of the Ancients. In answer to A Critical Enquiry into the Practices of the Antient Philosophers*. London: Printed for John and Paul Knapton, at the Crown in Ludgate-Street, 1747.

Taine, Hippolyte. *The Ancient Regime*. Translated by John Durand. Vol. 4. New York: Henry Holt, 1876.

Tamas, G. M. "The Legacy of Dissent: Irony, Ambiguity, Duplicity." *Uncaptive Minds* 7, no. 2 (Summer 1994): 19–34.

Tanguay, Daniel. *Leo Strauss: An Intellectual Biography*. New Haven: Yale University Press, 2007.

Tessitore, Aristide. "A Political Reading of Aristotle's Treatment of Pleasure in the *Nicomachean Ethics*." *Political Theory* 17, no. 2 (1989): 247–65.

Themistius. *Analyticorum Posteriorum Paraphrasis*. Edited by M. Wallies. In vol. 5.1 of *Commentaria in Aristotelem Graeca*. Berlin: Reimer, 1900.

———. *Libros Aristotelis de Anima Paraphrasis*. Edited by R. Heinze. In vol. 5.3 of *Commentaria in Aristotelem Graeca*. Berlin: Reimer, 1899.

Thoreau, Henry David. *Walden*. Edited by Stephen Fender. Oxford: Oxford University Press, 1997.

Tigerstedt, E. N. *Interpreting Plato*. Stockholm: Almqvist & Wiksell, 1977.

Tocqueville, Alexis de. *Democracy in America*. Translated by Harvey C. Mansfield and Delba Winthrop. Chicago: University of Chicago Press, 2000.

Todorov, Tzvetan. *On Human Diversity: Nationalism, Racism, and Exoticism in French Thought*. Cambridge, MA: Harvard University Press, 1993.

Toland, John. *Clidophorus*. London: J. Brotherton & W. Meadows, 1720.

———. *Pantheisticon*. London: Sam Patterson, 1751.

Toynbee, Arnold. *A Study of History*. Vol. 7. London: Oxford University Press, 1939.

Usener, Hermann. *Epicurea*. Cambridge: Cambridge University Press, 2010.

Velkley, Richard. *Heidegger, Strauss, and the Premises of Philosophy: On Original Forgetting*. Chicago: University of Chicago Press, 2011.

Verbeke, G. "Plutarch and the Development of Aristotle." In *Aristotle and Plato in the Mid-Fourth Century: Papers of the Symposium Aristotelicum Held at Oxford in August, 1957*, edited by Ingemar During, 236–47. Göteborg: Elanders, 1960.

Vianu, Lidia. *Censorship in Romania*. Budapest, Hungary: Central European University Press, 1998.

Vlastos, Gregory. "Further Lessons of Leo Strauss: An Exchange." *New York Review of Books*, April 24, 1986.

Volkov, Solomon, ed. *Testimony: The Memoirs of Dmitri Shostakovich*. Translated by Antonina W. Bouis. New York: Harper & Row, 1979.

Voltaire [François-Marie Arouet]. *Essai sur les moeurs*. Vol. 1. Paris: Garnier, 1963.

———. *Histoire de l'établissement du Christianisme*. In vol. 31 of *Œuvres complètes*, edited by Louis Moland. Paris: Garnier, 1877–83.

———. "Letters, Men of Letters, or Literati." In *Philosophical Dictionary*, translated by Peter Gay. New York: Basic Books, 1962.

———. *Les œuvres complètes de Voltaire*. Edited by Theodore Besterman et al. Geneva: Voltaire Foundation, 1968.

———. *Philosophical Dictionary*. Translated by Peter Gay. New York: Basic Books, 1962.

———. "Toleration." In *Philosophical Dictionary*, translated by Peter Gay. New York: Basic Books, 1962.

Wade, Ira O. *The Clandestine Organization and Diffusion of Philosophic Ideas in France, 1700–1750*. Princeton, NJ: Princeton University Press, 1938.

Walsh, Sean Noah. *Perversion and the Art of Persecution: Esotericism and Fear in the Political Philosophy of Leo Strauss*. New York: Lexington Books, 2012.

Walzer, Richard. *Greek into Arabic: Essays on Islamic Philosophy*. Cambridge, MA: Harvard University Press, 1962.

Warburton, William. *The Divine Legation of Moses Demonstrated, in Nine Books*. Vol. 2 of *The Works of the Right Reverend William Warburton, Lord Bishop of Gloucester, in Seven Volumes*. London: Nichols & Cadell, 1788.

Wayman, Alex. *The Buddhist Tantras: Light on Indo-Tibetan Esotericism*. New York: S. Weiser, 1973.

Webster, H. *Primitive Secret Societies: A Study of Early Politics and Religion*. New York: Macmillan, 1908.

Weisberger, Richard. *Speculative Freemasonry and the Enlightenment: A Study of the Craft in London, Paris, Prague, and Vienna*. Boulder, CO: East European Monographs, 1993.

White, Nicholas P. *A Companion to Plato's Republic*. Indianapolis: Hackett, 1979.

Wood, Gordon. "Conspiracy and the Paranoid Style: Causality and Deceit in the Eighteenth Century." *William and Mary Quarterly* 39 (1982): 403–41.

Wootton, David. "Narrative, Irony, and Faith in Gibbon's *Decline and Fall*." In *History and Theory* 33, no. 4 (December 1994): 77–105.

———. *Paolo Sarpi: Between Renaissance and Enlightenment*. Cambridge: Cambridge University Press, 1983.

Xenophon. *The Shorter Socratic Writings*. Translated by Robert Bartlett. Ithaca, NY: Cornell University Press, 1996.

Xenos, Nicholas. *Cloaked in Virtue: Unveiling Leo Strauss and the Rhetoric of American Foreign Policy*. New York: Routledge, 2008.

Zagorin, Perez. *Ways of Lying: Dissimulation, Persecution, and Conformity in Early Modern Europe*. Cambridge, MA: Harvard University Press, 1990.

Zaharna, R. S. "Understanding Cultural Preferences of Arab Communication Patterns." *Public Relations Review* 21, no. 3 (1995): 241–55.

Zeller, Eduard. *Aristotle and the Earlier Peripatetics*. New York: Russell & Russell, 1962.

Zuckert, Catherine H., and Michael P. Zuckert. *The Truth about Leo Strauss: Political Philosophy and American Democracy* (Chicago: University of Chicago Press, 2006.

Zuckert, Michael. *Launching Liberalism: On Lockean Political Philosophy*. Lawrence: University Press of Kansas, 2002.

Montaigne, Michel de: on ancient philosophers' religious imposture, 188; on ancient philosophers' writings about pleasure, 191; on Aristotle's concealed skepticism, 375n73; Bayle's admiration for, 318; classical republican virtue and, 186–87; on disadvantages of book learning, 213, 214; on disadvantages of truth, 162, 163; dispersal strategy used by, 318; on incompatibility between wise man and the crowd, 139, 141; indirect criticism of Christian teaching, 303; on most souls not profiting from philosophy, 117; on necessary dissimulation, 137; on Plato's noncommittal teaching, 20; on Socrates's approach to death, 198; stories and quotations used by, 308

Montesquieu, Charles de Secondat, Baron de: accused of excessive caution, 272, 402n65; anonymous publication by, 248; associated with the Masons, 248; d'Alembert on voluntary obscurity of, 161–62, 220; dispersal technique used by, 317; fighting on the side of reason, 254; on his own esotericism, 261, 317; on how to read a book, 296–97; on maintaining social role for religion, 276; on making the reader think, 214, 221; on Plato's protection of philosophy, 156; *Spirit of the Laws*, 221, 317, 324; terseness used by, 307; as writer of history, 263

morality: citizen-foreigner distinction in, 194–95; historicism/cultural relativism and, 200–201; modern state impervious to large beliefs about, 201; politics in classical world and, 183, 184; republican virtue and, 185

Mornet, Daniel, 247

Mortier, Roland, 277

Mozart, Wolfgang Amadeus, 248

Mubarak, Hosni, 133

multilevel writing, 4; of Aristotle, 34, 36–38, 41, 44, 46, 374n61, 376n81; hermeneutically conservative approach to, 112; for stages of student's education, 218

Mussolini, Benito, 339

Myanmar. *See* Burma

Mydans, Seth, 132

mystical turn of major philosophers, 329

mystical version of esotericism, 2, 368n2; used to deny Aristotle's esotericism, 26, 373n49. *See also* Neoplatonists; Neo-Pythagoreanism

mysticism, as esoteric mask of secular philosophers, 395n17

myths: of citizen-foreigner distinction, 195; as esoteric technique, 54, 307; fear of subverting, 3; founder of a nation resorting to, 241–42; Greek religious teachings in, 213; of just origins, 193; national, 164; of natural division of labor, 196; noble lie as, 192–96; of ordinary life, 197–99; rulers' authority based on, 195–96; as source of illusion, 185. *See also* illusion

narrative, postmodern, 330

natural law: Cicero on, 190; Hobbes on, 305

natural philosophy: Socrates's ambiguous relation to, 155, 156, 393n90; technological progress and, 89, 103, 381n18. *See also* science

natural religion, 264–65, 266; Hume on, 372n45

Natural Right and History (Strauss), 342

nature: esotericism of, 234; modern negative posture toward, 361; philosophy as pursuit of, 185; technological mastery of, 89, 103, 381n18

Nazi Germany, 130–31, 136, 304

Nekrasov, Nikolai, 304

Neoplatonists: commentaries on Aristotle influenced by, 35; esoteric interpretation of Aristotle by, 37–38, 42, 371n36, 375n73, 376n83; esoteric interpretation of Plato by, 28, 371n36, 376n83; extreme esotericism of, 29; "legend" of esotericism and, 26, 395n17; mysticism of, 2, 29; open esotericism of, 165; opposing Alexander of Aphrodisias, 39, 40–43, 46

Neo-Pythagoreanism, 2, 26, 35, 36

Neuberger, Joan, 132

Newton, Isaac, 14, 248

Nicomachean Ethics (Aristotle): Aquinas's commentary on, 324, 374n54; Cicero's lack of access to, 377n84; on "exoteric arguments," 31–32, 374n54; on pleasure, 190–91, 262–63; silent on immortality of the soul, 43; teleology in, 46; traditional gods mentioned in, 44, 45, 378n91

Nietzsche, Friedrich: on appeal of obscure writers, 219, 220–21; attack on Socrates, 353; continuity of Western rationalism and, 349; crisis in Western thought since, 327; historicist perspective and, 331, 334, 335,